MW01096536

Citizenship between Empire and Nation

Citizenship between Empire and Nation

Remaking

France

and

French Africa,

1945–1960

FREDERICK COOPER

Princeton University Press

Princeton and Oxford

Copyright © 2014 by Princeton University Press

Published by Princeton University Press, 41 William Street, Princeton, New Jersey 08540

In the United Kingdom: Princeton University Press, 6 Oxford Street, Woodstock, Oxfordshire OX20 1TW

press.princeton.edu

Jacket photograph: Women voting in elections in Dakar, Senegal, 1956. Documentation Française: Information AOF

All Rights Reserved

ISBN 978-0-691-16131-0

Library of Congress Control Number: 2014935568

British Library Cataloging-in-Publication Data is available

This book has been composed in Baskerville 120 and John Sans Lite Pro

Printed on acid-free paper ∞

Printed in the United States of America

10 9 8 7 6 5 4 3 2 1

CONTENTS

LIST OF ILLUSTRATIONS

PREFACE

This is a book about politics, in two senses. First, it is about politics as the art of individuals and organizations getting people to do things they did not think they wanted to do, about how the entry of different people into political debate changed the frameworks in which politics took place. It focuses on a moment of acute uncertainty after World War II, when the future of colonial empire was in question and a small group of African elected deputies pried open the cracks in the imperial edifice of France. They claimed for their constituents—who had been relegated to the diminished position of French subject—the status and the rights of French citizens. In the ensuing years, Africans used citizenship in order to claim political, social, and economic equality with other French citizens, and they sought, and sometimes succeeded, to change the institutions through which France governed its empire. Hence this is a book about give-and-take in the political arena. The second sense is conceptual. It is a book about citizenship, nation, empire, state, and sovereignty, but it is not a book about political theory in the formal sense. It is about how these concepts were deployed—and queried and transformed—in the course of political action.

I came to this topic via a particular pathway. After working for over a decade on labor history in British East Africa, I undertook in the 1980s and 1990s a comparative project on the labor question and decolonization in British and French Africa. As I looked into sources in France and Senegal, I was struck by how much the rhetoric that trade unionists deployed to make claims invoked the concept of citizenship, a concept much more salient in French than British Africa. Some time later, around 2000, I decided that a comprehensive focus on citizenship in France and French Africa would allow me to explore the tensions intrinsic to political life in heterogeneous and unequal political structures: between claims to material resources and demands for social and cultural recognition, between working within existing networks and institutions and seeking new forms of political order, between insistence on equality and demands for autonomy. I began to examine how Africans tried to make use of citizenship, as individuals and as members of collectivities. My project on citizenship became a study of political rhetoric and political action in France and French Africa.

This is a study of political elites, of French and African political actors confronting each other and trying to mobilize followers in a context where workers, peasants, and students, men and women, were voting in ever larger numbers, writing for African newspapers, and holding meetings and demonstrations in which the nature of political power was being contested. Coming from a study of African workers who were claiming the wages and benefits enjoyed by French workers, I was not caught up in the common narrative that presumes that what colonial people most wanted was necessarily their own nation-state. Most political activists, it turned out, were determined critics of colonial rule, but open to a range of alternatives, including forms of federal or confederal institutions that balanced, or so they hoped, desires for autonomy and cultural expression with an interest in participating in a wider ensemble that in some sense remained French. And the governing elites of France were so anxious to preserve a political entity larger than metropolitan France that they became caught up in debate with African leaders over what institutional forms such a composite polity could take. This is a story that has largely been written out of both French and African history.

This book describes only some of many forms of politics. There are other perspectives that deserve the attention of scholars—in a variety of languages and idioms, in different kinds of spaces. The focus here is on a space that was mutually intelligible to French and Africa political elites, who were pushing and pulling against each other.

Because political discourse is central to the theme and arguments of this book, I have tried to give a flavor of the give-and-take of debates. The debates were so extensive and intense that I have had to be selective, and this text contains a small fraction of the arguments presented in the legislative debates, newspapers, books, surveillance reports, official correspondence and reports, and other sources I have consulted and an even smaller fraction of the material that exists. The reader will observe a focus on figures whom I consider to be the most influential in framing big issues. Others might put the emphasis elsewhere, and there is no question that widening the scope will produce a richer and more nuanced picture. Because one can take for granted neither continuity nor change in any actor's way of thinking and arguing, I have brought out certain arguments that recur consistently as well as those that shift, incrementally or sharply.

Readers might also observe a certain Senegalocentrism in this account, although the rest of French West Africa, especially Sudan and Côte d'Ivoire, figure prominently in it. That bias reflects not only the inevitable compromises that researchers make in studying large and differentiated spaces—and the unevenness in the quality of research materials available—but a historical process. It was an older model of citizenship, developed in the Quatre Communes of Senegal, that became the basis for the citizenship provisions affecting all of overseas France after 1946, and the Senegalese deputies to the assembly that wrote the postwar constitution played important roles in writing those articles. In exploring the politics of citizenship from the Constitution of 1946 onward, I have looked at the range of forms it took in different parts of French West Africa, but with particular attention to the examples of Senegal and the Mali Federation. Some personages from French Equatorial Africa also figure in my discussion of the debates over the future of overseas France, but I leave to others the analysis of political action and discourse within that region. I hope this book will help other scholars pose questions about the complex politics of French Africa, and further study will no doubt greatly enrich—and perhaps contradict—the story told here.

The research for this book took place over more than a decade, mainly in France and Senegal. Along the way, I accumulated numerous debts. The first is to archivists in both countries: the Archives Nationales Françaises (Paris), Archives d'Outre-mer (Aix-en-Provence), the Archives Diplomatiques, formerly at the Quai d'Orsay, now at La Courneuve, the Archives Diplomatiques de Nantes, the Centre d'Archives Contemporaines (Fontainebleau, but now integrated into the archival center at Pierrefitte), the Fondation Nationale des Sciences Politiques (Paris), the Archives du Sénégal (Dakar), and the Service Régional des Archives–Dakar. The richness of the archival collection of the Archives du Sénégal has been particularly important to this study. I made extensive use of the Bibliothèque Nationale de France and also worked in Bobst Library of NYU, the New York Public Library, the library of IFAN in Dakar, and the library of the Hoover Institution at Stanford.

Most of my trips to archives were supported by research funds from NYU. Writing over several years was facilitated by fellowships—and the highly supportive staffs—from the Remarque Institute of NYU, l'Institut d'Études Avancées de Nantes, and the Wissenschaftskolleg zu Berlin, as well as by a grant from the American Council of Learned Societies. The congenial working environment and the interaction with other fellows and staff members at these institutes have been stimulating and have made the experience of writing this book much more rewarding than a relationship between author and computer. To Alain Supiot and Luca Giuliani, a special word of thanks.

Since this project has been in gestation for a long time, I have had the chance to air basic arguments as well as more specific parts of the text at conferences and lectures too numerous to list. As a convert, over some decades, from a student of economic and social history in British East Africa to a student of political history in France and French West

Africa, I have benefitted enormously from colleagues in France and those who study the French Empire, who have included me in conferences, invited me to give presentations, and talked to me about their work and mine. A nonexhaustive list, in no particular order, includes François Weil, Emmanuelle Saada, Emmanuelle Sibeud, Jean-Claude Penrad, Camille Lefebvre, Séverine Awenengo Dalberto, Didier Fassin, Eric Fassin, Jacques Revel, Cécile Vidal, José Kagabo, Alessandro Stanziani, Jean-Frédéric Schaub, Romain Bertrand, Jean-François Bayart, Achille Mbembe, Laura Downs, Florence Bernault, Isabelle Merle, Benoît de l'Estoile, Laure Blévis, Noureddine Amara, Marie-Noëlle Bourguet, Jean-François Klein, Pierre Singaravélou, Helène Blais, Yerri Urban, Jane Guyer, Todd Shepard, Gregory Mann, Alice Conklin, Gary Wilder, Odile Goerg, Robert Aldrich, Saliha Belmessous, Charles Tshimanga, Didier Gondola, Mary Lewis, and Catherine Coquery-Vidrovitch. The École des Hautes Études en Sciences Sociales has played a particularly important role in my integration into French scholarly life.

Friends and colleagues have kept me looking beyond Paris and Dakar. My long-standing interest in labor history has remained active thanks to my association with the Re:Work research unit based at Humboldt University in Berlin. Its director, Andreas Eckert, the fellows of Re:Work, and the PhD students at the Re:Work conferences and "summer academies" have kept me on my toes. Numerous conferences on empires, at the Institut des Hautes Études Internationales (Geneva), Humboldt University, Oxford University, Trinity College Dublin, Duke University, the Autonomous University in Madrid, the School of Social Sciences in Lisbon, New York University, Columbia University, Harvard University, Birkbeck University, Université de Paris 8, the University of Massachusetts, Yale University, UCLA, and other institutions have widened my perspective, as have conferences on decolonization at the Netherlands Institute for War Documentation, the University of Cologne, the University of Texas, the École des Hautes Études en Sciences Sociales, and the Institute of Social Sciences in Lisbon, plus a conference on sovereignty at the University of Wisconsin–Milwaukee and one on civil registration at Cambridge University. My students at NYU have made sure that I keep rethinking African history, and several of their dissertation projects— especially those of Michelle Pinto, Elisabeth Fink, Muriam Davis, Rachel Kantrowitz, and Jessica Pearson-Patel, as well as that of Brandon County of Columbia University—are illuminating different aspects of the recent history of French Africa that are discussed in this book. I also had the pleasure of participating in the defenses of two theses on citizenship questions in New Caledonia and Côte d'Ivoire, by Benoît Trépied (École des Hautes Études en Sciences Sociales) and Henri-Michel Yéré (University of Basel).

My biggest debt is to Mamadou Diouf. We first met in Dakar in 1986, and he has mentored me in the study of Senegalese history ever since. We have been colleagues at the University of Michigan and neighbors in New York. I timed my research trips to Dakar so that I could be there with Mamadou, and we have worked side by side in the archives. Mamadou's research on citizenship in the Quatre Communes before 1940 complements my own, and conversations with him have helped shape the questions I ask in this book. I have also enjoyed visiting his family compound in Rufisque and meeting Senegalese intellectuals through Mamadou. I have also over the years benefitted from the company and insights of Ibrahima Thioub, Omar Guèye, Babacar Fall, and Mohamed Mbodj in Dakar, Ann Arbor, Nantes, and elsewhere.

Earlier versions of this manuscript have been revised with help from thoughtful readings by Emmanuelle Saada, Mamadou Diouf, Alice Conklin, and Eric Jennings. Greg Mann deserves a special word of thanks for sharing with me some of his many insights into the politics of Mali and the draft of his forthcoming book. Jessica Pearson-Patel did an extremely thorough job of checking the citations and footnotes in the manuscript against my archival notes, digital images, photocopies, and other sources. I greatly appreciate the encouragement and good advice that Brigitta van Rheinberg of Princeton University Press has given me.

These words—and the final revisions on the manuscript—are being written in Sapporo, Japan. Following Jane Burbank halfway around the world, as she took up her fellowship at the Slavic Research Center of Hokkaido University, has brought me another of many experiences we have shared, as we worked on our own research and writing as well as on projects we have done together. She has given me close and valuable critiques of portions of this manuscript and, with insights coming from her own research on Eurasia, has pushed me to keep in mind that the range of political possibilities that exist in the world is wider than that coming from scholarship that focuses on Western Europe and its overseas colonies in the nineteenth and twentieth centuries. Jane's colleagues at the Slavic Research Center here have been welcoming and generous to a visiting Africanist. I am also grateful to Yoko Nagahara and her colleagues who brought me to a stimulating seminar among Japanese Africanists at Tokyo University. Living in a country that has resisted the imperialism of the English language and places a writer in the situation of living as an illiterate is perhaps a fitting way to bring the journey that this book has entailed to a close.

Frederick Cooper
Sapporo, August 2013

NOTES ON LANGUAGE AND ABBREVIATIONS

I have translated most words from the French, except where a nuance of meaning or tone makes it imperative to use the original. Some words are untranslatable (except by a long phrase explaining them). One is "ressortissant," meaning a person under the jurisdiction of a state. It means more than "inhabitant" and less than "citizen." Another is "état-civil," referring to a system of registering by the state of the main life events of individuals—birth, marriage, filiation, divorce, death. Whether the system applied to "ressortissants" or "citizens" overseas was in question. The term "Renseignements," as used in the notes, refers to the reports of security services, usually based on informants. I use the word "African" to refer to people living in territories south of the Sahara, except where more precision is required. The regional distinctions of "North," "West," and "Equatorial" Africa do not bear much analytical weight, but they do reflect common terms of discourse.

In the text, I have translated the most commonly used designations of French officials (e.g., Minister, Governor General, Governor) but have not translated titles that have rather particular meanings. If the word "Minister" is used without further specification, it refers to the Minister of Overseas France (Ministre de la France d'Outre-Mer). The title High Commissioner (of AOF or AEF) was used interchangeably with Governor General until 1956, when the title of Governor General was dropped. I usually use the untranslated designation Conseil de gouvernement—referring to a council exercising executive functions and responsible to a legislature—and while it usually can be translated as Council of Ministers, it was used in discussions of government in African territories before the title of Minister was conferred in 1957.

In the footnotes, I more often use untranslated titles for officials to make it clearer to the reader who might want to pursue an archival source exactly what the reference is, but I have used English for the most obvious official titles that are also used in the text. Where English and French names of institutions are nearly identical, I use them interchangeably in the text, but otherwise use institutional names in the original.

In the text and notes, I use these French acronyms:

AEF   Afrique Équatoriale Française
ANC   Assemblée Nationale Constituante

AOF	Afrique Occidentale Française
BDS	Bloc Démocratique Sénégalais
CGT	Confédération Générale du Travail
CGTA	Confédération Générale du Travail–Autonome
IOM	Indépendants d'Outre-mer
MFDC	Mouvement des Forces Démocratiques de Casamance
MRP	Mouvement Républicain Populaire
PAI	Parti Africain de l'Indépendance
PCF	Parti Communiste Français
PDCI	Parti Démocratique de la Côte d'Ivoire
PDG	Parti Démocratique de Guinée
PFA	Parti de la Fédération Africaine
PRA	Parti de Regroupement Africain
RDA	Rassemblement Démocratique Africain
UGTAN	Union Générale des Travailleurs de l'Afrique Noire

Abbreviations used in notes:

ADLC	Archives Diplomatiques, La Courneuve
ADN	Archives Diplomatiques, Nantes
ANF	Archives Nationales de France, Paris
AOM	Archives d'Outre-Mer, Aix-en-Provence
AS	Archives du Sénégal, Dakar
AUF	Assemblée de l'Union française
CAC	Centre d'Archives Contemporaines, Fontainebleau
FOM	France d'Outre-Mer
FPR	Papers of Jacques Foccart, Private, Archives Nationales de France
FPU	Papers of Jacques Foccart, Public, Archives Nationales de France
GM	Papers of Gaston Monnerville, Fondation Nationale des Sciences Politiques, Paris
IGT	Inspection Générale du Travail, Archives d'Outre-mer
MD	Papers of Michel Debré, Fondation Nationale des Sciences Politiques, Paris
SRAD	Service Régional des Archives–Dakar

Citizenship
between
Empire
and Nation

the colonies of French West Africa, eight small states with populations ranging from half a million to four million, were doomed to poverty and subordination if they tried to survive as independent nation-states. French West African political leaders sought instead to transform colonial empire into another sort of assemblage of diverse territories and peoples: a federation of African states with each other and with France.

Charles de Gaulle's very name evokes the idea of a strong French state. Yet in 1946 and 1947 he was saying that such a state could not be unitary. It would have to acknowledge the diversity of the territories that constituted it. In calling for a federal state, he did not need to tell his listeners that fewer than half of the 110 million French people he referred to lived in European France.

De Gaulle's federalism was not the same as Dia's. It put more emphasis on the federating state—France—than on the federated states. Neither federalism was classic, for neither posited a fully equal relationship among the federated components. Dia was more interested than de Gaulle in setting a political process in motion—as a movement *toward* the equality of African and European components of the federation. De Gaulle was above all interested in the federation remaining French, even if he recognized that not everyone would be French in the same way.

Why were such views *imaginable* in the 1940s and 1950s, 150 years after the creation of the French Republic as the incarnation of the French nation, at a time when Africans and Asians were seemingly striving for the kind of state Europeans supposedly had? If the basic narrative of transition from empire to nation-state is right, de Gaulle should have been defending a resolutely French France, with colonies as wholly subordinate entities, and Dia should have been claiming national independence.[2] Yet most political activists in French West Africa—from the radical Sékou Touré to the conservative Félix Houphouët-Boigny—sought some variant on the federal theme. Our expectations of what their history should have been are a backward projection of an idealized post-1960 world of sovereign nation-states.[3]

---

[2]Great Britain and the Netherlands were also considering different forms of federation as a response to the crisis of empire at the end of World War II, both to make regional development more manageable and to give a new legitimacy to an imperial polity. Michael Collins, "Decolonisation and the 'Federal Moment,'" *Diplomacy and Statecraft* 24 (2013): 21–40; Jennifer Foray, "A Unified Empire of Equal Parts: The Dutch Commonwealth Schemes of the 1920s–40s," *Journal of Imperial and Commonwealth History* 41 (2013): 259–84.

[3]John Kelly and Martha Kaplan also see the nation-state as a concept that became salient only after World War II, projected backward to fit a narrative that portrays it as natural and modern. "Nation and Decolonization: Toward a New Anthropology of Nationalism," *Anthropological Theory* 1 (2001): 419–37.

We can easily miss the kinds of approaches that political actors were pursuing. We know some turned into dead ends; the people involved did not. This book tells the story of how it happened that in 1960 the political actors of France and French West Africa ended up with a form of political organization that neither had wanted during most of the previous fifteen years.

In France, the colonial past was for some decades marginalized from even the best historical scholarship. By the 1990s, it was reappearing in some fine research, mostly by younger scholars making use of new archival sources.[4] More polemical works were also taking their place in public discourse, turning upside down French self-representations as the people of the rights of man. In such a perspective, colonial exploitation and oppression were not mere sidelights to French history, but an intrinsic part of French republicanism, its evil twin.[5] The critique of France's colonial past brought out anxieties among French intellectuals: about a French population divided between the descendants of "colonizers" and "colonized," about a society made up of multiple ethnic communities.

These debates have raised serious issues and include thoughtful works, but they have become so focused on defending or attacking the concept of "the colonial" or "the postcolonial" that they have moved away from the lived experiences the concept was supposed to elucidate.[6] The best way, to my mind, to move beyond this state of play is to get directly to the point: not the arguments of 2014 but those of 1945 to 1960; not what we now think people should have said in a colonial situation, but what they actually said, wrote, and did; not the supposedly immanent logics of preidentified types of political regimes, but the give-and-take of political actors in a time of profound uncertainty,

[4] See for example Raphaëlle Branche, *La torture et l'armée pendant la guerre d'Algérie 1954–1962* (Paris: Gallimard, 2001) or articles collected in the special dossier "Sujets d'empire," *Genèses* 53 (2003/4). Some of the best analyses of colonialism focused on the erasure of the subject from historical memory. See for example Benjamin Stora, *La gangrène et l'oubli: La mémoire de la guerre d'Algérie* (Paris: La Découverte, 1998).

[5] Examples include Pascal Blanchard, Nicolas Bancel, and Sandrine Lemaire, *La fracture coloniale: la société française au prisme de l'héritage colonial* (Paris: La Découverte, 2005), and Olivier Le Cour Grandmaison, *La République impériale: politique et racisme d'État* (Paris: Fayard, 2009).

[6] This tendency toward abstraction can be found in the contributions to the debate over France and postcolonialism in *Public Culture* 23, 1 (2011). For a French scholar's attack on postcolonial studies, see Jean-François Bayart, *Les études postcoloniales. Un carnaval académique* (Paris: Karthala, 2010). Useful discussions include Marie-Claude Smouts, ed., *La situation postcoloniale: Les Postcolonial Studies dans le débat français* (Paris: Les Presses de Sciences Po, 2007), and Romain Bertrand, *Mémoires d'empire: La controverse autour du "fait colonial"* (Paris: Éd. du Croquant, 2006). On the connections between colonialism and "immigration" today, see Charles Tshimanga, Didier Gondola, and Peter J. Bloom, eds., *Frenchness and the African Diaspora: Identity and Uprising in Contemporary France* (Bloomington: Indiana University Press, 2009).

the words and actions of people who were trying to figure out what they wanted and what they might possibly obtain.

What lies between the "colonial" and the "post"? Not an event, not a moment, but a process. For some fifteen years, people struggled—and sometimes fought—over alternative visions of how to transform the French colonial empire, to make it more durable, to make it more democratic and progressive, or to bring it to an end. Positions changed during this time of interaction and conflict. To see this period in the history of sub-Saharan Africa as the confrontation of an obdurate French colonialism against a resolute African nationalism would be to focus on the positions that were the *least* defended at the time. Even in Algeria, what the French government was defending with extreme brutality was—in the minds of much of the top leadership—France's control of the process of modernizing Algerian society.

This book explores concepts that have abstract meanings—citizenship, nationality, sovereignty. But I examine their specific—ambiguous and changing—meanings given them by actors at the time, and I emphasize the stakes people had in them: whether or not an African would be able to claim as a citizen a right to enter and seek work in European France, whether an African postal worker in Bamako could demand the same rights to sick leave and union representation as a worker from Toulouse, how a politician could assert a claim to state resources and use them to mobilize supporters.

Citizenship, in most contemporary formulations, is a relationship between a state and individuals. Two of its features make it a particularly volatile framework. First, it defines inclusion—in a formal sense of membership in a polity and a more subjective sense of belonging—and therefore it also defines exclusion. Second, citizenship melds a person's rights and his or her obligations to a state, so that a state that wishes to enforce obligations—military service, tax payments, obedience to laws—faces the fact that the same set of expectations and rhetorics on which its power is based also underscore the claims of individuals to certain rights. Such a conception leaves open fundamental questions: On what basis are the boundaries of inclusion and exclusion determined—and what sort of state includes or excludes certain categories of people from the status of citizen? What rights and obligations are associated with citizenship, and what combinations of state authority, judicial institutions, and actions by citizens—be they in the street or the voting booth—shape what those rights will be?

Citizenship is the object of a contemporary critique of liberal or republican governance—not least its entwinement with a history of colonial conquest and repression and of national liberation. If citizenship marks a liberation from forms of monarchical and autocratic government, if a rights-bearing citizen chooses his or her leaders, does the very act of individualistic participation separate people from their particular social connections and their particular histories, producing anonymous individuals linked to the anonymous state?[7] Does liberation from monarchs, oligarchs, aristocrats, and colonialists also separate politics from community?

If at an abstract level citizenship seems like a relationship of individual and state, in practice citizens act as members of communities and participants in networks, and the men and women whose actions constitute "the state" mobilize and organize their followers in the context of such relations. The notion of "belonging" that is intrinsic to citizenship might crystallize around collectivities that are both smaller—based on ethnic affinity—or larger—notably the possibility of citizenship in an imperial or multinational political entity that is the principal subject of this book.[8]

There is a specifically French dimension to such debates: French constitutions going back to the late eighteenth century proclaim the Republic to be "one and indivisible." Interpreting such a pronouncement is no easy task. Some argue that the Republic cannot recognize any distinction among citizens without threatening the fundamental principle of equality. One version of this argument is a radical defense of the equivalence of all citizens; another is a critique of citizens who seem to willfully refuse to integrate themselves into French society. Communitarianism appears in the latter argument as the current enemy of republicanism. Muslim "immigrants" are the principal target of such contentions.

Whatever the merits and shortcomings of these present-day arguments, the conceptual framework for both the egalitarian and the exclusionary versions presumes a singularity of republican thought that flattens French history. In the quite recent times that are the focus of this book, people actively debated the relationship of equality and diversity. The Constitution of 1946 referred to the "peoples and nations" of the French Union—in the plural—and, after much argument in which African deputies played an active role, it recognized that overseas citizens, within the Republic, could be citizens in different ways. They could vote in elections and have equal rights to education and to positions in the civil service, but unlike the citizens of European

[7] Long before the postcolonial and poststructural critiques of modern governmentality, Reinhard Bendix noted that citizenship "involves at many levels an institutionalization of abstract criteria of equality which give rise both to new inequalities and new measures to deal with these ancillary consequences." *Nation-building and Citizenship: Studies of Our Changing Social Order* (Berkeley: University of California Press, 1977 [1964]), 126. Recent scholarship on citizenship—and its increasing sensitivity to variety and complexity in studying different parts of the world—can be traced through the journal *Citizenship Studies*.

[8] Useful here is the notion of "meaningful citizenship" focused on the uneasy overlap of ethnic and national affinities in Lahra Smith, *Making Citizens in Africa: Ethnicity, Gender and National Identity in Ethiopia* (Cambridge: Cambridge University Press, 2013).

France, their civil affairs—marriage, inheritance, filiation—did not have to come under the French civil code.

To say that a person could be French in one or in many ways is to make an argument.[9] I am less interested in attempting to pinpoint, attack, or defend an essence of republican citizenship than to understand how such concepts were changed as they were deployed and contested in a specific historical context. One of the great debates of the postwar years among politicians and intellectuals in European and African France was how to reconcile a universalistic, egalitarian conception of citizenship with the particularity of African culture or cultures. This fundamental problem underlay controversies over numerous issues facing the French state: how to write a constitution for a France with metropolitan and overseas components, how to organize political participation and allocate legislative authority between metropolitan and overseas institutions, how to regulate labor or education within a varied and unequal political entity, and how to record the life-course events of citizens who had different conceptions of marriage, family, and inheritance.

In 1945, the demand for an inclusive citizenship in empire was revolutionary. The overwhelming majority of Africans—like Algerians—were then considered French nationals and French subjects but not French citizens. They could become French citizens only if they gave up their personal status under Islamic or "customary" law, accepted the rules of the French civil code over marriage and inheritance, and convinced administrators that they had fully accepted French social norms. Few chose to do so; fewer still were accepted.

But there was a notable exception. In the Quatre Communes (Four Towns) of Senegal the original inhabitants—*les originaires*—had since 1848 at least some of the rights of the citizen, including the right to vote, while keeping their personal and family affairs under the jurisdiction of Islamic courts. This situation was referred to as "citoyenneté dans le statut," a citizenship that recognized the particular personal status of the *originaire*. In these colonial enclaves, dating to the seventeenth century, French and local merchants forged ties to each other, often founding mixed families, and they gave shape to a culture of close interaction within a small world connected by sea to France and the Americas and by land and rivers to a large continent that lay beyond European knowledge and control. For French administrators, ensuring cooperation within the Quatre Communes was more important than defending the boundaries of Frenchness, and flexible

---

[9]As Niraja Gopal Jayal emphasizes in another context, "Every single dimension of citizenship is contested in contemporary India. . . . There are countless ways of being a citizen." *Citizenship and Its Discontents: An Indian History* (Cambridge, Mass.: Harvard University Press, 2013), 2, 6.

citizenship provisions made sense. Some French officials considered that the *originaires* were "électeurs" (voters), not "citoyens," with only some of the rights of the citizen. At last, in 1916, the French legislature made it explicit that they *were* citizens. For *originaires*, *citoyenneté dans le statut* made sense in a different way: as a means to defend a specific way of life. The established families spoke both French and Wolof; many were literate. Their status as rights-bearing individuals in French law was a bulwark in defense of a community that was not culturally French.[10]

By the time their citizenship status was secured, the people of the Quatre Communes had become a tiny minority in a large empire, as France conquered more and more of Western and Equatorial Africa. The large majority of conquered people were incorporated into a French imperial polity as subjects. For them—like most of the indigenous inhabitants of Algeria and other parts of the French Empire—the consequences of denial of citizenship were severe: lack of political rights, a separate system of justice known as the *indigénat* that placed arbitrary power in the hands of a local administrator, routine use—overt or masked—of forced labor. Throughout the history of the French Third Republic (1871–1940), some legislators repeatedly argued that a distinction between a citizen and a subject violated republican principles dating to the Revolution. But the distinction was already ingrained in both law and practice before the Third Republic was installed; governing different people differently was what imperial systems did. This book focuses on the last years of what had been an argument over the reach of citizenship—whether national or imperial—that had been going on for a long time, indeed since the French Revolution.

World War II created an opening in French politics that Africans were able to pry wider. France's defeat at the hands of Germany in 1940, the installation of a collaborationist regime in France itself, its loss of effective control over Indochina to the Japanese, and the destruction of the war left French politicians with the task of reinventing their country. One part of the empire had refused to participate in the collaborationist regime—French Equatorial Africa. It was no coincidence that that man who became its Governor General, Félix Éboué, was one of few men of color—he was from Guyana—to achieve high rank in the colonial service. His adherence to the government in

---

[10] Mamadou Diouf, "The French Colonial Policy of Assimilation and the Civility of the Originaires of the Four Communes (Senegal): A Nineteenth Century Globalization Project," *Development and Change* 29 (1998): 671–96; Hilary Jones, *The Métis of Senegal: Urban Life and Politics in French West Africa* (Bloomington: Indiana University Press, 2013). The other exceptional citizenship regime was also an enclave colony—the French establishments in India. See Damien Deschamps, "Une citoyenneté différée: sens civique et assimilation des indigènes dans les Établissements français de l'Inde," *Revue Française de Science Politique* 47 (1997): 49–69.

exile of Charles de Gaulle provided a symbolic rallying point: France's honor was saved by its empire. Troops from North and sub-Saharan Africa contributed greatly to the reconquest of southern France from the Nazis.[11] As an Allied victory appeared within sight in 1944, the leadership of the Free French knew that they had to inaugurate a new—Fourth—Republic. Writing a constitution meant that the entire organization of the state was up for debate in a situation where the alignment of political forces was uncertain. There, defenders of the old order and advocates of reform—incremental or revolutionary—would collide.

The following pages trace the struggle of African political leaders to turn empire into something else, above all to turn a system of invidious distinction into a polity that was inclusive, diverse, and egalitarian. Remarkably, it was the Senegalese system of citizenship that through heated arguments became the basis of French constitutional law. The citizens of 1946, as they became known, obtained the "quality"—and the rights—of the citizens of 1789, but they did not have to abandon the legal marker of their social and cultural distinctiveness, their personal status.

In 1946, France's African subjects acquired the right to have rights, the right to make claims.[12] African leaders whose activism was critical to the process became icons of liberation. The extension of citizenship overseas became known as "the Lamine Guèye law," the act abolishing forced labor as "the Houphouët-Boigny law." But to what extent could a young generation of African leaders turn citizenship into an effective basis for making wider claims?

The argument was not just over an individual's relationship to a French state that was trying to portray itself as no longer "colonial." It was over what kind of community Africans could participate in. Leading African activists argued that each territorial unit within France should be able to express its "personality." They soon began to insist that territories should become internally self-governing, but still belong to a larger, more inclusive unit that would remain French. Empire would become federation or confederation, and the once-dominated colonies—Senegal, Dahomey, Niger—would become equal partners with European France.

Their arguments ran into practical and subjective objections from metropolitan elites who took their superior mastery of the arts of governance for granted. But these arguments could not easily be dismissed if France wanted to hold together some form of "grand en-

[11] Eric Jennings's forthcoming book on Equatorial Africa and the Free French will shed new light on this episode.

[12] The phrase "right to have rights" originates with Hannah Arendt, who was thinking about stateless people more than the colonized. *Origins of Totalitarianism* (New York: Harcourt Brace Jovanovich, 1951), 177. On the right to make claims, see below.

semble" at a time when the naturalness and justice of colonial rule was being questioned around the world. Would citizenship push Africans into a homogenizing Frenchness, or could it provide them with political tools to make good their claims to a status that was equal but different? And if Africans were to participate in a politics of citizenship, would they do so through the territorial entities—Senegal, Dahomey, and so on—that French colonization had created or as members of a larger collectivity representing what Léopold Sédar Senghor referred to as "Negro-African civilization"? These questions were debated continuously from 1945 to 1960—and beyond.

The citizenship that French West Africans were claiming in the postwar years was not that of a nation-state, but an imperial citizenship—in a composite political entity, built by conquest, governed in a way that had subordinated and denigrated its subjects, but which was, activists asserted, to be transformed into a structure that would ensure the rights and cultural integrity of all citizens.[13] Such a conception both assumed the history of colonization and transcended it.

African politicians were in part thinking in practical terms, that the territories of French Africa were too small (unlike India or Algeria) and too poor to survive as nation-states—one people, one territory, one government. But they also had a deeper conviction of how politics was evolving in their time. They saw themselves as part of an interdependent world. Reformed empire offered Africans the chance to associate not just with a rich country but also with each other. They saw the heritage of France as valuable too, especially the tradition of the rights of man and of the citizen. If African peoples were to find their way in the postwar world, these activists insisted, they needed to develop and synthesize the best of the traditions that France and Africa had to offer.

The imaginations of political actors in French West Africa were far from imprisoned in a "derivative discourse" or a "modular nationalism" stemming from the world's prior history of nation making.[14] The

[13] What Sukanya Banerjee writes about British India at the end of the nineteenth century applies to French Africa in mid-twentieth century as well: "it was the empire, rather than a preexisting prototype of nation, that generated a consciousness of the formal equality of citizenship." *Becoming Imperial Citizens: Indians in the Late-Victorian Empire* (Durham, N.C.: Duke University Press, 2010), 17. See also Jayal, *Citizenship and Its Discontents*, and Daniel Gorman, *Imperial Citizenship: Empire and the Question of Belonging* (Manchester: Manchester University Press, 2006).

[14] My argument differs from that of Benedict Anderson. I see "imagined communities" in the twentieth century taking on a variety of forms—including ideas of imperial or postimperial communities and that of multinational states—rather than a single modular form originating in the late eighteenth and early nineteenth centuries. In distinction to Partha Chatterjee's early critique of nationalism as a discourse derived from European sources and his later attempt to locate a specifically non-European (in his case Indian) path to the nation, I stress the original, nuanced, and interactive nature

possibilities debated between 1945 and 1960 were varied. We need to understand what those possibilities were, what different people felt each had to offer, and why, late in this period, those possibilities were narrowed. If we think from the start that we know what citizenship is and where it is located, we might not even look into such issues.

And if we begin with a premise that sovereignty means a division of the world into distinct and equivalent political entities, we will miss the ambiguities and conflicting conceptions that surrounded the concept in the mid-twentieth century. As James Sheehan points out, "As a doctrine, sovereignty is usually regarded as unified and inseparable; as an activity, however, it is plural and divisible."[15] It was this divisibility of sovereignty that gave both African and French leaders the possibility of dismantling colonial empire without having to choose between French colonialism and national independence, between assimilation and separation.

In positing federalism as a route out of empire, African and French leaders were trying to invent new political forms that would preserve some kind of assemblage while giving a degree of autonomy to the former colonial territories. How much autonomy and how the assemblage could be governed were in question.[16] In two efforts at constitution writing, in 1946 and 1958, political leaders could not agree on what—if any—form of federalism was acceptable in both African and European France. They came up with words—first "French Union,"

---

of the arguments of African intellectuals and politicians. Benedict Anderson, *Imagined Communities: Reflections on the Origin and Spread of Nationalism* (London: Verso, 1983); Partha Chatterjee, *Nationalist Thought and the Colonial World: A Derivative Discourse?* (London: Zed, 1986); Chatterjee, *The Nation and Its Fragments: Colonial and Postcolonial Histories* (Princeton: Princeton University Press, 1993). For a critique of Anderson emphasizing the multiple forms of anticolonial politics, see Manu Goswami, "Rethinking the Modular Nation Form: Toward a Sociohistorical Conception of Nationalism," *Comparative Studies in Society and History* 44 (2002): 770–99.

[15] James J. Sheehan, "The Problem of Sovereignty in European History," *American Historical Review* 111 (2006): 2. Sheehan (3–4) conceptualizes sovereignty as a "basket" of different rights, powers, and aspirations, all components of which are subject to claims and counterclaims. As John Agnew notes, there is nothing new about such conceptions: sovereignty has long been a varied notion with an ambiguous relationship to territory. *Globalization and Sovereignty* (Lanham, Md.: Rowman & Littlefield, 2009), 98–99. For studies of sovereignty that look beyond Europe, see Douglas Howland and Luise White, eds., *The State of Sovereignty: Territories, Laws, Populations* (Bloomington: Indiana University Press, 2009), and Lauren Benton, *A Search for Sovereignty: Law and Geography in European Empires 1400–1900* (Cambridge: Cambridge University Press, 2010).

[16] The entry on "federalism" in the 1937 edition of the *Encyclopedia of the Social Sciences* [ed. Edwin R. A. Seligman and Alvin Johnson (New York: Macmillan, 1937) 5: 169–72] terms it "a tendency to substitute coordinating for subordinating relationships." The author of this entry, Max Hildebert Boehm, thought that, in practice, federalism in international politics offered only a "vague outline," but it was this outline that Senghor and others were trying to fill in a decade and a world war later.

then "French Community"—to signify overlapping goals while allowing arguments over their institutional manifestation to continue. The uncertainty was intrinsic to what political theorists have pointed to as the ambiguity of the federalism concept itself.

What forms of political organization can reconcile autonomy and association? Since at least Samuel von Pufendorf in the seventeenth century political theorists have tried to answer such a question, and it was at the heart of debates over how to unite the former colonies that became the United States of America. Some have pointed to two possibilities: federation, in which only the federal unit is recognized internationally and in which the division of powers between federal and federated units is regulated by constitutional law, and confederation, in which the relationship among the units is governed by treaty and each retains a sense of national identification and international recognition. Among the political actors who worked with this distinction was Léopold Sédar Senghor of Senegal. Long concerned with reconciling equality and difference within an inclusive political system, he by the mid-1950s refined his argument into a plan for a three-level political structure: individual African territories (Senegal, Côte d'Ivoire, etc.) with local autonomy, a federation embracing all the French West African territories (or perhaps a wider federation among Africans) with legislative and executive authority, and a French confederation, in which the West African federation, European France, and whatever other units chose to join would participate as free and equal member states. The middle tier, the "primary" or "African" federation, was for Senghor intended to both express and develop national sentiment among Africans and give Africans a stronger position in relation to European France. Not all African statesmen agreed. Félix Houphouët-Boigny of the Côte d'Ivoire opposed the middle layer. He wanted each African territory, individually, to join metropolitan France in a federation of equals. The dispute between Senghor and Houphouët-Boigny became known in the late 1950s as the battle of federation and confederation.

Both federation and confederation assume in principle the equivalence of their component parts. But that was not the situation that Senghor and other African leaders faced. Not only had France been a colonial power, but it was rich and large, with a well-educated population. And it had the great advantage of actually existing as an internationally recognized state. African states had to be created. The reality of whatever kind of ensemble France and its former colonies created was their inequality in resources and standard of living. Senghor referred to the need for both "horizontal solidarity"—of Africans with each other—and vertical solidarity—of Africans with France. And France was no disinterested, benevolent partner; its elites had their interests, prejudices, and anxieties.

Theorists have been telling us that the distinction between federation and confederation is artificial. If sovereignty is relational, the issue is not whether federated states do or do not have it, but just what the relationship among them is. The point is to recognize that the larger unit should be both "a people" and a plurality of peoples, that rights—including that of maintaining distinct cultural practices—need protection at different levels, that institutions need to balance common and local interests, that sovereignty is itself a bundle that can be allocated and shared in different ways.[17] Both the quarrel of federation and confederation and the euphemisms of Union and Community reflect the importance and the difficulty of imagining and turning into reality a complex political structure emerging out of a history of colonization and the quest for liberation. Senghor, de Gaulle, Dia, and Houphouët-Boigny were not theorists, but they were working with the intellectual and political tools they had—and with their quite different notions of what a Franco-African community should mean and whose interests it should serve.

In the first years after World War II, the question of African federation took a back seat to the immediate aim of virtually all African political actors: to obtain the rights of the citizen. Imperial citizenship was neither an oxymoron nor an unequivocal benefit to those who acquired it. For Africans, citizenship implied a claim on vitally needed resources, but what made the claim powerful was also what made attitudes toward it ambivalent—it was *French* citizenship.[18] And leaders in the French government were ambivalent about the basic characteristics of imperial citizenship—the equivalence of all citizens and the differences among them. They both welcomed and feared the consequences of the social and economic dimensions of citizenship: that Africans would become increasingly productive, useful, cooperative members of a French polity and that they would demand equality with their more affluent metropolitan brethren. They saw that France's recognition of the diversity of its citizens represented its best chance for survival as a world power, but could not quite accept that the different civilizations to which they belonged were on a par.

[17] Olivier Beaud, *Théorie de la fédération* (Paris: Presses Universitaires de France, 2009); Jean L. Cohen, "Federation," Political Concepts: A Critical Lexicon, www.political concepts.org/2011/federation; Jean L. Cohen, "Whose Sovereignty? Empire Versus International Law," *Ethics and International Affairs* 18 (2004): 1–24; Radhika Mongia, "Historicizing State Sovereignty: Inequality and the Form of Equivalence," *Comparative Studies in Society and History* 49 (2007): 384–411.

[18] As Sheehan puts it, "A claim is neither a request nor a demand. . . . To make a claim is to appeal to some standard of justice, some sort of right, but it is also to assert a willingness to back up this appeal with some sort of action." "Problem of Sovereignty," 3.

A Very Brief History of Citizenship

That citizenship has had shifting meanings over the sweep of history is not surprising; that its parameters were still uncertain in the mid-twentieth century is not so obvious.[19] Citizenship was associated with the Greek polis and the Roman Republic, with the notion of belonging to a unit of political solidarity, in which the people—or rather those who were adult, male, and free—would be ultimately responsible for governing that unit. When Rome expanded, citizenship was extended selectively—one did not have to be from the original city-state to become Roman. It entailed obligations—military above all—and rights, including that of being tried, if accused of a crime, in a Roman tribunal. Whether citizens could actually govern the empire was very much in question, but Roman emperors did not have to come from Rome. The empire included a diverse body of citizens, but also noncitizens, who had not desired or had not been accepted to a status that had become increasingly desirable as Rome's power grew. Then, in AD 212, the emperor Caracalla declared all free, male inhabitants of the empire's territories to be Roman citizens. Citizenship did not mean cultural conformity or that Rome was the exclusive focus of people's sense of belonging. One could be a Gaul and become a Roman.[20]

Citizenship was not the only form of belonging—it was precisely the specificity of its application that distinguished some Romans from others and distinguished Rome from other polities. It remained an exclusionary concept—excluding women and slaves within the empire and the "barbarians" without, although barbarians could become Romans and citizens.[21] In the centuries after Rome, citizenship was neither a general characteristic of "Western" polities nor a concept with a fixed meaning.[22] In fifteenth- and sixteenth-century Spain, it was associated with cities. In the France of Louis XIV, it referred to the king's assertion of power over people resident in its territory, not to their participation in governmental functions or decision making.[23]

The citizenship of the French Revolution was thus a major break, because it entailed a specific codification of rights, including the right

---

[19] Dominique Colas, *Citoyenneté et nationalité* (Paris: Gallimard, 2004).

[20] Greg Woolf, *Becoming Roman: The Origins of Provincial Civilization in Gaul* (New York: Cambridge University Press, 1998).

[21] Paul Magnette, *Citizenship: The History of an Idea*, trans. Katya Long (Colchester: ECPR Press, 2005).

[22] J. G. A. Pocock, "The Ideal of Citizenship since Classical Times," in Ronald Beiner, ed., *Theorizing Citizenship* (Albany: State University of New York Press, 1995), 29–52.

[23] Tamar Herzog, *Defining Nations: Immigrants and Citizens in Early Modern Spain and Spanish America* (New Haven, Conn.: Yale University Press, 2003); Peter Sahlins, *Unnaturally French: Foreign Citizens in the Old Regime and After* (Ithaca, N.Y.: Cornell University Press, 2004).

to elect representatives to an assembly that would represent the will of the people. A republic of citizens implied equality among them, but just who the citizens were and what dimensions of equality it entailed were not so clear.[24] Almost immediately after the Declaration of the Rights of Man and of the Citizen in 1789 the question of the domain of application of citizenship was posed. At home, the Revolutionary assemblies distinguished between an "active" citizen—who had to be male—and a "passive" citizen, whose person and property were protected by the rights regime but who did not participate in politics. It would take until 1944, when the female half of the population got the vote, for universal citizenship to entail universal suffrage.[25]

To some, the French "nation" was a bounded entity located in Europe. But the boundedness of the revolutionary nation was thrown open by events in the empire. In 1789, the white planters of Saint-Domingue—France's richest colony, the world's greatest producer of sugar, and the home to thousands of slaves, mostly African-born, living and working under miserable conditions—sent representatives to Paris to insist that the rights of the citizen applied to them. Moreover, they should have the right to govern their own colony, since the conditions of a slave society were not familiar to metropolitan legislators. Next came a delegation from the "gens de couleur," property-owning, slave-owning people born in most cases of French fathers and mothers of African descent; they too claimed that they should have the full rights of citizens. The assemblies in Paris could not make up their mind about these demands. Then, in 1791, a slave revolt erupted in Saint-Domingue, and among its complex strands was a demand by slaves for freedom and citizenship. The revolutionary government was threatened by royalist reaction, by the invasion of rival empires (British and Spanish), and by the slave revolt. It was for pragmatic reasons—not just revolutionary rigor—that the Republic decided to grant citizenship rights to free gens de couleur in 1792 and finally, in 1793, to free the slaves and make them citizens. It hoped to create an army of citizens to defend the revolution. The revolution, like most social movements that advance very far, brought together people across social categories in a complex struggle. Not everyone fought for the same goals, but an important part of the leadership sought to make France into a different sort of polity from what it had been, an

---

[24] David Diop, "La question de la citoyenneté dans l'*Encyclopédie* de Diderot et de d'Alembert: de l'irreductibilité de l'individualisme 'naturel' dans la société civile," in Claude Fiévet, ed., *Invention et réinvention de la citoyenneté* (Aubertin: Éd. Joëlle Sampy, 2000), 137–53.

[25] Pierre Rosanvallon, *Le sacre du citoyen: Histoire du suffrage universel en France* (Paris: Gallimard, 1992).

empire of free citizens. The great hero of the slave rebellion, Toussaint L'Ouverture, became for a time a Commissioner of the Republic.[26]

Empire citizenship was ended by Napoleon, who reinstated slavery in 1802. At that point the revolution in Saint-Domingue turned from remaking France toward exiting from it. Napoleon's army was defeated by a combination of rebel armies and tropical microbes.[27] The proclamation of the independent republic of Haiti in 1804 was the flip side of Napoleon's restoration of slavery in other French colonies in the Caribbean.

France itself was ruled by people calling themselves king or emperor for three-quarters of the postrevolutionary century. Under monarchical or republican government, the line between a national France and an imperial France was frequently blurred. In 1848, the definitive abolition of slavery in French colonies turned an entire category of people of African descent into citizens rather than slot them into an intermediate category. It was in 1848 as well that the *originaires* of the Quatre Communes of Senegal obtained much of the rights of French citizens without giving up their personal status under Islamic law.

But by then, the course of colonization was moving in a different direction. After the conquest of Algeria, beginning in 1830, French officials, initially claiming to respect the arrangements of the previous imperial ruler—the Ottoman Empire—insisted that Muslims could keep their status under Islamic law. But as the conquest of the region proceeded with escalating violence and as the government promoted the settlement of peoples of Christian confession from around the Mediterranean to create the nucleus of a settler society under French control, recognition of difference turned into invidious distinction.

The colonization of Algeria was initially the work of the monarchies that ruled France from the fall of Napoleon until 1848. The republic that briefly followed the revolution of that year, while also making citizens out of the slaves of the Caribbean, declared Algeria to be an integral part of the Republic, without making clear what that meant for its diverse peoples. It was the Second Empire (1852–70) that brought a kind of clarity to the situation—in the terms of a frankly self-proclaimed empire. Napoleon III famously said, "Algeria is not a

[26] See the classic text of C.L.R. James, *The Black Jacobins* (New York: Vintage, 1963 [1938]), and the more recent books of Laurent Dubois, *Avengers of the New World: The Story of the Haitian Revolution* (Cambridge, Mass.: Harvard University Press, 2004), and *A Colony of Citizens: Revolution and Slave Emancipation in the French Caribbean, 1787–1804* (Chapel Hill: University of North Carolina Press, 2004).

[27] Likewise, both the North and South American revolutions were struggles within the British and Spanish Empires before they became struggles against empire. The Spanish Constitution of 1812, with its attempt to sew together an imperial polity on both sides of the Atlantic, can be compared to the French Constitution of 1946, which will be discussed in this volume. See Jeremy Adelman, *Sovereignty and Revolution in the Iberian Atlantic* (Princeton: Princeton University Press, 2006).

colony, properly speaking, but an Arab kingdom. The natives like the settlers have an equal right to my protection and I am as much the emperor of the Arabs as the emperor of the French." Napoleon III had no qualms about defining distinctions among the people he ruled, and the rationale for differentiating among them drew on the notion of personal status.[28]

From the Second Empire onward, Muslim Algerians were considered French nationals and French subjects, but not French citizens.[29] The idea that personal status could preclude citizenship applied to Jews as well until 1870, when a new decree placed them collectively under the civil code and in the category of citizen. Muslim Algerians would have to apply as individuals—renouncing their "Islamic" personal status—if they wished to become citizens. The "colons"— settlers of European origin—of Algeria made full use of their own status as citizens to keep Muslim subjects a clearly demarcated—and denigrated—population.

In the 1880s and during World War I some deputies in the French legislature argued for extending "citoyenneté dans le statut" to Muslim Algerians. They failed.[30] More successful during the Great War were the efforts of Blaise Diagne, the first black African to sit in France's legislative body, the Assemblée Nationale. Promising to foster the recruitment of his constituents on the same basis as other French citizens, Diagne convinced the Assemblée to pass a law that made clear that the *originaires* of the Quatre Communes did not simply have certain rights of the citizen but *were* French citizens, even though they kept their Islamic personal status.[31] This law was not the work of jurists working with abstract notions of citizenship and status, but a political act, overcoming the opposition of politicians who did not think that

[28]The quotation is from Napoleon III's letter to his Governor General, 1863, http://musee.sitemestre.fr/6001/html/histoire/texte_lettre_a_pelissier.html. On status and citizenship in Algeria, see Laure Blévis, "Sociologie d'un droit colonial: Citoyenneté et nationalité en Algérie (1865–1947): une exception républicaine?" (Doctoral thesis, Institut d'Etudes Politiques, Aix-en-Provence, 2004). A forthcoming dissertation for Université de Paris I by Noureddine Amara will shed new light on the notions of nationality and citizenship in Algeria in relation to the succession of empires, Ottoman and French.

[29]That all the inhabitants of French colonies were French nationals is attributed by some jurists to Napoleon. Roger Decottignies and Marc de Biéville, *Les nationalités africaines* (Paris: Pedone, 1963), 15n1.

[30]Blévis, "Sociologie d'un droit colonial"; Alix Héricord-Gorre, "Éléments pour une histoire de l'administration des colonisés de l'Empire français. Le 'régime de l'indigénat' et son fonctionnement depuis sa matrice algérienne (1881–c. 1920)" (Thèse de doctorat, European University Institute, 2008). Emmanuelle Saada, focusing on people of mixed origins, provides an insightful analysis of law, culture, status, and citizenship in the broad sweep of French history. *Empire's Children: Race, Filiation, and Citizenship in the French Colonies*, trans. Arthur Goldhammer (Chicago: University of Chicago Press, 2012).

[31]G. Wesley Johnson, *The Emergence of Black Politics in Senegal: The Struggle for Power in the Four Communes, 1900–1920* (Stanford: Stanford University Press, 1971).

originaires, as a collectivity, were worthy of the title. The reforms did not go beyond the Quatre Communes, an indication that France, like most empires, was engaging in a politics of distinction making, deciding which people had which rights.

In the 1920s, the politics of imperial citizenship shifted in the direction of exclusion.[32] As military veterans of North and sub-Saharan African origin asserted that they had paid the "blood tax" and deserved the pensions and other benefits of French citizenship, the government tried to emphasize that colonial subjects were firmly immersed in their own cultures and that citizenship was not only inappropriate but detrimental to their cultural integrity.[33] Officials proclaimed France's genius in recognizing the diverse cultures of its empire as they strove through "traditional" authorities to keep subjects in their place—socially, politically, and geographically.[34] Meanwhile, the government rejected proposals to take a more active role in the economic development of the territories, not just because they did not want to face the costs but because they feared disruption of the colonial order.

In this imperial context, some African intellectuals—including Senghor from Africa and Aimé Césaire from the Caribbean—argued that people of African descent all over the world should recognize their shared cultural heritage—their "négritude"—and the contribution their civilization brought to humanity. They developed such ideas in both poetry and political writing, but they were running up against a widely held view that difference implied a lesser sort of Frenchness.[35] The Minister of Colonies, in 1931, was explicit about the status of

[32] Mahmood Mamdani's book *Citizen and Subject: Contemporary Africa and the Legacy of Late Colonialism* (Princeton: Princeton University Press, 1996) has much to say about subjecthood but little about citizenship, and its attempt to explain current problems on the basis of "colonialism" leapfrogs over the changes and conflicts of the period discussed here. For critical discussion of Mamdani's book, see the section "Autour d'un livre," in *Politique Africaine* 73 (1999): 193–211, with commentaries by Ralph Austen, Frederick Cooper, Jean Copans, and Mariane Ferme and Mamdani's response.

[33] Alice Conklin, *A Mission to Civilize: The Republican Idea of Empire in France and West Africa, 1895-1930* (Stanford: Stanford University Press, 1997).

[34] From the early 1900s through the 1930s, suggestions were made in the Ministry of Colonies and the Assemblée Nationale either to admit more Africans into citizenship or to create new categories intermediate between subject and citizen. Such proposals were rejected on the grounds that Africa was too diverse or that citizens might pose too many challenges to colonial rule. See Ruth Dickens, "Defining French Citizenship Policy in West Africa, 1895–1956" (PhD diss., Emory University, 2001).

[35] Gary Wilder, *The French Imperial Nation-State: Negritude and Colonial Humanism between the Two World Wars* (Chicago: University of Chicago Press, 2005). Although I am not persuaded by Wilder's characterization of the interwar French colonial state, his interpretation of négritude usefully puts it in the context of the colonial situation and leads into the book he is now completing on the political thought of Senghor and Césaire, *Freedom Time: Negritude, Decolonization, and the Future of the World*. See also the biography of Janet Vaillant, *Black, French, and African: A Life of Léopold Sédar Senghor* (Cambridge, Mass.: Harvard University Press, 1990).

subjects who did not come under the civil code: "They are French, but 'diminuto jure' French," that is, of diminished juridical status.[36]

Extending citizenship to certain categories of Muslim Algerians was considered again under the Popular Front (1936–38), only to be blocked by lobbying from settler interests and other defenders of the colonial status quo. The Popular Front also considered applying to French West Africa some of the social legislation—including the forty-hour week and the expansion of trade union rights—it had implemented in the metropole, but local officials and business interests pushed back, insisting that Africans were too backward to benefit from such provisions. Even these limited initiatives disappeared along with the Popular Front in 1938. Forced labor was soon revived, the very idea of applying social legislation to Africans ridiculed.[37] Then came the war. French West Africa came under Vichy rule, while French Equatorial Africa, thanks to Félix Éboué, proclaimed its loyalty to the Free French of Charles de Gaulle.

Empire in the 1940s: Governing Different People Differently

Well before the chronological focus of this book, citizenship was a permeable barrier, and the question of who would pass through it was not simply a juridical but a political question—hence one that was and would continue to be debated.[38] But could Africans have a say in the debate? And could the debate advance far enough to put an end to the invidious status of "sujet" or "indigène" (native)? The terms in which those questions were debated in 1945 and 1946 reflect the uncertain and fungible quality of concepts most French people think they understand—nationality and sovereignty.

Africans' status as French subjects and potential citizens should be considered in relation to a broader spectrum characteristic of empires. With the establishment of French protectorates from the 1860s over parts of Indochina, in 1881 over Tunisia, and in 1912 over Morocco, another category became an important part of the imperial frame: the fiction of protection implied the submission of the sovereign (the Prince of Cambodia, the Bey of Tunis, the Sultan of Morocco, and so

[36] Minister of Colonies, Circular to Governors General and Commissioners, 7 September 1931, B/20, SRAD.

[37] Frederick Cooper, *Decolonization and African Society: The Labor Question in French and British Africa* (Cambridge: Cambridge University Press, 1996), chap. 3.

[38] The importance today of different trajectories in constructing citizenship regimes was emphasized in the pioneering work of Rogers Brubaker, *Citizenship and Nationhood in France and Germany* (Cambridge, Mass.: Harvard University Press, 1992). For a more recent perspective, see Patrick Weil, *Qu'est-ce qu'un Français? Histoire de la nationalité française depuis la Révolution* (Paris: Gallimard, 2005).

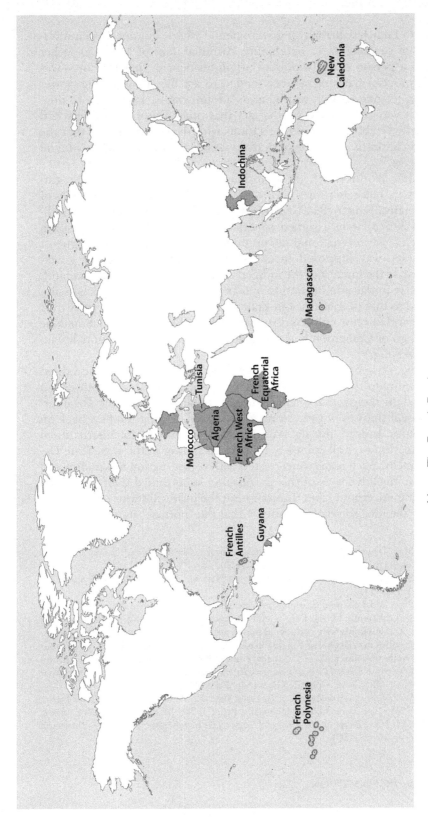

Map 1. The French Empire, ca. 1945.

on) to French control over governmental affairs, but not the renuncia-tion of sovereignty or nationality. An inhabitant of Morocco—other than a person of metropolitan origin resident in that territory—was a Moroccan national. France tended to act like a colonizing power in protectorates—that was what its administrators knew how to do—but it was constrained by the fact that other European powers had already established binding relations with the sovereign and that the juridical status of protected persons was distinct from that of colonial subjects.[39]

After World War I, the victorious empires added yet another cat-egory to their repertoires of power: the mandate. In Africa, colonies of Germany (Tanganyika, Togo, Cameroon, Rwanda, Urundi, and South-west Africa) were assigned to Britain, France, Belgium, and South Africa. The international community—represented by the League of Nations—was supposed to ensure that certain standards of gover-nance, in the interest of the indigenous population, were maintained.[40] The day to-day administration of mandates was in most respects assim-ilated to that of colonies, but France neither assumed sovereignty over its mandates nor conferred its nationality on their people. Someone in Togo or Cameroon had a Togolese or Cameroonian nationality-in-the-making.[41]

The existence of multiple forms of imperial governance added flexibility to the French government's potential strategies, but it also posed the danger that one form might contaminate another. The inter-national statuses of protectorates and mandates might reflect back on colonies. Indeed, during World War II, arguments for international trusteeship over all colonies surfaced, including in the U.S. State De-partment. Such ideas were greeted with consternation in London and Paris. The advocates of this proposition soon pulled their punches—fearing uncertainty and disorder—but the juridical status of mandates gave the idea some plausibility.[42] That the "normal" status of colonial

[39] Mary Dewhurst Lewis, *Divided Rule: Sovereignty and Empire in French Tunisia, 1881–1938* (Berkeley: University of California Press, 2013).

[40] Susan Pedersen, "Back to the League of Nations," *American Historical Review* 112, 4 (2007): 1091–1117.

[41] Syria and Lebanon, Ottoman provinces mandated to France after the war, were classified differently by the League and considered closer to self-government. By the 1930s, its inhabitants were considered Syrian and Lebanese citizens. Elizabeth Thomp-son describes the claims that activists made in the name of citizenship and the tensions between those claims and the paternalist ethos of French administrators and Syrian and Lebanese elites. *Colonial Citizens: Republican Rights, Paternal Privilege, and Gender in French Syria and Lebanon* (New York: Columbia University Press, 2000).

[42] W. R. Louis, *Imperialism at Bay: The United States and the Decolonization of the British Empire, 1941–1945* (New York: Oxford University Press, 1978); Mark Mazower, *No Enchanted Palace: The End of Empire and the Ideological Origins of the United Nations* (Princeton: Princeton University Press, 2009).

empires was beginning to be questioned in international opinion lay in the background as French leaders considered the rewriting of their constitution in 1946.

The takeoff point for debates on the status of individuals and territories in overseas France after World War II was thus a complex polity in which different territories were governed differently and in which multiple juridical statuses were possible. Multiple statuses for territories and individuals implied the possibility of shifts among them. Could sovereignty be considered an absolute when some people who had it (the Sultan of Morocco) could not exercise it and a power that acted like a sovereign was not (France in Cameroon)? And if some French nationals in overseas territories possessed the rights of the citizen—consistent with the interests of the French Empire—could not those rights be extended further, in the interest of reforming and perpetuating the empire?

At the end of 1945, the new government repudiated the name "French Empire" in favor of "French Union," a recognition that the future of a complex and unequal polity depended on reconfiguring the relation of its components. These relations did not easily dichotomize into colonizer and colonized, but fell into six categories.

1. The metropole (European France)
2. Algeria, divided into Muslim non-citizens, and non-Muslim citizens
3. Old colonies, mainly in the Caribbean, but also the Quatre Communes of Senegal, where citizenship had been extended along with the abolition of slavery in 1848
4. New colonies, including most of French Africa, as well as Pacific islands, where most people remained subjects

All four of these forms were considered part of the French Republic and their inhabitants were considered "Français."

5. Protectorates—Morocco, Tunisia, the states of Indochina
6. Mandates—Togo and Cameroon

Such a structure is typical of the composite—and often flexible—structure of empires.[43]

French West Africa (AOF) and French Equatorial Africa (AEF) not only occupied a particular place in this composite structure, but were themselves composite. They were often referred to—misleadingly—as federations. They were in fact administrative units, established in 1895 and 1910 respectively, grouping separate colonies with the aim of coordinating economic policy and facilitating efficient governance. AOF consisted of Senegal, Côte d'Ivoire, Sudan, Mauritania, Guinea,

---

[43]Jane Burbank and Frederick Cooper, *Empires in World History: Power and the Politics of Difference* (Princeton: Princeton University Press, 2010).

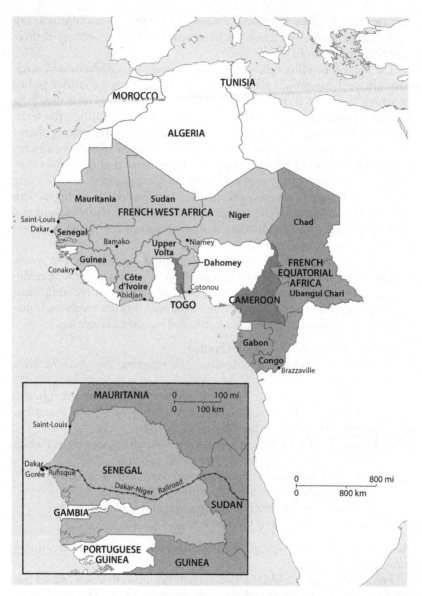

Map 2. French Africa.

Upper Volta, Niger, and Dahomey, while AEF incorporated Gabon, Congo-Brazzaville, Chad, and Ubangui-Chari. Each "federation" was headed by a Governor General, a powerful figure in the French colonial hierarchy, while each colony was administered by a senior official termed at different times Lieutenant Governor, Governor, and Chef de Territoire. African elites were affected by the experience of working within these two units. Some of the people who appear in the story told here—including Mamadou Dia of Senegal and Modibo Keita of Sudan—had attended the school, the École William Ponty, aimed at educating a small coterie of Africans who would bring French ways and their own esprit de corps to the different regions of AOF. Civil servants and teachers were often posted to different territories within AOF or AEF. And some had spent time in Paris.

AOF provided a model for Africans who were thinking beyond the level of the individual territory—if only an administrative unit could be turned into a political one, governed democratically, pooling resources, and expressing Africans' "horizontal" solidarity with each other. But not all West Africans experienced life in AOF in the same way. Its headquarters was in Dakar, in Senegal, but the territory with the best agricultural resources was Côte d'Ivoire. Landlocked territories like Niger and Sudan were poorer than their coastal neighbors and dependent on transportation links through them. Political activists would thus have to confront not only the differentiated nature of imperial governance, but the different levels of connection within French Africa.

Not just the best educated elites circulated around AOF or the empire. There were major streams of migrant agricultural labor—from Sudan to Senegal, from Upper Volta to Côte d'Ivoire—and dockers, seamen, clerical workers, and others moved about too. Military service imparted a wider experience of empire, for Africans served in other parts of the empire and on different fronts during two world wars. And while educated Africans had for some time been meeting up with people from across the empire in Paris, labor migration was picking up in the years after the war. Mobility defined a set of connections to something larger than the individual territory.[44]

Algeria, the North African protectorates, the Indochinese states, and the sub-Saharan colonies would all follow different paths through the transformation of empire and eventually out of it. France's lack of sovereignty over Morocco and Tunisia turned out to be an obstacle to its attempt to include them in a new order, but rendered less painful their eventual exit from empire. That Algerian territory and some of its

[44] This point is consistent with Anderson's contention (*Imagined Communities*) that the "circuits" of people shape the way they imagine communities, but those circuits were not specifically "national."

people were fully integrated into the French Republic made Algeria's path especially violent and traumatic. Sub-Saharan Africa was part of the Republic, but not an equal part. African political leaders were conscious of the weaknesses—especially poverty and territorial divisions—with which colonization had left them, and they understood that they had something to gain if they obtained the quality of citizen and made good on claims to equality with their fellow citizens. They did not face such a determined veto group as did their fellow ex-subjects in Algeria, but their own assertion of citizenship would mean no more than what their political actions could make of it.

We trace in the following pages the attempts of political and social activists in AOF to insist on the social and economic—as well as political—equivalence of all citizens and at the same time to seek recognition of cultural distinctiveness and the right to political autonomy within a wider French community. European France was an essential reference point for such claims: for what full political participation should mean and what a decent standard of living included. Africans, Senghor said in 1952, had a "mystique of equality." By the late 1950s, African leaders were also referring to a "mystique of unity" among themselves and a "mystique of independence," and the relationship among these objectives was far from clear. For French leaders, the question was whether they could reconfigure the multiple components of the French Union—including changing their juridical status and adjusting rights regimes—to give overseas citizens incentives to stay within the system, while retaining enough control in Paris to make the Union's preservation worthwhile. By the mid-1950s, they were caught in a dilemma: too much resistance to demands from sub-Saharan colonies risked opening a second anticolonial movement alongside the war in Algeria, but too full a response to demands for equality would lead to enormous expenses, as the people of impoverished former colonies sought equality with other French citizens in the era of the welfare state in Europe.

For Africans, the question of changing their relationship with France was made more complex by the uncertainties of their relationships with each other. In trying, in Senghor's terms, to conjugate "horizontal" and "vertical" solidarities, African leaders recognized that their mutual connections were based not only on a perceived common experience as Africans, but on relationships that passed through Paris and experience in French institutions, from schools to the Assemblée Nationale to the administrative structures of AOF. And they were acutely aware how much all these institutions—not just the formal structures of rule—had to be transformed if Africans were to have meaningful political voice in France in their territories, to achieve social and economic progress, and to ensure Africa's place among world civilizations.

That the power of the French state—and of the other western European powers—was badly shaken after World War II led African political leaders to believe that they could alter the power relations of empire. Before the war, some French Africans—relatively well educated and well traveled—had participated in networks of activists from around the world who challenged colonialism. On the ideological level, they had raised doubts about the seemingly ordinary nature of colonial empires, but their visions of a more just world ran up against the hard realities of imperial power. At war's end, the broad scope of internationalist anti-imperialism was becoming less salient, for the basic reason that political movements in different regions were achieving a degree of success, place by place. The colonial state was a moving target, deploying new strategies in response to pressures put on it and leading political movements to focus on goals that seemed increasingly attainable.

To understand how the ending of colonial domination was experienced we begin with the places where different people and territories stood in the complex and composite structure of French Empire at the end of World War II. We explore a dynamic of claims and counterclaims and of attempts to mobilize followers and shape the terms of debates—from the streets of Dakar to the legislative chambers of Paris. We need to set aside our assumptions of what a story of national liberation should be in order to understand the openings, closures, and new possibilities as people perceived them and in terms of which they sought to act. We explore what different people meant by citizenship, nationality, sovereignty, and state, and what they meant by France, Africa, Senegal, Côte d'Ivoire, and other categories of political belonging.

CHAPTER 1

FROM FRENCH EMPIRE
TO FRENCH UNION

World War II created a situation of uncertainty in which African political activists, among others, could work to pry a small opening into
a larger one. All concerned were inventing new political forms as they
went along. But they were well aware that the starting point for rethinking France was the concept of empire: an unequal and composite
political structure.[1] The politics of metropolitan France were also uncertain; the relative strength of different political formations and their
projects for reforming French society remained to be seen. But, after
the disastrous period of defeat and rule by a collaborationist, antire-
publican regime, the French political elite assumed that—in the metropole at least—the new order would be governed by legislative bodies
elected under universal suffrage. That a new constitution would be
required for a new Fourth Republic meant that there would be single
forum at which the reorganization of political life would be debated.
The question was not only how far such a debate could go but who
could take part in it, not least the people of France's empire who did
not have the status of citizen.

The initial propositions that French leaders made in regard to citizenship in overseas France were conservative, stopping well short of
extending the category of citizen across the empire. But the issue was
on the table as early as 1943. Most participants in the discussions were
aware that one could not go back to colonial business as usual, and African voices were making themselves heard, in Dakar as well as Paris.
In this and the following chapter, we look at a dynamic process by
which African leaders succeeded by October 1946 in inserting themselves into the debate over the place of empire in the new Republic
and used that place to insist on a new vision of citizenship.

---

[1] The jurist Pierre Lampué discussed the constitution of 1946 under the rubric "From
Empire to Union," writing "the constituents found themselves having to modify the
portrayal of the empire, right up to its name." "L'Union française d'après la Constitution," *Revue Juridique et Parlementaire de l'Union Française* 1 (1947): 1–39, 145–94, 2 quoted.

Toward a Postwar Empire

What distinguished the first phase of thinking about changing the status of colonial subjects was the absence of the people most concerned. The colonial establishment slowly came to realize it had to take into account the fact that Africans might want to shape their own future. But if the colonial subject purportedly had no voice and the republican citizen an equal voice, there were no evident criteria for deciding just how much voice overseas peoples would have.

The war was still raging when leading administrators gathered in Brazzaville, in the French Congo, in January 1944. Charles de Gaulle himself addressed the gathering. The conference was largely inspired by Félix Éboué, Governor General of French Equatorial Africa (AEF), the highest-ranking man of color in the colonial service.[2] His refusal to submit to Vichy had made him the symbol of the patriotism of overseas France, but Éboué's vision of colonial rule was in its own way a conservative one.[3]

The conferees—all of whom were administrators—wanted above all else to preserve the empire, and they accepted that in order to do so, they had to identify colonial rule with progress—for the colonized as well as the colonizers. But the "evolution" of African people, they argued, should take place within the framework of "traditional" societies. The Brazzaville delegates deplored past French policy for overtaxing peasants and subjecting them to forced labor. But Africans still had to be taught about the value of work, and their labor was needed to expand production. So the officials gave themselves five years to wean colonial Africa from forced labor. They pushed the idea of "a planned and directed economy," but insisted that Africa's vocation was to remain predominantly peasant; industrialization would have to be "prudent."[4]

Africans, they agreed, had to have a say in how they were governed. Those best educated in French terms could join the discussions of postwar policy, but not too many of them. If "notables évolués"

[2] Brian Weinstein, *Éboué* (New York: Oxford University Press, 1972).

[3] In 1941, Éboué had written, "The native has a comportment, laws, a *patrie* that are not ours. We will not bring him happiness, either according to the principles of the French Revolution, which is our Revolution, or by applying to him the Napoleonic code, which is our code. . . . We, on the contrary, will bring about his equilibrium by treating him as himself, that is not as an isolated and interchangeable individual, but as a human personage, bearing traditions, member of a family, a village, and a tribe, capable of progress in his milieu, and probably lost if extracted from it." *La nouvelle politique indigène pour l'Afrique Équatoriale Française* (Paris: Office Français d'Édition, 1945 [printed version of circular of 8 November 1941]), 12.

[4] On positions taken at Brazzaville in regard to political economy and labor, see Frederick Cooper, *Decolonization and African Society: The Labor Question in French And British Africa* (Cambridge: Cambridge University Press, 1996), 178–82.

(members of the educated elite) might vote in legislative elections in each colony, most of the "population non-évoluée" would be represented by their betters.[5]

Officials of the Colonial Ministry, in several documents prepared for Brazzaville, warned of the "danger of too much liberality in the concession of 'citizenship,' even local, for the future of our still coherent native societies." It was important "to avoid the rush toward 'citizenship' and in consequence to preserve from disaggregation those autochthonous cadres that are still solid and capable of being perfected." Access to citizenship should continue to be an individual affair, limited to people who could prove their personal merit. In the distance lay the possibilities of a more federal France—in which the diverse components of overseas and European France would exercise a degree of autonomy and share in the exercise of overarching authority—but that could be only "the long-range goal of our imperial policy." For now, a vague promise of "the most generous status" was offered to Africans, whose cultural integrity would be protected from too hasty an impact of France's individualistic, progressive, and republican society. And without question, officials insisted, "our national sovereignty over our colonies must remain intact."[6]

Despite the theoretical possibility for individual subjects to be accepted into the category of citizen, very few West Africans actually were. Between 1937 and 1943, only 43 people were considered for elevation to citizenship by "plein droit"—as an entitlement stemming from having won a Legion of Honor or other award or marriage to a French woman in certain circumstances—and 30 received that status. Only 233 applied for "voluntary" admission to citizenship—by convincing the administration that they deserved it—of whom 43 were accepted and 63 rejected, while 127 dossiers were classified as "without

[5] Summary of "les grandes lignes du débat" by the Commissaire aux Colonies, Conférence de Brazzaville, Procès-Verbal de la séance du 4 février 1944, AP 2288/2, AOM. De Gaulle had earlier proclaimed a special status of "notable évolué" for AEF limited to people who were literate in French, who had served France, and whose moral qualities were "above the average level for natives." They were freed from the indigénat and other indignities and given a vote in local elections. Decree of 29 July 1942, AP 873, AOM. Such a category was needed because "the intellectual and moral level as well as habits and social organization of nearly all natives does not yet allow us to envision their accession, en masse, to the quality of French citizen, as could be done in the old colonies." Comité National, Commission de la Législation, Report on Decrees Presented by Governor General of AEF, 11 April 1942, AP 873/2, AOM.

[6] Unsigned paper on stationery of Comité Français de Libération Nationale, Algiers, 20 November 1943, in preparation for Brazzaville conference, AP 2288/4, AOM; "Conférence de Brazzaville, Politique Indigène, Rapport No. 1," 17G 186, AS. For the conclusions of the conference, see La conférence africaine française. Brazzaville 30 janvier-8 février 1944 (Brazzaville: Éditions du Baobab, 1944).

result."[7] No wonder few applied. But those who did reveal some of the pathos of the citizenship process. Olympio Abdul, a clerk in the post office in Dakar, declared that he lived "in a European manner," could read and write French, and had been awarded a "colonial medal." Léonard Adotevi, an "auxiliary doctor," had served ten years outside his territory of origin (Togo). Tobie Gaston Ateba, from Cameroon, wanted to know the fate of his application made five years earlier and was told it was refused. Few Muslim names appear among the files of applicants in 1945–46; among those, Boubakar Diallo was refused and Saliou Diallo was still waiting, as he had been since 1940. A note in the file explained that delays were caused by the need to have the governor of the territory sign off, in addition to inquiries by the police, demands for proof of schooling, military service, and professional accreditation, and testimony about moral and political conduct.[8]

Yet citizenship categories could be adjusted—if doing so would foster state interests. Shortly after Algeria was liberated from the Nazis, de Gaulle decided to "attribute immediately to several tens of thousands of French Muslims their full rights as citizens, without implying that the exercise of these rights can be prevented or limited by objections based on personal status."[9] The Ordinance of 7 March 1944 applied to former military officers, holders of certain diplomas, active or retired civil servants, current and former members of chambers of commerce or agriculture, certain councilors, holders of various civilian and military honors or medals, members of councils of indigenous cooperatives, and several categories of auxiliaries to the administration. Such individuals did not have to give up their personal status under Islamic law in order to exercise the rights of the citizen. The number of people concerned was small, perhaps sixty-five thousand of Algeria's nine million Muslims, but the ordinance, without saying so, extended the Senegalese model elsewhere in the empire.[10]

---

[7] Direction Générale des Affaires Politiques, Administratives et Sociales, Note complémentaire, 21 January 1944, 17G 76, AS.

[8] Files may be found in AP 1083 and AP 1090, AOM. Comments on delays come from Affaires Politiques to Chef de Service à l'Administration Centrale, 7 May 1947 [that is a year after the new citizenship law made the process outdated], AP 1083.

[9] Speech at Constantine, Algeria, 12 December 1943, 4AG 518, ANF; record of the decision by the Comité Français de Libération Nationale, meeting of 11 December 1943, Commission des réformes musulmanes, 25 January 1944, Paul Giacobbi, "Rapport sur le problème politique présenté à la commission chargée d'établir un programme de réformes politiques, sociales et économiques en faveur des Musulmans français d'Algérie," 31 January 1944, BB30/1724, ANF. The limits of the reform were justified by worries about the "massive incorporation" into France of "8,000,000 Africans, foreigners by race, morals, civilization, whose religion is exclusive and imperative and whose evolution is still little advanced." "Note du Général Catroux relative au projet Valleur," nd [1944], BB30/1724, ANF.

[10] The text of the ordinance is in 4AG 518, ANF.

The relationship of empire, government, and citizenship was even more uncertain in Indochina. With Indochina under Japanese control, the Colonial Minister of de Gaulle's government declared on 24 March 1945—with more theoretical than actual effect—a new configuration for the empire:

> The Indochinese Federation forms with France and other parts of the community a "French Union" whose external interests will be represented by France. Indochina will enjoy, within this union, a liberty of its own. The inhabitants of this Indochinese Federation will be Indochinese citizens and citizens of the French Union. In these terms, without discrimination of race, religion, or origin and given equality of merit, they will have access to all federal positions and employment in Indochina and in the Union.[11]

The French Union would not acquire a juridical basis until the finalization of the new constitution in October 1946 and the meaning of the declarations about citizenship and federation were far from clear or generally accepted. But a new name for empire had been introduced, the formula of federation had been invoked, and the possibility of an inclusive citizenship had been put on the table.

In Algeria, as the cloud of Vichy repression dissipated, political movements among Muslims emerged with new militancy. They had for some decades been asserting the existence of an Algerian nationality, complicated by assertions of connections to wider left-wing and trade union movements on the one hand and to Islamic and Arab nationalist movements on the other. At war's end, French officials were trying to figure out with whom, if anybody, they could cooperate. Dr. Mohamed Bendjelloul was willing to work within French institutions to push for extending citizenship rights to all Muslim Algerians, but it was not evident how much support he had. Against the militant nationalist Messali Hadj, some French officials hoped to attract the "federalist" Ferhat Abbas. They worried that the new resolutions from Abbas's "Amis du Manifeste" (1943) dropped earlier calls for "a federative system under the aegis of France" and simply demanded an Algerian parliament and government. But, officials thought, the followers of Abbas were "sincerely attached to France." Given the divisions among Algerians, France might find allies. At the same time, the

---

[11] Declaration of French Government, 25 March 1945, 17G 176, AS. Robert Delavignette considered these citizenship provisions "comparable to the famous edicts of Caracalla" of AD 212. "L'Union française à l'échelle du Monde, à la mesure de l'homme," *Esprit* 112 (July 1945): 229. On the Indochinese context of federation, see Christopher Goscha, *Going Indochinese: Contesting Concepts of Space and Place in French Indochina*, 2nd ed. (Copenhagen: Nordic Institute of Asian Studies, 2012), David Marr, *Vietnam 1945: The Quest for Power* (Berkeley: University of California Press, 1995), and Pierre Brocheux and Daniel Hémery, *Indochine: La colonisation ambiguë 1858–1954* (Paris: La Découverte, 1995).

Governor General worried that "relying on repressive methods" might alienate "the last sympathies that remain for us in the Muslim milieu." In the margins of the letter in the National Archives (stamped "read by the General") somebody wrote in pencil, "this is what a governor general signs!"[12] Here was an indication how uncertain the government in Algeria felt about its own authority.

The Algerian situation soon took a turn for the worse. A demonstration at Sétif in May 1945, beginning with a peaceful march by Algerian political organizations, turned into a massacre by police, military, and settlers, plus killings by the other side. French officials lumped the Abbas faction with more radical elements and blamed them for an "insurrection," while the atrocities perpetuated against Algerian Muslims took much of the ground away from advocates of a middle position between federation and secession.[13]

Some of the people most concerned were already in metropolitan France at the time of liberation—some sixty-five to eighty thousand Muslim North Africans, three-quarters of them Algerian. French leaders sought their labor to contribute to reconstruction. Officials interpreted the Ordinance of 7 March 1944 as implying that Algerians as French nationals had the right to come and stay. In European France—but not in Algerian France—Algerians came under ordinary French law and were entitled to the same identification cards as French citizens. Moroccans, with their own nationality, had the status of a foreign worker, but they could enter on a "simple passport."[14] People were moving about imperial space, taking their nonequivalence with them.

Some officials wanted to assert that the concessions made in Indochina or Algeria had been taken "without pressure or bargaining but in light of the full sovereignty of France, which understands and accepts this responsibility."[15] More realistic were the reflections of Henri

[12] Governor General to de Gaulle, 3 April 1945, 3AG 4/18/2, ANF.

[13] Ministre de l'Intérieur to de Gaulle, 28 May 1945, 4AG 4/18/2, ANF. Army leaders reached into their arsenal of stereotypes, claiming the events had the character "of a holy war, of jihad." General R. Duval to General Henry Martin, 19 May 1945, 4AG 4/18/2, ANF.

[14] Ministre de l'Intérieur, circular to Commissaires de la République et Préfets, 20 February 1946; Directeur Général de la Main d'Oeuvre, circular to Inspecteurs Divisionnaires et Directeurs Régionaux du Travail et de la Main d'Œuvre, 5 December 1945, 770623/83, CAC; Sous-secretariat d'État aux Affaires Musulmanes, "Note au sujet de l'immigration des travailleurs nord-africains en France," 3 January 1946, and Note by Colonel Spillmann, Secrétaire Général du Comité de l'Afrique de Nord, to Président de la République, 30 October 1946, F/60/865, ANF. Despite the new legal situation, police followed old habits of surveillance and at times harassment of Algerians in the metropole. See Alexis Spire, *Étrangers à la carte: L'administration de l'immigration en France (1945-1975)* (Paris: Grasset, 2005).

[15] Declaration of French Government, 25 March 1945, and telegrams from Ministère des Colonies to Governor General, Dakar, 20 and 25 March 1945, 17G 176, AS.

Laurentie, a high official in the Ministry of Colonies. He recognized the signs of nationalism in Vietnam and saw that they could develop elsewhere, but in a form that "is not necessarily virulent or exclusive." The problem lay in France:

> Given conditions as a whole, taking into account that France now finds itself almost entirely deprived of its navy, its air force, and, one could say, its army, without speaking of its economic means, which have become quite feeble, it is a question of knowing if we will be able to resolve the contradiction: populations' aspirations for independence, on the one hand, and on the other hand the weakness of France that permits it with difficulty to lead, with continued authority, a liberal but progressive policy.

Here was an expression of French weakness as frank as one is likely to see from a government official.

Laurentie leaned toward the inclusive rather than the repressive pole of empire. Evolués needed to be turned from a threat into an asset—"a means of our action, as well as an absolute necessity of our future." It was also necessary to appeal to the "masses"—from which elite nationalists were often distant—and social reform was necessary to reach "a population that is evolving rapidly from traditional institutions that were unique to it to modern forms of collective organization." The distinction between citizen and subject was an obstacle; former subjects had to be integrated into a political and social fabric. He asked his colleagues to accept that "the liberty of colonies will be considerably augmented in the coming years" and maintain "a durable equilibrium" among elements of society. "Our old colonial privileges" had to be given up.[16]

Laurentie's perception of weakness proved all too accurate when Ho Chi Minh declared the independence of Vietnam on 1 September 1945, shortly after the Japanese surrender. France would now have to recolonize the territory in the face of a movement that had laid claim to the state and possessed a popular following and armed fighters. The government tried to find a way to convince Ho's regime that it could take its place within the Indochinese Federation and the French Union. Ho was not a likely candidate for such a role, but as the negotiations dragged on into the spring of 1946, the impasse was used

---

[16] Speech of Laurentie, Directeur des Affaires Politiques, to "cours d'information sur l'Indochine," copy sent by Minister to Governor General of AOF, 26 June 1945, 17G 8, AS. On the limits—personal and institutional—faced by a would-be imperial reformer, see Martin Shipway, "Thinking Like an Empire: Governor Henri Laurentie and Postwar Plans for the Late Colonial French 'Empire-State,'" in Martin Thomas, ed., *The French Colonial Mind* (Lincoln: University of Nebraska Press, 2011), 219–50.

by politicians opposed to reform to emphasize the need for a strong French hand.[17]

Events in Indochina and Algeria would shape the debate over extending citizenship to Africans, but in contradictory ways. The conflicts led some to conclude that French control had to be more rigorous and others to emphasize the need to make overseas subjects feel included in an imperial community. Sub-Saharan French Africa, where conflict seemed muted, offered an opportunity to demonstrate the benefits of imperial inclusion. In the early postwar years, however, most members of the government wanted to approach the restructuring of empire in a comprehensive way, as a reconfiguring of all its parts.

Rethinking was going on not just behind ministerial doors, but also before a wider public, with government officials intervening to shape a political agenda. The journal *Renaissances*, based in Algeria after it was taken over by the Free French, published a series of articles beginning in November 1943 calling for "a politico-administrative reorganization of our empire." Up to that point, the editorial noted, an individual "inhabitant of the empire" could become a citizen depending on his degree of "evolution"; it was imaginable that "at a perhaps quite distant date" all of them would be able to do so.[18]

An influential Governor, P.-O. Lapie, spelled out the case in terms that would shape debate for the next seventeen years: turning empire into federation. He argued that it was necessary that "France brings the colonies into a French federal system, following in this respect the international movement toward federation that is particularly well illustrated by the British Empire, Soviet Russia, and, in one form or another, by North America and China." The federal idea sprang from a concept of empire—and Lapie was still using that word—as something more complex than a dichotomy of metropole and colony, as a political entity with multiple components, each with a distinct relationship to France. He wanted each colony or group of colonies to have more "initiative" and "autonomy" while Paris would still exercise a measure of "control."

But Lapie could not bring himself to look beyond his belief that while the colonies included some people with a degree of evolution, "feudal or still primitive populations" predominated. Primitive people could not simply be brought into the institutions of republican France—universal suffrage or trial by jury for example. Instead, "it is appropriate to have natives evolve in the midst of their own institutions by choosing and developing those which over many years will lead native societies little by little to a status in which they are capable

---

[17] Brocheux and Hémery, *Colonisation ambiguë.*

[18] Editorial note to article of P.-O. Lapie (see below), *Renaissances*, November 1943, 29–30.

of understanding what we consider wisdom, because we practice it." Empire would thus turn into federation, but not of equals. European France would retain a tutelary role. Decentralization and autonomy would not necessarily take the form of each African territory choosing its own form of rule, but rather of distinct institutional forms being given recognition and supervision—and slowly being transformed by French authority.[19]

The magic word "federation" was also the focus of the intervention of Paul-Emile Viard, dean of the law faculty at Algiers, where jurists had made the law of empire into a specialty. He counseled "extreme prudence" in creating a federal system. A federation would reflect the "diversity of the Empire," and all its people, "whether they be of European or native origin," should be represented in a federal legislature. He thought that having a voice in metropolitan institutions—not independence—was what overseas peoples wanted. Here Viard sounded a theme that would be heard again and again: overseas peoples could be in Parliament, but "the Metropole must not be crushed by an excessive number of extra-metropolitan deputies."

Viard proposed that legislators from overseas should sit not in the Chamber of Deputies but in the Senate, intended to represent "circonscriptions" and social groups, whereas the Chamber represented citizens, proportional to their numbers. Protectorates, being themselves "states," would participate in an "Imperial Council." Overseas territories would have assemblies and more power over local affairs; the federal government would have defined domains of competence. This complex structure would establish "the French community." Viard was reflecting a conception common to much of the center-right: that this community was made up of collectivities, not just individuals, and Africans' place would be in the assembly of groups.[20]

These articles from 1944 were prefaced by René Pleven, one of de Gaulle's most influential followers, who would occupy the highest posts in subsequent governments. He frankly stated that "it is now that France is without doubt more conscious than she has ever been of the value of her 'Empire' and the duties which that implies." The act of colonizing, for him, meant "liberation from the great plagues that ravage primitive societies, whether called sickness, superstition, ignorance, tyranny, corruption, exploitation, or cruelty." He reassured his readers and himself that metropole and colonies would solve their problems together: "The French colonies, like the other provinces

[19]Gouverneur P.-O. Lapie, "Pour une politique coloniale nouvelle," *Renaissances*, November 1943, 29–34, and October 1944, 16–20.
[20]Paul-Emile Viard, "Essai d'une organisation constitutionnelle de la 'communauté francaise,'" *Renaissances*, October 1944, 21–41, 31–32, 41 quoted.

of France, want to help rebuild the house of France."[21] Here was a major theme in French history, particularly strong among Bretons like Pleven: European France as itself a composite of diverse territories and people, of "petites patries." Pleven thought such a conception extended overseas.

But not seamlessly. Pleven set his France of many provinces against a colonial past that had to be overcome; it was necessary to "suppress the racism to which we have already drawn attention and which remains the most delicate aspect of politics of this country." His ideas clearly reflected the experience of surviving the war: "the Empire remains intact under the integral sovereignty of France. . . . All this was possible only because of the loyalty, the attachment of the indigenous populations, African, Malagasy, Oceanic." What France owed these people was "reform of structures, and especially those that respond to the current development of our Empire." These ideas fit into his evolutionary conception of the world: France's role was an essential one: "to lead the masses to modern life."[22]

When it came to how reform was to be implemented, Pleven accepted that colonized people, including noncitizens, had to be represented in the institutions that would prepare the new republic. He did not say how or in what numbers. He was thinking about expanding citizenship, but not very far. He raised the possibility of "either a local citizenship or a citizenship of empire," but no decision could be made until representative institutions had been created. He wanted to co-opt into the process "non-citizens who have acquired, within indigenous society, an eminent place, because of either their intellectual activity or their economic activity."[23] That was how far, in 1944, one of the most influential Gaullists would go. But at least one specific point was clear: some indigenous voices would be heard as a constitution for a new republic was debated.

Ideas about forging a community of diverse peoples were coming from overseas as well. In 1945 appeared a book titled *La Communauté impériale française*, whose coauthors were from the European, Southeast Asian, and African parts of that "community." Léopold Sédar Senghor used the same word—province—as Pleven to evoke the shared fate of metropolitan and overseas France: "The colonial problem is fundamentally nothing but a provincial problem, a human problem." If parts of the volume bordered on pious evocations of the loyalty of the empire to France, Senghor's chapter was more far-reaching. His title,

[21] René Pleven, "Préface," dated 16 March 1944, published in *Renaissances*, October 1944, 5–8.
[22] Pleven to Governor General, AOF, 3 July 1944, 17G 127, AS; Press conference by Pleven with Paris Journalists, October 1944, Pleven Papers, 560AP/7, ANF.
[23] Press Conference, October 1944, and speech to Assemblée Consultative Provisoire, 15 March 1944, 560AP/7, ANF.

"Vues sur l'Afrique noire, ou assimiler non être assimilé" (Perspectives on Black Africa, or assimilate, don't be assimilated), went to the heart of the relationship between two "civilizations" caught in a profoundly unequal relationship with each other.[24] To European France, Senghor stressed the contributions of Africa to world civilization—a theme of his "négritude" writing from the 1930s. To African France, he pleaded, assimilate, don't be assimilated. Africans should integrate the best of what European culture had to offer into their own ways of life. Colonization was a "historical fact" whose implications had to be recognized and overcome, not by imitation or rejection of everything French but by a considered reconfiguration of the relationship.

Turning a long relationship based on violence and subordination into something that could be labeled community depended on giving the provinces voice, autonomy, and equality. Senghor—sensitive early on to metropolitan anxieties—denied that he wanted to impose "fleets of colonial deputies" on the French legislature. Instead, "It is a question of *citizenship of Empire*, an idea that over several years is making progress in France." He wanted Africans, Asians, and others in the French Empire to have equal rights wherever they were in French territory—rejecting ideas of some officials of a citizenship valid only within an individual's own territory—but such a notion of rights did not mean one citizen, one vote. Rather, he thought that the unit of representation should be "colonial nations" based on current groups of colonies, such as his own AOF. He claimed his idea was rooted in the familial structure of Africa: village chiefs would designate representatives, who would choose representatives for each colony, who would choose members of a federal assembly at the level of the AOF or other such group of colonies. This body would have legislative authority, although the executive would be a Governor General appointed by Paris. In European France would sit an "imperial Parliament" whose domain would be limited to matters of common interest, such as defense and foreign affairs. "Far from weakening the unity of the Empire," he wrote, "it would solidify it, just as the orchestra conductor would have for his mission, not to stifle, in covering the voices of different instruments with his, but to direct them in unity and to permit the least important country flute to play its role."[25]

"Citizens of Empire"—that was what Senghor sought to create. He had begun his essay by asserting that "since 1940, the word 'Empire'

[24] Robert Lemaignen, Léopold Sédar Senghor, and Prince Sisonath Youtévong, *La communauté impériale française* (Paris: Alsatia, 1945), 57–98, 58 quoted. Lemaignen was a wealthy businessman with colonial interests, part of the "grand patronat." He favored a sort of "citoyenneté impériale," but one that would not convey even a limited right to vote. Catherine Hodeir, *Stratégies d'Empire: Le grand patronat colonial face à la décolonisation* (Paris: Belin, 2003), 249.

[25] Senghor, in *Communauté impériale*, 59, 84–86.

has acquired an almost magical prestige," not least because the empire had proven faithful to the ideal of a French Republic when European France had come under German domination. Now the task was for France to renew and redefine itself. Senghor concluded by returning to a passage from the iconic figure of French imperial rule in Morocco, General Lyautey, which he had quoted as an epigram at the beginning of his article: a vision of empire as a "spectacle of humanity grouped together, in which men, so diverse in origin, habits, professions, and races pursue, without abdicating their individual conceptions, the quest for a common ideal, of a common reason to live." But if Lyautey's view of grouped humanity was at variance with colonial reality, Senghor's article had sketched out both a plan for a federal structure in which Africans would run their own affairs and a rationale for such a structure—the difference and equivalence of African and European civilizations.[26]

Senghor and the relatively progressive members of the colonial administration were starting from overlapping premises: empire as a complex polity, embracing different civilizations governed in different ways, that now needed to be transformed into another kind of complex polity, less hierarchical, more integrative. Henri Laurentie, for one, repudiated the notion of "the *colonies*, considered as possessions of the metropole, exploited for its profit, a conception that it outdated, condemned." Like Senghor, he embraced as a sequel to empire, "la Communauté française." And he drew a conclusion of immediate political relevance: the overseas population had to be represented in writing "the federating Constitution." Laurentie wanted to preserve the notion of empire as an "ensemble," softening its imposed, starkly unequal nature while maintaining France's tutelary power.[27]

Laurentie's transitional logic lay behind the circular sent by his Minister to the Governors General, Governors, Commissioners, and other top officials in overseas France in October 1945:

> It is necessary for us to substitute for colonization a form of "association." . . . It is certain, in effect, that the large majority of colonial elites aspire, if not to independence, at least to autonomy, and that these aspirations have been met with general sympathy in the world that the colonial powers must necessarily take into account. Not knowing how to adapt the French Empire to this difficult evolution that brings dependent peoples to a more individual and freer life is the greatest danger that threatens our colonial project.

[26] Ibid., 57, 98.
[27] Henri Laurentie, Lecture to École de la France d'Outre-Mer, 13 November 1944, and "De l'Empire à l'Union française," note for M. Walter, nd [1945], in Laurentie Papers, 72AJ 535, ANF.

France had to "integrate the people she directs into the nation, but an enlarged nation, in which all people, equal in law, will have the liberty to give themselves the institutions that are appropriate to their personality as well as their particular needs." The French government would still "direct" its diverse components, but those components would participate in both levels of governance. The Minister made clear that the proclamation of the Federation of Indochina in March 1945 took in the African territories as well. The empire as a whole was now being called the "Union française," and colonies were being referred to as "territoires d'outre-mer." Along with the official repudiation of colonialism came a repudiation of racism: "It is essential that we cease to give the impression of believing ourselves superior to any kind of indigenous race."[28]

As another leading intellectual figure of the Ministry, Robert Delavignette, wrote in a July 1945 article, the change in vocabulary did less to define a new way of thinking than to acknowledge uncertainty:

> Empire, French Federation, Imperial Community, French Union; we see in the variations of vocabulary only a groping step by which we try to capture and fix very new relationships that need to be presented together in spirit. There are no more colonies in the old sense of the word. There is even no more colonial Empire considered in relation to the metropole and as an object different from the metropole.[29]

But could this repudiation of colonial domination and these general ideas about an inclusive French community be turned into a functioning framework acceptable to most of the French political spectrum and to someone like Senghor, who saw himself socially, culturally, and politically in an ambiguous middle ground between French and African cultures, between a desire for incorporation and for autonomy? The starting point for people from Senghor to Laurentie was not an abstract view of a world of equivalent nations, but rather a conception of sovereignty as complex, divisible, and transformable. They were well aware, of course, that empire had its enemies around the world. The USSR had posed at various times as an anti-imperial power, even though it also described itself as a polity consisting of multiple national republics. The United States was a more immediate worry, for

[28]Circular (printed) of Minister of Colonies, 20 October 1945, 17G 15, AS. The Governor General of AOF asked his governors to distribute this statement to all administrators. Circular of 3 January 1946, 17G 15, AS.

[29]Delavignette, "L'Union française à l'échelle du Monde," 230. He repeated this statement in the 1946 edition of an earlier book, now titled *Service Africain* (Paris: Gallimard, 1946), 271. Delavignette's title change was revealing; the old version was *Les vrais chefs de l'empire* (Paris: Gallimard, 1939). Delavignette and Senghor frequently cited each other's articles and knew and respected each other.

the Roosevelt administration had made some anticolonial noises during the war, directed at both Churchill and de Gaulle, although it had not followed through. Americans, the French ambassador to Washington reported, did not understand the nature of France's policies overseas. "The terms Colonies and Empire provoke unfavorable reactions in all milieux but for different reasons, but particularly among liberals and people of color." He noted that American reporters who had in early 1945 visited AEF formed "very unfavorable impressions, with much commentary about the fact that only 36 blacks from AEF are French citizens."[30]

These tensions became more acute with negotiations over the founding of the United Nations, for France and Britain feared pressures to apply the model of mandates to all colonies, giving the UN a supervisory role. Even short of that, the possibility that the UN might encourage trust territories (the new name for League of Nations mandates) to claim independence could mean trouble when France refused such a change to its own colonies. The mixed nature of imperial repertoires in that case could turn out to be a problem, not an element of flexibility. The UN, like the United States, was not ready to upset the imperial apple cart, but the Foreign Ministry drew its own lesson from the very fact that such ideas had become discussable: France had to show that its own way of doing things was consistent with principles of the rights of man.[31]

International pressures at this time remained in the background, something to be aware of while French elites worked within their own frameworks. But there was another aspect of the international situation that was rarely commented on. Not only was France weakened by the war, but so were all the European powers, Germany most obviously. Empire was still a resource, but interempire rivalry was no longer the factor that it had been for centuries.[32] In the debates about how to reconfigure the empire, the possibility that a territory seceding from the French Empire might fall into the camp of another power was occasionally suggested, but no one could point to evidence that rivals actually coveted French territory or might exclude France from

[30]Ambassador Bonnet to Ministère des Colonies, 6 March 1945, K.Afrique 1944–1952, Généralités/1, ADLC.

[31]Affaires Politiques, Ministère des Affaires Étrangères, "Note pour le Ministre: L'Amérique et les Colonies," 12 March 1945, Ambassador of France to trusteeship conferences, April–June 1945, report on "Régime international de tutelle," K.Afrique 1944–1952, Généralités/1, ADLC. On the United Nations and the fate of colonial empires after 1945, see Mark Mazower, *No Enchanted Palace: The End of Empire and the Ideological Origins of the United Nations* (Princeton: Princeton University Press, 2009).

[32]On World War II as a break point in an interempire history, see Jane Burbank and Frederick Cooper, *Empires in World History: Power and the Politics of Difference* (Princeton: Princeton University Press, 2010), chap. 13.

access to overseas resources. The outside world appeared most often in the form of potential models for federalism or other forms of complex sovereignty—the British Commonwealth, the Soviet Union, the United States, Switzerland, as well as the former empires of Rome or the Austro-Hungarians (see below). The debate focused on how to maintain a complex and differentiated French polity and on how to avoid secession by any of its components.

In the uncertain moment when victory over Germany was in sight but institutions for a postwar polity were still an open book, de Gaulle's government set up formal structures to rethink the organization of France's empire. René Pleven spoke before a new body, which he chaired, whose ponderous name made clear its good intentions: "the commission charged with the study of measures to assure the Colonies of their just place in the new French Constitution." He set the agenda: "Everybody is convinced by the events of 1940 and by all the developments since 1940 that the new constitution that must be given to the Republic should include representation of the Empire and not simply leave, to the sole discretion of the metropolitan power, the life and political role of the Empire."[33] Colonial governance had long made use of commissions of various sorts, members chosen by the government, in part because the Ministry needed advice and legitimation while governing largely through decrees. Now, could these ad hoc bodies of wise men direct the empire in a more democratic direction?

Pleven's commission, meeting between May and August 1944, confronted the problem of making France appear *inclusive* when it could not be *egalitarian*. Pleven laid out the fundamental objection to his own proposal: "there are 60 million colonials for 40 million French people, a corresponding proportion of colonial representatives inside the metropolitan parliament would make the physiognomy of the French parliament into a parody." He was willing to see the state—if not the republic—as divisible, or at least not homogeneous: "I also believe that, quite often, one confuses the notion of the Republic and the notion of France one and indivisible as if Flanders could have the same structure as the territories of the Congo." He sought a diverse assembly, in which both colonial and metropolitan representatives would participate, though not in proportion to population or chosen by the same means. He also opened up the possibility that new statuses would be created "to shift the populations of the colonial territories

---

[33]Commission chargée de l'étude des mesures propres à assurer aux Colonies leur juste place dans la nouvelle constitution française, record of first session, 1 May 1944, copy in papers of Gaston Monnerville, Fondation Nationale des Sciences Politiques, GM 26, dossier 1. A copy of this document is also in AP 214, AOM.

from 'subjects' to 'citizens'" without saying what those statuses would be or how long the passage would take.[34]

Some delegates thought New Caledonia, the "old colonies," or the Quatre Communes could be assimilated into French departments; some thought Morocco and Tunisia could be autonomous states forming part of a federation. In the latter case, France was not free to act as it chose for such territories, since protectorates had "distinct international lives." Pleven intervened to say that federation did not mean equivalence of all components: "A Federation consists of France and all French overseas territories, France being recognized by all as the most meritorious member, the most important of the Federation." The tutelary relationship was still at the fore, but it now had to be defended explicitly against the implications that federalism implied equivalence among the federating units.

René Cassin, a leading figure in postwar French politics, put the inhabitants of Equatorial Africa at the "bottom of the scale," people with a "great attachment to France but whose primitive character implies that they are not in a state to create a true unity." But Morocco and Tunisia had their own sovereigns; they would benefit from "a bit more self-government." Henri Laurentie wanted to give each of France's diverse possessions its "own liberty, they must be able to breathe." Yet the tie of each to the metropole must remain "indissoluble." All this required innovation. A federation required federal institutions, such as an assembly in which each possession would be represented as a unit. He noted that the Dutch were thinking the same way; the Queen had promised its colonies a federal status.[35]

The specifics started to look difficult. Would the metropole have its own parliament in addition to France's federal parliament? Would the federal parliament include Algeria? The old colonies? Would the chief of state of the Republic—that is, the metropole and whatever territories were assimilated to it—also be the head of the federation? Would the federal assembly be consultative or would it have legislative authority? Would the republican parliament or the federal one have ultimate authority? And where would sovereignty lie, given that some components of the federation (like Morocco) had sovereignty and others (overseas territories) came under French sovereignty but lacked a voice in making sovereign decisions? If the metropole retained power over as foreign affairs while allowing devolution of power over local matters, would the people of New Caledonia, for example, have

[34] Ibid. Since the Congo was juridically part of the Republic, Pleven was saying (perhaps unintentionally) that the Republic was divisible but "France" was not.

[35] Commission, session of 9 May 1944. Federal institutions were among the possibilities considered for postwar reforms by the Dutch government in exile and resistance leaders. See Jennifer Foray, *Visions of Empire in the Nazi-Occupied Netherlands* (Cambridge: Cambridge University Press, 2012).

a special say in negotiating with their neighbors in Australia and New Zealand?

The deeply entrenched habits of mind in colonial situations, faced with the prospect of colonial subjects coming into French institutions, came into the open when commission member Jules Moch—a socialist—stated of the French of the metropole, "I do not accept that they be put into a minority by Negro chiefs ['chefs nègres']." Laurentie gently elided the racist tenor of Moch's remark, turning his words into a way of looking at federation as an assemblage of different peoples: "Negro chiefs, as M. Moch says with a certain scorn, are not bureaucrats; they represent a people." But the bottom line was that one could not leap from colonial distinction to republican equality. Delegates agreed that universal suffrage would not work.[36] The Ministry inferred from this discussion that reform could be politically difficult; Moch's remarks were indicative of "the repugnance of a metropolitan spirit—a repugnance shared by many French people," to making suffrage too universal and overseas representation too reflective of population.[37]

Despite such fears, no one was actually advocating that everyone from Djibouti to Brest participate as an equal voter in a French polity. Where, between complete domination and complete submersion, European France would lie was in question. If some commission members kept finding more and more areas where the metropole had to exercise strict control—foreign affairs, defense, economic coordination—others saw that a "notion of community between the Metropole and its colonies" could not be developed if the metropole claimed all decision making for itself.[38]

Some participants in the debate wanted colonial subjects represented in the main legislative body, others in "a sort of colonial senate"—a federal legislature alongside a purely metropolitan one. There were doubts that metropolitan politicians would give up significant power to the overseas territories and worries that too much decentralization could lead territories to go their own way, fostering "a certain tendency toward separatism."[39] Few participants could conceive of a community of equals. Nevertheless, any idea of Africans participating

[36] Another delegate, Sanglier, thought that Negro chiefs in any case had a special role in government: "They represent something as important as those elected by universal suffrage." Commission, session of 9 May 1944. Moch proved a recidivist, declaring the next week, "I do not want at all that a Negro king decides the balance between two French fractions." Ibid., 16 May 1944.

[37] "Note sur le rapport concernant la place des colonies dans la constitution française à venir" by l'Inspecteur Général des Colonies Lassalle-Séré," 25 July 1944, CAB 56/366, AOM.

[38] Lassalle-Séré, Commission, session of 23 May 1944.

[39] Lapie, Commission, session of 27 June 1944; Laurentie, 27 June, 4 July 1944; Lassalle-Séré, 16, 30 May 1944.

alongside European French people in a common project represented a significant change from past and current practices.

The federalists ran into not only the perception that Africans were too primitive to be good legislators, but also the idea that the people of the seemingly more advanced protectorates, such as Morocco, did not fit a republican legislative scheme. Would the Sultan of Morocco—who was repeatedly referred to as sovereign, king, or even emperor—accept to have his representatives sit in a legislature alongside Africans, whom he "considers much less important"? What would such a monarch think of being part of a greater France whose ideal was for citizens to choose their representatives?[40] Given that protectorates' status was determined by treaty, might not their participation in whatever constitutional structures France devised be considered voluntary? And were there not dangers in Algeria's place in a federal structure—from giving too much autonomy either to self-interested settlers or to "the Muslims of Algeria" who exhibited "little maturity"?[41]

The anxieties and possibilities about turning France into something other than the empire it had been were more durable than the committee's conclusions, which were not binding on the government. The report at least made clear that as a principle the federal idea had achieved widespread support. The commission declared its intention to "make manifest and active the principle of the French Community," giving equal weight to "the solidarity of these French countries [pays] and the notion that their personality and independence are accepted." The notion of "France and its colonies" would give way to the idea of an ensemble in which each territory had its independent vocation, but over which "the power of France is exercised with rigor and precision."

The ensemble would continue to have distinct components, which would now be considered as follows:

1. "Exterior provinces": Algeria, Réunion, Martinique, Guadeloupe, Guyana. They would be considered a "prolongation of metropolitan territory" and be represented in Parliament as well as in a federal assembly, while retaining a "large administrative liberty."
2. "Federal *pays*": Indochina, New Caledonia, Madagascar. These units, each with multiple components, were considered to have more "maturity" than other overseas territories and would be allowed to develop a "political personality" and elect deputies to a federal assembly.

[40]Cassin and Ballay, Commission, session of 20 June 1944. That neither the rulers nor the people of Morocco and Tunisia would accept representative institutions was repeatedly asserted by the Ministry of Foreign Affairs, for example in "Représentation des protectorats à l'Assemblée Constituante," 24 July 1945, CAB 56/366, AOM.

[41]Laurentie, Commission, session of 4 July 1944.

3. "Federal territories": AOF, AEF, Togo, Cameroon, Oceania, French Somalia. These territories would remain "under supervision" ["sous tutelle"], but as they matured, they would acquire more political "personality" and eventually choose their representatives to the federal assembly.
4. "International protectorates": Tunisia, Morocco, New Hebrides. Under international law, they possessed sovereignty and nationality, but the commission saw a "spontaneous movement" among them toward "the French community." They too would have a place in the federal assembly.
5. "French Establishments" in India. They would keep their "current colonial status" but with more liberties at the local level.[42]

We see here continuity in viewing the French state as a composite polity, containing nonequivalent components. The new idea emerging, from discussions in public and in government bodies, was to give them political voice, to different degrees and through different methods, in the institutions of the French state, probably including a federal assembly. Unresolved was the question posed during the commission's meetings: just who would be considered a citizen, and with what package of rights and duties?

Officials in Paris, used to exerting their authority, worried about the implications of federalism. Would it mean a whole set of federal ministries, responsible to a federal legislature, diluting the power of the Ministry of Colonies? Would a federal budget be acceptable to metropolitan taxpayers or to individual territories? Would particular territories object to being classified in different categories of the Commission's schema, or in the same one? How could one reconcile diversity with citizenship if all people of the empire were made into French citizens? But citizenship, an influential Inspecteur des Colonies remarked, was exactly what many "evolués indigènes" wanted.[43]

The most powerful voice for a France that would remain "intact" but whose organization "will not be the same as before the drama we just went through" came from Charles de Gaulle himself, speaking in July 1944—with decisive battles of the war now being fought on French soil. He put much stress on the loyalty and contribution of

[42]Report of Commission, Algiers, July–August 1944, GM 26. The Ministry itself saw these distinct statuses as a result not of ethnic or cultural distinction "but of the date and historical conditions of the establishment of French authority over their territory." It called for "a new charter" to replace these "diverse statuses, built up morsel by morsel, old and unadaptive." Ministère des Colonies, *Bulletin Hebdomadaire d'Information* 345 (9 July 1945): 1–2, clipping in AP 2147/2, AOM.
[43]Directeur du Cabinet, Ministère des Colonies, "Observations sur le rapport concernant la place des colonies dans la future constitution française," 28 July 1944, Inspecteur Général des Colonies Lassalle-Séré, "Note sur le rapport concernant la place des colonies dans la future constitution française," 28 July 1944, CAB 56/366, AOM.

overseas territories to the war effort: "not a soul refused the effort of the war for the liberation of France and the freedom of the world." He referred to "l'Empire français" in the present but applied the federal concept to the future: "I believe that each territory over which floats the French flag should be represented within a system of federal form in which the Metropole will be one part and in which the interests of everyone can be heard."[44]

Turning all this into reality would require writing a constitution. The basic method was familiar and generally accepted. An Assemblée Nationale Constituante (National Constituent Assembly) would be elected by all eligible voters and it would in turn appoint a constitutional commission to draft the text, with advice from other relevant committees. The assembly as a whole would debate, amend, and approve the text, which would then go before a popular referendum. But who—from the diverse components of the empire—would get to choose the deputies, how many would represent each territory, what roles would colonial deputies play in the actual writing, and who would vote in the referendum on approval of the text? It fell to the Comité Français de Libération Nationale, the political and military leaders around de Gaulle, based in Algiers before the recapture of France, to give the definitive answers to these questions. Government leaders were very conscious of the need to produce a legitimate document via a legitimate process, and they worried about the thorny issues that had emerged in committee meetings and public discussions. French leaders had come to realize that they needed, in some form, acquiescence in the overseas territories to the new constitution. The French government was becoming aware that there was and would continue to be pressure from below, as we shall see in the following discussion of an episode in Dakar in 1944 and 1945.

Aux Urnes, Citoyennes?

In 1944, over a century and a half after the Declaration of the Rights of Man and of the Citizen, French women obtained the right to vote. Recognized as citizens, the women of the Quatre Communes of Senegal should have been among them: Senegalese men had been voting since 1848. In the French Caribbean, where most of the electorate was of partially African descent, the change in gender rules produced little controversy. But in Senegal, the issue led to conflict.

The Governor General of AOF, Pierre Cournarie, wrote to the Commissioner of Colonies in June 1944 that applying the law to the

[44]Extract from de Gaulle's press conference, Washington, 10 July 1944, AP 214, AOM.

women of the Quatre Communes was consistent with "our republican principles," but not with "local realities and necessities." He was unhappy with the 1848 and 1916 laws on which the franchise of male *originaires* was based not because African men were voting, but because the vote was extended to all such inhabitants "on conditions immediately identical to those applied to the metropole, with no discrimination based on the observed degree of evolution." He did not argue with allowing women who were "exceptionally advanced [évoluées]" to vote, but he sought an alternative to applying the provisions to all women.

Cournarie thought women particularly backward and lacking in independence from their husbands. And he feared that the vote of residents of European origin would be diluted by doubling the vote of African citizens. As of 1941, he reported, Senegal had about twenty-seven thousand European citizens and eighty thousand African citizens, while the rest of French West Africa had fifteen thousand and five thousand, respectively—counting only male citizens.[45]

The Commissioner replied that it was important that future delegates elected to the provisional assembly that was to prepare the restoration of republican government be "lucidly and energetically French. Your influence should be exercised in this direction so that the colonial delegates will give a demonstration of the absolute unity of France and her Empire." His generalities only implicitly responded to Cournarie's concern. Nonetheless, in November the Government General decided to suspend the application to Senegal of the law extending the vote to female citizens.[46]

In February 1945, Lamine Guèye, the best-known *originaire* politician and stalwart of the Socialists in Senegal, began a campaign "in favor of the vote of Senegalese women."[47] Born in 1891 into the Muslim elite of Saint-Louis (one of the Quatre Communes), jurist, author of a 1921 thesis at the Université de Paris on the legal and political status of the *originaires* of Quatre Communes and its implication for civil law, Lamine Guèye was a strong defender of republican and egalitarian values.[48] With political activism returning to Senegal after being frozen during the period of Vichy rule, political parties were recruit-

[45] Governor General to Commissioner of Colonies, Alger, 1 June 1944, 20G 25, AS.

[46] Colonies (René Pleven) to Government General, Dakar, telegram, 13 June 1944, Governor, Senegal, to Governor General, telegram, 6 November 1944, 20G 25, AS. Some officials worried what to do about people of mixed origin or about women of color from the metropole or the Caribbean who would have the vote in their place of origin but who happened to be resident in Senegal. Directeur des Affaires Politiques, Administrative, et Sociales to Governor General, 3 January 1945, 20G 25, AS.

[47] Governor General to Commissioner of Colonies, telegram, 7 February 1945, 20G 25, AS.

[48] Lamine Guèye, *Itinéraire africain* (Paris: Présence africaine, 1966).

ing followers and making an issue of the status of French subjects. Lamine Guèye wrote to the Governor General protesting against the exclusion of Senegalese women from the voting, pointing to the humiliation of their knowing that European, Caribbean, Guyanese, Algerian, Malagasy, and New Caledonian women were going to the polls. The Governor General telegraphed Paris, "It is certain that he has succeeded in creating agitation on the subject and he is being followed." The security services reported protest meetings in Saint-Louis and Dakar in early March.[49]

Police sources described a meeting in Saint-Louis on 8 March at which women spoke. Verkha Seck, described as very influential in her quarter, stated, "There is no reason why European women vote and we are deprived of that right. We categorically refuse this injustice. We will vote or we will prevent European women from voting." Police spies reported that about one hundred adult women were present at this meeting in addition to about one hundred to one hundred fifty men. The women were "richly dressed and wearing beautiful jewels." At another meeting in Saint-Louis, a woman named Anta Gaye asserted, "We will barricade European women on election day if we are forbidden to vote like them."[50]

A letter by a Senegalese intercepted by security also described the March meetings in Saint-Louis: "all the women of Saint-Louis were represented. . . . The women made a public declaration that they intended to vote if French women voted. The atmosphere was aboil." Another letter pointed out that "the population is indignant" at the refusal to let female *originaires* vote. Meetings were held to arrange for delegation "composed of women and men" to the Governor.[51]

Cournarie panicked. He telegraphed Paris, "Agitation on subject of vote for Senegalese women continues at Dakar and Saint-Louis and reaches a certain degree of violence." He still thought that "Senegalese women not yet ready to participate in political life and that they are completely disinterested in the question. But agitators have taken over the issue and use it as an arm against France whose prestige was lost during the Vichy period. Given these considerations, I am led to propose to extend the vote to Senegalese women." That was a quick turnabout. Paris replied that it was Cournarie who had insisted that

[49] Renseignements, Dakar, 14 February 1945, Lamine Guèye to Governor General, 10 March 1945, Governor General to Colonies, Paris, 2 March 1945, Renseignements, Saint-Louis, 3 March 1945, Dakar, 6 March 1945, 20G 25, AS.

[50] Renseignements, reports of public meetings, Saint-Louis, 7, 8, 9, 11 March 1945, 20G 25, AS.

[51] Diallo Cherisse, Saint-Louis, to Alassane Diallo, Rufisque, 6 March 1945, and Keke A. Lamine, Saint-Louis, to N'Diaye Amadou Lamine, sergeant, 9 March 1945, 17G 415, AS.

women should not vote, and the Ministry did not want to go over the question again.[52]

Things were heating up. A committee in Saint-Louis was formed to press for the vote for women, and it sent a telegram to Paris. It claimed that three thousand male and female citizens had attended a protest meeting. A delegation went from Saint-Louis to Dakar to join a protest there. A white, Socialist politician in Senegal, Charles Cros, went off to Paris to talk to the Minister, and Lamine Guèye later did likewise.[53] Petitions were circulating. The Governor of Senegal met political leaders in Saint-Louis and was told that the government's decision was unacceptable and protests would continue. He feared "grave incidents." Several African politicians, according to reports on a meeting on 14 March, also warned of violence. Senegalese men who belonged to French patriotic organizations, such as the Front National de Lutte pour la Libération et l'Indépendance de la France (National Front for Struggle for the Liberation and Independence of France), spoke at meetings and sent petitions to the government. They evoked the patriotic record of Senegalese and deployed the language of republicanism: the suppression of the vote for women was contrary to republican legality; it was a sign of "racism." Senegalese political institutions, like the Conseil Colonial and Municipal Councils, had not been consulted by the Governor General. Female citizens of the metropole and Caribbean were getting the vote; it was insulting that Senegalese were not.[54]

A week later, security forces reported that protests were still going on. Political parties were calling for all Africans to boycott the next election. Another petition from citizens in Dakar came to the Governor General. Cournarie was still agonizing, and Paris telegraphed him that it was his responsibility to avoid violence.[55] Lamine Guèye's newspaper described the atmosphere in Dakar as "feverish agitation that goes beyond what is normal." And Fatou Diop, a Senegalese woman writing in the same issue of *L'AOF*, thought the Governor General was about to give way, and pointed out that the government had mistakenly assumed that Muslim Senegalese women were like North African women, whereas "here we are not veiled, we go out freely; there is

[52] Governor General to Paris, telegram, 7 March 1945 and letter, 8 March 1945; Paris to Governor General, telegram, 11 March 1945, 20G 25, AS.

[53] Governor General to Ministry of Colonies, 26 May 1945, 17G 132, AS.

[54] Petition to Governor General from Gaspard Ka Aly, 10 March 1945; Memorandum of meeting of 14 March between Governor, Malick Mustapha Guèye, President of Conseil Colonial, and others; Compte rendu of meeting, 5 April 1945, Renseignements, 12 April 1945, 20G 25, AS.

[55] Sûreté, Renseignements, 21 March 1945, Petition of délégués de la population de Dakar et banlieux to Governor General, 21 March 1945, Colonies to Governor General, telegram, 8 April 1945, 20G 25, AS.

no harem or gynaeceum." Women lived among men and took part in their activities.[56]

The Governor General had in fact already—this was mid-April—telegraphed to the Ministry that it was best to "accord the right to vote to Senegalese women without further delay and above all without waiting for incidents to take place." There was little time to draw up lists in time for elections, but officials would have to try.[57] The Commissioner of Colonies then drafted a decree annulling the one that had denied Senegalese women the right to vote and declaring, "Female French citizens are voters and eligible for office in the same conditions as male French citizens."[58] Charles Cros wrote from Paris, "We have just carried off a beautiful victory." The security services in its summary of political events in March noted the "movements of opinion" and the "protest campaign," but decided that, after all, "at no moment was order troubled."[59]

Some whites in Senegal complained in letters intercepted by the police that they would have to vote alongside "the most ignorant and stupid negresses."[60] But Cros and Lamine Guèye were welcomed on their return from Paris with a "triumphal" celebration.[61] A Senegalese sergeant in the army wrote, "Now, life in Senegal flourishes again." He was excited about the upcoming election for the reason officials feared, mainly that African women's votes would be added to men's: "racial unity constitutes a solid bloc, homogeneous, true, and crushing, plus women voters are on the side of Lamine."[62]

That was how the female citizens of Senegal got the vote. Political mobilization had made a difference; without it the Governor General would have made the women of the Quatre Communes stand aside as their sisters around the empire went to the polls.[63] Alsine Fall wrote

[56] Mohamed N'Fat Touré, "À propos de l'Union française," and Fatou Diop, "Les dés ne sont pas encore jetés," *L'AOF*, 20 April 1945.

[57] Governor General to Colonies, telegram, 12 April 1945, 20G 25, AS.

[58] Colonies to Governor General, telegram, 17 April 1945. The Governor General passed this on to the governors of all the colonies of AOF, telegram of 18 April 1945, 20G 25, AS.

[59] Cros to Ibrahima Seydou N'Dor, Dakar, 21 April 1945, 17G 415, AS; Sûreté, Sénégal, Bulletin de Renseignements Politiques de mars 1945, 20G 25, AS.

[60] R. Gayraud, Trésor, Dakar, to M. et Mme. G. Mounot, Etrechy, France, 30 April 1945, 17G 415, AS.

[61] P. Vidal, Saint-Louis, to Alice Galtier, Courbevoie, France, 3–4 June 1945, intercepted letter, 17G 415, AS.

[62] Sergeant Cissé, Oukam, to Brigadier-Chief William Alphonse, 19 June 1945, 17G 415, AS.

[63] The Governor of Cameroon later expressed a position similar to that earlier espoused by his West African counterpart: "I remain convinced that we should rule out the participation of native women, who do not participate at all in the political life of the country." He thought letting women vote would be "very badly received" in

an article in *L'AOF* titled "To My Senegalese Sister Voters" exhorting them to vote, adding, "You will thus demonstrate that the exercise of political rights should not and cannot lead to any perturbation in our morals or in our customs as some would seem to fear."[64] Women quickly queued up to register to vote in the upcoming municipal elections in Dakar. Afterward, Fatou Diop wrote in her article "Civisme féminin" that women had been told that politics had been of no interest to them, but now she was able to say to the women of Dakar that "your success" would show the capacity of women citizens to fulfill the "duty of the citizen."[65] The Governor General had learned his lesson, writing, "The Government General is happy to extend lively congratulations to the men and women voters of the Communes of Dakar, Rufisque, and Saint-Louis who just took part in municipal elections."[66] This mobilization was part of a wider ferment in Senegal of which officials there and in Paris were quite well aware as they pondered, over the course of 1945, the institutional future of the French Empire.

Doing Politics: Senegal, 1945

Lamine Guèye's campaign in favor of female suffrage in early 1945 was consistent with positions he had taken earlier and would continue to defend: advocacy of equality among citizens, a principle that was both general and deeply associated with the history of the Quatre Communes in which lay his roots and his electoral base. In 1943, he spoke before a large and enthusiastic meeting in Dakar about the three-hundred-year effort by Senegalese citizens to "obtain rights absolutely equal to those of metropolitan French people, including notably access to all civil service positions and absolute equality of wages in administration and commerce." He wanted to see "the complete disappearance of that odious racism anchored in the hearts of too many French people."[67] He was not alone. In 1943 and 1944, various organizations were writing to the new Free French government to claim

indigenous society. Governor, Cameroon, to Colonies, Paris, telegram, 26 July 1945, CAB 56/366, AOM. But things had by then moved beyond this point.

[64]Alsine Fall, "A mes sœurs électrices Sénégalaises," *L'AOF*, 22 June 1945.

[65]Fatou Diop, "Civisme féminin," *L'AOF*, 20 July 1945.

[66]Governor General to Governor, Senegal, telegram, 2 July 1945, 20G 3, AS. Lamine Guèye, after his victory, wrote the Minister to praise him for his responsiveness to grievances coming from "our distant province that has been so deeply French for over three centuries." He went on to raise other issues of discrimination in commercial establishments and workers' benefits. Lamine Guèye to Minister, 2 May 1945, AP 974, AOM.

[67]Lamine Guèye, speech to meeting of 31 December 1943, from police information, 17G 410AS. He raised similar points in a petition to Charles de Gaulle, 21 January, 1944, 17G 127, AS.

equal treatment: "if the native wants to remain French he intends to be so totally."[68]

Lamine Guèye's actions were also a step toward consolidating his leadership. In the municipal elections of June 1945 in Dakar, he handily won: 8,590 votes to 954 and 236, respectively, for his two opponents. He deployed simultaneously a republican rhetoric—insistence on equality for all "citoyens, citoyennes"—and an assertion of his African roots. He called himself "a child of the country" and his political party the Bloc Africain. His supporters labeled the opposing faction the "Bloc Français." His ally from Saint-Louis in the campaign for the vote for African women, Charles Cros, found himself on the right side of republican ideology but the wrong side of community mobilization. Lamine Guèye backed an African ally over Cros, and his candidate won the Saint-Louis mayoralty. Officials reported that "native women voted in imposing numbers, calmly and with discipline," while European women stayed away from the polls. The result, officials realized, was "a triumph for the Bloc African party."[69] As the municipal campaigns gave way to legislative campaigns, the Socialist Party of Senegal, of which Lamine Guèye was the leading figure, issued its manifesto calling for "the equality of races and peoples" and for "the accession of all Africans to citizenship."[70]

Senghor, in a letter of May 1945 intercepted by French security, took up the theme of equality, calling for universal suffrage and eligibility for office for "all citizens and non citizens." "Naturally," he argued, "the principle on which we constantly rely is the equality of races and peoples." In what was perhaps a reflection of his roots outside the Quatre Communes, Senghor argued that equality between Africans and Europeans also implied "the same equality among Africans." Like his patron Lamine Guèye, he thought political parties in Africa should be based on "loyal Franco-African cooperation" but under African leadership.[71]

French officials were also hearing citizenship talk from other parts of AOF. Dahomean politician Sourou Migan Apithy worried about

[68] Union Républicaine Sénégalaise to Commissaire des Colonies, 10 August 1943, 17G 228, AS. The Association Professionelle des Fonctionnaires des Cadres Supérieures de l'AOF described its members as "French citizens under the same obligations as all other functionaries" and protested against "racial discrimination of which we are victims." Letter to Commissaire des Colonies, 10 August 1943, 17G 228, AS.

[69] Monthly Political Report, 16 July 1945, 17G 132, AS; Renseignements, 25 June 1945, 20G 3, AS.

[70] Monthly Political Report, 13 October 1945, 17G 132, AS.

[71] Senghor, intercepted letter written in Paris to A. de Saint Jean of the journal Clarté, 5 May 1945, 17G 415, AS. Security reports refer to Senghor's correspondence as "monitored." The officers concluded that he was "a partisan of the French Union, but with absolute equality." Inspection régionale des contrôles techniques de l'AOF, "Synthèse d'informations générales bimensuel," 1–15 May 1945, 17G 414, AS.

the continued existence of "the spirit of domination and hegemony" in France. Born in Porto Novo in 1913, student of politics and administration in Paris, artillery officer in the French army in 1939–40, accountant, protégé of a Catholic missionary, Apithy began his political career in mid-1945, running for the Assemblée Nationale Constituante. But earlier, in May, he published an article in the Dahomean press emphasizing the importance of universal suffrage and the abolition of any political distinction between citizens and noncitizens. He thought that the discussions going on in France had reached the point where extending the vote to Africans was "accepted," but the conditions under which they would vote were not. Therein lay the struggle. His position was clear: a single electoral college, universal suffrage, and representation proportional to population.[72]

The ferment was not limited to an elite. Workers, especially in the public service, made clear over the course of 1945 their expectations that the end of the war would bring them both benefits and respect.[73] Officials on the scene and in Paris were conscious not only of the burst of demands for wages and benefits, but also of the rhetoric of social movements which put equality and citizenship to the fore. Strikes of schoolteachers in Senegal, of postal workers in Soudan, Guinea, and Senegal, and strike threats by railroad workers throughout AOF all worried officials.

What shook the colonial establishment most profoundly was a series of strikes in Senegal beginning in December 1945, culminating in a general strike in Dakar, Saint-Louis, and other Senegalese cities in January 1946—all coinciding with the opening of the Assemblée Nationale Constituante in Paris. It began with dockers striking for higher wages and gathered momentum as first the dockers, then others, won modest concessions from the government. By mid-January, workers from manual laborers to civil servants were on strike, and the event took on the aspect of a mass movement as well as a labor action: daily meetings were held in a sports terrain, European-owned stores were boycotted, women joined men. Some workers were striking for an increase in the minimum wage, and labor unions, in negotiations, introduced the argument that calculating subsistence needs should be done on the assumption that the needs of an African worker were the same as those of a European. For civil servants, the key issue was benefits, especially family allowances, equivalent to those of Europeans. The slogan "equal pay for equal work" became the hallmark of the strike. Union leaders showed mastery not only of techniques of

[72] Sourou Migan Apithy to Joseph Santos of the newspaper *Voix du Dahomey*, 10 May 1945, 17G 415, AS.

[73] Cooper, *Decolonization and African Society*, chapter 6. Nor had the massacre in December 1944 by the French military of returning African soldiers protesting conditions at the Camp de Thiaroye near Dakar been forgotten.

organization, but also of the rhetoric of republican citizenship, visible for example in this letter to the Governor General from government workers in Dakar: "What we want is the total disappearance of racial prejudice, the application of republican principles that have made the grandeur of France," followed by a detailed list of benefits to which they laid claim.[74]

Officials realized that some striking workers were from the Quatre Communes—hence citizens—and others were migrants from the interior—hence subjects. Any way out of the conflict would involve both categories. Fearful that repressive tactics would drive Africans out of the labor market, officials on the spot were unsure how to act, and so they called in a labor expert from France to help them. He arrived with his formulas and his tactics based on metropolitan and West Indian experience. He helped to bring the movement to an end by negotiating, category by category, with union leaders, making major concessions on wages and benefits. The breakthrough was in the realm of imagination as well: solving a conflict in a colonial situation by treating it as an industrial relations issue, entailing negotiations and contracts in familiar, metropolitan forms. Manual workers did not obtain as much of a wage increase as they wanted, but the principle of a living wage was agreed upon; civil servants did not get the same family allowances as their metropolitan equivalents, but they did get allowances in the same form and based on the same rationale—that encouraging family formation among this category of population was socially beneficial. The 1946 strike was more than a watershed in labor history: it revealed the fragility of a colonial order and the potential of defusing conflict by treating African workers in similar terms as European ones—a fiction, obviously, but a more useful one than that of Africans' unbridgeable alterity.

Bringing Subjects In

Let us return to Paris. The one point of agreement seemed to be keeping the different components of the empire—in some of which serious conflicts were erupting—together. The Minister of Foreign Affairs in April 1945 described the goal as "to put together in the midst of the

---

[74] Frederick Cooper, "The Senegalese General Strike of 1946 and the Labor Question in Post-War French Africa," *Canadian Journal of African Studies* 24 (1990): 165–215; Cooper, *Decolonization and African Society: The Labor Question in French and British Africa* (Cambridge: Cambridge University Press, 1996). The quotation is from the Délégués des Syndicats et Associations Professionnelles des Travailleurs Indigènes du Gouvernement Général to Governor General, 18 December 1945, K 405 (132), AS.

'federal French Union' the whole of the territories belonging under diverse guises to the French community."[75]

We have already seen how the debates in the committee on the "just place" of colonies in the new constitutional order (May–June 1944) brought out both the possibility of incorporating colonial subjects into constitution writing and legislating and anxieties that such people would dilute French control, if not French civilization. In the interim in which French governance stood between the collapse of Nazi power in France in 1944 and the opening late in 1945 of the assembly that would also write a new constitution, France was governed in a somewhat ad hoc manner by leaders close to de Gaulle, influenced by former resistance organizations, business organizations, labor unions, and other associations, as well as by a semilegislative body whose title gives away its status—the Assemblée Consultative Provisoire (Provisional Consultative Assembly). The colonial question went before this body.

That consultative assembly, meeting from late 1943 to August 1945, focused on the immediate issue of representation of colonies in the soon-to-be-chosen constitution-writing body, the Assemblée Nationale Constituante (ANC). It included only one Muslim Algerian, Mohamed Bendjelloul, and one West African, Ely Manel Fall.[76] Here and elsewhere the inconclusive discussions had an effect: raising expectations on the part of colonial politicians who participated in them.

In its first session in Paris, delegates referred to themselves repeatedly as "we, citizens of the Empire," and to France as an "empire," "an imperial community," an "ensemble of all the lands over which the French flag floats." One delegate cited Robert Delavignette: "France no longer has an Empire, but she is an Empire." The distinction makes clear that for him the French state meant the entirety of the assem-

[75] Minister of Foreign Affaires to Minister of Colonies, 19 April 1945, dossier Afrique-Levant/Afrique-Généralités/37, ADLC. Protectorates, unlike colonies, came under the Ministry of Foreign Affairs, and it was worried about the difficulties of including sovereign entities like Tunisia in "a French imperial community." "Note sur la situation de la Tunisie au regard de l'Union française," 16 May 1945, and General Mast, Resident General of France in Tunis, to Minister of Foreign Affairs, 5 June 1945, ibid.

[76] Ely Manel Fall was Senegalese. He had attended the special school for sons of chiefs and became a teacher, later a chief. Lamine Guèye noted that Fall had been a civil servant for thirty years, but "he has not yet been admitted to the rank of French citizen like the most modest peasant or worker in France and the old colonies, even if illiterate." "Parlons sérieusement des choses sérieuses," L'AOF, 23 March 1945. Fall was defeated by Senghor in the elections to the Assemblée Nationale Constituante in October 1945. Joseph Roger de Benoist, L'Afrique occidentale française, de la conférence de Brazzaville (1944) à l'indépendance (1960) (Dakar: Nouvelles Éditions Africaines, 1982), 29, 519.

blage.[77] Delegates hesitated between their recognition of the need for people of the colonies to be represented in governing institutions and concern that their "degree of evolution" was not sufficient for the task.[78] One delegate, Marcel Poinboeuf, asserting that French people were "the most universalist people," drew the inference that creating "a true community" among diverse people implied that social laws would have to be extended overseas.[79]

Mohamed Bendjelloul was all too well aware of his isolation, and he stuck to his goal of extending citizenship to "the entire Muslim population of Algeria" and to bring his constituents out of the "economic and social morass" in which they found themselves.[80] His biggest challenge was to obtain support for the representation in the future constitutional assembly of Muslim Algerians "at the same time and on the same terms as the representatives of the non-Muslim French." Bendjelloul insisted that the personal status of Muslims was nothing more than "a pretext" to exclude them, operating only "in the private domain of marriage and inheritance." To make personal status a matter of distinction in public life would put "the French democratic tradition in contradiction with itself."[81]

The general principle of representation of all overseas territories was endorsed by Minister of the Colonies Paul Giacobbi in the name of the government.[82] Roger Deniau, speaking for the Assembly's Commission de la France d'Outre-Mer (Overseas Committee), claimed that "everyone seems to agree on the principle of representation of the overseas territories in the Constituent Assembly." He mentioned the loyalty of overseas subjects during the war and then concluded,

> But the essential element in favor of this representation is the affirmation of the principle of the fundamental equality of all men and of all races whose union constitutes the great French community. Only this principle clearly affirmed and resolutely

[77] Maurice Chevance, Assemblée Consultative Provisoire, *Débats*, 20 March 1945, 591. Paul Giacobbi, Gaston Monnerville, and others spoke in the same vein; *Débats*, 19 March 1945, 561, 20 March 1945, 595. De Gaulle's conception, stated briefly at the conclusion of the discussion on 20 March, put the accent in a different place: he agreed on the need for "cohesion" between metropolitan and overseas France in an ensemble, but stated "and tomorrow, it is to the French nation, in collaboration with her overseas daughters, to whom the task falls to construct it." Ibid., 596.

[78] Interventions of Gaston Monnerville, Pierre Guillery, Pierre Lebon, 19 March 1945, ibid., 561, 565–66, 567.

[79] Ibid., 20 March 1945, 589.

[80] Bendjelloul to Ministre d'État Jeanneney, 12 October 1944, 3AG 4/18/2. Bendjelloul pointed out that he alone represented eight million Muslims, while six Europeans represented the seven to eight hundred thousand colons of Algeria.

[81] Mohamed Bendjelloul, Assemblée Consultative Provisoire, *Débats*, 2 August 1945, 1767.

[82] Paul Giacobbi, ibid., 29 July 1945, 1612.

applied can allow for the construction of a French union of which France will be the focus. For diverse reasons, the committee decided unanimously that all French men and women—citizens, subjects, protected persons, administered persons—who inhabit the overseas territories will be represented in the National Constituent Assembly.

He added, "People seem to still ignore that we have an empire, and an empire without which, we should repeat, the return of France will not take place and without which the position of France will never be as important." The logic of imperial inclusion was still at work—now enlisted in the cause of extending political rights.[83]

Bendjelloul emphasized inclusion, not empire: "We want our share in the common patrimony."[84] There seemed to be agreement on the principle—but not on the number of representatives who would come from overseas, and some deputies—including Jules Moch, who had earlier railed against "Negro chiefs"—wanted to keep the numbers low. The principle of representation was agreed to only by leaving the numbers question in abeyance.[85]

De Gaulle's government appointed yet another committee (March 1945) to study the representation of colonies in the future constituent assembly. This time the chair was Gaston Monnerville, a métis from Guyana, deputy from that territory from 1932 to the fall of France, figure in the resistance against Vichy and the Nazis for which he received the Croix de Guerre 1939–1945 and the Rosette de la Résistance, and an experienced student of French politics (and future deputy, Senator, and President of the Senate). The old politics of commissions was being invigorated by the appointment of a man of his origins and distinction.[86] Its members included Senghor, described as Professeur de Lettres. Africa, the Antilles, and Vietnam were included in the committee's purview, but Morocco and Tunisia were not on the grounds that they were internationally recognized polities.[87] Although its conclusions would not bind the government, they would have a predictably strong effect on framing the subsequent debate.

After meeting in April and May, the committee, reporting in July, advocated the vote for noncitizens as well as citizens, insisting that

[83] Ibid., 2 August 1945, 1769–70.

[84] Ibid., 1768.

[85] Ibid., 1767–73.

[86] The choice may have been influenced by the heroic stature of Monnerville's fellow Guyanese, Félix Éboué after he swung AEF into de Gaulle's camp (he died in 1944).

[87] Minister of Foreign Affairs to Minister of Colonies, 17 March 1945, Afrique-Levant/Afrique généralités/38, ADLC. The Ministry nonetheless insisted that what was at stake was "a revision of the relations that unite the metropole with *all* the member countries [*pays membres*] of the French community." Minister of Colonies to Minister of Foreign Affairs, 5 April 1945, ibid.

such an action was "as justified as it is indispensable." The conclusion stemmed from its basic premise of equality of all people and races. The majority favored universal suffrage for noncitizens and citizens, insisted that both should vote within a single electoral college, and acknowledged that there would be great technical difficulties, owing to lack of censuses and the état-civil, the registers by which the French state kept track of who its individual citizens were, recording births, marriages, and deaths. To meet these difficulties, noncitizens would vote indirectly—choosing, presumably within manageable communities—electors who would in turn vote alongside citizens. Two committee members, both jurists, wanted to add guaranteed representation for French citizens living overseas—Europeans in other words—who would be minorities within their territories. Three other members agreed that all should be represented, but did not think that subjects, especially in Africa, were evolved enough for universal suffrage. They worried that noncitizens would outnumber citizens, and they denied that the double college (separate voter rolls for citizens and noncitizens) represented racial discrimination; it was a distinction based on status, and people could change their status.[88]

The principle of equality was strongly defended in the Monnerville Committee, by Africans among others. Sourou Migan Apithy, from Dahomey, stated his goal: "Our mission is to profit from this revolutionary period to create something new." He saw any distinction between citizens and noncitizens as "old conceptions," and he resented efforts to co-opt "blessed évolués." There could be no differentiation by civil status, no distinction between electoral colleges. Senghor asserted that the conservative arguments were based on "undisguised contempt for black Africa." He warned that if Africans did not participate "on the basis of equality" in constitution writing, they would oppose the constitution. Vietnamese delegates expressed doubts about the adequacy of plans for an Indochinese Federation with the French Union; they demanded full equality with European French citizens. Monnerville tried to conciliate their anger and assure his fellow committee members that they had influence, while Laurentie reassured everyone that "the principle of equality must be the only philosophical motif for the resolution which the committee is in the process of making."[89]

Meanwhile, the Ministry of Colonies was coming up with rough drafts for the sections of a new constitution on the French Union. The Union would include the metropole, overseas departments (including

---

[88] "Rapport de la commission chargée de l'étude de la représentation des territoires d'outre-mer à la future assemblée constituante," 18 July 1945, Afrique-Levant/Afrique généralités/38, ADLC.

[89] Transcript of session of 3 May 1945, ibid.

the Antilles), protectorates (relabeled "pays-unis"), and overseas territories (to be called "territoires-unis"). The draft vaguely stated that the people of each of these units would be "citizens of the French Union under conditions set out by laws." The metropole would be in charge of defense and international relations, but the components of the Union would—depending on their degree of evolution—exercise autonomy in regard to local affairs. A federal assembly would be able to write and revise laws governing the relationship of the components, including promoting "territoires-unis" to either "département d'outre-mer" or to "pays-unis," depending on their evolution and their desires—that is, toward either greater integration or greater autonomy. The vagueness was in some ways the point of the draft: to allow change, presumably in the course of evolution of heretofore backward people, but with the presumption of a heterogeneous France incorporating the diverse and changing elements.[90]

French jurists—sitting on still another committee—had their own perspective. They had their doubts about the federal idea that up to this point had been invoked by leading Gaullists and Africans alike. Some of the lawyers did not believe French people would give up the preeminence of a metropolitan parliament or that colonial subjects were up to a major legislative role, even in an assembly devoted to overseas matters. Settlers and metropolitans would have to have a majority there. Perhaps the people of the colonies would be content with more power in their own territories and a consultative role at the center.[91] The jurists feared "any centrifugal force" that might tear apart "the unalterable integrity of the French patrimony." Most important was their fear that the political cohesiveness and organization of territories, especially in Africa, was insufficient for these units to be combined in a federation: "One can only federate that which exists," commented their report.[92]

The lawyers had put their fingers on something important: they saw the new structure deriving not from abstract notions of federation or ideas of equality among French citizens, but from a history of empire that was evolving in new directions. The jurist Henry Solus—author of numerous prewar treatises, including on colonial law—wanted to call the new entity "l'Union impériale française," but Laurentie—from the

[90] Ministère des Colonies, "Schema d'un avant-projet de constitution de l'Union française," 12 April 1945, ibid. See also "Sous Commission Colonies," Report, 27 April 1945, ibid.

[91] Bureau d'Études, transcript of sessions of 2, 16, and 20 March 1945, in Monnerville Papers, GM 26/2 (also in Afrique-Levant/Afrique généralités/38, ADLC).

[92] Report of commission of experts, included in circular of Secretary General of Ministère des Colonies, 4 April 1945, Afrique-Levant/Afrique généralités/38, ADLC.

political side—thought this choice of words was "inopportune," suggesting bad associations with "the idea of imperialism."[93] But Professor Pierre Lampué, a specialist on law in the colonies, made much of the imperial roots of the new formation in a memorandum. He even thought that the word "empire" had the "the advantage of experience [ancienneté]." He went on to say, "It is true that the word Empire sometimes signifies colonies to the exclusion of the metropole. But, in general, it includes all countries that belong on whatever basis to the central government. Nothing implies therefore that the word Empire could not be retained despite changes in the internal structure and local organization that intervenes." Abandoning the word in favor of "Federation" or "Union" might, however, have political advantages, including "to mark the will to increase local privileges and to associate the colonies with the political life of the ensemble."[94]

Laurentie, who had been advocating a sharp break with past practices from within the colonial administration, remarked that the proposals coming from the jurists would create "a gap between the metropole and the Empire."[95] But while awaiting the process of constitution writing, the real power lay with a narrow group around de Gaulle. They were hearing not only from the committees they had appointed, but also from lobbyists, some of whom were defending the old colonial order with the usual arguments about the incapacity of noncitizens to govern themselves.[96] As late as October 1945, as the final plans for the ANC were being finalized, Laurentie sought an audience with de Gaulle, insisting to the General's Cabinet director that he did not know what the government's colonial policy was, even though he was among the people who were supposedly making it. Indochina was in turmoil (Ho Chi Minh had declared independence in September), but the administration there was doing nothing to resolve the situation. Violent incidents had occurred in Algeria, Cameroon, Senegal,

[93] Constitutional experts, 2 and 15 March 1945, in ibid. Henry Solus's many publications include *Traité de la condition des indigènes en droit privé. Colonies et pays de protectorat (non compris l'Afrique du Nord) et pays sous mandat* (Paris: Société anonyme du "Recueil Sirey," 1927).

[94] Pierre Lampué, "Observations sur la réforme constitutionnelle de l'Empire Coloniale," nd but with papers from May–June 1945, GM 26/2.

[95] Bureau d'Études, transcript of sessions of 20 March 1945, in Monnerville Papers, GM 26/2.

[96] Comité de l'Empire Français (signed by F. Charles-Roux) to Minister of Colonies, 16 July 1945, 3AG 4/22/1, ANF. The letter argued, "The entrance into these assemblies of native, non-citizen elements taking the place of settlers who founded and developed the Empire, of natives who, by their merit and degree of evolution, acceded to citizenship, would mark a disturbance of the entire imperial edifice that creates the force and pride of France."

and Syria. "I have come to doubt that we will retain the Empire." The Director promised to communicate with the General.[97]

Meanwhile, the government was working in the ambiguous field that had been laid out. De Gaulle's advisor Pierre Ruais, in a series of memoranda in July and August, noted that there was little agreement beyond including in one way or another "all the territories." There were worries about too much noncitizen representation or the wrong—that is too nationalist—representatives getting elected, but he pointed out that relatively open elections might not turn out so badly for the government, for in the overseas territories "the means of which the Administration disposes to back a suitable candidate are infinitely more varied and efficacious than in France."[98] In other words, the government could allow a more inclusive system of representation—and manipulate it. But an inclusionary text was a political necessity: "any distinction between citizens and non-citizens established in a law intended to transport this community into the realm of political reality would introduce a destructive element into that community. The gap between citizens and non-citizens should instead be overcome." But not necessarily right away: the first step was to open voting to people with certain qualifications: "a significant mass of people with competency to vote and be eligible for office who would become if not French citizens or citizens of personal status, at least for now, voters."[99]

Ruais knew that Monnerville, whose committee wanted to bring noncitizens into the voting process as equals, would defend his report in the Assemblée Consultative Provisoire. Anything short of a common electoral college would bring charges of trying to "institute a mode of voting based on inequality between citizens and noncitizens." But leading colonial officials feared too many voices of "natives still little evolved" and wanted the double college. And they wanted representation for noncitizens limited to évolués and indigenous elites of various sorts. What Ruais was working with was the possibility of a process, opening the door to growing participation by noncitizens, but not letting everyone in at once.[100]

The Assemblée Consultative Provisoire indeed voted in favor of a resolution, based on the Monnerville Committee report, calling for representation of all territories and universal suffrage (indirect in the

[97] Laurentie to G. Palewski, Directeur du Cabinet, 3 October 1945, 3AG 4/22/1, ANF. On Laurentie's frustration with the government's backsliding on the recommendations of the Monnerville Commission, see Shipway, "Thinking Like an Empire."
[98] Note pour le Général de Gaulle, 30 July 1945, 3AG 4/22/1, ANF. This point had been made before by an Inspecteur de Colonies, Lassalle-Séré, who wanted advocates of universal suffrage to be aware that it might produce conservative results. Notes, 25 July 1944, CAB 56/366, AOM.
[99] Ruais, Note pour le Général de Gaulle, 30 July 1945, 3AG 4/22/1, ANF.
[100] Note pour le Général de Gaulle, 1 August 1945, 3AG 4/22/1, ANF.

case of noncitizens).[101] But the government did not have to follow either the Assemblée or the Monnerville Committee. It admitted that the principle of universal suffrage, for noncitizens as well as citizens, was "the most satisfactory" mode of representation. For citizens overseas—in Africa, the Antilles, and elsewhere—the principle could be implemented without particular difficulty, for citizens were already enumerated and on voter lists. In the overseas territories, notably Africa, the problem was practical.

> Noncitizens are not always registered by name, and the size of these populations, their dispersal, the state of their administrative organization, the lack of the état-civil, and finally the short time lapse that separates us from the date fixed for the general election make it provisionally impossible to establish electoral lists and put in place even approximately the electoral technology that universal suffrage, at one or several degrees, requires.

So the government accepted universal suffrage for citizens, but delayed its implementation for noncitizens. Electoral rights would be limited to "certain categories of people who are the most representative of the autochthonous population." The government insisted that this system of "limited suffrage" would not be a precedent.[102]

The government adopted a middle ground on representation: all territories—and subjects as well as citizens—would be represented. But not in proportion to population and not chosen on the same criteria. There would be two colleges. Six deputies would represent West Africa's fifteen million Africans (including Togo and the largely African citizens of Senegal), whereas twenty-one thousand citizens (almost all European) in West Africa would elect four. French Equatorial Africa and Cameroon ended up sending three deputies of European origin, two of African, and one (Gabriel d'Arboussier) of mixed parentage. Algeria's citizens (mostly European) would elect the same number of representatives as the vastly larger body of Algerian noncitizens (overwhelmingly Muslim). The European populations of Morocco and Tunisia would choose a total of five delegates, their indigenous populations none. Indochina was not included at all. The entire overseas empire would have 64 seats out of 586.[103]

[101] Assemblée Consultative Provisoire, *Débats*, 29 July 1945, 1611–14, 1631.

[102] Minister of Colonies, "Exposé des motifs for a draft ordinance on the mode of representation in the Assemblée Nationale Constituante," nd [1945] CAB 56–369, AOM.

[103] De Benoist, *L'Afrique occidentale française*, 42; D. Bruce Marshall, *The French Colonial Myth and Constitution-Making in the Fourth Republic* (New Haven, Conn.: Yale University Press, 1973), 141. As Marshall points out, the exclusion of the Associated States left out an important segment of nationalist opinion, while important Algerian nationalists were detained for their alleged role in the Sétif rising. Ferhat Abbas did join the second Constituante. Marshall, however, underestimates the autonomy and importance of

The list of technical difficulties sounds like an excuse, although the challenges were real enough. They in fact marked the limits of the knowledge and power of a colonial government at the time of World War II. The administration did not know who lived in its territories: not their names, not their places of residence, not even their numbers. What they knew in most of French Africa was a set of people with whom they worked: chiefs, "local notables," former soldiers. Such people would be allowed to vote in the "second" (noncitizens') college on 21 October 1945. The état-civil was compulsory only for citizens in AOF. Since the 1930s, the law had provided for an "état-civil indigène," but it was not compulsory and few Africans saw a need to use it. In 1944, 105,000 entries had been made across AOF, mostly births. That certainly would not help in identifying voters in a population estimated at nearly sixteen million.[104] Over the ensuing years, officials would continue to emphasize the need for a functioning état-civil and prove unable to do much about it (see chapter 3).

But the capacity of the administration to determine the outcome even in operating with known figures was limited. Officials were not entirely happy with seeing Lamine Guèye—given his campaigns for republican equality—go to the Assembly in Paris, but they knew beforehand he would be elected in Senegal. His protégé Léopold Senghor was elected too, defeating Ely Manel Fall, who had long worked with the administration. Most strikingly, the second college (noncitizens) in Côte d'Ivoire elected Félix Houphouët-Boigny, despite machinations of the governor in favor of a more conservative rival. Houphouët-Boigny had since 1944 been organizing African cocoa farmers, competitors of the *colons* (European settlers), and campaigning against forced labor, in which the administration had been conniving for decades. His platform called for "the concession of citizenship to all natives." All these figures would play influential roles in the battles that were to come.[105]

Where African organization had been less developed in advance of the first elections, notably in Equatorial Africa, connections to the administration and to missions were more of a factor, so that the elections produced their own context rather than the other way around. Even so, some of the deputies proved dynamic critics of the colonial establishment, for example Gabriel d'Arboussier, elected in Gabon-Congo, son of a French colonial administrator and an African mother.

West African deputies, and he misreads their political strategy for transforming empire into federation as their working within a colonial "myth."

[104] Procureur Général de l'AOF to Governor General, 3 July 1946, 23G 6, AS.

[105] De Benoist, *L'Afrique occidentale française*, 42–47. Houphouët-Boigny's platform from 1945 may be found at http://www.fonds-baulin.org/ouvrages/la-politique-interieure-d/annexes-32/article/annexe-4?artsuite=1&lang=fr (accessed 29 October 2013).

Figure 1. Félix Houphouët-Boigny addressing a crowd in Treichville, Côte d'Ivoire, 1945. ©AFP/Getty Images.

In his platform he described himself as the "link" between his European and African sides. He went on to say, "No French Nation without the French-Empire Community, but no French-Empire Community without the just human weight of the overseas territories."[106]

It is easy to dismiss the composition of the ANC as tokenism—especially after the pious talk of equality and the proposals for a single college and universal suffrage from the Monnerville Committee. But for a colonial empire, it was a breakthrough. The *principle* of representing all subjects and citizens had received much support. Not just one

---

[106]Florence Bernault, *Démocraties ambiguës en Afrique Centrale: Congo-Brazzaville, Gabon: 1940-1965* (Paris: Karthala, 1996); Gabriel d'Arboussier, "Programme électoral," elections of 21 October and 18 November 1945, AP 2199/18, AOM.

or two, but a bloc of representatives from Africa, Algeria, and the Antilles were now in an assembly in Paris charged with writing a constitution and meanwhile passing legislation. There were nine Africans (and three Malagasy); before the war there had been one.

They had several assets despite their small numbers. Facing the fact that Vietnam was sliding into war and that Algeria was a powder keg, well aware of the strike movements and political organizing in West Africa in 1945–46, all too concerned with France's political, economic, and military weakness, top officials and at least some politicians knew they had to make a significant gesture toward giving colonial subjects a stake in empire. They recognized—and this would prove a critical factor later on—that any constitution that did not have at least the acquiescence of most of the deputies from the colonies would have no legitimacy. French legislators were divided, and every vote counted, so the politics of coalition building and breaking were humming. And perhaps most important, the African deputies cared above all else about the provisions concerning the overseas territories; metropolitan deputies were often indifferent, often absent from the assembly when colonial issues were debated. And what African deputies cared about greatly was citizenship.

They were, however, not the only people who cared. *Colons* from Senegal, Côte d'Ivoire, Guinée, Sudan, and Cameroon met in Doula, Cameroon, in September 1945 to organize the defense of their interests, calling themselves—trying to evoke the French Revolution—the États Généraux de la Colonisation. The president of the Association des Colons de l'AEF, Georges Pacques, thought the Brazzaville conference was an exercise in demagoguery for offering "the title of voter to these poor blacks." He sought a "return to normalcy" after "this folly"—all the talk of a "native labor code, elections, eligibility for office." The États Généraux sought their own "political emancipation" via the creation of a legislative chamber in each territory, divided into two colleges, the first for French citizens, the second for "citizens of empire," who would be selected by "evolved natives, chosen by a committee composed of equal numbers of civil servants and settlers."[107] The idea of a second-order citizenship for at least some current subjects—in this case selected by white people—would become a recurring theme of those who opposed the extension of full citizenship overseas.

The defenders of colonialism in France, such as the Comité de l'Empire Français, had already gone on record considering the exten-

[107]"États Généraux de la Colonisation," mimeographed document including opening and closing speeches by President Pacques, 5, 8 September 1945, and the declaration of the assembly of 8 September 1945, copy in Bibliothèque Nationale de France, côte 4-LK11–2194.

sion of citizenship "en bloc" an "immense error." They worried that the modest extension of citizenship to a few tens of thousands of Muslim Algerians was being interpreted there as "a new edict of Caracalla." Certainly, "to associate natives with French life" was a worthy goal, but citizenship "must not be accorded without being merited." To be French meant "to participate in the blood, the spirit, the soul of Joan of Arc, Sully, Richelieu, Louis XIV, Colbert, Napoleon, Clemenceau." A rather tall order for an African.[108]

Publications associated with colonial interests kept up the drumbeat against extending French citizenship—"a dangerous absurdity," according to an article in *Marchés Coloniaux* in early 1946.[109] Less contemptuous of Africans and those who favored giving them citizenship was *Climats* (weekly journal of the Communauté Française), which wanted to "reinforce union among all the populations of the French Community" but to do so by emphasizing the "preeminence and permanence" of French sovereignty throughout the union. The journal continued,

> Instead of an ill-considered and ineffective extension of French citizenship to all *ressortissants* of the overseas territories, it would be better to recognize membership [droit de la cité] in the French Community; they would be declared along with French citizens "citizens of the French Union" without effect on their personal status, which they could keep, along with their traditional institutions, as long as they remained attached to them; this disposition would have the effect to confer upon them essential democratic liberties: freedom to come and go, freedom of work, freedom of the press, freedom of conscience, freedom of assembly, trade union freedom, freedom of association.[110]

Citizenship of the French Union—distinguished from citizenship of the French Republic—would remain for a time the fallback position for people who did not think Africans worthy of full inclusion. The list of rights that *Climats* wanted to convey appears substantial and would have made a considerable difference to people subject to the *indigénat* and forced labor, but for advocates of citizenship it fell short on two counts: it did not include the right to vote and it was a distinct list, conceded by French legislators who presumably could give or take

[108] "Projet d'une Constitution de l'Empire Français," annexe to transcript of meeting of 14 November 1944 of Conseil Consultative de l'Empire Français, 100APOM/898, AOM.

[109] Claude Vion, "La citoyenneté impériale est un problème constitutionnel," *Marchés Coloniaux*, 9 February 1946, 124–25, 124 quoted.

[110] *Climats*, 28 February 1946.

away anything without its affecting their own metropolitan constituents. Yet among at least some defenders of colonial hierarchy, there seemed to be a sense that a French community had to be reaffirmed, even if colonial subjects should not expect to be equal to French citizens within it. Whether extended to a few or to many, a second-tier citizenship was what a segment of the political spectrum wanted to offer. As the discussion of the place of the French Union in the new constitution came under discussion in Paris, the lines between equal and second-tier citizenships were being drawn.

◢

CHAPTER 2

A CONSTITUTION FOR
AN EMPIRE OF CITIZENS

Whatever the arguments in 1944 and 1945 over Africans' capacity to act like any other voters and legislators, a basic change in political imagination was becoming evident: the taken-for-granted quality of white men dominating black men and women no longer held. With the opening of the Assemblée Nationale Constituante (ANC) in December 1945, a small block of deputies came with clear determination to represent the interests and desires of people who had been colonized. They would face the task of influencing, as a small minority, the writing of a new constitution as well as writing immediately necessary legislation. The Africans included the following from AOF: Lamine Guèye and Léopold Senghor from Senegal, Fily Dabo Sissoko from Sudan, Félix Houphouët-Boigny from Côte d'Ivoire, Sourou Migan Apithy representing both the overseas territory of Dahomey and the mandate of Togo, and Yacine Diallo from Guinea. From AEF came Gabriel d'Arboussier and Jean Félix-Tchicaya from (Gabon-Moyen-Congo). Alexander Douala Manga Bell represented Cameroon, and Joseph Raseta, Joseph Ravoahangy, and Said Mohamed ben Cheikh Abdallah Cheikh were elected in Madagascar. The African territories also had their representatives of European origin, some of them defenders of the status quo, others—such as Louis-Paul Aujoulat of Cameroon—more open to change.

Two embodiments of French colonial oppression—forced labor and the *indigénat* could not survive the arrival of the new legislators.[1] No sooner had the ministers responsible to the ANC taken office at the end of 1945 than first decrees abolishing the *indigénat* came out of

---

[1] Lamine Guèye brought up both the *indigénat* and forced labor at the very first meeting of the Assembly's Commission de la France d'Outre-mer, extracting from the Minister (Jacques Soustelle) promises that decrees were being prepared to end the former and the latter would end by 1 April 1946. Soustelle called ending the *indigénat* a "gesture" to "representatives of noncitizens" taking their seats in the Assembly. ANC, Commission de la France d'Outre-Mer (FOM), Session of 12 December 1945, 27 February 1946, C//15293, ANF; Minister, telegram to governors general, 10 December 1945, AP 937, AOM.

the Colonial Ministry; the rest of the structure of separate justice was dismantled by February. African deputies, led by Félix Houphouët-Boigny, introduced a bill abolishing forced labor. No one was then willing to defend this sordid practice, and the law was passed unanimously in April 1946, shortly before the final vote on the first version of the constitution.[2] Also in April, the Assembly accomplished something that had been proposed in the 1920s, again in the 1930s, and even by the Vichy government in the 1940s but had come to naught each time: to create a fund for economic development, paid for by the metropolitan taxpayer. Development planning and funding, advocates insisted, would bring the riches of the overseas territories to fruition, employ labor more efficiently, and provide the resources "without which liberty and fraternity are only an illusion."[3]

The constitutional debates went on from December 1945 to September 1946 and present us with a story of politics in action whose outcome at times hung in the balance.[4] This chapter is about a legislative drama. It took place on three stages.

The Commission de la France d'Outre-mer (Committee on Overseas France) was at first chaired by Marius Moutet, long the Socialists' colonial specialist. Moutet was more open to colonial reform than most of his generation; he was a proponent of "democratic colonization." As a deputy during World War I, he had proposed (in vain) extending *citoyenneté dans le statut* to Muslim Algerians. He was a leader of the Ligue des Droits de l'Homme in the 1920s. Between 1936 and 1938, he served as Minister of Colonies in the Popular Front government, during which time he tried, with limited success, to extend parts of the Front's social legislation to the colonies and to wind down

---

[2] In February, the new Minister, Marius Moutet, told deputies that the *indigénat* was abolished and governors were moving away from compulsion in public works. As deputies expressed concern about the timetable, Moutet agreed with their suggestion that passing a law was the best way to get rid of forced labor altogether. That was what African deputies accomplished. ANC, Commission de la FOM, 27 February 1946, C//15293, ANF; Frederick Cooper, "Conditions Analogous to Slavery: Imperialism and Free Labor Ideology in Africa," in Frederick Cooper, Thomas Holt, and Rebecca Scott, *Beyond Slavery: Explorations of Race, Labor, and Citizenship in Postemancipation Societies* (Chapel Hill: University of North Carolina Press, 2000), 107–50.

[3] ANC, *Débats*, 12 April 1946, 1756–58; Report for the Commission de la FOM by Gaston Monnerville, on proposed law "tendant à l'établissement, au financement et à l'exécution du plan d'organisation, d'équipement et de développement des territoires relevant du ministère de la France d'Outre-Mer," ANC, *Documents*, April 1946, Annex 891, 867.

[4] Previous scholarship on colonialism and the making of the Fourth Republic includes D. Bruce Marshall, *The French Colonial Myth and Constitution-Making in the Fourth Republic* (New Haven, Conn.: Yale University Press, 1973); James I. Lewis, "The MRP and the Genesis of the French Union, 1944–1948," *French History* 12 (1998): 276–314; and Véronique Dimier, "For a Republic 'Diverse and Indivisible'? France's Experiences from the Colonial Past," *Contemporary European History* 13 (2004): 45–66.

forced labor.[5] When Moutet returned to the Ministry—now called the Ministère de la France d'Outre-mer (to be referred to as the Overseas Ministry)—the chair of the Assembly's committee passed to Lamine Guèye, Deputy from Senegal. Deputies from the colonies, including Africa, were well represented on the committee—twenty-two out of forty-two members, including such luminaries as Lamine Guèye, Léopold Senghor, Gaston Monnerville, and Aimé Césaire.[6]

In the Commission Constitutionnelle (Constitutional Committee), the actual drafting committee, only a handful of colonial deputies were present, but they included Senghor, who would exercise considerable influence on issues concerning the French Union—so much so that the first version of the constitution was sometimes called "La constitution Senghor."[7]

The assembly as a whole debated and voted on each article as well as on the whole text. Wording of articles was sometimes bounced back and forth among these three bodies, and behind these fora was both the "government"—that is the ministers and their cabinets, responsible to the Assembly as a whole—and networks among the deputies, including an important grouping of overseas deputies.

The Assemblée Nationale Constituante: Different Voices

As deliberations began in the Committee on Overseas France in December 1945, Moutet, then chairing the committee, laid out the message of the discussions of the previous year: "Nowhere where our flag floats should the persons under its protection have the feeling that they are citizens of an inferior race."[8] From the earliest committee drafts of the constitutional provisions on the French Union, the deputies seemed to agree that all subjects should acquire the "quality" of French citizens (a favorite phrase, but which jurists would later make clear was indistinguishable from being a citizen). And they should have the rights of the citizen without having to give up their personal status.

The colonial administration, meanwhile, was saying that it favored a liberal view of granting citizenship, disingenuously interpreting the positions taken at Brazzaville to mean more than they did. A circular to West African governors in December 1945 stated, "The general tendencies of French policy, as specified at the Brazzaville conference,

[5] Jean-Pierre Gratien, *Marius Moutet: Un socialiste à l'Outre-Mer* (Paris: L'Harmattan, 2006).

[6] Lamine Guèye had good personal relations with Moutet and with Henri Laurentie, director of political affairs at the Ministry. Marshall, *French Colonial Myth*, 164–65.

[7] Lewis, "MRP and the Genesis of the French Union," 283.

[8] Testimony before Commission de la FOM, 12 December 1945, C//15293, ANF.

give us, in effect, the duty to facilitate, to a large extent, the accession to the quality of the citizen to those who seek it, thus attesting to their desire for complete integration in the national community, under reserve that their attachment to France be established and that they fulfill other essential conditions explicitly imposed by law."[9] In fact, this circular said nothing new; the onus was still on the individual to prove how French he or she had become. The chance for change now lay in the Assembly.

Propositions for constitutional provisions were soon under discussion in this committee, and the head of the Constitutional Committee, André Philip, promised to get the overseas committee's ideas before proceeding. He was amenable to "proclaim for the colonies the same principles as for the metropole" and to ensure that each colony would have an elected council with "considerable decision-making power in relation to the administration." Meanwhile, colonies would be represented in "the sovereign assembly," leaving open the question of whether there would be a special consultative assembly for overseas territories.[10]

Lamine Guèye and the "intergroupe coloniale de l'Assemblée National Constituante"—the informal grouping of most non-settler deputies from overseas—presented already-formulated proposals to the Overseas Committee.[11] His text departed from the premise that "France constitutes with the overseas countries and territories a union whose members enjoy all the essential human rights and liberties." There would be universal suffrage, civil and military employment would be open to all under the same conditions, and the "original inhabitants of the overseas countries and territories" could keep their "personal status" unless they chose to renounce it.

Lamine Guèye was applauded. Discussion began. A right-wing deputy, René Malbrant, insisted that "natives" were not ready for universal suffrage and elections would be too hard to organize in the absence of the état-civil. He proposed simply to make suffrage universal only where it was "technically possible." Senghor would not accept this argument, pointing out that when Frenchmen began to exercise the right to vote, most of them were illiterate, and Sourou Migan Apithy noted that technical difficulties were not invoked when it came to collecting taxes. Monnerville, citing his committee's previous work, made the fundamental point: "we are building for the future." Aimé Césaire added that when citizenship and the vote were extended to newly freed

---

[9] Governor General, AOF, circular to governors, 21 December 1945, B/20, SRAD.
[10] Commission de la FOM, 19 December 1945, C//15293, ANF.
[11] The intergroup also had an audience with de Gaulle. Note pour le Général de Gaulle, 19 December 1945, 3AG4/3/2, ANF.

slaves in 1848, they had "conditions of life similar to those of animals." Now it was time to make "the same gesture for the Africans."[12]

In January, discussion of the intergroup's text led to agreement that it should include mention that the "the union will be a union freely agreed to"—a statement that made a politically powerful point at the expense of historical accuracy and which would become a point of controversy. It added to the original proposal—which had discussed the substance of citizenship without using the word—the clause "each member of he Union has the quality of citizen and enjoys the entirety of the rights attached to it." A sensitive issue had come up: would people be citizens of the French Union and something else too? Apithy wanted overseas citizens to "conserve their quality of Togolese or Cameroonian." Senghor pronounced himself "favorable to a single citizenship, but the question could be posed of the mandated territories or Indochina. It is necessary to be able to consult them." From there followed a discussion of the Union's diversity. Even Indochina, Moutet pointed out, was an assembly of "separate states"—representing "khmer" or "annamite" civilizations. The possibility of double citizenship was raised, but opposed on the grounds that it would compromise absolute equality."[13]

The committee was wrestling with basic issues facing a heterogeneous polity. Defining institutions of government was even more complicated. The intergroup proposed dividing power between a federal state and territorial states, but federation in this case would emerge not out of the fusion of equivalents but out of the extremes of inequality characteristic of colonization. Moutet echoed the jurists' committee of the previous year: "One only federates something that exists. Now, we create." The committee decided that the concept of "union" was more realistic than that of "federation" or "community." There would be a common assembly, but it would not be called federal. There would be universal suffrage, but not necessarily direct. There would be legislative assemblies in each territory, but they would have "delegated legislative power," recognizing the legislative supremacy of the Assemblée Nationale in Paris while providing autonomy in actual operations.[14]

Gabriel d'Arboussier, the jurist representing the French Congo, spoke to the committee about the basic constitutional problem: "The overseas territories are attached to France under *very diverse* conditions." Because the old colonies (Martinique, etc.) had long been represented in the Assemblée Nationale (and were by then en route to the status of a French department), so too should be the overseas

[12]Commission de la FOM, 26 December 1945, C//15293, ANF.

[13]Ibid., 15 January 1946. The terms "khmer" and "annamite" both commonly represent in French discourse an ethnicization of political and territorial units—protectorates of Cambodia and a part of Vietnam, incorporated into Indochina.

[14]Ibid., 15 January 1946.

territories but not Morocco, Tunisia, and Vietnam, which possessed "true national sovereignty." Their peoples did not necessarily have the same desire as those of the overseas territories. Togo and Cameroon could lean toward either more integration or more autonomy. Hence, there had to be two sorts of assemblies in Paris, one for the Republic, including its overseas territories, and one for the Union, including the protectorates.[15]

Louis-Paul Aujoulat, a citizen (European) deputy from Cameroon, conscious no doubt of the fears expressed earlier of submerging metropolitan France in its overseas people, thought that the territorial legislatures should have greater authority than provincial councils in the metropole, compensating for underrepresentation relative to population in the Paris assemblies. The committee agreed on the representation of the overseas territories in the National Assembly, but left open the question of the participation of Associated States (protectorates). The details would have to be spelled out in laws. All agreed that rights should apply to everyone. Houphouët-Boigny persuaded his colleagues to agree that the interdiction of forced labor for private interests should be added to the list of rights.[16] In this committee—with its strong but not exclusive membership from overseas—there seemed to be agreement on the basic structure of the French Union and shared concerns about the problems of constructing such a complex entity.

The problem of political equality confronted the deputies in several ways. The number of overseas deputies was one question: proposals on the table in February suggested one deputy per seventy-five thousand people in the Antilles, one per four or five hundred thousand in Africa. The question of separate colleges for different electors—if no longer between citizens and subjects, then between citizens who came under the French civil code and citizens who did not—would prove highly divisive. Senghor and other Africans were adamantly opposed to the double college, which they considered a form of racial distinction. Europeans from the colonies worried that they would be submerged in a black majority in each territory, and they did not accept assurances from Senghor and Houphouët-Boigny that Africans would not vote along racial lines. The issue, some claimed, was not race but representation: whites in the colonies deserved representation, their situation being equivalent, apparently, neither to that of whites in the metropole nor to that of blacks in the colonies. The committee was

[15] Ibid., 23, 24 January 1946. Departmental status for the old colonies was no longer controversial. The committee unanimously approved such a law, based on a report submitted by Césaire, on 6 February 1946, and the law was enacted in March. *Le Monde*, 15 March 1946.

[16] Commission de la FOM, 24 January 1946, C//15293, ANF.

not persuaded by this deviation from equality: it voted sixteen to two (with one abstention) in favor of the single college.[17]

The committee decided that two years was long enough for a transition to universal suffrage. At first, people in designated categories—those best known to the state—would vote: "notables évolués," members of local or territorial councils, members of cooperatives and unions, people with state honors, civil servants, military veterans, "merchants, industrialists, planters, artisans," chiefs of villages, and anyone with two years of formally recognized employment in a commercial, industrial, artisanal, or agricultural enterprise.[18] Lamine Guèye asserted, "Everyone in the colonies will vote. . . . Cooks will vote, kitchen hands, gardeners, launderers, all who in order to work must have a work card." Governor Lapie joined the consensus for inclusivity while indirectly noting a basic problem, the state's lack of knowledge of who its citizens were: "In sum, all men or women who can present to the electoral bureau a document proving their identity can be voters."[19] Both men were getting ahead of themselves—voting rights would remain a contentious issue—and both had indicated an important qualification: only some Africans had documents to prove who they were. But they both captured the excitement of the moment: if the projected constitution went through ordinary people would vote.

One can at least see here what serious political actors in 1946 could *imagine*. Deputies from African France showed no interest in independence, but a great deal in political rights and in political autonomy. Their counterparts from European France were not defending absolute control of a unitary republic over subordinate colonies but confronting a France of nonequivalent parts, each of which might participate to greater or—some of them insisted—lesser extent in its own governance.

How did the proposals for a Union of citizens—different but equal—fare in the less supportive environment of the Constitutional Committee? There were real arguments. Votes on several articles were close; positions changed; alliances shifted. Momentum changed as committee proposals were debated in the full assembly and went back to committee; deputies close to the government shuttled between committee and cabinet members. The outcome was anything but predetermined.

When Moutet and d'Arboussier presented the views of the Overseas Committee to the Constitutional Committee, they emphasized

[17] Ibid., 22 February 1946.
[18] Ibid., 1 April 1946.
[19] Ibid., 10 April 1946. The Minister alluded to the possibility of forming the electoral body "on the one hand individually by all who can be identified and on the other hand collectively by those who are not identifiable." He was suggesting the possibility of indirect voting, that is, community leaders voting on behalf of their brethren with no documents.

the importance of repudiating "conscious or unconscious racism" and the difficulties of balancing unity with the distinct juridical status of different parts of the empire and their "cultural traditions."[20] Their propositions were taken up in these terms. The need to protect the rights of overseas populations—vulnerable to exploitation by "local magnates" as well as by the metropole—was brought up, and Moutet responded by emphasizing what remained a crucial aspect of citizenship ever since, that all inhabitants could protect themselves against the exercise of power in a particular location by the right to move anywhere in French territory: "The committee intended above all that a black could freely leave his village, that nothing prevents an Algerian to come to France to work. It is above all freedom of movement that it is important to recognize and to ensure the end of certain abuses." He went on to make clear that "indigènes" coming to European France would have the same rights as anyone else, including the right to vote, although the modalities of suffrage would be variable in their own territories.[21]

The first point of contention came quickly. Paul-Emile Viard, the jurist from Algiers (chapter 1), pronounced himself in favor of the double college, and Moutet replied that this was impossible "if one does not want to see the extra-metropolitan territories detach themselves from France. . . . The deepest aspiration of the autochthonous populations is to feel that they are being treated on the basis of equality. . . . If the maintenance of separate colleges prevails, we will have to expect the resignation of these representatives." But Viard thought that if this were so, then personal status should be treated the same way throughout the French Union. Moutet disagreed: "Men of different religions can perfectly well be united in the same electoral college."[22] That point would be debated for the next eight months.

Would representation in the National Assembly be proportional to population? Moutet knew the stakes behind the question: such a rule "would end up producing a majority of overseas representatives in the national assembly." What he wanted instead was a double assembly, one in which the overseas territories, but not the Associated States, had a voice, but not a large one, plus a second assembly devoted to issues affecting all the overseas components of the French Union. Moutet wanted to leave open different paths of evolution: possibly to transfer more power to local assemblies in the territories or to turn the National Assembly into something more federal. The second assembly would "allow us to hear the voices of representatives of Associated

---

[20]Commission de la Constitution, *Comptes Rendus Analytiques*, session of 25 January 1946, 258–64.
[21]Ibid., 264–65.
[22]Ibid., 264–66.

States (Tunisia, Morocco), which would not accept to be seated in a political assembly with a national character."[23]

Such a "chamber of countries and nationalities" worried deputies on the left. Pierre Cot thought it would encourage "separatism." But one could not go to the other extreme—assimilation. The second assembly had to become "a true association of free peoples, of nationalities that have become conscious of themselves." Moutet claimed that an assembly devoted to overseas problems, with all categories of the Union represented, would be part of a process: "Federalism cannot be created by law; it is the result of historical elements and historical evolution."[24] A skeptic replied, "Federalism presumes that the different federated territories have attained the same degree of civilization."[25] We come back to the difficulties of building federal structures on the basis of a colonial history.

The colonial status quo had its defenders in the Constitutional Committee. Jacques Bardoux, presenting the ideas of the Académie des Sciences Coloniales, argued that the constitution should "reaffirm" the nationality of "all the inhabitants of the French community," but citizenship would be acquired by conditions to be determined by governors or residents general and approved by "the grand council of the French community." Others labeled the proposal "very reactionary," and it got little attention.[26] More difficult was an argument between those who favored the committee proposal for conferring "la qualité de citoyen" on all members of the Union and those, including Viard, who wanted to declare "every person of French nationality is a citizen." The latter seemed more definitive, but the former's vagueness about what "qualité" meant was considered by others to be an asset in a Union that was multinational. By following the word "qualité" with specification that such a person would "enjoy all the rights and liberties that are essential to the human personage," the original text would guarantee rights without constituting "an imposed French citizenship."[27]

Africans, members noted, were French nationals, but Moroccans, Vietnamese, and Tunisians were not. And Africans might prefer to become more autonomous rather than more integrated, so the vaguer formulation left the door open for the "particularity and originality of each people." Too national a concept of citizenship might also alienate Algerians, who might see it as a disguised policy of assimilation—denying their own forms of identification—while too "union" a form of citizenship might seem to citizens of European France to dilute

[23] Ibid., 25 January 1946, 266–67.
[24] Ibid., 267–68.
[25] Remark of Jacques Fonlupt-Esperaber, ibid., 269.
[26] Bardoux, ibid., session of 5 February 1946, 325, and remarks of Pierre Cot, 6 February 1946, 331.
[27] Valentino, ibid., 6 February 1946, 332.

their sense of Frenchness. René Capitant had the wisdom to suggest that the Assembly "institute a single citizenship, but without characterizing it."[28] Although some thought the text was making a distinction (whether positive or negative) between citizens of the Union and citizens of France, the text remained ambiguous. After some close votes on amendments to the language, the committee agreed on the text: "All nationals and *ressortissants* [people under state jurisdiction] of the metropole and overseas territories enjoy the political rights attached to the quality of the citizen by the present constitution."[29] There seemed to be general agreement that in the overseas territories people could enjoy the quality of the citizen without renouncing their personal status, but Capitant worried that while "the maintenance of personal statuses is a sign of liberalism . . . it is necessary nevertheless to avoid 'crystallizing' these statuses by constitutional texts."[30]

After the texts were bounced back and forth between the Constitutional Committee and a subcommittee, the Socialist Guy Mollet, presiding, summarized the discussion as concluding that people in the overseas territories—French nationals—would be given both civil and political rights, while nationals of the Associated States civil rights only. Jacques Fonlupt-Esperaber thought this implied "a double nationality: one imperial, the other of a country. For example, one could be Sudanese and French." To do so was to admit that a "national sentiment" might exist among people who were juridically French nationals—like the Sudanese or Algerians—as well as among Moroccans. Between acknowledging such a sentiment and creating a second-order citizenship, there was a fine line to walk. Léopold Senghor put this clearly, speaking about the constituents who had sent him to Paris: "Senegalese accept the French Union. But if they are politically French, they are not culturally French."[31] The line, he was suggesting, could be walked: it was *political* belonging that the constitution had to codify. Accepting different sentiments of belonging did not have to threaten other people's collective sensibilities or citizens' political position within a French community.[32] An edited version of the citizenship clause was approved by a vote of twenty-three to eighteen.[33]

[28] Ibid., 6 February 1946: Fajon 334, Capitant 332.

[29] Ibid., 335.

[30] Ibid., 335.

[31] Guy Mollet, Jacques Fonlupt-Esperaber, and Gilbert Zaksas, ibid., session of 22 February 1946, 442.

[32] Senghor, ibid., 443. Senghor proposed an article specifying a right of "all the peoples and all the collectivities" within the Union to "independence and flourishing of their language, their culture, their civilization and their spiritual life." Session of 26 February 1946, 451.

[33] Ibid., session of 22 February 1946, 444.

Heated—and in retrospect quite remarkable—was the debate over whether the constitution should declare the French Union "a union freely consented to." It obviously was not; it had been created by colonial conquest. The real question was whether there would be a right of secession. Given the demands coming from Algeria and Madagascar (see below)—not to mention the de facto independence of northern Vietnam under Ho Chi Minh—the issue was immediate. The Committee on Overseas France clearly hoped that such a declaration would enhance the attachment of diverse peoples—including those with nationalities other than French—to France. Others feared that the right of secession, unlike the recognition of cultural and political diversity, was a threat to the integrity of the French Union. The "free consent" doctrine carried the committee and would in April carry the ANC as a whole, only to be removed after the defeat of the constitution in the May referendum and the election of a more conservative Constituante.[34] But the idea would resurface—in the constitution of 1958.

One of the more striking interventions in the early debate came from Daniel Boisdon, a member of the center-right Mouvement Républicain Populaire (MRP). He compared "the current situation of France to that of the Roman Empire, when the latter accorded the right of citizenship to all its subjects, which, moreover, did not make local civilizations disappear."[35] Boisdon was underscoring the diversity of civilizations that could flourish under the French Union, and he did so by a reference to a history of empire—the Emperor Caracalla decree of AD 212 declaring all free, male inhabitants of the empire to be Roman citizens. In the committee and again on the floor of the Assembly, empire references would be invoked repeatedly: to the British Commonwealth, to the Austro-Hungarian Empire. So too would federal systems: the United States, Switzerland, and even, by noncommunists, the multinational structure of the Soviet Union.[36]

The Roman reference constituted a framework for debate off the floor as well. The progressive colonial official Robert Delavignette thought that the French Union in itself implied a kind of "new citizenship," which he compared to the edict of Caracalla.[37] In March, *Marchés Coloniaux*, the periodical of the colonial business lobby, made the opposite argument: "A new edict of Caracalla would be by virtue

[34] Ibid., 5 February 1946, 322–23. When the article referring to free consent went through another round of discussion, on 22 February 1946, there seemed to be little dissent. Ibid., 444–41.

[35] Ibid., 5 February 1946, 328.

[36] These references are analyzed in the context of a long-term history of empire in Jane Burbank and Frederick Cooper, "Empire, droits et citoyenneté, de 212 à 1946," *Annales: Histoire, Sciences Sociales* 63, 3 (2008): 495–531.

[37] Robert Delavignette, *Service Africain* (Paris: Gallimard, 1946), 271.

of its universality a lazy solution, for our Empire has neither the geographic unity of the Roman Empire nor the ethnic and moral unity of the British Empire, to which only the Indies are an exception."[38] But even this journal saw positive aspects of a Roman-like notion of imperial unity. A week earlier, it had praised the Muslim deputy from Algeria, Mohamed Bendjelloul, and his followers for *wanting* French citizenship: "They only ask, as has been repeated now for two millennia: 'Civis romanus sum.'"[39] Later in the debate, the Foreign Ministry also expressed doubts about a new "edict of Caracalla," thinking that it would offend people in the Associated States who did not regard themselves as part of a Rome-like empire and that it presumed a "civic unity" whose existence was "uncertain."[40]

The article-by-article discussions in the Constitutional Committee abutted on problems that had been evident from the first discussions of the French Union. The Committee was faced with proposals coming from the metropolitan parties as well as deputies from the West Indies, Algeria, Madagascar, and sub-Saharan Africa.[41] They were not all pushing in the same direction. The Antillian deputies, notably Aimé Césaire, with the experience of nearly one hundred years of citizenship as well as continued discrimination, were pushing for fuller integration into France, at least for themselves. This they achieved: the "old colonies," by a law passed in March in the midst of the constitutional debates, achieved the status of departments, equivalent to those of metropolitan France. Muslim Algerians proposed their own bill for Algeria, recognizing its "national" status and providing it substantial autonomy under a government elected by its citizens—old and new—stripping away most of the privileges of the colons. A similar proposition came from two deputies from Madagascar (Joseph Ravoahangy and Joseph Raseta), who asserted that Madagascar had been a state before the French conquest in 1896 and deserved the status of a state once again. Their bill would proclaim Madagascar a "free and independent state, administering its own budget, possessing its own army, ensuring its own external representation," but remaining "integrated into the French Union." Their claim to prior statehood had a basis in history, but played down the fact that this

[38] René Malbrant, "Un nouvel edit de Caracalla ne résoudrait rien," *Marchés Coloniaux*, 30 March 1946.

[39] René Malbrant, "Citoyenneté total ou union librement consentie entre peuples libres," *Marchés Coloniaux*, 23 March 1946.

[40] "Note sur la situation de la Tunisie au regard de l'Union française," 16 May 1945, and General Mast, Resident General of France in Tunis, to Minister of Foreign Affairs, 5 June 1945, Afrique-Levant/Afrique-Généralités/37, ADLC.

[41] The different approaches in the constitutional committee are summarized in Marshall, *French Colonial Myth*, 218–22.

state, like most, was built on conquest and hierarchy. Not everyone identified with a Malagasy nation in the same way.[42]

The debates were taking place in the shadow of tension outside of the Assembly. Having declared the independence of Vietnam in September 1945, Ho Chi Minh had not burned his bridges with France and he was involved in negotiations with the French government over achieving autonomy, in some form, within the French Union. On 6 March 1946, an agreement was signed by which France recognized the Republic of Vietnam as a "free" state—the word "independent" was avoided—with its own government, parliament, and army within the Indochinese Federation and the French Union. The agreement provided for Vietnamese and French armed forces to cooperate in maintaining order and for further negotiations. The agreement left much in abeyance, including the question of exactly where sovereignty lay.[43]

The Constitutional Committee did not welcome—or even seriously consider—the proposals coming from Madagascar and Algeria—and the Vietnamese situation was in the hands of negotiators (Indochinese states, like Morocco and Tunisia, were not represented in the ANC). Metropolitan deputies, meanwhile, had their own concern with federalism. The left had welcomed calls for liberty for the colonies, but their major goal was a unitary government in European France. They wanted a single legislative chamber, providing a clear voice of "the citizen," instead of a division of power that would give presumably more conservative rural communities a bigger voice. The right was afraid of just that, so it sought a bicameral sovereign assembly in France. Collectivities would be represented in the second chamber and would constitute a check on the first. This sense of France as an ensemble of communities led some relatively conservative politicians to favor a second chamber representing the "collectivities of the Metropole, but just as much the collectivities of the Empire."[44] But it was not clear

[42]The Minister was worried by such claims, and he thought that the deputies had been elected by a very small college of elite citizens, from "a single race, the Hova race, that in the past exercised a sort of predominance over the island." Lamine Guèye had similar concerns. Commission de la FOM, 16 April 1946, C//15293, ANF.

[43]Marshall, *French Colonial Myth*, 198–201, stresses the importance of these negotiations to the constitution writers. See also David Marr, *Vietnam 1945: The Quest for Power* (Berkeley: University of California Press, 1995), and Pierre Brocheux and Daniel Hémery, *Indochine: La colonisation ambiguë 1858–1954* (Paris: La Découverte, 1995).

[44]"Note sur le problème constitutionnel" for de Gaulle (stamped "lu par le général), August 1945, 3AG 4/2/1, ANF. The memo pointed to the need to represent local, familial, trade union, artisanal, entrepreneurial, scholarly, and artistic communities—a "grand council of all the French collectivities," a phrase lifted from the pioneer of the Third Republic, Léon Gambetta.

that all deputies on the right thought that overseas communities were the kind of collectivities they wanted to see represented in a senate.

In this cauldron of conflicting visions, the African deputies, few in number, had room for maneuver. They had a nuanced position on the federal/unitary question. As we have seen, Lamine Guèye and Léopold Senghor strongly defended republican principles—the rights of all citizens—and the particular civil status that the *originaires* of the Quatre Communes enjoyed. The January strike in Senegal had made clear the value of thinking of France as a single unit: that was the basis for claims for equality of wages and standard of living. Africans, more than practically anybody in the empire, needed the resources of the French Union as a whole. But the desire for autonomy, or at least an expression of Africans' sense of themselves as a collectivity, was there as well, and Senghor and Lamine Guèye understood the aspirations of Algerians and others for an expression of belonging. Hence they looked to a middle ground between federal and unitary institutions: a strong center capable of aiding the territories—and providing a reference point for economic and social claims as well as political rights—and enough autonomy to protect the interests of an African majority in each territory and to express collective sentiments.

The African deputies were not unhappy with compromises that left the composition of territorial legislatures and the precise matters over which they had control to laws rather than constitutional articles. They themselves saw possibilities of evolving in either of two directions, more toward the West Indian model of full incorporation into France—in which case demands for equality would escalate—or toward the Moroccan or Indochinese model of state autonomy. Such suppleness, however, would turn out to be a double-edged sword.

The details of the commission debates are too intricate for analysis here. But let us pause over a revealing document that was put on the record in early April—Léopold Senghor's report on the constitution's treatment of the French Union, requested by the Constitutional Committee after a series of discussions in the committee and in several subcommittees.

Senghor evoked the heritage of the French Revolution, quoting the words of the decree of 16 pluviôse an II (1794) that had abolished slavery and gone on to declare "all men, without distinction of color, resident in our colonies, are French citizens and enjoy all the rights ensured by the Constitution." He condemned the 1802 decree of Napoleon—"the dictator"—reestablishing slavery, and he lauded the revolutionary government of 1848, which had definitively made slaves in the colonies into citizens. Now, after World War II, came "the necessity to free the overseas people from the modern slavery of the *indigénat*, a regime of occupation." That is why all "nationals and *ressortissants*" of the metropole and overseas territories had to have the political rights and qualities of the citizen. This was, he repeated, "the spirit, if not the terms, of the decree of 16 pluviôse an II."[45]

The situation was now different. In 1798 and 1848, "the Jacobin tradition was vital." The only possible political stance was that of assimilation. But since 1848, there had been progress in sociology and "especially ethnology." France had discovered "the brilliant Arab civilization" through which Greek civilization had been transmitted, the metaphysics of India, and the social humanism of China and Indochina, as well as the "collectivist and artistic humanism of black Africa." The vigor of these civilizations and their importance within the French Empire "went against a brutal integration that risked breaking a French equilibrium and the equilibrium of these new worlds."

To codify a France that respected simultaneously difference and equivalence meant a compromise between federal and unitary visions of government, and here he brought to the constitutional debate his phrase "assimilate, don't be assimilated." His report proposed that all French subjects be defined simply as "simply citizens without specifying whether they are 'French citizens' or 'citizens of the French Union.' Usage will decide the label, which in any event, is of secondary importance."[46]

Senghor's report was adopted by the committee, and he later presented it to the Assembly as a whole. The studied ambiguity of the clause on citizenship was, he made clear, the point: to leave open to "the peoples of the Union . . . the possibility to take themselves, according to their wishes and their own genius, toward either assimilation and integration or association and federation." He stressed the unanimity within the committee on the texts and hoped for the same in the ANC.[47]

Outside the Assemblée, critics of extending citizenship made their case known at the same time that Senghor was making his. *Climats* published a long article that took note of the different "categories of French people" recognized at law: citizens "de plein exercise" (full citizens), those—in Senegal—who kept their personal status, certain citizens in Algeria whose citizenship was not heritable, and noncitizens,

[45] ANC, "Rapport Supplémentaire de la Commission de la Constitution" on Union française, Léopold Senghor, reporter, 5 April 1946, in ANC, *Documents*, Report 885, first annex, 2–4, 6. His oral presentation to the Assemblée made similar points. *Débats*, 11 April 1946, 1713–15. Jacques Soustelle took up Senghor's allusion to the liberation of 1794 by suggesting that if this effort had been maintained, perhaps Toussaint L'Ouverture and Dessalines, instead of being heroes of the independence of Haiti, would have been "great statesmen of the French Union." Ibid., 12 April 1946, 1775.

[46] Senghor, Report, 4, 6.

[47] Commission de la Constitution, *Comptes Rendus*, 8 April 1946, 667–69; ANC, *Débats*, 11 April 1946, 1714. *Libération*, 12 April 1946, reported, "It was a black man, a qualified professor in the lycées of Paris, M. Léopold Sédar Senghor, who read, in an impeccable manner, the report that was so well written."

some with limited political rights, others without. It advocated a citizenship of the French Union "superposed" over the status the person had in his or her part of the French Union, be it French citizenship or another status. French citizenship, *Climats* insisted, had to be linked to the "rules of common private and public law of the French state," but citizenship of the French *Union* "does not affect personal status." Union citizenship "could include men of extremely different civilization, culture, stage of evolution. Being different from French citizenship, it allows envisioning different modes of suffrage that will respect the social and customary rules until such a time when the development of a political sensibility among voters justifies proceeding to the ballot." The position came out of a fundamentally imperial notion of governing different people differently, with an evolutionary language betraying the notion of hierarchy rather than mutual acceptance.[48]

The citizenship clause was by now the bottom line for the overseas deputies.[49] They had already made a compromise on the federal principle that some of them had favored, for their Socialist and Communist allies were adamant on having a single chamber legislature and hence a unitary principle of law making. Some deputies from overseas, such as the West Indian Paul Valentino, later expressed regret over compromising the federal position, but hitching their constitutional aspirations to a position that was not theirs was the price of working closely with parties of the left.[50] Deputies hoped that citizenship and some form of legislative representation would at least give new citizens of the former colonies a base from which to push for desirable legislation and improved institutions, even if the Union fell short of a federation of equivalent territories.

When constitutional proposals came before the ANC as a whole, the question of how seriously the many pious words about rights, liberties, and equality should be taken emerged quickly. As the draft Prologue was introduced, Bendjelloul wanted to be sure the drafters meant what they said. His Algeria had long been ruled under "special" laws, so now he asked, "But would we be freed of all special laws?

[48] "L'Assemblée sera-t-elle capable de donner la vie à l'Union française?," *Climats*, 11 April 1946. A government survey charted responses in metropolitan France to the question, "In your opinion should natives of the colonies vote?" In all, 59 percent said yes, 24 percent said no, and 17 percent had no opinion. The yes opinion reached 79 percent among Communists and 77 percent among socialists, but 35 percent on the "right" and 49 percent for supporters of the MRP. SSS, 15 April 1946, AP 2147/2, AOM.

[49] Lamine Guèye later wrote, "In coming to sit in the National Constituent Assembly the overseas deputies had as their primary objective the abolition of the *indigénat* and the establishment of equal rights for their constituents." Quoted in Marshall, *French Colonial Myth*, 221.

[50] Paul Valentino, ANC, *Débats*, 16 April 1946, 1917.

Freed from any regime of exception? Placed on the same footing of equality as the inhabitants of the metropole?" He wanted the assembly to affirm "that all peoples possess the absolute right to independence and to the flourishing of their culture, language, civilization, and spiritual life." He hoped that the right to independence would not have to be exercised and that the new constitution would bring in "a new era of justice and peace, of equality, of liberty, for Algeria, for France, and for democracy."[51]

Pierre Cot, a leading figure on the left, speaking on behalf of the Constitutional Committee, underscored the breakthrough of his committee's draft. It would

> extend the field of democracy. . . . Its principal advantage, in my eyes, is to put an end to the colonial regime. The colonial empire of our country is no more. In its place we want the French Union: we are putting together this community of people freely associating and striving to realize by common effort the best of our democratic traditions. . . . Up to now, France consisted of 40 million citizens and 60 million subjects; she will find herself enriched, ennobled, and expanded, for tomorrow she will have 100 million citizens and free men.[52]

When it came to specifics, Cot put a lot of weight on the "Conseil de l'Union française," which he saw as a "chamber of reflection," a balance to the unicameral Assemblée Nationale. In effect, the Union would be a check on the nation.[53] The weakness of the proposal was noted quickly: the Conseil de l'Union was consultative only; it could not pass legislation. The sovereignty of the Assemblée Nationale raised the stakes of the overseas representation in it, for the territories needed to bring "the necessary impact" to the debates over issues concerned with their relationship to metropolitan France. Such a situation risked to compromise the very democratic initiative, as well as the "unity of the French Union" that the constitution was intended to promote.[54]

Of particular concern was whether the election of the President—which all agreed would be indirect—should include the Conseil de

[51] ANC, *Débats*, 8 March 1946, 646. See also his intervention of 19 March, 865–66.
[52] Ibid., 9 April 1946, 1620.
[53] Cot was specific that this assembly would "compenser les inconvenients du régime de l'Assemblée unique." Ibid., 1622.
[54] Intervention of François de Menthon (MRP, member of Constitutional Committee), 9 April 1946, 1624, 1626. The Communists were adamant about not creating a "new Senate," out of the Conseil d'Union française. They acknowledged that while overseas deputies would be a presence in the Assemblée Nationale, they would not be there in proportion to population. This was of "secondary importance" compared to that of ensuring that the Assembly would be the voice of the people. Etienne Fajon, ibid., 1628.

l'Union or just the Assemblée Nationale. Paul Coste-Floret, from the center-right MRP, wanted to give a bigger voice to the Conseil. The President, after all, was chef d'État, distinct from the head of government, and that meant he should be chosen by "the representatives of the citizens and the representatives of local collectivities."[55]

The idea of representing communities was part of Coste-Floret's political credo: "We believe that the time of individualist democracy is over. . . . We are today partisans of a pluralist democracy, that is to say a democracy of groups, one that is not content with approaching the citizens as such, but that also seeks to approach the people organized in their territorial collectivities, in their professions, and in their families." For him, if the Assemblée Nationale incarnated "the citizen," another assembly had to represent "the different social groups."[56] It is clear that he was thinking of the community—rural, centered on family and local institutions, perhaps on the Catholic Church—as a more conservative element to offset the mobilized citizen voting one by one for deputies to a National Assembly. But the draft constitution spoke of the "territorial communities" as "communes and departments" and "overseas territories and federations" in the same breath.[57]

René Pleven was more explicit on this point. He too favored bicameralism, but for him the problem was precisely on the level of the Union. He defended the "federative idea" as he had earlier (chapter 1), although—perhaps thinking of his native Brittany—he now preferred to call it the "regionalist idea" in contrast to the "unitary idea." He wanted the federal assembly to have real power. Taking up the difference in "personality" of the overseas territories, as well as their variety of "political statuses," he feared that the mixture of political entities was undermined by the consultative nature of the proposed assembly. The components—including the metropole—should rule themselves in regard to domestic matters and rule together in regard to defense, foreign affairs, and communications. He wanted to see a new assembly evolving out of "a federal, imperial, intercolonial assembly." In mixing these words, he was accepting the historic evolution from empire to federation. The counterpart of his assembly was that there should be

[55] Coste-Floret, ibid., 1639. The alternative in question was election by a two-thirds majority of the Assemblée Nationale.

[56] Coste-Floret, ibid., 1640. Coste-Floret had undoubtedly thought through the implications of his group argument on overseas territories. A jurist who had taught law at the Université d'Alger, he had written in 1939 an article on personal status in the colonies that concluded that "the accession of the French subjects in Algeria to political rights" implied a rethinking of "purely technical juridical problems." Paul Coste-Floret, "Jus sanguinis, jus soli et statut personnel dans les rapports de la Métropole, de l'Algérie et de l'Étranger," *Revue Critique du Droit International* 34 (1939): 201–14, 214 quoted.

[57] Rapporteur général, citing article 111 of draft Constitution, ANC, *Débats*, 9 April 1946, 1645. See also the argument in favor of the rights of collectivities of influential MRP member Daniel Boisdon. Ibid., 7 March 1946, 607.

no representation of the overseas territories in the Assemblée Nationale: Why, he asked rhetorically, should voters overseas elect deputies to "a metropolitan legislative assembly"? Why should they vote on the budget for European France, when citizens of the metropole were not sitting in the legislatures of African territories?[58]

The alternative to a federalism, in Pleven's or Senghor's variant, was a unitary structure representing the will of a single French people, and such a structure could have given overseas politicians a firm position to demand reform, but only if they had sufficient voice in the center. Such an alternative ran into the fears in European France of a colonial majority. The federalist solution might allow each territory to express its personality and its interests—but only if the territorial legislatures were given real authority, something that caused deputies to worry about the loss of sovereignty.[59] The situation became even more complicated when it came to the Associated States—for they *did* have sovereignty, and French constitution writers were not sure that the Constituante had the power to determine their status or that the republican ideal of rights was compatible with the conceptions of the monarchs of those states. Making the French Union democratic came up against the underlying heterogeneity of the empire, in which autonomy and democracy were sometimes at cross-purposes.[60]

The Algerian deputy Mohamed Bendjelloul kept pressing on what citizenship would actually mean to his constituents. He acknowledged the breakthroughs of the text—"the recognition of the same rights and freedoms for Muslim Algerians as for French people, the enjoyment of the rights of citizens, accession to all civil and military positions, respect of personal status." But the electoral law, being considered at the same time as the constitution, took away part of what was being conceded: the double college left Algerian Muslims "twixt and between the full citizen and the former French subject." Algeria remained a "land of exception and still under special laws!" He pointed to the contradiction between the draft constitution's affirmation of "universal, equal, direct, and secret suffrage" and another clause giving the

[58] Pleven, 11 April 1946, 1720–21.

[59] For Jacques Soustelle, a decision-making Conseil de l'Union française was needed to give substance to the French Union. Ibid., 15 April 1946, 1857, 1864. The Algerian jurist Paul Viard rejected federal structures because the territories possessed "no characteristic of sovereignty," but he admitted that the unitary state he preferred was inconsistent with the diversity of personal statuses in the empire. From the opposite direction of Senghor, the advocate of federalism, he ended up also advocating "a middle solution." Ibid., 11 April 1946, 1715–17.

[60] The dilemma of including the Associated States in the new constitutional structure came up early and awkwardly when two deputies proposed a resolution affirming the "legitimate place" of those states in the French Union. The ANC could agree only to a bland resolution asking the government to consider the situation. Ibid., 11 April 1946, 1721–23.

Assemblée Nationale the job of making rules for elections. Bendjelloul raised the possibility of abstaining or even voting against the constitution if his constituents received anything less than full electoral rights.[61]

The Assembly, in the end, could agree that overseas subjects would be made into citizens, but not on a federal structure in which those citizens could govern themselves. It voted against giving the Conseil de l'Union française the status of a second chamber of Parliament. It continued to debate the powers to be ascribed to the Assemblée Nationale and to the elected councils in departments and overseas territories, leaving much of the details to future laws. Had the constitution taken a truly federalist turn, a federal assembly would have stood at a "preeminent and superior" level to the legislative bodies of the federated states, including the Assemblée Nationale, but in the end the only federal body was relegated to a consultative role.[62]

The traps of history were most clearly revealed as the debates in the ANC wound down. Lamine Guèye wanted to have written into the constitution a guarantee that the voters (électeurs et électrices) of the overseas territories could vote their approval or disapproval of the constitution. Coste-Floret pointed out that the amendment was itself unconstitutional: the inhabitants of the overseas territories would become voters only by virtue of the constitution, so they would have no right to vote until it had passed. Lamine Guèye was indignant. He insisted that the government could by decree admit everyone to the category of citizen and allow them to vote. Not to do so would be to tell the people of the territories, "Whatever we have done had neither the scope nor the significance that you attached to it. Legislating for the overseas populations outside of what they would want is almost to say: to legislate against them."[63] But by law Coste-Floret was right, and while assembly leaders promised to study Lamine Guèye's proposal, it was not accepted.

In the final speeches before submitting the draft constitution to a referendum—from which most Africans would be excluded—deputies from all sides lamented the compromises that had gone into the constitution: a "cocktail" the head of the Constitutional Committee called it.[64] Left and right accused each other of sabotaging federalism, an idea both had at earlier points claimed to support but about which both had substantial doubts.[65] From different places in the political

[61] Mohamed Bendjelloul, ibid., 11 April 1946, 1718.

[62] A point made clearly by Viard, ibid., 1716.

[63] Lamine Guèye, ibid., 18 April 1946, 2021–22.

[64] Ibid., 19 April 1946, 2068. The reporter said bluntly, "This constitution is not very good." But it was the best that could be done under the circumstances. Ibid., 2066.

[65] Reporter General, ibid., 2065. He squarely blamed the MRP for pushing the rest of the Constitutional Committee away from truly federalist principles.

spectrum came applause for "the admission, about which we all rejoice, of our overseas brothers into the national community,"[66] for the creation of a French Union that "eliminates the primitive notion of colonialism as the Third Republic understood it,"[67] for proclaiming "the equality of rights of the peoples of the overseas territories and those of the metropole."[68] But René Pleven, who had articulated the case for imperial federalism as the war was ending, expressed his "sadness" at the results: "We will vote against this constitution because it does not accomplish in a reasonable manner what we expected of it, that is the integration of the overseas countries [pays]." He repeated that those countries should have their place in a Union assembly that had the power to vote on defense and other such matters and to have a role in choosing the President of the Republic, but he did not want the National Assembly to include "deputies who will vote on laws not applicable to the people who will have elected those deputies." With more than the Union in mind, he declared that a single chamber legislature could lead to dictatorship.[69]

And a final exchange occurred on the subject of citizenship. Paul Viard of the MRP criticized other parties for refusing to affirm "the unity of the French Republic," and he insisted that it was the position of his party that "all the overseas French are declared citizens." When the reporter read the text, "All French nationals and *ressortissants* of the metropole and the overseas territories enjoy the rights of the citizen," Viard replied, "It does not say French [citizen]."[70] The tension between having the rights of a French citizen and being a French citizen expressed the dilemma of turning an empire that was both incorporative and hierarchical into a union that was egalitarian and diverse. MRP leaders were saying that the legislative structure was too centralized, but not French enough. With the MRP and others on the right voting against the constitution, and Socialists, Communists, and most overseas deputies voting for it, the constitution of 19 April 1946 was approved by a vote—disappointing to its authors—of 309 to 249.[71]

The newspaper *Libération* issued a particularly strong statement of what the ANC had accomplished.

It above all accomplished a revolutionary endeavor of exceptional breadth: the establishment of the French Union. The Empire, that was a beautiful old word. Overseas France, a happy formula. The French Union, put in the form of texts, consecrated

[66] Edouard Herriot, ibid., 2058.
[67] Daniel Mayer (Socialist), ibid., 2059.
[68] President of the Commission, ibid., 2069.
[69] Pleven, ibid., 2062.
[70] Viard and Reporter General, ibid., 2069.
[71] Ibid., 2081–82. The deputies from Madagascar abstained.

by the Constitution, is the end of the colonial regime, of native forced labor, it is the free entry into the French community of sixty million new citizens, emancipated in a single gesture, and suddenly called upon to participate in the rights and duties common to the French of the metropole.[72]

The Lamine Guèye Law, the End of Colonialism, and the Practicalities of Voting

Lamine Guèye made another—crucial—move before the first ANC adjourned and the campaign for ratification began. Fearing that the draft constitution might be defeated in the referendum on its approval scheduled for 5 May, he asked the Assembly to put in the form of a law the constitution's provisions on citizenship. In explaining his bill, he underscored the importance of declaring "without waiting for the results of the referendum that will give force to the Constitution, that the *ressortissants* of all the French overseas territories are proclaimed to be citizens, by means of ordinary legislation." The single article of the bill proclaimed that "all *ressortissants* of the overseas territories (including Algeria) have the quality of citizen in the same respect as French nationals of the metropole or the overseas territories. Specific laws will establish the conditions under which they will exercise their rights as citizens." Lamine Guèye saw the bill as summarizing what all parties had agreed upon in earlier discussions, and if the bill maintained the nuanced language of not exactly saying that overseas *ressortissants were* citizens or were citizens *of France*, there was no such nuance in his statement that the act would abolish "all the barriers that still exist among the men whom we want to proclaim equal."[73]

The bill passed unanimously. Lamine Guèye was right that consensus had been reached during constitutional debates on this approach to citizenship. His bill became known as the law of 7 May 1946 or, more tellingly, the Lamine Guèye law.

The Ministry of Overseas France saw the unanimity of the vote as critical, especially when, as Lamine Guèye had feared, the constitution was rejected by referendum: "The rejection could not be brought about by a question that had received the unanimous votes of the deputies. In addition, during the course of the campaign for the referendum, no objection was raised on any measure relative to the rights of the inhabitants of the Overseas Territories." Moutet made much of the spirit in which the law was passed. "The law of 7 May 1946 proclaims above all the principle of equality: there are no more subjects,

[72] *Libération*, 29 April 1946.
[73] *Documents de l'Assemblée Nationale Constituante*, Annexe No. 1198, 25 April 1946, 1177.

Figure 2. Socialist Party Leaders, December 1946,
with Lamine Guèye in the back center. ©AFP/Getty Images.

there is no colonial regime." He cited Senghor's deliberate ambiguity over what former subjects were citizens of, but he pointed out to his High Commissioners in the overseas territories that from now on former subjects would have equal access to jobs in the civil service. Pay and benefits could not reflect personal status, only conditions of service. There could be only one labor code, for metropolitan and "autochthonous" workers alike. There could be no separate codes of justice, no deviation from the principle of equality in public rights. The clause pertaining to special laws spelling out how the law would be applied was taken to refer to the need for a law governing elections, not differential civil rights. Now that all were citizens and potential voters, but with different personal statuses, it was "indispensable to organize their état-civil." They would have to be made to register births, marriages, and deaths "on the same basis as all French citizens." He returned to the implications of the law's proclamation of equality: "It remains for us to bring this equality to fruition, to take it from the domain of theory to that of realities."[74]

[74]Minister to Governor General, 14 June 1946, and AOF, Directeur Général des Affaires Politiques, Administratives, et Sociales, "Note au sujet de la loi du 7 Mai 1946," July 1946, 17G 152, AS.

For the moment, the Lamine Guèye law was promulgated in all the overseas territories, although not in the mandated territories of Togo and Cameroon or in the Associated States because of uncertainty among jurists over whether it could apply to territories whose populations did not have French nationality (see below).[75] The law allowed France to assert itself in international circles that were becoming critical of colonialism:

> A law of last 7 May made all the *ressortissants* of these territories into citizens, on the same basis as French nationals of the metropole. The dependence, the non-autonomy of the territories in question is thereby notably attenuated, if not abolished, not by their transformation into free states, but because they are becoming part of an ensemble, which is first of all the French Republic, the French Union in a wider framework, parts whose autonomy will soon be as real, as complete as that of a French department, for example.

The Ministry had to admit that the territories had no international status, but officials thought they had at least a claim to being on the progressive side of the colonial divide, although it was a leap to assert that France had eliminated "all traces of the colonial status."[76]

The Constituante had debated not only the broad principles of a remade empire, but the specifics of how to elect representatives and run legislative bodies at different levels of the whole. The law on Territorial Assemblies of 9 May 1946 was intended to give overseas territories a serious voice in local affairs, going beyond the consultative (and often European-dominated) colonial councils and the municipal governments that had existed in only a few "communes de pleine exercise." Each territory got its elected assembly, and its purview included the local budget and levying taxes, as well as oversight over many economic activities. The law of 13 April 1946 dealt with elections. Its most important and controversial provision for the overseas territories was the single college: citizens of French civil status, mainly Europeans, would not be able to elect their own representatives.[77] The law did not, however, go as far as universal suffrage, and officials expressed acute

[75] Conférence des Hauts-Commissaires et Gouverneurs Généraux, "Rapport sur l'électorat politique dans certains Territitoires d'Outre-Mer," 16 July 1946, AP 216/1.

[76] Minister of FOM to Minister of Foreign Affairs, 30 August 1946, K.Afrique 1944–1952, Généralités/33, ADLC. Jurists in the foreign ministry were more skeptical about claims to nondependence. "Consultation de M. Gouet, Juriconsulte, sur la définition à donner au terme Territoire non-autonome," 25 September 1946, ibid.

[77] The often-heated debate on the election law took place on 5 April 1946, and can be seen in ANC, *Débats*, starting on p. 1504. The electoral law, the Ministry worried, provided for forty-two deputies for the overseas territories, elected by citizens who were mostly illiterate and hard to identify, a possible logistic nightmare, possibly manipu-

anxiety about not only the overseas population's lack of familiarity with elections, but also their own lack of knowledge of the overseas population. Administrators did not have the kinds of lists election officials used to keep track of voters. They did not know who their new citizens were.

Deciding who could vote began with what a government in a colonial situation actually knew. First, chiefs were supposed to know their people, so forms of indirect suffrage were considered: votes would be organized by community to choose representatives who would in turn vote in the general election alongside the more civic-minded citizens, who would vote directly. Second came the people whom the state did know: ex-soldiers, trade union officials, members of agricultural or trade cooperatives, merchants, educated people, employees of the state or of French-run corporations (but not "ordinary wage workers," who were too numerous). The "capacitaires"—the people who met such criteria—could vote directly, others in what was referred to as an election "in two degrees."[78] Officials estimated, however, that the number of voters would expand to something like six or seven times the number of 1945.[79] While some officials and legislators worried about backward, rural people voting, Laurentie worried about the capacitaires, as privileged and hence unrepresentative Africans. He referred to their potential predominance as "la sénégalisation," in apparent reference to the limiting of voting rights to a small elite under the prewar regime in Senegal. Instead, he wanted to rethink the laws on territorial assemblies and on voting: "universal suffrage, in effect the voting of villages, should replace the monstrous system we created."[80] In fact, the laws on both electoral arrangements and territorial assemblies had to be revisited, for they were based on the assumption that the April constitution would be ratified. It was not.

Saving Citizenship: The Second Constituent Assembly

All this was thrown into contention by the vote on the constitutional referendum. The campaign against the referendum was not focused on the colonial question. The most substantive issue was the single-chamber legislature, notably the fear on much of right and center of the political spectrum that the left might dominate such a chamber

---

lable by elements officials regarded as demagogic. Affaires Politiques, Note pour M. le Ministre, 16 July 1946, AP 216/1, AOM.

[78] Conférence des Hauts-Commissaires et Gouverneurs Généraux, "Rapport sur l'électorat politique dans certains Territitoires d'Outre-Mer," 16 July 1946, AP 216/1, AOM.

[79] Henri Laurentie, "Note pour le Ministre," 1 July 1946, AP 216/1, AOM.

[80] Laurentie, "Note personnelle pour M. le Ministre," 4 June 1946, 72AJ/535, ANF.

and use it as the basis for establishing a socialist dictatorship. De Gaulle's voice was only the most powerful calling for defeat of the constitution. *Marchés Coloniaux* proclaimed, "We will try to save the Empire by voting: NON!" Its main argument was that if the constitution were accepted, the pressure to make representation proportional to population would be irresistible and sixty million "provincials" would outvote forty million "native Europeans"—shaping metropolitan as well as overseas legislation.[81]

In Algeria the vote on the referendum turned out to be relatively close, largely because the reforms of 1944 had put a significant number of Muslim Algerians onto the voter rolls. The Antilles favored the constitution. In most of Africa, where the large majority of citizens were settlers, the vote was about two to one against the constitution, but in Senegal, where most citizens were Africans, the vote was 28,915 to 2,666 in favor.[82] That African opinion seemed to favor the constitution overwhelmingly led officials to fear a disappointed, perhaps violent, reaction to the referendum's defeat.

The "non" vote in the referendum on 5 May brought about a reconfiguration of the politics of remaking empire. It led to new elections for a new Constituent Assembly in June and, following the rightward momentum, a new alignment of parties—one less sympathetic to voices from the colonies. The MRP, as James Lewis has shown, was largely responsible for the shift. Its leaders—influenced by a social Catholicism focused on family and social integration as an alternative to socialism—had been sympathetic to colonial aspirations for inclusion. Hesitating between federalist and unitary approaches to governing the French Union, MRP politicians had not followed a rigid line in the first Constituent Assembly, negotiating with overseas deputies and with leftist parties. But defeating the unicameral legislature was the bottom line for the MRP, and its members voted against the final version of constitution and campaigned for its defeat in the referendum. Some of the MRP's most ardent followers of social Catholicism (such as Louis-Paul Aujoulat of Cameroon) wanted a more vigorous approach to social betterment. But with increased representation—but short of a majority—in the new assembly, the MRP now looked to its right for allies, including to deputies close to colons or advocates of a strong, centralized France ruling over its dependencies. The deteriorating situation in Vietnam gave more pertinence to this last argu-

<hr />

[81] René Moreux, "Au référendum du 5 mai, tous les coloniaux répondront: 'NON,'" *Marchés Coloniaux* 27 April 1946, 389.

[82] Marshall, *French Colonial Myth*, 171. A disciplined campaign for a "oui" vote is described in Senegal, Monthly Political Report, April, May, June 1946. See also Dahomey, Monthly Report, May 1946.

ment, as negotiations failed to arrive at a modus vivendi between a Republic governed by Ho Chi Minh and a federation run from Paris.[83]

In the wake of the constitution's defeat, de Gaulle attempted—in his famous speech at Bayeux on 16 June—to frame the subsequent debate. In the opening passages of his speech, he made clear that behind his arguments lay the experience of war and the concepts of state, nation, empire, and federalism. "It is here on this soil of the ancestors that the State reappeared: the legitimate state, because it rests on the interest and sentiment of the nation . . . [,] the State, capable of reestablishing around itself national unity and imperial unity, to assemble all the forces of the *patrie* and the French Union." Empire and nation, imperial unity and national unity, were in his thinking separate but joined. The state drew its strength from the unity and confidence of its citizens. The proposed constitution had not met such criteria. A second legislative chamber was needed to represent the different parts of France; a strong presidency was required. "The future of the 110 million men and women who live under our flag is in an organization in federative form." Sixty million of those men and women lived overseas, and they would remain part of "a free nation grouped under the aegis of a strong State."[84]

Over the summer, colons mobilized for a constitution more to their liking. The Comité de l'Empire Français declared, "It is above all the law of last 7 May on citizenship that must be reformed."[85] The États Généraux de la Colonisation met in Douala, Cameroon, and set out an explicit defense of a colonial order. This body attacked the extension of citizenship across the empire and insisted that access to the status of "citizen of empire" should be awarded only on an individual basis. "It is not by the stroke of a pen that one can turn millions of entirely uncultured beings into conscious and organized citizens." The États Généraux also complained loudly about the abolition of forced labor—which had served settler interests directly in places like the Côte d'Ivoire—a move that by then did not add to their credibility, for if there was any aspect of colonialism of which government officials needed to wash their hands, this was it.[86]

Marchés Coloniaux turned its campaign against the first constitution into an argument for its own version of federalism: "The Empire can still be saved by federalism." Each territory should have its own legislature with authority over purely local affairs and the double

[83] Lewis, "MRP and the Genesis of the French Union," esp. 285–88.

[84] Discours de Bayeux, 16 June 1946, reprinted in Charles de Gaulle, *Discours et messages 1940-1946* (Paris: Berger-Levrault, 1946), 721–27.

[85] Comité de l'Empire Français, Section de l'AOF, meeting of 11 July 1946, 100APOM907, AOM.

[86] Conclusion of meeting of les États Généraux de la Colonisation, *Le Monde*, 25–26 August 1946; *Climats*, 1 August 1946.

college would ensure "the legitimate representation of settlers." Only citizens—under the old rules—would vote for deputies to the Assemblée Nationale; a second, federal assembly, would include native deputies "who enjoy imperial citizenship." It continued to argue for "coherent colonial policies," unapologetically using the terminology officials had repudiated. It published as well statements from the Comité de l'Empire français, which denied that "évolués" truly represented African communities and claimed that "the true elite of the latter consists of their customary notables." Africans, in short, belonged in their tribes, while the empire needed "an advanced direction and control which must be the fact of responsible Frenchmen." A "colonial manifesto" issued jointly by the Académie des Sciences Coloniales, the Comité de l'Empire Français, the Comité de l'Afrique Française, *Marchés Coloniaux*, and several other empire-boosting organizations rejected "the concession of French citizenship to the ensemble of overseas territories," while calling for more autonomy for territorial councils in which the double college would protect settler interests. The drumbeat continued throughout into the summer.[87]

Belittling the political capacity of colonial populations could take place in respectable circles, such as an article by an influential demographer and architect of the metropole's social policy, Adolphe Landry, in *Le Monde*. He argued that giving citizenship to indigenous people would be "a major error, concerning populations that for the most part have no état-civil and which for the most part have no notion of the political or other problems which are debated in our assemblies."[88]

In Africa, the government was trying to say the opposite. Officials, after the referendum, reassured Africans that the constitution had been rejected for reasons not concerning the overseas territories and they should not worry about losing the rights they thought they had acquired. But the fact that new elections were conducted under previous election laws without the votes of people who thought they had acquired political rights was hardly reassuring. The June election, however, went smoothly, and those Africans allowed to vote expressed their determination by turning out in large numbers to return the main authors of the earlier document to office.[89] Henri Laurentie wrote to

[87] René Moreux, "Repenser toute notre politique coloniale et refaire la Constitution de l'Empire," *Marchés Coloniaux*, 25 May 1946, 493–95; "Un important Manifeste Colonial: Pour une politique coloniale cohérente," *Marchés Coloniaux*, 1 June 1946, 521–23. See also *Marchés Coloniaux*, 4, 25 May, 13 July, 27 July, 10 August, 28 September 1946.

[88] Adolphe Landry, "France et l'Union française: Il y faut deux citoyennetés," *Le Monde*, 17 September 1946.

[89] Secretary of Government, General, Digo, telegram to Ministry, Paris, 6 May 1946, Moutet, telegram to High Commissioners, 8 May 1946, Governor General, "Rapport sur le Référedum et élections (5 mai, 2 et 30 juin 1946) en AOF" [nd], AP 486/2, AOM.

Lamine Guèye in July, on behalf of the Minister, assuring him that "the overseas territories are part of the French Republic and benefit from all the liberties inscribed in her constitution. . . . The system of local liberties remains out of discussion."[90]

The top official in AOF, Governor General René Barthes, was more forceful. At a meeting of high officials in July, he "declared himself absolutely partisan of the project of the first Assemblée Nationale Constituante in regard to the French Union. A change of status would constitute, in this sense, a grave political error. He declared that the suppression of the *indigénat*, of native justice and forced labor as well as the possibility of accession to citizenship constitute social progress that will bear its fruits sooner or later." The conference concluded that the constitution approved by the first Assembly "constituted a supple system."[91]

For African activists, the course of action was clear: defend the Lamine Guèye law. Senghor said exactly that as soon as the new Constituent Assembly began work: there was no going back on this "essential disposition" of the former project.[92]

During the summer, African political leaders in Senegal were holding meetings. They reminded people that the Lamine Guèye law had passed unanimously. Representatives of different political tendencies called for a united front. The Union des Syndicats, the umbrella trade union organization, joined the call for unity. "Are we FRENCH CITIZENS?" asked a headline in the left-leaning Dakar newspaper *Réveil*.[93] In Côte d'Ivoire, officials reported anxiously that the Syndicat Agricole Africaine—Houphouët-Boigny's organization—was developing networks across the territory to defend what they thought they had gained. From rural districts came reports of demonstrations against chiefs, of chasing chiefs from a village, of refusals to give chiefs their usual prestations, and even of the eleven wives of a chief leaving him for their lovers—all of which were associated with the efforts of Houphouët-Boigny's followers to supplant local administration.[94] Houphouët-Boigny, even as the second ANC was deliberating in

[90]Laurentie to Guèye, 22 July 1946, AP 216/4, AOM. Officials were clearly concerned that politics could heat up in West Africa in the summer of 1946. Some North African nationalists, including Messali Hadj, had visited Dakar, and police worried that they might stir things up. Renseignements, Paris, 22 August 1946, AP 2147/2, AOM.

[91]Compte rendu de la conférence des Hauts Commissaires et Gouverneurs Généraux des Territoires d'Outre-mer, 5 July 1946, F/1a/3253, ANF.

[92]ANC, Commission de la FOM, 5 July 1946, C//15313, ANF.

[93]Mamadou Diawara, *Réveil*, 1 August 1946. See also the 25, 29 July issues.

[94]Sûreté, "Note sur la situation en Côte d'Ivoire," 13 July 1946, Governor, Côte d'Ivoire, to Governor General, telegram, 15 September 1946, Administrator in Chief, Haute Côte d'Ivoire, to Chef de la Subdivision Centrale de Bobo-Dioulasso, and latter's reply, 19 September 1946, Report on "incidents de Bobo-Dioulasso du 10 Septembre 1946," 17G 556, AS.

September and October, was working to turn these networks into a political party in the Côte d'Ivoire and then to bring it together with other territorial parties to form a political organization—the Rassemblement Démocratique Africain (RDA)—embracing all of French Africa (see chapter 4).

In the Ministry in Paris during the summer of 1946, there was no die-hard defense of the status quo, but serious doubts about the new proposals, and the old ones as well. Laurentie worried that people had high expectations of the Union without it being defined: The Union "has passed into the vocabulary, into opinion and even into law and it is from now on forbidden to avoid the consequences." But the Union "has no institutions; it is a soul without a body, a juridical virtuality."[95]

Laurentie now thought that the Union had to be considered a "confederation of states presided over by France," containing diverse entities, some of whose status was in flux toward either more integration into France or a status of association. But for now the overseas territories were part of the Republic and should be represented in Parliament, although their deputies should not be "excessively numerous." He recognized that the opposition of Europeans overseas to the single college and indigenous peoples to the double college were irreconcilable. He hoped that citizenship provisions could recognize both federalist and assimilationist arguments by leaving nationality "in the shadows." Citizens of the French Union could also be "Algerian, African, Malagasy citizens." Federalism implied according French citizenship "where it is still demanded, notably in Black Africa (assimilation)." The last point indicated his belief that most African politicians were more intent on equality with metropolitan France than on autonomy, while Algerians and Malagasy were more intent on national autonomy. He was trying to accommodate both tendencies inside a structure that would somehow remain French.[96]

The Associated States came under the jurisdiction of the Ministry of Foreign Affairs, not the Ministry of Overseas France, and its officials realized that the question of citizenship rights for the people of those states was going to be a headache. Someone else was the sovereign in

[95] Note by Yvon Gouet for Minister of FOM, 20 July 1946; Henri Laurentie, "Note sur la necessité d'une constitution de l'Union française," June 1946, Laurentie, "Note pour le Ministre," 12 June 1946, AP 216/2, AOM. One idea of the Foreign Ministry was to have separate constitutions for the République and the Union—the latter minimalist, in deference to the sovereignty of the associated states. "Note sur la nécessité d'une constitution de l'Union française," June 1946, Afrique-Levant/Afrique généralités/37, ADLC. Law professor Georges Scelle also argued for two constitutions, the Union version to be written by its own constituent assembly. "Le problème de l'Union française," *Le Monde*, 12, 13 September 1946.

[96] Henri Laurentie, "Schema d'un programme général concernant l'organisation politique, administrative et économique d'outre-mer," 25 June 1946, AP 216/1, AOM.

the Associated States. The notion of rights, officials in the Ministry noted, was "incompatible with the political status of Morocco. Any negotiation engaged on such a basis with the Sultan would necessarily end up a failure."[97]

There was also a question over whether the Lamine Guèye law applied to mandated territories. The Foreign Ministry's legal expert thought it did not: "with the goal to raising the juridical and political condition of all members of the great French family, the law of 7 May 1946 proclaimed as citizens the *ressortissants* of the overseas territories." But the people of Togo and Cameroon, he claimed, were not French, just as Moroccans were not. They belonged to distinct political entities. "If the inhabitants are not and cannot be French, it is evident that they cannot become French citizens. . . . The observation is valid for the quality of *French citizen*. One can conceive of, for 'people administered under a French mandate' a status equal to that of natives of our colonies, but not identical."[98] The Overseas Ministry's jurists disagreed: they thought that the people of Morocco and other Associated States were *ressortissants* of France, and therefore the Lamine Guèye law applied broadly.[99] But the problem was posed: the mix of French sovereignty, Moroccan sovereignty, and the partial autonomy of ex-colonies created a legal thicket, but it was also the point of building the French Union.

The first round of constitutional debate had produced studied ambiguity on crucial questions of what former subjects were citizens of and how their newfound rights would be exercised. The more polarized political climate after June 1946 made it harder to be fuzzy on such questions.

When the next attempt to write a constitution began in July, the MRP initially tried to seize the federalist high ground, consistent with its view of a France of communities. The key idea was a Union assembly with more power than the April version and in which the overseas territories had half the seats, but with overseas representatives excluded from the Assemblée Nationale. The proposal immediately became a sore point with African deputies.[100] As the first debates in

[97] Note pour M. Jordan, from Direction d'Afrique-Levant, sous-direction des protectorats, June 1946, Afrique-Levant/Généralités/37, ADLC.

[98] Noël Henry, "Note pour la direction d'Afrique-Levant," 14 May 1946 on the application of the Lamine Guèye law to Cameroon and Togo; Henry, "Note pour la direction de l'Afrique-Levant," 29 August 1946, Afrique-Levant/Généralités/37, ADLC. He pointed out that the law, by conferring the quality of citizen rather than citizenship, was all the more unclear.

[99] Yvon Gouet, "Note pour M. le Ministre," 20 July 1946, AP 216/2, AOM. Henry's second memo was a response to Gouet.

[100] For reactions to the proposed exclusion of overseas deputies from the National Assembly, see Commission de la FOM, 17 July 1946, C//15313, ANF, interventions of Yacine Diallo and Lamine Guèye, as well as session of 7 August, intervention of

the Committee on Overseas France (on 17 July) revealed, the MRP seemed to be taking away something from the overseas territories—participation in the National Assembly—without saying what it was going to create in its place, since the authority of territorial governments capable of participating in a federal legislature was not yet specified. The MRP was advocating a strong central government capable "of taking care of questions of federal interest" without making clear how much input those outside of metropolitan France would have on that government.[101] Senghor asserted that the MRP plan was not "a true federalism," since it did not declare that the government would be responsible to a federal parliament.[102]

The next week, a group of self-styled "autochthonous" deputies—which became known as the intergroup[103]—presented through Sourou Migan Apithy their own proposal for a French Union that "renounces any unilateral sovereignty over colonized peoples. It recognizes their liberty to govern themselves and to manage democratically their own affairs." Lamine Guèye turned around an argument used against African participation in a federal government to make it into a call for giving each territory its own status and its own assembly: "One cannot federate what does not exist. In fact, nothing exists." And he reminded everyone of the centrality of rights and liberties in the April constitution; the new one also had to guarantee "the absolute equality of all within the union, of whatever origin." The Committee went around and around on these and other proposals. At the end of the session, it voted fifteen to thirteen with two abstentions for the intergroup plan. Africans could get a hearing.[104]

But not necessarily their way. The Constitutional Committee had begun to talk about the MRP proposal. Senghor declared, "I am astonished that one wants to go back on texts that were voted on unanimously." Coste-Floret made clear what he thought the difference was: Senghor wanted an "evolved federalism"—for the present—while Coste-Floret wanted a "progressive federalism," on the grounds that "the different states of the Union are not sufficiently evolved to allow for such a brutal entrance into federalism." Coste-Floret's idea was to have a federal assembly with "very extensive consultative powers" for

Houphouët-Boigny. Aujoulat, a member of the MRP, argued that the territories would be better represented in the Union assembly, where they would be half the members, rather than in the National Assembly, where they would be few.

[101]The MRP presentation to the Commission de la FOM was made by the R. P. Bertho, 17 July 1946, C//15313, ANF.

[102]Ibid.

[103]*Le Monde*, 24 July 1946. The intergroup was presided by Lamine Guèye and included Ferhat Abbas and Gaston Monnerville. A self-styled "intergroup" had presented proposals to the Commission de la FOM the previous December (see above).

[104]Commission de la FOM, 23 July 1946, C//15313, ANF.

the period during which a future structure of the Union was being considered. But with a powerless assembly, such a structure risked reproducing the domination of metropole over overseas territories instead of something more egalitarian, and if one side feared one outcome, the other side feared its opposite.[105]

Even Coste-Floret recognized that the Assembly could not unilaterally make decisions for the Associated States. But if they were given a choice on the matter, he feared, they could take themselves out of the Union as easily as they could stay in.[106] And overseas territories might, as they "evolved," become more like Associated States, making federalism and secession more plausible alternatives. Senghor was willing to live with uncertainty if it was to give his constituents choice, but that made all the more important in the meantime the problem of guaranteeing individual rights—political and civil. He thought that in ten or twenty years a new constituent assembly might produce a federal assembly that would in fact control the government, putting European France under the same ruling structures as other parts of the Union.[107]

The MRP insisted it was not going back on the rights accorded by the April constitution, and Coste-Floret got a unanimous vote to that effect out of the first committee session devoted to the French Union.[108] But such assurances were not necessarily credible, given that prosettler elements and some groups in the assembly had pushed for a second-tier citizenship or for retention of the prewar exclusions.[109] Ferhat Abbas, the influential Algerian leader newly elected to the Assemblée, noted that in a diverse union—including territories like his own Algeria that had lost their sovereignty but "independently of your will have kept their personality"—"there cannot be citizens of the first zone and citizens of the second zone." One had to "put an end to the equivocation, even hypocrisy, of double citizenship."[110]

The proposal of the Committee on Overseas France came before the Constitutional Committee. MRP leader Jean-Jacques Juglas made clear that it had garnered only a bare majority. He referred to the ongoing negotiations with Ho Chi Minh, which the government hoped

[105]Commission de la Constitution, *Comptes Rendus*: interventions of Coste-Floret, Senghor, Fonlupt-Esperaber, Ferhat Abbas, and Cot, 3 July 1946, 31, 34, 36, 37, 40, 41. On fears of domination by the former colonies, see René Malbrant, ibid., 12 July 1946, 116.

[106]Coste Floret, ibid., 3 July 1946, 32, 12 July 1945, 114.

[107]Ibid., 12 July 1946, 114. Apithy put it this way: "It will also be necessary to allow the overseas territories to seek their true nature; some want autonomy, others assimilation." Ibid., 119.

[108]Ibid., 3 July 1946, 39.

[109]One such proposal for a second-tier citizenship came from the Gauches Républicaines, annex to session of 26 June 1946, ibid., 25–26.

[110]Ibid., 12 July 1946, 118.

would produce a mutually acceptable federation in Indochina that would remain within the French Union, suggesting that the stakes of incorporating Associated States was particularly acute.[111] Lamine Guèye presented the project of his intergroup: their plan would have given the "peoples of the Union" the right to "dispose freely of themselves," specifically the possibility to opt, within twenty years, for "the regime of their choice," that is between fuller integration or the status of an associated state. From the start, all would have the same rights and duties.[112]

Senghor, on behalf of the Socialist Party, proposed another openended variant: he agreed that time was needed—but not twenty years—to decide whether overseas territories would move toward integration or association. Meanwhile, local assemblies elected under universal suffrage would administer the interests of individual territories, while a High Commissioner would coordinate services of each group of territories, giving stability to the system. After one year, an elected assembly of metropolitan and overseas territories would meet to decide on the structure of the Union. But he warned that colonial interests were counterattacking, calling for "the suppression of citizenship."[113]

Some European deputies and Lamine Guèye renewed their battles over specific representation for people of French civil status living overseas.[114] Coste-Floret, sensing that the debate was turning into a retrospective of the pros and cons of colonization, refused to identify himself with "colonialism" but reminded his colleagues that he had lived in North Africa and taught at the law faculty in Algiers. He opposed the "project presented by the intergroup of autochthonous representatives." He did not like the fact that metropolitan deputies had not been involved in writing it and he did not like the text. He preferred the Socialist text, but he did not believe one could leave the organization of the Union up in the air; if everyone agreed on "the federal solution," it was necessary to define it.[115]

[111] Juglas, ibid., 24 July 1946, 180–81. Indochina remained a source of anxiety during the subsequent debates over the French Union. Opinion leaders feared not only a weakening of France, but the possibility that other powers would encroach on its empire. *Libération*, 8 August 1946.

[112] Lamine Guèye, Commission de la Constitution, *Comptes Rendus*, 24 July 1946, 181–82, and text of project, ibid., 195. He acknowledged that components of the federation had to be created, and he wanted those units to be the AEF and the AOF, not individual territories. Ibid., 182.

[113] Senghor, ibid., 25 July 1946, 198–99.

[114] Colonna, ibid., 25 July 1946, 202–3; Guèye, ibid., 203. Ferhat Abbas warned against subordinating the interests of France to 140,000 Frenchmen living in Tunisia, compared to three million Tunisians. Ibid., 206.

[115] Coste-Floret, ibid., 25 July 1946, 209.

By this point, the Overseas Ministry was beset with anxiety: its own control over the overseas territories seemed to be slipping away in the various proposals to create or to defer a federal structure. A Comité interministeriel (representing different ministries), under Alexandre Varenne—an old-timer, Governor General of Indochina in the 1920s—came up with another plan and set it before the Constitutional Committee. Criticizing the "juridical virtuality" of the status quo, it followed Laurentie in proposing a Union with a President—who would be the President of the Republic—a Haut Conseil (Upper Council), and an Assemblée de l'Union française (Assembly of the French Union). The Haut Conseil would consist of the heads of the Associated States and the French Republic, who would meet regularly; the Assemblée would be a body of indirectly elected representatives from each of the Union's territories. Neither body would have the capacity to enact laws or decide policy. Varenne's committee wanted to be sure that the Union would not govern the Republic (as federal governments usually stand above federated states). The Union would be "an intercontinental juridical construction, external to the French Republic," including "very dissimilar parts, some unitary, some federal." The government should set out general principles for the Union in a "Charte de l'Union française," but institutions should not be defined too precisely.[116]

In such a plan, the overseas territories, as opposed to the Associated States, would be "an integral part of the French Republic." They would therefore be represented in the French legislature (in whatever numbers) as "delegates of the public powers of the French Republic and not at all as delegates of each of the diverse overseas countries." Territories, as such, would be represented in a future Assemblée de l'Union Fédérale.[117] After consulting the Foreign Affairs Ministry, the committee thought it could not "impose" on the Sultan of Morocco or the Bey of Tunis their entry into the Union; they would have to decide to do so as an "extension of their current sovereignty."

The Varenne committee was tightening its grip on former colonies, while loosening the structure of the Union. It acknowledged, citing Laurentie, that there was no going back on citizenship.[118] Its message was communicated to the Constitutional Committee on 25 July. Coste-Floret did not entirely agree with the government's report and wanted his committee to vote on whether to include institutions of the

[116]Comité Interministeriel pour le Statut de l'Union française, "Note résumant les vues exposées au Comité dans sa séance du 22 Juillet 1946," AP 216/1, AOM.

[117]Ibid. In this document in the Archives d'Outre-Mer the word "Confédérale" between "Assemblée" and "Union" is crossed out. The structure was, arguably, confederal, but somebody at least did not want to use the word.

[118]Ibid. It was at this point that Laurentie had written Lamine Guèye giving him similar reassurances. Laurentie to Lamine Guèye, 22 July 1946, AP 216/4, AOM.

French Union in the constitution. The vote was twenty-one to nineteen in favor, with the overseas members, Socialists, and Communists voting no. The idea that one should wait one year or twenty was also rejected—barely—and the question now was which of the competing proposals for Union institutions would prevail.[119]

The long discussions produced compromises. Territories, it was proposed, could change their status "in the framework of the French Union," splitting the difference between the idea of the ex-empire as durable and as flexible but not making explicit a right of secession. Ferhat Abbas was at pains to say "we reject separatism" for sentimental and practical reasons, although he approved of the provision of the intergroup text for reconsideration of the nature of the Union in twenty years. Coste-Floret, for his part, assured his colleagues that he saw the Union as "a contract freely agreed to." He thought secession should entail not just an ordinary law, but a referendum in the territory concerned. Paul Bastid, however, was loath to organize "separatism in advance."[120] The committee's text contained the portentous words assuring territories of the "free disposition of themselves," the possibility of moving either toward the status of a "free state linked to France by an international treaty, political autonomy, or complete integration into the Republic."[121]

The question of citizenship came up early in the Constitutional Committee—on 26 July—and was not resolved until late: should the constitution convey "the quality of the French citizen" or "the quality of the citizen of the French Union"? Senghor worried that if any distinction was made between different citizenships, "one will use this argument to deny access to us in all sorts of situations." Lamine Guèye proposed that the constitution reproduce the law that bore his name. Coste-Floret accepted this argument—pointing out that it did not apply to Morocco and Tunisia, which had their own nationalities. The text was accepted unanimously, but when the question of a citizenship of the Union grouping together the new citizenship with those of the Associated States, came up, the tension returned. The proposition of René Malbrant, a defender of *colons*, creating a citizenship of the French Union produced a tie vote, twenty-one to twenty-one, and was therefore not adopted.[122] It would resurface later.

On many subjects, whether it was the organization of a Union assembly or the election of a president, members ran up against the problem that Associated States were not represented in the current assembly and overseas territories were not yet organized as political

[119] Commission de la Constitution, *Comptes Rendus*, session of 26 July 1946, 216–21.
[120] Ferhat Abbas, Coste-Floret, Paul Bastid, ibid., 26 July 1946, 228–30.
[121] Ibid., 230–31. Ferhat Abbas and two colleagues voted against this text.
[122] Ibid., 31 July 1946, 233.

bodies. The MRP refused to have a subsequent assembly devoted to such tasks, while Senghor did not want a structure dictated to the overseas territories.[123] Henri Teitgen pointed out that not only did members disagree with each other, but the ideas of each faction were incoherent. He hoped federalism would emerge out of a process: "The best solution would be to remain there and hope that a federal solution will emerge from the local organization of each territory and subsequent evolution."[124] In the end, much would be left undecided or vague, giving rise to both the relatively peaceful decolonization of sub-Saharan Africa and the violent one of Algeria.

The committee came up with a report, which Coste-Floret presented to the ANC on 2 August. He claimed the mantle of the federalist conception, respecting "the different degrees of evolution of the diverse overseas peoples while giving them the maximum freedom compatible with this evolution." Rather than develop a full institutional structure for the Union, the constitution, he argued, could define its goals and its overall composition. It would consist of departments, territories, and states, giving them a choice of how to evolve "in the framework of this Union." The "situation" of each state or federation of states would depend on the act that defined its union with France (i.e., treaties, presumably renegotiable). Most important, the constitution would "give to all French nationals or *ressortissants* of the metropole, the overseas departments and territories the rights and liberties attached to the quality of citizen."

Explaining why the constitution would refer to the qualities of the citizen rather than just say they were citizens, he stated, "If French citizenship is not explicitly accorded to them, it is because the committee had the scruples to respect the freedom of those who would not intend to acquire French citizenship. On the other hand, in a gesture of liberation that constitutes one of the fundamental characteristics of this draft constitution, the committee proposed to give to forty million subjects all the rights and liberties attached to the quality of the French citizen." He asserted, as had Senghor during the first Constituante, that the new constitution echoed that of 16 pluviôse an II, of the French Revolution. Like Senghor, he claimed to be doing one better: "The rights of citizenship that it confers, it confers them *dans le statut*," that is, the *originaires* of the overseas territories could keep their personal status unless they chose to renounce it. His report went on to claim that the projected constitution would give assemblies in each territory "very large local autonomy." They would be chosen by direct election under universal suffrage, and laws would spell out the

[123] Ibid., 31 July 1946, 245.
[124] Ibid., 31 July 1946, 252.

details.[125] Coste-Floret claimed near unanimity in the Constitutional Committee for a federalist approach, admitting differences about how much should be left as general principle and how much specified in the text.[126]

Coste-Floret and Senghor claimed different brands of federalism, but federalism nonetheless. If Senghor wanted an open framework that would allow territories to choose degrees of integration and autonomy, he feared that Coste-Floret's open framework would allow the French government to use "evolution" as an excuse to reinstate a colonial situation. Both Coste-Floret and Senghor distinguished between having the rights of the citizen and *being* a French citizen. Senghor may have realized more clearly than Coste-Floret that in an open-ended institutional arrangement, the rights-bearing citizen, able to organize politically, was the likely source of future possibilities. The MRP's "progressive federalism" might actually turn out to be more progressive than its architects intended. But for now African deputies had to defend their version of citizenship and prevent constraining interpretations of electoral rules from getting enshrined in the constitution.

As the discussion was about to move to full floor debate, the Committee on Overseas France received a telegram of protest from an African trade union organization, the Union des Syndicats du Sénégal et de la Mauritanie, a member of the Confédération Générale du Travail (the trade union federation linked to the French Communist Party): "Black Africa indignant at MRP attempt to sabotage acquired rights of overseas populations protests with last energy and makes known ready to use all means including violence to maintain freedoms, democratic forces united meeting Saint-Louis Wednesday 24 July make known that if liberties attacked will demand resignation of colonial deputies and will consider act as end of cooperation." A Cameroonian trade union organization protested too.[127] The Senegalese newspaper close to Lamine Guèye, *L'AOF*, informed people of the debates going on in Paris and warned of moves to abrogate the law of 7 May—a "racist campaign," wrote Senghor in one article.[128]

But there were also warnings in the French press against conceding too much to the overseas territories: giving them a high degree of autonomy might turn the French Union into an "exit antechamber," a step out of the French Empire toward independence, or worse still, into

[125] "Rapport fait au nom de la Commission de la Constitution," Annexe II-350, session of 2 August 1946, *Documents de l'Assemblée Nationale Constituante*, 295–96.

[126] ANC, *Débats*, 20 August 1946, 3189.

[127] Meeting of 21 August 1946, C//15313, ANF.

[128] Léopold Senghor, "L'Union française (Racisme ou Démocratie?)," *L'AOF*, 9 August 1946. He noted that opponents advocated a "local citizenship different from French citizenship." See also *L'AOF*, 16 August 1946.

the hands of other "big empires" interested in "these again-available territories."[129] The world, in some eyes, was still a place of interempire rivalry, and the French Union had to be organized accordingly.

The Colony of Its Former Colonies?

When the provisions on the Union went before the Assembly as a whole, the most vigorous initial attack came from a respected, old-line defender of French republicanism, Edouard Herriot. He was angered by references in the draft texts to colonial oppression (which said only that France repudiated oppression, not that it had practiced it). He thought that bad colonialism had ended in the eighteenth century and praised the icons of France's colonial history—Ferry, de Brazza, Gallieni, Lyautey. Colonization, he said, had been "a work of intelligence and, to a large extent, a work of goodness." He claimed to favor federalism, but "organized federalism, that is not acephalous, not anarchistic." In other words, he wanted a strong central government capable of acting across the French Union. Coste-Floret's project lacked "a federalizing organ."[130] He disliked the idea of keeping the status of overseas territories open—doing so could give them the idea of going their own way, maybe even signing up with another power. But the remark that had the biggest impact concerned citizenship. If all people of overseas France were to join in the normal activities of the citizen, then—taking account of the numbers involved—"France will thus become the colony of its former colonies." At this, Senghor jumped up to reply, "This is racism!"[131]

But Herriot's point had been made before, in practically every discussion of citizenship and electoral participation since 1944, and it would be made again—including by Senghor himself. A unitary conception of French politics—one citizen, one vote—would indeed make the deputies of European France a minority, but Senghor and his colleagues wanted a pluralist, federal France, in which each component, European France included, would exercise power over its own affairs and express its own personality. Yet Herriot had made it hard to paper

[129] Rémy Roure, "Union ou séparatisme?" *Le Monde*, 24 August 1946. Henri Teitgen similarly referred to the danger of creating an "exit vestibule." Cited in *Le Monde*, 24 August 1946.

[130] ANC, *Débats*, 27 August 1946, 3333. Herriot thought the Soviet Union was a model for a "well-constituted federalism," recognizing plural republics but with a strong "central power." Ibid., 3334.

[131] Ibid., 3334. Herriot claimed that overseas citizens under the committee draft would have more rights than those of the metropole, "since we, citizens of the metropole, do not have the right of secession, happily so." Ibid., 3335.

over the difficulties of the citizenship issue: would everyone really have equal political rights in an empire of citizens?

Herriot's speech put the debate on hold.[132] The same day as Herriot spoke, de Gaulle issued a declaration to the press also highly critical of the texts that were then being debated. He particularly opposed the principle of "libre disposition"—the fiction that membership in the French Union was voluntary and territories could choose to withdraw. He saw this provision leading "to agitation, to dislocation, and finally to foreign domination." The territories' "solidarity with France" and the responsibility of France should be "unquestioned." At the same time, de Gaulle reaffirmed his advocacy of federalism, calling on each territory "to develop according to its own character," which included the possibility of "autonomy proportional to its development."[133] The MRP—the center-right party—was put in the awkward position of appearing to be giving away too much: too much choice for overseas citizens to go their own way, too much influence by them on the metropole.

Re-creating Colonialism?

But even as government officials and constitution writers put their heads to writing a more rigorous text, the Ministry was worried about the dangers of appearing to re-create colonialism. A paper circulating in the Ministry for a "draft government declaration" stated, "Empires belong to history; the age of imperialism is over." Now, the time belonged to "great federative projects, continental or intercontinental." Among such systems was the French Union, grouping "people distinguished by their ethnic origins, their religions, their manners, but closely united in a common attachment to these libertarian and egalitarian ideals." Even such a self-congratulatory document revealed an important dimension of official thinking: the genie of citizenship was out of the bottle.[134]

[132] Even the Communist leader Jacques Duclos agreed shortly after Herriot's speech that the text had to be rethought; 27 August 1946, 3342. Herriot's fear of numbers was echoed in *Climats*, 29 August 1946 and *Le Figaro*, 15–16 September 1946. The threat had already been noted in *Marchés Coloniaux*, 27 April 1946, 389.

[133] "Déclaration à la Presse le 27 août 1946," reprinted in Charles de Gaulle, *Discours et messages 1940–1946* (Paris: Berger-Levrault, 1946), 735.

[134] Mimeographed paper, "Projet de declaration gouvernementale," attached to note for Minister, 4 September 1946, AP 216/2, AOM. Meanwhile, federalism had its defenders in the press: the only choice, wrote René Capitant, "if colonialism and assimilationism are equally condemned." For Capitant, federalism emerged out of empire; a federal system would give "suppleness and new force to our imperial system." "La force irrésistible de l'idée fédérale," *Le Monde*, 6 September 1946.

But the proposals before the Constituante did not offer to the Ministry a useable blueprint for a postimperial France. An internal memo dated 23 August complained of the proposed design, "It is neither a federation nor a confederation, nor even a society of nations." The Minister, Moutet, would use this phrase when he went before the Constitutional Committee. The Union needed to treat overseas territories as integral parts of the Republic, and the Republic's representatives should be their administrators, even if there was less "tutelage" than in colonial times and more decentralization. The institutions of the territories would be spelled out by organic laws passed by the Assemblée Nationale in which the territories were represented. It would be a different story with Associated States: "on the spot, the Associated States are masters of their representative institutions." There would be a Council with representatives of heads of these states, presided by the President of the Republic, and an elected assembly of the entire Union, which Associated States would join if they wanted to. The memo left open the question of whether the Union would eventually develop ministries responsible before the Assemblée de l'Union.[135]

Before the Overseas Committee on 4 September, Moutet now waffled on the question of citizenship: "Can we look to a citizenship of the Union or an extension of the law of 7 May 1946, which made French citizens out of the overseas *ressortissants*? This, said the Minister, is to be examined. But what is certain is that all individuals grouped in the French Union must enjoy the same liberties and rights guaranteed by the Constitution—and be constrained to the same duties." Pressed by Lamine Guèye on whether the government was going back on the law that bore his name, Moutet replied that it was not, but "one can think of citizenship of the Union for the populations of the Associated States—French citizenship for the populations integrated into the French Republic."[136]

The next week, coming before the Constitutional Committee accompanied by Varenne, who had headed the interministerial committee, Moutet spoke in sterner tones than he had used before. The existing draft was inadequate. He told the committee, article by article, what he wanted, following his Ministry's memo. He was adamant that there had to be a local administration responsible to the French government: "One cannot suppress what one is not sure to be able to replace." Once structures were in place in the territories and Associated States, the possibility of a federal assembly would come open. But for now "most territories are only administrative entities that unite

[135] Affaires Politiques, Note pour le Conseil des Ministres, 23 August 1946, AP 216/2, AOM; Commission de la Constitution, *Comptes Rendus*, 11 September 1946, 480.
[136] Moutet, Commission de la FOM, 4 September 1946, C//15313, ANF. Moutet was particularly concerned about the "sovereignty of the Bey or of the Sultan."

populations that are different and often very opposed to each other." Any assembly would be built from territorial assemblies, not for an ensemble of territories like AOF, which he thought too centralized and too far from the "milieu of the populations."

On citizenship, Moutet now took a much weaker position than the one he had once shared with Senghor and Lamine Guèye: to concede to the peoples of the Union "the quality of citizen of the French Union." Citizens of the Union could keep their personal status unless they chose to renounce it, and they could acquire French citizenship under conditions defined by law. He concluded with an anecdote more interesting for its language than its contents: Deputies from Madagascar had recently been traveling in Natal (South Africa). They were refused entry to a hotel. According to Moutet, "they replied, as long ago, 'civis romanus sum,' 'I am a French citizen.' These were Malagasy autonomists who are the first to invoke in front of Great Britain the quality of the French citizen that the law of 7 May conferred upon them." He considered that this episode showed "that we have not done so badly."

He did not say that the law of 7 May referred to qualities of the citizen, not qualities of the citizen of the French Union. But his invocation of the precedent of the Roman Empire revealed more than he perhaps intended. It was an imperial vision of citizenship that he was proposing. He was twitting the deputies from Madagascar, who had gone further than their continental African colleagues in claiming national identification for their territory, suggesting that when push came to shove, being part of the French imperium was what did them the most good.[137] But his overall message was to put the overseas territories in their place: with vaguely defined autonomy, no meaningful form of federal legislative authority, and a second-tier citizenship.

The government text, members pointed out, was quite different from what the committee, for all its differences, had been discussing. Citizenship immediately became an issue. Challenged by Lamine Guèye, Moutet claimed nothing had been taken away from people, like Senghor, Houphouët-Boigny, and Lamine Guèye, who possessed the quality of the French citizen. Union citizenship was intended for the people of the Associated States, who had their own nationalities. The text "in no way entails the loss of the quality of French citizens recognized by earlier laws." He did not mention that citizenship in the French Union would be guaranteed by the constitution, the French citizenship of Africans by an ordinary law that presumably could be repealed by another ordinary law.[138]

[137] Commission de la Constitution, *Comptes Rendus*, 11 September 1946, 477–89. The anecdote is on 489.
[138] Ibid., 492.

Senghor and Guèye challenged Moutet on another point that would remain in contention: that in local assemblies, all elements of the population would be represented. Did that mean the double college, guaranteeing seats for a European minority by means of voter roles separated by status? No, said Moutet and Coste-Floret. But what do you mean by "different elements of the population"? asked Senghor. Minorities, Moutet said, but he was clearly talking about European minorities.[139] Ferhat Abbas accused Moutet of maintaining divisions among people while talking about the Republic one and indivisible. Moutet's reply was paternalistic: the more Algeria was like a French department, the more its people participated in legislative assemblies, "the more Algeria will be close to its larger emancipation and I am convinced that a different system would take you away from liberty and emancipation." Refusing Abbas's assertion that Moutet's proposals were more assimilationist than federalist, he insisted that it gave territories the choice of "assimilation for those who desire it," and other statuses within the Union if that was what they wanted.[140]

But Lamine Guèye would not let him off the hook and pushed Moutet once again to promise that the law of 7 May 1946 "survives entirely." Citizenship of the Union, Moutet repeated, did not concern West Africans: "This provision is only applicable to French-protected persons; it is superfluous to say to a French citizen that he is also citizen of the French Union, because that adds nothing to his quality."[141]

Near the end of the session Coste-Floret told Moutet that the government's proposals seemed "timid." He wanted the Assemblée de l'Union française to have real power, while Moutet's proposal left it with merely a consultative role. Without such power, one was not creating "a true federation." He promised to improve the text, but Moutet was not taking the bait: "We are not creating a federation, but the French Union."[142]

The next day, Coste-Floret repeated that the government text was "timid." The committee decided to use it as a base but to amend it.[143] Ferhat Abbas was bitter: the government "announces the rights of the colonized man." Now, Coste-Floret defended the proposal as real progress.[144] The debate went off into myriad complexities, but what

[139] Ibid., 495.

[140] Abbas and Moutet, ibid., 499–500. *Marchés Coloniaux*, which opposed Abbas on most things, claimed to agree with him on federalism, but did not mention that Abbas wanted a federation of equals. What the journal wanted to beat down was assimilation and equality. René Moreux, "La pertinente leçon de M. Ferhat Abbas," *Marchés Coloniaux*, 27 July 1946, 747.

[141] Lamine Guèye and Moutet, Commission de la Constitution, *Comptes Rendus*, 501–2.

[142] Coste-Floret and Moutet, ibid., 503, 505.

[143] Ibid., 12 September 1946, 507–8.

[144] Abbas and Coste-Floret, ibid., 509–10.

provoked passionate exchanges was a proposed requirement that seats be reserved for French nationals living in all parts of the Union, including Associated States, whose own populations would not be represented in the Assemblée Nationale. The emotion was intense because of a basic concern: enshrining a distinction in the constitution between two portions of the population—a "wall of China" Pierre Cot called it. Coste-Floret and his allies tried to insist that the distinction was of nationality, not of race, but they did not convince. Lamine Guèye was categorical: "We must renounce particular representation."[145] Why not put in the constitution "the possibility of particular representation"—not requiring it or naming who would be represented—suggested Paul Bastid. For now, the committee rejected any mention of special representation, but Bastid's suggestion would later provide a way out of an impasse that nearly made it impossible for overseas deputies to accept the constitutional text.[146]

The proposal that a representative appointed by the government would be the "depository of the powers of the Republic" also brought back charges of reimposing a new version of the colonial governor. The representative could be "an autochthon," chimed in René Malbrant, while Pierre Cot accepted the need for such representation now but wanted the door open to an administration run by local people. A compromise was reached: there would be a "delegate responsible for the interests of the French Union."[147]

And once again, citizenship: Lamine Guèye wanted to replace the clause on Union citizenship with a text that said the opposite: "All nationals and *ressortissants* of the French Union have the quality of the French citizen and enjoy the rights and liberties attached to it." Malbrant opposed him. But Cot pointed out that the combination of local and Union citizenship made sense for Associated States, not elsewhere. Coste-Floret reminded everyone that the Lamine Guèye law did not actually make anyone a French citizen, but "simply a citizen," and that Senghor's report had said that usage would decide what this citizenship actually meant. France's history of discrimination would not leave the room: Houphouët-Boigny and Jean Félix-Tchicaya (Congo-Gabon) reminded everyone that distinctions among French people led to differences in pay and terms of service in the army and civil service. Félix-Tchicaya asked, "What, in short, do you want to make of us? Citizens of the second zone or super-natives?"[148] A solution emerged: in effect to give constitutional status to the

[145] Fajon, Cot, de Tinguy, Coste-Floret, and Guèye, ibid., 517–19.

[146] Paul Bastid, ibid., 520. For the committee's votes, see ibid., 522–23.

[147] Jean Félix-Tchicaya, Houphouet, Césaire, Cot, Malbrant, Boisdon, and others, ibid., 544–46.

[148] Lamine Guèye, Malbrant, Senghor, Cot, Coste-Floret, Houphouet, and Félix-Tchicaya, ibid., 17 September 1946, 551–53.

Lamine Guèye law, applied as it was to overseas territories, leaving in abeyance just what citizenship would mean in the Associated States. The committee, probably tired to the bone, approved, with no votes against and two abstentions.[149]

There were pressures in the opposite direction. In an article in *Le Monde* at this time, Georges Scelle wrote as if the language of empire were still current: "the French colonial empire must have its constitution." He wanted that constitution to be entirely distinct from that of the Republic, and he did not like the presence of colonial representatives in writing the latter. Asking rhetorically about the participation of Muslims in a debate about religious liberty, he wrote, "I must be dreaming!" He wanted a completely metropolitan legislature, then a "superposed" federal structure in which overseas peoples could participate in accordance with their "degree of maturity and civilization." *Le Figaro* editorialized against extending citizenship to "all men and women of the Empire who never heard of France, who have not even changed from the mores of ancient slavery. . . . French people would thus soon find themselves put into a minority inside their own political assemblies."[150] But if the top political leaders believed such arguments, they were by now careful to avoid calling an empire an empire and worried about the legitimacy of any constitution overseas.

The next week Moutet and Varenne were back before the Commission making their old demands. They still claimed that the Lamine Guèye law would still operate in favor of the overseas territories even if it was not in the constitution and that citizenship in the French Union would benefit people like Syrians, Lebanese, Togolese, and Cameroonians, as well as nationals of the Associated States.[151] No minds were changed, but committee members clearly felt the pressure to conform to the government's wishes. Some members tried to reassure overseas deputies for the *n*th time that recognized rights were not in question.[152] Ferhat Abbas once again brought the conflict to its historical roots: it was being subject to special laws that drove Algerians to want autonomy. "The current system cannot be maintained. 'One can do anything with bayonets,' said Napoleon, 'except sit on them.' Do you want to go back to periodic killings?" He cited the examples of repressive violence in 1871, 1884, 1914, and 1945. He still thought there was a way out: "For us, the problem is to find a form that allows

[149]Ibid., 553–54.

[150]Georges Scelle, "Le problème de l'Union française: II," *Le Monde* 13 September 1946; "L'Empire en danger," *Le Figaro* 15–16 September 1946. See also Adolphe Landry, "France et l'Union française: Il y faut deux citoyennetés," *Le Monde*, 17 September 1946.

[151]Moutet, Commission de la Constitution, *Comptes Rendus*, 18 September 1946, 566–67. Philip referred to Moutet's proposition as a Union citizenship that "is superposed on the citizenship of each inhabitant of the Union." Ibid., 569.

[152]Ibid., 573.

us to integrate Muslim nationalism with French politics and the best form seems to us to be federalism." On the other hand, "by not listening to us, you will make clear your intention to keep the native in his native condition and thereby your refusal to see in him a man like others." Coste-Floret replied, "We cannot let you say that."[153]

But Coste-Floret went on to note that Ferhat Abbas's proposals "link up, on several points, with ours," specifically in advocating "federal organs." Senghor helped bring things back to earth: A "true federalism" was "in the present state of things only a goal," and meanwhile the deputies had a constitution to write. He and other colleagues got Ferhat Abbas to withdraw his counterproposal in favor of amending the government's version.[154]

The same day, the committee still up in the air, the entire Assemblée Nationale was beginning to talk in general terms about the French Union. Conflict emerged there too. Coste-Floret, caught between the Ministry and overseas deputies, presented an amended version of his report. He said he was going further in creating "federal organs" for the Union—the presidency, the Haut Conseil ("the embryo of a federal government"), and the Assemblée de l'Union française, which he might well have called an embryo as well, since it had only the power to give advice. The members of the latter would be elected by territorial assemblies (half coming from overseas France), leading him to evoke "perfect parallelism" between the Union assembly and the second chamber (Conseil de la République) that came out of the right's drive for bicameralism at home.

There was in fact nothing perfect about the parallelism. The Conseil de la République, also known as the Senate, had real power to amend legislation passed by the Chambre des Députés, forcing a second vote by the Chambre. The Assemblée de l'Union française, as it emerged from the debates, had to be consulted on matters affecting overseas France, but it had no power to legislate. But Coste-Floret's point is revealing of a certain way of thinking: he was in effect contending that what he had earlier called a "democracy of groups" applied all over the French Union. African territories, as collective entities, should be represented, as should the communes of rural France. But they would not be represented according to population in the Chambre des Députés or the Conseil de la République, and the body in which they were more fully present would have no real power. Coste-Floret's proposal also contained some of the elements overseas representatives most disliked: a strong administrator in each territory responsible to Paris, little precision about how territorial assemblies would be elected and

[153] Ferhat Abbas, ibid., 18 September 1946, 576–78; Coste-Floret, ibid., 578.
[154] Ibid., 579.

what powers they would have, guaranteed representation for European French settlers overseas. On citizenship, he insisted that nothing would be taken back.[155]

Such assurances were not satisfactory to Senghor, for the proposed constitution would fix in place two kinds of citizens. He saw in second-tier citizenship an old argument about culture, as if some members of the Union were "cannibals" or "primitives." He attacked the incivility of the "pretend defenders of civilization." Instead of "an imperialism that sterilizes civilizations, there should be a conjunction of civilizations, a melting pot of cultures." He was arguing neither for separation nor for a federation of full equals—France would retain "its role as guide" for some time—but he was seeking to initiate a process that would turn colonial hierarchy into "cooperation among civilizations."[156]

The importance of the past's connection to the future was underscored by Aimé Césaire, who brought out an alternative reading to the history of benign colonization promoted by Herriot: a history of enslavement continued by forced labor. By driving people of the colonies to despair, the new constitution could provoke the very secession movement it was trying to prevent. He joined Senghor in insisting that the people of overseas France feared having their hopes dashed as they had many times since 1789.[157]

Lamine Guèye challenged the Assembly to reject him personally: Would you take away my citizenship, he asked? "One speaks of Union citizenship; we say right away, we do not want it." Foreign countries would see a passport marked "citoyen de l'Union" as a badge of inferiority. The proposed text, said the deputy from Madagascar Joseph Ravoahangy, "would constitutionalize colonialism." Ferhat Abbas agreed: "We want France without colonization and without colonialism."[158]

Jean-Jacques Juglas, speaking for the MRP, tried to assure his colleagues that he understood their "worries." He defended the text for the possibilities it offered for the future. If it was not federalism, it permitted federalism to be built. Later, under questioning, he may have given away something about his evolutionary time frame: "If in thirty, forty or fifty years we are obliged to reconsider, that is possible." He thought that the French "community of culture" did not exclude "the maintenance of natural diversities" while saying that the basis of the Union was "the French culture of which we are proud."[159]

[155] ANC, *Débats*, 18 September 1946, 3785–86.
[156] Senghor, ibid., 3791–92.
[157] Césaire, ibid., 3795–97.
[158] Lamine Guèye, ibid., 3799, 3801; Joseph Ravoahangy, 3802, Ferhat Abbas, 3803–4.
[159] Juglas, ibid., 3804–5, 3817.

Prosettler deputies wanted less ambiguity—and fewer promises. René Malbrant's bottom line was the representation in all assemblies of "citizens of French status." To do so, he insisted, was not to "constitutionalize differences of rights; it is a question of constitutionalizing the presence of France." Still, his argument, in terms of rhetoric, overlapped that of his foes; the constitution should allow "each country to maintain its originality and to evolve."[160] In effect, the same text that would allow Africans to move toward autonomy would allow settlers in Algeria and elsewhere to defend their own ways and their own power.

The problem of Associated States remained. Antoine Colonna, a deputy representing "French citizens of Tunisia," said frankly what more progressive politicians did not want to say aloud: "Do not forget, the essence of the sovereignty of the Sultan of Morocco and the Bey of Tunis is necessarily the opposite of our constitutional law. Between the two is the difference between a monarch with divine rights and a democracy based on popular will." But Colonna was not so much interested in the rights of most Tunisians—only of his own constituents, "a true provincial French cell."[161]

More nuanced was the intervention of Louis-Paul Aujoulat, the social Catholic deputy from Cameroon. He admitted that he was elected by "a handful of Europeans," but he denied representing either "big business" or reactionary colonialists, and he realized that the single college had become, in the last few months of debate, "the symbol of the rights and liberties promised to overseas populations and also the confirmation of their access to citizenship and the prerogatives it supposed." He had tried unsuccessfully to convince his white constituents of the merits of a more egalitarian electoral system, but they still deserved to be understood and represented. The solution, he thought, was not to inscribe in the constitution either the single or the double college. In the long run, he went on to argue, it might be better for overseas representatives to sit in a federal rather than a national assembly, but "in the current state of things," they belonged in the Assemblée Nationale. He admitted that "everywhere in the overseas territories and thanks to the war one observes a certain taking hold of territorial, even national, consciousness. We in no way want to stop it. We consider, on the contrary, that it is wise to permit its normal expression in institutions that allow its expression in liaison with us."[162] Aujoulat recognized the myopia of his own constituency and by a mixture of compromise and temporizing hoped to find an accommodation with African politicians—and with history.

[160] Malbrant, ibid., 3793–94. See also Devinat, ibid., 3806–7.
[161] Colonna, ibid., 19 September 1946, 3836.
[162] Aujoulat, ibid., 3839–41.

The previous day, Pierre Cot had warned that the majority in the assembly was risking the legitimacy of the constitution if they produced a document unacceptable to the overseas representatives.[163] But the head of government, Georges Bidault, wanted his way, and he turned the committee's effort to find compromise language into a confrontation. The government asked to interrupt the evening session of the ANC on 19 September so Bidault could appear before the Constitutional Committee. He came with a hard-line message: "The text of the government is, I repeat, the text of the government. It creates a citizenship of the French Union. I ask the commission to hold to its principle and not to go beyond it." Challenged by Senghor, Bidault seemed to want to split his opposition between those who already had citizenship rights from those who hoped to get them: "There is no question of going back on acquired rights, for the four communes on Senegal, for example." Overseas *ressortissants* who had French civil status, and Algerian Muslims who had become citizens in 1944 (he said in response to Ferhat Abbas) would keep their French citizenship, but they would also have Union citizenship, as would people from the Associated States and the metropole. He did not use the word, but he was saying that Union citizenship would be superposed on both French and other citizenships. On representing French citizens overseas, Bidault was equally adamant. They would choose their own representatives. Whatever the theories, Bidault said, what mattered was practice, and whether it was in Algeria, Morocco, or Tunisia, "France must remain the guide and guarantor of these peoples." The head of the committee asked the Assembly to suspend its session the next morning to allow the Constitutional Committee to meet.[164]

First came an evening session of the Assembly: more concerns from representatives of Madagascar and French Equatorial Africa that the promised gains were being taken away, that promises of equality were proving hollow, that Africans were being accused of being incapable of governing themselves. The double college and the ambiguity of provisions on citizenship remained the sorest of sore points. Houphouët-Boigny saw behind the efforts to dilute African rights the hand of colonial interests hoping to reestablish forced labor. He asserted that it was not overseas deputies who threatened the unity of the French Union, but those who sought to divide the French population into

[163] Pierre Cot, ibid., 18 September 1946, 3815.

[164] Bidault, Commission de la Constitution, *Comptes Rendus*, 19 September 1946, 587–91. Marshall (*French Colonial Myth*, 282–86, 301) points to attempts at deal making during the second Constituante—support for one side's domestic concerns in exchange for support on the Union. But Bidault's hard line broke such understandings—and in the end he did not get his way. Such is politics.

"metropolitans and autochthons, autochthonous citizens of French status and autochthonous citizens of Muslim status, race from race, territory from territory."[165]

The next day, the committee took up the government's demands. Acceptable wording was found for a few articles. But as soon as a clause guaranteeing representation in the Assemblée de l'Union française to persons of "French" status came up, Senghor made clear that if those words remained, he would vote against the constitution. Houphouët-Boigny pleaded, "do not constitutionalize racial discrimination." Senghor repeated the theme: "We cannot constitutionalize any form of racism. We stand firm on this point."[166]

The "intergroup" that Lamine Guèye had earlier organized now proclaimed its intention to insist on the maintenance of the rights and liberties recognized by the first Constituent Assembly.[167] On 20 September, the intergroup's members on the Constitutional Committee—Lamine Guèye, Senghor, Houphouët-Boigny, and Ferhat Abbas—walked out after they could not get the special representation for citizens of "French" status living in overseas France written out of the constitution. They and their colleagues in the intergroup would attend neither Committee nor general sessions of the Assembly.[168] The absence of the overseas members of the Committee, a member commented, "would take away all significance from the texts voted on the French Union." Coste-Floret agreed.[169]

But the other members of the Constitutional Committee were still talking to each other. They got something done, and it was not what Bidault had demanded. The draft of the citizenship article before them on 20 September said "all nationals of the French Republic have the quality of citizens of the French Union. The *ressortissants* of the territories under French mandate enjoy the same rights and prerogatives as the citizens of the French Union." But the President of the Commission thought the article "unclear" and suggested instead that one

[165] Raseta, ANC, *Débats*, 3845, and Félix-Tchicaya, 19 September 1946, 3645–47, Houphouët-Boigny, 3849–50. Houphouët-Boigny's accusation was far from paranoid, for the États Généraux de la Colonisation, which was now combating the citizenship clauses, had also objected to the law abolishing forced labor.

[166] Senghor, Houphouët-Boigny, and others, Commission de la Constitution, *Comptes Rendus*, 20 September 1946, 597–600.

[167] *Le Monde*, 11 September 1946, referred to the members of the intergroup as "colonial parliamentarians," an interesting choice of word.

[168] *Libération*, 21 September 1946; Lamine Guèye, *Itinéraire africain* (Paris: Présence Africaine, 1966), 163–64. Aimé Césaire did not walk out, for he wanted to be present for debate over an article with which he was particularly concerned, but he associated himself with his colleagues' protest. Commission de la Constitution, *Comptes Rendus*, 20 September 1946, 600.

[169] Etienne Fajon and Coste-Floret, ibid., 609.

should simply constitutionalize the Lamine Guèye law. Coste-Floret replied "there is in addition a considerable moral advantage to constitutionalize the Lamine Guèye law." After some hand-wringing about the absence of overseas deputies, the committee decided to do what the absent members would have liked, substituting, "all *ressortissants* of the overseas territories have the quality of citizen on the same basis as the French nationals of the metropole." A separate article specified that the people of the overseas territories could keep their personal status without forfeiting any rights, unless they chose to renounce that status. And another, applying to the Associated States, made clear that they would have the quality of the citizen of the French Union with rights attendant upon that status.[170] The committee's new version would turn the general assurances of government leaders that the rights promised under the Lamine Guèye law would continue into a firm constitutional provision. The argument that Coste-Floret had been making all along, that the *ressortissants* of the Associated States wanted to have the rights of citizens, not to be citizens, was accepted at the same time as was the stronger provision for *ressortissants* of the overseas territories.

The issue of the double college remained. But a way out had been proposed by Paul Bastid even before the walkout: to refer only to the "possibility" of representation for people of a particular status, without requiring such representation or saying who would benefit from it. The very principle of enshrining distinction among voters by status had been too much for Senghor and his colleagues, but later that day Bastid's amendment became the basis of consensus among remaining deputies, now convinced that they had to come to agreement. The government got its way in ensuring that its administrative powers would be represented in each territory, only the title "représentant" was changed to "dépositaire des pouvoirs de la République." The "depositary" would in effect be a governor.[171]

Later that day, 20 September, the Assembly learned of the "new and grave fact" of the walkout. Shortly thereafter, the discussion was adjourned at the Overseas Minister's request to allow discussion of matters that were "a bit delicate."[172] The African parliamentarians met with Bidault and, according to Lamine Guèye's account, told him in no uncertain terms that their constituents would not accept to be considered "in their own countries as diminished citizens."[173]

[170] Ibid., 607–8.

[171] Jacques Bardoux and others, ibid., 611–12. Moutet joined the later session that day, 614–18. The newspaper *Le Populaire* (21 September 1946) described the committee session as "stormy" during the day and reaching "détente" at night.

[172] ANC, *Débats*, 20 September 1946, 3888, 3889.

[173] Guèye, *Itinéraire*, 161–62.

The Assembly resumed its deliberations late that that evening. The counterproject prepared by Ferhat Abbas was discussed—in his absence—and dismissed.[174]

When the offending article on the representation of people of French status in the Assemblée Nationale came up, Moutet now stated that he wanted to replace the clause on that representation with the simple statement that an organic law would determine the representation of "diverse parts of the population." Personal status—French or otherwise—was not mentioned by name; privileged representation would not be enshrined in the constitution. The President of the Constitutional Committee indicated his acceptance. Moutet said he would abide by the accord. The Assembly accepted the new version. A similar agreement prevailed in regard to territorial assemblies; their composition would not be fixed in the constitution but left to law.[175]

Challenged by a Communist deputy from Algeria who wanted to put territorial assemblies on a par with the metropolitan one, Coste-Floret refused to compromise state sovereignty. In his terms, "each organ finds its place in a constitutional hierarchy," with the Assemblée Nationale on top.[176] Likewise, the government refused renewed demands to put territorial administration under someone responsible to the legislature of that territory rather than an appointee of the government in Paris. Moutet insisted, "We will see what those local assemblies will be, but they do not yet exist. Meanwhile, the current administration must be maintained with the authority it now has."[177] The exchange made clear that the Republic remained sovereign overseas: overseas peoples would now have voice—in Paris and at home—but not power in their territories.

Moutet was at the same time defensive—giving an emotional account of his efforts to rid the overseas territories of the *indigénat* and forced labor—and insistent on a process. One had to first create local assemblies by law, then let them mature, and only then give them administrative and legislative authority within a system that, at last,

[174] The proposal was presented by Abbas's colleague Ahmed Francis. The text called for France to "renounce all unilateral sovereignty over colonized peoples." Francis accused the government of putting the "notion of empire" into the constitution. In the counterproject, each "people" would have the right to decide on its own what its status would be—integration or autonomy and federation. The head of the Constitutional Committee pointed out that the counterproject had been discussed in committee and rejected. Ferhat Abbas, returning, declared that he advanced his project "for France for the overseas peoples." He insisted on a vote and lost. ANC, *Débats*, 20 September 1946, 3893–96.

[175] Ibid., 3897, 3906. Another try for special privilege—this time for French citizens in the Associated States—was set aside. Ibid., 3907.

[176] Sportisse, Apithy, and Coste-Floret, ibid., 3900–3901.

[177] Moutet, ibid., 3902.

could be called federal.[178] Jacques Duclos, the Communist leader, intervened to support this position, stating that his party like all others wanted to "ensure the permanence of the presence of France in the diverse places of the world where the flag of our country floats. If France were absent, its absence would signify other presences."[179] Socialists and Communists were advocating not decolonization, but progressive empire, within a world of rival imperial ambitions. And most of the arguments were about just how progressive empire could be.

The last act of the citizenship debate was played out in the Assembly, but it had already been decided by the agreement worked out by Lamine Guèye's intergroup. The draft article now conferred the "quality of citizen" on "all *ressortissants* of the overseas territories," with the conditions of exercise of those rights to be spelled out by law. A deputy representing French citizens in Morocco, Jean Jullien, wanted to amend the text to say that *ressortissants* of the overseas territories could accede to French citizenship by renouncing their personal status. Coste-Floret saw no reason to do so since the people concerned already had "French citizenship." Jullien complained about letting two citizenships "be superposed." Coste-Floret replied that the texts did not create a double nationality, but did create a double citizenship, one for the overseas territories with the same qualities as the citizenship of the Republic, and the other for the Associated States, which had their own nationality and citizenship but would now share in "a common federal citizenship." He did not want to upset the apple cart: the new article, he said, was the "reproduction pure and simple of the text of the Lamine Guèye law, which had been greeted overseas with enthusiasm, as you know." Lamine Guèye himself took the floor to state, "I am happy to take the occasion that is thus offered me to thank the unanimous committee for having willed to accept to constitutionalize the text of the law of 7 May 1946. This law, in effect, lays out that all nationals of the Republic, consequently the inhabitants of the overseas territories, are citizens on the same basis as those of the metropole."[180]

Jullien's amendment was defeated and the Lamine Guèye law became an article of the constitution. A second article ensured that "all *ressortissants*" of the French Union would have the quality of the citizen of the Union and "enjoy the rights and liberties guaranteed by the preamble of the present constitution"—an article that would mainly affect the Associated States and perhaps the mandates, which lay outside

[178] Accused implicitly of defending a colonial status quo via the continued presence of a governor-like figure, Moutet remarked, "Excuse me, I am perhaps a bit sensitive on this point." Ibid., 1905.

[179] Duclos, ibid., 3905.

[180] Julien, Coste-Floret, and Guèye, ibid., 3908.

the domain of the previous article. And a final article on citizenship established the right of overseas citizens who did not have "le statut civil français" to keep that status unless they chose to renounce it. Eugénie Éboué-Tell, the widow of Félix Éboué and a deputy, asked to add a clause making clear that this status could in no case be applied to limit or refuse "the rights and liberties attached to the quality of French citizen." Coste-Floret accepted the amendment on behalf of the Constitutional Committee. The assembly also accepted the amendment, and it passed the articles on citizenship.[181]

At the end of the momentous session, Edouard Herriot, whose intervention of 27 August had brought out French anxieties of submergence under an empire of citizens, expressed his approval of not just the outcome of the debate, but the process. He acknowledged the importance of Lamine Guèye's role. He thought the best proof of France's civilizing action was in the interventions of the overseas deputies: "The nuances of our French style were utilized by you in speeches that greatly interested us" and honored the Assembly's tribune. The contributions of the overseas deputies revealed "a new enrichment of French civilization, which in the course of its history and progress, having received contributions from many directions, will from now on profit from all you offer in spirit, youth, and faith." At first glance patronizing, Herriot's words take on a different meaning if one remembers that he had not previously had the experience of working with more than one African deputy, was for the first time experiencing intense debate with such individuals, and seemed to be reciting a lesson on the mutual benefits of dialogue among civilizations that had been taught on the floor of the Assembly by Léopold Senghor.[182]

As deputies made their final statements about the constitution as a whole, Coste-Floret claimed only to have introduced "the embryo of federal government." Ferhat Abbas lamented that the constitution did not "introduce that breath of liberty, solely able to raise enthusiasm and bring about the adhesion of hearts." He deplored a missed opportunity to associate an Algeria that could remain Algerian "while uniting for their own grandeur and the true renaissance of the new France in a loyal and egalitarian politics of association."[183] But the deputies from West Africa had constitutionalized citizenship and prevented the constitutionalizing of racial distinction, even if they would have to live for a time with protected seats for white minority overseas

---

[181] Ibid., 3809.

[182] Herriot, ibid., 3909.

[183] Ibid., ibid., 4230, 4233. The entire document had to go through a second reading, but Coste-Floret was careful to keep Union issues out of serious debate. Ibid., 4190, 4212–13.

under regular legislation. The African deputies voted for the new constitutional text; Muslim Algerians abstained.[184]

Let us review the final result. Three articles on citizenship would set the stage for future struggles over what it meant for former subjects to participate in a France that was now claiming to be postcolonial and postimperial:

Article 80: "All *ressortissants* of overseas territories have the quality of citizen, on the same basis as French nationals of the metropole or of the overseas territories. Specific laws will establish the conditions under which they will exercise their rights as citizens."

Article 81: "All French nationals and *ressortissants* of the French Union have the quality of citizen of the French Union which assures them of the enjoyment of the rights and liberties guaranteed by the preamble of the present Constitution."

Article 82: "Citizens who do not have French civil status maintain their personal status unless they renounce it. This status can in no case constitute a motive to refuse or limit the rights and liberties attached to the quality of French citizen."

Moroccans and Tunisians would have a special kind of citizenship superposed on the nationalities and citizenships that they already had. They would not *be* French citizens, but they would have at least some of the rights of French citizens. Africans (and Algerians) had the quality of French citizens, without specifying that this meant that they were citizens of the French Republic.[185]

Article 82 made it plausible for the French Overseas Ministry to maintain, as it had in July, that "the legislature wanted to mark the perfect equality of all in public life, but not the perfect identity of the French of the metropole and the overseas French."[186] The jurist Pierre Lampué described the provisions of the constitution as "a remarkable transformation of even the notion of French citizen."[187]

The second version of the constitution dropped the pretense of the first version that the French Union was a free association of states and people and—more substantively—dropped the implication that territories could in some circumstances take themselves out of it. But the

[184] Lamine Guèye cabled to Dakar that the assembly had kept or even extended the rights voted by the previous assembly. "Une heureuse nouvelle," *L'AOF*, 4 October 1946.

[185] The text was less than explicit about its applicability to Algeria, but jurists thought there was little doubt that it applied. Pierre Lampué, "L'Union française d'après la Constitution," *Revue Juridique et Parlementaire de l'Union Française* 1 (1947): 148.

[186] AOF, Directeur Général des Affaires Politiques, Administratives et Sociales (Berlan), note, July 1946, 17G 152, AS.

[187] Lampué, "L'Union française d'après la Constitution," 154. He considered article 82 to be based on the idea of "citoyenneté dans le statut" of the 1916 law applied to the Quatre Communes and the 1944 law that gave certain categories of Algerians citizenship rights without their losing Islamic status, "now generalized." Ibid., 150–51.

preamble to the new constitution still contained some plurals that, from present-day assertions about the nature of the French Republic, are quite remarkable: "France forms, with the overseas peoples, a Union founded on equality of rights and duties, without distinction of race or religion. The French Union is composed of nations and peoples who put together or coordinate their resources and their efforts to develop their respective civilizations, to improve their well being and ensure their security." One can see in this phrase the effects of arguments made in the Assemblée by Paul Coste-Floret and others that France was a "democracy of groups"—an assemblage, a composite. As Lampué remarked, a year later, the text mixed "two different ideas, which are that of the equality of individuals and that of the association of peoples."[188]

The next sentence of the preamble also mixed posturing—repudiation of the arbitrariness of colonialism without admitting that France had ever practiced it—with a specific promise: "Faithful to its traditional mission, France intends to lead the peoples of whom it has taken charge to the freedom to administer themselves and to manage democratically their own affairs; repudiating any system of colonization based on arbitrariness, she guarantees all equal access to the civil service and the individual and collective exercise of the rights and liberties proclaimed or confirmed above." The promise of rights and eventual self-government would be a basis for claims; the promise of equal access to the civil service would become a more specific foundation for claims to equality of public employment anywhere in the Union, including metropolitan France itself.

Another clause in the preamble carried potential for the future: "On the understanding of reciprocity, France agrees to limitations on its sovereignty necessary for the organization and defense of peace." That sovereignty was neither absolute nor indivisible was thus inscribed in constitutional law. It remained to be seen how the principle would be put to use.

The constitution that emerged at the end of September 1946 was approved in a referendum in October.[189] Few Africans could vote, since the old rules applied until the approval process was complete. But by all indications it was well received in Africa.[190] Lamine Guèye, Senghor, and their colleagues understood the ambiguity of the document that had resulted from their efforts: it did not provide for universal

[188] Lampué, "L'Union française d'après la Constitution," 18.

[189] De Gaulle opposed the second constitution as he had the first. He did not think "la France et l'Union française" could protect their independence without stronger state institutions than those provided. *Libération*, 1 October 1946. But 54 percent of the voting electorate did not take his advice. The MRP split. The left, despite misgivings, was largely in favor. Ibid., 14 October 1946.

[190] *L'AOF*, 4, 7, 11, 18, 25 October 1946.

suffrage, the single college, strong territorial assemblies, or executive authority responsible to elected legislators in the territories. The institutions it created were far from constituting a polity that was egalitarian, multinational, or federal. The real power lay in a legislature located in Paris—now containing two chambers, one elected directly, the other chosen by elected bodies representing particular communities. The new legislature was national, but it was not entirely metropolitan, since overseas deputies sat in both chambers. They were a small minority. The President of the French Republic was President of the French Union, but in the latter role he had no cabinet and no ministries. The ministers were responsible only to the National Assembly—and hence to the interplay of party politics, in which Africans would not necessarily play a big part.[191] The assembly that most resembled a federal body had a consultative role only. But Africans, who had wanted something better, were not opposed to what they got: the constitution was not an obstacle to legislation that could provide for the single college, universal suffrage, and stronger territorial assemblies.

African leaders, as Senghor had made clear during the debates, could live with uncertainty, for what they wanted was to set a process in motion. They knew they could not expect to achieve all they wanted in one step. A small minority of deputies from overseas had forced down ministers who had wanted different provisions on citizenship and elections. Their defense of citizenship, if not exactly a triumph, closed a phase of the debate over the rights of the imperial citizen that had begun in France in 1789 and opened a new chapter in the struggle for equal political, social, and economic rights.

[191]The absence of federal ministries and the vulnerability of the French Union to the "rolling sea" of party conflict were emphasized by Rémy Roure in *Le Monde*, 15–16 September 1946. De Gaulle considered the system a "simulacrum" (*un faux-semblant*) of federalism. *Le Monde*, 20 September 1946.

CHAPTER 3

DEFINING CITIZENSHIP, 1946–1956

Having worked hard to keep in place the citizenship clauses that they thought they had won in April and were almost taken away in September, the deputies from French Africa knew that things could evolve for the better or change for the worse. They would be fighting repeated battles with individuals and groups that wanted to restore old-style colonialism. Even people who wished to see a more egalitarian, more participatory polity emerge out of colonial empire were not necessarily sure how, or if, respect for difference and assertions of equality could be reconciled.[1] If we are to understand this period, we need to recognize the uncertainty of the times. What mattered most was not the intrinsic nature of citizenship but how it was *used*.

Some scholars want to read the colonial policy of the Fourth Republic as a sham, a false promise of reform concealing a reality of continued colonial oppression, postponing the only realistic and legitimate outcome, the creation of independent nation-states.[2] But the actors in this chapter—like those of the previous chapter—did not perceive their alternatives that way. People thought they could make a difference and they were operating within frameworks that were theirs, not those of a more recent time.

In this and the following chapter, two dimensions of claiming citizenship are at the forefront.[3] One concerns political citizenship: could the limitations of the Fourth Republic's institutions be transcended,

---

[1] Two leading jurists wrote in 1952 that the Constitution's sections on the French Union were "a view of the future" more than a design for governing the Union. Louis Rolland and Pierre Lampué, *Précis de droit des pays d'outre-mer (territoires, départements, états associés)* (Paris: Dalloz, 1952), 77.

[2] France's record in this regard is sometimes compared unfavorably to that of Great Britain. The classic statement of this position is Tony Smith, "A Comparative Study of French and British Decolonization," *Comparative Studies in Society and History* 20 (1978): 70–102. More satisfactory, because of the question mark, is Tony Chafer, *The End of Empire in French West Africa: France's Successful Decolonization?* (Oxford: Berg, 2002).

[3] Existing scholarship on citizenship after 1946, none of which goes into great detail, plays down the breakthrough without addressing how African political and social movements actually used the concept. Catherine Coquery-Vidrovitch, "Nationalité et citoyenneté en Afrique occidentale français: Originaires et citoyens dans le Sénégal colonial." *Journal of African History* 42 (2001): 285–305; James Genova, "Constructing Identity in Post-War France: Citizenship, Nationality, and the Lamine Guèye Law, 1946–1953," *International History Review* 26 (2004): 55–79.

giving Africans a fuller voice in their own affairs? The second concerns social citizenship: could the formal equivalence of all French citizens become the basis for obtaining equality of life chances, in the workplace, in schools, in civil service positions? In both cases, we need to consider how citizenship discourse was invoked and political mobilization organized, by politicians in Paris and by individuals and organizations in the cities and countryside of Africa. The focus of the current chapter is a series of debates, largely conducted in Paris, in which African deputies participated vigorously but with considerable frustration over the design of the French Union: how to conduct elections, how to bring the majority of Africans into the état-civil, how to provide a legal framework by which Africans could exercise their right to exercise or renounce their personal status. Chapter 4 examines the process of claiming citizenship in French West Africa itself, looking at two exemplary confrontations, over party politics in rural Côte d'Ivoire and over questions of social equality in the domain of labor, and it examines how African leaders tried to bring together the two continents by claiming voice in a kind of political ensemble that was entering the realm of imagination and became known as "Eurafrica."

Defining Citizenship

The Ministry of Overseas France, even before the passage of the October Constitution, had gone out on a limb to inform the administration of AOF that the Lamine Guèye law had proclaimed a "principle of equality" and the end of the colonial regime: "A return to that regime is no longer possible: no text, including a legislative one could go against the principle that the law of 7 May 1946 was intended to put forward."[4] The Ministry had to abandon projects for legislation—including a proposed labor code—for "indigènes" because that category no longer existed. Any labor or other regulations for overseas France would have to treat people of metropolitan and African origins in the same manner. The Ministry recognized that the equivalence of citizens would give strong impetus to demands for equality in all dimensions and that deviation from such principles could produce conflict: "Any labor conflict now presents not only an aspect of class struggle, but also an aspect of 'colonized versus colonizers.'"[5] Existing bodies of legislation such as that "on emigration and circulation of natives" lost juridical basis. An African's freedom of movement

[4] Minister to Governor General, 14 June 1946, 17G 152, AS.

[5] Directeur des Affaires Politiques, Administratives et Sociales, "Note au sujet de la loi du 7 mai 1946," July 1946, 17G 152, AS. On the labor code, see below and Frederick Cooper, *Decolonization and African Society: The Labor Question in French and British Africa* (Cambridge: Cambridge University Press, 1996), chap. 7.

anywhere in the French Union could no more be restricted than that of a metropolitan French citizen.[6] The Ministry told High Commissioners to remind their administrators that government policies "forbid all racial discrimination" and that, insofar as the law permitted, they should punish people who "inflict vexatious treatment on natives in hotels, cafés, restaurants, and theaters."[7] France had become, officially at least, an antiracist state.

But there was ambiguity in the Constitution's treatment of citizenship.[8] For one, under Article 80, all inhabitants of overseas France acquired the "quality of the citizen," but it did not say that they were *French* citizens. The Ministry, in June 1947, felt the need to clarify matters for the benefit of the Government General of AOF, but it concluded that there was no need to label citizenship as French because there was nothing else it could be. "There is no 'citizenship of empire' and 'French citizenship.'" The "*ressortissants*" and the "nationals" mentioned in Article 80 possessed, without ambiguity, "French citizenship." Any backtracking from such a position would be taken as "a sign of our duplicity" and would be "exploited against us."[9]

Juridically, then, the people of French Africa were French citizens.[10] But not everybody in the administration in Africa got the point. In

[6] Laws that applied specifically to indigenous people governing their consumption of alcohol, ownership of firearms, or circulation had to go. Directeur Général des Affaires Politiques, note, July 1946, 17G 152. Eventually there were complaints in the Assemblée de l'Union française that the repeal of such laws was going too slowly and a "complete overhaul of colonial legislation" was needed. Paul Alduy, *Débats*, 25 July 1950, 1127, plus annex listing laws to be abrogated, 1138–39.

[7] Minister (Coste-Floret), circular to Haut Commissaires, Commissaires, Gouverneurs, et Chefs de Territoire, 15 December 1947, 17G 152, AS.

[8] Constitutional ambiguity was recognized by procolonial elements, who saw the need to mount a campaign to resolve uncertainty in their favor. Comité de l'Empire Français, Section de l'Afrique Occidentale, session of 14 November 1946, 100APOM/907, AOM.

[9] Minister to Governors General, 13 June 1947, 17G 176. The Minister's gloss on citizenship drew on the analysis of his legal expert, Yvon Gouet, who wrote "it is clearly a question of an identical citizenship in regard to its basis and which is common to all French citizens, before and after the law of 7 May 1946." He emphasized the Constituante's "wish to establish strict equality among all French people." Note pour M. le Directeur des Affaires Politiques, 13 January 1947, AP 3655, AOM. Gouet's argument was also published as "Le nouveau statut des originaires des territoires d'outre-mer dans l'Union Français," *Penant* 57, 555 (1947): 71–78. Robert Delavignette made much the same point. "Note sur le statut des originaires des territoires d'outre-mer dans l'Union française," 23 October 1947, AP 3655, AOM. See also Pierre Lampué, "L'Union française d'après la Constitution," *Revue Juridique et Parlementire de l'Union Française*, 1 (1947), 147.

[10] The citizens of 1946, if traveling in non-French territories, were thus entitled to the full protection of France on the same basis as any other French citizen and therefore should not be treated as a "native" in any foreign country or colony. Minister of FOM to Minister of Foreign Affairs, 31 March 1948, and Minister of Foreign Affairs to Minister of FOM, 2 December 1949, Afrique-Levant/Afrique Généralités, ADLC.

1949, the Minister had to warn his High Commissioners not to confuse noncitizens with citizens "who have kept their special personal status." Administrators should be careful to employ "a juridically correct terminology."[11] As late as 1954, no less a figure than the Governor General of AOF told his officials that passports issued to "citoyens français de statut personnel" should say "citoyen de l'Union française." The Ministry had to correct him, explaining that under the Constitution *ressortissants* of France were "all French and French citizens.... If the expressions used in the constitutional text are fairly ambiguous, there is no doubt about the intention of the legislator." The Dakar administration had to issue a circular repeating the formula: "There are no *'ressortissants* of the overseas territories,' but only *ressortissants* of France who are all French and citizens." The passports of citizens should simply say "Français."[12]

Then there was the problem of Article 81, which did define another citizenship, that of the French Union. Everybody in the metropole, overseas departments and territories, Algeria, trust territories (Togo and Cameroon), and Associated States possessed such citizenship, but for those outside the last two categories, it meant little because they had something better, French citizenship. People in the Associated States and trust territories did not have French nationality, but they were guaranteed, as citizens of the French Union, the rights specified in the preamble of the Constitution, the general statement of rights to free speech, protection from arbitrary arrest, and other rights of the individual. But the body of the Constitution, specifying among other things how people would be represented in Parliament, did not apply to them. Moroccans, Tunisians, Vietnamese, and so on were not represented in the Assemblée Nationale. Their precise status came under treaty relationships with the sovereigns in the Associated States or with the United Nations (taking over the mandates issued by the League of Nations) in the case of trust territories. Officials admitted there was some confusion here; in Indochina, where the colony of Cochinchina had in effect been dissolved to become part of the

[11] Minister, circular to High Commissioners of Territoires d'Outre-mer, 20 December 1949, 950236/24, CAC.

[12] Governor General to Minister, 24 February 1954, Minister, Circular, 21 June 1954, and Directeur des Affaires Politiques, Dakar, to Directeur des Services de Sécurité, 2 July 1954, letter circulated to all governors by the Governor General, 3 August 1954, 23G 93, AS. However, identification cards (see below) were supposed to mention either "Statut personnel" or "statut civil métropolitain de droit commun." The Governor of Senegal had heard that such cards often had the incorrect expression, "African" or "Muslim." Governor, Senegal, circular to Commandants de Cercle, 28 May 1954, 1D/10, SRAD. Applications to change status were filled with errors. For example, the space for nationality in the file of Ernest Sampah Kassi, from Côte d'Ivoire, was filled in with "citoyen de l'Union française," but he clearly was "citoyen français." Dossier in 23G 98, AS.

Associated State of Vietnam created out of Annam, Tonkin, and Cochinchina, the situation was fuzzy.[13] In the case of Togo and Cameroon, France conferred representation in Parliament and the same rights as those of French citizens even though the Ministry did not think it had to (although the original mandate specified that people in mandated territories should be treated as well as those in colonies).[14]

The Ministry's advisors referred to citizenship of the French Union as "a superposed citizenship"—superposed on Moroccan or Tunisian citizenship or on French citizenship for French nationals, in Europe or in Africa or over an ambiguous status for inhabitants of Togo or Cameroon ("citoyens administrés français"). Union citizens would have access to civil service jobs and schools in France as well as the rights specified in the preamble of the constitution.[15] As the influential MRP politician Daniel Boisdon put it, "The constitution has created a citizenship of the French Union without having created a corresponding nationality."[16] As we will see, the fact that Morocco and Tunisia had their own sovereigns—men capable of exercising willpower—mattered a great deal.

The relationship of citizenship and personal status was summarized in the following chart loosely based on one prepared by the French military in 1948 for its own understanding:

[13] François Borella, *L'évolution politique et juridique de l'Union française depuis 1946* (Paris: Librarie Générale de Droit et de Jurisprudence, 1958), 166–67, points out that France's giving up sovereignty over Cochinchina was a unilateral act of the French government, not a decision shared with the states of Indochina.

[14] The Governor of Togo thought that "the Togolese, particularly the Togolese of the south, is ferociously particularist. To try to give him suddenly the quality of the French citizen would be seen by him not as an act of benevolence on our part, but as a French attempt to assimilate Togo and its inhabitants into some sort of colony, not considering their quality of 'protected person.'" A Togolese or Cameroonian who wanted French nationality would have to be naturalized. Governor, Togo, to Minister, 20 July 1946, AP 3655, AOM; Note by Directeur des Affaires Politiques to Chef du Service des Affaires Sociales, September 1953, 950236/1, CAC; Garde des Sceaux to Minister of FOM, 16 January 1958, 950165/13, CAC; Robert Delavignette, "Note sur le statut des originaires des Territoires d'outre-mer dans l'Union française," 23 October 1947, AP 3655, AOM; Lampué, "L'Union française d'après la Constitution," 162.

[15] Delavignette, "Note sur le statut des originaires," 23 October 1947, Minister of FOM to Ministre de la Guerre, 27 August 1947, Affaires Politiques, "Note au sujet de la citoyenneté," 5 February 1952, AP 3655, AOM; Gouet, "Le nouveau statut," 76–77; Rolland and Lampué, *Précis de droit*, 251. For government jurists' attempts to figure out what French Union citizenship meant in the Associated States, see Service Juridique, Ministère des Affaires Étrangères, "Note pour le Secretariat des Conférences," 18 March 1948, Afrique-Levant/Afrique Généralités/37, ADLC.

[16] Daniel Boisdon, *Les institutions de l'Union française* (Paris: Berger-Levrault, 1949), 83.

Citizens of French Union				
Citizens of French Republic				Citizens of Associated States
French Civil Status		Personal Civil Status (overseas)		
Metropole	Overseas	Voters	Nonvoters	

The chart suggests the multiple ways in which a person could be a citizen, a "French" citizen as well as a "Union" citizen. Before the war millions of people—in Algeria and the colonies—had been French nationals without being French citizens; now, all French nationals were French citizens, and one could be a French citizen (of a certain sort) without being a French national.[17]

Early on, the Ministry encountered two problems that it would never solve. One followed from the provision of Article 82 that guaranteed citizens in the overseas territories the right to keep their personal status without prejudice to their exercise of political rights, unless they chose to renounce that status. The problem was in the implicit recognition that such citizens had the right to renounce their personal status under Islamic or "customary" law. Officials wondered if they should "act very liberal" and allow people to change status by simple declaration. Or should there be "strict and precise conditions that guarantee effective adhesion to French civil status"? Were the "life conditions, beliefs and milieu" of the person acquiring "French" status consistent with the civil code? The practice that worried the Ministry the most was polygamy—something forbidden under the French civil code. So the question was how to control the renunciation process itself, "guaranteeing the *solemnity, the authenticity*, and *the seriousness* of this renunciation, while avoiding anything arbitrary in the application of the intervening texts."[18] The texts did not intervene, because legislators could not agree on what they should say.

The second problem was a practical one, important to the manner in which citizenship rights could be exercised: generalizing and

[17] État-major de la Défense Nationale, Section Coloniale, "Fiche a/s statuts des personnes dans l'Union française," 10 May 1948, AP 3655, AOM. The État-major's chart has an error in it, misusing the term "national français."

[18] Paul Coste-Floret to Mathurin Anghiley, Conseiller de la République, 8 July 1948, Yvon Gouet, Note to Direction des Affaires Politiques, 13 January 1947, AP 3655, AOM.

systematizing the état-civil. If citizens eligible to vote were to be distinguished from noncitizens, they would need to be identified, and if citizens, in certain instances, were entitled to social benefits, the individual would have to be tracked. But registration of births, marriages, and deaths had been effectively implemented—and was compulsory only for citizens under the old regime, not the "citizens of 1946." Officials were stumped about how such vital information as marriage and filiation could be recorded when the nature of marriage and recognition of the paternity of a child were regulated in many different ways in different African communities.[19] I will return to both these problems later in this chapter.

There was another ambiguity in the text that the Ministry was anxious to clear up. Article 80 said that "particular laws" would regulate the application of the citizenship provisions. That could potentially mean that the law could take away much of what the Constitution conferred. But the Ministry wanted to dispel such fears, remembering full well the emotion attached to the issue. Its lawyers decided that the phrase "particular laws" referred only to voting and the nature of representation in Parliament. It was only in this domain "that the Constituents drew back before the practical consequences of absolute equality." They did not want to "bend a principle vigorously affirmed elsewhere." No law could restrict the exercise of the rights of speech or assembly. No more could the status of "indigène"—or a religious or racial designation—figure in decrees or laws, nor could personal status be an obstacle to the exercise of any right, with the notable exception of the right to vote.[20] The Conseil d'État in April 1947 confirmed that *ressortissants* of the overseas territories, as well as Togo and Cameroon, were eligible for public employment anywhere in the metropole, the overseas territories, and the trust territories.[21] All citizens had the legal right to enter any part of the French Union where they chose to go: "The circulation of French people (all citizens since 1 June 1946) and

[19]The need for an effective and universal état-civil was recognized even before the constitution was approved, as a consequence of the Lamine Guèye law and the extension of the vote to some categories of people who did not have French civil status. See Minister to Governor General, 14 June 1946, 17G 152, AS.

[20]Minister to Governors General, 13 June 1947, 17G 176, AS. The Ministry's lawyer, Yvon Gouet, wrote that there could be no discrimination against citizens from the overseas territories "relative to equal access to children and adults to education and professional training or to equal access to public service." He insisted that discrimination against citizens of the French Union (that is from Associated States) was also forbidden. Gouet to Directeur des Affaires Politiques, 14 October 1946, AP 3655, AOM.

[21]"Extrait de registre des délibérations," Commission de la Fonction publique, Conseil d'État séance du 23 avril 1947, AP3655, AOM.

French administered persons, who are citizens of the French Union, can no longer be limited inside the Republic." The right of such citizens to come to the metropole could not be contravened even if their doing so caused "grave problems."[22] The "current regime of freedom of passage" produced anxiety in official quarters in the next decade and a half—particularly in regard to Algerians—and officials tried to figure out ways to at least keep track of people whom they regarded as potential dangers or social burdens. At times they tried to focus social services on such migrants.[23] But they were constrained by the constitutional right of all French citizens to "travel under the same conditions as all ordinary passengers and [they] are only obliged to present an official identity card and pay for their tickets."[24]

For a time at least, suffrage would not be universal, the double college would remain in place, overseas territories would not be represented in the Assemblée Nationale in accordance with their population, and territorial assemblies would have limited powers in the face of the sovereign authority of the Assemblée Nationale in Paris. Nonetheless, many Africans saw in citizenship something to celebrate. Governor General Barthes told his fellow high administrators in early 1947 that the citizenship clause was "so important" that he had been asked by some African politicians to declare a national holiday to celebrate it. He did not do so, but the newspaper *Paris-Dakar* reported in June 1948 that "the anniversary of the Lamine Guèye law was joyfully celebrated."[25]

[22] Affaires Politiques, note on "le droit d'aller et de venir," May 1953, 950236/1, CAC. In 1950, officials noted that French citizens from Africa seeking to enter France were subject to "no regulation," although metropolitans going to Africa had to meet certain conditions (presumably legal under older regulations because their status had not changed in 1946). They wanted to ensure that Africans coming to European France could pay their way back, but the proposal was not implemented. Exposé des motifs from Ministry, 30 May 1950, F60/1382, ANF.

[23] On the ways in which the police in metropolitan France maneuvered between the constitutional provisions of citizenship and their perception of Muslim Algerians as dangerous, see Alexis Spire, *Étrangers à la carte: L'administration de l'immigration en France (1945-1975)* (Paris: Grasset, 2005), and Emmanuel Blanchard, *La police parisienne et les Algériens (1944-1962)* (Paris: Éd. Nouveau Monde, 2011).

[24] Governor General, Algeria, to Ministre de l'Intérieur, 16 September 1947, Governor General, Algeria, to Ministre du Travail, 3 June 1948, F/1a/5056, ANF. For attempts to observe and provide social services to Muslims from French North Africa to metropolitan France, see the minutes of the Commission interministerielle de coordination pour les affaires sociales musulmanes, 18, 24 March 1954 (and thereafter), F/1a/5044, and Robert Montagne, "Rapport provisoire sur l'émigration des musulmans d'Algérie en France," 1954, F/1a/5047, ANF.

[25] Transcript of Conférence des Hauts-Commissaires et Gouverneurs, session of 24 February 1947, 106, 19PA/3/34 (Delvignette Papers), AOM; *Paris-Dakar*, 2 June 1948.

Claiming Political Rights in the Paris Legislature

African legislators, for the next ten years, would keep their focus on the political and social dimensions of citizenship, seeking to give Africans equality of voice and equality of opportunity. Let us begin with the legislative side. The successful defense of the Lamine Guèye law in 1946 gave way to considerable frustration, as the possibilities the constitution allowed for change proved difficult to get through a fragmented Assemblée Nationale. The main dynamic of electoral change was the gradual increase in the franchise, slowly turning elections into events of mass mobilization, changing the nature of constituencies to which African politicians had to cater. Most legislators claimed, at least in public, to believe in universal suffrage, but not necessarily right away.[26] The gradual extension of the franchise until universal suffrage was achieved in 1956 contrasts to the blockage that occurred in regard to the double college and the power of territorial assemblies, a blockage that produced continual tension and kept the question of race in political debate. But African legislators were not entirely frustrated in the postwar decade, and their proudest achievement was in the realm of social citizenship, the Code du Travail of 1952, a subject I will take up in the next chapter.

Rather than follow the ups and down of legislators' attempts to reform the electoral system and remedy the shortcomings of the Constitution—they were almost continuous until 1956—let us describe the general conditions under which reform was stalled. With a divided polity and no clear majority in the Assemblée Nationale, politics depended on maintaining unity within parties and coalitions among them. Up until 1947, the Communist Party (PCF) was part of a government coalition, but after labor unrest and growing polarization, the party was excluded from government, so the MRP and the Socialist Party were no longer seeking to appease a left ally. Neither of those parties had a consistent position on colonial questions, the most contentious of which concerned Indochina and Algeria. The MRP included a number of "social Catholics" who were sympathetic to colonized peoples, particularly in regard to issues of welfare and family life. But if the party wanted to keep a share of power, it needed the votes of elements that can be characterized as "colonialist"—deputies elected by the colons of Algeria, supporters of overseas businesses,

[26] Even the procolonialist *Marchés Coloniaux* could claim to favor universal suffrage and admission of Africans to the first college "as the work of school, missions of all confessions, doctors, social assistants will transform in depth the backward masses." René Moreux, "Le suffrage autochtone universel, mais à deux degrés, en Afrique noire, pour les non-évolués," *Marchés Coloniaux*, 15 May 1948, 751.

and other defenders of empire as it had been.[27] The Socialist Party had African members in the Assemblée—Lamine Guèye most notably—and some of its members embraced the idea of making the overseas territories a showcase of progress, but Socialists at times needed the support of pro-colon factions.

The PCF, especially after its expulsion from the government in 1947, stood clearly for advancing the cause of political participation and social progress in overseas France, but was ambivalent on the question of colonialism itself, with much of the party hoping to revolutionize the entire French Union.[28] The uncertain nature of Fourth Republic politics both opened up possibilities for political maneuver by African deputies and made it difficult to bring about systematic change in the political structure of the French Union.

The Minister of Overseas France in 1946 and 1947, Marius Moutet, was a Socialist who, as we have seen, had preached the gospel of equality within a Greater France. James Lewis describes as "tragic" the fact that as a member of a divided party in an even more fragmented coalition, he had to make one compromise after another.[29] When he left the Ministry, the chances of electoral reform diminished. Nonetheless, Africans and other former subjects were finding ways to exercise political voice inside and outside of legislative institutions. The wiser heads in the French government were aware of the risk of alienating overseas citizens too much. No less a figure than the Governor General of AOF, René Barthes, warned that being relegated to the "second college" left the West African feeling like "a diminished citizen, an incomplete citizen. . . . Moreover, I tell you, 'take care, these diminished

[27] For the views of influential socially minded Catholic organizations and leaders, see Semaines Sociales de France, *Peuples d'Outre-Mer et civilisation occidentale* (Lyon: Chronique Sociale de France, 1948). MRP leader Paul Coste-Floret claimed to favor enlarged powers for both territorial assemblies and the Assemblée de l'Union française, expanded suffrage, and the phasing out of the double college, but when push came to shove, the party did not back such reforms in parliamentary debates. See his declarations in "Autorité, travail, amour, principes de la politique de l'Union française," *Marchés Coloniaux*, 15 May 1948, 753–56.

[28] The PCF was unsure how far it should go in supporting Ho Chi Minh in the Indochina war, in criticizing the repression of the 1947 Madagascar revolt, or in backing the nationalist cause in Algeria until the middle ground became untenable in 1956. Its hesitancy had much to do with ambivalence over reintegrating itself into the mainstream of parliamentary politics in alliance with part of the Socialist Party or positioning itself as a militant opposition. See Irwin Wall, *French Communism in the Era of Stalin: The Quest for Unity and Integration, 1945-1962* (Westport, Conn.: Greenwood, 1983). Even in 1956, a PCF spokesman could state his party's goals as "a true French Union." Léon Feix, cited in ibid., 187.

[29] James I. Lewis, "The Tragic Career of Marius Moutet," *European History Quarterly* 38 (2008): 66–92.

citizens number fifteen million, the others some tens of thousands, that is all.'"[30]

The fact that citizens in one or another part of the empire, at any given time between 1945 and 1962, were engaged in parliamentary politics, strikes, public discourse, localized mobilizations, and armed conflict concentrated the minds of policy makers on avoiding the more dangerous forms of struggle.[31] They worried too that international opinion, no longer taking for granted the normality of colonial rule, could lead to interference in France's way of doing things. The best defense against interference was the argument that France was not keeping its overseas population in a state of dependence—that everyone was a citizen, enjoying "complete equality" and participating in governing the French Union.[32]

The Constitution, as we saw, neither enshrined nor prohibited the double college, so it remained a burning issue until it was finally abolished for sub-Saharan Africa in 1956. The power of territorial assemblies had no constitutional definition either, so the Assemblée Nationale would have to determine their makeup and authority. The Ministry, and especially Moutet, had throughout the summer of 1946 opposed the double college and favored if not immediate universal suffrage, at least a relatively inclusive franchise.[33] Laws providing for relatively strong territorial assemblies elected by a single college had been approved by the first Assemblée Nationale Constituante and retained support in the Commission de la FOM in the second.[34]

Lamine Guèye and others had expressed great emotion (chapter 2) during the first Constituante at the possibility of ordinary Africans, at least those with some form of written identification, voting. The defeat of the first constitution invalidated the April 1946 electoral law. The coalition that had supported colonial reforms had frayed by the second Constituent Assembly. The tactic of the boycott that had kept

[30]Transcript of Conférence des Hauts-Commissaires et Gouverneurs, session of 24 February 1947, 12–13, 19PA/3/34, AOM.

[31]Had a strong part of the procolonialist lobby had its way, it would have eliminated Africans from the French legislature. See for example the demands formulated at the meeting of 29 April 1947 of the Conseil Consultative du Comité de l'Empire francais, 100APOM/898, AOM.

[32]See for example Minister of Foreign Affairs, circular to "agents diplomatiques et consulaires de France à l'étranger," 12 June 1947, Minister of Foreign Affairs, to Ambassadeur au Conseil de Tutelle, 18 August 1947, K.Afrique 1944–1952/Généralités/33, ADLC.

[33]Moutet wrote to the Governor General of AOF on 4 August 1946 (telegram) that he was working on a law "to institute direct universal suffrage in Africa and Madagascar." Such a law would require developing voter rolls, tables of the état-civil, lists of people on tax rolls, etc. 17G 176, AS. See also Directeur of Affaires Politiques, Note, July 1946, 17G 152, AS.

[34]Commission de la FOM, 10 April 1946, C//15293, ANF; Lamine Guèye, ANC, *Débats*, 5 October 1946, 4712, reporting on behalf of the Commission de la FOM.

the citizenship provisions of the Lamine Guèye law in the constitution and the double college out of it could not be used very often.

On 4 October 1946, a few days after the final vote on the second version of the constitution, the Assembly took up the question of how deputies would be elected to the Assemblée Nationale from overseas.[35] First came the question of the vote in Algeria, and the demand for political voice for Muslims ran into explicit defense of the privileges of European French citizens. Muslim Algerians, notably Ferhat Abbas, were not at this time opposing the double college, for they had another goal: a federal system, in which Algerians would have their own assembly with considerable powers. "Our goal . . . is not to invade the metropolitan national Assembly with Muslim representatives from Algeria" but to "leave you at your ease" to govern the metropole, while Algerians governed Algeria insofar as internal matters were concerned. But Algerians did need a minimum of deputies to protect their interests. While Kaddour Sator (a Muslim Algerian associated with Abbas) argued that Algeria's eight million Muslims—compared to 800,000 people of French civil status—should by strict proportionality have had 106 deputies in the Assemblée Nationale, they were asking for only 35, against 20 for the deputies of the first college (citizens of French personal status). The number was important, because a minimum of 25 deputies was needed to constitute a group in the assembly, and the Muslim Algerians wanted to be able to act. Now, the government and prosettler deputies were proposing 15 and 15.[36]

What is striking is the reasoning. François Quilici, a deputy from Algeria, wanted no part of Abbas-style federalism, but he did not want one person, one vote either, fearing "an invasion" of Muslim deputies that would lead "to the submersion of the metropolitan assemblies, that is to say the sovereignty of the French nation." He insisted that his argument was not racist, but based on "the only remaining difference, the civil statuses of the two communities." Those Muslims "who have the most contact with our civilization, those who have proven themselves the most capable" (that is, those who either had renounced their Muslim status or came under the limited provisions of the law of 7 March 1944) could enter the first college. "We take the 'cream,' in a sense, of the second college," said Quilici.[37] The counterargument,

[35]The law allocating seats and setting voting procedures for the Assemblée de l'Union française generated little controversy and was approved by voice vote. It was not intended to be "an assembly representing all the territories equally" but "an assembly on the basis of parity between on the one hand the metropole and on the other hand the overseas French Republic and the Associated States." M. de Tanguy on behalf of Commission Constitutionnel, ANC, *Débats*, 2 October 1946, 4391, 4393.

[36]Ibid., 4 October 1946, 4550–51. The now-invalid April law had provided for fourteen deputies from the first college and twenty-one from the second.

[37]Quilici, ibid., 4547.

expressed strongly by Ferhat Abbas, Sator, and also the metropolitan deputy Pierre Cot, was that the law was defining "two sorts of men."[38] Paul Viard, the jurist from Alger, wanted to exclude even the "cream" of Muslim Algerians who had joined the first college, on the grounds that the category was adequately represented by the second college, but the government made him back off. But he had made his point: "each category of the population will have its place."[39]

Unlike the situation in Senegal, where protests in 1944–45 had made the government back down from its intention to exclude Muslim women from the extension of the franchise to women, Muslim women in Algeria remained disenfranchised. Ferhat Abbas wanted women to vote under the same conditions as men. Sator asked for an explanation of why Muslim women in Algeria, alone in overseas France, were excluded from the vote. He received neither explanation nor satisfaction. Abbas's proposal was rejected 379 to 158. Muslim Algerian men would elect their fifteen deputies, the same number as the men and women of the first college who represented a tenth as many people.[40] The assembly majority—by its blatant disregard of principles of equality or justice expressed in the constitution it had approved days before—may well have helped to push Algeria down the road to war.[41]

When it came to Africa's place in the Assemblée Nationale, Moutet had been pushed to cut a deal.[42] Some overseas citizens would get to vote in a single college, some in the double college. For the overseas territories as a whole, the representation in the ANC of twenty-six would increase to thirty-four, nineteen from territories with a single college, while the territories with the double college would elect nine from "un collège d'autochtones" and six from colleges of "citoyens de statut français." West Africa would benefit from the single college, French Equatorial Africa and Madagascar would be stuck with the double college. Perfectly well aware that this proposal was a step back from what had been approved in the first Constituante and was still favored by the Overseas Committee, government spokesmen asked for patience. Jean Félix-Tchicaya, deputy from Congo-Gabon, wanted to amend the brokered bill to provide the single college for French

[38] Ibid., 4548–50. Cot quoted, ibid., 4549.

[39] Viard, ibid., 4552.

[40] Ibid., 4552–53.

[41] Ferhat Abbas presented to the President in October 1948 a pamphlet that a high French official interpreted as "vigorous, attractive," presenting "federal doctrines" for a relationship between an Algerian republic and the French Republic. He saw this plan fitting within a federalism that had "partisans across the political spectrum" Wishful thinking, perhaps, but maybe also a sign of the opportunities being missed in Algeria. Chérif Mecheri (in charge of relations with Associated States and one of few high officials of Muslim Algerian origin), note for President, 21 October 1948, 4AG 527, ANF.

[42] Moutet, ANC, *Débats*, 4 October 1946, 4556.

Equatorial Africa, pointing out not just the violation of the principle of equality but the fact that it was discriminating against precisely that part of the French Empire that had stood up for a free France during World War II. The head of the Committee could say only that he found these arguments "very pertinent." To the consternation of the right, Félix-Tchicaya's amendment passed on a voice vote. Opponents tried to raise procedural objections, and the outcome hung in doubt. Meanwhile, Joseph Ravoahangy of Madagascar tried to get rid of the double college for his island, insisting, "One cannot proclaim the abolition of racial distinction and maintain it in practice. One cannot accord French citizenship to all *ressortissants* of the overseas territories and annihilate this disposition by creating citizens of the first and second zones."[43] It was here that Moutet entered his plea: he had made a deal. The appeals from Equatorial Africa and Madagascar were rejected.

All citizens participating in the first college—those with "French" civil status—would obviously be eligible to register and to vote. For the citizens of 7 May 1946, the question was more delicate, for even people in favor of a universal or relatively inclusionary franchise thought that without a generalized état-civil, it would be hard to tell who was a legitimate voter—from the territory in question, of the proper age, untainted by a disqualifying criminal conviction. Top officials of the Ministry agreed on the necessity to get everybody inscribed in the état-civil, but meanwhile the question was who could vote under actual conditions. The answer was in the system included in the abrogated election law passed by the first ANC (chapter 2): a list of "capacities" for the eligible voter, in single or double colleges. The problem was *individualization*, to make up voter lists out of people who were identifiable, as opposed to the heretofore dominant conception of Africans in terms of the communities to which they belonged, identifiable via the vertical channels of imperial command, via chiefs, elders, or other such leaders familiar to the French officials.

The list of enfranchised categories now considered by the Assemblée included "notables évolués" recognized officially as such; members and former members of local councils of various sorts; members or former members of cooperatives, unions, or rural cooperatives; recipients of the Légion d'honneur or other medals for military or civilian service; civil servants; people with "permanent employment" in an commercial, industrial, artisanal, or agricultural enterprise "on a legal basis or possessing a certificate of regular work"; assessors and other personnel of indigenous courts; ministers of religion; soldiers and former soldiers, including those in the deuxième portion du contingent (civilian service in lieu of military); "all merchants, industrialists,

[43] Ravoahangy, ibid., 4555.

planters, artisans or in general all holders of a license"; chiefs; owners of a building with a property title; anyone with a hunting permit or driver's license.[44] This rather odd combination of people shared the attribute of having written evidence of who they were.

Explaining why he would vote against the bill as a whole, Lamine Guèye focused on the injustice of the double college. But the other side also had its words to say. Quilici, who had defended the settlers of Algeria, now defended the double college for much of Africa. There were not many people of French civil status who lived in Equatorial Africa, he admitted, but "these are the territories where the indigenous populations are the most backward. . . . In addition, in all our overseas territories, the European minority is the leading minority. It is it which brings and dispenses the benefits of civilization and of democratic liberties." Straying from the bill at hand, he came back to Algeria: "It is honestly impossible to contend that outside of an elite, trained moreover in our schools, the political consciousness of the Muslim masses is equivalent to that of European masses. The Muslim masses are still docile to traditional influences or specifically Islamic appeals." "You are practicing racism," interjected Arthur Ramette, a Communist deputy from the north of France. "No," replied Quilici, "this is not racism. It is a reality."[45]

The debate over what became the electoral law of 5 October 1946, taking place between the Assemblée's vote on the constitution and the referendum that put it into effect, brought out the split in the assembly between open defenders of white privilege and defenders of the principle of equality. And it reveals as well the importance of political machinations. Quilici's view of reality was self-evidently racist; Moutet's arguably was not, and he was clearly going against his better—or at least his previous—judgment on the franchise, the single college, and the powers of the assemblies. He was part of a government that was trying, rather desperately, to hold itself together. When the constitutional text passed muster with the electorate (that is, citizens eligible under the old rules, excluding most Africans) and new elections were held, the Parliament remained divided. The defenders of a principled, inclusive, nonracial approach to political participation ran up against both out-and-out racism and political opportunism.

An African writing in the newspaper *Réveil* after the electoral apparatus was set up in October made clear his astonishment, after the Lamine Guèye law, to see "the enumeration of categories that vote and of others that do not vote."[46] But in the ensuing years, voting turned out to be a dynamic element of politics. The criteria were expanded

[44] Ibid., 4 October 1946, 4557.
[45] Quilici and Ramette, ibid., 4 October 1946, 4560.
[46] Moussa Deme, "À propos de la loi electorale," *Réveil*, 24 October 1946.

slightly—adding mothers of two or more men who had served in the military as well as people literate in French or Arabic, for instance.[47] The real change was that people did whatever it took to get on the voter rolls. In the first election under the electoral law, in November 1946, just fewer than eight hundred thousand people in French West Africa were counted as legal voters, out of a population of perhaps fifteen million. Around three million voters were registered by June 1951, rising to six million by January 1956. It was only then that universal suffrage and the single college were instituted (see below and chapter 5). By the time of the first election under universal suffrage, in March 1957, ten million people were on the rolls, over half of the population.[48]

The law of 5 October 1946 applied to elections to the Assemblée Nationale. The day after this debate, so disappointing and painful to deputies from Algeria and sub-Saharan Africa, the question of the powers and mode of election of territorial assemblies came up. The Overseas Committee proposed with near unanimity a law similar to that adopted unanimously in April but which had to be redone in the light of the new constitution. Now, the government announced that it did not even want to discuss such a law. It pleaded lack of time and proposed to act by decree until at the latest 1 July 1947, by which time a law governing the territorial assemblies would have to be voted on.[49] The government—probably uncertain that it would get a bill to its liking out of the Assemblée—would itself determine the composition, mode of election, functioning, and competences of the assemblies.[50] Félix-Tchicaya, Houphouët-Boigny, Apithy, and others expressed their consternation at the backsliding from an earlier consensus and commitments made by the Minister in May and August to protect the rights promised during the first constitutional discussions. They pointed out that African deputies had accepted their underrepresentation in the Assemblée Nationale as a trade-off to giving territorial

[47]Gregory Mann suggests that even the small gesture to mothers of soldiers gave the Union Soudanaise, the most dynamic political party in the Sudan, a new target to mobilize in elections, turning upside down what the government perhaps hoped for in making this concession—that such voters would be a conservative influence. "The End of the Road: Nongovernmentality in the West African Sahel" (manuscript), chap. 2.

[48]Joseph Roger de Benoist, L'Afrique occidentale française, de la conférence de Brazzaville (1944) à l'indépendance (1960) (Dakar: Nouvelles Éditions Africaines, 1982), 513.

[49]The Commission's proposal was presented by Lamine Guèye, and the government's refusal to accept or even discuss the law was announced by Jean Letourneau, Ministre des Postes, Télégraphes et Téléphones in the absence of Moutet. ANC, Débats, 5 October 1946, 4712. See the discussions in the commission on 25 September 1946, C//15313, ANF.

[50]The possibility of defining the local assemblies by decree had been brought to the Commission de la FOM on 25 September 1946, and it was unanimously rejected. C//15313, ANF. See Lewis, "Tragic Career of Marius Moutet."

assemblies real power to run the affairs of their territories. Now, there was no guarantee that the quid pro quo would be honored. Jean Félix-Tchicaya warned that such backsliding "risks provoking, in my country, sentiments of reprobation, distaste, and contempt."[51] They spoke in vain.

The Ministry indeed proceeded to act by decree.[52] And—a sign of Moutet's weakness—it decided that members of the territorial assemblies would be elected in two colleges. In each assembly, the majority of councilors (in most cases by a ratio of between 1.5 and 2 to 1) would come from the second college. The Ministry had consulted with the Conseil d'État—the "sages" who advised on constitutional matters—and they had come out on the side of those who wanted to protect people of French civil status. The Conseil held that Senegal could keep the single college, because it had long voted that way, but elsewhere

> the Conseil d'État believes that while it is normal to give a certain majority to the population of personal status, it is indispensable to avoid that citizens of French status are completely eliminated from local assemblies where elections done under a single college would risk giving a crushing majority to citizens of personal status, although the general interests of citizens of French status, without being opposed to those of the citizens of personal status, are nevertheless not the same and present more complexity.[53]

White voters had the right to a voice in the assemblies to protect their unique interests; never mind that this implied a diminished voice for black voters. Houphouët-Boigny bitterly referred to "this caricature of local assemblies that the socialist Moutet has just given to Africa."[54]

[51] *Débats*, 5 October 1946, 4713–15. The government claimed that it would act in the interests being defended by the overseas deputies.

[52] When discussing possible decrees before a displeased Commission de la FOM, Moutet pleaded, "We thus have behind us an important accomplishment and I ask of you, when you will be back home, not to insist on what you have not obtained, but make evident that your presence among us has not been irrelevant to this accomplishment." On the double college, he stated, "You know my sentiments—but there is resistance that is difficult to overcome." Members of the Commission, at the end of the session, issued a press statement expressing their regret over the text of the decrees and their intention to reserve "their complete freedom of action." Session of 8 October 1946, C//15313, ANF.

[53] Conseil d'État, section des finances, extrait du registre des délibérations, 21 October 1946, AP 998, AOM. When a related issue came up a year later, the Conseil d'État stuck to its reasoning. Note of Conseil d'État, 6 February 1947, AP 998, AOM, and extract from deliberations, 5 June 1947, AP 984, AOM. Part of its reasoning in both decisions was that there should not be disparities in how territorial assemblies were elected, and since Algeria had two colleges, others should as well.

[54] Letter to Gabriel d'Arboussier (apparently intercepted), 4 November 1946, in Robert Delavignette Papers, 19PA/4/58, AOM.

In 1947, the relationship among citizenship, voting, and the place of African legislatures in the French Union remained the focus of controversy and anger. In January, the territorial assembly of Senegal, enraged at its own weakness, suspended work and refused to act on the budget or other (very limited) matters on which it was required to pronounce. Its members passed a resolution referring to itself as "a pseudo-deliberative assembly," and demanded that it have the power to "deliberate effectively on all questions relevant to the life of the country." In June, it was still refusing to act in the absence of a law giving the assemblies "real powers." It gave up the protest in July.[55]

African political parties, including Houphouët-Boigny's Rassemblement Démocratique Africain (RDA, to be discussed in chapter 4), kept up a steady stream of criticism of electoral laws, coming from its representatives in Paris and party operatives in African cities. The party's strategy was to start with gains that had already been achieved and keep pointing to the "contradictions . . . between the principles proclaimed in the preamble [of the Constitution] and the inequality instituted by certain constitutional provisions and aggravated by the policies of the current government."[56] Houphouët-Boigny proposed to the Assemblée Nationale new legislation that would have given territorial legislatures more authority and more democratic electoral procedures. Lamine Guèye, a Socialist, proposed a law to give the territorial assemblies "a real power of decision and control over the quasi-totality of the affairs of the country." Other parties responded by acknowledging the malaise in Africa but watered down Houphouët-Boigny's submission. The Overseas Committee of the Assembly, reviewing these proposals in a report prepared by Houphouët-Boigny, called the ending of the double college "the essential question," for it was "always considered by overseas peoples as racial discrimination and the negation of these passages of the Constitution." For the committee, universal suffrage remained an essential goal as well, and while it admitted that the absence of the état-civil made such a goal difficult to achieve at the moment, it proposed that the government give itself a time limit of four years to set up the état-civil, meanwhile expanding the categories of eligibility to vote to all who could read or write or produce certain documents.[57]

The colonial deputies were not the only ones to hold strong opinions. The Rassemblement de Gauche—in which colons were represented—

[55] *Réveil*, 26 January, 5 June, 14 July 1947.

[56] Pamphlet, "Le Rassemblement Democratique Africain dans la Lutte Anti-imperialiste," 1948, copy in "West African Political Ephemera, 1948–62," University of Wisconsin, microfilm 2169, available through CAMP.

[57] Assemblée Nationale, Proposition de loi No. 952, 18 March 1947, and Report by Commission de la FOM, Document 2245, 5 August 1947; copies of both documents as well as other proposals for electoral reform may be found in F60/1399, ANF.

equated any diffusion of power to the territories to a move from "aban-donment to abandonment." It insisted that the double college was a "security lock" without which the French Union would fall apart, and it wanted "to restore the authority of the metropole."[58]

One reason for government caution on the power of assemblies was that it feared, probably correctly, that what assemblies wanted most was to control the allocation of forest, agricultural, and mining concessions. Moutet claimed to oppose such devolution because he wanted to coordinate economic planning, but the desire for such con-trol sounds suspiciously like the "pacte colonial."[59] The government got its way to continue the regime of decrees, leaving bitterness in its wake. It accepted some minor changes in who could vote, but gave itself a new deadline—1 July 1951—for deciding the serious questions concerning the assemblies. In the end, it would fail to do even that.[60]

Government officials in Africa were of two minds concerning elec-toral reform. The Governor of Senegal seemed annoyed that African politicians wanted to turn territorial assemblies into "little parlia-ments," and he feared that extending Senegal's single college more broadly in West Africa would only reinforce such tendencies. He thought that Senegal's citizens from the Quatre Communes looked down their noses at the "neo-citizens of 1946 from the interior" and manipulated the electoral system in their favor. He wanted to guard against the dangers of a territorial assembly elected on universal suf-frage by creating a second chamber of "traditional chiefs, chambers of commerce, agriculture and industry, professional organizations"—a view of Africa through the lens of French corporatism. The Governor General, however, thought that the status quo of limited franchise and limited powers for the territorial assemblies was dysfunctional. Put-ting all legislative powers in Paris was part of the "especially central-izing character of the current system" which complicated the efficacy and legitimacy of the current government. He thought the current sys-tem of "restricted suffrage" put power in the hands of a largely urban

[58] *Le Monde*, 24 July 1947, reporting on actions in the Assemblée Nationale and in article by Rémy Roure for Rassemblement des Gauches. As the newspaper reported, the Commission de la FOM had voted for a bill that included abolition of the double college, but that had raised a storm among procolonial deputies in the Assembly.

[59] Conférence des Hauts-Commissaires et Gouverneurs, session of 24 February 1947, 5–6, 19PA/3/34, AOM. Robert Delavignette saw assemblies seeking to become "a rival of the national parliament." Ibid., 17.

[60] *Le Monde*, 24 July, 5, 6, 13 August 1947. The overall sequence of events is summa-rized in Lewis, "Tragic Career of Marius Moutet," 74–76. While doing little to empower the territorial assemblies, the Minister wanted to be sure that any assembly for AOF (or AEF) as a whole would be weaker still. The local assemblies should be the "dominant powers," and the assembly of the group would have a role in regard to "common inter-ests" but would not be "a super-assembly" and should not come between the territories and Paris. Commission de la FOM, 5 March 1947, C//15406, ANF.

minority and discouraged participation in politics. He favored the single college, not least because the Europeans elected in their separate college did little except protect their own interests. The political affairs specialists in Paris also thought that in the absence of universal suffrage, leaders were able to "create for themselves an electoral clientele. . . . It results from this that the young colonial leaders quickly occupy the scene and block the passage to elements coming from the masses and authentic native society."[61]

Officials worried that if African politicians went back to their constituents empty handed, the French political position could become more difficult to sustain. They were realizing by the early 1950s that once even a contained program of electoral politics was allowed, friendly political elites had to demonstrate that their brand of politics paid off. The Ministry, for these pragmatic reasons, was aware that it could not block the door to all reform. Officials were thinking that some form of "decentralization" and "deconcentration"—taking authority out of Paris and putting it in territories where elected politicians would have a voice—had to be considered.[62] In short, part of the official mind saw a more democratic Africa as more conducive to French interests than the patchwork of openings and closures of the status quo.

But the Ministry was not free to strategize on its own. The single college and universal suffrage remained blocked in the French legislature. The nadir of the African quest for electoral justice occurred in 1951–52, when, knowing that they lacked the votes for total abolition of the double college and for universal suffrage in elections for the Assemblée Nationale and the territorial assemblies, colonial deputies tried to go partway and were repulsed. Senghor and his allies had proposed to enlarge the list of eligible voters, put in place electoral commissions independent of local administrators, and extend the single college for elections to the Assemblée Nationale from AOF to AEF and Cameroon (but not Madagascar, where tension between settlers and local people made it too difficult for the moment). They ran into a frank defense of the double college, although Coste-Floret tried to take a middle position, favoring the elimination of the double college in some places.[63]

[61] Governor, Senegal, Response to questionnaire from Ministry on territorial assemblies, enclosed Secretary General of Senegal to Governor General, 25 July 1952, and Governor General, circular to Governors, 20 June 1950, AOF/Dakar/251, ADN. Henri Laurentie, "Développements récents de la politique coloniale française," lecture at King's College London, 28 November 1946, Laurentie Papers, 72AJ/535, ANF.

[62] Such an argument is particularly clear in Directeur des Affaires Politique, "Note pour Monsieur le Ministre," 21 March 1952, AP 2187/6, AOM.

[63] Assemblée Nationale, *Débats*, 24 April 1951, Senghor, 3839–40, Henri Caillavet, 3841, René Malbrant, 3844–47, Paul Coste-Floret, 3859–60.

Figure 3. Léopold Sédar Senghor, 1949.
Photo by Felix Man/Picture Post/Hulton Archive, © Getty Images.

The Assemblée Nationale passed a modest bill along Senghor's lines, but the upper house, the Conseil de la République, initiated a wholesale assault on the single college, on widening the franchise, and on any increase in the minuscule number of seats allotted to overseas territories. During the debate, Raphaël Saller, senator from Martinique, former high colonial official, and one of few men of color in the body, laid bare his colleagues' defense of racial privilege:

> You have the sentiment that the overseas populations are not ripe for democracy, that their knowledge of the workings of the modern world is insufficient, that they do not know at all how to make use of the electoral instruments of universal suffrage or to use the thousand advantages of science put at their disposal, and finally they do not have sufficient patriotic conviction to defend France in all circumstances et never to align against her. From this point, you think that they will need European direction for centuries, the direction of a father to his children, of a master to his servants. And, according to you, the best means of ensuring the indispensable presence of France overseas is not to give to the inhabitants of these countries the quality of French person in all its fullness, but to place French people of the metropole in all command posts, that is to say to give to a tiny minority, whatever its intellectual or moral weaknesses, as many or even more rights than the enormous majority of autochthons.[64]

Saller insisted that the only way to maintain the unity of France was the opposite—equality for all.

His colleagues were unconvinced. Under pressure of impending elections, the government forced the lower house, on the second reading of the bill, into a take-it-or-leave-it approach to the bill that the Conseil de la République had gutted. In the end, Félix-Tchicaya said on the floor of the Assembly, "it is a shameful act for Parliament."[65]

Equally shameful was the handling of a bill later that year that left Africans—faced with the possibility that the territorial assemblies would be left without any legal basis at all—having to accept a bill that reinforced the double college in territorial elections and did little to make the assemblies more meaningful legislative units.[66] The double college was maintained in Algeria as well, despite pleas in the Assemblée de l'Union française to end this form of "racial discrimination."[67]

[64] Conseil de la République, *Débats*, 22 May 1951, 1943.

[65] Ibid., 1937–60; Assemblée Nationale, *Débats,* 22 May 1951, 5729–36; Assemblée Nationale, Commission de la France d'Outre-Mer, session of 22 May 1951, C//15408, ANF.

[66] Assemblée Nationale, *Débats*, 22–23 November 1951, 8335–44, 8417–26, 25 January 1952, 356–400.

[67] AUF, *Débats*, 21 December 1951, 1180, 1187, 1192.

In 1952, reacting to another member who asked the Assemblée de l'Union française to proceed to the single college "by stages," Gabriel d'Arboussier exclaimed angrily, "The last five years are now almost six and you are still for the status quo."[68] Such journals as *Marchés Coloniaux* continued to defend the double college as a matter of principle. In a series of articles, Pierre Singly attacked "the myth of universal man and unique civilization." He went on about the essential qualities of African social life, especially its orientation toward the group. If institutions were introduced based on European individualism, "there are a thousand chances against one that we do more harm than good."[69] During these years, government ministers would periodically come before the Overseas Committee to hem and haw about the double college, concluding that the time was not yet ripe to eliminate it.

Institutional reform stagnated, but African voters did not. They voted in increasing numbers between 1945 and the reforms of 1956, and they voted often. Beginning with the elections for the Constituent Assembly, they voted five times for deputies to go to Paris, and they voted three times for territorial assembly members. There were replacement elections and referenda. Territorial assemblies voted for members of the Grand Conseil de l'AOF, which began to meet in December 1947, and for the Assemblée de l'Union française, which commenced in 1948. Lamine Guèye saw the opening of the Grand Conseil as a big step toward the "establishment of a federal system thanks to which the different territories of AOF and AEF now enjoy a large economic and financial autonomy."[70] Campaigning for elections became a regular feature of West African life.

Whereas some African intellectuals expressed disillusionment, others saw progress out of the dark days of colonialism. Replying to an argument that the Lamine Guèye law had been a "sham," Boubacar Obèye Guèye, writing in the Socialist newspaper *L'AOF* shortly after the law's second anniversary, reminded his readers how bad things had been in the days of forced labor and the *indigénat*. He concluded, "I prefer instead to mark this date as a step toward real equality which must be conquered after juridical equality insofar as it is true that a legal text, no matter how generous the impulse that inspired it, is only

[68] AUF, *Débats*, 30 October 1952, 1040.
[69] *Marchés Coloniaux*, 30 November 1946, 1265 quoted, 14 December 1946, 1, 15 February, 3 May, 2 August 1947, 3 May, 547 quoted. See also "Les élections doivent se faire sur le principe du double collège," *Marchés Coloniaux*, 26 July 1947, 1008–10. The journal claimed its arguments were not racial and that "bit by bit with their social elevation," indigenous people could join the first college. Ibid., 1008. The procolonial lobby would in fact have liked to roll back some of the provisions of the Constitution, for example, reducing the tiny number of deputies from the overseas territories.
[70] *Paris-Dakar*, 4 October 1947. See also Ruth Schachter Morgenthau, *Political Parties in French-Speaking West Africa* (Oxford: Clarendon, 1964), 56–67, and Borella, *Évolution politique*.

a legal text."[71] In 1950, the anniversary of the Lamine Guèye law was again celebrated in Senegal.[72] African politicians kept plugging away through 1956 for the single college, universal suffrage, and real power for territorial assemblies—in short to make citizenship into a political reality.

Federalisms

Much of the debate, from different points in the political spectrum, concerned the meaning to be given to federalism, as a way of inserting the unequal components of an empire into a greater whole of a new design.[73] Charles de Gaulle was still speaking in federalist tones in May 1947, as he had in June 1946 (chapter 2): "Each overseas territory must be considered to have its own character and, consequently, be organized on its own account." Of the French Union's diverse components, "Each, in the framework of French sovereignty, should receive its own status, depending on the very variable degree of its development, regulating the ways and means by which the representatives of its French or indigenous inhabitants debate among themselves internal affairs and take part in their management. . . . We will not be able to bring the French Union to life without institutions of a federative character."

But there was no question about the place of France in de Gaulle's federal scheme: "The French Union must be French, which implies that the authority, and I mean the authority of France, will be clearly exercised on the ground, and that her duties, rights, and responsibilities remain beyond question in the domains of public order, national

[71] Boubacar Obèye Guèye, "Autour de la loi Lamine Guèye," *L'AOF*, 24 June 1948. He was replying to Doudou Guèye "Une duperie: La loi du 1er juin dite loi Lamine Guèye," and "Amertume d'un anniversaire la Loi du 1er Juin." *Réveil*, 14, 28 June 1948, who argued that democratic laws were being sabotaged by the administration, that the "pacte colonial" remained in place, that African civilian and military personnel were discriminated against, and that people were being killed in Madagascar and Indochina. He personally criticized Lamine Guèye for not standing up to officials.

[72] Amadou Saliou M'Baye, "Anniversaire de la loi Lamine Guèye," *L'AOF*, 1–12 June 1950.

[73] Jurists recognized how far the Constitution of 1946 was from any true federalism. Pierre Lavigne saw the relationship of the metropole and the Associated States as "confederative" and "therefore not different from what it was under the Empire." "La Constitution de l'Union française," *Penant* 57, 558 (1947): 89–102, 99, 101 quoted. See also Lampué, "L'Union française d'après la Constitution," 35, and for more discussion of federalism, René Pleven, "The Evolution of the French Empire towards a French Union," address to the Anti-Slavery Society, 21 July 1949, published by the Society, 12–13; Louis Jovelet, "L'Union française sera-t-elle fondée?," *Le Monde*, 19, 20/21,22, 23, 24, 25 April 1947, and further articles in ibid., 17 January 1950, 28–31 August, 3–4 September 1951.

defense, foreign policy, and the common economy." France must be "a strong state to which everything else is attached."[74]

Even for people who held condescending, if not downright racist, views of Africa, it was difficult to think through the problem of holding France together without a variant on federalism. In a series of articles in *Le Monde* in 1951, titled "Where Is the French Union Going? Diverse Solutions to the Colonial Problem," Pierre Frédérix rejected any fuller participation of Africans in French legislative institutions by evoking the specter of "two hundred polygamous men in a position to regulate the status of French families." Going on about the ignorance of Africans, their subordination to "gerontocracies," their need of social services to be provided by a generous France, and the supposed fact that "the rural masses ignore the ABCs of citizenship," he nevertheless concluded that there was no choice but "to divide legislative powers between overseas assemblies and the federal assembly. We are not there yet. But it is difficult to see any other perspective that could, sooner or later, offer sufficient advantages and attractions to our overseas associates to persuade them to remain."[75]

A quite different reaction to the diversity of the imperial community emerged as the Overseas Ministry and some legislators, from both overseas and metropolitan constituencies, sought to portray France as "a great Muslim power." A large number of French citizens, especially in North and West Africa, were Muslims. As Gregory Mann and Baz Lecoq point out, the attempt by the administration to help organize, subsidize, and observe the pilgrimage of Muslims from West Africa to Mecca after 1946 was part of an effort to put on display "an image of a new imperial citizenry in which simultaneously holding membership in the Union *and* Muslim civil status represented not a historical anomaly but a vision for the future."[76] Islam—and especially worldwide networks among Muslims—posed both a danger and a diplomatic opportunity.

Tiémoko Diarra, speaking as a representative of the "Muslim populations of Africa," reminded his colleagues in the Assemblée de

[74]Charles de Gaulle, speech in Bordeaux, reported in *Le Monde*, 17 May 1947. De Gaulle was not in government at the time, but his pronouncements carried great weight with those who were.

[75]Pierre Frédérix, "Où va l'Union française? Des diverses solutions du problème colonial," *Le Monde*, 28, 30, 31 August, 3/4, 5 September 1951.

[76]Gregory Mann and Baz Lecoq, "Between Empire, *Umma*, and the Muslim Third World: The French Union and African Pilgrims to Mecca, 1946–1958," *Comparative Studies of South Asia, Africa and the Middle East* 27, 2 (2007): 367–83, 369 quoted. The idea of France representing itself as a "Muslim Power" had roots in the prewar era. See James McDougall, "The Secular State's Islamic Empire: Muslim Spaces and Subjects of Jurisdiction in Paris and Algiers, 1905–1957," *Comparative Studies in Society and History* 52 (2010): 553–80.

l'Union française in July 1952 that half the population of AOF was Muslim and that issues of Arabic education and of equality—and especially "respect of the human personage"—had to be faced. France had to keep its promises and ensure that "constitutional principles [are] applied to the letter." The Assembly, taking seriously the idea of France as "a Muslim Power," voted to ask the government to work out a policy toward its own Muslims and those of the rest of the world.[77] Here we have an echo of France's thinking like an empire, drawing its prestige from the diversity of its populations—now a population of citizens.

Sub-Saharan Africa was the part of the French Union where things were going the least badly. Indochina was at war, Algeria caught between eight million Algerians whose leaders were insisting that they constituted an Algerian nation and eight hundred thousand well-connected colons who insisted that they were part of a French nation. The political situation of the trust territories was unclear, and in Cameroon quite dangerous. But where the logic of the composite system of the French Union was most clearly not working was in regard to the Associated States, formerly protectorates, Laos, Cambodia, Vietnam, Morocco, and Tunisia. The fact—noted but finessed during the constitutional debates—that France could not legally impose its constitution on these states was now becoming a real problem.

Chérif Mécheri, the prefect in charge of administering the French Union on behalf of the President and himself of Algerian origin, put the problem frankly in terms of a transition out of empire: "The states in question form part of the French Union not because of a new right but because of a previous right stemming from treaties. They were, following the treaties parts of the Empire; the Union having succeeded the Empire, they are necessarily part of it." Officials in the Foreign Ministry could not find anything in the treaties saying that France could "resolve the question of the entry of Morocco and Tunisia into the French Union by a unilateral decision."[78]

Morocco and Tunisia refused to participate in the institutions of the Union; they did not send representatives to the Haut Conseil de l'Union française, where Union affairs were supposed to be discussed. Nor did French officials think they could be induced to do so.[79] Noted the French Resident in Morocco, Eirik Labonne, "the sovereign never misses an occasion to invoke the conventions of Algeciras and the

[77] AUF, *Débats*, 3 July 1952, 732, 8 July 1952, 763-64, 11 July 1952, 894-95, 903.
[78] Note of M. Mecheri to President, 20 November 1947, "Note de la Direction d'Afrique-Levant pour le Ministre," 13 March 1947, 4AG 518, ANF.
[79] The jurist Pierre Lampué wrote, "the constitution only allows us to propose to the governments of the Associated States their participation in the formation of common institutions." "L'Union française d'après la Constitution," 27.

international character" of the "Cherifian empire."[80] An interesting choice of word—a top French official was giving Morocco the status of an empire. With Morocco and Tunisia refusing to participate in Union institutions, the Associated States of Laos, Cambodia, and Vietnam were what was left, and France was prosecuting an ugly war in Vietnam. The truncated Haut Conseil met a few times from 1951 to 1953 and once in 1954, and then, after France lost its war in Vietnam and Morocco and Tunisia kept their distance, it faded out of existence.[81]

From the time of the passage of the constitution onward, it was far from clear what Union citizenship would mean in these states. Could France tell sovereign states that their citizens had certain rights because they were also citizens of the French Union? As Labonne put the problem, "The rights that follow from the citizenship of the Union conferred on Moroccan subjects by Article 81 might be in opposition with Moroccan public law or the Islamic religion, which we have engaged to respect. This citizenship superposed on Moroccan nationality can only be conceived in an explicit act of cherifian sovereignty." Morocco was not a republic; its ruler did not see power emanating from the people but from him. Labonne continued,

> The rights enumerated in the preamble of the Constitution are moreover susceptible to get a mitigated reception. Some of them are incompatible with the personal status or the economic and social organization of the Moroccan population or with the international status of Morocco: the equality of rights, in all domains, of men and women, trade union freedom, the collectivity's appropriation of monopolies or enterprises with the character of public, national service; social security for all.[82]

Reflecting in 1950 on citizenship in the French Union, the jurist Lampué concluded that while the concept of citizenship of the Republic—including the overseas territories—was clear enough, Union

[80] Quoted in Note de la Direction d'Afrique-Levant pour le Ministre, 13 March 1947, 4AG 518, ANF. Chérif Mecheri referred to the head of state of Vietnam as "l'Empereur Bao Dai," note for the President, 29 March 1952, 4AG 518, ANF. According to jurists consulted by the Ministry, Tunisia and Morocco should be considered Associated States even though they refused to participate in the institutions designed for such states. Avis du Comité Juridique relatif à la représentation des protectorats de l'Afrique du Nord au sein des organes centraux de l'Union française, 4 February 1948, AP 217/1, AOM.

[81] Gérard Peureux, *Le Haut-Conseil de l'Union française* (Paris: Librairie Générale de Droit et de Jurisprudence, 1960). Peureux analyzes the failure of this institution, and with it—he argues—the failure of the French Union to become a composite of different kinds of political units affiliated to France. See also Borella, *Évolution politique*, 347–48.

[82] Notes on "Le Maroc et l'Union française: Aspects diplomatiques de la question," and "Aspects juridiques de l'entrée du Maroc dans l'Union française," 23 December 1946, accompanying Ambassadeur et Résident Général, Rabat, to Ministre des Affaires Étrangères, 23 December 1946, 4AG 518, ANF.

citizenship was a new and untested idea. It ran directly into the problem of mixed sovereignties, being "superposed" on top of an Associated State's nationality. When Article 81 conferred on such citizens the rights specified in the preamble to the Constitution, it said something different from referring to rights enumerated in its body. Preambles were, Lampué thought, statements of principles, not necessarily enforceable judicially. But the Assemblée Nationale Constituante could not have done more than it did, lacking under international law "the power to impose rules in a direct and unilateral manner." France could only propose that Associated States enforce the rights enumerated in its Constitution.[83] There were specific rights that could be conveyed by French fiat, such as the right to enter and reside in metropolitan France since Moroccans and Tunisians were not foreigners on French soil. But in other respects, the significance of Union citizenship was what Morocco and Tunisia—by "laws internal to the two countries"—chose to make of it.[84]

In 1955, the constitutional guardians of the Conseil d'État argued that because the sovereign of Morocco had rejected participation in the Union, Moroccans were not really "ressortissants" of it and could not benefit from Article 81 of the Constitution. The court acknowledged that the right of free circulation applied to "ressortissants de l'Union française" but insisted that France could not unilaterally impose such a status and that the "Empire chérifien" had expressed its "clear refusal to participate in the central institutions of the Union."[85] The decision soon became irrelevant: the next year Morocco and Tunisia became independent states.[86]

---

[83] Pierre Lampué, "La citoyenneté de l'Union française," *Revue Juridique et Politique de l'Union Française* 4 (1950): 305–36, 311, 318, 319 quoted. The situation was different in regard to trust territories, he argued, even though they too were detached from French nationality. France had the obligation to treat them equivalently to the people of its own overseas territories, and the latter now had the quality of the French citizen.

[84] Ibid., 333. An influential legislator, Daniel Boisdon (MRP), noted that "Tunisians and Moroccans are the subjects of absolute monarchs" and the guarantee of rights to their subjects was "a dead letter." Boisdon tried to get the administration and the Assemblée de l'Union française to clarify what Union citizenship meant, but the government did not want clarity. It did not want to be accused of "French interference" or treat the Associated States on the basis of full reciprocity (as Boisdon suggested), contending that they were not at "a comparable level, politically, economically and socially" to France. Boisdon did not get much traction. Note by Ministère des Relations avec les États Associés, 9 February 1951, and Minister's letter to Boisdon, 19 April 1951, 4AG 561, ANF; AUF, *Débats*, 12 November 1952, 1110–18; Daniel Boisdon, "La citoyenneté de l'Union française," *Union Francaise et Parlement* 28 (1951): 12–13; Boisdon, *Les institutions de l'Union française*, 83–84.

[85] Conclusions of Conseil d'État, 18 March 1955, published in *Penant* 65, 626–27 (1955): 67–82, 71 quoted.

[86] For recent analyses of the routes of Morocco and Tunisia out of empire, see Adria Lawrence, *Imperial Rule and the Politics of Nationalism: Anti-Colonial Protest in the French Empire*

Since 1946 Africans had been making something of their citizenship. Africans were voting and parties were mobilizing to channel their interests. The right of free circulation was being used by growing numbers of Africans seeking work in France, and more and more were entering institutions of higher education in France. But political institutions had opened up only so far; the organization of the French Union had not evolved into a truly federal structure; electoral systems were far from equitable; the relationship of the sovereignties of the Associated States and the Republic was at an impasse; and violent conflict was ongoing in Vietnam and brewing in North Africa. By the early 1950s, the French Union had still not proven itself a viable successor to empire, but it was clear that Africans were going to be active players in its future evolution. They were insisting that an inclusive citizenship be pushed further. And meanwhile, officials in France were beginning to wonder if citizenship, and all the claim making it entailed, might have gone too far, especially in the social domain. These are topics to which I will return.

Registering Citizens

Whether the lack of an état-civil for the indigenous inhabitants of AOF was a reason or an excuse for restricting their voting rights, it became a source of controversy and uncertainty that was never resolved. A look at the politics of reforming the état-civil reveals the ambivalence of French leaders about the place of difference and equality in their reformed empire. Officials saw this institution as both necessary and inappropriate for Africa: "The metropolitan état-civil corresponds to a society that is solidly organized and whose evolution has ended, which is not the case in French West Africa."[87]

Even as the constitution was being debated, the Ministry was adamant that the expansion of citizenship required a comprehensive état-civil: "While the citizens of the law of 7 May 1946 maintain their personal status, it seems, however, indispensable to organize their état-civil. It would be inconceivable that citizens would not be con-

(Cambridge: Cambridge University Press, 2013), and the epilogue to Mary Dewhurst Lewis, *Divided Rule: Sovereignty and Empire in French Tunisia, 1881–1938* (Berkeley: University of California Press, 2013). See also Daniel Rivet, *Le Maghreb à l'épreuve de la colonisation* (Paris: Hachette, 2002).

[87] Directeur Général de l'Intérieur and Directeur Général Adjoint des Affaires Politiques, "Rapport concernant la pluralité d'État-Civil en AOF, en réponse aux observations faites par M. Monguillot, Inspecteur Général de la France d'Outre Mer," 6 June 1952, 23G 34, AS. The sentence quoted was apparently picked up from an earlier note from Affaires Politiques, February 1947, 23G 33, AS.

strained from now on to make note of and have registered, by an officer of the état-civil, births, marriages, and deaths, on the same basis as any French citizen."[88]

Officials associated the état-civil with the concept of individualism. They wanted to convince Africans to present themselves to the state in such a guise, and they had to convince themselves that they could develop a direct relationship of state and individual, rather than work through the vertical channels of European command and "chiefly" authority by which the state had long defined its relationship with African collectivities. As the Minister put it in 1951, "French citizens have a right to an état-civil and the right to certain identification; it is necessary for them to have an identification that is not only invariant despite the events that might mark their existence, but transmittable, which is an element of proof of filiation, and hence the individualization of persons."[89] The état-civil is above all a "means to prove the identity of a person and register the acts which modify his juridical individuality."[90] Registering births in the état-civil was a prerequisite for establishing identification documents, notably a card that was theoretically—but not practically—required of anyone leaving his or her home district after 1949. Such a card, noted one official, would "serve as the basis of integration of the individual into a modern society."[91]

The citizen was not only an individual who—actually or potentially—could vote, but also a person who as a result of his or her particular situation might be entitled to certain social benefits. But without the état-civil to track individuals over their life course, the state could not ensure that a pensioner was the same individual who had worked, that children were enrolled in school at the proper age, or that family allowances went to those people who were entitled to them. Even in regard to former soldiers—who after all had paid the "blood tax" individually—the government did not know where they were or even

[88] Minister of Overseas France, circular to Governors General, 14 June 1946, AP 3655, AOM.

[89] Minister to Governor General of AOF, 21 September 1951, 23G 6, AS. The Minister went on to worry that African naming practices—especially the absence of a patronymic—made it difficult not only to identify individuals, but to prove filiation. The Ministry lawyer, Yvon Gouet, referred to people within the categories of the electoral law of 5 October 1947 as "individualisables." Note for Directeur des Affaires Politiques, 13 January 1947, AP 3655, AOM.

[90] Directeur Genéral de l'Intérieur and Directeur Général Adjoint des Affaires Politiques, "Rapport concernant la pluralité d'État-Civil en A.O.F., en réponse aux observations faites par M. Monguillot, inspecteur general de la FOM," 6 June 1952, 23G 34, AS.

[91] Délégué du Chef de territoire du Sénégal à Dakar to Chef de la Sûreté locale, Dakar, 27 April 1957, 1D/17, SRAD.

how many of them there were, and so could not tell what its pension obligations were, let alone how to allocate them properly.[92]

There were two fundamental obstacles. The obvious one was that it took considerable literate and trained personnel and considerable expense to create and maintain records on every individual in a large and widely dispersed population. Contrary to myths of "modern" colonial government as bureaucratic and controlling, it was in all but a few areas thinly spread, ad hoc in its daily actions, dependent on African intermediaries. As the Governor of Senegal put it, "A compulsory état-civil is a necessity, above all with the new laws on citizenship, but putting it into practice demands means which we do not yet have." The Governor of Sudan thought that a compulsory état-civil in his territory of 3.1 million people would generate 312,000 acts each year, recording births, deaths, and so on. In addition, it would have to issue "jugement supplétifs" (retrospective registration of a life event) for the over three million acts it had failed to record in the past. Such tasks, he concluded, could be accomplished only for the sedentary part of his population, step by step, and at high cost. Getting chiefs to do the work of bureaucrats would not be simple: most, officials thought, were illiterate.[93]

The other obstacle was more fundamental—uncertainty in official circles about how to proceed. Should there be one état-civil or two, or many, corresponding to the diversity of personal status regimes overseas? There existed an "état-civil indigène" in Algeria, parts of French West Africa, and a few other places, but—given that the état-civil was seen to embody the unity of the French population—a dual system was contrary to the spirit of the times. A "distinction between two états-civil would only consecrate racial discrimination," wrote the Governor of Senegal in 1951. But others insisted that a distinction in status was not a distinction of race, and feared that a single état-civil would obscure the rules of marriage or inheritance that particular acts were supposed to represent. Perhaps a single set of registers could make note of the status regime under which marriage or inheritance took place, but even that practice would go against the idea of the state refusing to recognize status distinctions.[94] And while Algeria was—in official

[92] Gregory Mann, *Native Sons: West African Veterans and France in the Twentieth Century* (Durham, N.C.: Duke University Press, 2006), 123. The government began a survey in 1947 to figure out the situation of ex-soldiers. Ibid., 125–26.

[93] Governor of Senegal, Rapport Politique, 1945–46, AP 2142/3, AOM; "Rapport concernant l'organisation de l'état civil obligatoire au Soudan français," included in Governor of Sudan to Governor General, 1 December 1948, Governor, Côte d'Ivoire, to Governor General, 17 June 1949, 23G 33, AS.

[94] Governor of Senegal to High Commissioner, 6 February 1951, and Governor General to Governor of Senegal, 2 March 1951, 23G 34, AS; Governor General to Minister, 25 August 1949, 23G 33, AS. The Grand Conseil of AOF adopted a resolution supporting "the principle of the native état-civil in all the territories." *Paris-Dakar*, 18 December

thinking at least—a bifurcated society, sub-Saharan Africa was even more diverse.[95] Africans were mobile; people who married according to one set of rules might live in a town where most people followed different ones; mixed marriages were common. Who would keep the books for each form of marriage and inheritance? Who would know enough to confront the social complexities that lay behind life events? The practical problem of ensuring that act corresponded to the correct rules of marriage, inheritance, or recognition of children would not be solved by attaching an ethnic name to a personal identification.

From 1946 through the mid-1950s, officials complained about the difficulty of identifying voters. As the Governor General of AOF insisted in 1946, "This identification is impossible to realize given the current state of the état-civil indigène. . . . The état-civil is ignored, I would add *willfully ignored*, by the masses."[96] No less an advocate of African voting rights than Léopold Senghor also admitted in 1951 that "it is impossible, because of the insufficiency of the état-civil, to institute universal suffrage in the overseas territories where it is not yet in place by the time of the next election."[97]

The provisional solution, used from the first elections to the Constituent Assembly in the fall of 1945, in effect remained in place for a decade: the designation of voters by "capacities," on the basis of such identifying documents as labor contracts or hunting licenses (as described above).[98] Voting, in the absence of the état-civil, could even

---

1947. The Ministry's jurist Yvon Gouet argued for a single état-civil with mention of the status regime relevant to each act. "Remarques sur une réorganisation éventuelle de l'état-civil dans les parties d'outre-mer de la France qui connaissent le régime de la pluralité des états civils et dans les territoires sous tutelle," *Revue Juridique et Politique de l'Union française* 8 (1954): 492–585, esp. 507–10, 518, 551–55.

[95] Délégué du Gouverneur à Dakar to Governor, 27 June 1956, G/13, SRAD; report from Directeur des Affaires Politiques, Ministère de la France d'Outre-Mer, "Étude en vue d'une réorganisation de l'état-civil dans les territoires dépendant du Ministère de la France d'Outre-mer qui connaissent le régime de la pluralité des états-civils," nd [May 1956], 23G 33, AS; Yvon Gouet, "L'Article 82 (paragraphe 1) de la Constitution relatif à l'option de statut et l'élaboration de la 'théorie des statuts civils' de droit français moderne," *Penant* 67 (1957), section doctrine, 1–94.

[96] Governor General to Minister, 3 March 1946, 17G 139, AS. See also Governor of Togo to Minister of Overseas France, 20 July 1946, and Minister of Overseas France to Minister of Foreign Affairs, 29 October 1949, AP 3655, AOM; Governor, Sudan, to High Commissioner, 17 September 1946, Minister, circular to High Commissioners, 13 June 1947, Governor, Niger, to High Commissioner, 17 August 1946, 23G 96, AS.

[97] Commission de la FOM, meeting of 11 April 1951, C//15408, ANF.

[98] See "Instructions à MM. les présidents des commissions de distribution des cartes électorales," 1955, F/15, SRAD. A person seeking an electoral card could present in addition to a notice from the état-civil or a jugement supplétif, documents stemming from military service, regular employment, a university diploma or identification card, a railway pass, etc.

create the presumption that one was a French national—the reverse of how things were supposed to be.[99]

The big expansion of voting occurred not among citizens of "French" civil status—for whom the état-civil was both compulsory and extensively used—but in "the second college," for people of particular status. Even when universal suffrage and the single college were implemented in 1956, the basic problem of identification was still unsolved. Ministry officials and legislators, particularly in the Assemblée de l'Union française, were still trying to extend the état-civil, without agreeing on how to do so.[100]

The issue went beyond identifying voters—and that helps to explain why it proved so intractable over so long a time. In 1947, Mamadou Kamara, a member of the territorial assembly in Guinea, submitted a resolution pointing out Africans' need for birth and marriage registration for numerous acts in daily life, and hence the need for an "état civil indigène." He pointed out, "To take account of the polygamy that exists in Africa, [it] should be set up in a manner to permit the registration of acts of the état civil concerning four wives." But in 1953, the territorial assembly of the Côte d'Ivoire, faced with what it saw as discrimination, voted a resolution calling for Africans to be allowed to use the "registres de l'état civil européen."[101] It was between these two arguments—one for recognizing difference (through multiple états-civil), the other insisting on equality (through a single état-civil)—that officials in the Ministry of Overseas France and legislators were hesitating for the entire postwar decade.[102]

Meanwhile the "état-civil indigène" was being more widely used. After a debate in the Grand Conseil de l'AOF in June 1950, the government issued in August the orders that expanded the record-keeping centers (adding largely rural secondary centers to the largely urban primary ones) and required people living within ten kilometers of such centers to register births and deaths. These orders were seen as a temporary measure while waiting (in vain) for the legislature in Paris to

[99] Minister, Circular to High Commissioners, 9 September 1947, 23G 93, AS.

[100] Draft of text for Minister of FOM to deliver to Commission Permanente du Grand Conseil de l'AOF on voyage to Dakar, 21 July 1956, AP 2292/10, AOM; reports and correspondence for the AUF, session of 1955, in C//16323, ANF, and the discussion in *Débats*, 29 November 1955, 1025–42; Assemblée Nationale, *Débats*, 25 January 1951, 386, 392; report by the Commission de la FOM of the Assemblée Nationale, No. 2245, 5 August 1947, copy in F60/1399, ANF; Yvon Gouet, Note pour M. le Directeur des Affaires Politiques, 13 January 1947, AP 3655, AOM.

[101] "Voeu no. 55," présenté par M. Mamadou Kamara, le Conseil Général de la Guinée Française, 8 November 1947, and "Voeu no. 35–53/AT," Assemblée Territoriale de la Côte d'Ivoire, 14 August 1953, both in 23G 33, AS.

[102] The attempts and the debate are reviewed in Roger Decottignies, "L'état civil en AOF," *Annales Africaines 1955*, 41–78, and Gouet, "Remarques sur une réorganisation éventuelle de l'état-civil."

act.[103] Registering marriages was not made compulsory because, said the Governor General, "marriage in Africa is in effect an institution that is too unstable and presents, depending on the region, characteristics that are too different for it to be the object of general regulations."[104] In 1951, administrators reported that there were fifteen hundred centers recording acts for the état-civil, most kept by canton chiefs. Officials were trying to get schoolteachers and nurses, as well as chiefs, to staff these centers. Between 1948 and 1953, the annual number of births, deaths, and marriages recorded in the état-civil rose from 119,000 to 356,000, but that was not a lot for a region with a population estimated at 17 million. The overwhelming majority of the registrations were of births—253,000. Only 23,000 marriages and 80,000 deaths were registered.[105] Given the disparity between recorded births and deaths, the state could not know how its living population was changing. Procedures were ad hoc, depending on local administrators and chiefs who were not properly trained.

Officials complained that many acts were registered long after the fact—a sign that people used the état-civil when a reason arose for them to do so.[106] When, for example, people needed to prove a child was of the correct age to enter school, they could get a "jugement supplétif," a decision by a low-level court certifying a birth—and approximating its date—based on the testimony of two witnesses. These judgments thus entailed quintessentially social processes—calling on one's neighbors—and they entailed initiative on the part of the person concerned. Documenting who was a citizen was not just an affair for a surveillance-minded state.[107]

[103] Grand Conseil de l'AOF, *Bulletin*, commissions reports, 25 and 31 May 1950, and discussion, 9 June 1950, 27–34. The upshot of this effort was the arrêté of 16 August 1950. In the absence of a law coming from the Assemblée Nationale in Paris, the juridical standing of this measure was questionable. See Gouet, "Remarques sur une réorganisation éventuelle de l'état-civil," 511.

[104] Governor General to Minister, 25 August 1949, 23G 33, AS.

[105] Premier Président de la Cour d'appel, chef du service judiciaire pi, A. Laget, to High Commissioner, AOF, 28 February 1955, 23G 34, AS. The ratio of declarations to population varied from eight births and four deaths per one thousand in AOF as a whole, to thirty-nine and eleven, respectively, in Dakar. Report from Directeur of Affaires Politiques, May 1956, 23G 33, AS, p. 70.

[106] Premier Président de la Cour d'appel, chef du service judiciaire pi, A. Laget, to High Commissioner, AOF, 28 February 1955, 23G 34, AS; Directeur Général de l'Intérieur, Service des Affaires Politiques, "Note sur l'extension et la réorganisation de l'état-civil en AOF," August 1951, 23G 33, AS. See also comments on implementing the état-civil indigène in Senegal in various reports from different districts from the early 1950s in 11D 1, AS.

[107] For examples of jugements supplétifs, see 11D1/1450, AS. For official awareness of how registration was being used, see Mission 1951–52, M. Monguillot Inspecteur Général des Colonies, "Rapport concernant la pluralité d'état-civil en AOF," 14 May 1952 and observations of Directeur Général de l'Intérieur and Directeur Général

Officials also tried, via a decree of October 1949, to make Africans venturing outside of their "circonscription" of origin carry identification cards. But the effort did not go well: the materiel needed was not getting to the districts; the information needed to establish identity was not there; Africans ignored the requirement. Administrators also found that the ID was being used creatively. Political parties, realizing that the cards provided the kind of individualized documentation needed to get on the electoral rolls, were distributing them—to people likely to vote as the party desired. The attestations needed for identification, in the absence of the état-civil, could be cooked up.[108]

Changing Status

There was another issue: changing status. The Constitution stated that a person could exercise the rights of citizenship without giving up his or her personal status, unless he or she chose to renounce that status. The Ministry saw this article as quite progressive: "This principle gives to the *originaires* of the overseas territories a very large measure of liberty in the domain of private law. They can for example remain polygamous and continue, in regard to property law, to make use of collective traditional property. And the fact of remaining within their personal status implies no inferiority."[109] But how would an individual proceed if he or she wanted to come under the French civil code? The Constitution mentioned the possibility of renunciation but did not provide a mechanism to exercise it. Initially, the Ministry decided that "accession"—the procedure for obtaining citizenship prior to the Lamine Guèye law—would be "the normal procedure for opting for the status of French private law."[110] But that made little sense once all the inhabitants of the overseas territories were already citizens. A legislative act would be needed to set out a new procedure, and a record would have to be kept of each renunciation of personal civil status.

The stakes of changing status had been lowered by the Constitution, but they were not negligible. In most of Africa, French civil status, through 1956, was necessary to vote in the first college; discrimi-

Adjoint des Affaires Politiques, 6 June 1952, 23G 34, AS; Conseiller Technique, Affaires Politiques, Paris, circular to High Commissioners, 22 August 1952, 11D1/897, AS.

[108]Governor, Senegal, circulars to Commandants de Cercle, 4 February 1950, 6, 24 February 1953, Chef de Sûreté, Dakar, to Délégué du Gouverneur, 5 February 1954, 1D/10, and report of Inspecteur Aujas, Commissariat Central, Bureau des Cartes d'Identité, to Commissaire Centrale de la Ville de Dakar, 10 August 1954, 1D/17, SRAD. A copy of the arrêté of 17 October 1949 is in 1D/17, SRAD.

[109]Minister to Mathurin Anghiley, Conseiller de la République, 8 July 1948, AP 3655, AOM.

[110]Governor General, Circular to Governors, 29 November 1946, B/20, SRAD.

nation in terms of hiring existed—illegally—in military and civilian employment; and some Africans might simply have wanted to express their adherence to the religious or civil order represented by French status or to change the way their property would be inherited. The question then was whether to treat renunciation as a simple declaration, subject only to verification of competence and absence of fraud, or whether acquiring "French" civil status required evidence that the person involved lived according to the rules implied by that status. Inclusive pluralism and invidious distinction were again in tension with one another.

Repeated proposals for a law regulating renunciation of personal status were made. In 1947, the Minister of Overseas France noted that the government could conceivably give every applicant French civil status on demand, but to do so lacked "realism." People were so attached to local customs "such as polygamy" that were inconsistent with French civil law that there would be a "very dangerous divergence" between law and practice. Any candidate for common civil status would have to be single or monogamous, or else repudiate any wife beyond the first. The implications of renunciation on family members and on inheritance had to be sorted out.[111] The Conseil d'État at the time agreed: to be granted French civil status, one had to have "habits and style of life approaching that of people with civil status."[112] While retaining personal civil status was not supposed to diminish the rights conveyed by the Constitution, some legislators worried that law and practices still made "distinctions among French citizens of different statuses."[113] Yet the Constitution seemed to imply that renunciation of personal status was a right.

The government of AOF brought before one of the earliest meetings of the Grand Conseil a bill requiring people seeking to renounce their personal status to meet a modest number of criteria demonstrating they were capable of living according to the French civil code. The proposal met with a chilly reception. Lamine Guèye argued that

[111] Minister, circular to High Commissioners, 13 June 1947, F60/1401, ANF. There was no question in official thinking of going from French to indigenous status or from one indigenous status regime to another. Garde des Sceaux to Ministre de la Population et de la Santé Publique, 2 January 1947, 950236/24, CAC.

[112] Statement of Conseil d'État in regard to bill on renunciation of personal status, 13 July 1949, F60/1401, ANF.

[113] AUF, Commission de la Législation, de la Justice de la Fonction publique, des Affaires administratives et domaniales, Rapport No. 154, séance of 15 June 1950; Avis de l'Assemblée de l'Union française, 13 July 1955; AUF, Rapport de la Commission de la Législation, No. 20, 27 January 1955, Overseas Minister to Secrétaire Général du Gouvernement, 13 June 1949, F60/1401, ANF; Note of C. Deschamps, Chef du Bureau des Affaires Administratives, "sur la citoyenneté des ressortissants d'AOF," 14 May 1952; Minister, circular to High Commissioners, 13 June 1947; Note "sur la citoyenneté des autochtones" by Avocat Général, Dakar, April 1947, 23G 96, AS.

renunciation could be "tacit": one would simply conduct one's affairs (marriage, inheritance) in accordance with the civil code. One report for the Grand Conseil argued that "except for the first (to be monogamous or single) the other proposed conditions are not essential. The individual, having the full capacity to choose, must be able to do it with complete freedom." Another report signed by Houphouët-Boigny and Almamy Ibrahima Sory Dara went further. "We are black and proud of the color of our skin. We would not want to change our personal status for anything in the world. Like any nation, we have our past, to be sure more or less glorious, but it should not be underestimated. We have our religion, our customs, to which we are enormously attached." The renunciation bill entrenched the very distinction citizenship was supposed to erase. Africans, the report argued, were in effect being told, "Like me, you are only citizens in the voting booth, on election day; like me, you often come to ask in the course of daily life whether you really are citizens." Some Dahomeans argued in favor of the bill, on the grounds that it would clarify matters, but the majority of the Conseil expressed its opinion that the draft law was "useless" for overseas citizens seeking to renounce their personal status, for they "have the possibility of tacitly renouncing this status."[114]

Proposals to regulate renunciation came up later and in other fora—it was something of a cause for Daniel Boisdon of the Assemblée de l'Union française—but African legislators repeatedly objected.[115] The skeptics were not wrong about the kind of thinking behind efforts to enact a system of renunciation of personal status. As Boisdon himself pointed out, the change of status "is only possible in one direction." He admitted, "If the diversity of customs is respected in the short run, it is with the secret hope that, progressively, their disappearance will be accomplished." He asked critics of renunciation legislation if they wanted to "wall in" Africans in traditional social units. "If you want to raise the level of our autochthonous fellow citizens, give them the possibility to enter the rhythm, the current of modern life by submitting themselves to a status of universal character, and that is

[114] The debate and the reports are in AOF, *Bulletin du Grand Conseil*, 20 December 1947, 52–53, 55–56. The argument also went on in newspapers. N'Diawar Sarr argued that renunciation of personal status for a Muslim meant renouncing the religion. "Le Statut personnel devant le Grand Conseil de l'A.O.F.," *L'AOF*, 6 January 1948. Doudou Guèye argued that the renunciation law would create two categories of citizens. *La voix du RDA*, in *Réveil*, 26 December 1947.

[115] AUF, *Débats*, 25 July 1950, 1133. The committee on legislation of the AUF discussed the renunciation question at its meetings of 10, 17, 24, 31 May, 2, 14 June, 22, 27 November 1950 (C//16170, ANF), and the Assembly as a whole debated it on 27 July 1950 (*Débats*, 1160–69, 1184–88), without results. For more attempts, see debates on 7 July 1955, *Débats*, 655–69, and request from Assemblée Nationale to Assemblée de l'Union française for opinion on a bill, 23 October 1956, copy in 23G 96, AS.

precisely the character of French civil status."[116] Officials in the Ministry had a similarly evolutionist view:

It is finally by reference to our law that it is possible to direct the evolution of customs and it is possible, notably, to direct evolution against traditional mores, to favor monogamy, to struggle against bargaining in regard to bridewealth, and to recognize that the widow is free to dispose of herself. Accepting the equality of statuses and the consequences that follow from it would be to reverse the course of evolution, renounce in part our civilizing actions and compromise the results already attained.[117]

Anxieties about the nonequivalence of personal status had a gender component too, evident in an unsuccessful attempt by a deputy from Madagascar to get the French legislative apparatus to intervene in regard to marriages that crossed status lines. Currently, a woman of local personal status who married a man of "French" personal status gave up her own status for the French one, and a man of local personal status who married a woman of French personal status gave up his status for that of his wife. The deputy objected: "Since the deepest antiquity, the statutory primacy of the husband constitutes an immutable rule of life among most peoples." The current practice therefore constituted a "deplorable diminution" of the husband. This proposal would have reinforced the old hierarchy of gender by rejecting the French hierarchy of statuses.[118]

African deputies objected not only to their colleagues' sense of the superiority of one status but to the fact that renunciation could be only a one-way street. They saw here a return to the doctrine of assimilation that they thought had been buried in the Assemblée Nationale Constituante's recognition of multiple status regimes, and they feared that personal status could demarcate a "citizenship of the second zone."[119] Opponents thought that verifications that an African was living in accordance with the civil code turned the right to renounce personal status into a favor. Proponents feared that letting people come under

[116] Daniel Boisdon, *Les institutions de l'Union française* (Paris: Berger-Levrault, 1949), 74; statement to AUF, *Débats*, 27 July 1950, 1164. Boisdon added that there were thirty or forty "customs" in French West Africa alone, while in France, marriage practices were as much "Western" as "French." Ibid., 1162, 1165.

[117] Affaires Politiques, "Rapport à Monsieur le Ministre," 5 May 1955, AP 492, AOM.

[118] Demande d'avis from President of Assemblée Nationale to AUF regarding the law proposed by M. Ranaivo to determine the "statut personnel des époux dans le mariage et celui des enfants," No. 112 of 1953, 17 March 1953, C//16291, ANF. The file is labeled "out of date." Jonah Ranaivo was a deputy from the second college of Madagascar, serving 1951–55.

[119] An expression used by Ya Doumbia of Sudan, AUF, *Débats*, 27 July 1950, 1166. See also the interventions of Soppo Priso of Cameroon and Djim Momar Guèye of Senegal, 1167–69, 1187–88.

the civil code whose family life did not conform to it would produce only conflict and unhappiness.[120] Proposals to regulate renunciation were frequently made and invariably sidetracked until the implementation of territorial autonomy in 1956 and independence in 1960 took the question out of French hands.

The renunciation proposals thus crystallized a conflict over culture that constitutional compromises had not resolved. At least some elements in the Paris Ministry maintained their civilizing mission by criticizing African marriage practices: polygamy, bridewealth, uncertainty about the bride's consent.[121] Africans, now taking active roles in the debate, were defending their right to maintain their own practices. But the constitution did signify, at least, that Africans had an element of choice in the process—they could or could not renounce their personal status—and their representatives had a voice. And if some Africans opposed the very idea of renunciation, others wanted to take advantage of the constitutional possibility to mark their conversion to Christianity or to get away from indigenous inheritance rules. The dossiers of candidacy for "statut de droit commun" contain formulaic expressions to the effect that the applicant "has approached French civilization by his manner of life and social habits"—similar to the formula once used by subjects trying to become citizens.[122]

Take the application of Ernest Sampah Kassi, from the Côte d'Ivoire. His form declared, misleadingly, that he was "citizen of the French Union." He was monogamously married to a French citizen, probably meaning a citizen of "French" civil status (statut civil de droit commun). His marriage and his children's births were duly registered in the état-civil. Working in the "cadre local des commis-expéditionaires" (clerks-forwarding agents) he had a salary that allowed him to live "decently." He could read, write, and speak French. The report on him

[120] Ibid., 1162, 1165, 1167; AUF, Commission de la Législation, 2 June, 22 November 1950, C//16170, ANF. Once a person changed status, "difference" was no longer a discussable question, for the civil code applied "uniformly to all French citizens with the statut civil de droit commun." For this reason, some people thought there should be a possibility for partial renunciation—of polygamy only—but that proposal went nowhere. AUF, Commission de la Législation, 22 November 1950, C//16170, ANF, and AUF, Avis No. 266, 7 March 1957, C//16352, ANF.

[121] See 23G 102, AS, for a large file of official correspondence, from 1945 to 1957, about the possibilities and dangers of regulating marriage in Africa. Some officials felt that if the state was to record marriages, regulate changes of personal status, and pass out benefits on the basis of family status, it had made African marriage its business and could act to change its forms.

[122] See the applications in 23G 98, AS and 2D/1, SRAD. The legal uncertainties and conflicting jurisprudence over renunciation are pointed out in G.-H. Camerlynck, "De la renonciation du statut personnel," *Revue Juridique et Parlementaire de l'Union Française* 3 (1949): 129–45, and François Luchaire, "Le champ d'application des statuts personnels en Algérie et dans les territoires d'outre-mer," *Revue Juridique et Parlementaire de l'Union Française* 9 (1955): 38–44.

commented that he "lives with his family in an apartment in permanent material constructed in a European style. The rooms are kept in a clean state and are furnished in European style. Along with his family, his style of life and social habits fully approach those of French civilization." He had manifested no hostility to France, had no criminal record, and had been exempted from military service. In short, the application looked as if he was applying for a citizenship he already had.[123] But not many people were following his route: according to Boisdon, there had been only 138 applications to obtain statut civil de droit commun in 1954, of which 18 had received a favorable response, 2 had received a negative one, and 118 were pending.[124]

In November 1955 the Conseil d'État reminded everyone that under the constitution, accession to French civil status was a right, not a favor: "The facility recognized for natives by the Constitution to benefit from this status cannot be negated by the silence of the legislator."[125] The Ministry sent around circulars based on that decision instructing administrators that personal status is "an opportunity available to any citizen who is not placed in a situation that prevents him from using it and is an opportunity whose exercise depends on a declaration." The process was supposed to be "easy for the person making the declaration."[126] The government had failed a test of both constitutional rigor and fairness, ten years after the Constitution gave overseas citizens the possibility of choosing whether to retain their old civil status or opt for the "French" one.[127]

Conclusion

Citizenship opened the door to claim making and to controversy over the status and political situation of the new citizens. The limited nature of African deputies' victory at the Assemblée Nationale Constituante came out quickly and persistently in the ensuing decade in the blockages in the French legislature over universal suffrage, the single

[123] Case of Ernest Sampah Kassi, including report by Commandant de Cercle, Abidjan, 21 October 1955, 23G 98, AS. Métis continued to apply for French civil status under a 1930 decree seemingly rendered obsolete by the constitution. Owen White, *Children of the French Empire: Miscegenation and Colonial Society in French West Africa 1895–1960* (Oxford: Clarendon, 1999), 147–48.

[124] Boisdon, AUF, *Débats*, 7 July 1955, 669.

[125] The text of the decision, dated 22 November 1955, is printed in *Revue Juridique et Politique de l'Union Française* 12, 2 (1958): 350–52.

[126] Directeur des Affaires Politiques, Paris, circular, to High Commissioners in Africa, 25 April 1956, 23G 96, AS; Garde des Sceaux, circular to Procureurs Généraux, 7 March 1957, 23G 98, AS. Yerri Urban, "Race et nationalité dans le droit colonial français 1865–1955" (Doctoral thesis, Université de Bourgogne, 2009), esp. 562–68.

[127] See correspondence over proposed legislation from 1956 in 23G 96, AS.

college, and powers for the territorial assemblies. The constitution had placed African deputies where their voices could be heard, and they did not hesitate to speak. But their efforts ran into the efforts of other politicians to defend, with varying degrees of explicitness, the privileges of metropolitan citizens overseas—particularly those of Algeria—and the anxiety of officials about losing control. Many of those officials were in fact of two minds, and they were concerned that a regime of half measures would be ineffective. So there was an element within the Ministry of Overseas France favorable to universal suffrage, to greater decentralization of decision making, and to ending practices like the double college that Africans correctly perceived as perpetuating a regime of racial distinction that had, on the surface, been repudiated.

But the problem lay deeper, emerging most clearly in the unresolved debates over the extension of the état-civil and the regulation of renunciation of personal status. African politicians did not all agree among themselves: some opposed any distinction among French citizens, while others saw different statuses and different versions of the état-civil as a way of protecting Africans' right to difference. French officials and legislators did not agree either, and it was their uncertainty that above all prevented legislative solutions to the controversies. Behind their disagreement over enacting one or multiple systems for the état-civil and their inability to specify criteria for Africans who wanted "French" civil status lay a profound unease with the apparent acceptance of diverse ways of being French in the Constitution of 1946. Much of the French elite could not, in their heart of hearts, accept that African ways of marriage and affiliation were equivalent to French norms. Their acceptance of "citoyenneté dans le statut" had been an act of state, a way of reconciling diversity and equality as a matter of constitutional law, a form of thinking through and beyond empire. But the decade-long legislative paralysis over voting rights and civil status revealed both the political and the ideological limits of the reforms of 1946.

CHAPTER 4

CLAIMING CITIZENSHIP

French West Africa, 1946–1956

The politics of citizenship played out in African cities and countryside as well as in Paris, in popular mobilization as well as legislative controversy, in regard to issues of livelihood, of institutional change, and of basic conceptions of political life. This chapter considers different instances of African claim making, and it hardly exhausts the locations, participants, and idioms of African politics. First, we look at the effort of the RDA in the Sudan and especially the Côte d'Ivoire to build up its political apparatus across the territory and the efforts of the government to combat what it saw as a countergovernment. We will see how both the party and the government learned about the limits of what they could do. Second, we focus on the social and economic significance of citizenship by looking at the efforts of labor unions to turn the abstract notion of the equivalence of citizens into concrete gains for their members. We then turn to ways in which African political leaders sought to change the very terms in which future politics was discussed—to rethink the meanings of nation and sovereignty. They were thinking about different levels of political belonging and political action—the territory, French Africa as a whole, the French Union. And as France entered into discussion of creating a European community, they were thinking of expanding the idea of a "Franco-African" political ensemble into something even wider, into "Eurafrica."

Citizenship in a Colonial Situation:
The RDA and the Threat of Parallel Government

African politicians faced the problem of whether they could delve deeply enough into largely rural, spread-out populations to win elections and undertake a range of political activities to challenge the French government on all the levels at which it operated, from the locality to the French Union as a whole. Political leaders like Senghor and Houphouët-Boigny had learned what they could and could not accomplish during the ANC and the debates over electoral laws. Could they now build large, durable organizations capable of organizing diverse communities? For the French government, the question was what limits they could set on African political organization, now that the fact of African political participation had been given constitutional sanction.

The founding of the Rassemblement Démocratique Africain (RDA) represented the most striking effort of African politicians to construct an organization with breadth as well as depth. In September 1946, with the citizenship issue still unsettled in the ANC in Paris, Houphouët-Boigny and Gabriel d'Arboussier drafted a manifesto calling on territorial parties in all of AOF and much of AEF to group themselves into a new ensemble. Delegates from the parties assembled in Bamako from 18 to 21 October 1946. The manifesto of the RDA was signed by Houphouët-Boigny, Lamine Guèye, Jean Félix-Tchicaya of Gabon-Congo, Sourou Migan Apithy of Dahomey-Togo, Fily Dabo Sissoko from Sudan-Niger, Yacine Diallo of Guinea, and Gabriel d'Arboussier from Gabon-Congo, all deputies except the last (who had been in the first assembly but not the second).

The manifesto made clear the intensity of the struggle for citizenship and a meaningful form of federalism. It condemned the false federalism of the then most influential French political party, the MRP, calling its stance "the mask of an authoritarian regime." But it went on to argue, "Our adhesion to the French Union, which we solemnly proclaim, is justified by a realistic view of the world's problems," by confidence in Africa, and by "the certitude that despite reaction, we will obtain the liberal, democratic, and human conditions that will allow the free development of the original possibilities of African genius." The idea of uniting territorial parties stemmed from the structure of French Africa, with its two grand—but at the time administrative—federations, and the need to fight for African interests and democratic principles across the French Union.[1]

The founders made their goal precise: "We have taken care to avoid equivocation and not to confuse PROGRESSIVE BUT RAPID AUTONOMY within the framework of the French Union with separatism, that is immediate, brutal, total independence. Doing politics, do not forget, is above all to reject chimeras, however seductive they may be and to have the courage to affront hard realities." The manifesto concluded, "Vive l'Afrique Noire, Vive l'Union française des Peuples Démocratiques."[2]

[1] Joseph Roger de Benoist, *L'Afrique occidentale française, de la conférence de Brazzaville (1944) à l'indépendance (1960)* (Dakar: Nouvelles Éditions Africaines, 1982), 67–69, and Frédéric Grah Mel, *Félix Houphouët-Boigny: Biographie* (Abidjan: CERAP, and Paris: Maisonneuve et Larose, 2003), 280–86. The Manifesto, dated 12 September 1946, is reproduced in de Benoist, *L'Afrique occidentale française*, 559–61.

[2] De Benoist, *L'Afrique occidentale française*, 559–61; *Réveil*, 30 September 1946.

The Overseas Minister at the time, Marius Moutet, feared that the new African political formation was too radical, too close in rhetoric to what communists were saying, but behind his anxiety was a more mundane political calculation: Moutet was trying to line up African deputies behind his own party, the Socialists, and the RDA was setting itself out as an alternative, a specifically African alternative. Moutet put pressure on his closest African allies like Lamine Guèye to dissociate themselves. Senghor did not even go to Bamako, later admitting he had made a mistake. Moutet ended up promoting what he wanted most to prevent, for by keeping Socialists out of the RDA, he left the field open to the French Communist Party to develop an alliance with an important African party (despite misgivings within the RDA), leaving the Senegalese Socialists relatively isolated outside their home country.[3] Senghor himself would soon break with Moutet's (and Lamine Guèye's) Socialists, even sooner than the RDA broke with the Communists.

Administrative pressure and personal rivalries led to defections of Sissoko, Apithy, and others, but the RDA sought a coherent African strategy. Only one party in each territory could claim the RDA mantle. The RDA branches set about making themselves into veritable machines in the territories, and despite administrative connivance with its opponents, succeeded well in Côte d'Ivoire, Guinea, and the Sudan, while becoming competitive elsewhere in AOF with the exception of Senegal and Mauritania. There was infighting between personal factions within the RDA in some territories and rivalries with other parties, but on the relationship of the territories to France, the RDA position remained consistent with its original manifesto for at least a decade, trying to make citizenship—social as well as political—into a meaningful construct across French Africa.

The RDA was a loosely structured organization, owing much of its coherence to the respect in which its founding president, Houphouët-Boigny, was held. Meanwhile, the Ivorian branch, the Parti Démocratique de la Côte d'Ivoire (PDCI) set about building on its rural base to mount an effective challenge to administrative control. And the party's branch in Sudan, the Union Soudanaise, was also confronting the basis of administrative power in the countryside by challenging the authority of chiefs. It was led by Modibo Keita, a schoolteacher, graduate of the elite training program at the École William Ponty near Dakar, posted in a town in an agricultural region of the southern Sudan.

Let us begin with a small incident in the town of Sikasso, Sudan. In 1946, Modibo Keita persuaded the local section of the Union

[3] Ruth Schachter Morgenthau, *Political Parties in French-Speaking West Africa* (Oxford: Clarendon, 1964), 89.

Soudanaise to mobilize people, especially former soldiers (tirailleurs) against local chiefs who were abusing their authority. He had considerable success. An administrative inspector noted that chiefs were no longer being obeyed. But he admitted that Keita and his followers had a point, for the local French administrator of the district (Cercle) had tried to conceal from his charges the recent reforms, including the suppression of forced labor.

Some months later, the chiefs were still not being obeyed, and the Union Soudanaise was gaining the loyalty of villagers and collecting dues. The inspector reported that "the Union Soudanaise in the Cercle of Sikasso constitutes a veritable state within the state. Nothing can get done in this Cercle without the local leaders of the Union Soudanaise giving their consent. In fact, the Union Soudanaise works against our authority and paralyzes our actions."[4]

Keita, while acting locally, was also appealing through official channels, jumping the hierarchy directly to the Governor General in Dakar with a telegram in November 1946 denouncing "slave regime that Administrator Rocher has sustained in Cercle Sikasso." He claimed that it was Rocher who had "reduced the population to revolt." The Governor General asked local authorities to consider whether Keita could be prosecuted for sending this "insulting" telegram.[5] Keita also contacted one of the deputies from Sudan in the Assemblée Nationale, Mamadou Konaté, who in early 1947 sent a dossier on the affair to Marius Moutet, the Minister of Overseas France, insisting that Sudanese activists in his area had been calm and disciplined, but were being prosecuted because of Keita's telegram. Another deputy, Henri Lozeray, had earlier written to Moutet complaining that Keita's lieutenant Seydou Traoré had been sentenced to nine months in prison for outrage to a magistrate, adding "a citizen of metropolitan origin never would have been investigated for such a letter addressed in moderate terms to an authoritative civil servant." To him, administrators' actions recalled the *indigénat*.[6]

Governor Louveau had written in December to the Governor General in Dakar that Modibo Keita "has succeeded in having a quasi-absolute authority, unquestionable personal influence over former soldiers, some of the civil servants and an important portion of the pop-

[4] "Rôle de l'Union Soudanaise et ses procédés," extract from report of Inspecteur des Affaires Administratives Cande, nd 1947, 28PA/3/168 (Moutet Papers), AOM. There is some confusion of dates in the papers in this dossier, and what I have set out here represents the most logical sequence.

[5] Modibo Keita, pour le Comité local section soudanaise Rassemblement Démocratique Africain, Sikasso, to Governor General, Dakar, telegram, 20 November 1946, 28PA/3/168, AOM.

[6] Mamadou Konaté to Minister, 6 February 1947, Henri Lozeray, membre de la Commission de la FOM, to Minister, 26 December 1946, 28PA/3/168, AOM.

ulation." Keita was using his authority against the chiefs and the administration, and even appointing his own canton and village chiefs. The Union Soudanaise apparently had eight thousand dues-paying members, and one of the top leaders of the RDA, Gabriel d'Arboussier, had visited the area, an occasion for which Keita had brought out his "small army" of ex-tirailleurs and one thousand supporters. He thought of transferring Keita to another district and his principal lieutenant Seydou Traoré to yet another one. He admitted there was a problem with "an old-style and tired administrator M. Rocher," but he still wanted to act against the movement's leaders.[7]

Moutet wrote the governor saying he was surprised by Keita's arrest, which seemed to him to have a "political character," and he told Konaté that he had asked the prosecutor to lift the mandate of arrest.[8] But later in 1947, Moutet telegraphed the Governor General that the actions of the RDA were "analogous to those which preceded trouble in Madagascar."[9] What had occurred in the meantime was a major insurrection in rural Madagascar, whose connection with the mobilizing efforts of the most popular political party there appears murky today but was compelling in officials' minds. The insurrection had been put down by French forces with tremendous loss of life. The file in Moutet's papers, on which these paragraphs are based, peters out at this point, but we know the eventual outcome: Modibo Keita, the schoolteacher in Sikasso, built the Union Soudanaise-RDA into the major political party in the Sudan, and in 1960 he became the first head of the government of the Mali Federation.

Whether or not an African political party in a small town in Sudan had truly constituted itself as a parallel administration, important officials thought it did. They worried about communist politics in Africa, but even more about the danger that, as Moutet put it to a meeting of top administrators, "these populations, of which the largest number are still in a relatively primitive state" might be stirred up by political parties.[10] But by now, the administration could not just go its repressive ways free from critical eyes. A local party leader could mobilize people, including men with military experience and jobs in local administration. He had access to the Assemblée Nationale in Paris, and African deputies could at least make a Minister think twice about arresting activists on flimsy charges. A Minister might still display

[7]Governor, Sudan, to Governor General, 1 December 1946, 28PA/3/168, AOM.

[8]Ministre to Governor, telegram, nd [February 1947?]; Moutet to Konaté, 24 February 1947, 28PA/3/168, AOM.

[9]Moutet to Governor General, telegram, 20 September 1947, 28PA/3/168, AOM. The standard account of the revolt in Madagascar is Jacques Tronchon, *L'insurrection malgache de 1947: essai d'interprétation historique* (Paris: Maspero, 1974).

[10]Moutet to Conference of High Commissioners and Governors, 21 February 1947, 28PA/3/93, AOM.

his prejudices about primitive Africans and dangerous agitators in a closed meeting, but it was no longer colonial business as usual—not in relation to local activism, not in relation to parliamentary politics.

The incident contributed to officials' fear that authority in rural areas was diminishing; so too did a similar incident in Kankan, in rural Guinea, in 1947.[11] As Robert Delavignette put it, the Minister had once exercised "*imperium* on behalf of the Republic, by the intermediary of a hierarchy of European functionaries and indigenous authorities." But now, "the powers of the hierarchy have also been diminished. The colonial administrator has lost his disciplinary code of the *indigénat*, and above all has been dispossessed of his quality of magistrate of indigenous tribunals. Finally, the native chiefs have seen their traditional authority blown apart. The abuses they could have committed have served as a pretext for agitation, which has also been full of excesses." Delavignette saw the change as not entirely a bad thing—going from rule by decree to a situation where legal procedures shaped overseas policy was a positive step—but the loss of day-to-day authority was a worrisome matter.[12]

A larger-scale and longer-lasting confrontation took place in the Côte d'Ivoire, but it had the same origins as the one described above—in successful mobilization by an African political party with roots in rural Africa and connections in Paris, and in administrative fears that alternatives were being developed to the vertical channels characteristic of imperial power. Houphouët-Boigny's political machine, which would dominate politics in Côte d'Ivoire for a half century, had developed primarily among African cocoa planters in the southern part of the territory. In 1944, farmers possessing at least two hectares of coffee or three of cocoa under cultivation had set up the Syndicat Agricole Africain (SAA). They were aggrieved that white planters benefitted from government services—particularly forced labor recruited in the northern Côte d'Ivoire or neighboring French territories—while African planters were discriminated against on a racial basis. The SAA forged a network not only among planters, but among chiefs of northern areas from where potential workers could come—if they could be

[11] Ex-soldiers played a big part in the demonstrations, which included a siege of the administrator's office by fifteen hundred men and protest marches of two to three thousand. The leader was a Muslim cleric, and grievances were focused on abuses of authority by chiefs and local administrators. The Guinea branch of the RDA would later make a major effort to mobilize rural dwellers. Elizabeth Schmidt, *Mobilizing the Masses: Gender, Ethnicity, and Class in the Nationalist Movement in Guinea, 1939–1958* (Portsmouth, N.H.: Heinemann, 2005), 46–48, 106; Elizabeth Schmidt, *Cold War and Decolonization in Guinea, 1946-1958* (Portsmouth, N.H.: Heinemann, 2007), 51–55.

[12] "Rapport sur la situation politique dans les États et territoires relevant du Ministre de la France d'Outre-mer," 4 September 1948, Delavignette Papers, 19PA/3/30, AOM, p. 33.

freed from the yoke of forced labor. At this time, a relatively progressive Governor, André Latrille, saw forced labor as not only detestable in itself and a demeaning stain on his administrators, but as a practice with no future. The SAA furnished him an alternative—a network capable of supplying labor by means other than coercion, or at least by means in which French administrators were not complicit. With the first postwar elections, the SAA converted itself into a political organization and successfully backed Houphouët-Boigny's candidacy for the Assemblée Nationale Constituante. That the SAA offered a more promising, and less politically costly future than maintenance of the forced labor regime helped to convince the Ministry not to oppose the initiative of Houphouët-Boigny in the Assemblée Nationale Constituante to abolish forced labor. With the passage of his bill in April 1946, Houphouët-Boigny established himself, in and beyond the Côte d'Ivoire, as the emancipator of French West Africa's workers.[13]

Over the next decade or so, African cocoa planters became the motor of AOF's most dynamic economy, and the SAA, transformed into the PDCI—branch of the RDA—became one of Africa's most successful political parties.[14] In the summer and fall of 1946, incidents of disobedience of chiefs, including a violent demonstration, were reported in the northern Côte d'Ivoire. Local officials feared that the Parti Démocratique, along with the communist-connected Comité d'Études Franco-Africaines, were taking over "the political direction of the bush." Police reported that "the natives no longer recognize the authority of canton chiefs." Governor Latrille thought that the violence might have something to do with a chief forcing people to work for him when it was no longer legal, and he was critical of the local administrator.[15]

Two new developments in 1947 from outside the region produced a more constricted atmosphere: the drift to the right of the French

[13] Frederick Cooper, "Conditions Analogous to Slavery: Imperialism and Free Labor Ideology in Africa," in Frederick Cooper, Thomas Holt, and Rebecca Scott, *Beyond Slavery: Explorations of Race, Labor, and Citizenship in Postemancipation Societies* (Chapel Hill: University of North Carolina Press, 2000), 107–50. Security agents thought Houphouët-Boigny considered himself "le Gandhi de l'Afrique." "Note sur la situation en Côte d'Ivoire," 13 July 1946, 17G 556, AS.

[14] Aristide Zolberg sees the origins of the PDCI as an amalgam of social groups, the SAA most prominenet among them, but by 1947, he argues, it was turning into a "monolith," with a strong central committee and a cell-like organization. *One-Party Government in the Ivory Coast* (Princeton: Princeton University Press, 1969), 113–17.

[15] Governor, Côte d'Ivoire, to High Commissioner, telegram, 15 September 1946, Commandant de Cercle Lequer, to Governor, 29 September 1946, Chef de Subdivision Centrale de Bobo-Dioulasso, reply to questions 19 September 1946, Chef de Brigade Mobile Bobo-Dioulasso, to Chef de la Sûreté, 9 July 1946, Governor to High Commissioner, 4 October 1946, Moutet Papers, 28PA 8/175/3, AOM; Governor to Governor General, 4 October 1946, Governor General to Minister, 19 October 1946, 28PA 8/168, AOM.

political spectrum, especially the exclusion of the PCF from the governing coalition (in May) and the Madagascar revolt (March–April) and its bloody repression. The former brought to the Overseas Ministry Paul Coste-Floret, anxious to preserve central power and strongly anticommunist, who contributed to a complex whereby every rural stirring was often seen as a second Madagascar that had to be nipped in the bud.[16] But the on-the-ground politics in Côte d'Ivoire did not correspond to predetermined images of either communists or bloodthirsty natives.[17]

On the government side, the hard line began with settlers persuading officials to replace Latrille, seen as too pro-PDCI, as Governor. Governor Georges Orselli, in charge for a time in 1948, later told an investigatory commission that he had been told by Coste-Floret, "You are going down there to suppress the RDA."[18] He did not do it and was replaced by Laurent Péchoux, who took on the task with zeal.

The incidents began with riots in Treichville, a working-class suburb of Abidjan, that followed RDA members' disruption of meetings in January and February 1949 of what they felt was a government sponsored political party. Pro-RDA crowds apparently roughed up opponents and pillaged their property. The police took this to be an occasion to crack down hard, arresting RDA followers and leaders (Houphouët-Boigny, who was there at the time, was protected by his parliamentary immunity). Thus began a pattern repeated in several smaller towns around the Côte d'Ivoire, which appear as riots in official accounts and as police violence in those of the RDA members. The hearings of a committee of the Assemblée Nationale in 1950 provide oral testimonies supporting both versions.[19]

In the course of 1949 incidents multiplied. The RDA called for a variety of mass actions, many of them directed against the economic

[16]The second Madagascar thesis was embraced by the hard-line Governor Laurent Péchoux and the more progressive Robert Delavignette. Testimony of Péchoux, 25 July 1950, 221, and of Orselli (reporting conversation with Delavignette), 4 July 1950, 98, in Assemblée Nationale, *Impressions, projets de lois, propositions, rapports, etc. tome CXXVII, Session de 1950, No. 11348, "Incidents de la Côte d'Ivoire"* (Paris: Imprimerie de l'Assemblée Nationale, 1951). This volume contains the testimonies in the Assemblée's official inquiry into the incidents, referred to below.

[17]Alexander Keese puts more weight on French officials' fear of communism (and less on their concern with the RDA's parallel administration) than I do. Governor Péchoux and various officials were prone to find—or at least to say they found—communists throughout Côte d'Ivoire, but Keese overestimates the coherence and consistency of French thinking about the relationship of communism and anticolonial movements in AOF. "A Culture of Panic: 'Communist' Scapegoats and Decolonization in French West Africa and French Polynesia (1945–1957)," *French Colonial History* 9 (2008): 131–45.

[18]Orselli, "Incidents," 98.

[19]There is a good account, largely based on testimonies from the above investigation, plus newspapers, in Morgenthau, *Political Parties*, 188–202. See also the long report by G. Delamotte, Procureur de la République, Grand Bassam, 16 July 1951, 17G 554, AS.

position of Europeans: boycotts of commercial houses, strikes of house servants and gardeners, refusal to sell fruits and vegetables to Europeans. There were also mass demonstrations, including several by women. "I was afraid of the women," testified the Commandant de Cercle of Dimbokro, after an incident in which a crowd of women, throwing rocks at the police, tried to free someone from a jail.[20] Ex-soldiers played a part in some demonstrations.[21] The towns of Grand Bassam, Dimbokro, and Bouaflé and smaller interior towns like Zuenola, Grand-Labou, Ngokro, Motobe, Daloa, D'Issia, and Katiola were sites of mobilization.[22] Officials accused the RDA of ordering its members to destroy the houses of opponents.[23] Some of the mass actions were directed against the wave of detentions by which the government was cracking down on—and provoking—the unrest. In a number of cases, police fired on and killed demonstrators—fifty-two by one count. Some three thousand people ended up in jail. Prisoners engaged in hunger strikes.[24]

What bothered officials the most was that the RDA seemed to be setting up a "parallel administration" in some towns and rural chiefdoms. Péchoux himself told the investigatory committee that "RDA forces of order existed alongside the legal policy." He insisted that the RDA had created its own "clandestine tribunals" and a "parallel jurisdiction." One such court, he said, had heard two hundred cases over two years and fined people for corruption and other crimes. The RDA, he alleged, was telling people to pay their taxes to the party instead of the government. Farmers were being told to market crops through parallel channels, not through European commercial houses, and RDA members attacked markets and market sellers in towns like Bouaflé. Crop exports fell. Officials were convinced that the movements were being coordinated from the top of the RDA—by Houphouët-Boigny, Gabriel d'Arboussier, Ouezzin Coulibaly, and others.[25] A French

[20] Pierre Montel, "Incidents," 2 August 1950, 668. A demonstration of women who paraded into town, attacked customers and sellers in the market, and tried to take over the prison in the town of Daloa is described in the telegram of Commandant de Cercle, Daloa, to Governor, 6 January 1950, 17G 554, AS. He warned that "disorder is spreading."

[21] Houphouët-Boigny, "Incidents," 28 June 1950, 70.

[22] Incidents in the interior are catalogued in the Delamotte report, 16 July 1951, 17G 554, AS. For waves of incidents in December and then in January, see Governor, Côte d'Ivoire, to Governor General, 31 December 1949, 7 February 1950, 17G 554, AS.

[23] Governor General to Minister, 28 February 1950, 17G 554, AS.

[24] Morgenthau, *Political Parties*, 198–99.

[25] Péchoux, "Incidents," 25, 27, 29 July 1950, 219, 310–13, 537–38; Governor General, report to Minister, 26 January, 1 February 1950, and telegrams, 7, 12, 13 February 1950, 17G 554, AS. A circular (if authentic) to all sections of the RDA from Gabriel d'Arboussier stated "only the action of resolute masses can bring to fruition our cause, in parliamentary as well as juridical terms"—an interesting argument for seeing the

prosecutor claimed that the RDA had created "village committees" that were intended to supersede the authority of the administration at the village level. He concluded, "the RDA had tried to insert itself directly into the local scene by undertaking actions that belong either to administrative or judicial authority."[26] The investigating committee, later touring towns in the Côte d'Ivoire, collected a number of testimonies of RDA members alleging harassment by the administration and from a number of other Africans alleging harassment by RDA members.[27]

If the story told by most officials during the parliamentary inquiry was one of an RDA parallel government, with its police and courts, and of rock-throwing women and interference with Africans and Europeans trying to do business, the story told by RDA members depicts a program of government intimidation. Behind the harassment, they saw the maintenance of a "mercantile" economic order and the failure of the government to live up to its constitutional promises of equal treatment of citizens. Houphouët-Boigny brought the discussion down to the level of the petty exactions of a local French administration. District officials had been

> simultaneously administrators, judges, accusers and directors of cooperative societies. They indiscriminately inflicted fines, appointed and fired chiefs at their pleasure. Messieurs les commandants, who could obtain for free cows, sheep, chickens, [now] saw themselves constrained to pay like others, like the poor, can I say; because they, as the best paid civil servants, did not pay for food products! The occasion was ripe to retake their exorbitant powers! . . . Down with the RDA! Down with communists! Down with the agents of Moscow![28]

The two versions are not mutually incompatible. The RDA had, over a period of five years, established good networks across small towns; its campaign against forced labor had won the support not only of workers but of African cocoa planters. It gave people in a variety of social niches reason to believe that the RDA could deliver on its promises. Its top leaders had prestigious posts in Paris, and when the local administration tried to go after RDA leaders, Houphouët-

---

ultimate goal of mass action to be parliamentary and juridical. Circular of 19 December 1949, copy in 17G 554, AS.

[26] Guy Delamotte, "Incidents," 29 July 1950, 497–99. The Commandant de cercle at Daloa also testified about "clandestine tribunals" that judged misdemeanors and even felonies and made convicted people pay fines that were divided among the judges. Ibid., 11 August 1950, 895.

[27] Assy N'Gho, "Incidents," 31 July 1950, 636–68, Mamadou Koné, 31 July 1950, 651.

[28] Houphouët-Boigny, "Incidents," 21 June 1950, 46, 28 June 1950, 71.

Boigny played his two cards successfully: he could use his parliamentary immunity to avoid the tyranny of the local administration, and if an official overstepped his bounds—and one tried to serve a warrant on him—he could surround himself with a crowd of people who could prevent such an official from acting.[29] At the same time as the RDA could stay in motion with boycotts, demonstrations before jails, and interference with commerce; shifting from town to town, it could act like an established political movement, its deputies issuing protests, calling in the Assemblée Nationale for investigations of the Côte d'Ivoire administration, getting articles published in African newspapers.[30]

The administration, for its part, tried to portray the movement as riot, disruption, and communist conspiracy, but it also kept harping on the theme of parallel government—something that acknowledged the capacity of the RDA. It used the standard techniques of colonial repression—mass arrests and a degree of deadly violence—but it also, if RDA testimony is to be believed, engaged in a sort of politics that was new to French Africa but would have its place in the ensuing decade: meddling with electoral lists to reduce the number of RDA voters.[31] But for all the possibilities the administration had to lean on its own African personnel to work against the RDA, it did not mount a credible threat to its electoral success. And it pulled its punches: when a local prosecutor tried to arrest Houphouët-Boigny, his superiors made him back off.[32] Governor Péchoux lobbied vigorously for the government to ban the RDA altogether; the Ministry refused.[33] The RDA

[29]Governor General to Minister, 7 February 1950, 17G 554, AS; Georges Chaffard, *Les carnets secrets de la décolonisation* (Paris: Calmann-Lévy, 1965–67), 1:112–16.

[30]Houphouët-Boigny and Coulibaly sent a telegram directly to the Minister to complain of police methods "worthy of the Gestapo used against population Region Zuenoula," and they threatened to take the information to the UN and the press. The Minister duly informed the Governor General of this telegram, and the Governor General predictably denied the charges. Ministry to Governor General, telegram, 21 January 1950, and letter, 24 January 1950; Governor, Côte d'Ivoire, to Governor General, telegram, 17G 554, AS. When the Governor General tried to get governors in other territories to ban RDA meetings, another deputy, Mamadou Konaté of the Sudan, complained to the Minister, who got officials in West Africa to refrain from a general ban on RDA meetings, without admitting they had done wrong. Governor General to Ministry, telegram, nd (February or March 1950), and Ministry to Governor General, telegram, 9 March 1950, Governor General to Minister 19 March 1950, Governor, Côte d'Ivoire, to Governor General, telegram, 24 March 1950, all in 17G 554, AS. The RDA-connected newspaper *Réveil* (19 December 1949, 27 February, 3 April 1950) called attention to the "repression" in Côte d'Ivoire.

[31]Houphouët-Boigny, "Incidents," 21 June 1950, 53, 28 June 1950, 58.

[32]Governor Péchoux to Governor General, 31 January 1950, Governor General to Minister, 7 February 1950, 17G 554, AS.

[33]Governor to Governor General, telegram, 14 February 1950; AOF, Direction Générale de l'Intérieur, Service des Affaires Politiques, "Note sur les activités illégales du

pulled its punches too: Côte d'Ivoire did not turn into a second Madagascar. And even in May 1950, after months of fighting off police repression and courting arrest himself, Ouezzin Coulibably concluded a
speech stirring up his militants, "The RDA does not want France's departure, on the contrary. It wants to collaborate in the French Union,
a fraternal union."[34]

The pushing of limits on both sides occurred in towns across much
of the southern Côte d'Ivoire in 1949 and into 1950. In the summer of
1950, after insistence by the RDA and some of its friends in Paris, an
investigatory committee from the Assemblée Nationale looked into
the situation, hearing from Houphouët-Boigny and Péchoux, and numerous others; the transcript of testimonies is over eleven hundred
pages long. But there was one arena where compromise was possible:
the RDA's legislative alliance with the PCF. Houphouët-Boigny later
seemed rather amused that someone as bourgeois and traditionalist
as he was—property owner, businessman, Catholic, scion of a chiefly
family—could have been considered a communist. At the time, he denied that the RDA was a communist movement and insisted that its
relationship to the PCF was a legislative alliance only, conditioned by
the willingness of the PCF to vote for measures regarding the French
Union that the RDA supported.[35] It was, in other words, a pragmatic
relationship that could be jettisoned when it did more harm than
good. That was the origin of the famous "désapparentement," the
breakup of the relationship between the RDA and the PCF.

The deal was made quietly and personally, between Houphouët-
Boigny and François Mitterrand, then the Minister of Overseas
France.[36] The RDA—the overall organization, not just its Ivorian
branch—publicly announced its disaffiliation from the PCF in September 1950, and Mitterrand told his officers in Dakar and Abidjan
to call off their dogs. Governor Péchoux was transferred away from
the Côte d'Ivoire the next May. Some—including one of the RDA's
top leaders, d'Arboussier—thought the pact a betrayal of principle,

PDCI, 2 March 1960; Governor to Governor General, 6 March 1950; Minister to Governor General, 6 June 1950, all in 17G 569, AS.

[34]Reported by security services. Renseignements, Abidjan, 29 May 1950, 17G 555,
AS.

[35]Houphouët-Boigny, 28 June 1950, 70; speech in Grand Bassam, reported by
police, Renseignements, 20 December 1951, 17G 555, AS; speech at colloquium on
history of RDA, published in Rassemblement Démocratique Africain, *Actes du colloque
international sur l'histoire du RDA, Yamoussoukro, 18-25 octobre 1985* (Abidjan: CEDA Hatier,
1987), 1:10.

[36]The initial rapprochement between Houphouët-Boigny and the government owed
much to René Pleven, who became President of the Council of Ministers in July, and
who was more familiar than his Parisian colleagues with personalities in Africa. See
Chaffard, *Carnets secrets*, 1:121–24, and Joseph Roger de Benoist, "Le désapparentement
et ses lendemains," in RDA, *Actes du colloque*, 1:389–407, esp. 393.

but for other RDA leaders the relationship with the PCF had not had much to do with principle, or ideology, in the first place.[37] RDA leaders acknowledged that their ability to formulate a program for themselves had been hurt by the "savage repression" that they had experienced, but the break with the PCF, they argued, would now allow the party to pursue the "realization of its destiny by its own means, with its own voice" and it would no longer have to "adopt a priori positions." It was both liberated and constrained to undertake "a politics of the possible" and "as realists to look at the government that is in front of us, reactionary or not, with which we must deal to obtain the maximum."[38] Houphouët-Boigny compared his situation to that of Kwame Nkrumah in the Gold Coast, who, faced with having to work with a more conservative British government after 1951, made his arrangements, not taking issue with British policies that did not concern the Gold Coast. "He has his feet on the ground," noted Houphouët-Boigny, and that was where he proposed to keep his.[39]

The deal left in place what was, if anything, the more important problem that the RDA was posing to the French government—its local organization. The Administration still played dirty tricks in the 1951 election campaign—keeping RDA members off commissions supervising registration and voting, erasing RDA members' names from lists and padding opposition lists, and openly urging people to vote against the RDA. They knocked off some RDA candidates, but not Houphouët-Boigny, and the Administration thereafter gave up such strategies in the Côte d'Ivoire (but not elsewhere, for example Niger in 1958). In both the Côte d'Ivoire and the Sudan, the

[37] For others, the affiliation with the PCF was more profound, since they had entered the RDA via communist study groups and engaged in long debates over RDA-PCF relations. Alpha Oumar Konaré, "Le RDA, l'Union soudanaise et le désapparentement," in RDA, *Actes du colloque*, 1:173–88. D'Arboussier objected both to the nondemocratic way the decision to disaffiliate had been made and to the RDA's cooperation with a government that he regarded as still oppressive. Instead of Houphouët-Boigny's deal, he sought an "alliance of democratic African forces and democratic and progressive forces of the entire world, and first of all those of the French people in their common struggle against imperialism." *Le RDA est toujours anticolonialiste (lettres ouvertes à Félix Houphouët-Boigny)* (Dakar-Paris: Imprimerie pour le Commerce et l'Industrie, 1952), second letter, September 1952, 29, quoted, CAMP microfilm (University of Wisconsin Library, 2169). See also Morgenthau, *Political Parties*, 200–201. On the other side of the bargain, Mitterrand was beset by administrators, settlers, and their allies, who wanted to keep up the repression of the RDA. He felt compelled to explain later, "The Rassemblement démocratique africain was not communist." *Présence française et abandon* (Paris: Plon, 1957), 184, 194–98.

[38] RDA, "Rapport politique à toutes sections," Paris, 8 December 1950, 17G 572, AS. Sékou Touré initially opposed the break with the PCF, but came around and made his own move to break with the communist-affiliated French trade union. Schmidt, *Mobilizing the Masses*, 159–61.

[39] Quoted in Morgenthau, *Political Parties*, 98.

territorial branches of the RDA had developed into movements that the government would have to live—and negotiate—with. Police reports from the Côte d'Ivoire in 1951 pointed to evidence of militancy and antigovernment propaganda, but emphasized that the PDCI was taking care to remain within the law and maneuvering to bring potential rival parties into the RDA fold.[40] In 1953, government officials reported, the RDA in Côte d'Ivoire was so solidly entrenched that European planters and businessmen had decided to cooperate with it. By 1956, the PDCI-RDA was telling the government whom it could assign to posts in local administration and Houphouët-Boigny was sitting in the French cabinet.[41]

In Cameroon, the French government did, indeed, eliminate a political party—the Union des Populations du Cameroun (UPC) from the scene, driving it underground and into a guerilla conflict that began in 1955.[42] The UPC had after 1948 taken a radical stance on labor issues and it had called for independence at a time when such a demand was considered anathema. Some of the highest officials in the government would have liked to do eliminate the RDA from the Côte d'Ivoire, but they failed. The reason why Coste-Floret, Péchoux, and others wanted to destroy it was the reason why they failed: The RDA had, unlike the UPC in Cameroon, enracinated itself too deeply in too much of the Côte d'Ivoire. The government would have to deal with the RDA and reach compromises with its leaders.

Citizenship in a Colonial Situation: The Rights of Labor

Another kind of politics was played out between West Africa and France, in which the social meaning of citizenship was at stake. I have already described the strikes of 1946 in Senegal, in which the slogan "equal pay for equal work" became part of a well-coordinated social movement, embracing people from unskilled laborers to relatively privileged civil servants, winning important concessions on wages for some and family allowances for others, and above all pushing the state to accept that African workers and their representatives would have

[40] Service de Police de la Côte d'Ivoire, "La vie politique: le RDA," nd 1951, Governor General to Governor, 31 August 1951, Service de Police, Renseignements, 4 September 1951, 20 December 1951, 17G 555, AS.

[41] AOF, Affaires Politiques, Notes sur la Côte d'Ivoire, November 1954, AP 2257, AOM; Morgenthau, *Political Parties*, 201–3.

[42] Richard Joseph, *Radical Nationalism in Cameroun: The Social Origins of the UPC Rebellion* (Oxford: Oxford University Press, 1977); Achille Mbembe, *La Naissance du maquis dans le Sud-Cameroun, 1920–1960: Histoire des usages de la raison en colonie* (Paris: Karthala, 1996); Meredith Terretta, "Cameroonian Nationalists Go Global: From Forest *Maquis* to a Pan-African Accra," *Journal of African History* 51 (2010): 1–24.

a place within a system of industrial relations based on metropolitan principles. Over the course of 1946, citizenship and labor became intertwined.[43]

Of almost mythic proportions was the great railway strike of 1947–48, shutting down the major transportation system of French West Africa for five months.[44] The strike was about the *cadre unique*, the demand of African railway workers for a single, nonracial job hierarchy, with the same scale of benefits for all members. The young, militant leader of the AOF-wide union of "indigenous workers" on the railroad, Ibrahima Sarr, defined the issue in the language of citizenship, even while the constitution was being debated in Paris, calling for "the abolition of antiquated colonial methods condemned even by THE NEW AND TRUE FRANCE which wishes that all its children, at whatever latitude they may live, be equal in duties and rights and *that the recompense of labor be a function solely of merit and capacity.*"[45]

Sarr thought such ideas applied not only to the elite of railway workers, but also to the "auxiliaries," who worked without job security and other indemnities, and whom he wished to integrate into the "cadres," the permanent labor force. In April 1947 the union pulled off a theatrical coup. At the moment of a visit to Senegal by the President of France, it organized a strike. In such circumstances, the government could not publicly go against principles of equality. An official commission accepted the principle of the single cadre. But when management refused to follow through, the entire African labor force on the railway, across AOF, went on strike in October.

Governor General Barthes insisted that the strike was illegal; he would not negotiate. The strike remained remarkably solid until January, when the Abidjan-Niger region broke away and went back to work, largely because Houphouët-Boigny, whose constituency was strongest among cocoa planters being hurt by the strike, put pressure on the Ivorian branch to return to work. Even this defection did not lead the rest to lose heart.

Workers survived this long only because they were integrated into town-centered and family-centered networks, which gave them access to food supplies. Women played a crucial role in pulling together

[43] The subject of this section is discussed in much more detail in my *Decolonization and African Society: The Labor Question in French and British Africa* (Cambridge: Cambridge University Press, 1996).

[44] Frederick Cooper, "'Our Strike': Equality, Anticolonial Politics, and the French West African Railway Strike of 1947–48," *Journal of African History* 37 (1996): 81–118. Recent scholarship on the railway and the strike includes James A. Jones, *Industrial Labor in the Colonial World: Workers of the Chemin de Fer Dakar-Niger, 1881–1963* (Portsmouth, N.H.: Heinemann, 2002), and an ongoing Columbia University PhD dissertation by Brandon County.

[45] Renseignements, 29 May 1946, K 352 (26), AS.

such resources. The chief labor inspector commented, "Here the means of defense are very different—and singularly more effective—than in the case of metropolitan strikes."[46] The incompleteness of workers' absorption into proletarian society gave them more diverse roots than their French comrades had; they were part of Africa. But neither other African trade unions nor African political parties joined to build a solid front against the colonial regime. The railway union had itself failed to join the 1946 strike in Senegal; unions had different political affiliations; and, after the 1946 strike settlement, unions had a great deal to gain by working within professional boundaries. The RDA did not back the strike because the railway workers were not affiliated with it and because of the opposition of Houphouët-Boigny. The strike thus remained a railway strike, becoming neither a proletarian movement in general nor a focus of anticolonial action by political parties.[47]

The government's caution in using repressive means—arrests, requisition, ejecting strikers from railway housing—reflected the postwar conjuncture. Railway workers represented the best hope for the kind of stable, skilled workforce officials wanted to build. Finally in March 1948, a new Governor General decided to compromise. He sustained the railway on some of the issues, split the difference on others. There would be no punishment for striking. Many auxiliaries were slowly integrated into the single cadre.

The Administration now knew that restructuring the colonial labor system would involve African agency as much as imperial design. The principles of the equivalence of citizens could not be kept within a Parisian container. The government made its point too: African unions could fight and win, but within certain legal and institutional structures. The very battle brought both sides deeper into those structures, and the strike became neither a popular liberation struggle nor an exercise in colonial repression.

There were other major strikes between 1945 and 1950—a general strike in Conakry in 1950 and others in Senegal and Dahomey most notably. Sékou Touré made his name in Guinea by leading the labor movement through major strikes, culminating in one that lasted over two months in 1953. By pulling wage workers into the Guinea branch of the RDA, Sékou Touré, Elizabeth Schmidt argues, began to attract people from different social positions into a political movement that focused on issues of immediate, material concern—wages, veteran

[46] Inspecteur Général du Travail to Deputy Dumas, 6 January 1948, in IGT, Report, 24 January 1948, IGT 13/2, AOM.

[47] In an interview in 1994, a strike veteran used the phrase "our strike" to distinguish his memories from the version of the novelist Ousmanne Sembene, who subsumed it under an anticolonial rubric in *God's Bits of Wood*. See Cooper, " 'Our Strike.' "

benefits, education, and health facilities, as well as on the abuses of rural chiefs.[48]

As early as 1948, the labor movement in French West Africa—working with parliamentarians in Paris—was fighting its next battle: for a labor code, based on metropolitan models, applying to overseas France. The code would make certain conditions of labor into legally defined rights: minimum wages, the forty-hour week, paid vacations. And because it would also give workers the right to form and join unions and to strike—subject to certain procedures—it would make clear that workers had the right to *claim* rights.

Many administrators and business leaders also wanted to see a labor code in place, but for their own reasons: to promote and enforce orderly procedures. As noted earlier, the citizenship law of April 1946 had immediately forced the Ministry to give up its plan to implement a "code du travail indigène," since such a category no longer existed. Any code would have to apply to all wage workers in the overseas territories. With such a reach, the stakes in specifying rights and benefits were high.

For the government, and particularly the Inspection du Travail, the model for industrial relations was French. As a system of protection for the vulnerable, social security was based on "solidarity," and hence the presumed unity and universality of the French citizenry. In 1946, officials were talking about installing overseas "a system of social security . . . strongly resembling the current system perfected for the metropole."[49] But this universalistic vision had its limits when applied to the overseas territories: the focus was specifically on one category among citizens, the wage laborer. The African worker could be assimilated to the normative and institutional frameworks for industrial relations and social security in France, but the rural African, living in a "traditional" milieu, could not. Only slowly and with the revolutionizing of agricultural production would their way of life be transformed. The more immediate task was to ensure that urban workers could raise families in their places of work, producing a new generation of workers under the watchful eyes of doctors, urban planners, teachers, and civil servants. Codifying labor relations—and promoting wages sufficient to raise a family—were crucial to the process. It was above all the resistance of employers and their allies in the Paris legislature that dragged the process out.[50]

[48] Schmidt, *Mobilizing the Masses*, 56, 71–83.

[49] Inspecteur Général du Travail, Note, November 1947, K 461 (179), AS; Inspecteur Général du Travail, Paris, to Inspecteur Général du Travail, AOF, 17 December 1946, K 438 (179), AS.

[50] Cooper, *Decolonization and African Society*, 278–92; Omar Guèye, *Sénégal: histoire du mouvement syndical: la marche vers le code du travail* (Paris: L'Harmattan, 2011).

For African politicians, labor was a constituency, not the only one but important by virtue of its organization, its falling within the "capacities" specified by the election laws, and its strategic location in a colonial society that was fragmented along different axes. In each territory of AOF, individual unions were grouped into a "union des syndicats," and at the level of AOF as a whole these unions belonged to one of the major French union federations, the largest being the Confédération Générale du Travail (CGT). African trade unionists had their own priorities, but affiliation with union organization spanning the French Union as a whole provided resources and legitimacy within the French system.

The immediate passage of the Code du Travail—along with demands for equal wages and benefits for all workers—was the major theme of union meetings from 1946 to 1952. A Sudanese trade union newspaper made the case for a universal social security scheme with particular vigor: "In the face of danger, there is no difference between a FRENCHMAN born near the banks of the Seine or the Loire and a FRENCHMAN born near the banks of the Senegal or the Niger."[51] French officials both welcomed a well-organized labor force as part of the "modern" world and feared that it could be "a formidable element of social agitation, if, seriously discontented with their lot, they were taken in hand, supervised and guided by clever people without scruples. . . . The moral and material situation of these workers should necessarily remain among the most fundamental preoccupations of all."[52]

The Ministry, the Assemblée de l'Union française, and the Grand Conseil in Dakar talked about the need for a code from 1947 to 1950 before a proposed text made it to the floor of the Assemblée Nationale. It was backed not only by African deputies but also by a faction within the center-right MRP, mainly by social Catholics, who sought an integrative approach that would be supportive of African family formation and more important would be appealing enough to workers to fend off communist organizing. Backers were explicit about extending a French model of labor to Africa: the point was to extend "the majority of the social advantages accorded to metropolitan workers."[53]

African deputies focused on a form of work defined by the authority of the employer and the payment of a wage. They were content to leave "customary" laborers outside of its purview, a stance that no doubt appealed to the peanut growers who backed Senghor and the cocoa growers who were Houphouët-Boigny's constituency. Pro-colon

[51] *Barakela, organe de l'Union Régionale des Syndicats du Soudan*, 17 September 1951, 17G 272, AS; Cooper, *Decolonization and African Society*, 285–87.

[52] AOF, IGT, Rapport Annuel, 1951, 197–98.

[53] Report of the Commission des Affaires Sociales, AUF, *Documents*, Annex No. 12 to session of 26 January 1949, 23.

deputies tried to call Africans on that position, posing as defenders of African peasants and agricultural workers against exploitation by fellow Africans. Coming from where it did, the argument lacked credibility. When there seemed to be sentiment in the Assemblée to dilute provisions on the work week and overtime, Senghor cut to the key point: "As you know, Africans now have a mystique of equality. In this domain, as in others, they want the same principles to be applied from the first in the overseas territories as in the metropole."[54]

The debate—on and off in the Assemblée, bouncing between it and the more conservative upper chamber—went on for two years. It had some of the drama of the citizenship debates of 1946, and several provisions provoked tough fights and close votes. In the end, African deputies had to threaten to vote against the bill as a whole to save an article allowing for the future extension of the French system of family allowances to workers in the private sector (public employed already had family allowances).[55]

A key act of the drama took place in Africa. As the debate neared a climax, Abbas Guèye, veteran leader of the 1946 strike in Senegal and now a deputy allied to Senghor, wrote to the Comité de Coordination des Unions Territoriales des Syndicats de l'AOF et de l'AEF and to several constituent unions warning of delays and dilutions. His letter set off a chain of mobilizations, including a day of demonstrations and speeches on 28 October 1952 and a one-day general strike across AOF on 3 November, with more strike plans held in reserve.[56] Conservative deputies complained of being threatened, but the point had been made. Even Paul Coste-Floret, who as Minister had done battle with the RDA in Côte d'Ivoire, noted that the bill that emerged from all the turmoil was not at all inconsistent with "our law or the principles on which it is based, but, on the contrary, they recall the most authentic principles of our democracy."[57]

The code provided for a forty-hour work week, paid vacations, procedures to set minimum wages in different professions and locations, and the right to organize and (with limits) strike. Implementing the code led to some conflict, notably a strike in Guinea that lasted from

[54] Senghor, Assemblée Nationale, *Débats*, 22 November 1952, 5502–5. This phrase was picked up by Governor General Cornut-Gentille to let administrators know the sentiments they had to accommodate themselves to. Speech to Grand Conseil, 13 Octobre 1954, 20. It was also used up a leading authority on colonial law, for whom the words had a positive significance: "The mystique of equality brings us back to the mystique of the law." P.-F. Gonidec, "Une mystique de l'égalité: le code du travail des territoires d'Outre-Mer," *Revue Juridique et Politique de l'Union Française* 2 (1953): 176–96, 96 quoted.

[55] Assemblée Nationale, *Débats*, 22 November 1952, 5547–51.

[56] The mobilization is described in Cooper, *Decolonization and African Society*, 303–4.

[57] Assemblée Nationale, *Débats*, 6 November 1952, 4796.

September to November 1953 and made CGT leader Sékou Touré into a hero. Another round of agitation took place in 1955–56 over the implementation of family allowances. As before, Africans argued that anything less than full implementation would violate principles of equality among citizens. Social Catholics wanted to support family life, and many officials thought that working-class families were particularly worthy and needful of attention because they were likely to follow "modern" ways. Other officials feared disorder if African unions were stymied. The probusiness or pro-colon deputies made their habitual arguments about the peculiarity of the African, insisting that African families were not comparable to European ones. In 1956, African unions won their battle.[58]

There were, typically, maneuvers to compromise the effect of the code: indemnities for European workers for "displacement" and job classifications that put most African workers on the low end of the skill hierarchy. Most important, the code applied to wage workers only, not to "customary" labor. The work of family members on small farms was exempt, and that of tenants and clients fell into a gray area between regulated and unregulated forms of work. Whereas the Constitution and the code forbade discrimination among *workers*, the code made a distinction between types of *work*, separating a codified "French" realm from a noncodified "traditional" realm.[59] Thus if political citizenship would supposedly unite all French people, social citizenship could imply a separation between two categories of Africans.

When it came to the civil service, there was less room for maneuver, and indeed in 1950 the "second Lamine Guèye law" had built on the first Lamine Guèye law to guarantee public employees benefits equal to those of civil servants coming from the metropole. There were arguments about how fairly this law was implemented too, but officials knew they were in a quandary. They needed not only to respond to trade union pressure—and the civil service unions were the strongest—but also to take into account the fact that administration actions, from development to repression, depended on the loyalty and skills of civil servants.[60]

[58] Cooper, *Decolonization and African Society*, 305–21.

[59] The exclusion of "customary" labor relations from the code could be read as having to do with the personal status of the employer, and this created problems of jurisdiction—over what kind of tribunal could hear different kinds of work-related cases. See François Luchaire, "Le champ d'application des statuts personnels en Algérie et dans les territoires d'outre-mer," *Revue Juridique et Parlementaire de l'Union Française* 9 (1955): 45.

[60] The Commission des Affaires Diverses of the Grand Conseil de l'AOF reported that the second Lamine Guèye law enshrined the "principle of eliminating all discrimination in salaries and benefits of any nature based on difference of race, personal status, origin, or place of recruitment." But the decrees of implementation left certain inequali-

Numerous reports and correspondence referred to the problem of African "cadres" in the administration, for example in this comment of the Governor General of AOF in 1947:

> I am obliged to take into account the fact that very rapidly and increasingly, I will have Africans among the African cadres, in the cadres that serve the affairs of Africa. Africans do not accept that, because of being African, they have salaries inferior to the salary given to a European who came to take this place, who fills that role alongside them and does not fill it any better, with more conscientiousness or more experience.[61]

The problem was clear: civil servants in Africa were French citizens working for the French state; deviations from equality of treatment would be evident and galling. As we shall see in the next chapter, the government by the mid-1950s was realizing that the French reference point—above all in regard to standard of living—had become a dangerously important part of social and political action in an empire of citizens.

How high Africans could push in the hierarchy was also at issue: "It seems clearer each day that in the realm of practice the elites—or at least those that are usually called évolués—should be called upon to play ... a more assertive and efficacious role." These imperatives would soon be given a name—"l'africanisation des cadres"—and its implementation would reflect a demand both from current civil servants for advancement and from high officials who saw in the program a way of giving educated Africans a stake in the French Union. Whether the French government could control both the pace of change and its costs would become an increasingly difficult question.[62]

Here we have social citizenship in action: movement politics in Africa, parliamentary politics in Paris, in which coalitions formed among African deputies concerned with equality, social Catholics worried about the family, communists and socialists who favored progressive legislation overseas as in the metropole, and officials worried about

---

ties in place, a point underscored by Lamine Guèye himself. *Bulletin du Grand Conseil*, session of 6 November 1951, 17–18, 22. See also Cooper, *Decolonization and African Society*, chaps. 7 and 11.

[61] René Barthes, statement to Conférence des Hauts-Commissaires et Gouverneurs de la FOM, 22 February 1947,19PA 3/34, AOM.

[62] Minister to High Commissioners of Territoires d'Outre-Mer, circular 17 July 1951, 17G 641, AS. On "Africanisation des cadres," see Michelle Pinto, "Employment, Education, and the Reconfiguration of Empire: Africanization in Postwar French Africa" (PhD diss., New York University, 2013).

order.[63] The factionalization of French politics gave African deputies and their French leftist allies a chance to pick up votes on questions of social policy from MRP deputies who believed in such reforms, votes that were not available on issues of electoral reform in the early 1950s. One could make similar arguments about different domains of social policy—education, health, and veterans' benefits. The equivalence of citizens did not always carry the day, but in the mid-1950s it was an argument that had to be confronted.[64] The French government had staked its legitimacy on presiding over an empire of citizens, and when the citizens were as well organized as the West African labor movement, the logic of their claims and the potential for trouble if they were not met were hard to resist.

Toward a More Perfect Union?

The deputies and other political leaders from French West Africa were trying to put together diverse constituencies at a time when voter rolls were taking in an expanding portion of a diverse citizenry. They were well aware that the institutional structure in which they operated was a work in progress, and in basic ways unsatisfactory. Across Africa, there was a wide variety of forms of collective thought and action, to which the RDA and other parties were sometimes able to connect, sometimes not.[65] There was also in the early 1950s the beginnings of activism among youth groups, especially students. Meanwhile, the very nature of the French Union was in question, and African political elites were trying to figure out how—or even if—they could reorganize it.

A consistent vision of how France could be remade came from Senghor in the decade that followed 1946. On the occasion of a visit of French President Vincent Auriol to Senegal in April 1947, Senghor

[63] Officials thought that the labor code of 1952, like the 1946 citizenship provisions, made France look good in international circles. Still, the prevalence of poverty in much of French Africa left France vulnerable to accusations of failure to live up to promises of social and economic rights. See papers in the file K.Afrique, 1944–1952, Généralités/31, ADLC; Speeches of Minister, 26 February 1949, AP 219/1, AOM, and Cooper, *Decolonization and African Society*, chap. 9.

[64] Note the mitigated outcome—better than after World War I but well short of equality—in debates over veterans' pensions. Gregory Mann, *Native Sons: West African Veterans and France in the Twentieth Century* (Durham, N.C.: Duke University Press, 2006). On divergent views of educational reform, see Harry Gamble, "La crise de l'enseignement en Afrique occidentale française (1944–1950)," *Histoire de l'Education* 128 (2010): 129–62.

[65] For a recent study that links the formation of a particular rural Islamic community with party politics in the Côte d'Ivoire, see Sean Hanretta, *Islam and Social Change in French West Africa: History of an Emancipatory Community* (Cambridge: Cambridge University Press, 2009).

published an article in *Réveil* that took the Constitution as a point of departure. Even the second, less favorable version of the constitution did not freeze the situation of the overseas territories. By law rather than a constitutional revision, the territories could evolve toward either the status of a department or that of an Associated State. The electoral laws and decrees that followed the Constitution had given rise in Africa to "indignant stupefaction" for the "racial discrimination" that they enshrined. The goal was clear: these laws had to be revised: "We, Negro-Africans, will agree to remain in the French Union only on this condition. We do not want to be either dupes or accomplices."

Not just institutional structures, but society had to be reformed:

> We want less to rid ourselves of the tutelage of the metropole than of the tyranny of international capitalism. We think that an autonomy that simply brings us back to the feudal regime of castes would not solve the problem. We are not rebels, but revolutionaries. We want to construct a better world, better than the colonial world of yesterday, better as well than our world before the European conquest. We will build it taking inspiration from European socialism and the old African collectivism. We will thus reconcile modern technique and African humanism. For it is a question of building a new world where, in an organized society, men will be equal and fraternal "without distinction of race or religion."[66]

Here we have Senghor's way of articulating ideas: writing in a public forum, at a well-chosen moment, in a vein that combined immediate political issues and a philosophical position. Senghor's claims to building a new world and escaping international capitalism were complemented by his evocation of African humanism and French fraternalism. He was seeking not to re-create the African world before the French conquest, but to provide a synthesis of civilizations. In the immediate present was a straightforward demand: to reform the institutions of the French Union in the spirit of the Constitution recently accepted by the French electorate.

Senghor's idea of humanity constituted of diverse civilizations was written into the name of the newspaper he founded in February 1948, *La Condition Humaine*. Its opening editorial called for "the liberation of Africa in the framework of the French Union." From the conciliation of civilizations, he came down to the organization of an inclusive polity in which Africans could both express their personality and remain part of a larger whole: "We say that assimilation is an illusion in a world where peoples have become conscious of their personality; and we affirm that independence is a dream in a world where the interde-

[66] Léopold Senghor, "Les Négro-Africains et l'Union française," *Réveil*, 24 April 1947.

pendence of peoples affirms itself so manifestly." He was seeking "a new economic and social order," and it was such a transformation that he termed "revolution." His movement would be socialist, but following Marx more in spirit than to the letter.[67]

Aware of talk of European integration taking place, he worried about a new "pacte colonial" that would allow Britain and France to cooperate to more fully exploit their empires. The European connection, however, if used to support social and economic betterment, could prove valuable to Africans: "That is what we call 'vertical solidarity.'"

I will return to the subject of Africans' fears and hopes for a European connection broader than that to France, but now I want to underscore the importance of Senghor's notion of vertical solidarity. He was frankly acknowledging the reality of inequality—especially social and economic inequality. The vertical relationship was still a relationship Africans had need for such a connection, but only when vertical solidarity was combined with a different sort of relationship. There was "another solidarity, more real because based on ethnology and geography, that is 'horizontal solidarity' that ties together people of the same continent or the same condition." Horizontal solidarity needed to be organized "on the basis of equality among all peoples, whatever their race or religion. For that we need courage and imagination."[68] Behind this choice of words was a focus on the need for political action: vertical solidarity without the horizontal would be the old colonialism reincarnated, but horizontal solidarity without the vertical would be unity in poverty, a failure to understand the nature of interdependence in the world as it was.

It was in 1948 that Senghor broke with his mentor Lamine Guèye. He was making a personal as well as a political break against the "dictatorship of Lamine" that had dominated Senegal. It was also a reaction against the way in which the Senegalese Socialist Party had become subordinated in its vertical relation to the French party. The party had failed to work against the double college, obtain equal pensions for veterans, or bring about democracy in Algeria. Senghor insisted "we remain faithful to the socialist ideal," but he was founding a new party, the Bloc Démocratique Sénégalais (BDS).[69]

Unspoken was the change of political circumstance that was at least as much to Lamine Guèye's credit as to Senghor's, the expansion of the Senegalese electorate following the constitutional reforms of 1946. Lamine Guèye's base in the Quatre Communes was increasingly

[67] *La Condition Humaine*, 11 February 1948.
[68] *La Condition Humaine*, 11 July 1948.
[69] *La Condition Humaine*, 5, 19 October 1948. On party politics, see Morgenthau, *Political Parties*, de Benoist, *L'Afrique occidentale française*, and Christian Roche, *Le Sénégal à la conquête de son indépendance 1939–1960* (Paris: Karthala, 2001).

overshadowed by the new voters from the inland towns and countryside. Senghor had grasped the opportunity, and—even though he was a Catholic—he was working through the leaders of the Islamic brotherhoods—known as marabouts—who had great influence in rural Senegal. He was engaged in a kind of vertical politics he did not talk about—through power brokers with influence over rural voters, even as he set about cultivating other leaders, such as Ibrahima Sarr, hero of the railway strike of 1947–48.[70] The Lamine Guèye law was ultimately Lamine Guèye's undoing, as it provided new citizens, new voters, and a new political dynamic that Senghor grasped more quickly.

Senghor saw social rights—not just political ones—flowing from the French Constitution, and he specified what this meant: full access for overseas citizens to civil service jobs, equal wages, equal pensions, and other benefits, administration of enterprises by both metropolitan and indigenous people. None of this, he argued, had been realized, and French funding for development programs, while welcome, was "ridiculously low." The struggle both echoed a European history—seeking the kind of "social conquest wrested in the metropole from the French bourgeoisie"—and had a specifically African element—a struggle against "indigenous feudalities" as well as colonial exploitation.[71]

In the light of such aspirations, Senghor wrote on behalf of the BDS, "indigenous nationalism" was "like an old hunting rifle." The colonies were "poorly equipped" even in agriculture, while technology in the metropole was "more and more advanced." These considerations led him to his central theme: "Yes, it is good that the Constitution of the French Union allows us to help ourselves with the experience and resources of France, to develop at the same time, with our economic potential, our own Negro-African personality." But that personality was not closed in on itself. "We are no more racist than regionalist or nationalist. The BDS in defending the Senegalese and African man defends the man of the French Union and the universal man. The 'Human Condition' remains our definitive objective."[72]

He was equally emphatic about what the movement was not: "The Bloc Démocratique Sénégalais, I affirm once again, is not afflicted with Senegality." He reminded his readers that he had "many times

[70] See the excellent biography of Senghor, Janet Vaillant, *Black, French, and African: A life of Léopold Sédar Senghor* (Cambridge, Mass.: Harvard University Press, 1990).

[71] *La Condition Humaine*, 11 July 1948.

[72] Senghor, "Rapport sur la méthode du Parti," to Congress of BDS, 15–17 April 1949, *La Condition Humaine*, 26 April 1949. Modibo Keita was even more categoric in rejecting the idea that Africa "must evolve on her own." He considered this idea "an imbecilic sectarianism having as a consequence the birth of a retrograde nationalism." Report to 1947 congress of US-RDA, quoted in Konaré, "Le RDA, l'Union soudanaise," 177.

publicly condemned nationalism as an infantile illness that we have to cure."[73]

These principles were also enunciated by the grouping that Senghor helped to organize, beginning in 1948, inside the Assemblée Nationale, the Indépendants d'Outre-Mer (IOM). The IOM's policy declaration of 1948—repeated almost verbatim in 1951—rejected the goal of national independence: "The modern world has no room for small economic entities whose independence will be a myth if they are not adequately equipped and if they do not participate in a broader 'UNION.'" For the IOM, the "temptation of narrow nationalisms represents a grave danger." Its call, repeated in 1953, was for an "economic and social democracy" to be built on the "great emancipatory laws of 1946 crowned by the Constitution." The 1953 manifesto picked up Senghor's call for "vertical solidarity" between France and Africa as well as common action among African territories. As in 1951, it called for the revision of the Constitution in the direction of "an active federalism." The group sought "a double decentralization to the detriment of the central government and the governments general for the benefit of each territory, and then a deconcentration of powers that translates into a democratic extension of the prerogatives of the territorial assemblies."[74]

For Senghor, the issue was reforming the entire French Union. Throughout 1953 and 1954, Senghor's BDS kept calling for constitutional revision and "a great French federation."[75] But Senghor had to work with a constitution that gestured to federalism and concentrated power in the Assemblée Nationale, precisely the body that was unable to come to grips with electoral reform, Algeria, and other divisive issues. In the end, African deputies would find that their way out of the impasse depended on separating their future from Algeria, a bifurcating of pathways in the remaking of the French Empire, toward war in Algeria and a renegotiated relationship between France and sub-Saharan Africa.

But that is to get ahead of the story. If one looks at party manifestos, articles in African newspapers in the period 1948 to 1956, and legislative interventions by African deputies and councillors, one keeps coming back to claims framed by the Constitution of 1946 and directed toward remedying its inconsistencies, discriminatory structures—and most important—the lingering sense of humiliation that former colonial subjects perceived. Some Africans were still unsure that the con-

[73] *La Condition Humaine*, 29 November 1951.

[74] "Déclaration du groupe interparlementaire des Indépendants d'Outre-Mer (24 Décembre 1948)," and "Situation des Indépendants d'Outre-mer en 1950," copies in AP 2257/3, AOM; Statement of political parties, in Assemblée Nationale, *Débats*, 6 July 1951, 5909; *La Condition Humaine*, 25 February 1953.

[75] *La Condition Humaine*, 25 February, 2 April 1953, 21 December 1954.

cept of citizenship could work for them, as one can see in the eloquent intervention in July 1950 of Ya Doumbia, representative of the Sudan in the Assemblée de l'Union française (and like Modibo Keita a graduate of the École William Ponty). For him, "the question was whether the citizenship that has been conceded was viable and did not create a juridical impasse, for it seems a priori impossible to have the same rights and duties as metropolitan nationals and in addition retain a personal status that in many ways is opposed to French citizenship as an integral whole." In the absence of laws to make clear what personal status signified, there was a risk that citizenship would be limited to equal rights before the penal law and to political rights (themselves compromised by the electoral laws). There were still gaps between the treatment of soldiers and ex-soldiers of the two statuses—"citizens of the same country"—and "racial discrimination that is becoming more and more intolerable" in the pay and benefits of civil servants, depending whether they were of African or European origin or Africans "assimilated" to a "European" status. In some territories, Africans faced discrimination in access to restaurants and cinemas owned by Europeans. "What is the value of this citizenship?" Ya Doumbia asked.

And if one looked toward "citizenship extended to citizenship of the French Union" the juridical situation was confusing and contradicted the internal law of certain Associated States. There were, he argued, four types of citizens: of "metropolitan status," of the Quatre Communes of Senegal, of Associated States, and of former subjects or protected persons. All but the first were "citizens of the second zone," their secondary status marked by the double college. The inadequacy of "customary tribunals" weakened the effects of their right to keep their personal status under customary law. There was no clarity in regard to "indigenous property rights." And "in regard to the economic regime, political and social equality remain an empty word in the overseas territories."[76] But resolving the problem, Ya Doumbia and some of his colleagues insisted, was a matter of political will, not an inherent contradiction in the Constitution's conception of citizenship: "It is evident that one can be a citizen, a perfect citizen, under the same fiscal, military, electoral rules as other citizens without, nevertheless, being obliged to adopt the same modes of family life or inheritance regime as one's fellow citizens."[77]

[76] Ya Doumbia was presenting to the Assembly a report of the report of the Commission de la Politique Générale. AUF, *Débats*, 25 July 1950, 1122–25. It took the Ministry nearly four years to respond, in an internal memo, to Ya Doumbia's points. It claimed progress on most fronts and that further changes were under consideration. Section d'Études, Note pour M. le Directeur du Cabinet du Secrétaire d'État à la FOM, 2 March 1954, AP 217/1, AOM.

[77] Avis of Commission de la Législation, de la Justice et de la Fonction Publique, des Affaires Administratives et Domaniales, on proposition of Darlan, Ya Doumbia, and

Ya Doumbia sat in a body that could contribute to the discourse on overseas governance, but not to governance itself, since it was a consultative unit only.[78] Giving the Assemblée de l'Union française real power in affairs concerning the Union as a whole—that is, making it into something more like a federal legislature—was therefore one point in the reformist agenda.[79] It ran head-on into the conception of a unitary French state held by many. But it was not a neat left-right issue, since de Gaulle, among others, remained a consistent advocate of some kind of federalism, albeit a federalism with French teeth, while many on the left feared that conservative elements in overseas territories as well as the metropole would undercut a reformist agenda.

The situation offered a potential dynamic. Most French leaders wanted to integrate Africa more closely into France to avoid the dangers of the French Union flying apart. Most African leaders wanted more equality. In a general debate on overseas policy, a social Catholic, MRP-member, Louis-Paul Aujoulat could speak of the need for a "reinforcement of integration" and "reaffirmation of French sovereignty," and still insist that territories should have more power "to administer themselves all the while remaining fully within the Republic." The solution, Senghor argued, was not just giving Africans more voice, but democratizing executive authority. However, he noted, there was not one Minister from overseas territories in the government. The centralizing hand on the reigns of power was responsible for the continued existence of the "pacte colonial" and the extremes of economic inequality.[80] The Minister of Overseas France at the time, Louis Jacquinot, replied to these arguments by emphasizing the progress made in "our large community," especially the extension of citizenship, which "the people . . . knew how to use wisely." He promised more power to the local assemblies, so that "the territories can and must develop their own personality." He raised the "possibility to re-

---

others to ask government to propose laws "specifying the conditions under which the *ressortissants* of the overseas territories exercise their rights as citizens." AUF, *Documents*, No. 184, session of 4 July 1950, 219.

[78] Other African legislators complained that even as a French parliamentarians, they faced racial insults in their home territories: "returning home, any 'petit blanc,' as we call them, drags us in the mud," said a councillor from Cameroon. AUF, Report by Commission de la Législation, No. 104, 6 April 1949, copy in 950236/2, CAC, citing the words of M. Okala. Assembly members advocated legislation to ban racial discrimination in such instances, but all they got was a questionable assertion that discrimination was not tolerated any longer. See Minister (Coste-Floret) to High Commissioners and Governors, circular, 15 December 1947, 17G 152, AS.

[79] The President of the Assembly, Daniel Boisdon, claimed it was "an Assembly of Civilizations." What an assembly of civilizations could actually do was not so clear. "Nous sommes une Assemblée de civilisations," *Marchés Coloniaux* 3, 111 (27 December 1947), 1845–48.

[80] Senghor and Aujoulat, Assemblée Nationale, *Débats*, 6 April 1954, 1913, 1925–26.

form Title VIII of the Constitution," claiming this was the first time a Minister had suggested such a possibility.[81]

It did not happen. There were some reformist successes: steps toward equalizing the rates of pay and benefits of civil servants in 1950, the labor code of 1952, more Africans voting in elections.[82] But attempts to advance universal suffrage and end the double college ran into a stone wall, and more fundamental revision of the Constitution was caught in the instability of governments in the Fourth Republic. And there was also an element of distrust that led even African deputies to wonder if universal suffrage might be used against them. Houphouët-Boigny—even before the conflict in the Côte d'Ivoire became acute—worried about the "meddling of the local administration in elections": chiefs, themselves not chosen by the local inhabitants, might intervene, so that enrolling more rural voters might produce an electorate more under the thumb of the administration. He did not think universal suffrage would be possible until the état-civil was fully extended, and meanwhile he preferred extending "conditions of capacity"—presumably focusing on people whose ability to register and vote freely was less subject to manipulation. In 1951, it was Senghor who was arguing that universal suffrage, for practical reasons, took time to install, and he too invoked the inadequacy of the état-civil and the impossibility of putting it into place before the next electoral cycle.[83] But as we have already seen, the process of generalizing the état-civil was itself hung up, and indeed universal suffrage would be implemented before an état-civil had been put in place.

What went on beyond AOF was on people's minds. In 1951, Kwame Nkrumah's Convention People's Party won legislative elections in the Gold Coast, and Nkrumah emerged from detention to become Leader of Government Business, a kind of apprentice prime minister. He would lead his country to independence in 1957. In 1954, the French government—under pressure from the UN Trusteeship Council as well as from local politicians—reformed the government of Togo in a way that many Africans desired. A Conseil de gouvernement (Cabinet), with half of its members coming from the Territorial Assembly, took charge of administering the country, with the Governor presiding over the council but with limited powers to act independently of it. Nicolas Grunitzky, deputy from Togo, pointed out

[81] Ibid., 9 April 1954, 2023, 2025.

[82] The party newspaper *La Condition Humaine* (2 May 1950, 15 March 1952) gave Senghor credit for some of the advances.

[83] Commission de la FOM, sessions of, 6, 11 April, 22 May 1951, C//15408, ANF. Lamine Guèye blamed his loss in the 1951 elections in part on irregularities in the hastily arranged process of registering new voters. Notes de M. Mecheri à l'attention de M. le Président, 2 July 1951, 4AG 518, ANF.

in Paris that the project for Togo's government had originally been presented in 1952. In the meantime, he noted, "the installation of the Nkrumah government has become for Africans, and especially for Togolese, a true pole of attraction."[84] And looming above the politicians who wanted to reform the French Union was the French defeat in Vietnam in 1954 and the situation in Algeria, where war began in earnest in that same year. Things were moving across the French Union, but would they move together or along separate paths?

Rethinking Sovereignty

To rewrite the Constitution meant to think about the Union as a whole. By focusing on this level, African leaders pushed the Ministry and leading French politicians to ask themselves whether they wished to think systematically about the questions left unanswered in the Assemblée Nationale Constituante in 1946 or else about the mix of reform and repression that would keep each component in the Union. It was not clear in the early 1950s that the French Union was viable at all.

The comprehensive approach was most clearly expressed by Senghor in an article in the journal *La Nef* in June 1955. He cited the contradiction in the Constitution between the preamble, which stressed equality, and the body, which conferred power on institutions dominated by the metropole. Subsequent governments had insisted on the unity and indivisibility of the Republic—a "sterile" formula, unsatisfactory to the people of Asia, Africa, or North Africa. With no progress toward federalism, it was necessary to think differently, and Senghor turned to the concept of confederation—an ensemble that would recognize the national personality, not just the autonomy of component parts. That Morocco and Tunisia seemed headed toward independence raised "the possibility for France to create, with other 'independent states' a confederation to which all would concede limitations of sovereignty." Senghor was putting other states of the former empire on a par with France and making the crucial point that all—Morocco, Tunisia, and a reformed France—could cede some of their sovereignty to the confederation.

Senghor spelled out institutional arrangements to make a confederal government work. The French Republic would become a federal republic within the confederation, and making it federal would entail increasing the representation of Algeria, the overseas territories, and the overseas departments in Parliament. Here he alluded to the noto-

---

[84]Assemblée Nationale, *Débats*, 3 November 1954, 4692, 4694. Senghor made a similar point about the importance of neighbors acceding to internal autonomy, and used this as an argument for reform of Title VIII. Ibid., 30 November 1954, 5618.

rious words of Herriot from 1946, insisting that overseas citizens did not want France to become the colony of its former colonies. They did not want France to lose its personality any more than they wanted to lose theirs: "African nationalism is willing to renounce the nation, but not the African *patrie*."

Senghor was distinguishing, as he had in his literary writing, between nation—a political creation—and patrie, the sentiment of belonging. His notion of the "petite patrie" had both African and French roots—his own Serer origins and resentment against the larger and more domineering Wolof of Senegal melded with the romance of the "terroir-province" in France.[85] It was the place of the nation in political institutions that had to be rethought. To do so meant rewriting the Constitution to transform the "the unitary Republic, centralized and centralizing into a federal Republic, on the model of Canada, Switzerland, or West Germany." Algeria and the overseas territories and departments would have internal autonomy within this federal republic: "The *nation* and sovereignty would be the French state," even if the "patrie" lay in more diverse sentiments. The federal government would be in charge of foreign affairs, defense, money, and economic coordination. Everything else would be the concern of local governments and their legislatures. And the individual territories would be free to federate among themselves within the Republic. The already diverse Republic could then join Morocco and other former Associated States as partners in a confederation.

He came back to a theme he had earlier articulated for his African audience: the choice between "total independence" and "assimilation" was a "false dilemma." Nationalism was in "complete contradiction" with technology and science. Different people lived with their "complementarity."[86]

---

[85] Etienne Smith, "'Senghor voulait qu'on soit tous des Senghor': Parcours nostalgiques d'une génération," *Vingtième Siècle. Revue d'Histoire* 118 (2013): 97–100.

[86] Léopold Senghor, "Pour une solution fédéraliste," *La Nef* Cahier 9 (June 1955), 148–61. This issue also included pieces on the future of the French Union by Gaston Monnerville, René de Lacharrière, J.-M. Domenach, Maurice Duverger, and François Mitterrand. Mitterrand must have angered Senghor by asserting, "African youth does not have morally, professionally, or civically perspectives that are large enough, varied enough, complete enough in the current limits of our system" to make nationalist aspirations possible to fulfill. But he also wrote, "It is in effect difficult to hold to the notion of a unitary Republic from Lille to Brazzaville and from Pointe-Noire to Fort-Lamy." So one had to "soften the unitary Republic" and federate associated states. "Paradoxes et promesses de l'Union française," *La Nef* Cahier 9 (June 1955): 223–31, 229, 230, 231 quoted. Duverger despaired of both the assimilation of the left and the paternalism of the right and concluded his essay by asking, "will the ruin of the Empire be completed before the generations can undertake its transformation into a Commonwealth?" "Une course contre la montre," *La Nef* Cahier 9 (June 1955): 212–22, 222 quoted.

In the midst of uncertainty, Senghor had sketched out a program for remaking state and nation in a multitiered structure. He was aware of the different ways in which liberty could be exercised, and he could at the same time celebrate the extension of citizenship to ex-slaves in the 1790s and criticize the Jacobin framework in which this move had been made. His own thinking about federation and confederation was evolving. In 1948, he had used the word "confederation" to emphasize a composite polity that recognized difference among its components, whereas "federation" presumed equivalence of the units being federated.[87] In 1953, he was not making much of this distinction, but rather trying to argue for a supple form of federation itself: "Within the French Union, organized in a flexible federation—or in confederation—would be, alongside the kingdoms or republics of Asia and Africa, a *federal French Republic*." The "flexible federation" or "confederation" would include this federal republic, plus the Associated States of Laos, Vietnam, Cambodia, Morocco, and Tunisia.[88] In 1955, he had become explicit. He was advocating a three-way structure, beginning with individual territories or states: the federation would embrace citizens of the Republic, in both Africa or Europe. The confederation would be multinational—Moroccans, Vietnamese, French, and so on. As we shall see, after 1956, his position would shift again: he would then advocate an *African* federation, which would take its place in a confederation alongside France and whatever other parts of the former French Empire chose (freely) to remain or join.

The pattern reflects an increasing assertiveness of a distinct African vocation within the French Union, but he was consistent in regarding the French Union as an ensemble of nonequivalent components, descended from empire's mode of governing different people differently. Senghor took such a complex entity as a historical fact. For him, the Union posed the immense danger of discrimination and exploitation and the immense possibility of interconnection, of mutual learning, and of social progress.

The most radical challenge to these reformist arguments came from student groups, particularly from Africans in Paris. They were not a large part of the overseas student population in Paris: of students from the French Union in French universities, only 251 came from AOF, 38 from AEF, compared to 1,123 from Algeria, 764 from Tunisia, 532

---

[87] *La Condition Humaine*, 5 October 1948. He was reacting in this instance to a publication of the Socialist Paul Alduy, "Confédération et Fédération."

[88] "Socialisme, Fédération, Religion," from Rapport sur la méthode to Ve congrès du BDS, 3–5 July 1953, reprinted in *Liberté II: Nation et voie africaine du socialisme* (Paris: Seuil, 1971), 105.

from Morocco, 890 from the states of Indochina, 707 from the Caribbean region, and a scattering from elsewhere.[89]

The Association des Étudiants du RDA had, according to police, close connections to the PCF and had opposed the RDA leadership's decision to end the parties' legislative alliance. By 1952, the monthly bulletin of the association, the *Voix de l'Afrique Noire*, published in Paris, was setting forth a clear call for "the liquidation of the entire colonial system of imperialism" and for "political, economic, social and cultural emancipation in view of national independence." The students, with a bit of sarcasm probably directed at Senghor, stressed the integrity of their own effort "that does not depend essentially on the claim-making eloquence of such and such a deputy in a European Chamber or Assembly." Their manifestos were anticapitalist as well as anticolonialist, emphasized the need to jar rural Africa out of its "ignorance," and called for an effort to forge among Africans "a modern mentality (the only guarantee of adaptation to current life) without being obliged to pass through foreign modes of expression, which would be illusory." But the students writing for the *Voix de l'Afrique Noire* did not forget who they were: "We do not have the right to forget that our particular task as students is to pursue our studies and bring them to a conclusion." They were concerned with scholarships as well as liberation, and both were on the agenda at meetings when students came from France to Senegal on vacation. The police were keeping a careful eye on all this activity, and duly noted the militancy of the group's main leaders, Cheikh Anta Diop and Amadou Mahtar M'Bow, who by 1958 would become important figures on the radical side of Senegalese politics. Police reports, however, do not suggest that the radical movement was yet extending much beyond the student milieu.[90]

If the student movement's most important linkage was to the PCF in France, Senghor and his colleagues were engaged in a dialogue with other parts of the French political spectrum. In books and journals, intellectuals were willing to ask fundamental questions about the nature of the French state in their uncertain times, reflections that both overlapped and differed from those coming out of Africa. A book published in 1950 by a high civil servant, jurist, and political journalist, Henri Culmann, brought out a postimperial perspective—

[89] AFP bulletin, 17 February 1953, citing the Bureau Universitaire de Statistiques, AP 2265, AOM.

[90] *La Voix de l'Afrique Noire, Bulletin Mensuel d l'Association des Étudiants RDA*, February 1952, copy in 21G 209, AS. For reports on meetings of the association and other police surveillance, see Chef de Sûreté, A. Laporte, "Étude sur les revendications et les activités politiques des étudiants Africains," 23 August 1951; Direction des Renseignements Généraux, Sûreté Nationale, Section "Union francaise," report on "Activités des étudiants africains en France," nd [1951]; Renseignements, 22 July 1952, 28 November 1952, 29 December 1953, 21G 209, AS.

thinking through empire to something new.[91] Culmann wrote, "The French Union was not born in 1946 by a promulgation but in 1636, by the arrival of the first Frenchman in the first colony and his encounter with the first inhabitant."[92] The question for him was how a highly unequal structure created by empire could evolve. Societies within the Union should have their own laws and legislatures "on an equal footing." His precedent for such legal pluralism was the Ottoman Empire: "This organization functioned for 388 years in the Turkish empire, which extended from Algeria to Tibet, through the regime of capitulations."[93] But the present Union had a contradiction at its core: all people within it were in theory equal, but only as individuals, while the overseas territories, not being self-governing, had a status that had only slightly changed from that of colony. But what sort of entity was the French Union? "It is this ensemble—this collective unity one might say—that has the quality of a state. Metropolitan France is not by itself a state."[94]

Not everyone agreed that the French Union was a state, and the French Republic was not.[95] But for Culmann the metropole was not a discrete state, but part of something bigger and more diverse—a consequence of the "colonial fact." In a world that now demanded "the universal equality of men in rights and freedom" such a nested polity had to be transformed by dividing power among its different levels.[96]

Socialist politician Paul Alduy also set out his thinking about sovereignty and the state in a book published in 1948. He saw the French Union as "a sort of super-state harmonizing the metropole-colony relationship, transposing overseas these principles of liberty and equality that the French seem hitherto to have jealously guarded for themselves alone. . . . If the French want to base a long-term politics on the free consent of peoples, they do not have a choice of the means. There is only one of them: efface oneself before the sovereignty of

[91] Henri Culmann, *L'Union française* (Paris: Presses Universitaires de France, 1950). See also Boisdon, *Institutions de l'Union française*; René Jacqmin, *États-Unis de France: Ce que doit être l'Union française* (Paris: Larose, 1953); Paul Alduy, *L'Union française: Mission de la France* (Paris: Fosquelle Editeurs, 1948); A. Fauchon-Villeplée, *Constitution et Union française* (Paris: Berger-Levrault, 1953).

[92] Culmann, *L'Union française*, 133.

[93] For an interempire perspective, see Jane Burbank and Frederick Cooper, *Empires in World History: Power and the Politics of Difference* (Princeton: Princeton University Press, 2010).

[94] Culmann, *L'Union française*, 17, 31, 34, 72–73, 131.

[95] The jurist Borella wrote in 1958, "The French Union is not a state, but an international community composed of entities recognized by international law." Borella, *Évolution politique*, 54.

[96] Culmann, *L'Union française*, 125–26, 135.

the Union recognized as superior to that of France."[97] Culmann and Alduy, by locating state and sovereignty above the French Republic, were reversing the current constitution's vesting ultimate sovereignty in a *national* assembly. Much as both of them differed from Senghor, they were all trying to develop a political form that did not fit into either the framework of empire or that of equivalent states. Such views were now thinkable among respectable members of the French political establishment.

In 1953 and 1954, as things were going from bad to worse in Vietnam, Algeria, and Morocco, the journal *Politique Étrangère* published a series of articles on the dangers and possibilities facing the French Union. Opinions ranged from the complacent defense of French accomplishments overseas by General Georges Catroux to a biting indictment of French failures to live up to promises by Léopold Senghor. But when it came to the future, both ends of the spectrum were calling for a similar solution: "that the French Republic and the Associated States should remain in a federation run by a true federal system and that the autonomy conceded within the French Republic should become effective" (Catroux); "the true solution to the problem is a Federation" (Senghor). Catroux's federation would be headed by a France that was "disinterested" and a "tutelary guide," but it would have to give up its pretensions to be a unitary state. Senghor denounced the very idea of "la République une et indivisible": it would not only be "the death of autochthonous civilizations" but of France itself, for it would imply that "three hundred Arab-Berber and Black deputies" would come to Paris—the Herriot problem once again. The solution was his combination of federal and confederal structures, but above all a step-by-step process of "raising the former colonies to the level of the metropole, on the basis of equality of rights and duties, which is the principle of the Federation."[98]

But could the high officials of the government entertain such a thorough rethinking of state and sovereignty? The Minister of Overseas France, Louis Jacquinot, on a visit to West Africa in March 1954, admitted that constitutional reform was necessary. Even the double college had to be considered anew, although he made no promises to get

[97] Alduy did not worry that by diluting its formal power France would in practice give up too much, for it would retain "the preponderant role justly conferred on it by her economic and military power, the size of her population, the quality of her elites." Alduy, *L'Union française*, 23, 32, 83, 86–90.

[98] Georges Catroux, "L'Union française, son concept, son état, ses perspectives," *Politique Étrangère* 18, 4 (1953): 233–66, 262, 264 quoted; Léopold Sédar Senghor, "L'avenir de la France dans l'Outre-Mer," *Politique Étrangère* 19, 4 (1954): 419–26, 421, 423 quoted. In this series, see also XXX [Anonymous], "Union française et institutions européennes," *Politique Étrangère* 18, 4 (1953): 267–76, and P.-O. Lapie, "Conception unitaire ou conception pluraliste de la Communauté française," *Politique Étrangère* 19 (1954): 437–44.

rid of it. He understood that the Union would have to evolve as some kind of complex structure, with powers located in different places: "Our century has largely gone beyond the stage of narrow nationalisms. The future of the world belongs to large economic and political ensembles." African voices would have to be heard, and this would mean that "particular issues" would be decided by "different collectivities," including communal, territorial, and federal assemblies. But about sovereignty, he brooked no ambivalence: the Assemblée Nationale "should naturally conserve its entire sovereignty." On matters that applied to all citizens, including public liberties, criminal penalties, military recruitment, and "political organization," its power would remain intact. Perhaps local assemblies could make decisions in more domains, but subject to review in Paris.[99]

Within the Ministry, officials were questioning the centralization of administrative authority more than sovereignty. Ministry inspectors, evaluating how policies were being implemented, drew attention to the need for what as early as 1948 was called "bureaucratic decongestion." Citizenship had widened the domain in which Paris thought it should act and contributed to administrative blockages. The lack of authority of territorial legislatures made things worse. Personnel all over AOF now had to be administered through the same mechanisms under the same rules.[100]

The Ministry, as of 1953, was of two minds about centralization. The federations of AOF and AEF, with their ability to coordinate policy over multiple territories under the eyes of a powerful High Commissioner, had been in place since 1895 and had became even more relevant as a unit of planning in postwar circumstances. They combined diverse resources and the possibility of economies of scale, and they were consistent with an alleged "historical evolution tends toward the creation of large political units." Decentralization might seem to bring government closer to the people, but a strategy of focusing on "small territories," some of them very poor in comparison to others, was risky. Territorial autonomy could lead to a "centrifugal tendency of nationalism" or perhaps to "regionalism" (in one document in the archives, "nationalism" is crossed out and "regionalism" substituted). In the

<hr>

[99] Jacquinot, speech to Grand Conseil de l'AOF, 2 March 1954, text in 17G 518, AS.
[100] "Rapport sur la Décentralisation en AOF," by P. Chavuet, Inspecteur Général des Affaires Administratives, 29 May 1948, 18G 281, AS; Inspecteur Général de la FOM, Chef de la Mission d'Inspection en AOF, to High Commissioner, 14 August 1954, along with enclosed reports, 18G 238, AS; Robert Delavignette, Note for the Minister, 25 November 1950, AP 492, AOM. In 1950, the Minister noted the calls for decentralization and asked the High Commissioners for their views, but pointed out that the principle of "Governments General is not and should not be put in question." Six years later they were in question. Minister to High Commissioners, AOF and AEF, 7 June 1950, AP 218/1, AOM.

opposite argument, AOF and AEF were portrayed as "a screen" between Paris and the territories that might slow communication, raise expenses, and make the work of a governor more difficult.[101]

But if the Ministry was thinking inconsistently about administrative decentralization, African leaders were campaigning for *political* decentralization—for real power to be located in African legislatures. Senghor had called in 1951 for "a double decentralization to the detriment of the central government and the governments general for the profit of each territory, followed by a deconcentration of power that takes the form of a democratic extension of the prerogatives of the territorial assembles."[102] Senghor was ahead of French officialdom in seeing decentralization as a fundamentally political problem, but he was getting ahead of himself in not focusing on the implications that relocating power to territories would have on his hopes for federal and confederal structures—an issue that would come to haunt him after 1956. We will take up these issues in the next chapter.

Meanwhile, African deputies and some of their allies—still trying to improve the political structures in which they operated—submitted to the Assemblée Nationale in April 1955 a proposed resolution calling for revision of Title VIII of the Constitution that would ensure territories were "integrated—in stages—*into* a federal French Republic." The deputies were quite sure what they did not want: "It would be folly for poor territories of 500,000 to three million inhabitants to wish to constitute themselves in so-called independent nations." Put together, the different parts of the Union would create "a confederation of Associated States, based on principles of equality and non-discrimination." The revised constitution would specify general principles, and organic laws would fill in the details. Such an entity would take fifteen years to create. The Assembly agreed that Title VIII needed to be "revised," but the discussion did not make clear how.[103]

Officials in the Ministry knew that Title VIII was flawed. But officials also knew that the process of constitutional revision was long, and they could not agree whether to devolve more power to territorial institutions or maintain a centralized planning process and authority to bring about reforms. They almost instinctively argued that the power of Governors and High Commissioners had to be preserved. And they were well aware of the pressure from Africans to cede ground

[101] Ministère de la FOM, Section d'Études, "Note sur la décentralisation," 2 December 1953, AP 492, AOM. This report even raised the possibility of breaking up AOF into two federations, Dahomey-Niger-Togo vs. the more western territories, each seen to be a more coherent geographic unit.

[102] Assemblée Nationale, *Débats*, 24 July 1951, 6044.

[103] *La Condition Humaine*, 22 April 1955; Assemblée Nationale, *Débats*, 24 May 1955, 2943–45, 2962.

to the territorial assemblies.[104] With the situation in the Associated States and Algeria falling apart around them, they were not sure that any constitutional reform could apply to the French Union as a whole.

"Eurafrique"

There was another perspective from which sovereignty and authority were being rethought in the early 1950s: Europe. Already in 1949, African leaders were becoming aware that their French compatriots were talking with other European leaders about some sort of framework for common institutions. There was a long way to go before arriving at the confederal structure and shared sovereign functions of the European Union today, but the possibility was on the table early on. The first concrete step was the Coal and Steel Community, agreed to in 1951, followed by the European Economic Community in 1957. But even before 1950, the possibility of European political cooperation—perhaps based on a confederal structure with a European parliament of some sort—was being discussed in French political circles. In 1949, Senghor felt he had to remind the Assemblée Nationale that, as France considered its position in Europe, "in terms of the Constitution, the French Republic is not just composed of the metropole, but also of overseas departments and territories." France was not, in short, a European country. On this point, government officials agreed: "France is not a European power. It is a world power."[105]

In 1950, Senghor sent to the Minister of Overseas France a resolution of the IOM, then representing forty of the sixty-seven overseas deputies in the Assembly, expressing their concern that negotiations over Europe were going on over their heads and that French African territories risked becoming "an international colony." Instead, they insisted "that Eurafrica, notably, which we believe to be necessary and possible, should be conceived of only as a form of economic association, freely conceived on the basis of equality, where the present and future interests of Africa will be protected under the same conditions as those of Europe." Africans did not want their continent to become a "reservoir of primary material and an outlet for [Europe's] excessive production." Nor did they want to open it up to extensive European immigration. The Minister replied by claiming to share the IOM's preoccupations. He told them that the presence of Africans in Parliament

[104] Unsigned, undated paper reporting on meeting of Minister (Teitgen) and cabinet, 4 May 1955, AP 492, AOM.

[105] Senghor, Intervention in Assemblée Nationale, 18 September 1949, reprinted in *Liberté II*, 60; Directeur Général des Affaires Politiques, "Note sur la position des territoires d'outre-mer dans la question de l'intégration européenne," 14 October 1952, K.Afrique 1944–1952/Généralités/L'Europe et l'Afrique, ADLC.

and in local assemblies ensured that African interests would be represented. He thought access to a larger European market would benefit Africa and European immigration would be restrained. He anointed himself "your interpreter in respect of the Government to defend African interests."[106]

In August 1950, not long after the above resolution was sent to the Ministry, Senghor joined one of the bodies discussing how to put Europe together, the Assemblée Consultative Européenne (in Strasbourg) and, along with a British and another African colleague, submitted a resolution calling for "a constituent assembly for Africa and for the establishment of the United States of Africa." They proposed a European and African commission that would prepare for elections in each colonial assembly of representatives to a "Pan-African assembly" to study such possibilities. Senghor soon backed off the proposal, saying that he wanted these ideas discussed, not that he believed in them. What he wanted to get on the table was his conception of Eurafrica, growing out of his vision of horizontal and vertical solidarities:

> The only efficacious solution thus lies in federation. . . . In my opinion this federation must be made along two axes of solidarity. On the one hand, vertical solidarity between the overseas peoples and those of Europe on the model of the French Union. On the other hand, horizontal solidarity among the peoples of the same continent. . . . This is the only chance for Europe and Africa to save themselves, for these complementary continents, united by the same destiny, by history and geography. . . . Neither nationalist nor racist, I continue with men of good will the fight for Eurafrica. It is self-evident that the latter cannot be that of Hitler, but a federal, democratic Africa, in dignity and honor, that is in equality, the condition of fraternity.[107]

As Senghor well knew, Eurafrica was a concept with a past. It had been invoked in the 1930s by French ideologues eager to gloss the complementary destinies of Europe and Africa in a particular way: a combination of African resources in raw materials and raw labor and European resources in technology, manufacturing, and governance. The idea appealed to Vichy, and to Nazis as well: a Eurafrica of combined and uneven development. For some defenders of the French presence in North Africa after the war, Eurafrica was an appealing notion, for Algeria, Morocco, and Algeria could be the linchpin of a vast regional economic system, and perhaps the benefits accruing to

---

[106] "Résolution du Groupe Interparlementaire des Indépendants d'Outre-mer à propos des décisions de la conférence de Londres," enclosed Senghor to Minister, 16 May 1950, and Minister (Jean Letourneau) to Senghor, 9 June 1950, AP 219/3, AOM.
[107] *Le Monde*, 15, 26 August 1950.

its inhabitants would give a bit of legitimacy to a continued French presence.[108]

Senghor was turning the idea around: Europe's claim to Africa was Africa's claim on Europe. The issue was practical, but also civilizational, the complementarity between European and African modes of being, the former rationalist, the latter intuitive. He saw Eurafrica in such terms—as long as colonialism was thoroughly repudiated.[109] For Africans, the difficulty of integrating France's African territories into a European community was also the interest in doing so: the huge gap between the standard of living on opposite sides of the Mediterranean and the hope of allocating resources to bring about greater equality and more balanced forms of economic interaction.[110]

The call for a United States of Africa was a false alarm perhaps, but the resolution submitted to the Assemblée Consultative Européenne frightened the Overseas Ministry. "The idea of a United States of Africa is dangerous," contended a study group in the Ministry. "It would lead to the dislocation of the French Republic whose overseas territories would separate in order to become, from then on, a part of an African confederation." But if France wanted to keep pan-African unity out of discussions of pan-European unity, it had to give its Africans a place in those discussions. Overseas territories could participate in "a Eurafrican community," the study group insisted, only "by the intermediation of the French Republic." Still, Africans had to be consulted on such a process and they "would without doubt react very violently" if such a community were constructed over their heads.[111]

Everyone concerned was on uncertain terrain. Indeed, the idea of Europe—let alone Eurafrica—generated confusion as well as passion. Some sort of economic and political community appeared to many in the late 1940s to be a way of ensuring that the history of two world wars would not repeat itself; economic cooperation promised bigger markets, more secure supplies of raw materials, and an alternative to economic nationalism. But many French leaders worried about giving up too much sovereignty and especially that Germany might play too

[108] Charles-Robert Ageron, "L'idée d'Eurafrique et le débat franco-allemand de l'entre-deux-guerres," *Revue d'histoire moderne et contemporaine* 23 (1975): 446–75; Papa Dramé and Samir Saul, "Le projet d'Eurafrique en France (1946–1960): quête de puissance ou atavisme colonial?" *Guerres mondiales et conflits contemporains* 216 (2004): 95–114.

[109] Senghor made the connection between civilization complementarity and Eurafrica in "L'Afrique et l'Europe: Deux mondes complémentaires," *Marchés Coloniaux*, 14 May 1955, reprinted in *Liberté II*, 148–57.

[110] Such an argument for historical interdependence and the need for future development was the gist of a speech given by the Senator from Senegal Ousmane Soce Diop to the assembly in Strasbourg, a copy of which he sent to the Minister of Foreign Affairs, 22 August 1950, K.Afrique 1944–1952/Généralités/subdossier L'Europe et l'Afrique, ADLC.

[111] Affaires Politiques, Section d'Études, Note, 26 March 1952, AP 219/3, AOM.

big a role. Opinions on Europe did not divide neatly along left-right lines.[112]

Many advocates of European cooperation did not want to be seen as jettisoning Africa in favor of Europe; they argued for integrating the two. Some saw Eurafrica as a way of extending social democracy over much of the world; others were more interested in expanding Europe's access to Africa's raw materials.[113] Some saw a federal Eurafrica as an alternative to the Soviet and American blocs. But there were doubts about how much of the costs of developing and defending Africa France's European partners would be willing to undertake, how willing they would be to listen to Africans' opinions, and how much they expected to get from an enlarged economic community. Some French leaders embraced Europe because they thought that the burdens of empire could be shared, while others feared that France's European partners could benefit from Africa's markets and leave France with the costs.[114] Some thought that integrating Africa into Europe would give Africans incentives to cooperate and save France from losing its influence overseas; others feared that integrating Africa into Europe would allow African politicians to act in cooperation with European politicians whose interests diverged from those of the metropole. There was uncertainty in different parts of the political spectrum over whether European integration would upset the cohesion of the French Union or whether including the overseas territories would undermine the cohesion of Europe. The upshot in the early 1950s was that France proved cautious about European integration even as it was debating how to reconfigure its empire. A negotiated European defense pact was refused ratification in the Assemblée Nationale; eco-

[112]The divisions—and shifting alliances—are too complex to be analyzed here. See Yves Montarsolo, *L'Eurafrique, contrepoint de l'idée de l'Europe: Le cas français de la fin de la deuxième guerre mondiale aux négociations des Traités de Rome* (Aix-en-Provence: Publications de l'Université de Provence, 2010), and Marie-Thérèse Bitsch and Gérard Bossuat, eds., *L'Europe unie et l'Afrique: de l'idée d'Eurafrique à la convention de Lomé I* (Brussels: Bruylant, 2005). Some advocates of European integration believed they could get support in France only if they ensured that the overseas territories would have a place within it. Anne-Laure Ollivier, "Entre Europe et Afrique: Gaston Defferre et les débuts de la construction européenne," *Terrains et Travaux* 8 (2005):14–33, esp. 20. Business interests gave Eurafrica mitigated support, seeing possibilities for profit but fearing loss of control. Catherine Hodeir, *Stratégies d'Empire: Le grand patronat colonial face à la décolonisation* (Paris: Belin, 2003), 273, 278.

[113]Jean-Marie Palayret, "Les mouvements proeuropéens et la question de l'Eurafrique, du Congrès de La Haye à la Convention de Yaoundé (1948–1963)," in Bitsch and Bossuat, *L'Europe unie et l'Afrique*, 185–229, esp. 193–200, 205.

[114]The economist Jacques Lecaillon emphasized that France lacked the means to respond to the "growing demands" of the overseas territories. But the thrust of his analysis was that he could not imagine France without the overseas territories or Europe without France. "L'intégration de l'Union française dans l'Union européenne et les enseignements de la théorie économique," *Annales Africaines 1954*, 19–48, 19 quoted.

nomic cooperation was limited for the time being to steel and coal. The Common Market would only come into being under the Treaty of Rome of 1957.

It was into this realm of disagreement and uncertainty that African politicians stepped with their insistence that they had to have a place in whatever institutions were governing Europe. As Senghor told the Assemblée Nationale in 1952, "Eurafrica will not be built without the consent of Africans." If the government wanted to negotiate to protect French agriculture—or to enlarge its markets—it could not forget the overseas territories. And Africa had much to offer to France's position within Europe: "Eurafrican France of 88 million inhabitants will be in the first place, as much by the number of its inhabitants as by its resources of all varieties."[115]

Senghor kept up his involvement in European fora, appearing before the "Ad hoc assembly charged with developing a draft treaty instituting a European political community" in January 1953. He insisted that under the French Constitution overseas territories were an integral part of the Republic, and therefore "enter by right in the European political community." He insisted, "I am impassioned by the Eurafrican idea." And that meant overseas participation in European institutions. There was talk of creating a Chambre des Peuples that would be a key element of a federal Europe, and Senghor proposed that the overseas departments and territories be allotted twenty seats, with sixty-three going to the metropole, a modest proposal, he thought, given that the overseas and metropolitan populations were relatively equal. Europe had to be faithful to its own ideals—the value of the "human person"—and it could therefore not exclude millions of persons. And he had a warning, put in terms of one of his favorite phrases: "Africa has the mystique of equality in cooperation. If you refuse to satisfy it, the men of good will that we are will become tomorrow, in twenty or thirty years, 'collaborators' in the eyes of the young generations." Africans supported the European Community, notably the reconciliation of Germany and France, but they refused to be "the pages that carry the bride's veil, we refuse to be the wedding presents or the china" of the household. Participation in governing institutions was a matter of shared humanity, but also of interests, which were not

---

[115] Senghor to Assemblée Nationale, 17 January 1952, reprinted in *Liberté II*, 91, 93. The Groupe des Indépendants d'Outre-Mer had earlier issues a manifesto insisting that the entry of French Africa in "an expanded European union . . . can be imagined neither without the consent of Africans nor at the price of economic or industrial stagnation of their territories nor without the active participation of Africa in the advantages of the system." Statement of IOM at opening of session of Assemblée Nationale, *Débats*, 6 July 1951, 5909.

necessarily the same for overseas and metropolitan citizens: "Cultur-ally, politically, we are French, we expect to be French, we want to enter into the Community in the French framework, but economically [our] interests are not the same."[116]

Senghor's intervention caused consternation in Paris.[117] The Political Affairs section of the Ministry recognized its dilemma. If France joined a larger European entity without its overseas territories, it was effectively breaking up the French Union. If it joined with them, then African representatives would participate actively, bringing problems before European bodies. "Up to the present our Republic made itself understood with one French voice." But now they faced the reality that there were multiple French voices. Officials claimed that over-seas representatives would pose demands on behalf of their territories, making "a harmonious development plan" harder to achieve. Overseas representatives to a European institution could find non-French al-lies, leaving representatives of metropolitan France wondering if they had become "the colonies of Europe." The study group of 1953 con-cluded that it needed to build "a solid barrier" against proposals like those of Senghor. Worried as well about Africans' connections to each other, it fell back on a notion of a unitary—but presumably Franco-African—state: "The only counterweight to separatist Pan-Africanism is the unity of the Republic and not a federalism that carries the seed of disaggregation."[118]

Africans' insistence on participation in any European venture had a solid constitutional basis, which Senghor did not hesitate to make explicit: sovereignty lay in the people, and Africans were among the people. Africans deputies, including Senghor, Abbas Guèye, and Jean-Hilaire Aubame, kept reminding their colleagues that Africans

[116] Senghor's interventions before Assemblée Ad Hoc chargée d'élaborer un projet de Traité instituant une Communauté Politique Européenne, Strasbourg, 8–9 January 1953, AP 219/3, AOM. Later that year, Senghor worried that French officials were trying to construct "a resolutely European Europe." Speech in Assemblée Nationale, 18 November 1953, cited in *La Condition Humaine*, 10 December 1953.

[117] However, some MRP leaders, notably Pierre-Henri Teitgen, shared Senghor's de-sire to integrate Africa into the European Community. Teitgen was at loggerheads with many of his colleagues. See Montarsolo, *L'Eurafrique*, esp. 104–5, 137–39.

[118] Directeur des Affaires Politiques, "Note: La République française et la Fédération européenne," 28 January 1953, AP 219/3, AOM. The Juriconsulte of the Ministry, not-ing that the project for Europe constituted a confederation, pointed out that it would in effect create a "common citizenship" of Europe, in which citizens of each member would have rights in the others—something on a European scale like the citizenship of the French Union. Note pour M. le Directeur des Affaires Politiques, 9 February 1953, AP 219/3, AOM.

insisted not only on having the benefits of integration, but on participating in developing and managing it. Senghor warned that failure to include the French Union in Europe would lead "directly to the secession of the overseas countries."[119] One of the most influential Socialist leaders and future Minister of Overseas France, Gaston Defferre, grasped the stakes: "The exclusion of the overseas countries, particularly the overseas departments and territories, that is the territories of the Republic, in the event of the integration of the metropole into a European community could only be considered by the peoples of these countries as an act of discrimination of a colonial, even racist, character."[120]

The race word had been spoken, the danger of splitting apart the French Union invoked. For Defferre, Europe could not be built at the expense of the French Union: "Let us not forget either that France without the French Union would no longer be a nation of world importance, would become a small nation whose population, economic resources, territory, strategic positions would be all the more limited given that she finds herself in Europe faced with powers that are expanding and might not, perhaps, take their time to dominate us." A convinced Europeanist, he thought that the only way to proceed was to make the new community more inclusive but less ambitious in its initial goals: specific agreements for cooperation on the line of the Coal and Steel Community, rather than a full-blown common market, would allow for the working out of a positive relationship between Europe and overseas France.[121]

The opening of the European question was forcing an ongoing reconsideration of the Union question, just at a moment when some were arguing that only federalism would keep the Union from falling apart. Might Eurafrica be a better alternative than "France" to the nationalist movements threatening in Algeria, Morocco, and Tunisia? But the question kept coming back to that repeatedly raised by Senghor and others from AOF: who would run the show in the big tent? To some members of the French elite, too much of a political role for Africans now seemed to give Africans a chance to make their own relationship with Europe, bypassing Paris, or too much power to Europeans to

[119]Assemblée Nationale, *Débats*, 18, 24, 27 November 1953, 5249–50, 5487, 5629–30. See also Senghor, "L'intégration des pays d'outre-mer dans la Communauté européenne," *Le Monde*, 6 October 1953. Gaston Monnerville also warned of the dangers of the secession if African territories were not given full voice in Eurafrica. Speech in Brussels, 1 March 1954, 4AG 528, Dossier II, ANF. The argument for inclusion as a requirement of constitutional law was also put forward by the jurist P.-F. Gonidec. "L'Union française et l'Europe," *Union Française et Parlement* 52 (July 1954): 6–10.

[120]Defferre, Assemblée Nationale, *Débats*, 17 November 1953, 5210–11.

[121]Ibid., 5212.

make their own relationship with Africa. The Europeanization of Africa worried the author "XXX"—presumably an official hiding behind anonymity—entering the discussions of the Union's future in *Politique Étrangère*: to remain a "world power," France had to integrate with both continents, but it could not give up its own authority over Africa. "We have no right," insisted XXX, "to transfer the moral obligation that the trusteeship of overseas populations represents to other nations that cannot, to the same degree as France, claim a liberal tradition founded on the principle of equality of races."[122] But if France were to tie together both continents on such a basis, it had to make good on its promise of equality, that is, solve the problem of the French Union as well as that of Europe.[123] That was a tall order, as the more insightful officials like Robert Delavignette realized, recommending caution in balancing European and African objectives.[124]

The Dahomean deputy Sourou Migan Apithy was weighing the balance of France's European and African priorities. In a report to the Assemblée Nationale on behalf of its Overseas Committee, he took a critical view toward the proposed treaty establishing a European Defense Community. He saw the pooling of resources within Europe conflicting with the Constitution's provision for the French Union to pool its resources for defense. France consisted not of forty-four million Europeans, but of eighty-seven million people overseas and in Europe. The treaty writers considered overseas territories as "annexes of the metropole," as if they were in "a secondary position, without even anticipating if they are being annexed to Europe, 'given as dowry,' or if the lines attaching them to European France will be loosened." A common European defense pact implied a "progressive diminution of French sovereignty," and he saw this effort "to surmount nationalism" as positive.

Here he made an insightful connection: "This is an effort of the same kind as that which is asked of diverse territories of the French Union that are supposed to overcome their local particularisms to integrate themselves from one day to the next more freely into the

[122]XXX, "Union française et institutions européennes," 272, 275. See also René Servoise, "L'Union française devant l'intégration économique européenne," *Politique Étrangère* 18, 4 (1953): 277–306. The North African dimensions of Eurafrica are emphasized in Dramé and Saul, "Le project d'Eurafrique" and, with emphasis on the late 1950s, in the forthcoming dissertation at New York University by Muriam Haleh Davis.

[123]"At the moment when we try to found Europe . . . let us first found the French Union," pleaded Daniel Boisdon. AUF, *Débats*, 12 November 1952, 1113.

[124]Robert Delavignette, "Notre double vocation: L'Europe et l'Afrique," Agence France Presse, 4 January 1954, cited in Louisa Claire Rice, "Reframing Imperialism: France, West Africa, and Colonial Culture in the Era of Decolonization, 1944–1968" (PhD diss., Rutgers University, 2006), 30.

Republic." The layering of sovereignty within the French Union was analogous to the layering of sovereignty proposed for the European Defense Community. But did one preclude the other? Apithy worried that some provisions of the proposed treaty tended to create "a sovereign state that would govern and administer only non-European French people." Overseas France, partially governed by European institutions, "would become a bit German, a bit Italian." But if the overseas territories were not integrated into Europe, then France would be divided into "two distinct zones, one European, with diminished sovereignty, the other extra-European, with full sovereignty." In this scenario, European France would cede some of its sovereignty to Europe, and only overseas France would remain fully French. Apithy concluded that priority should go to ensuring the full participation of the overseas territories in French sovereignty: "In any case, we would like—it is our great ambition—to be better French people and more fully in the French community before becoming European French people." For him, it was a choice between two systems of layered sovereignty, and when advocates of the defense community termed one "European," he assumed they meant what they said. And that left out Africa. It was the other form of layered sovereignty, labeled French, that gave Africans a clear place.

Twenty-four members of the Overseas Committee backed Apithy. Fifteen opposed him. The treaty was voted down in the Assemblée Nationale, 319 to 264. Senghor and Apithy were on opposite sides. Houphouët-Boigny abstained.[125] Senghor and Apithy both wanted to reform the French Union, but Apithy had a more focused view on the relationship of France and its African territories, Senghor a broader vision of both Europe and Africa.[126] But Europe was not about to be constructed overnight. The relationship of French Union and European Union would surface from time to time throughout the 1950s. But the flurry of argument in the early 1950s draws our attention to the relationship of two confederal ideas, either of which would have constituted a historical break: one turning a three-hundred-year history of colonial domination into a federation or confederation of equal states, the other turning a fifteen-hundred-year-old history of rivalry for power in Europe into a confederation of equal states. We know how the story turned out: a Eurafrican confederation did not come to pass, but European leaders eventually decided that they liked the idea of confederation for themselves.

[125] Assemblée Nationale, *Débats*, 29 August 1954, 4419–22, 4471.

[126] Senghor remained worried that if Africans did not fully participate in European institutions, accords among Europeans could "open the door to German colonization." Commission de la FOM, 20 December 1954, C//15640, ANF.

Conclusion

Doudou Thiam, Senegalese, French-trained jurist, future Minister in Senegal, published in 1953 a pioneering book-length analysis of the citizenship that overseas peoples had won seven years earlier. He had no doubts about the importance of the citizenship of 1946: "The great innovation of the Fourth Republic is to have generalized what was only an exception."[127] For all the subtlety of his juridical analysis of the less-than-clear constitutional text, he ultimately saw the extension of citizenship to Africans in human terms, a relationship of two civilizations that had up to then been unequal. He asked, "To say to an African or a Malagasy that he is a French citizen, is it not to ask him in a sense to grow a new skin, to get rid of the sum of traditions that make his personality?" But then he answered his question in the negative: "But in fact the problem is no longer posed entirely in those terms. It is posed less under the angle of assimilation of one civilization by another as under that of an exchange of cultures." Europe and Africa, he said, could learn from each other's way of doing things, ways which a common citizenship put into juxtaposition—"a junction between two humanities." Contrary to the usual thinking about citizenship, the Constitution did not make all citizens subject to the same laws; different rules applied to Africans' marriages and inheritance. It did not quite entail equality of political rights, because it left open the possibility—which the government was insisting on exercising—of leaving Africans not fully enfranchised and underrepresented in electoral institutions. But citizenship should be seen not just as what it was in 1946 or 1953, but also in terms of the extremely unequal structure out of which it had emerged and the direction in which it was moving. "In sum, citizenship is a *tendency*, a notion in movement, and not a definitively fixed notion."[128]

That was how some of the African legislators who had helped to write the citizenship clauses had seen the significance of the text in 1946—as an act of becoming—and that is how they were still finding it in the early 1950s, an often-frustrating attempt to realize citizenship's potential for raising once-colonized people to the political and juridical stature of their colonizers, of providing a basis for claiming social and economic equality with their more affluent, better-educated fellow citizens. They had learned how vigorously their effort to make "a tendency" into a reality was being opposed, out of the habits and interests of the old colonial system and out of the inertia and opportunism that characterized the Republic created in 1946.

---

[127] Doudou Thiam, *La portée de la citoyenneté française dans les territoires d'outre-mer* (Paris: Société d'Éditions Africaines, 1953), 13.

[128] Ibid., 81, 157–58, 174.

The political structure in which they lived and acted, the French Union, was a peculiar sort of entity. It had attributes of a super-state, of which the French Republic was a component, and attributes of an extension of the French Republic. Historically, it emerged out of empire, and its rulers were divided over whether they wanted to retain the power in an imperial center or share it among the different sorts of components which made it up. In 1947, Prime Minister Paul Ramadier told a meeting of High Commissioners that this "great union, in which we believe as a categorical imperative, has not yet found its definitive formula, that she searches for its soul." It was essential that it find not only its soul but its body: "France by itself would be France enslaved. That is why, gentlemen, the problem of the French Union, the imperial problem, has become not that of the aggrandizement of France, of the growth of France, but the problem of the life and existence of our country."[129]

In 1955, the Union was coming apart at both its softest and most rigid points, the Associated States and Algeria. The crisis in the Associated States exposed the basic fallacy of the Union as a supra-national structure, for the Constitution of 1946 had been written unilaterally, without revision of the treaties by which the protectorates had, while retaining international sovereignty, ceded much of their sovereign prerogatives to the protecting power. When the Sultan of Morocco and the Bey of Tunis refused to participate in the institutions designed for them, the Haut Conseil and the Assemblée de l'Union française, there was little the French government could do. In a world context, where colonial power had lost its taken-for-granted aspect, the international status of these territories counted for more than it had before, and the political movements that wanted to make real the sovereignty that nominally they had never lost had a good opportunity to stake their claims. The French war in Vietnam was lost by 1954, and whether Indochinese sovereigns would continue to play a role in the Union was no longer so sure.

The war in Algeria started in 1954. In reality, Algeria was experiencing two kinds of empire conflicts at once. The Front de Libération Nationale (FLN), which launched the war, was following in the footsteps of Vietnamese and Indonesians in a struggle for independence, conducted in the name of an Algerian nationality. Some Algerian leaders, notably Ferhat Abbas, had tried to reconcile the claim to Algerian nationality with continued participation in the French Union. Any such possibility ran into the second struggle, one with echoes of the process leading up to the North American Revolution of 1776 or the revolutions in Spanish America of the early nineteenth century (or in the

[129] Prime Minister Paul Ramadier, speech to Conférence des Hauts Commissaires, 21 February 1947, 28PA/3/93, AOM.

future white Rhodesians' Unilateral Declaration of Independence of 1965): a settler movement, taking things into its own hands, claiming to be plus français que les Français, and standing in direct opposition to the attempt of the French state to convince the majority of the colonized population that it had a stake in continued membership in the French system. In this case, the fragmented nature of French politics gave settlers sufficient voice in key French parties to conduct an effective operation within French institutions. Later, when the French government gave indications that it might turn against settler domination of Algerian policy—in 1958 and then in 1961–62—elements of the settler population and their supporters in the French military were willing to engage in acts of insurrection against the state they claimed to epitomize. The fiction that Algeria was an integral part of the French Republic was repeatedly invoked by people at various points of the political spectrum to set a sharp limit on the kinds of adjustments that could be made. A number of people on the center and left managed to convince themselves that France could be an agent of social and economic progress in Algeria, if only the rebellion could be put down and settlers marginalized. The Fourth Republic proved unable to resolve—or even think through—its double challenge in Algeria.

But in Africa, the lines of struggle were not so sharply drawn. Most African leaders were well aware of the immense need for resources that the continent faced, of the small size and inadequate level of education of each territory. Most saw the French Union as providing a connection not only to France and its resources but to each other— Senghor's horizontal and vertical solidarities. They had accepted that the Constitution and the Union were works in progress. Yet Africans were chafing at the failure of the political promises of 1946 to be met, and they had run into obstacles to reform, from the opposition of defenders of racial privilege to officials concerned about their loss of control, to the indecision and short-term deal-making characteristic of the Fourth Republic's legislature. Nonetheless, African trade unions had shown their vitality; movements like the RDA had weathered political repression; and African intellectuals were proposing solutions to the political impasse in which the Union stood. Perhaps sub-Saharan Africa could be the core of a reformed structure—respectful enough of multiple nationalities to be attractive even to militant Moroccans and Algerians—or perhaps it should be treated as a special case, the part of the former empire to which inclusion in a larger entity offered the most.

CHAPTER 5

REFRAMING FRANCE

The Loi-Cadre and African Federalism, 1956–1957

The loi-cadre—framework law—of 1956 is widely recognized as a turning point in the history of French Africa. To some African intellectuals today, it is the moment when Africa's fate was sealed. Africa was "balkanized," as Senghor said at the time. The territorially bounded system of government entrenched by the law would become the basis for the independent states of former French Africa. Those states have, in the past fifty years, produced a deeply troublesome record on the issues that concerned African political actors in 1956: democratic elections, equality, rights, economic development, education. However, for Africans at the time the loi-cadre constituted a victory. They won their most important political demands of the previous decade: universal suffrage, the single electoral college, and territorial assemblies with real power. The loi-cadre made elected assemblies in each territory responsible for the budget and for its own civil service, and it thus broke with the centralizing tendencies of French rule.

The loi-cadre was not intended to create nation-states. For African advocates of federalism it did not end the quest to be included in some sort of "grand ensemble," and for French leaders it was not "decolonization." So to get from the territorial structures of the loi-cadre to francophone African states as we have known them in the past fifty years, we will have to keep following the historical vicissitudes of the period between 1956 and 1960.

The loi-cadre was passed in the same year as Morocco and Tunisia shed their status as Associated States to become fully independent. Algeria was at war. The loi-cadre, although drafted by the previous government, was put into law by the same government under Socialist Prime Minister Guy Mollet that decided to escalate the war in Algeria, and in some sense the two acts are mirror images. As it slid deeper into the quagmire of Algeria, the government was trying to prevent a second anticolonial war, both by responding partially to the demands of African political movements and by reducing the role in colonial politics of the Assemblée Nationale, where governing coalitions' dependence on prosettler factions from Algeria had blocked meaningful reform overseas.

The loi-cadre was an attempt to reconfigure the place of Africa in the French Union, not an attempt to reconfigure the Union. It was a law, not a constitutional revision as had been demanded by most African political leaders. A "loi-cadre" was a particular type of law, sketching only the outlines of reforms, allowing the government to fill in the details via decrees. The government could then implement the principles of the law in its own way and on its own schedule, not subject to the typically glacial pace of legislative action. The Assembly would have to vote within a set period if it wished to block a decree. The government was still trying to hold together an extended, supra-national France, but the loi-cadre was a comedown in terms of thinking about empire systematically. The government was adjusting to a situation in Africa that was becoming untenable, an attempt to reach a trade-off with African elites both to avoid the kind of political polarization it faced in Algeria and to escape from escalating social demands by conceding African elites more political power.

The loi-cadre was the product of politics—of different actors pushing on each other, trying to get what they could and concede what they had to. Within two years, politics would enter a new phase, but one framed by the ways in which African politicians had adapted to the new configuration that the loi-cadre introduced.

The Possibilities, Dangers, and Costs of a Reformed Union

In 1955 and 1956, there was wide agreement that the French Union was working badly and little agreement on how to change it.[1] Senghor continued to push for system-wide transformation, for turning the Union into a federal or confederal structure. He was confronting a variety of arguments: that constitutional change was too complex and time-consuming, that federalism weakened the gains that citizenship had extended, that federated states were likely to fall into demagoguery or secession, and that reforms had already proven themselves too costly.

In the summer of 1955, Mamadou Dia, who was becoming Senghor's second in command in his political party, wrote in *La Condition Humaine* that there was no realistic alternative to federalism. Dia was in his early forties, five years younger than Senghor, influenced by his Islamic upbringing, his education at the elite teacher-training college École William Ponty, socialist thought, and social Catholic

[1] Africa was sometimes singled out as the region where there was some hope. Former Minister of Overseas France Jean-Jacques Juglas praised the African deputies in the Assemblée Nationale and the work of the territorial assemblies in Africa. "Faut-il réviser le Titre VIII de la Constitution?," *Union Française et Parlement* 60 (March 1955): 6–7.

conceptions of economy and society. As he put it, "Other than federalism, [the choice] is either colonialism or total independence, in other words, two extremes that are no longer part of our world." He went on to make a more far-reaching point: "It is necessary that the imperialist concept of the nation-state give way definitively to the modern concept of the multinational state."[2]

For Dia, the nation-state was neither modern nor desirable. Large, inclusive, diverse ensembles of people were the wave of the future, and political institutions had to reflect that fact. At around the same time, in July 1955, the Minister of Overseas France, Pierre-Henri Teitgen, responded in the Assemblée de l'Union française to yet another proposal to revise the constitution in terms that both acknowledged the justice of the demands and sought to contain them: "The issue is a request addressed to France from all the elites of our overseas territories, avid for freedom, dignity, and pride. They ask every day to play a bigger role in the management of their affairs, to assume responsibilities, to feel themselves engaged and personally responsible for the destiny of their territories. . . . How could we not respond affirmatively to such requests?" Teitgen worried about going too far in the direction of decentralization and the danger of not going far enough, rapidly enough. And he set out an argument that would have decisive importance later on: giving territories authority to manage their "purely territorial" affairs implied that they should control the civil service that would implement them. But he worried that until their economies had, with France's help, developed further, the metropole would be stuck with the bill. In a journal article, he was arguing meanwhile for a "modern federalism," one that gave a considerable legislative role to territories while keeping the authority needed for economic planning and development at the center. He called for giving the territories "a sort of secondary legislative power," an expression he would be careful to avoid later on. Africans should acquire political experience at the "base" rather than starting at the "top."

He also had an important suggestion about procedure, given the stalled efforts at amending the constitution: the Assemblée Nationale could "content itself with framework laws [lois-cadre]." Teitgen was suggesting a centralized mode of decentralization, keeping the process under the control of the Ministry even if the goal was to devolve significant power to the territories, avoiding the complications of legislative debates while responding to inevitable and justified demands of African elites. For Teitgen, a "classic federalism" was not practical,

[2]Mamadou Dia, "L'Afrique Noire devant le nouveau destin de l'Union française," *La Condition Humaine*, 29 August 1955. For Dia's background, see his autobiography, *Mémoires d'un militant du tiers-monde* (Paris: Publisud, 1985).

and the "renewed federalism" he advocated meant, although he could not quite say so, something other than a federation of equals.[3]

But the federalist option now met vigorous opposition, notably in an article jointly written in January 1956 by Paul Coste-Floret, MRP deputy, former Minister, influential veteran of the constitution writing of 1946, Fily Dabo Sissoko, deputy from the Sudan, Henri Guissot, deputy from Upper Volta, René Maran, Caribbean novelist and a key figure in the négritude movement, Maurice Viollette, former Minister, and others. They called federalism a "panacea." It contained, they said, a double illusion: that the poor territories had the resources for a meaningful autonomy and that such an autonomy would encourage them to remain part of the French Union. The authors feared that in each federated territory, a narrow elite would dominate its institutions. A durable federalism, they thought, required geographic contiguity, relative ethnic homogeneity, and a considerable common store of traditions and political experience. Senghor's insistence on grouping African territories together—AOF and AEF in particular—within a federal France was especially dangerous, the article asserted, because the groups would be both an obstacle to administrative decentralization and a focus of loyalty competitive to that of the French federation. Instead, Coste-Floret and his coauthors wanted to build "on a common French patriotism and on the desire of the masses for equality and social justice." French nationality and citizenship across the Union had given specific meaning to these sentiments and aspirations. It was through the deepening of institutions of citizenship that a "fusion" of the various parts of France could take place: full equality in terms of military service and employment opportunities, including the Africanization of the civil service; a single état-civil, "since only the precise individualization of citizens can allow them the full exercise of their rights"; a coherent regime of land tenure; the education of the entire population; the development of health facilities overseas; the full application of social and work legislation; the employment of professional magistrates in all administrative jurisdictions. They also called for the augmentation of overseas representation in the French Parliament and the end of the double college, and they thought the

[3] Teitgen, AUF, *Débats*, 7 July 1955, 676–78; Pierre-Henri Teitgen, "Le Fédéralisme moderne est un mariage sous le régime de la communauté," *Union Française et Parlement* 64 (July 1955), 1–4. The Assemblée de l'Union française and the Assemblée Nationale kept getting more proposals for constitutional change into 1956. Even the conservative Conseil de la République discussed the need for reform, without specifying what it would be. AUF, *Débats*, 7 and 8 July 1955, 680–711; Assemblée Nationale, *Documents*, No. 10199 of 23 February 1955, 407, and No. 660, of 21 February 1956, 468–69, proposal No. 1042 of 1955–56, 7 March 1956, 714–15; Proposition of Jacques Fourcade to revise articles 71–74 of constitution, *Documents*, No. 2208, 15 June 1956, 1769–70; Conseil de la République, *Débats*, 19 July 1955, 1835–51.

talk about France being colonized by its former colonies was nonsense. Economic development, including the industrialization of overseas territories, was vital. The task would be expensive, and it would be "quasi revolutionary."[4]

What is remarkable about this Afro-French document is that French citizenship is at its core, especially coming from a lead author who, ten years previously, had been inclined to see France as an assemblage of groups. The collective experience of citizenship and nationality had to be solidified to make the Union work.[5] The individual citizen—properly registered and actively exercising rights—was as much a focus as state institutions and economic development. Because French Africans *were* citizens, their demands for equality in all respects were legitimate and inescapable, even if meeting them was extremely costly. Here, from a rather diverse cross-section of the French elite, was an alternative to federalist reforms: a unitary France—fully integrating overseas citizens and improving their conditions of life.

But a unitary citizenship promised to entail even higher costs for the French taxpayer than Teitgen's unequal federalism. And the costs of imperial citizenship were beginning to get attention in the press. In an article in *Le Monde* in October 1954, René Servoise (political scientist and official in the Overseas Ministry, Algeria, and other government services) wrote, "Whoever says 'French citizen' expresses a claim to a standard of living equal to that of metropolitans and similar social benefits." France was taking on "many difficult, heavy, unprofitable tasks." It was obliging itself "not only to pull the overseas peoples out of their relative misery, but to fix implicitly as an objective our own European standard of living and our western norms of civilization." Neither Britain nor Belgium had comparable ambitions. Servoise saw that what he termed France's "assimilationist philosophy" had taken an economic and social turn—a claim to equality of standard of living.[6]

[4] Paul Coste-Floret, Amadou Diop, Fily Dabo Sissoko, Yvon Gouet, Henri Guissou, Iba-Zizen, Marie-Hélène Lefaucheux, René Maran, Jean Scelles, and Maurice Viollette, "Un programme pour une nouvelle politique française outre-mer," *Union Française et Parlement* 69 (January 1956): 5–11.

[5] For a related argument focused on citizenship, see Jules Ramarony (deputy and former minister), "La Constitution de l'Union française doit être repensée avec les États intéressés et cimentée par une citoyenneté commune," *Union Française et Parlement* 60 (March 1955): 12–13.

[6] René Servoise, "La métropole ne pourrait supporter les charges qu'entraînerait une politique d'assimilation des Territoires d'Outre-mer," *Le Monde*, 14 October 1954. See also the same author's "Introduction aux problèmes de la République Française," *Affaires Étrangères* 19, 4 (1954): 379–418. He also brought back the argument that citizenship implied a big increase in overseas representation in parliament and that the logic of assimilation would "slip unnoticed into all domains." Ibid., 392–93. On the cost of empire and the inefficiency of the imperial economy, see also Jacques Lecaillon, "L'intégration de l'Union française dans l'Union européenne et les enseignements de la

This argument would, a couple of years later, resurface in a more highly publicized critique from the right of the cost effectiveness of colonialism. But for now, as a group from the Centre d'Études de Politique Étrangère that included Servoise put it,

> the Metropole cannot by itself bear the burden of development if the territories are only "demanders." To the sharing of rights must correspond a sharing of expanded responsibilities. The local assemblies—at all levels—must bit by bit become aware of the financial impact of their exigencies in the social realm. The primacy of the social, the application overseas of measures intended for metropolitans must not lead to the ruin of an economy in the process of being reborn, at the risk of leading the pilot-state and the overseas territories into the same failure. Only greater responsibility in the management of public affairs, from the municipal to the federal level can make the autochthons aware of economic problems.[7]

Conflicting arguments for ending the impasse on reforming the French Union were on the table at the beginning of 1956. France could pursue the integrative logic of citizenship, but then it would have to face the costs. Or France could distance itself from the social and economic implications of equality among citizens, but to do so required giving Africans political responsibility. In between lay the egalitarian federalism of Senghor and Dia that posited a large devolution of power and the unequal federalism of Teitgen that kept more power in Paris. Something had to give. How much power had to be devolved to African territories to induce leaders to lower their demands for social equivalence with the metropolitan population, and how much power was France willing to give up to shield itself from such demands?

Territorializing the Empire

The Overseas Ministry was trying to think through the dangers and benefits of both administrative and political decentralization. And it was becoming increasingly anxious about the political dangers it faced. Behind the demanding politicians was the potential at least of even greater militancy. As in the preceding years (chapter 4), officials got reports of organizations like the Rassemblement des Jeunesses

---

théorie économique," *Annales Africaines 1954*, 19–48, and Pierre Chauleur, "Les Territoires d'Outre-mer apportent-ils à la métropole plus qu'ils n'en reçoivent?," *Le Monde*, 4 April 1954.

[7]Centre d'Etudes de Politique Étrangère, Groupe d'étude des institutions, "L'Afrique Noire et la République Française," nd [1954], copy in 4AG 528, dossier II, ANF.

Démocratiques Africaines, connected to the RDA and European communist parties. They had been following the journals *L'Etudiant d'Afrique Noire* and *Voix des Jeunes*, with their mix of complaints about the conditions facing African students in France and radical demands for political change, including independence. Youth were becoming "uncontrollable elements." At the same time, officials seemed to think that in several territories a dominant party was keeping politics, at least in the formal sense, under its control. Well aware of what was going on elsewhere in the world, they worried about "the contagion of universal emancipation," coming out of Bandung, Algiers, Accra, and Cairo. More specifically, and using the same metaphor, they claimed that the calls for independence set out in youth publications and political rallies stemmed from "a virus infiltrating from North Africa."[8]

The various forms of politics that were emerging in cities, towns, and countryside across AOF—whether based on local idioms, religious linkages, or radical internationalism—merit further research, but officials in Dakar and Paris were most often reacting to the people they understood best: elected representatives in Dakar or Paris, party leaders, trade unionists, writers. Over the past five years, stated a long report in the Ministry of Foreign Affairs, the government's hope was "to gain the time needed for the formation of an intermediate African stratum of moderate nationalism, consistent with normal evolution, enjoying a liberty of expression breaking with the previous silent obedience, but accepting in exchange to enact loyally and openly the Franco-African role." There had been some "good results." But danger lay in the ambitions of the same people on whom the hopes rested: "At a time close to the conquest of responsible posts by the 'new men,' elements of escalation, connected to the contagion of external events, seriously menace to ruin the work undertaken to lay down balanced bases for a Franco-African community." Political ferment was occurring in the context of disappointing results in the project of economic development, and stagnation was a "new cause of aggravation in facts and spirits."[9] With the risk of agitation from outside—or perhaps more seriously from below—the government faced with new urgency the classic problem of empires, giving intermediary elites enough of a

[8] *Voix des Jeunes*, September–October 1955, copy in AP 2265, AOM; Direction des services de Sécurité of AOF, Dakar, 11 July 1955, 21G 210, AS; "Situation politique, économique et sociale de l'AOF en 1956," 15 May 1956, Afrique-Levant, 1953–1959/AOF/11, ADLC.

[9] "Situation politique, économique et sociale de l'AOF en 1956," 15 May 1956, Afrique-Levant, 1953–1959/AOF/11, ADLC. Officials' growing awareness of the tension between the immediacy of social demands and the slowness of economic development is spelled out in Frederick Cooper, *Decolonization and African Society: The Labor Question in French and British Africa* (Cambridge: Cambridge University Press, 1996), chap. 10. See also Jacques Marseille, *Empire coloniale et capitalisme français: Histoire d'un divorce*, 2nd ed. (Paris: Albin Michel, 2005).

stake in the system to keep them cooperative without giving them the idea that they could take over the whole thing.

What these elites seemed to want was, in official eyes, too much. The High Commissioner of French West Africa objected in 1954 to Senghor's proposal to create Conseils de gouvernement (governing councils) in the territories. He saw this idea as a "kernel of a future local executive" that would be responsible "before the local parliament." That of course was exactly what Senghor wanted. But this high official found such a move unacceptable, for by creating "exorbitant, abnormal powers in regard to the constitution, it would break the equality of rights among citizens of the Republic in favor of African citizens." Africans would be "supercitizens": they would have representation in two levels of parliaments, in Paris and at home, while metropolitans would have only one. As for a Conseil de gouvernement, there was no point. Executive power lay in the governor, and there was no question of such an official being responsible to a territorial legislature. The Assemblée Nationale in Paris was the only body with legislative authority under the Constitution. He ended up in a defense of the Republic one and indivisible. In any case, such reforms were "premature," African legislators were not sufficiently experienced. One should perhaps start with municipal reform and let Africans gain experience in municipal councils—never mind that legislation on municipalities had not gone very far.[10] What is interesting about these shopworn arguments is how rapidly the administration would do what its highest official in Africa said it could not.

Precisely the forms that were being dismissed for West and Equatorial Africa were being considered for Togo and Cameroon, where UN oversight made French leaders particularly eager to show that they were on a progressive course. A Conseil de gouvernement with a mix of elected and appointed members was now in the cards.[11] And the developing revolt of the UPC in Cameroon—which turned into armed conflict in 1955—and the overlapping populations of Togo and the already self-governing Gold Coast pushed officials to undertake reform in the trust territories. As the changes went into effect there, officials understood that there would be a clamor for them in AOF.[12]

Should the Ministry try to reform the Union systematically—entailing a constitutional revision—or focus on the specificity of each territory? Officials hesitated. They understood that the people of AOF "want above all no longer to be submitted to a narrow subjection to

[10] High Commissioner, AOF, cited in report on draft of a proposed law on "assemblées locales et du statut financier des groupes de l'AOF et de l'AEF," 12 May 1954, AP 491, AOM.

[11] Ibid.

[12] Pierre Messmer, "Note de présentation d'un projet de Conseil de Gouvernement pour le territoire de la Côte d'Ivoire," 10 August 1955, AP 491, AOM.

the metropole, to the Administration above all." But they could not go to the other end of the spectrum, putting the territories "on an equal footing to the metropole." Repeatedly returning to the fear of "secession," the policy makers wondered if they could lighten the "administrative burden"—conceding a degree of autonomy to territorial assemblies while maintaining "French ties" by keeping in place "personnel du commandement" (governors), training functionaries, providing technical assistance, maintaining certain state services (justice, treasury), economic improvements, and closer trade ties. They were sufficiently aware of what was going on around them to realize that they had to persuade Africans of "the well-understood interest of AOF to remain attached to France, against the closest cultural, political, and economic attraction which it is bound to: the nature of economies, the geography and even the history, which over time, form nations."[13]

By 1955, Ministry officials were focusing on the economic dimensions of the problem: the "general poverty" of West Africa" and the "incredibly small revenues" that it produced. AOF consisted of mostly poor territories, "against a minority of rich territories." The necessary services of the former could come either from the latter, via the Government General, or from France itself. If the borders of the territories—and hence the unevenness of natural resources and ease of communications—were arbitrary, so too would be the redistribution of resources through central institutions. Even calculating where revenue was coming from—given that products and the people who produced them moved across territorial borders—was to a significant extent arbitrary.[14] The High Commissioner thought that Niger, Upper Volta, the Sudan, Dahomey, Guinea, and Mauritania "could not, under any circumstances, constitute viable entities."[15]

Such a problem risked confounding any strategy of decentralizing authority. So too did the apparent dearth of qualified personnel in some of the territories.[16] But decentralization was desired not only by African politicians, but also by an administration that was coming to realize how much of a burden it had placed on itself once it had hitched its legitimacy to ideas of development and equality among citizens. Now, officials in the Ministry of Overseas France wanted territorial governments to "do their apprenticeship in public respon-

[13]"Mémoire sur la réforme des structures de l'AOF," Dakar, 11 July 1955, AP 491, AOM.

[14]Affaires Politiques, section d'études, note pour M. le Ministre 27 November 1953, AP 217/4, AOM; "Rapport sur les finances de l'AOF," 15 January 1954 by R. Lassalle-Séré, AP 491, AOM; Cornut-Gentille to Inspecteur Général de la FOM, 19 July 1954, AP 491, AOM.

[15]High Commissioner to Minister, draft letter, early 1956, 18G 273, AS.

[16]Direction Générale du Personnel, Note for Directeur du Cabinet, 8 October 1954, 18G 238, AS.

sibilities," and matching tax revenue and expenses was the first responsibility. "It is necessary that each of the collectivities has itself the power to impose taxes without obstacle or limit, to cover the expenses for which it must be judged, in the framework defined in advance by law."[17] Whereas the individual territories would have trouble facing their own costs, officials worried that the three-layer administrative system that was then in place (territory, AOF, Paris) was cumbersome and expensive.[18]

High among the burdens was the cost of the civil service. Since all civil servants were French functionaries, and the two Lamine Guèye laws (1946 and 1950) prohibited discrimination on the basis of status or origins, all had to be paid on French scales. "The desire for equality, one of the strongest sentiments that animate the natives as soon as they arise, pushes them to claim equality of remuneration. . . . In the current state of affairs, there is no basis from which to resist claims when they go beyond the limit, already too high, at which the charge becomes too heavy for the budgets."[19]

Recent progress in bringing Africans into the civil service made the question even more difficult: Africans now constituted 85 percent of the cadres, including 23 percent of the cadres généraux (the highest levels) and 70 percent of the cadres supérieurs. To be sure the cadres généraux included some corps (veterinarians, doctors' assistants, pharmacists, and midwives) that were all African, and the highest positions were still largely occupied by metropolitans. But as a personnel question, the administration had to come to grips with the fact that its actions depended on men who were both "Africans" and "employees" of the state and who might pose demands accordingly. And the problem was not simply the logic of equivalence among citizens, but the activism of social movements: "It is easy, from here, for the African unions to take on the Administration at its own game, and far from demanding the abolition of the privileges of Europeans, to base individual and collective demands on the quest for assimilation to the most favorable situation. . . . The public service in AOF is impregnated by the spirit of pure assimilation: to stay on this base creates a misunderstanding that can only become aggravated on the level of race."[20]

[17] "Mémoire sur la réforme des structures de l'AOF," 11 July 1955, AP 491, AOM.

[18] Ibid.

[19] Ibid. See also Inspection Générale de la France d'Outre-mer, "Mission d'Inspection en AOF 1953–1954, Étude d'une réorganisation administrative éventuelle de l'AOF," 20 June 1954, AP 491, AOM.

[20] Direction des Services de Législation Générale, de Contentieux et de Liaison, "Memorandum sur le problème de la fonction publique en Afrique Occidentale Française," 15 January 1955, 18G 268, AS; Michelle Pinto, "Employment, Education, and the Reconfiguration of Empire: Africanization in Postwar French Africa" (PhD diss., New York University, 2013). See also Cooper, *Decolonization and African Society*, chaps. 7 and 11.

"Race" again—officials had trouble getting away from their fear that anything short of equality among citizens would push Africans to see their grievances in racial terms.

There was a way out of this trap: "The solution consists of giving to those in charge of receipts, that is, the elected representatives of taxpayers, the power of decision on questions of status and remuneration of the cadres of the territories. Only they can accept an increase in the budgetary burden for only they have the responsibility of voting on the tax that will cover it."[21] There would still be common services that would remain on the French account, but at least those functions specific to each territory could be devolved to that territory and its assembly.

The implications of these arguments within the Ministry was that the French government had to devolve real power to territorial assemblies—to tax, to decide on a budget, and to set the conditions of employment in the civil service. All this was being thought out in the context of anxiety about whether the territories could actually afford to take on such burdens and with fear that public sector unions—and political agitation in general—might soon mean that the French government would lose control over the situation. The generalization of citizenship had located issues of equivalence at the level of the French Union—and hence standards set in the metropole itself. And the problems were not just economic. Promised equal justice as citizens of France, Africans might think that letting territories write laws and employ magistrates would create a justice of the "second zone," so the issue of centralizing or decentralizing government posed a dilemma of another sort.[22]

We do not see in the government thinking within the Ministry in mid-1955 a conscious effort to carve up French West Africa so as to keep its territories poor and weak. The problem was that their being poor and weak posed inescapable dilemmas to any form of federalism as a successor to empire. Officials were casting about for a solution

[21] "Mémoire sur la réforme des structures de l'AOF," 11 July 1955, AP 491, AOM. The memo suggests that the Ministry perceived the immediate problem was financial and fiscal, rather than the imperial nature of the economy per se. French consumers paid more than world market prices for African commodities, and African consumers paid more than world prices for manufactured goods; the balance may well have come out in favor of the metropole, offsetting some of the costs of development finance (much of which ended up getting spent for goods and services in the metropole). But a commercial balance in favor of the metropole did not remedy the cause behind the fiscal burden on the French state—the poverty of Africa.

[22] This issue was brought out in "Rapport de développement sur les compétences et les possiblités de déconcentration concernant: 'La Justice et la legislation autochthone,'" 19 August 1954, by X. de Christen, Inspecteur de la FOM, AP 491, AOM. See also Inspection Générale de la FOM, Mission d'Inspection en AOF 1953–1954, "Étude d'une réorganisation administrative éventuelle de l'AOF," 20 June 1954, AP 491, AOM.

to a problem that was both economic—the gaps between metropole, "rich" territories, and poor territories—and political, the tension between a wish to maintain central control and avoid its financial burdens, and the demands coming from the territories for both equality and autonomy.

In between Paris and the territories was Dakar, and several reports agonized over the extent to which it constituted a burden—soaking up revenue, distributing it arbitrarily, distancing government from African voters, placing too much power in the hands of a sort of "superprefect"—or else provided services more efficiently than eight separate governments.[23] The Ministry, in late 1955, had gone as far as to have a Technical Councilor draft a proposal for a law to abolish the Government General of AOF, devolving most of its powers to the territories. Each would have its "moral personality and financial autonomy." It would be governed by a territorial assembly and an executive council, half of whose members would be appointed by the governor to take charge of specific functions, half of whom would be chosen by the elected assembly. There would, under such a plan, be some interterritorial institutions to coordinate policies, but there would be no more government in Dakar—and certainly no legislative and executive institutions uniting French West Africa.[24]

The Ministry was not yet ready to go that far. It was also hearing warnings about devolving too much power, notably from the Governor General of AEF, who feared that the elites of his domain were not numerous and educated enough to run territorial governments, that Governors and Conseils de gouvernements would clash, and that the diminution of his own powers and unclear divisions between the territories and the AEF as a whole would lead to "real dangers." But even he saw the creation of a Conseil de gouvernement, half of whose members would come from elected representatives, as a "normal evolution" of territorial governance.[25] His counterpart from AOF, Bernard Cornut-Gentille, also worried about loss of central control over financial matters and incoherence in the actions of eight different legislatures and governments, but he warned that any decentralization

---

[23] "Étude d'une réorganisation administrative éventuelle de l'AOF," 20 June 1954; Affaires Politiques, "Note au sujet des suggestions faites par M. l'Inspecteur Sanner sur la réforme de la structure de l'Afrique Occidentale Française," 12 August 1955; Pierre Messmer, "Note en réponse à la note en forme de rapport de Monsieur l'Inspecteur Sanner," 15 October 1955; Governor General to Minister, 7 May 1955, all in AP 491, AOM.

[24] "Avant projet de loi relatif aux institutions des territoires de l'AOF," from Conseiller Technique of Ministry, 30 November 1955, AP 492, AOM. This file includes discussions and comparisons of various proposals for decentralization of administration and different forms of legislative and executive authority in the territories, from the late 1940s to 1955.

[25] Governor General, AEF, to Minister, 13 January 1955, AP 491, AOM.

that did not give real authority to assemblies and councils in the territories "can only bring about disappointments and incite demands." So in considering the plans for reform, he recommended something "much more profound." But the next year, realizing that France "will not have decided what she wants in Black Africa, whether total territorialization or federalism," concluded that no proposal to reconfigure the relation of central, federal, and territorial institutions could be "anything other than empirical."[26]

Out of all this uncertainty among officials in Paris and Dakar, the Minister, Teitgen, had come up with his idea for an unequal federalism—a highly select devolution of power to territorial assemblies—that he had set forth in July 1955 before the Assemblée de l'Union française. In private discussions within the Ministry he had been more frank. France had been trying to avoid political decentralization, but it had found that it could not. "Federalization" was the only alternative. The French government had to hold onto the essential: army, diplomacy, "economic power," including money, credit, planning, tariffs. But "all the rest must go to the federal level and can thus from now on be decentralized." The territorial assemblies would have to have a larger role, but executive authority had to come from Paris through the appointment of High Commissioners, governors, and their underlings, although it was not necessary that "the man who commands at the bottom of the scale is always a metropolitan." And he was thinking that the Ministry needed to move quickly, while revising constitutional reform would require "a certain time."[27] It was on this basis that Teitgen's Ministry set about devising a plan for decentralizing the administration of African territories, but it remained unclear how much power Paris could cling to if it wanted to get African leaders to back off their demands for economic and social equality.

Toward the Loi-Cadre

In July 1955, the single college and universal suffrage were yet again being discussed in the Overseas Committee of the Assemblée Nationale, as was increasing representation from overseas in that body. Once again, advocates of reform saw themselves representing "the federal tendency." The Committee voted by large majorities in favor

[26]Governor General, AOF, to Minister, 7 May 1955, AP 491, AOM; High Commissioner to Minister, early 1956 (draft of letter), 18G 273, AS. It is not clear whether Cornut-Gentille actually sent this letter, but it does indicate his thoughts.

[27]Statements of Minister at meeting of his cabinet and governors general, 4 May 1955, AP 492, AOM. One official present, Pignon, remarked that it was important that the government was not considered "as an occupying administration, but that of Africans themselves."

of such reforms—including revision of the Constitution—but the issue got sidetracked by changes of government.[28]

In 1955 Edgar Faure, President of the French Council of Ministers, asked Senghor to chair a committee to look into modifications of the constitution. Senghor's report, dated July 1955, was comprehensive. He pointed to the "constitutional confusion" in which France was operating. Of central importance was its "unilateral" character in regard to the Associated States. The constitution should set out only general principles of a relationship—confederal in Senghor's terms—leaving the rest to negotiations and treaties. He even suggested that the confederation's name should be "Union," not "French Union," and he saw the Commonwealth (whose name he insisted was not "British Commonwealth") as a model. Senghor thought that overseas opinion was now "less concerned with enlarging parliamentary representation than to obtain local autonomy." A new structure would turn the territories into states, but in a federal, not international, sense. Each would have legislative and executive authority.

But there still was the problem of how to devise a legislative assembly at the federal level in which France would be only one component: "the metropole would undoubtedly have the impression of losing its sovereignty, submerged under the political rights of the overseas territories and becoming, in the words of President Herriot, 'the colony of its colonies.'" Acknowledging the legitimacy of a position he had called racist in 1946, Senghor sought a way out by reconfiguring the chambers of Parliament, so that overseas representatives would remain a minority in the Assemblée Nationale, and the upper house would consist of two sections, one of which would contain exclusively metropolitan representatives deliberating on metropolitan affairs and the other a combination of overseas and metropolitan representatives.[29]

Here is where the Ministry stepped in. For all its uncertainties and disagreements, it had come up with a plan—but not for rewriting the constitution or changing the structure of French legislative bodies.

[28] Meetings of 29 October, 2, 9 November 1955, C//15640, ANF. In February, the Committee appointed a subcommittee to study revisions of Title VIII. Meeting of 15 February 1956, C//15767, ANF. See also several proposals to the Assemblée Nationale in its *Documents*, session of 1955–56, for example, Nos. 11618, 10199, 10295, 10398, 11831 (1955), 1042, 660 (1956). Old arguments for the double college now had to be hidden behind a facade of multiculturalism: a defender of reserved seats for settlers suggested that instead of the double college, overseas territories should have a "plurality of colleges," one for each ethnic group. Raymond Dronne, "La querelle du double collège et du collège unique en Afrique noire," *Union Française et Parlement* 67 (November 1955): 19–20.

[29] See the two reports of the Commission Senghor, "Note sur le problème de la revision du Titre VIII," and "Note sur les modifications à apporter à la constitution de la République française," 6 June 1955, 4AG 528, ANF, and the published summary by Senghor, "Pour une République fédérale," *Politique Étrangère* 21, 2 (1956): 165–74.

Quite the contrary, the Ministry was seeking a reform specific to the overseas territories—that is, Africa—but it was in its own way addressing Senghor's concern with autonomy. The plan was first drafted under the leadership of Teitgen (MRP), but with a change of government, the Minister became the Socialist Gaston Defferre, and it was he who came before the Overseas Committee of the Assemblée Nationale on 2 March 1956.[30]

The timing was significant. On 6 February the newly installed Prime Minister, Guy Mollet, had been shocked by settler demonstrations during his visit to Algiers, and in the ensuing crisis had—because of a combination of pressure and his own belief that social reform and development in Algeria required the suppression of the revolt—decided to escalate France's repressive effort. On 12 March, the Assemblée Nationale voted "pleins pouvoirs"—giving the government and especially the military a free hand in prosecuting the war. The pattern of torture and forced relocation of villagers—and a campaign of violent acts by the FLN against civilian populations especially in Algiers—had already emerged.[31] Meanwhile, France had signed (on 2 March) an agreement with Morocco that would lead to the ending of the protectorate on 7 April. Tunisia became independent on 20 March. The debate over changing political institutions in the overseas territories would take place against this background, and the context undoubtedly focused the minds of officials on solving the political problems of sub-Saharan French Africa, even if those north of the desert were proving intractable.

The proposed law to "bring about the evolution of the overseas territories" was not, Defferre told the Committee, a partisan product. He cited the need to act quickly; he could not wait for constitutional reform or for the Assembly to deliberate line by line what the reforms would be. He wanted legislative authority to issue decrees, which could be rescinded only if Parliament acted within certain time limits. He told the Committee—in which Africans were well represented—that the goal was "a true decentralization and a true deconcentration." Territorial assemblies had over the past nine years shown their maturity. It was time for them to have more power. Each assembly would name members to a Conseil de gouvernement that would sit alongside the Governor "who will occupy himself with the problems of the exec-

[30] At the time of the drafting of the loi-cadre, Senghor was on the outs with the administration. Mollet resented his resignation from the Socialist Party, Defferre was close to Houphouët-Boigny, and the High Commissioner, Cusin, did not get along with him. Roland Colin, *Sénégal notre pirogue: au soleil de la liberté. Journal de bord 1955–1980* (Paris: Présence Africaine, 2007), 61.

[31] Martin Evans, *Algeria: France's Undeclared War* (Oxford: Oxford University Press, 2012); Raphaëlle Branche, *La torture et l'armée pendant la guerre d'Algérie 1954–1962* (Paris: Gallimard, 2001).

utive." Here was a concession of executive authority that the Ministry had been reluctant to make. African territories would have a cabinet responsible to their legislatures.

The second dimension of the reforms concerned the civil service, entailing both "l'africanisation des cadres" (Africanization of the civil service hierarchy) and a distinction between "cadres territoriaux et les cadres généraux," that is, between civil servants assigned to a territory and those serving in overseas France as a whole. He was careful to say that the reform would not trample on the "acquired rights" of current civil servants, but he thought that Conseils de gouvernement could exercise real power only if the control of the civil service was in their hands. He thought the current institutions of the Union gave representatives from overseas many places in which to speak, but not to act, contributing to "discontent." The new law would provide for universal suffrage and the single college.[32]

Questioned about the status of AOF, Defferre said the Ministry had been confronted with two theses, "one of the breakup pure and simple of federation—each territory becoming purely and simply autonomous, which is an extreme thesis—and that of maintaining the situation as it currently exists." He wanted to split his ticket, giving each territory more autonomy, the High Commissioner of AOF less authority. He was not sure what the relationship of the Grand Conseil de l'AOF and territorial assemblies should be.[33]

A few days later, the Committee discussed the proposal among itself. Senghor had constitutional doubts; the form of a loi-cadre gave the government powers that were not constitutional. Teitgen, the original author, saw the powers as limited and necessary; it had taken Parliament three years to act on a related project that concerned only Togo. He stressed that giving each territory control of the civil service was essential to making the other reforms effective. He knew functionaries were worried about losing the entitlements they had won in the French system, and like Defferre he implied that current, but not future, civil servants would have their acquired rights protected. He was worried about the meager financial resources of the territories and thought that getting rid of the Government General of AOF would help.

Apithy, like Senghor, opposed giving so much authority to issue decrees to the government. Above all, he wanted to give power to territorial assemblies, at the expense of both the Grand Conseil of AOF and the "central administration," although he did not object to "services of sovereignty" like defense, diplomacy, and money remaining

[32] Commission de la FOM, Session of 2 March 1956, C//15767, ANF.
[33] Ibid.

French concerns.[34] Senghor kept objecting to special powers for the government, and he pointed out that there were no Africans in the offices of the Ministry. Only a federal structure would give Africans a chance at running their own affairs and expressing "our local personality."[35]

The proposed civil service reforms made African deputies anxious. Sékou Touré noted the "worry that now reigns in the overseas civil service milieu." Diawadou Barry wanted to be sure that the State Services, not just the territorial civil services, would be Africanized. Defferre insisted that the point was for each Conseil de gouvernement to have a "true managerial authority over the services that are under their orders." If all was in place by March 1957, he promised, elections could be held under the single college. And he wanted a "crushing majority" in the Assemblée Nationale to show that the reforms would go on regardless of the outcome of the next election.[36]

Apithy had proposed to amend the original text to do away with the Grand Conseils in AOF and AEF. Senghor opposed this move, warning that it would "risk leading to a 'balkanization' of Africa," a term he would repeatedly invoke. The discussion, as near as one can tell from a transcript, was notably unpassionate, with deputies more inclined to express concerns than opposition. They had, after all, been demanding for years much of what the loi-cadre offered. The Commission voted twenty-eight to ten with four abstentions in favor of the government's proposed law.[37]

The vote in the Assemblée de l'Union française, after a relatively brief debate, was 124 to one in favor. Before that body, Defferre again stressed the need to act rapidly in the face of the "malaise" in Africa. He put the most emphasis on decentralization, on the augmented powers of the territorial assemblies, on more localized assemblies—what he termed the organization of "la brousse" (the backcountry)—and on the reform of the civil service. His one applause line was a promise not to take away any of the benefits current civil servants had acquired at the time of their entry into service.[38] Daniel Boisdon wanted to know if universal suffrage—which he claimed to have long favored—could be put into effect without long delay since it was still necessary to

[34] Sessions of 7 and 14 March 1956, C//15767, ANF.
[35] Session of 14 March 1956, C//15767, ANF.
[36] Sessions of 14, 16 March 1956, C//15767, ANF.
[37] Session of 16 March 1956, C//15767, ANF. Barry's amendment on the civil service passed twenty-five to eighteen. Interviewed in *Afrique Nouvelle* (20 March 1956), Senghor said, "I personally warned some of my colleagues against the 'balkanization' of Black Africa."
[38] AUF, *Débats*, 13 March 1956, 249–92, esp. 249–50, 292. The Assembly was under pressure from the Ministry to act rapidly. Defferre to Albert Sarraut, 5 March 1956, and Sarraut to President of Commission de la Politique Générale, 7 March 1956, C//16333, ANF.

"organize seriously the état-civil." And he warned that if the single college went into effect in sub-Saharan Africa, it would have to do so in
Algeria as well. Muslims in Algeria would not tolerate that Muslims in
Niger were voting in a single college, whereas they were not.[39] This was
an issue the government preferred to leave in abeyance; confining the
issue to sub-Saharan African territories was basic to government strategy. But the government knew it could not get the support of African
deputies without providing universal suffrage and the single college.

Guirandou-N'Diaye, who had repeatedly criticized the government's stance on electoral laws over the years, now stated that he and
his fellow Socialists would vote for the law because it is "an effective
instrument to speed up the evolution of the overseas territories by ensuring the putting into place of institution that have long been demanded." A big majority would "demonstrate in the eyes of the world,
and above all to Africans, that France makes no distinction among her
children."[40]

The main act was in the Assemblée Nationale, but it was not a particularly dramatic one. The Socialist Paul Alduy, reporting for the
Overseas Committee, applauded the proposed reforms and put them
in the context of threats to order: "We must not let ourselves be overtaken and dominated by events only to give in to claims when they
are expressed in violent fashion." He wanted to transform rather than
abolish the governments general, for fear of leading to "that which
our most eminent colleagues were able to call the 'balkanization' of
Africa." He saw the restructuring of the civil service as linked to the
"africanisation des cadres."[41]

Senghor stepped in to say he had at first opposed the project, but
with some modifications, it was now acceptable to him. The issue was
still the power the government was allocating to itself. But, he admitted, the current situation was "extraordinary"; he had "confidence"
in the present government but not in Parliament. And he agreed
completely with the key reforms of universal suffrage and the single
college. The creation of territorial civil services was essential; without
such a move autonomy would be "illusory." In the end, he would vote
for the law because "it contains several dispositions that we cannot
renounce"—a statement that says more about the blocked goals of the
previous ten years than a conviction that the new law was the breakthrough its advocates insisted it was.[42]

It was Pierre-Henri Teitgen, former Minister and initiator of the
bill, who laid bare why the Ministry was willing to break the logjam

[39] AUF, *Débats*, 13 March 1956, 259.
[40] Ibid., 291.
[41] Assemblée Nationale, *Débats*, 20 March 1956, 1065–68.
[42] Ibid., 1070.

on suffrage and territorial autonomy. For him, the issue was getting away from assimilation. He argued that assimilation had passed from a concept premised on the superiority and supposed attractiveness of French culture to a focus on the French standard of living. He made much of the new turn: "We will totally change the orientation, the spirit, the objectives of our overseas policy." There was a cultural dimension to his rejection of assimilation: "our compatriots from each of our overseas territories have a history different from ours, a past different from ours, traditions, structures, psychological reactions different from ours, a mentality, as some philosophers say, different from ours. They are less Cartesian, less logical, less juridical, more sensitive, more affective"—some lines that could have been quoted from Senghor.

But the fundamental issue was that it is "impossible that the metropole would be ready to accept all the consequences of assimilation. Why not have the courage to say so?" Assimilation had once meant, "Be, like all of us, citizens of the one and indivisible Republic, with the same rights as ourselves; you will have from this fact immediate satisfaction, you will by these means obtain dignity, freedom, independence, and autonomy." At that point, Félix Kir interrupted to say, "Assimilation is not demanded by the overseas territories. They prefer federation."

But now, Teitgen went on, assimilation meant something else:

> When you speak of assimilation to our compatriots from the overseas territories, they mean first and foremost economic, social assimilation, assimilation of standard of living. And if you say to them that France wants to bring about assimilation overseas, they reply to you: then give us immediately equal wages, equality in labor legislation, in social security benefits, equality in family allocations, in short, equality of living standards. . . . What would be the consequences? It would be necessary to attain this goal that the totality of French people consent to a reduction of 25 to 30 percent in their standard of living for the benefit of our compatriots of the overseas territories.

That the citizens of metropolitan France would not do. It was necessary to "turn the page." One had to think of other demands coming from overseas:

> demands for freedom, independence, pride, dignity, administrative autonomy, and in consequence to consecrate and develop the juridical, political, administrative, and economic personality of each of our territories, therefore to give to local, territorial representatives of the population of our territories, the management and the mastery of interests specific to these territories and territorial services that represent these particular and local interests.

Hence the need to empower assemblies and to separate territorial services—but not the "services de souveraineté," which should remain in the hands of the government in Paris. Such services of sovereignty should not be on the budget of the territories, and one could not expect for a territory like the Côte d'Ivoire to pay the expenses of Niger or Upper Volta. It was therefore necessary to "dissociate the federation," to reverse the centralizing tendencies focused on Dakar. Such a move was necessary politically as well as administratively and economically, for it was necessary to involve the "African in the bush" in politics, and Teitgen was convinced that the man of Côte d'Ivoire, Dahomey, or Guinea would find it hard to engage in "this adventure that develops far away from him."[43]

For a leading MRP politician, the road traveled was a long one. The centralizing tendencies of French policy, the focus on France as a reference point for cultural and social practices, the insistence on la République une et indivisible were being set aside, and a set of basic powers of government—but not all—were being entrusted to elected African governments. The MRP's ambivalence about the single college that had stymied African attempts at electoral reform for a decade fell by the wayside during the debate, with only brief criticism from predictable sources.[44] Teitgen himself was frank about the reasons for his change of heart. The indivisibility of the Republic had translated into the indivisibility of the French standard of living. African political and social movements had been too effective in their claim making, and stonewalling them was too risky in the current political climate.[45]

Other participants in the debate alluded to political danger—even though, with the exception of Cameroon, there was little violence in sub-Saharan Africa. But the war in Algeria, tension and violence in Morocco and Tunisia, and the recent loss of the war in Vietnam were in the background. One speaker referred to the Bandung meeting of 1955, where heads of new states had tried to produce a united "Third World" movement: "The spirit of Bandung blows across Africa. Watch

[43]Ibid., 1072–76.

[44]René Malbrant, ibid., 1080–81. Near the end of the debate, Defferre agreed to an amendment by a conservative deputy that would delay the institution of the single college until the Conseils de gouvernement had been put in place. African deputies insisted that getting rid of the double college was a matter of principle, vitally important to their constituents, and it should be abolished immediately. Defferre backed down and the Assembly decided that the single college should go into effect immediately except in Madagascar. Assemblée Nationale, *Débats,*, 22 March 1956, 1205–7.

[45]Personnel costs were as high as 58 percent of the budget in Senegal, 51 percent in Sudan. Comments of Torre, Secrétaire Général de l'AOF, Conférence interterritoriale des Vice-Présidents du Conseil, Chefs de Territoire, et Hauts-Commissaires, Dakar, 28 November 1957, 18G 298, AS. Lecaillon ("L'intégration," 22–23) gives the figure of 62 percent for AOF as a whole.

out."[46] Alduy, in his committee report, had referred to the moves toward self-government in British Africa. African deputies warned that "troubles could perhaps break out."[47]

Senghor had spoken on behalf of the Indépendants d'Outre-mer, with some reserve, in favor of the bill. Gabriel Lisette spoke more enthusiastically on behalf of the RDA, mentioning the reforms that "will allow overseas elites to accede to responsible posts." He affirmed his attachment to the French Union and the "communauté franco-africaine." Although he came down on the same side as Teitgen, he did not agree with the latter's contention that the loi-cadre would ease the financial burdens of empire. The entire reform would be "a failure, a failure creating an even graver situation than that which we face today if a powerful economic and social effort is not undertaken to give a strong foundation to the local governments."[48]

The Dahomean deputy Sourou Migan Apithy used the occasion to press the case for devolving all power to the individual territories, contrary to Senghor's and others' desire to give AOF and AEF a share of the power being given up by France. His argument was a cultural and political one: "Africans, like all populations of the overseas territories, have the strongest sentiment of belonging to a collectivity, a country, a 'patrie locale'—Senegal, Sudan, Dahomey, Chad, Gabon, etc.—which forms part of the French Republic, but distinguishes itself from the other members of the French community by its geographic, historical and human originality, by the conditions of its economic, psychological and religious life." He did not want to repudiate the "cohesion of the ensemble that they form with the people of France," but he feared that unless the Government General and the Grand Conseil de l'AOF were cut down to size, if not eliminated, the powers of the new territorial governments would not be effective. Those governments needed to retain "the integral part of their fiscal resources." He proposed another set of articles—virtually a new bill—as an alternative to the Teitgen-Defferre version. His proposal was voted down, but an African argument against African federation had been given prominence.[49]

African deputies, sensitive to the influence of civil service unions, wanted—and got—assurance that current functionaries would not be aversely affected and wanted assurance that Africanization of the civil service was a priority. Defferre insisted that Africanization was a priority, but he would not promise Sékou Touré that recruits for the ter-

[46] Paul Devinat, Assemblée Nationale, *Débats*, 20 March 1956, 1089.

[47] Alduy, ibid., 1065–68; Philibert Tsiranana, ibid., 1084.

[48] Lisette, ibid., 1090–91.

[49] Apithy, ibid., 21 March 1956, 1119–23. The Assembly also voted down an amendment to limit the Governments General's role to "general coordination." Defferre did not want to go so far, leaving to the Governments General "a right of inspection, coordination, and arbitration." Ibid., 1132.

ritorial services would have the same conditions as those in the State Services (those that remained under French control): the point was to give territorial assemblies the power to make such decisions. He did not say that those assemblies, elected by local taxpayers, would have an incentive to keep salaries below French standards.[50]

The law committed the government to "promote economic development and social progress" without making clear how such a commitment could be enforced. Discussion proved an occasion for speakers both to boast of what France had done so far and to warn of how expensive further social progress would be. Social development, some metropolitan deputies insisted, required a concomitant increase in agricultural and industrial production, a way of saying that if Africans wanted the social conditions of Europeans they had to produce like Europeans.[51]

One of the domains of long-blocked progress came up in the debate. Sékou Touré proposed an amendment to the loi-cadre requiring the "organization of the état-civil" so that inhabitants of the territories could have an identification document within a year. He cited all the trouble Africans were having to get appropriate documents and the need for better documentation given that the law provided for universal suffrage. Defferre insisted that he shared Sékou Touré's concerns, but "much time and effort is necessary." His Ministry would try to act as fast as possible, but Sékou Touré's proposal "would put me in a delicate situation if, because of material difficulties that could arise, it was not possible for me to meet the deadline fixed by this amendment." He asked Sékou Touré to withdraw his amendment, and Sékou Touré did so. Neither pointed out that one consequence of the transfer of functions to territorial governments would be that the état-civil would be their problem.[52]

As the vote neared, Saifoulaya Diallo, on behalf of the RDA, made clear how important the abolition of the double college was and concluded that the law "raises one more time a great hope in the overseas territories." The bill passed 477 to 99.[53] It had smooth sailing in the Conseil de la République, where more modest attempts at electoral and institutional reform had previously been blocked.[54] The loi-cadre was finally approved in June 1956.

[50] Sékou Touré, Diawadou Barry, and Defferre, ibid., 22 March 1956, 1173–76.

[51] A point emphasized by Robert Buron and accepted by Defferre. Ibid., 1189–93.

[52] Ibid., 1193–94. This issue also came before the Conseil de la République (*Débats*, 12 June 1956, 1073). Hassan Gouled pointed out how little had been done to advance the état-civil in the past five years. He wanted action to revise voter lists by the end of 1956, but in the end he withdrew his amendment.

[53] Assemblée Nationale, *Débats*, 1208–11.

[54] Conseil de la République, *Débats*, 7, 8, 12 June 1956, 955–92, 1018–30, 1044–74. The reporter for the Conseil's Commission de la FOM (Yvon Razac) called universal

Figure 4. Senegalese women voting, 1956.
Documentation Française: Information AOF.

In the most recent elections for the Assemblée Nationale (January 1956), 3.3 million West Africans had voted (out of 6 million inscribed on the voter lists). The number was twice that of the previous election. In the first elections after the loi-cadre—for territorial assemblies across AOF in March 1957—the number of voters jumped to 4.8 million people, out of over 10 million on the voter rolls. They were now voting under universal suffrage and in a single college.[55] In 1957 voters in each territory elected representatives who in turn chose the members of an executive council, including a "vice président du conseil," who would become in effect a junior prime minister, serving with the Governor (now referred to as Chef de Territoire) appointed by the

suffrage "the normal final step of the evolution begun at Liberation" and predicted that the single college would be "greeted with joy by all the overseas peoples." Ibid., 958. The strongest opposition came from Luc Durand-Réville—a supporter of colonial business interests—who thought that the autonomy being conceded to territories would be a step to federalism, which would be a step toward secession. He wanted more authority to remain with governors and for business interests to be represented on a council. Ibid., 966–68. The vote for a slightly modified bill was 194 to 63, with Africans voting for it. Ibid., 1076. The Assemblée Nationale (*Débats*, 19 June 1956, 2743) voted on second reading for the modified bill 446 to 98.

[55] Figures from Joseph Roger de Benoist, *L'Afrique occidentale française, de la conférence de Brazzaville (1944) à l'indépendance (1960)* (Dakar: Nouvelles Éditions Africaines, 1982), 529, 543.

French government. French West Africans had taken a big step toward governing themselves, within the French Union.

Implementing the Loi-Cadre, Debating Federalism

The implementation of the loi-cadre turned out to be more controversial than its enactment.[56] The conflict among different conceptions of territorialization and federalism became sharper. Senghor had injected into the debate the concept of "balkanization." He was invoking an earlier imperial breakup: that of the Austro-Hungarian Empire after its defeat in World War I into nation-states that were apparently too small, too poor, and too weak to stand up in the power struggles of Europe.[57]

The debate over federalism had gone public in Africa while the loi-cadre was under discussion in Paris. Sourou Migan Apithy published in the Dakar-based newspaper *Afrique Nouvelle* an article favoring federation at the level of the French Union, not AOF. Bertin Borna attacked Apithy's argument under the title "We Want Unity: We Refuse a Divisive Federalism!" He insisted that AOF—which Apithy wanted to dismantle—should be "the dream of all," providing a unity needed to combat exploitation and plan for economic change. Amadou Gaye joined in, arguing that the territories were artificial units and the loi-cadre would "reduce [AOF] to powder." Such a solution might satisfy the "egoism" of the rich territories, but leave the poor ones in the lurch. Apithy replied, "Individualize first, integrate afterward."[58] Not all Dahomeans agreed. In its Assemblée Territoriale, Emile Zinsou used Senghorian language to argue for "a federation of two directions,

[56] The procolonial right had all but given up on the defense of their sacred cows—a success for Teitgen and Defferre's strategy. One of their main lobbies now expressed the hope that Africans voting in a single college would continue to elect Europeans, that "the golden rule of interdependence of peoples" would result in cooperation of French and African elites, and that "wise men like Houphouët-Boigny" would keep everything on an even keel. Comité Central de la France d'Outre-mer (former Comité de l'Empire Français—the name was changed in 1947), Section de l'Afrique Occidentale, meeting of 20 December 1956, 100APOM 907, AOM.

[57] While Africans were worried about the risks of the loi-cadre, Aimé Césaire—the great advocate of departmental status for the "old colonies" of the French Caribbean—was thinking that the loi-cadre approach might be better than the status he had won. He was disappointed in the results of departmentalization, seeing the advantage of autonomy and an executive at the territorial level. Statements in Commission de la FOM of the Assemblée Nationale, 20, 27 June, 1 August 1956, C//15769, ANF.

[58] Sourou Migan Apithy, "Une seule solution valable: le Fédéralisme," *Afrique Nouvelle*, 24 April 1956; Bertin Borna, "Nous voulons l'unité: nous refusons un fédéralisme diviseur!" *Afrique Nouvelle*, 5 June 1956; Amadou Gaye, "Plus celà change . . . ," *Afrique Nouvelle*, 26 June 1956; Sourou Migan Apithy, "Individuer d'abord, intégrer ensuite," *Afrique Nouvelle*, 10 July 1956.

'vertical solidarity' with France and 'horizontal solidarity' with other West African territories, English- or French-speaking."[59]

Senghor's political party in Senegal, the BDS, was worried that the debate was going against its conception of federalism. Mamadou Dia, in his report to the May meeting of the party, railed against some African elected officials who "under the pretext of decentralizing in favor of the territories do not hesitate to look toward the suppression of the federations." The danger was "balkanization," "crumbling into bits," making each territory into a "closed space of isolated experiences." Against this tendency he argued that "Senegalese democracy will not be viable except in a larger framework of proletarian African democracy, integrating itself at the highest level, in the even larger framework of a *democracy of united working peoples.*" The world was in the process of closer integration "first, necessarily, horizontally, vertically only second." Africans had to unite, then the French Republic would be made into a federal republic, the French Union into a confederal state.[60]

To each his own federalism. Houphouët-Boigny gave a speech in France calling for "a relatively supple federal system. Let us give to the world this example of an assemblage of races and of people of diverse religions building in brotherhood a common house."[61] In Paris, he asserted, "The nationalisms of 25 years ago are outdated, we are in the era of interdependence of nations. And we want to build with the French people, despite differences of race, civilizations, and religious convictions, a fraternal community."[62]

Houphouët-Boigny's federalism was focused on the relationship of each territory to France, but it was the Governor of his Côte d'Ivoire—Pierre Lami—who gave a frank description of what was at stake. His territory, although it had only 13 percent of AOF's population, accounted for 37 percent of its external commerce and 49 percent of its exports. Lami did not object to having Ivorian revenues help out the poor countries of AOF, but he insisted that his budget was "ridiculously insufficient," especially given the new demands under the loi-cadre. He wanted more revenue to come to Abidjan, not Dakar.[63] And Houphouët-Boigny figured in the French government's plans to promote its interpretation of the loi-cadre. He sat in Guy Mollet's

[59] Dahomey, Territorial Assembly, 27 August 1956, cited in Affaires Courantes, Dahomey, to High Commissioner, Dakar, telegram, 30 August 1956, AP 2199/17, AOM.
[60] Mamadou Dia, "Rapport Moral" to VIIIe Congrès Annuel du BDS, *La Condition Humaine*, 31 May 1956.
[61] Speech reported in *Abidjan-Matin*, 19 June 1956. He had earlier praised the loi-cadre, in part for its suppleness. He applauded its extension to the territories of universal suffrage, the single college, Conseils de gouvernement, and budgetary autonomy. "Qu'apportera la loi-cadre?," *Afrique Nouvelle*, 15 May 1956.
[62] *Paris-Dakar*, 15 October 1956.
[63] *Abidjan-Matin*, 10 July 1956.

cabinet and his support was valued by the government. As a political analyst in the Ministry put it, "I believe, in effect, that it is essential that the RDA be committed, by the authority of its chief, a member of the government, to accept the reforms realized by the loi-cadre."[64]

The Grand Conseil of AOF was meanwhile defending its very existence. On 2 July its Commission Permanente adopted a motion demanding that the federal character of AOF be reaffirmed and that it—not just the territories—benefit from having a Conseil de gouvernement. Some services could be decentralized, but others should be kept at the level of the AOF. It sent a delegation to Paris to plead to such an effect with the Ministry.[65]

By year's end, relations between the Grand Conseil and Paris had deteriorated. The Grand Conseil claimed it was not being told about financial consequences of the loi-cadre and that it was being reduced to an "organ of coordination," the opposite of the desire, expressed by most of its members, for it to be a true legislature of the AOF. In protest, it refused unanimously to examine the budget for 1957, one of its main duties.[66] As the decrees implementing the loi-cadre came out, members perceived that they tend "to suppress the political and administrative entity that the AOF constitutes." Another delegation went off to Paris. Even RDA representatives close to Houphouët-Boigny thought the decrees would have "disastrous consequences," including the undermining of "federal solidarity, the asphyxiation of impoverished territories, the resurrection of tribal rivalries, and the birth of frequent conflicts among the territories."[67] Territorial assemblies in Senegal and Dahomey—but not Côte d'Ivoire—expressed solidarity with the Grand Conseil. Finally, in January, the High Commissioner gave the Grand Conseil enough assurances that its concerns would be taken seriously that it resumed its budgetary deliberations, passing a "transitional budget" about ten days later. The protesting territorial assemblies did likewise. The Grand Conseil would continue to have a role. The delegation to Paris reported the surprise in the Ministry at the dissatisfaction brewing in Africa; officials had thought the decrees of application would have been greeted with enthusiasm.[68]

[64] Pignon for Direction des Affaires Politiques, note to Minister, 4 October 1956, AP 491, AOM.

[65] *Afrique Nouvelle*, 29 June, 3 July 1956; Draft of text for High Commissioner to deliver to Commission Permanente du Grand Conseil de l'AOF on voyage to Dakar, 21 July 1956, AP 2292/10, AOM.

[66] *Paris-Dakar*, 20 November, 4, 5, 6, 10 December 1956.

[67] *Paris-Dakar*, 13 December 1956; *Afrique Nouvelle*, 18 December 1956; *L'Unité*, 29 December 1956.

[68] *Paris-Dakar*, 10, 16, 21 January 1957. See also Senegal, Assemblée Territoriale, *Débats*, 14 December 1956, 23–31. The issue of a government with an executive for Afrique Equatoriale Française was, according to its High Commissioner, of no particular

The malaise had broken into the open; it would turn out to be as much a conflict among African politicians as between Dakar and Paris.

When Teitgen presented on 22 January 1957 a report on the decrees to the Overseas Committee of the Assemblée Nationale, Senghor confronted him with the political storm that had arisen in the African assemblies.[69] They should have been consulted before the decrees were drafted. The decrees were producing the reverse of what he wanted: if some services went from the responsibility of the AOF to the territories, others—like post and telegraph and customs—went to Paris, as State Services. Modibu Keita (of the Union Soudanaise-RDA) evoked the disappointment of high hopes and threatened that government intransigence would lead the territories of AOF to demand still more autonomy, such as that conceded recently under the UN's gaze to Togo. Teitgen's reply hardly clarified the larger question of where power was to be located, but did make explicit that having spun off part of the burden of the civil service to the territories, he wanted to keep some means of exercising power close at hand:

> The decree defining State Services is the keystone of the political reforms proposed to apply the loi-cadre. A question of principle must be posed at the start: to know if one wants to commit to a federal-style system or a confederal-style system. If one intends to bring about a confederal system, it is necessary to give territories authority over all services necessary to organize true autonomy, the Republic assuming only obligations of exceptional nature. If one, on the contrary, wants to bring about a federal system, it is necessary to give the Republic all services necessary to maintain the coherence of the ensemble and all whose activities can only be efficient at the level of the Republic. My personal preferences go toward a federal system, the other system necessarily becoming a powder of small, impotent units.

He was using Senghorian language against Senghor—favoring a large ensemble, but one centered on Paris, not Dakar.[70]

Behind the scenes, the Minister was continuing to talk about the high costs of personnel—66 percent of the budget in Dahomey, 43 percent in Côte d'Ivoire—"the outer limit of their possibilities." And the

---

urgency. Gabon was opposed to any such move and enthusiasm elsewhere varied. High Commissioner, AEF, to Minister, 28 May 1958, AP 493, AOM.

[69] For the decrees proposed by the government, see Assemblée Nationale, *Documents*, Nos. 3424 to 3435 (3 December 1956), 887–915. The Socialist Paul Alduy, who had spoken for the loi-cadre in the Assemblée Nationale, now thought that Senghor's warnings were justified: "An excessive deconcentration would risk ending up in political fragmentation, a sort of new tribalization of the black continent." Assemblée Nationale, *Débats*, 29 January 1957, 365–66.

[70] Commission de la FOM, Session of 22 January 1957, C//15768, ANF.

government could not just reflect on the problem in peace, thanks to "the existence of organized unions controlling the quasi-totality of civil servants and agents of the administration, having at their disposal competent cadres and well-informed experts and coordination of their actions over the AOF as a whole. It is certain that the unions will not give up their current organization, strongly centralized, and will see their actions largely favored if they find in front of them an insufficiently coordinated Administration."[71] Defferre was not sure that territorial governments were up to the task of taking on the unions. As we shall see, they proved quite capable of doing so.

Senghor was worried what spinning off AOF's civil servants to the territories would signify for future possibilities of federation. He wanted at least to keep the door open to the development of interterritorial services. He and Teitgen argued before the Overseas Committee about whether territorial taxes should pay part of the cost of State Services and compromised on their paying no more than 10 percent. Teitgen would accept interterritorial services but not interterritorial cadres. The AOF would have to employ cadres seconded from the territories (or possibly from Paris), not its own civil servants. Senghor still wanted the decrees to give AOF's institutions real functions as embodiments of West African solidarity. Teitgen replied that "solidarity must be desired by the territories and not imposed." Lisette and Apithy agreed with Teitgen, not Senghor. In the end, the Committee agreed—with twenty-four voting in favor against thirteen abstentions—to refer to "coordination in economic, social, and cultural" matters and the role of AOF to "develop and manage their common interests and property." The Committee debate underscored the difficulty Senghor was facing: the argument against a federal structure for French West Africa was opposed not just by French leaders trying to keep power in Paris, but by African politicians trying to gain a strong piece of it for their own territories.[72]

But how much power would lie with the politicians chosen by their assemblies to sit on the Conseil de gouvernement? Apithy, drafting the report for the Committee, pushed for an all-elected Conseil, not one mixing elected and appointed members, and he wanted members to have the title of Minister, including a Prime Minister. In the end, he settled for Vice-Président du Conseil, conceded to the appointed Governor the right to preside over the Council, but argued that what counted was the powers attributed to the Vice-President. All seemed to agree that the Assembly and the Conseil should have jurisdiction over economic regulation of internal commerce, organization of

[71] Note, 24 December 1956, apparently a draft circular to the Chefs du Territoire, 18G 301, AS.

[72] Commission de la FOM, Session of 22 January 1957, C//15768, ANF.

markets and fairs, support for production, representation of economic interests, "the organization of chieftaincies," circumscriptions, rural collectivities, and most communes, the "creation of centers for the état-civil," and the development of basic education. Most important, Apithy's report on the government's draft decree said the assembly and the council would have charge of the "statutes of territorial civil servants, the systems of remuneration, holidays, social benefits, and retirement."

Here came the critical argument facing politicians in territories where public sector unions were a strong power base but whose electorates now included all citizens. Modibo Keita saw the dangers to newly elected African politicians:

> Initially directed at the Chef de Territoire [governor], workers' discontent will turn toward the Conseils de gouvernement which in fact will not be responsible and we will see a real tearing apart between cabinet members, territorial assemblies, and workers and opposition between different social strata of the population. . . . We agree to be the target of the discontent of our brothers, but on the condition that we have real responsibilities and that we can make them understand that when one aspires to the management of the benefits of these affairs one must in counterpart accept the difficulties.

Sékou Touré expressed similar concerns. If, as an elected official, he was going to take the heat from disappointed civil servants, he wanted to be sure that he was doing so on the basis of full responsibility before the territorial assembly.[73] Here, from the perspective of African deputies, was the trade-off that was at the heart of the loi-cadre: real power for African elected politicians in exchange for breaking the link between French salary scales and African ones, for the largest sector of salaried employees. They were not happy with the continued role of the Chef de Territoire in administration, and they were trying to get as much of a role for the elected council and its chosen leaders as they could possibly squeeze out of the French government.

Sékou Touré, Modibo Keita, and their colleagues would of course be running in electoral units defined by territory. They might face opposition in territorial elections organized by civil service unions, but they would also have powers of patronage and rights to allocate considerable resources. It was no coincidence that at the same time as this debate was going on Sékou Touré was trying to reorganize the French African trade union movement—to make it a specifically African organization (see below).

[73] Ibid., 22, 31 January 1957.

In the decrees that the government proposed, the Chef de Territoire—responsible to the government in Paris—represented French sovereignty, and the Vice-Président du Conseil represented the authority of the territorial assembly to enact, implement, and enforce laws. The tension between sovereignty and power was thus exposed in a way it was not in more unitary polities.

Defferre was quite clear where the responsibility for the civil service of each territory would lie: "The civil servants of the territorial services, when they have a claim to make, will be perfectly able to go to their elected representative in the territorial assembly and tell him: Here is what we demand. The territorial assembly will make its decision with total freedom." He added, "M. Sékou Touré, trade unionist, knows as well as I that any claim by workers has a financial impact and that it is not for the executive to decide but the deliberative assembly, which votes on the budget." That was what the Socialist Minister, like his MRP predecessor, wanted most to do: to let African elected officials take on the trade unions, to let African taxpayers pay the bills for an increasingly Africanized civil service.

Defferre recognized that for government to function well required "Franco-African collaboration. . . . Today, as we start practically from zero, if this collaboration is not established between the governor, the Conseil de gouvernement, and the territorial assembly, the first step will not be taken."[74] But the debate on the floor of the Assemblée Nationale on the implementation decrees had a different tone from that on the law itself. Senghor insisted that the decrees simultaneously gave too much power to Paris and "balkanized" Africa by undermining AOF and AEF. The government was conceding only "a semiautonomy, I do not want to see a semblance of autonomy; not the reality but the appearance of power." Frustrated that the metropolitan majority kept backing the government as various articles were challenged, he claimed there was "a real dispute between the metropole and the overseas territories, especially those of Black Africa." The President of the session tried to tell him that all present were "French deputies, with no other title." Senghor went on, "We have no intention either to appeal to the UN or to resort to violence, because we condemn it. . . . One solution remains to us: to use our right of refusal."[75]

Teitgen maintained his argument that the division of services was the "keystone" of the entire reform and that the State Services had to include foreign relations, security, ensuring "the respect of the liberty of citizens," courts, the Inspection du Travail, the police judiciaire,

[74] Ibid., 31 January 1957.
[75] Assemblée Nationale, *Débats*, 29 January, 1 February 1957, 371, 485–86. Senghor repeated his objection made earlier in Committee that the territorial assemblies—which were supposed to benefit from the decrees—had not been consulted in their drafting.

services that ensured the cohesion of all and "social and cultural progress," monetary services, and external communications. The French state would pay for all that; its functionaries would administer them.[76] The argument was partly about the list, but more fundamentally about the disappearance of the middle: those services that were not specific to each territory but that were claimed by Paris, whereas Senghor insisted that they belonged at a West African level. Senghor wanted the federation to have at least a piece of the action in regard to postal services, telephone, and telegraph, and higher education, but his proposals were voted down.[77] Yet even those deputies like Apithy who opposed the West African federation did not like the fact that the reforms left too much power with the Chef de Territoire, while the administrators of the State Services were not responsible to the territories at all.[78]

Robert Buron tried to find a middle ground: the territories were free to federate themselves—if they so chose—but first they had to establish their autonomy. Perhaps AOF and AEF might want to go in different directions. Apithy supported this argument—one must first establish "elements at the base," rather than see federalism imposed by the Assemblée Nationale or the Grand Conseil de l'AOF.[79]

Defferre understood the disagreement among Africans about a federal ensemble for West Africa. He did not want to go too far in either direction, and he did not like Apithy's plan to make the Vice-Président du Conseil into a Prime Minister and weaken the authority of Chefs de Territoire. Such a move would turn the territories into "veritable states," contrary to the Constitution. Teitgen agreed. Neither the current nor the former Minister could foresee that only two years later, the venerable title of "state" would be given to these territories as part of a new constitution.[80]

The arguments over the decrees circled round the central issue: African demands for the "democratic management of their own affairs." Mamadou Dia enlarged the context: Nigeria was heading toward some form of self-government; the trust territories of Togo and Cameroon were gaining more autonomy than was being conceded to West Africa. There had been talk, he said, about a "Cameroonian citizenship" (a reasonable proposition, since Cameroonians did not have French nationality and were citizens of the French Union, not the Republic). But his current demands were moderate: "We are not there yet. We do not demand for the overseas territories a citizenship of Dahomey, of the Côte d'Ivoire, or of Senegal. We thus remain behind the status of

[76] Ibid., 29 January 1957, 363–64.
[77] Ibid., 31 January 1957, 442, 446.
[78] Ibid., 29 January 1957, 366–67.
[79] Ibid., 30 January 1957, 396–97.
[80] Defferre, ibid., 30 January 1957, 406–9; Teitgen, ibid., 425.

Cameroon and Togo." In fact as of August 1956, the *ressortissants* of Togo became Togolese citizens, while effective April 1957, those of Cameroon became Cameroonian citizens. Both citizenship decrees stated that the citizens of these new entities would, at least while they remained under UN trusteeship, still enjoy the rights of French citizens, while French citizens in those countries would enjoy the rights of Togolese or Cameroonian citizens.[81] The interlayering of citizenship rights in parts of the Union upped the ante for the other African territories.

The details of organizing the Conseils de gouvernement produced close votes in the Assemblée Nationale. Africans did force the administration to ensure that the councils would have room to operate and that they would reflect the will of the territorial assemblies. The administration refused to back down on setting two kinds of civil services on different trajectories, and the advocates of a West African federation failed to get a civil service attached to such an entity. In the end, the government was allowed to go ahead with decrees fairly close to what it wanted. It had conceded real power to the territories, and it had distanced itself from some of the burdens of an empire of citizens, especially of a civil service of people claiming the right to equal salaries and benefits.

Senghor was bitter over the undermining of AOF. Dia thought "we find ourselves at an impasse," but he still wanted an elected Conseil de gouvernment and therefore, "We wish despite everything that the reform goes through." Other African deputies thought they had done well. Apithy saw the bill opened up new possibilities: "I am convinced that this instrument, imperfect as it is, can nonetheless be used to concrete ends and that all the hopes we have placed in voting for this text would not be disappointed." RDA leader Ouezzin Coulibaly thought that African efforts had injected "a bit more of the democratic spirit and to do this we struggled while taking into account African realities." He reminded everyone that Africans had ten years of experience working in assemblies; they knew what compromises were and they had avoided "the politics of all or nothing, which would be the politics of the worst."[82]

The debate in Paris had only just begun when Mamadou Dia published in *Afrique Nouvelle* an article under the title "Une Afrique Unie." He described the past ten years of action by elected African

[81] Dia, ibid., 422–23. The decrees he was referring to are Decree 56–847 of 24 August 1956, *Journal Officiel du Territoire du Togo*, 30 August 1956; Decree 57–501 of 16 April 1957, *Journal Officiel de la République Française*, 18 April 1957, 4112–13. On the complexities of the situation, see Roger Decottignies, "La condition des personnes au Togo et au Cameroun," *Annales Africaines 1957*, 7–52.
[82] Assemblée Nationale, *Débats*, 2 February 1957, 555–57.

representatives in Paris as a failure, and he attributed the failure to a lack of a coherent doctrine:

> The worst is that in the majority of territories, even where the RDA or the IOM extends its influence, political groups are often only electoral committees whose principal role is investiture, and the leaders, fetish-men, [are] more solicitous of ensuring their authority and the growth of their prestige than to educate the masses politically. . . . The triumph of "electoralism" cannot accommodate itself to the in-depth work that puts the person elected under the control of the voter and enlightens his choice.

Dia understood quite well how his own political apparatus functioned. The electoralism he condemned was likely to get stronger once elected politicians had more resources to seek and to distribute.

To get beyond this narrowly focused brand of politics required the creation of "a great socialist federation." Overseas citizens needed to "save the situation by imposing an indispensable revolution in French politics." Unifying African political parties was "the only means for us to accomplish our mission in regard to France, in regard to the world."[83] He had put his finger on the crucial danger emerging from the loi-cadre—of territorially focused "electoralism." He and Senghor would indeed try to take the step of unifying parties across French Africa to work for federation, but it would not be easy.

The French Connection versus African Unity: Trade Union Controversies

In proposing the loi-cadre, Teitgen and his colleagues were trying to tame one of the most successful claim-making efforts of African social movements since the passage of the Constitution—for equal pay and benefits for wage workers. Unions of civil servants had been the largest and best organized, and for them the demand for equivalence among all citizens working for the government had been powerful. By creating territorial civil services, the loi-cadre broke into this logic of equivalence and put African politicians within each territory in the position of deciding how much of union demands would be met and figuring out how to pay for them.

---

[83] Mamadou Dia, "Une Afrique Unie," *Afrique Nouvelle*, 15 January 1957. Dia feared that European France, far from providing a solution to the problem, was itself heading in a dangerous direction, developing in response to the Algerian war "a neo-nationalism, worthy of Maurras and his epoch."

But the top leadership of African trade unionism were themselves stepping off the pathway they had successfully pursued. Most major African unions were affiliates of the French confederations—large groupings of diverse unions. The largest was the West African branch of the Confedération Générale du Travail (CGT), the union close to the French Communist Party. Some scholars have argued that the effort to break this connection paralleled other aspects of decolonization: the CGT treated African workers as if they needed French tutelage. Yet African trade unionists were as capable of using French comrades as the other way around—for their experience and resources, for the legitimate place within French industrial relations. The federations of African unions had a record of success in the battle for social equality. Why then would they seek to go in another direction?

I have discussed this history in detail elsewhere, and so will be brief.[84] For some African political leaders in the mid-1950s, notably Sékou Touré, trade unions were a springboard; for others, like Houphouët-Boigny, they were of minor interest compared to the relatively prosperous farmers who were his base; for Senghor, labor leaders had a place in a broader movement with himself at the apex. Seeking to move beyond his working-class base, Sékou Touré was trying by the mid-1950s to find a broader ideological basis for his political campaigns. Aware that political power was increasing attainable, trade union leaders increasingly emphasized the African side of their affinities. Sékou Touré began to speak of the "personality of African trade unionism." The Senegalese CGT voted in November 1955 to form a new central organization, the Confédération Générale du Travail-Autonome (CGTA), independent of the French CGT and cooperating with Senghor's political party. Guinea's Union des Syndicats—linked to Sékou Touré Parti Démocratique de Guinée (PDG)—joined the CGTA in May 1956. By year's end the CGTA had nearly matched the CGT's sixty thousand members.[85]

The old CGT now realized that the attractions of autonomy had to be confronted, while the new CGTA saw unity as necessary in its struggle against colonial authority. The rivals eventually decided—at the very time of the debates over implementing the loi-cadre in Paris—to form a new exclusively African association, the Union Générale des Travailleurs d'Afrique Noire (UGTAN).[86]

[84] What follows is largely based on my *Decolonization and African Society*, chap. 11. See also Babacar Fall, *Le travail au Sénégal au XXᵉ siècle* (Paris: Karthala, 2011); George Martens, "Le syndicalisme en Afrique occidentale d'expression Française: de 1945 à 1960," *Le Mois en Afrique* 178–79 (1980): 74–97 and 180–81 (1980–81): 53–83; Andras November, *L'évolution du mouvement syndical en Afrique occidentale* (Paris: Mouton: 1965).

[85] Martens, "Le syndicalisme en Afrique occidentale," 54–61; November, 93–94, 97–100.

[86] Cooper, *Decolonization and African Society*, 414–15.

In the first elections for territorial assemblies under the loi-cadre, many UGTAN leaders joined the electoral competition and some won seats. Victorious party leaders were anxious to have a labor leader in the Conseil de gouvernement, for purposes of co-optation and constituency building. In eight of the nine territories of AOF and Togo, trade union leaders were named Minister of Labor or Minister of the Civil Service.[87]

French officials expected that the entry of African labor leaders into ministries would tame them and above all curb the CGT. To a significant extent they were right. UGTAN in some instances intervened to cool off strike movements. UGTAN itself witnessed a vigorous debate over whether their comrades, now in power, were failing to support the union cause. Much of the rank and file focused on typical issues—revisions of the minimum wage, equalization of benefits, and the status of the civil service under the "territorialization" policies of the loi-cadre.[88]

CGTA and UGTAN, even before the entry of leaders into the ministries, had begun to articulate an ideology that subordinated "class struggle" to "national liberation." At a CGTA meeting in February 1956, Sékou Touré argued, "Although the classes of metropolitan and European populations battle and oppose each other, nothing separates the diverse African social layers [couches sociales]." Hence there was no social basis from which to contest the actions of the governing elite. The CGTA denied that the international working class had an interest in African problems.[89] As UGTAN was born, its leaders began to insist that the struggle against colonialism should "take pride of place over the class struggle."[90]

The closer Sékou Touré got to power, the less like a trade unionist he sounded. In February 1958, he told trade unionists that a strike against "the organisms of colonialism" or against employers—such as the 1947–48 railway strike—was "just," but now an elected assembly "is sovereign for all questions relevant to the world of work. . . . But when [a strike] is directed against an African Government, it affects African authority. . . . Trade unionism for trade unionism's sake is historically unthinkable in current conditions, trade unionism of class just as much. . . . The trade union movement is obligated to reconvert itself to remain in the same line of emancipation."[91]

[87] Martens, "Le syndicalisme en Afrique occidentale," 88–89.

[88] Cooper, *Decolonization and African Society*, 415–17.

[89] AOF, Service de Sécurité, Bulletin d'Information, February 1956, 17G 627, AS; Senegal, Renseignements, 21 February 1956, 21G 215, AS; Senegal, Renseignements, 2 August 1956, "Rapport Moral et d'Activités" to Comité Générale de l'Union CGTA of Senegal-Mauritania, 7–8 July 1956, 17G 610, AS.

[90] Governor, Dahomey, to High Commissioner, 22 January 1957, K 421 (165), AS.

[91] Exposé de M. le Vice Président Sékou Touré à l'occasion de la conférence du 2 février 1958 avec les résponsables syndicaux et délégués du personnel RDA, "Le RDA

The argument that the existence of a semiautonomous African government preempted the claims of workers was a notable dimension of the post-loi-cadre political scene. When a strike broke among civil servants in Sudan in early 1958, unions accused the government of refusing the "just demands of workers." But the party newspaper insisted that unionized workers should give the governments the space it needed "to find the most appropriate means to perfect the semiautonomy of management, to have perspectives of the future, to envision the possibilities for disentanglement given our budgetary possibilities. To deny them the right and this will would be a blow to their freedom of initiative, an alienation of their action, an obstacle to governing with intelligence, a desire to confine them into routine." It soon upped the ante by warning unions against becoming "instruments of sabotage of the new institutions."[92]

Although colonialism was the arch-villain in the rhetoric of the autonomists, some French officials considered UGTAN "favorable to our future in Africa"—not without risks of its own, but still preferable to communist-connected trade unionism.[93] So much did they think they needed an alternative to the kind of trade unionism they had been facing that they badly underestimated Sékou Touré's determination to practice politics his own way (see chapter 6).

The Inspecteur Général du Travail predicted in April 1957 that as RDA members, with their UGTAN connections, entered ministries, they would provide workers "very meager satisfaction in regard to the demands they are now expressing." Workers would soon be "caught between their search for a rapid and substantial improvement in their material conditions and their respectful fear of local African authorities, who will not lack means to make their point of view prevail."[94]

A bitter confrontation occurred in Dahomey where the demands of different groups of workers came together at the end of 1957 into a strike movement. The Minister of Labor, Guillaume Fagbamigbe—formerly of the Dahomean CGT and later UGTAN—was criticized for having "betrayed the cause of the working class." A speaker at a union meeting commented that "it was easier to obtain satisfaction

et l'action syndicale dans la nouvelle situation politique des T.O.M.," PDG (9)/dossier 7, Centre de Recherche et de Documentation Africaine, Paris.

[92] *L'Essor*, 14, 21 February 1958. Mamadou Dia, years later, also used the word "sabotage" to describe what the unions had done by going on strike in 1959. Dia, *Mémoires d'un militant*, 99.

[93] "Note sur la situation du syndicalisme C.G.T. en A.O.F.," March 1956, 19PA/3/37, AOM; IGT, "Evolution de la situation syndicale en A.O.F.," 28 July 1956, 17G 610, AS; Minister to High Commissioner, draft of a letter, not sent, dated 8 February 1957, AP 2264/8, AOM.

[94] AOF, IGT, "Note sur l'évolution du syndicalisme en A.O.F.," 19 April 1957, IGT 11/2, AOM.

from a European Labor Inspector than it is now from an African Minister." Similarly, when some UGTAN leaders in Senegal took their grievances to Mamadou Dia, Vice-Président du Conseil, he told them huffily that the "particular struggle of the workers to resolve secondary contradictions risks compromising the general struggle engaged by the Conseil de gouvernement, the Unions, and the Senegalese People" to ensure real autonomy from France.[95] UGTAN's top officials tried to convince workers that the local administrations were not "organisms to combat systematically, but organisms elected by the populations, and which should be served to advance the historic march of Black Africa toward its unity and its development."[96]

Of course there was much to be debated about the respective interests of wage workers, peasants, fishermen, merchants, and others in an African polity committed to social betterment. But Dia—let alone Sékou Touré—was trying to shut off a dialogue, not open one up. The Guinean trade unionist David Soumah eloquently warned of the danger: "A unity which ends up in reality in subordinating trade union action to the good will of governments and employers, which submits trade unionism, the very expression of liberty, to a too narrow obedience toward political parties and political men, neutralizes the action of the masses for social progress."[97]

There is no evidence that the movement for autonomous African trade unionism arose from a spontaneous nationalism of the mass of African workers. The creation of UGTAN was initiated from the top down, and individual unions, even after the turn in the leadership's orientation and the inauguration of African governments in the territories, often pursued the familiar goals of better wages and benefits and equality with French civil servants. After trade union leaders like Sékou Touré became candidates for territorial office, they were seeking to subsume workers' interests in a broader constituency and to control the agenda of social intervention themselves. Once African politicians, including former trade unionists, entered political office, the insistence on unity of action had both resources and threats behind it. The appeal to African unity was not necessarily unifying.

[95] Dahomey, Renseignements, October 1957 to April 1958, in 17G 588, AS; Governor, Dahomey, to Minister, 30 January 1958, AP 2189/12, AOM; Sûreté, Bulletin d'Information August 1957, 17G 631, AS; Renseignements, April 1958, 17G 633, AS.

[96] Alioune Cissé to UGTAN Congress, Bamako, 8–10 March 1958, reported in AOF, Service de Sécurité, Bulletin d'Information, March 1958, 17G 633, AS; reports on the Réunion Interterritoriale de la Fonction Publique, Dakar, in AOF, "Renseignements d'activtiés communistes et apparentées," 18 January 1958, 17G 620, AS; Afrique Nouvelle, 14 February, 21 March 1958. More generally, see Cooper, Decolonization and African Society, 420–23.

[97] Report of David Soumah, Secretary General, to Congress de la CATC, Abidjan, 10–12 March 1958, 17G 610, AS.

"Balkanization" or Federalism in French West Africa?

The elections to the territorial assemblies in March 1957 brought into place representatives who could not just speak for their constituents but who could choose a Conseil de gouvernement that would exercise power. With a Vice-Président du Conseil working alongside—and often in tension with—a governor, and with elected members exercising executive responsibilities in ministries with specific functions, the nature of politics had changed.[98] In Côte d'Ivoire, Guinea, Upper Volta, and the Sudan, territorial parties affiliated with the RDA won a decisive majority. In Senegal, Senghor's Bloc Démocratique Sénégalais (transformed into the Bloc Populaire Sénégalais after merging with other parties in early 1957) was solidly in control; so too was the Union Progressiste Mauritanienne in its territory. In Dahomey and Niger, the political scene was more divided. But in most of AOF, early efforts by political leaders like Houphouët-Boigny, Senghor, Modibo Keita, and Sékou Touré had pulled together political machines that incorporated local power brokers and acquired a momentum of their own.

The modus vivendi of African parties in the late 1950s and early 1960s attracted considerable attention from political scientists at the time—who saw the possibilities and limitations of a vigorous, self-consciously modernizing political process.[99] I focus on a question of political imagination: how, in the new political landscape, did political elites imagine the relationship of territory, French West Africa, and French Union?

In a series of interviews in the summer of 1957, *Afrique Nouvelle* showed its readers how leaders were staking out their positions in the aftermath of the loi-cadre. Lamine Guèye emphasized that the French Union was not functioning, and the only way to reconstruct it was by "something new inspired be federalism," not necessarily in a classic sense. Senghor was pushing his "confederal Union" to replace the French Union, and he chastised his colleagues on the French left for not giving up their "superiority complex." For them to do so would at last be to decolonize, and "decolonization is one of the prior conditions of the Franco-African Community." Houphouët-Boigny also

---

[98] Sékou Touré, taking office as Vice-Président du Conseil, sent a telegram to the President of the French Republic "to affirm his will to work toward the reinforcement of the fraternal ties between France and the territory and to work for the harmonious development of the Franco-African community." Telegram, 11 May 1957, AP 2187/7, AOM.

[99] See Ruth Schachter Morgenthau, *Political Parties in French-Speaking West Africa* (Oxford: Clarendon, 1964), Aristide Zolberg, *Creating Political Order: The Party States of West Africa* (Chicago: Rand McNally, 1966), and many studies of political change in the 1950s and 1960s in individual African countries. On AEF, see Florence Bernault, *Démocraties ambiguës en Afrique Centrale: Congo-Brazzaville, Gabon: 1940–1965* (Paris: Karthala, 1996).

spoke of a "Franco-African Community" and emphasized raising the African standard of living as a prerequisite, while cautioning about the difficulties of constitutional reform. Jean-Marie Koné of the Union Soudanais-RDA was more specific: he wanted the AOF to become a federation with its own executive and assembly. Ouezzin Coulibaly thought the loi-cadre had gone too far in the direction of decentralization, but that the territories should decide how much power they would concede to the federation. Apithy maintained his outright opposition to a federal executive for the AOF.[100] There was more agreement on both maintaining and transforming the relationship with France than on giving substance to the notion of African unity.

The thinking of Senghor and Dia was evolving as they confronted the new order's split personality, half territorial, half Parisian. Where they wanted to be was in between: "It is the federal state of AOF that would be integrated into the federal French Republic."[101] Faced with the dangers of territorial fragmentation, Senghor was now saying that there had to be two layers of federation, one in West Africa, the second the French Republic. Then would come the French Union, reconfigured as a confederation.

Here we have the two fronts on which African political elites would be engaged until overtaken by the events in Algeria and the crisis of the French Union in 1958: the old battle to redo the constitutional provisions on the Union and the emerging struggle among African leaders over how to organize political life among themselves. The latter was not just a question of parties jockeying for power or of jurists trying to define institutions: it was a question of where collective belonging, a sense of commonality, lay. In other words, where in Africa did one find a nation, or the potential of building a nation? And how did one translate such visions into political programs?

On the institutional front, the struggle to revise Title VIII of the Constitution continued up until the crisis of 1958. African representatives presented new proposals to the various Parisian assemblies; political parties included revision of the Constitution in their programs; African newspapers repeatedly called for constitutional revision. The new wrinkle came from experience—the frustrations of semiautonomous government, and particularly the tensions between Chefs de Territoire (governors) and Vice-Présidents du Conseil. Mamadou Dia, who took on the latter post after his and Senghor's party won the 1957 elections in Senegal, told the Territorial Assembly in December that his powers were "incomplete and insufficient." He referred to "the regime of *semiautonomy* and *supervised freedom*." He later referred to the loi-cadre as "a poisoned gift." Now, "strengthened by popular

[100] *Afrique Nouvelle*, 25 June 1957.
[101] *Afrique Nouvelle*, 6 November 1956.

suffrage," he was demanding "complete internal autonomy." French officials in Paris thought Dia's critique unfair and wanted the High Commissioner to cool him off, but not "to engage in a polemic with Mr. Mamadou Dia." The situation was made more difficult by what Dia termed the "French political crisis," entailing repeated changes of ministers in Paris and growing conflict over how to handle the Algerian situation, leading Dia to conclude "I was paralyzed in my actions." The Chef de Territoire, however, had a more positive view of Dia, recognizing in him someone for whom the Franco-African community was not "a soporific slogan" but "a necessity recognized by him and brought to fruition concretely and daily by his comportment and that of his ministers since they took up their posts."[102]

The situation remained in an important sense colonial.[103] The Chef de Territoire still represented French sovereignty. Some police functions were territorial, and the territory was expected to pay for them as well as to supply needed personnel to the Chef de Territoire, but security was ultimately a state—that is, French—responsibility.[104] The Assembly and the Conseil de gouvernement responsible to it fixed export tariffs except for minerals and oil and voted on a development plan. They controlled the situation of territorial civil servants, internal commerce, tourism, the état-civil, public hygiene, urbanism, jails, and so on. They oversaw rural collectivities. But the Chef de Territoire appointed Chefs de circonscription (local administrators), even though the Minister admitted that such officials had a dual role, representing French authority and the territorial executive.[105] The French government, as guarantor of constitutional rights and responsible for the appeals courts, retained control of the judicial process, but with some

[102] Dia, Speech to Assemblée Territoriale of Senegal, 20 December 1957, VP 114, AS; Directeur des Affaires Politiques, Note pour M. le Ministre, 24 December 1957; AFP report on conversation with Dia, 16 November 1957, AP 2292/1, AOM; Dia, *Mémoires d'un militant*, 70. Dia also complained directly to the High Commissioner about the latter's "literal, restrictive, and static interpretation . . . of the loi-cadre." Dia to High Commissioner (Cusin), 26 December 1957, VP 114, AS; Chef de Territoire to High Commissioner of AOF, 6 June 1957, AOF/Dakar/253, ADN.

[103] The Chef de Territoire, Pierre Lami, told Senegal's assembly of its powers and called for working together in the name of "our lost leaders," listing Lat Dior, El Hadj Umar, Amadou Bamba, and generals Blanchot and Faidherbe, in other words putting colonial conquerors and the people they repressed in the same category of memorialization. Assemblée Territoriale, *Débats*, 14 May 1957, 116–18.

[104] Minister to High Commissioners of AOF, AEF, and Madagascar, 24 July 1957, 18G 195, AS. Some members of the AUF tried unsuccessfully to pass responsibility for internal public order to territorial governments on the grounds that they should enforce the laws they had the power to make. Proposition of Robert Schmitt, Alfred Bour, and others (MRP), AUF, No. 190 of session of 1957–58, 25 March 1958, C//16374, ANF.

[105] Transcript of meeting of Presidents and Vice-Presidents of Conseils de gouvernement, Paris, 10 February 1958, VP 363, AS.

misgivings officials realized that assemblies would have to set penalties for violation of laws they passed.[106]

The High Commissioner of AOF, Gaston Cusin, wanted to be sure that African politicians learned a few lessons about the responsibility that went with their new power. Reminding the Grand Conseil that over 50 percent of the budgets went to personnel costs, he called such expenses "an unbearable burden on our budgets." L'AOF had to "slow down the growth of personnel expenses. Thus is offered to the territories the latitude to organize their civil service according to their conceptions and consistent with their means." The effort depended on "the Africanization of the civil service." Africanization in turn required "more and more effective social institutions . . . no economic progress without a social infrastructure, no infrastructure without resources." And that problem was not France's any more: "The responsibility for development of the economy, especially agriculture has been entirely transferred to the territorial governments."[107] It was the territories that faced the dilemma of needing economic development to pay the social costs necessary for that development to take place—and to muster the patience and the political will to let such a process unfold over time.

France would help, and it would therefore retain leverage. Its experts were needed in various domains of territorial government and through the State Services. As part of a large economic ensemble, French officials and most African politicians agreed, the impoverished territories stood a better chance of developing, even if they were assuming much of the financial burden and political risk. Such were the shifting balances of roles and power in the mid-1950s.[108] The authority of the appointed representatives of the French Republic was inscribed in the French Constitution, as was that of the Assemblée Nationale in

[106]Ministère de la FOM, "Réformes apportées dans les territoires relevant du Ministère de la FOM par la loi No. 56.619 du 23 juin 1956 dite loi-cadre, August 1957," 4AG 43, ANF; High Commissioner to President of Grand Conseil, nd [July 1958], 18G 272, AS; "Tableau indiquant l'extension des attributions des Assemblées Territoriales d'AOF et d'AEF," December 1956, AP 493, AOM; Ministre, Circular to High Commissioners of AOF and AEF, 15 May 1957, 18G 282, AS. The Ministry was careful to keep territorial ministers from having contact with foreign governments, except via the French government. Minister of FOM to Minister of Foreign Affaires, 20 August 1958, Cabinet du Ministre/Couve de Murville/110, ADLC.

[107]Cusin, Allocation to Grand Conseil, 21 June 1957, published as a pamphlet by the Grand Conseil; Cusin, speech to Grand Conseil, *Bulletin*, 16 November 1957, 32.

[108]Territorialization undercut the authority of the once-powerful Governor General, who no longer held that title but retained that of High Commissioner. He officially was the "depositaire" of the power of the Republic, and under the loi-cadre he delegated that responsibility to the Chef de Territoire. The Minister instructed each High Commissioner that he "cannot intervene in the management of the interests of the territories, that is in the functioning of the territorial services of the territories," but he could only act in relation to the "services of the Group" (i.e., of AOF as a whole). Circulars, 17 May, 8 August 1957, 18G 282, AS.

Paris, which had chosen to delegate some of its authority and could, presumably, take it back. To change such a division of sovereign authority would require amending the Constitution.

A revealing illustration of the tussles that ensued can be seen in regard to the Senegalese government's decision in 1958 to move the capital of the territory from Saint-Louis to Dakar. Mamadou Dia thought Dakar was much more in the center of things; the Overseas Minister was not happy with the expense of such a move, but more important—and hypocritically given that he was trying to dismantle the AOF—argued that since Dakar was the federal capital, Senegal should not move its offices into it without the consent of the rest of AOF. The Assemblée de l'Union française wanted to get involved too. The Minister did not help his cause by saying that "we are not yet at the point of maturity and precision" to take such a decision. Dia was irate. The location of the capital of Senegal was Senegal's business, and Dakar was "the flesh of our flesh."[109]

Dakar became the capital of Senegal. An African government could play tough and win. The loi-cadre was not just an instrument for decentralizing administration. It had given a measure of power to political bodies, conscious of their having been installed by an African electorate, exercising their new prerogatives, all too aware of the powers that they did not have.[110] Hence the demand for full autonomy, above all to get rid of the appointed Chef de Territoire and make the executive fully responsible to the Territorial Assembly and through universal suffrage to the people.

The question of an African federation did not go away after the setback of the loi-cadre. The Grand Conseil voted unanimously in early September 1957 to demand a federal executive for the AOF. But delegates from the Côte d'Ivoire soon complained that Senegal and its friends had fiddled the terms of the debate, and they dissociated themselves from it.[111] The scene was repeated in April 1958: the Conseil voted unanimously in favor of a federal executive for the AOF, and the Côte d'Ivoire delegation later objected to the way the debate

[109]AUF, reports and propositions No. 180 of 18 March 1958, No. 208 of 16 May 1958, C//16374, ANF; text of Dia's speech in Saint-Louis, 4 March 1958, 21G 223, AS. Dia also mentioned disagreements with the French government over the recruitment of teachers, the status of the civil service, and other subjects. Press conference, 5 March 1958, 21G 223, AS.

[110]For more on the tensions—but also efforts at cooperation—see Conférence interterritoriale des Vice-Présidents du Conseil, Chefs de Territoire, et Hauts Commissaires, Dakar, 28 November 1957, 18G 298, AS. Not least of the problems was that the territories faced growing responsibilities with inadequate budgetary resources. The High Commissioner admitted that for some years the burden "must be shared between the Africans on the one hand and metropolitans on the other." But African leaders, he said, had to know that if you give a subsidy, "it's on you."

[111]*Afrique Nouvelle*, 3 September 1957; *Paris-Dakar*, 4 September 1957.

was conducted. Sékou Touré, along with Tidjani Traoré, authored a resolution on behalf of the RDA criticizing the attitude of the Côte d'Ivoire delegation. His colleague from Guinea Moussa Diakité attacked "territorialism" and argued that an executive responsible to a West African legislature "will develop the fraternity and solidarity lying among Africans of all races and will be the only valid basis of the Franco-African ensemble in which we want to integrate freely by association."[112]

Houphouët-Boigny was just as firm in the opposite direction: "The Côte d'Ivoire has made its choice: whatever happens it will adhere *directly* to the Franco-African Community." Other territories, he said, could group themselves or not as they chose. He conceded only that there could be "a certain degree of economic coordination at Dakar." But he had to respond to the way others were framing the debate. He denied the charge that he was opposed to "African unity," stating, "We have brought about the unity of our tribes inside our territories. Just as Brittany has found its own unity in the midst of the French ensemble, we will bring about African unity within the vast framework of the federation"—the French federation that is. He denied his motives were economic or personal. He was all for a federal executive: "Yes, but in Paris, not in Dakar."[113] Mamadou Coulibaly, representative from the Côte d'Ivoire to the Assemblée de l'Union française, warned that the federal executive at Dakar would give rise to "federal superministries that are both onerous and inefficient." The Côte d'Ivoire was ready to quit the federation of AOF "to demand an entire autonomy of administration and management while waiting to be able to federate directly with France."[114] The Assemblée Territoriale of the Côte d'Ivoire indeed resolved in May 1958, in the midst of the government crisis in France, to demand "its autonomy within the federally based Franco-African community," adding that it rejected "any direction, assembly, or executive at the level of Dakar." It threatened that if the Grand Conseil ever brought up the question of the federal executive again, it would "withdraw again, purely and simply, from the Grand Conseil."[115]

[112]*Afrique Nouvelle*, 11 April 1958; AOF, Grand Conseil, *Bulletin*, 5 April 1958, 298–303.

[113]*Afrique Nouvelle*, 18 April 1958. On the same page was an article by Amadou Wade, "La Côte d'Ivoire n'est pas la vache à lait de l'AOF" [the Côte d'Ivoire is not the milk cow of AOF]. He was refuting an allegation made in the Territorial Assembly of the Côte d'Ivoire that this territory was paying a disproportionate share of the bills for AOF. He insisted that the Côte d'Ivoire got more than its share of infrastructural development and returns from the receipts of the AOF. He thought a federation of French West Africa could function without the Côte d'Ivoire.

[114]Mamadou Coulibaly, "Les raisons de la décision ivoirienne," *Afrique Nouvelle*, 2 May 1958.

[115]*Afrique Nouvelle*, 30 May 1958.

The argument was as much within the RDA as it was between the RDA and Senghor's political formation.[116] Jean-Marie Koné and Sékou Touré favored a French West African federation inside a Franco-African community. In the September 1957 RDA conference in Bamako, it became clear that Houphouët-Boigny was in a minority. The conference—and a later RDA meeting in April 1958 in Paris—tried to reach a compromise. The formula called for "territorial autonomy and the democratization of the existing federal executive," a phrase that the federalists could interpret as moving toward an executive responsible to an elected body and the antifederalists could interpret as tinkering with the status quo. There would be no "supergovernment in Dakar or in Brazzaville." But Sékou Touré added that there was still "the possibility for the territories to group themselves if they so desire," and he optimistically asserted, "We have decided to build the Franco-African Community, while maintaining the unity of Africa that is dear to it."[117] His astute choice of words could only paper over the gap.

Given the extent of disagreement, it was not a propitious time for political parties to consolidate across territories, but that was what Senghor, Houphouët-Boigny, and others thought they should do— to express their aspirations for African unity, to bring potential rivals into the fold. They referred to their goal as "regroupement."[118] There was even an attempt to bring Senghor's and Houphouët-Boigny's political formations into alliance (September–October 1957), but there were too many differences and too many personalities involved to make it work. The upshot was that the RDA remained a French-Africa-wide aggregation of territorial parties seriously divided over the issue of a West African federation, while Senghor tried to build an alternative West-Africa-wide formation embracing non-RDA, profederation parties. Its first incarnation was known as the Convention Africaine (January 1957), the later one Parti de Regroupement Africaine (PRA, March 1958), and still later the Parti de la Fédération Africaine (see chapter 6).

[116] In the Grand Conseil, Sékou Touré engaged in a little game of one upmanship with Senghor over who was a better proponent of a united AOF. He claimed that the RDA, as the only AOF-wide party, was the only one that could "unify Africa in making Senegal aware of the problems of Cameroon, Guinea aware of the problems of Sudan and Niger, etc." *Bulletin*, 21 and 22 June 1957, 11, 17.

[117] *Afrique Nouvelle*, 1 October 1957, 25 April 1958; Chérif Mecheri, Note for the President, 2 October 1957, 4AG 543, ANF; de Benoist, *Afrique Occidentale française*, 352–58. A French journalist reported on the vitality and seriousness of the discussions in Bamako, noting the mix of anticolonial militancy and support for a Franco-African community. André Blanchet, *Itinéraire des partis africains depuis Bamako* (Paris: Plon, 1958).

[118] For a combination of historical analysis, memoir, and documents, see Abdoulaye Ly, *Les regroupements politiques au Sénégal (1956–1970)* (Dakar, Paris: CODESRIA/Karthala, 1992).

In late 1956, Senghor launched a strong attack on the RDA, on Apithy, and on others whom he thought had let the French government get away with the "balkanization" of West Africa. He put territorialization in the context of the effort being mounted that would soon culminate in the European Common Market: "The Europeans find that 43 million metropolitans is too few and that it is necessary to 'make Europe,' but 20 million Africans together are too many and it is necessary to unmake Africa." Africans should know, he said, that "before putting together the 'Franco-African Community'" it is necessary to put together the "African community." It was essential to figure out a division of competences among the levels of government—territorial, federal, confederal. He maintained his position on the need for both connections among Africans—what he had earlier termed horizontal solidarity—and the French connection—vertical solidarity—both because of Africa's acute need for the resources of the wealthier part of the world and because of the complementarity of European and African civilizations, the one supposedly "rational," the other "intuitive." He concluded, "It is necessary to continue the fight." He did just that.[119]

In February 1957, as Senghor and Dia were reorganizing their political party in Senegal to contest the March elections, a student leader, Tidiane Baidy Ly, expressed surprise at the absence of the word "independence" from any party resolution. Senghor accused him of "a sin of youth." It was some months later, in September 1957, that the first French West African party with independence as a goal issued its first manifesto—the Parti Africain de l'Indépendance (PAI). The party's stated goal was "the conquest of the independence of Black Africa and . . . the constitution of an African socialist society."[120] It had its roots in student organizations, with such leaders as Cheikh Anta Diop and Amadou Mahtar M'Bow, who had been writing strong critiques of French colonialism since around 1950. There were meetings in Paris, and in July 1957 police spies reported on meetings organized by students returning to Africa from France during school vacations, with such goals as "to denounce the loi-cadre" and "unmask the cur-

[119] "Union française et fédéralisme," presentation to the Université des Annales, 21 November 1956, and "Les décrets d'application de la loi-cadre ou 'donner et retirer ne vaut,'" L'Unité Africaine, 5 March 1957, both reprinted in Liberté II: Nation et voie africaine du socialisme (Paris: Seuil, 1971), 197–215. On the founding of the Convention Africaine, see also Abdoulaye Guèye, "Le Congrès interterritorial de Dakar a fait avancer la cause de l'unité et de l'émancipation des masses africaines," L'Unité, 4 February 1957. Guèye claimed that the Socialists in Africa, notably Lamine Guèye, were standing in the way of unity because of their connection with the French Socialists Mollet and Defferre, who were responsible for the inadequacies of the loi-cadre.

[120] Report on Congrès Constitutif du Bloc Populaire Sénégalais, Dakar, 22–24 February 1957, 17G 629, AS; Direction des Services de Sécurité de l'AOF, Bulletin d'Information, September 1957, 17G 632, AS; Ly, Regroupements, 119–20.

rent political leaders." The PAI was centered in Dakar and Thiès, and there were other signs of radical student activity in Dahomey, Guinea, and the Côte d'Ivoire.[121]

The argument for immediate independence was a late entry into territory-wide political competition, with the notable exception of the UPC in Cameroon. In Senegal the PAI was no match for Senghor's well-organized political machine. After the March 1957 elections, security services reported, the focus of political activity across AOF was jockeying for position in the territorial governments about to take office.[122] Politics, often, is the art of the possible.

But if the proindependence party had trouble finding traction, the word was being heard more often and with a range of implications. Senghor's repeated warnings against a nominal independence let his listeners—not least those in Paris—know that independence was an option. And the notion of autonomy—a central part of West African political discourse since at least 1946—was being pushed further, into an ambiguous area where autonomy, independence, and sovereignty were all overlapping. From 1956, Senghor was using the expression "internal autonomy," and by 1957 it had become "the largest possible internal autonomy" or "complete internal autonomy." By early 1958, it had escalated to "total internal autonomy" and "internal sovereignty."[123]

RDA leaders—echoing a position largely maintained by African deputies in the constitutional debates of 1946—were arguing in 1957 that Africans wanted the *right* to independence, a right that they did

[121] Direction des Services de Sécurité de l'AOF, Reports, 11, 18 July, 10, 23 August 1957, 21G 210, AS; idem, Bulletin d'Information, September 1957, 17G 632, AS; idem, Bulletin d'Information, March 1958, 17G 633, AS; "Situation politique, économique et sociale de l'AOF en 1956," 15 May 1956, Afrique-Levant, 1953-1959/AOF/11, ADLC; Sûreté, Renseignements, 24 July, 2, 12 December 1957, 21G 213, AS. Historians are beginning to bring out the ideas and initiatives on the radical end of the West African political spectrum. See Elizabeth Schmidt, *Mobilizing the Masses: Gender, Ethnicity, and Class in the Nationalist Movement in Guinea, 1939-1958* (Portsmouth, N.H.: Heinemann, 2005) and Klaas van Walraven, *The Yearning for Relief: A History of the Sawaba Movement in Niger* (Leiden: Brill, 2013).

[122] Officials commented on the calm atmosphere and party focus of the 1957 election. Direction des Services de Sécurité de l'AOF, Bulletin Spécial d'Information sur les Élections aux Assemblées Territoriales en AOF, [March 1957], 17G 629, AS. On postelection politics, see idem, Bulletin d'Information, May 1957, 17G 630, AS.

[123] Chérif Mecheri claimed that Senghor used the expression "autonomie interne" for the first time in October 1956, although it is consistent with arguments he had been making for years. Note for the President, 9 October 1956, 4AG 543; Direction des Services de Sécurité de l'AOF, Bulletin d'Information on Congrès de regroupement des parties africaines, 11-13 January 1957, 17G 629, AS; Direction des Services de Sécurité de l'AOF, Bulletin d'Information, on Conférence de Regroupement des Partis Politiques Africains, 15-16 February 1958, 17G 633, AS.

not at present intend to exercise.[124] When Gabriel d'Arboussier referred in April 1958 to the "confusion over the notions of independence, sovereignty, federation, and confederation," he was trying to suggest that such notions were not hard and fast. Africans were now thinking of their territorial assemblies as "holders of sovereignty," but they wanted to maintain interterritorial solidarity and remain part of the Franco-African community. His was not a political theorist's reflection on the meaning of sovereignty, but a politician's effort to come to grips with a situation in which maintaining different kinds of political affinity was the only way forward.[125] Senghor was saying that sovereignty would lie with the French Republic, but only because the territories, having acquired the right to independence, were renouncing it. He knew that France was contemplating ceding some of its sovereign rights to Europe.[126] Sovereignty was not absolute and hard; it was supple, layered, shared.

In the discourse of RDA spokesmen (including those who favored and opposed an African federation) and PRA leaders, the word "independence," when spoken, appeared alongside interdependence, confederation, or association with France.[127] Such language sought to capture some of the militancy behind the emergence of the PAI and to both threaten and reassure French leaders.[128] Framing political goals in such terms addressed a problem that Senghor shared with someone as radical as Sékou Touré—how to keep alive the appeal of "African unity" when there was no fundamental agreement on how or whether the diverse territories of AOF should unite, except through their common participation in the institutions of the French Union.

[124]Chérif Mecheri, Note for the President on the Bamako conference of the RDA, 2 October 1957, 4AG 543, ANF. Mecheri claimed that this was the first time the right to independence "was affirmed in such a categorical manner."

[125]*Afrique Nouvelle*, 4 April 1958.

[126]See the subtle shift in his thinking in "Pour une solution fédéraliste," *La Nef* Cahier 9 (June 1955): 148–61, esp. 158, and "Union française et fédéralisme" (1956), "Les décrets d'application de la loi-cadre" (1957), from *Liberté II*, 197–15." See also Mamadou Dia "Une Afrique Unie," *L'Afrique Nouvelle*, 15 January 1957.

[127]See for example Apithy, *Afrique Nouvelle*, 24 April 1956; Sékou Touré and Djibo Bakary, *Afrique Nouvelle*, 8 August 1958; Modibo Keita, 26 February 1958, reported in Direction des Services de Sécurité de l'AOF, Bulletin d'Information, February 1958, 17G 633, AS. Noting all the militancy expressed in the RDA meeting at Bamako in September 1957, the Ministry reassured itself that "at no time was the principle of the Franco-African Community put in question by a speaker of the movement." "Synthèse politique concernant les Territoires d'Outre-mer, Cameroun, Togo," September 1957, 4AG 548, ANF.

[128]The threat was made explicitly by Modibo Keita: "if France allows the occasion to accomplish the Franco-African community to escape, Africa will inevitably commit itself to the only open path compatible with its dignity: the path to independence." *Le Monde*, 1 March 1958.

Such thinking had its own coherence, specificity, and strategy. It is only in retrospect, after political imaginations narrowed in the direction of national, territorial states, that it appears unrealistic. African leaders had to govern societies that were poor and socially fragmented, with tiny elites uncertain of their own basis of support in a newly enfranchised electorate.[129] They were quite conscious of the continuing impact of the colonial past—prejudice and condescension, economic structures that had not fully broken with the "pacte colonial," administrative structures that had not fully broken with a colonial command system. But they knew equally well how much French authority had broken down, how much they were part of a dynamic political situation in which new possibilities were opening up, from citizenship in 1946 to the new authority of the Assemblée Territoriale and the Conseil de gouvernement. In this sense, the attempt to build institutions of layered authority—at the level of the French Union, AOF, and the territories—responded to both the basic problems and the assets that African political movements actually had.

Senghor's version followed from positions he had long been articulating that were both practical and visionary. Such a community entailed not only diversity, but complementarity, of the intuitive thinking of the "Negro-African" with the analytical reasoning of the European. These essentialist conceptions have been much criticized in commentaries on his thought, but they grew out of his desire to counter the assimilationist, modernizing conception of culture change with a model that placed the interaction of the European and African citizens of France on a plane of equality. But in economic and social terms, the situation was not one of equivalence. He repeatedly emphasized that real independence meant coming to grips with poverty, illiteracy, inequality, and fragmentation within African territories. He sought a socialist economic policy, but was not very specific about what this entailed beyond a critique of the actions of capitalist trusts and the French government in maintaining a form of the pacte colonial.[130] He would later spell out his vision in a way that combined

[129] In an influential book published in 1957, the sociologist and anticolonial intellectual Germaine Tillion warned that Algeria—and sub-Saharan Africa as well—risked "clochardisation" (becoming beggers) if they had to face independence without French aid and the remittances of workers in France, given the current realities of their economic situation. *L'Algérie en 1957* (Paris: Ed. de Minuit, 1957). Similar worries about independence leaving African territories bereft of needed resources bothered other French intellectuals. See Paul Clay Sorum, *Intellectuals and Decolonization in France* (Chapel Hill: University of North Carolina Press, 1977), 84–88, 96–97.

[130] See for example Léopold Sédar Senghor, "Pour une République Fédérale dans une Union Confédérale," *Union Française et Parlement* 97 (1958): 5–11, esp. 6, 8. A more comprehensive analysis of his thought will appear in Gary Wilder's forthcoming *Freedom Time: Negritude, Decolonization, and the Future of the World.*

socialist notions of planning with the humanist economics of French social Catholics.

Combining the economically unequal and the culturally unlike, Senghor kept insisting in 1956, was the way forward for Africa: "All great civilizations were from cultural and biological mixture [métissage]." Africans only spoke of their "négritude so as not to come with empty hands to the rendezvous of the Union." But not just any union. Here he got specific. It was necessary to fix the anomalies of the Constitution, and he returned to his earlier proposals for how to integrate independent states with territories that were part of the Republic, how to balance metropolitan and overseas components of a federal legislature. The end was not "a classic federation"—which would not be acceptable to European France—but something more flexible. He did not push the logic of equivalence among citizens too far: if family allocations overseas had to be identical to those of metropolitan France, the charge would be beyond what the territories could afford and would have to be paid by the metropole. Pushing "local autonomies" rather than a "unitary and centralizing" Republic would allow for a more realistic balance. The overseas territories and departments, including Algeria, would become "states with internal law, integrated into the French Republic." The former protectorates, now independent, would negotiate their relationship with France. Assemblies at each level of the Union would ensure that each component, metropolitan France included, would exercise autonomy while common affairs would be debated among equals.[131]

His metropolitan interlocutors had no such comprehensive program. They were improvising, trying to appease African demands for autonomy and distance themselves from some of the burdens of common citizenship. They were badly shaken by the failures of the Union in Morocco, Tunisia, Algeria, and Indochina. The Ministry of Overseas France, for all the hope it had invested in the loi-cadre, knew that it had sidestepped the question that had animated African politicians for years: "Certain people would prefer first to modify Title VIII of the Constitution to pose the base of a federal French republic. But the loi-cadre has kept that position in reserve, since it is said explicitly in its Article 1 that it does not 'prejudge the expected reform' of the Constitution."[132]

From the Ministry's point of view, the results of the loi-cadre were uncertain a year or so after it was put into effect. Part of the problem was context: the Algerian war was making France's position in West

[131] Of the many expressions of Senghor's vision, a particularly well elaborated one is his presentation to the Université des Annales, 21 November 1956, reprinted in his *Liberté II*, 197–210.

[132] Draft of text for Minister to deliver to Commission Permanente du Grand Conseil de l'AOF on voyage to Dakar, 21 July 1956, AP 2292/10, AOM.

Africa more fraught, especially since thirty-five thousand troops from the ex-AOF were serving in this colonial war. Ghana, as of 1957, provided an actual example of an independent African state. But most important, officials feared the "weakening of the authority of the representatives of France and the State Services." Their worry was the mirror image of what was bothering Mamadou Dia and other Vice-Présidents du Conseil: that France retained too much of the old colonial hierarchy. French officials thought not only that the partial control of elected officials over the budget and territorial services eroded the authority of French officials in each territory, but that at the local level, party organizations were undercutting district administrators. Party bosses could, for example, ask the government to transfer a disliked Commandant de cercle somewhere else. A report cited High Commissioner Cusin to the effect that "it is not a question of 'divide and rule' because it is not a question of 'ruling.'"

Security services were keeping an eye out for communists or radical nationalists, and finding a few, but they did not have much evidence that either the PAI or communists in the RDA were much of a danger. They did see another tendency in party politics: that the PDCI-RDA in Côte d'Ivoire and the PDG-RDA in Guinea were establishing a "takeover," a "monolithic" control over their respective territories. They saw the developing monopolies of the leading party in several of the territories as evidence of "the African conception of a democracy of a totalitarian type." A government report recognized that some elements in West Africa wanted a real federal government for this large territory, but it did not think that any territorial government was likely to retrocede any of the powers it had just received. In these respects, the political analysts of the government would prove to have a point.[133]

The Benefits of Europe and the Cost of Empire: Eurafrica, 1956–1957

So the government was faced in 1957 and early 1958 with what it had faced before 1956: demands for revision of Title VIII, for territorial autonomy free from the supervision of Chefs de Territoire and High Commissioners, for some form of federalism.[134] However much the

---

[133]Cusin, cited in Cabinet of High Commissioner, "La situation en AOF," 5 June 1958, 17G 619, AS; M. Naves, Chef du Cabinet du Président de l'Union française, Note for the President, 3 December 1957, 4AG 543, ANF; Direction des Services de Sécurité de l'AOF, Bulletin d'Information, September 1957, 17G 632, AS; idem, 10 August 1956, 21G 210, AS.

[134]Coste-Floret reported on a round of proposals for revision of Title VIII in Assemblée Nationale, *Documents*, No. 4663, 26 March 1957; Senghor later submitted new proposals, No. 5822, 18 October 1957; Mitterrand proposed a conference to discuss

government was evasive in regard to confederation and federation in its former empire, it was thinking about just that in regard to Europe. We have already noted the beginnings, from the late 1940s, of government attempts to reconcile its two sorts of connections—one (to adapt Senghor's terminology) vertical, to its current and former overseas dependencies, the other horizontal, to other European nation-states. And we have seen concern in Africa over whether some form of European community would Europeanize colonial exploitation, shunt Africa aside, or perhaps multiply opportunities for trade and investment beneficial to Africa.

At the time of the loi-cadre, the Eurafrican question was entering a new phase. France was deep into negotiations that would produce the Treaty of Rome of 1957 and the European Common Market. In Paris, officials were balancing hope that its European partners would add to investment, development aid, and market opportunities in Africa and the usual fear of loss of control. One of the leading lights of the Ministry's economic team, Pierre Moussa, made clear the stakes in May 1956. If the overseas territories were not integrated with the rest of France into the Common Market, then France's economic zone would be cut in two, one Franco-African, the other European. France would then bear the costs of protecting Africa's fragile productive systems from cheaper imports while its own markets would be opened to European competition. France's European partners might object to France's special relationship to Africa. If, however, France were to enter the Common Market along with its overseas components, it would create a "Euro-African common market," and shared decision making among European members might "put in question French political sovereignty" overseas. France would have to persuade its partners to make overseas France subject to "special clauses" given its "underdevelopment." All things considered, Moussa thought, the only viable solution was for French Africa to be included, with special arrangements to favor its economic development.[135]

Among the French politicians most disposed to Eurafrica—in the face of many doubts—were two successive Ministers of Overseas

---

the structure of a "communauté franco-africaine," No. 6487 (4 February 1958). Copies of these documents, along with a "Note sur les propositions faites en vue de la révision du Titre VIII de la Constitution," April–June 1958, can be found in AP 218/1, AOM.

[135] Note from Directions des Affaires Économiques et du Plan, Ministère de la FOM, 3 May 1956, AP 2317, AOM. Pierre Moussa also presented his arguments in print, even declaring that France's already-existing "common market" with its overseas territories was a precedent for a Eurafrican common market. *Les chances économiques de la Communauté Franco-Africaine* (Paris: Colin, 1957). The overall story of the political battles over Eurafrica up to 1957 is told in Yves Montarsolo, *L'Eurafrique, contrepoint de l'idée de l'Europe: Le cas français de la fin de la deuxième guerre mondiale aux négociations des Traités de Rome* (Aix-en-Provence: Publications de l'Université de Provence, 2010), 197–258.

France, Pierre-Henri Teitgen of the MRP and the Socialist Gaston Defferre—the two authors of the loi-cadre. Defferre accepted Moussa's arguments. France's obligations would be shared through the "Europeanization of FIDES [the French development fund]." In this way, the Common Market would "remove the handicap which the burden of the Overseas Territories constitutes for France in the conjuncture of tight competition."[136]

Defferre, with some difficulty, persuaded Prime Minister Mollet to make the inclusion of France's overseas territories and departments a condition for France's acceptance of the economic community. Mollet was particularly concerned in 1957 to include Algeria in the Eurafrican common market. Eurafrica offered the hope that all of Europe would help develop Africa and give Algerians a sense of being integrated into a large ensemble that was both French and more than French. For Mollet, the Eurafrican possibility was a justification for repressing the rebellion that complicated such efforts. There ensued a year of bluffing and negotiation in which it was not clear whether a new Europe, a new Franco-African community, or a combination of the two would emerge.[137]

France's would-be European partners were skeptical of what they had to gain by including French Africa in Europe. Belgium alone of the five partners had major colonial interests in Africa, and for a time allied with France, but the Congo was already committed to a relatively open trade regime, and most investment came from private sources. Germany very much wanted the Common Market to succeed, but looked at Africa as a cost of France's entry rather than as a benefit; it would be expected to be a major contributor to the "European FIDES." Moreover, German leaders saw France's political situation in Africa—especially Algeria—as a mess in which it did not wish to get involved.[138] Much as Defferre and Mollet wanted an inclusive Eurafrica, weaving together its former colonies and its former rivals, it was not in a strong position to get it.

French officials worried as well that any agreement on equalizing social charges across Europe would be prohibitive if extended to

---

[136] Minister to Président du Conseil, 22 May 1956, AP 2317, AOM.

[137] Mollet's promise (dated 20 December 1956) was conveyed in the statement of Georges Monnet to the AUF, *Débats*, 15 January 1957, 13. The assembly wanted the overseas departments and territories to be included in the common market. *Débats*, 24 January 1957, 58-76, 80-92, 95-107. See also Montarsolo, *L'Eurafrique*, 203-5, and on the Algerian questions, Evans, *Algeria*, 194-96.

[138] Guia Migani, "L'Association des TOM au Marché Commun: Histoire d'un accord européen entre cultures économiques différentes et idéaux politiques communs, 1955-1957," and Guido Thiemeyer, "West German Perceptions of Africa and the Association of the Overseas Territories with the Common Market 1956-1957," in Marie-Thérèse Bitsch and Gérard Bossuat, eds., *L'Europe Unie et l'Afrique: de l'idée d'Eurafrique à la Convention de Lomé I* (Brussels: Bruylant, 2005), 233-85.

Africa, and they worried that if Europe adopted a principle for the "free circulation of people," people from Europe's poorer and more populated regions might migrate to Africa, to the disadvantage of indigenous people. Defferre acknowledged that sharing decision making and burdens with Europe could put French sovereignty in question. But on balance, he was favorable to the inclusion of the overseas territories in the Common Market; sovereignty was—we see once again—not an absolute.[139]

Defferre linked Eurafrica to the loi-cadre. The autonomy the loi-cadre conceded was likely to grow wider, and France needed new means to ensure that African territories would want to stay in France's orbit. The possibilities for markets, investment, and development aid that European integration offered seemed to provide that alternative. But it had to be managed delicately—lest France's partners assume the benefits but not the burdens of the Africa connection.[140] France's "general interests" might not always line up with those of the territories, which were now the domain of their own Conseils de gouvernement. Negotiators with European partners had to find a way to "safeguard at the same time the spirit of the loi-cadre" and "the profound desire for close cooperation, in mutual respect for respective needs and interests." A few months later, Defferre noted the tension between the territories' integration into Europe *via France*, and the possibility that the territories could evolve politically, including *away from France*. The solution, for now, was to keep the Eurafrican relationship focused on economic cooperation.[141]

Less salient in this phase of the discussion of Eurafrica was the issue that had preoccupied Senghor and others from 1950 to 1953: African voices in European institutions. Both because African governments were now preoccupied with their autonomous domains and because the project of European union had been redefined as of an economic rather than political nature, the issue was in the hands of technocrats like Moussa and the high-power elites involved in European negotiations, with Defferre the principal defender of African interests.[142] The African politician most involved was Félix Houphouët-Boigny, a

[139] Minister to Président du Conseil, 22 May 1956, AP 2317, AOM.

[140] Anne-Laure Ollivier, "Entre Europe et Afrique: Gaston Defferre et les débuts de la construction européenne," *Terrains et Travaux* 8 (2005), 14–33, esp. 26–28, 32.

[141] Minister, remarks to Commission de coordination économique métropole-outre-mer, session of 17–18 July 1957, AP 2317, AOM; Minister of FOM to Minister of Foreign Affaires, 22 October 1957, AP 2317, AOM. Later, a new minister, Jacquet, insisted that European integration would not affect the political future of the overseas territories: "The problem of eventual independence of the overseas territories does not concern our partner. It only concerns in fact the Franco-African Community." Testimony to Commission de la FOM of the Assemblée Nationale, 30 January 1958, C//15768, ANF.

[142] Hamadoun Dicko, taking up Senghor's earlier argument, wanted the territorial assemblies to be consulted on the treaty and have a say in European institutions, but

member of the Mollet government, who was enlisted both to explain to Africans the virtues of Eurafrica and to appeal to the other five European powers to take a part in African development.[143] He waxed eloquent on the possibilities that the Common Market offered:

If the Europe of Six succeeds, by virtue of a truly effective commercial and investment policy, to make the black populations feel that the Euroafrican association is capable of producing practical results, not only will the Franco-Belgian territories of this part of the African continent reject the influence of the Bandung group and that of the communists, but the Franco-Belgian territories will also constitute for neighboring colonies a symbol of prosperity. It is probable, then, that the former British colonies of Africa will ask for their association with the Eurafrican Common Market on the same conditions as Britain is now doing for the future European market.[144]

Not everyone was so taken. Senghor and others continued to worry that the political gains being made would be lost in a European community in which Africans had only a marginal voice. Senghor stated in 1957, "My friends and I declare ourselves, from the start, favorable to the idea of a European market; I say precisely 'to the idea.'" The substance was another story. He had "apprehensions" that decisions might be made even further away from the African continent, that African industries would go unprotected and European immigrants would descend on the continent, that France's partners would not be willing to address Africa's concerns.[145] Anxiety was expressed at the Assemblée de l'Union française, above all about decision-making authority becoming ever more distant from the Africans who, under the loi-cadre,

Defferre firmly refused. Montarsolo, *L'Eurafrique*, 213. On Senghor's hostility, see ibid., 236–37.

[143] Montarsolo, *L'Eurafrique*, 234–36.

[144] Quoted in Guia Migani, *La France et l'Afrique sub-saharienne, 1957–1963: Histoire d'une décolonisation entre idéaux euroafricains et politique de puissance* (Brussels: PIE Peter Lang, 2008), 56–57. See also Houphouët-Boigny's argument for Eurafrica in "A mes frères métropolitains," *Union Française et Parlement* 89 (1957): 2–4. The metropolitan counterpart of Houphouët-Boigny's optimism was Robert Schuman's contention that "Eurafrica will be a revolutionary political act with an economic base. Thanks to it, Europe and Africa will consolidate with each other a common enterprise of generalized cooperation." Schuman also saw Eurafrica as a barrier against the influence of Bandung or Moscow. "Unité européenne et Eurafrique: Politique révolutionnaire," *Union Française et Parlement* 79 (January 1957): 1–3, 3 quoted. Teitgen was more melodramatic: "what will be the future of Europe if Africa tilts toward the camp of anarchy, disorder, nationalist fever, misery, or the colonialism of the dollar, or even worse, in the Soviet camp? And what will be the chances of Europe if it separates from Africa?" Assemblée Nationale, *Débats*, 15 January 1957, 14.

[145] Assemblée Nationale, *Débats*, 18 January 1957, 166.

were expecting power to come closer to home.[146] Modibo Keita, the next year, argued forcefully that building Eurafrica depended on finding an acceptable basis for a Franco-African Community: "I affirm that Eurafrica will not be built if the Franco-African Community is not constructed, that the Franco-African Community will not be constituted without the affirmation of the African personality."[147]

In any case, neither Houphouët-Boigny's fantasy of Eurafrica nor Senghor's fears were actualized. France's European partners, especially Germany, did not want to take on the burdens of empire, which they guessed would be greater than the benefits. France had to back down from its insistence on including Africa within Europe (although it got Algeria included, hedged by numerous conditions, on the grounds that it was an integral part of France).[148] Overseas territories obtained the status of "associate" members of the European Economic Community. Germany and other partners were willing to contribute substantially—but a fraction of what the French government had asked for—to a European development fund, but it did not want the political onus of having French African territories within the Community. The territories of Africa would benefit from some European aid, a degree of tariff protection for their infant industries, and beneficial conditions for the sale of their products in Europe. Senghor grumbled but there was little he could do. The European Economic Community would indeed be European.[149]

The details of Africa's connections to Europe after the Treaty of Rome of 1957 are beyond the scope of our discussion. What is important in this context are the tensions and complementarities between two modes of supranational or supraterritorial thinking at this time, one focused on making a new Europe, the other on transforming an old empire. The same concerns appear for example in a flurry of correspondence in 1956 in regard to negotiations over Euratom, a program of European cooperation in regard to atomic energy. By then, ura-

[146]Assemblée de l'Union française, *Débats*, 15, 24 January 1957, 12–14, 58–76, 80–92, 95–107.

[147]Keita, remarks on visit of Minister of FOM to Bamako, 26 February 1958, 17G 633, AS.

[148]On Algeria and Eurafrica, the forthcoming research of Muriam Haleh Davis should be revealing.

[149]Montarsolo, *L'Eurafrique*, 243–58, Migani, *La France et l'Afrique*, 47–63. In presenting the treaty to the Assemblée Nationale, Foreign Minister Christian Pineau was still able to argue that Europe's help would keep Africa attached to France by undertaking tasks "that we could not do alone." *Débats*, 18 January 1957, 158. Senghor complained about the vagueness of provisions on Africa and the lack of assurance that Africa would continue to get French resources. Ibid., 166–67. Africans in the Assemblée de l'Union française expressed reservations about the treaty, but in the end favored it, largely because of provisions for freer circulation of goods and development aid. *Débats*, 24–25 June 1957, 602–78.

nium from Niger was being exploited. Having something to supply gave France a leg up in negotiations—in relation to the established Belgian uranium mining operations in the Congo—and cooperation would assure the overseas territories of a market as well as access to processing facilities, technical know-how, and patents for equipment. The Ministry saw another side: "The development of the African territories demands a gigantic effort that goes beyond our means." Working on a European scale would help provide an "army of soldiers of peace: economists, engineers, scientists." Nuclear energy would have a big role, the Ministry claimed, in African economic development. And because of the effort, "Europe must appear to African countries like a power with resources as great [as the United States and Soviet Union] and as sure of herself and her civilizing mission." The Ministry had realized that "African and Malagasy opinion, which remains very sensitive to anything that can be interpreted as survivals or resurgence of the 'pacte colonial,'" would object to "engagements conceived and taken without them."[150]

The Ministry acknowledged that participation in Euratom meant a certain "abandonment of sovereignty" for France, and hence for French Africans. It noted the "susceptibilities, not to say suspicions, that weight heavily on Euroafrican cooperation." But keeping Africa out of this and other mechanisms of European cooperation might carry even greater risks: "Participation in the Community *without* the Overseas Territories would separate in law as in fact the territory of the Republic into two distinct parts. . . . By the fact of such a separation these populations could justifiably fear becoming the appendix of a state, member of the Community, and promised by this fact to a European neocolonialism, of a discriminatory character." Parliamentarians from the territories would have a voice in ratification of any treaty; their opposition would be a serious problem, and so they had to be assured of both benefits and participation.[151]

As with the Common Market, the outcome of European negotiations on Euratom was not favorable to African inclusion in decision-making processes. Africans would supply uranium; Europeans would make policy.[152] But the interventions of the Minister of Overseas France made clear that he, at least, had learned something from the give-and-take of politics with his African colleagues. In the mid-1950s,

[150] Minister of Economic Affaires to Minister of FOM, 3 August 1956, and Minister of FOM, "Note au sujet du projet 'Euratom,'" 2 February 1956, Minister to Président du Conseil, 3 April 1956, AP 2316/5, AOM.

[151] Minister to Président du Conseil, 3 April 1956, and Minister to Minister of Economic Affaires, 3 April, 15 May, 1956, AP 2316/5, AOM.

[152] Gabrielle Hecht, *Being Nuclear: Africans and the Global Uranium Trade* (Cambridge, Mass.: MIT Press, 2012).

two forms of federation or confederation were in play. Their relationship had yet to be sorted out.

In considering both the Common Market and Euratom, French officials were confronting not just the complexities of decision making, but the burdens of welfare and development in a polity that was no longer colonial and not yet egalitarian. As mentioned earlier in this chapter, the articles of René Servoise from 1954 had raised the question of whether the costs of maintaining an inclusive polity might now exceed the benefits. Similar questions were being raised within the government, mainly by the Ministry's inspectors who were reporting on the high costs of development projects—including wages and benefits for unionized workers—and the relatively slow growth of private investment and export production. In 1956, the cost of maintaining colonies achieved a new notoriety and even a name—cartiérisme—when the well-known journalist Raymond Cartier published an article about the African empire in the popular magazine *Paris-Match*. Cartier's bottom line was negative; African colonies cost more than they brought in. He concluded, "It is necessary to transfer as fast as possible as much responsibility to Africans. At their risk and peril."[153] Cartier's article was too coldly calculating for many on both the left and right, and it was sarcastic and dismissive in relation to Africans' aspirations, but its conservative argument for decolonization weighed on people's minds.[154]

French leaders, assessing the possibilities and drawbacks of closer integration with European neighbors and African former colonies, had tried to achieve both. They had not convinced their European partners of the benefits of integrating French Africa into European institutions. And if most African leaders still thought they had something to gain from France—or perhaps Europe—the question of whether France had something to gain from Africa was now being posed with a clarity that had not previously been evident.

Personal Status and Territorialization

Integrating collectivities was complex and uncertain. Integrating individuals across the space of the French Union was another story. At the time of the loi-cadre, the French government had not solved the problem of how to incorporate different status regimes into the état-civil or that of defining the rules for changing personal status. Even

---

[153] Raymond Cartier, "En France noire avec Raymond Cartier," *Paris-Match* 383, 384, 386 (11, 18 August, 1 September 1956), 41 of last article cited. The growing pessimism of the inspectors is discussed in Cooper, *Decolonization and African Society*, chap. 10.

[154] Nathalie Ruz, "La force du 'cartiérisme,'" in Jean-Pierre Roux, ed., *La guerre d'Algérie et les français* (Paris: Fayard, 1990), 328–36.

as the Ministry was working on the text that became the loi-cadre, legislators as influential as René Pleven were trying to get a law passed to generalize a version of the état-civil that would make mention of an individual's personal status regime, complaining that even in 1956 only "a very small minority of évolués" were using the état-civil. Now, Pleven and colleagues—breaking with the legally and ideologically dubious idea of a separate état-civil indigène that was the best AOF could then offer—wanted a single register in which "alternative formulas" of marriage, divorce, adoption, and recognition of children could be recorded. Spouses could opt for monogamy or otherwise. Jurists did not think the matter was so simple, and in any case the bill was not enacted.[155]

Although the état-civil had been closely associated with *French* citizenship, organizing it was assigned, under the loi-cadre, to the territories on the grounds that "the rules in effect seem as if they must be very different according to the degree of evolution of the populations."[156] French legislators kept bringing up the lack of clear legislation on the état-civil, but there was little they could now do other than lament: "The decree of application transfers the responsibility for establishment of the état-civil to local governments, and I fear that progress will not be more rapid than in the past. The choice of system—including a single état-civil or two registers according to personal status—is still not decided."[157]

Proposals to regulate the renunciation of personal status also kept coming.[158] They too were becoming increasingly irrelevant. The Conseil d'État had ruled in 1955 that renouncing one's personal status was a

[155] "Proposition de loi tendant à compléter les actes d'état civil par l'indication du statut civil et de la nationalité des individus, ainsi qu'à généraliser et reorganiser l'état civil en Algérie, dans les Territoires d'Outre-mer et les territoires sous tutelle et à supprimer le régime de la pluralité des états civils," presented by René Pleven and others, Assemblée Nationale, session of 1955–56, Document 230, 27 January 1956, copy in C//16333, ANF. The Assemblée de l'Union française had voted in November 1955 in favor of generalizing the état-civil to the overseas territories, Algeria, and the mandates, with "indication of the civil status of the individuals." *Débats*, 29 November 1955, 1125–42.

[156] "Rapport de développement sur les compétences et les possibilités de déconcentration concernant la justice et la législation autochtone," 19 August 1954, by X. De Christen, Inspecteur de la FOM, AP 491, AOM; Minister to Garde des Sceaux, 9 December 1958, 950236/2, CAC.

[157] AUF, Report No. 28 of session of 1957–58, 12 November 1957, by Commission de la Législation, Justice, Fonction publique et des Affaires administratives et domainiales, written by Alfred Bour, copy in C//16350, ANF; AUF, *Débats*, 17 January 1957, 21–26.

[158] AUF, Proposal No. 292 of 1955–56, 31 May 1956, copy in C//16333, ANF. Whenever such proposals came up, discussions turned to whether French civil status was superior, whether indigenous statuses discriminated against women, whether polygamy was being encouraged or undermined, or whether conversion to Christianity was being given adequate or too much recognition. AUF, *Débats*, 7 July 1955, 654–69.

right, whether or not the legislature pronounced on the subject (chapter 3). Since then, a declaration before the nearest civil jurisdiction to a person's residence—made by someone over twenty-one, single or monogamous, duly informed of the irrevocable nature of the act—was what was required. Jurists regarded the story as one of legislative failure.[159] The major significance in public law of obtaining French civil status disappeared with the abolition of the double college in sub-Saharan Africa—in contrast to Algeria where "French Muslims of Algeria" remained a recognized category, a marker for discrimination both negative and, in respect to some social policies after 1958, positive.[160] In private law, something like Lamine Guèye's suggestion of 1950 that "tacit" change of status seemed to answer many people's needs, but officials did think there was a significant demand for status changes. Officials in the overseas territories were told by the court and the Ministry to make it relatively straightforward for someone to acquire "French" civil status by declaration before a local judicial authority.[161]

Meanwhile, high officials were perfectly capable of confusing the relationship of citizenship, nationality, and status. Not for the first time, the Minister had to rebuke the High Commissioner of AOF for writing that identity documents being considered should contain the mention "citizen of the French Union." The correct expression was "French citizen," and the "autochthons of AOF have the most absolute right to have their nationality inscribed on their passports, booklets, cards, and other identity documents . . . without distinction of origin or status."[162]

---

[159] René Pautrat, "Les vicissitudes du statut personnel," *Annales Africaines 1957*, 331–61, esp. 355, 361.

[160] Todd Shepard "Thinking between Metropole and Colony: The French Republic, 'Exceptional Promotion,' and the 'Integration' of Algerians, 1955–1962," in Martin Thomas, ed., *The French Colonial Mind* (Lincoln: University of Nebraska Press, 2011), 298–323. A Cameroonian politician, Andre-Marie Mbida, asserted he was the "first and only entirely autochthonous deputy from Cameroon" because the others were "of French civil status, whereas I keep my native Cameroonian status." Letter to President of Republic, 4 September 1956, 4AG 47, ANF.

[161] Garde des Sceaux, circular to Procureurs Généraux, 7 March 1957, 23G 98, AS; Direction Civile de Législation to President of Commission des Lois Constitutionnelles, de la Législation et de l'Administration Générale, Assemblée Nationale, 8 February 1960, 950236/24, CAC; René Pautrat, "Formes et conditions de la renonciation au statut personnel particulier," *Revue Juridique et Politique de l'Union Française* 12, 2 (April–June 1958): 350–57; Yvon Gouet, "L'Article 82 (paragraphe 1) de la Constitution relatif à l'option de statut et l'élaboration de la 'théorie des statuts civils' de droit français moderne," *Penant* 67 (1957), section doctrine, 1–94; Pierre Lampué, "La diversité des statuts de droit privé dans les États Africains," *Penant* 71 (1961), 1–10.

[162] Minister to High Commissioner, 26 April 1957, 950236/1, CAC. On the complications and confusions of applying nationality law overseas, see Roger Decottignies, "L'application du code de la nationalité française dans les Territoires d'Outre-mer

Africans, the Minister was saying, had a right to documentation. They had increasing need of it to vote, to send children to school, to collect benefits from salaried employment, and to exercise other rights, including that of free movement anywhere in the French Union.[163] Despite the inadequacies of the registration system, the citizens of AOF were voting in increasing numbers, going to school, collecting wages and benefits from regular employment, and seeking work in European France. To get papers required navigating between different systems of specifying people's social location, but Africans were taking the initiative to get a "jugement supplétif," the retrospective recording based on witnesses of a previously unregistered life event, when they needed to do so.[164] Police in metropolitan France complained that since people coming from Africa to work were citizens, they could not be made to meet specific requirements for documentation and registration. They were hard to track.[165] Africans were learning how to manage their encounters with bureaucracy. And the French state had, by 1957, passed on to other governments its effort to keep an eye on citizens over their life courses and to record—using the notion of multiple personal statuses—exactly where each individual or family stood in a spectrum of cultural difference.

(décret du 24 février 1954)," *Annales Africaines 1954*, 49–90; Henri-Louis Brin, *La nationalité française dans les Territoires d'Outre-mer (décret du 24 février 1953)* (Paris: Recueil Sirey, 1954).

[163] French officials were attached enough to the principle of free movement that as Associated States became independent they wanted to negotiate accords allowing "full freedom of circulation and residence to the nationals of each party," subject to "strict reciprocity." Président du Conseil to Ministers and Secretaries of State, Direction du Personnel, circular, 19 August 1957, and Minister of Foreign Affairs to Minister of FOM, 27 June 1956, 950236/1, CAC.

[164] Ministry, Circular to High Commissioners, 16 February 1955, 940227/81, CAC. The Ministry wanted to make it easier for Africans to get identification so as to get into the metropole. Minister of FOM to Minister of Interior, 14 July 1957, 940227/80, CAC. The bureaucratic maze and ambiguous social relations are depicted with poignancy by Ousmane Sembène in his film "Mandabi," showing the trouble an elderly Senegalese had in documenting his identity so that he could cash a money order from a relative working in France.

[165] For the history of migration, especially from the region near the Senegal-Sudan border, see François Manchuelle, *Willing Migrants: Soninke Labor Diasporas, 1848–1960* (Athens: Ohio University Press, 1997). In the 1950s, French officials' anxiety was above all focused on North African immigrants, who also had the right to be there. Special committees were created with the dual purpose of surveillance and focusing social services on "French Muslims in the metropole." See le Préfet, Chef du Service des Affaires Musulmanes et de l'Action Sociale, Ministère de l'Intérieur, Note à l'attention de M. le Ministre (de l'Intérieur), 25 February 1959, F/1a/5045, ANF. Especially during the Algerian war, the police did find ways to keep an eye on Algerians, although they were less worried about sub-Saharan Africans until the 1960s. See Alexis Spire, "Semblables et pourtant différents. La citoyenneté paradoxale des 'français musulmans d'Algérie' en métropole," *Genèses* 53 (2003): 48–66.

If French leaders thought they had preempted the debate over revising the Constitution with their concession of partial autonomy to elected governments in the territories, they soon learned otherwise. Even while the loi-cadre was moving toward adoption in June 1956, Senghor was pushing in the Assemblée Nationale for a revision of Title VIII of the Constitution under which "the French Union ceases to be solely French to be universal, in the manner of the Commonwealth, based as she will be on the sovereignty of all the states."[166] A report for the Overseas Committee agreed on the proposed name change: "Constituted of a plurality of states and nations, the Union was not founded on its French quality, rather than that of any other nationality of which it is composed. Moreover, from a political point of view, this term is not a happy one, because of the inequality it seems to consecrate. The states, which have acceded to independence do not accept it." Perhaps Morocco, Tunisia, Laos, Cambodia, and other former Associated States could be brought back to the fold. Even the idea that the French Union was French was open to debate.[167]

Within the overseas territories more powers would have to go to the Conseils de gouvernement, less to Chefs de Territoire. Several proposals for constitutional change were put forth and a subcommittee was appointed to sort it all out, with Senghor warning that disappointing Africans' aspirations for federalism would "run the risk of inciting claims for independence whose realization would be disastrous for the territories and for the metropole."[168]

Senghor and Dia, arguing against the "chopping up of Africa," proposed to locate authority in the group of territories—AOF notably—rather than the individual territory, but their proposal lost out on a fifteen to thirteen vote. The committee was more favorable to Senghor's plea that even "if African opinion does not demand independence it cannot any more renounce its right to independence." Several deputies praised the idea of a union based on "free consent"—as had been initially voted in 1946 only to be overturned in the second version of the constitution.[169] Discussions continued. In November, after wait-

---

[166] Assemblée Nationale, *Débats*, 1 June 1956, 2228.

[167] Commission de la FOM, meeting of 1 June 1956, C//15769, ANF.

[168] Ibid. There was also discussion in the Assemblée de l'Union française, focused on increasing the powers of the Assembly, *Débats*, 13–14 June 1956, 536–47, 552–62.

[169] Commission de la FOM, 27 June, 4 July 1956, C//15767, ANF. There was another round of debate on the question of groups like the AOF on 1 August 1956. On the floor of the Assemblée Nationale, Senghor declared that his party would vote against any reform of Title VIII that would "eliminate the federation of AOF and AEF or only refuse them federal executives." *Débats*, 13 May 1956, 2267. Mamadou Dia continued to argue that "we want only, for the future, 'to reserve the right of independence,'" but not at present to exercise it. Press conference, 5 March 1958, 21G 223, AS.

ing for other Assembly committees to weigh in, Overseas Committee members were complaining in the fall of 1956 of the "lack of hurry."[170]

A year later, Senghor and friends submitted another of their many proposals for constitutional reform, criticizing the regime of "semi-autonomy" coming out of the loi-cadre and insisting on the need for organizing "large spaces" for economic and social progress. They denied that they saw such spaces as a step toward independence. Only the enactment of a "federal constitution"—covering the metropole, the overseas departments and territories, and Algeria—would allow France to achieve "diversity in unity."[171] A few months later, François Mitterrand called for a conference to create "a Franco-African community" and decide on its basic institutions. Mitterrand argued, "This Franco-African ensemble, so much alive already in spiritual and affective terms, as well as economic and social, has no institutional reality." He worried about the alternative models—the independence of Ghana, the ex-British Sudan, Libya, Tunisia, and Morocco, as well as the politics coming out of Bandung and Cairo—but thought that the experience of African assemblies showed "the maturity attained by the overseas elites, thanks to their responsibilities." Successful federal institutions might attract former members of the Union to rejoin, and perhaps bring in others from Africa and Asia. He made the parallel with the effort to forge a European economic and political community.[172] Taken together, the two proposals reveal that the territorial focus of the loi-cadre had not put an end to the quest for federation or community beyond the level of the nation-state.

These and other proposals went into a legislative mill that had already furnished much evidence of how dysfunctional it was. There were more rounds of proposals and debate.[173] But time was not on the side of remaking the French Union. Not only were Tunisia and Morocco fully independent, but their relations with France had deteriorated as a result of the Algerian war. Throughout 1957 and into 1958, the National Assembly's Overseas Committee as well as the Committee on Universal Suffrage were considering texts for constitutional revision, while the Minister urged caution in constitutional revision.

[170] Alduy, Commission de la FOM, 7 November 1956, C//15769, ANF. The Commission du Suffrage Universel also had endless discussions in which the question of federalism once again appeared. See especially 7, 21 June, 12 July, 18 October 1956, 24, 31 January, 7, 14, 21, 28 February, 7, 14 March, 1 June 1957, C//15774, ANF.

[171] Assemblée Nationale, *Documents*, No. 5822, 18 October 1957, 13.

[172] Ibid., No. 6487, 4 February 1958, 827–28.

[173] See the records of debates in the Commission du Suffrage Universel, January–March 1957, C//15774, ANF, and in the Commission de la FOM, November 1957–January 1958, C/15768, ANF, as well as Coste-Floret's report on behalf of the former in Assemblée Nationale, *Documents*, No. 4663, 26 March 1957, 1890–99, and René Pleven, "L'avenir de l'Union française," *Union Française et Parlement* 84 (June 1957): 1–9.

Coste-Floret tried to claim that his desire for a "decentralized unitary state" was not that different from Senghor's federalism, but each man insisted on his own version.[174] In February 1958 Coste-Floret came up with a new report. But Senghor thought that governmental instability was so bad that a serious discussion was not possible. Others thought that the loi-cadre had made revision of Title VIII obsolete. Discussion was deferred.[175]

In February 1958, Coste-Floret brought the discussion to the floor of the Assemblée Nationale. He had recently published an article in *Le Monde* in which he called for a revision of the Constitution to create "a communitarian Republic in a confederal Union of freely adhering sovereign states." He was updating the position in favor of a "democracy of groups" that he had advocated in 1946 (chapter 2).[176] In the Assembly, the debate was chaotic. Coste-Floret criticized federalism but spoke of the urgency to create a "Franco-African community"; Senghor insisted on confederalism; others advocated community or federation or asserted that the entire discussion had become "a bit nebulous." Said Mohamed Cheikh, speaking for the Overseas Committee, noted that African political parties were in the midst of an intense discussion among themselves and wanted to put off debate on Title VIII. Senghor disagreed. Coste-Floret contended that Africans were both emphasizing the urgency of the issue and trying to put off decisions. The Assembly decided yet again not to decide.[177]

And so it continued into May and beyond.[178] Chérif Mecheri, the President's principal advisor on the French Union, had even earlier worried that the issue of constitutional change was producing "an atmosphere of escalation and demagoguery." He was also hearing complaints that the loi-cadre was already "outdated," but he thought most African leaders were more preoccupied with resolving practical problems in their new roles than in "putting in question the very structure."[179] However, events outside of AOF—in Algeria—were overtaking the debate and throwing the question of revising Title VIII into that of inventing a new French Republic.

[174]Commission du Suffrage Universel, 24 January 1957, 7 February 1957, C//15774, ANF; Commission de la FOM, 30 January 1958, C//15678, ANF.

[175]Commission de la FOM, 12 February 1958, C//15678, ANF.

[176]*Le Monde*, 4 January 1958.

[177]Assemblée Nationale, *Débats*, 12, 13, 18, 20 February 1958, 706–9, 738–40, 847, 914–22. See also AUF, Proposition 120, 28 January 1958, and Demande d'Avis, No. 141, 20 February 1958, C//16375, ANF and the series of articles on revising Title VIII by René Pleven, Paul Coste-Floret, François Mitterrand, and Léopold Senghor in *Union Française et Parlement* 91 (1958): 3–14.

[178]Assemblée Nationale, *Débats*, 13 May 1958, 2253, 2266–67; Commission de la FOM, 2 July 1958, C//15678, ANF.

[179]Chérif Mecheri, Notes for President, 14, 22 February 1958, 4AG 528, ANF.

Conclusion

The issues at stake in the constitutional debates were profound, as they had been when first broached over a decade earlier. There was general agreement through all phases that some form of Franco-African community should be held together. But providing it with institutions, or even a name, continued to elude politicians.[180] The issue was not—as so much literature on French colonial policy often portrays it—between a stubborn French colonialism and strident African nationalism.[181] The debate was in between. If one took the logic of the equivalence of citizens to its logical conclusion, then Herriot's nightmare would come to pass: French politics would be dominated by overseas voters, and the burdens of equalizing, across a space characterized by extreme economic inequality, the salaries of civil servants, the standards of education and health care, and the opportunities for productive jobs would be more than metropolitan taxpayers would tolerate. At the other extreme, independence was fraught with risks—of continued impoverishment, of political weakness, even of recolonization by the United States, the Soviet Union, or the European Economic Community. Africans leaders were trying to balance their need for resources with their desire for autonomy and recognition, their stated wishes for African unity with their desire to be part of a still wider ensemble.

The loi-cadre, however, was a real breakthrough. It responded to Africans' most important demands—for universal suffrage, the single college, and real power for territorial assemblies. It did not dismantle all of the colonial structure, for the notion of administrative command was still embodied in the person of the Chef de Territoire, as well as the bureaucrats of the State Services, over whom territorial assemblies had no control. The system was neither full autonomy nor a continuation of subordination. African political and social movements had their say, and their positions had to be taken seriously even when French officials did not like them.

Even as the place of "federalism" in constitutional reform was being debated, the very existence of the territorial governments set up under

[180] Some of France's best political theorists weighed in too. Maurice Duverger suggested that instead of revising the French Constitution, there should be a new constituent assembly elected by universal suffrage to write a Union constitution distinct from that of the Republic. Reprinting Duverger's article, *Afrique Nouvelle* (28 March 1958) questioned African politicians about the idea. Djibo Bakary and Sékou Touré liked it; Dia and Apithy did not.

[181] Even in regions where nationalist mobilization had a longer and deeper history, the relationship between nationalism and alternative conceptions of politics is complex, as recent studies are bringing out. James McDougall, *History and the Culture of Nationalism in Algeria* (Cambridge: Cambridge University Press, 2006); Adria Lawrence, *Imperial Rule and the Politics of Nationalism: Anti-Colonial Protest in the French Empire* (Cambridge: Cambridge University Press, 2013).

the loi-cadre was shaping future possibilities.[182] The governments had been put in power by political machines focused on territorial constituencies. Several territorial parties were affiliated with the RDA, others were independent, and Senghor was, in 1957 and 1958, trying to organize another umbrella party, an alliance that would both reflect and promote the idea of a French West African federation. That the territorial political leaders had resources of budgets and patronage at their disposal, while Senghor had an idea, did not bode well for his vision of the future.[183] But the last act had not yet been played.

In March 1957, Félix Houphouët-Boigny, returning from the independence celebrations of Ghana, wished the new country well and pointed to the juxtaposition of two political trajectories in the former British colony and the territories of French West Africa: "A bet is thus opened, between two territories, one having chosen complete autonomy, the other preferring the difficult route of the constitution with the metropole, of a community of men who are different but equal in rights and duties." He had confidence in the choices his party and his government had made: "An experiment without precedent in the already long history of peoples: a community of men, of different continents, races, religions, and degrees of civilization, but engaged in the same combat for well-being in justice, freedom, equality, fraternity. . . . We need France for our human and social emancipation, and France needs us to ensure the permanence of its grandeur, of its genius in the World."[184]

[182] The Ministry commented in the summer of 1957 that the "the politicians who have taken on executive responsibilities in the different territories are discovering every day a bit more of the variety and extent of their powers." Condescendingly, it asserted that the leaders were taking on these powers with "the ardor of neophytes, jealous of their missions and their prerogatives." "Synthèse politique concernant les Territoires d'Outre-mer, Cameroun, et Togo," July-August 1957, 4AG 548, ANF.

[183] Senghor and Dia of course organized a patronage machine themselves, distributing resources to influential marabouts in the countryside. Catherine Boone, *Merchant Capital and the Roots of State Power in Senegal, 1930–1985* (Cambridge: Cambridge University Press, 1992), 86–89.

[184] Speech of Houphouët-Boigny, 8 March 1957, AP 2292/10, AOM.

CHAPTER 6

FROM OVERSEAS TERRITORY TO MEMBER STATE

Constitution and Conflict, 1958

France, as it handed over power and burdens to African territorial governments, seemed to be trying to conserve what mattered most to it, sovereignty. A constitution that proclaimed the Republic to be one and indivisible remained in place, even if the relationship of the French Republic, overseas territories, French West Africa, and the French Union was ambiguous and contested.[1] At the same time, France was conceding a set of sovereign *functions* in a different direction—to Europe. Senghor thought France was doing in Europe what African territories should do: assert their autonomy and proceed to "abandonments of sovereignty." Independence on the basis of individual territories would produce "skeleton states" and lead to "a neocolonialism worse than the original because hypocritical." French West Africans, he kept arguing, should unite in a "primary federation" that would in turn be part of a confederation of equal nations, including European France.[2]

Not all in Africa agreed with Senghor, but by 1958 the cry of "African Unity" had become practically ubiquitous, heard from trade unions to political parties. Senghor, who had in 1952 spoken of Africans' "mystique of equality," argued in the spring of 1959 that in reaction to the "balkanization" of Africa since the loi-cadre, Africans were now imbued with a "mystique of unity."[3] Political parties believed that such a slogan would appeal to an electorate expanded by universal suffrage, not just to those in a position to compare their situation to that of people of metropolitan origin. The idea of African unity

---

[1] René Pleven argued that constitutional reform was necessary precisely because the notion of an indivisible republic was obsolete. "L'avenir de l'Union française," *Union Française et Parlement* 84 (June 1957): 1–9, 6 cited.

[2] Léopold Sédar Senghor, "Pour une République Fédérale dans une Union Confédérale," *Union Française et Parlement* 97 (1958): 5–11, 7, 9 quoted.

[3] *Afrique Nouvelle*, 3 April 1959. He added, "Our goal is the constitution of a Negro-African nation, a collectivity that beyond artificial frontiers and tribal diversities, comes into itself by integrating Negro-African values with the fertile contributions of France."

offered to the many people who had experienced the humiliations of colonial rule an alternative conception of who they were and how they could act. But for the top leadership, including Senghor, Houphouët-Boigny, and Sékou Touré, a united Africa should take its place in a "Franco-African community."

But African political leaders faced a double problem in reconciling African unity with the realities of post-loi-cadre Africa. First, they actually governed in their respective territories. They were responsible for difficult decisions that might or might not be popular with the people who elected them. Second, the institutions in which African leaders actually worked together to make policies and laws were above all in Paris, although Senghor (and Sékou Touré) were struggling to build them up in Dakar. The tensions between a political reality in which territory played a large part and an ideal of a strong and united Africa taking its place in the world would frame political debates among African political elites for the next several years.

But the politics of French West Africa changed fundamentally as a result of the ongoing struggle in Algeria. On 13 May 1958, four years into the war, a near–coup d'état against the French Republic occurred in Algeria, with elements of the army supporting settler activists who feared the government was on the verge of making compromises with the rebels and not defending "l'Algérie française." The events revealed that republican rule was not fully secured in France. Into this situation rode Charles de Gaulle as savior of France. He became the Président du Conseil (Prime Minister) and insisted that he be given special powers to deal with the situation. Much of this maneuvering was of dubious constitutionality, and principled members of the legislature protested. But many at various points of the political spectrum were so panicked by the threat of a coup that they put their faith in charismatic authority.

In the midst of the crisis, most of the political elite in both European and African France wanted *some* kind of federative structure to take the place of the French Union, based on a common citizenship and some combination of autonomy and overarching authority. Over the course of the debates over a new constitution for a new republic, African leaders were able to impose conditions on de Gaulle that he and his collaborators had initially rejected. Such was the give-and-take of politics. But Africans' political relationships with each other remained uncertain.

Reform Overseas and the Crisis of the Fourth Republic

In the months before the Algerian storm, the African party with an AOF-wide organization, the RDA, was deeply divided over the question of African federation. The voice that was becoming increasingly prominent within the RDA belonged to Sékou Touré, and he was coming down strongly on the side of an African federation linked to a Franco-African community. In March 1958, on the occasion of a visit by the Minister of Overseas France to Conakry, he called for "the integral decolonization of Africa: its people, its habitats, its economy, its administrative organization, in order to build a solid Franco-African community whose longevity will be all the more guaranteed in that it will no longer have in its midst the phenomenon of injustice, of discrimination or any cause of depersonalization and indignity." French governors in each territory should give way to prime ministers responsible to the legislature. Most important, AOF and AEF should have federal executives and legislatures. He saw the common citizenship of people across AOF as a fundamental basis of political unity, and he insisted the connection was economic as well: there were no "Guinean, Senegalese, or Ivorian markets, but an African market, common to all the territories of Africa under French influence." A government for AOF was the first step. The second was the creation of "the Franco-African Community whose competences will be limited exclusively to essential problems that can ensure the cohesion and effectiveness of the republican ensemble." He thought that most African political movements (except the PAI) agreed with him. But he warned that hesitation on the part of the French government could lead the people of Africa to push for independence, which he described as "a jump into the unknown."[4]

France's top official in AOF, High Commissioner Gaston Cusin, understood that his government had to come to grips with—and try to influence—the discourse about autonomy and independence. Among the Africans in "responsible positions" with whom had he been working, he had found "valuable interlocutors." He went on to say, "The current tendency in the evolution of institutions goes toward greater autonomy and toward independence as anticipated in the constitution. . . . It is necessary to judge the situation coolly and above all to take the politics and passion out of the word 'independence' to prevent its demagogic utilization." Europe and Africa would continue to cooperate, and Africans had to be aware of how much they needed such a framework. "It is the task of those who demand independence to judge the moment when they can exercise it, assuming they want to maintain the living standards they will have attained, or else accept sacrifices. . . . From the time that one recognizes the personality of a territory, there is no more common 'purse,' nor a common civil service. The metropole can no longer impose solutions but can conclude contracts establishing economic relations and anticipate periodic assessments."

[4] *Afrique Nouvelle*, 28 February, 7 March 1958.

Better, he told his African interlocutors, to remain part of a "great ensemble" in which France and its former colonies would interact "on the basis of equality" than to fall for "the illusion of believing in total independence." If at one level he was preaching to Africans that they had better understand the price of independence, at another he was engaging with the arguments coming out of Africa that refused the dichotomy of territorial independence and colonial subservience and sought concrete measures for exercising choice and autonomy. Perhaps on this basis, France could take at their word African leaders who had insisted since 1946 that having the right to independence did not mean that they would take it.[5]

African political leaders, through the first half of 1958, were complaining about the regime of "semiautonomy" and urging revision of the Constitution.[6] They were, meanwhile, trying to work within the limits of the loi-cadre, facing at times the hostility of African civil servants to the territorialization imposed upon them, including a series of strikes in Senegal that "seriously deteriorate the social situation."[7] There were strikes in the Sudan and Dahomey as well in early 1958.[8]

The parties—RDA and its opponents—were debating the "regroupement" of parties to express the desire for unity (chapter 5). By the end of March, the major non-RDA parties (with the exception of the proindependence PAI) were working on fusing into the AOF-wide Parti de Regroupement Africain.[9] As the PRA met to organize itself in April, the RDA coordinating committee tried to distinguish its position: "This is not the time to decide on regrouping." The territorial assemblies should first consolidate their role; they could then decide whether to form a group. But that was not how Sékou Touré was thinking: if a referendum were held, he said, "a huge majority of men and women of Black Africa would impose a politics of federal unity against any politics of dissociation among territories whose borders have no reference to the economic situation, social, human or cultural realities, or the political vocation of Africans."[10] Only six months

[5] "Égalité totale entre la Metropole et l'Outre-mer: Conclusions de la Conférence des responsables d'Afrique Noire," *Afrique Nouvelle*, 21 February 1958; " 'L'indépendance n'est pas un sujet tabou, mais toute libération politique réelle ne se conçoit qu'au fur et à mesure des possibilités économiques,' a déclaré M. Cusin, Haut Commissaire de la République en AOF," *Marchés Tropicaux*, 1 March 1958, 560.

[6] For another, fruitless, debate on the floor of the Assemblée Nationale over revising Title VIII, see *Débats*, 12, 13, 18, 20 February 1958, 702–9, 738–40, 847, 914–22.

[7] An opinion expressed both by the President (that is, the French Chef de Territoire) and the Vice-President (Mamadou Dia) of the Conseil de Gouvernement. *Paris-Dakar*, 25 February 1958.

[8] *Paris-Dakar*, 11, 14, 25 February, 1 March 1958.

[9] *Paris-Dakar*, 28 March, 5 April 1958.

[10] *Paris-Dakar*, 24, 25, 26 April 1958. The PRA constituted itself as a group within the Assemblée Nationale in Paris. *Paris-Dakar*, 14, 16 May 1958.

later Sékou Touré would take quite a different position in an actual referendum—without entirely giving up the ideas expressed here. And despite the agreement between Sékou Touré and the PRA on federalism, there were partisan clashes between RDA and PRA supporters in Guinea in early May, and incidents in Upper Volta as well.[11]

Neither agreement among African leaders nor a plan to reform the constitution was getting any closer when the crisis in Algeria hit. As one French government fell and an attempt—short lived—was made to put together another one, Senghor tried to find a long-term solution to an immediate crisis. In Algeria, part of the population saw itself as French, part as "Arab-Berber." The problem could not be solved if each expression required an independent state. But Africans were thinking in more nuanced terms:

> We agree, ourselves, to transcend the notion of independence by giving it positive contents. We accept to remain in the "French ensemble." Why do our fellow citizen of the metropole not in turn accept, like us, transcending this notion of independence? Why not desacralize it? The problem is not to know whether or not a country will be independent: it is to know if, whatever status it has freely chosen, its evolution will take place, until the final step, against or with France.

Overseas territories, perhaps including Algeria, might see themselves part of such an ensemble even if they rejected the Republic. To get beyond "independence," Senghor came back to the formulas he had worked out over the previous years: solidifying the federations of AOF and AEF, turning the "République une et indivisible" into a federal republic of which AOF, AEF, and metropolitan France would be components, and turning the Union into a voluntary confederation of states.[12]

As the near-coup unfolded in May, deputies from overseas—including Senghor, Apithy, Keita, Félix-Tchicaya, and Houphouët-Boigny—met to draft a letter to President René Coty expressing their "attachment to republican legality and democratic liberties." The President of the Grand Conseil de l'AOF, Gabriel d'Arboussier, called for the "defense of the Republic" and for progress toward a "Franco-African community."[13] Houphouët-Boigny made clear that Africans supported the Republic as part of a double set of expectations: to obtain via constitutional reform "absolute independence in the management of

[11] *Paris-Dakar*, 9, 12 May 1958.
[12] Assemblée Nationale, *Débats*, 13 May 1958, 2253, 2266. He was speaking on the occasion of designation of Pierre Pflimlin as prime minister.
[13] *Afrique Nouvelle*, 23 May 1958; *Paris-Dakar*, 19, 20, 21 May 1958. The PRA voted in favor of the government of Pflimlin as the "only legal government." *Paris-Dakar*, 17 May 1958.

our own affairs without the disadvantages and the servitudes of an illusory nominal independence" and "to obtain economic, financial, cultural, and technical assistance from the metropole until we are able to contribute by our own riches, made fruitful this way, to the general prosperity of the community."[14] Africans were raising their voices to defend French democracy at a time when it was under assault. But on the vote to invest de Gaulle as Président du Conseil, Africans split, and not along party lines: Houphouët-Boigny, Modibo Keita (RDA), and Apithy (PRA) voted in favor, while Gabriel Lisette, Sékou Touré (RDA), Senghor, Dia, and Diawadou Barry (PRA) decided not to take part in the vote.[15]

By the beginning of June, when de Gaulle was installed as head of government, the African demand to revise Title VIII had been folded into the government's plan to write a new constitution for the Fifth Republic. Houphouët-Boigny became a Ministre d'État in de Gaulle's government and was put on the Conseil interministériel (Interministry Council) that would have the first go at rewriting the constitution. Senghor was offered a ministerial post, but declined because, he said, he wanted to devote himself to his party—and no doubt because he wanted some distance between himself and a government in which his chief opponent on the federalism question had the ear of the leader. Sékou Touré, meanwhile, ventured into less consensual territory by demanding a referendum in the overseas territories for them to decide on a federal executive for themselves. The PRA also wanted a referendum specifically on the overseas dimensions of a new constitution. Senghor, after two conversations with de Gaulle, praised him as the man of Brazzaville, and thought him favorable to recognizing the autonomy of the overseas territories, while emphasizing that the PRA was pushing for the equality of those territories with the metropole.[16]

Africa and the Constitution of the Fifth Republic: Writing Behind Closed Doors

The constitution-writing process was more opaque than it had been in 1946. The process was under the supervision of Michel Debré, de Gaulle's Minister of Justice (Garde des Sceaux), jurist, resistance figure, longtime Gaullist, Senator, supporter of the French Union and keeping Algeria French. The Conseil interministériel on which

[14] *Le Monde*, 22 May 1958.

[15] *Le Monde*, 3 June 1958.

[16] *Paris-Dakar*, 22, 23 May, 2, 7, 13, 14 June, 2 July 1958; *Afrique Nouvelle*, 13 June 1958. Senghor was perhaps a bit too eager to find agreement with de Gaulle at his meetings, saying afterward, "I realized that there was no essential difference" between de Gaulle's ideas and the program for constitutional revision of the PRA. *Le Monde*, 3 July 1958.

Houphouët-Boigny sat was to come up with a draft to be presented to Parliament, rather than leaving the task to a committee of the Assemblée Nationale itself. A Consultative Committee with members from both the Assemblée and de Gaulle's governing circle would examine the draft. It was clear from the start that one man had a decisive word—Charles de Gaulle. Mamadou Dia early on expressed his "worries" about the process. No African political party, he said, would accept a constitution that did not reflect "a federalist perspective."[17] De Gaulle was reassuring on that point, declaring in a radio broadcast to the overseas territories, "In 1958 we must build new institutions, establish the connections of our union in a federal mode, organize a great political, economic, and cultural ensemble that responds to modern conditions of life and progress."[18] De Gaulle apparently was also hoping that the "countries under French influence that have become independent"—the former Associated States of Indochina and North Africa—would want to rejoin the reformed French entity.[19]

Among most Africans, the substantive positions on constitutional revisions remained much as they had been, but there was an evolution in language, probably due to fear of being outflanked by the PAI, UGTAN, and the vocal minority of students and politically active youth.[20] The "right to independence" had been invoked by Dia and others for quite some time now—with the insistence that Africans had no intention of exercising it. In March 1958, Modibo Keita insisted that France come to grips with what Africans wanted: "interdependence with France in a federal construction." Keita warned, "Africa has chosen, France hesitates." And if France continued to hesitate, Africans would follow "the only open path compatible with its dignity, the path of independence."[21] Africa, Keita was saying, had found a route to its future, combining independence and interdependence; it was now France's turn to decide if it would take such a path.

Could France agree to coexist with its once colonized territories as equals within a new kind of political structure? Could Africans resolve

[17] *Paris-Dakar*, 12 July 1958.

[18] *Paris-Dakar*, 15 July 1958. *Le Monde* (12 June 1958) commented that in proposing a federal structure in 1958, de Gaulle was taking returning to a theme of his famous speech at Bayeux in 1946 (chapter 2).

[19] *Paris-Dakar*, 16 July 1958.

[20] For an explanation, published early in 1958, of the radical, proindependence position by an activist of the Fédération des Étudiants d'Afrique Noire en France, see the book of the Dahomean Albert Tévoédjrè, *L'Afrique révoltée* (Paris: Présence Africaine, 1958). He was careful to stress the dangers of bringing independence to "a cut-up Africa." Ibid., 131.

[21] Speech in presence of Minister de la FOM, Bamako, reported by Direction des Services de Police du Soudan français, "Synthèse mensuelle de renseignements," March 1958, Bamako/Ambassade/1, ADN.

the quarrel over the African federation? And could such issues be faced in the context of founding a new Republic with a new constitution?

The Conseil interministériel began work in mid-June and presented a preliminary draft at the end of July. The Comité Consultatif Constitutionnel (Consultative Constitutional Committee), with sixteen members from the Assemblée Nationale, others from the Conseil d'État, and still others chosen by the government, then went to work. This committee included Senghor, Lamine Guèye, Philibert Tsiranana of Madagascar, and Gabriel Lisette of Chad.[22] Lisette would defend the thesis of a federal France, Senghor that of a confederal France containing an African federal state. Deliberations were attentively covered in the African press.

The difficult question, Houphouët-Boigny pointed out to his fellow ministers early in their deliberations, was over the nature of federal ties among not-equivalent units:

[Houphouët-Boigny] indicated that with quasi-unanimity the representatives of Black Africa are hostile to secession. . . . The entire difficult consists of the definition of federal linkages because the Franco-African ensemble includes countries of very unequal development. . . . A true federal state must be born that will substitute itself for the different autonomous states. That said, it is essential that the future Constitution be elaborated under conditions such that the overseas countries have the sentiment of having participated. . . . M. Houphouët-Boigny thinks that the Constitution should specify the framework but cannot do more because, notably, of the current uncertainty of knowing whether certain territories will federate directly with the French Republic or group themselves in federations that will themselves federate with the government of the French Republic. . . . M. Houphouët-Boigny intervened to make clear that the representation of the overseas countries in the National Assembly cannot be proportional to their population and that to the extent that one evolves toward a federal regime, the representations of overseas countries in the National Assembly, institution of the Republic, should disappear. . . . M. Houphouët-Boigny summarizes his position by saying that it is necessary to define clearly the federal principle, define clearly the rights of future federated countries, but that the enjoyment of those rights will take place in stages.[23]

---

[22]The government made sure that Sékou Touré was not on the Comité Consultatif. Lisette represented the RDA. Jean Foyer, *Sur les chemins du droit avec le Général. Mémoires de ma vie politique 1944–1988* (Paris: Fayard, 2006), 86.

[23]Compte rendu de la réunion constitutionnelle du 13 juin 1958 in Comité National chargé de la publication des travaux préparatoires des institutions de la Ve République,

Notable in his intervention is, first, that African territories were in the process of evolving in a state-like direction, so that they would be slowly withdrawing from their minority position in the national legislature of France. Second, he saw the ultimate future as federal, but he admitted that the argument among Africans over the form of federalism was unresolved, and he was not using his privileged position to impose his version over that of Senghor and Sékou Touré.

When Houphouët-Boigny intervened, de Gaulle had already given his own version of federalism. The presidency, slated to be a more powerful office than it had been under the Fourth Republic, "will immediately have a federal character, which is essential for the future." Election of the president would be indirect, through an electoral college containing a variety of representatives of legislative bodies, in which overseas representatives would play a significant role. The upper chamber of the legislature would have enhanced prominence, and de Gaulle envisioned it as a "federal Senate." It would have a section similar to that of the current Conseil de la République; another—reflecting a French corporatist tradition—would consist of representatives of "economic, social, and cultural forces"; and a third would have "a truly federal character."[24] The last section was where overseas France would be fully represented.

One problem that had bedeviled the Fourth Republic—a constitution unilaterally imposed on Associated States—led some people to propose to the constitution writers that France have two constitutions, one for France, the other for a "federation of associated peoples," of which France would be a member state. But if the legitimacy of a constitution for France as a state-in-itself was clear enough, the proposals ran into the problem that each of the entities of the federal unit might want to negotiate its own sort of relationship with the French Republic. Since some of those entities did not yet exist, one could not predict what they would want—perhaps not a federation at all.[25] The constitution writers were hearing repeatedly what their predecessors

---

Documents pour servir à l'histoire de l'élaboration de la Constitution du 4 octobre 1958 (Paris: La Documentation française, 1987), 1:248–49.

[24] *Documents*, 1:246–47. De Gaulle's aide Jean Foyer later wrote that while de Gaulle clearly thought the new order would be federal, in his conception "the federation cannot at the beginning be anything other than inegalitarian to be accepted by the population of what is still the metropole. But it must not be too much to fulfill the hopes of the Africans." *Sur les chemins du droit*, 84. De Gaulle also outlined his thinking about federalism in his Bastille Day speech of 1958, much to the disappointment of Dia, Sékou Touré, and other Africans who considered the speech vague and unresponsive to African demands. *Afrique Nouvelle*, 18 July 1958.

[25] "Note et projet d'articles établis pour M. Debré par MM. Louis Bertrand et Max Querrin au sujet d'un projet de Constitution fédérale," 17 June 1958, and "Note pour M. Michel Debré établie par M. Yves Guéna au sujet du projet de Constitution fédérale," 18 June 1958, *Documents*, 1:259–64.

of 1946 had been told but chose to ignore, that any idea of a French community had to be the joint creation of all concerned. The Minister of Overseas France, Bernard Cornut-Gentille, had grasped this point: Africans insisted on being part of the process and there were only two possible outcomes: "the overseas peoples expect either independence or equality with the metropole inside a union that is to be defined." Without institutional autonomy and an equal place in common institutions, "one risks the rejection of the Constitution by the overseas peoples."[26]

As soon as legal experts were consulted, the contradictory imperatives of the constitution writers emerged. A group headed by François Luchaire—on his way to a career as one of France's most distinguished jurists—pointed to the tension between the generally held goals of having a president "equipped with effective powers" and the demand for autonomy for overseas territories. If overseas territories were to participate fully and equally in French institutions, they would have a decisive voice in some decisions, a situation that "the metropolitan voter will not accept." But if they did not, "the overseas voter will not accept such a departure from equality, which to him has a mystical quality."[27]

The corporatist idea of an assembly representing economic interests had by late June been dropped; whether the proposed federal assembly had too much power or too little was still being debated.[28] Luchaire's group suggested that France work with the territories to establish "a *contractual* federation." It must avoid creating "a federation by means of authority." With a French constitution in place, the territories and France could negotiate a pact establishing common, federal, authority, defense, foreign policy, and monetary policies. "The signatories of this pact would commit themselves to respect the rights legitimately acquired under the previous regime (a disposition essential for the security of our investments)." Here was a consideration so delicate it was rarely mentioned: if there was to be an exit from empire, the property of French citizens overseas would have to be protected. The French government's desire for such protection would, in the end, give Africans a bargaining chip in independence negotiations.

Overseas voters, in Luchaire's scheme, would only provisionally be represented in French institutions, awaiting the implementation of the federal accords. Algeria would have to decide whether it wanted to be integrated into metropolitan France or have a special status in the

---

[26]"Notes du Ministre de la FOM à M. Michel Debré," 21 June 1958, *Documents*, 1:275–76.

[27]"Note sur l'état actuel des travaux constitutionnels établie par M. François Luchaire," 23 June 1958, *Documents*, 1:285.

[28]"Compte rendu de la réunion du groupe de travail établi par M. François Luchaire," 27 June 1958, *Documents*, 1:296.

federation. France could ask Tunisia, Morocco, Vietnam, Cambodia, Laos, Togo, and Cameroon if they wanted to have a relationship (and not necessarily the same relationship) with the new "community of associated peoples." The people of the overseas territories were part of the republic, but they might choose to become "associated peoples," in which case their place in the community would have to be reconfigured.[29]

The jurist was pointing to the inherent contradictions in the Gaullist project. What he did not say was that leaving so much to negotiation meant that the new federation might well lack any coherence. And he did not mention, until Debré brought it up at a later session in regard to overseas participation in the election of the president, a variation of the "Herriot problem." As Luchaire reported on 10 July, "The Minister of Justice believes that too great an overseas participation in the election of the head of state would destroy his authority in the metropole, because the latter would say he was elected by the Blacks."[30]

In the privacy of this meeting, there was no Senghor to inject "this is racism," as he had in the constitutional debate of 1946 when Herriot had warned against France becoming the colony of its former colonies. But the situation had fundamentally changed since 1946. The autonomy the overseas territories had acquired in 1956 over internal affairs gave them a place from which to a debate whether or how they would participate in the common affairs of the successor to the French Union. As Africans voted in increasing numbers and as social movements forced the government to concede much of their demands, a colonial situation was gradually becoming something else. Ending colonialism was not a single moment in French history; it did not occur in 1946, as the Ministry had claimed, or in 1960, as the conventional chronology of African history would have it. Not only would overseas populations vote to accept or reject a new constitution (unlike in 1946), but that they were slowly coming into a position to act *as states* to negotiate the contents of a new federation.

The debate went on over how much of a federal constitution would have to be the subject of interstate accords and how much could be laid out in advance.[31] As for the question of whether the overseas

[29]"Note établie par M. François Luchaire pour M. Louis Jacquinot au sujet de la réforme constitutionnelle à l'occasion du Conseil interministériel du 30 juin 1958," *Documents*, 1:310, 311, 317.

[30]"Compte rendu de la réunion du groupe de travail établi par M. François Luchaire," 10 July 1958, *Documents*, 1:403. Debré was not the only one to worry about the Herriot problem. René Servoise warned that the current system, because it insisted that the overseas territories were part of the Republic, might have the effect of "insidiously colonizing the metropole without frankly decolonizing the overseas territories." "Le 'préalable' à la réforme du Titre VIII," *Le Monde*, 6 May 1958.

[31]De Gaulle was apparently becoming impatient over the slow pace at which the committee, beset by disagreements, was working. *Le Monde*, 13–14 July 1958. A number

territories would participate individually or as groups in a French federation, Ministry Counselor Alain Plantey asserted, "It is necessary to let them solve the problem of their federation." France would impose neither "balkanization" nor a federation of AOF or AEF. Reversing a long-standing position, he argued that France could no longer treat economic development as "a common competence"; development issues would have to be negotiated bilaterally with each territory lest "France be accused of maintaining the overseas territories in a state of poverty."[32] Luchaire, however, thought it was unwise to make modest reforms now and leave basic decisions for future negotiations; if overseas territories did not get reforms now, they might prefer independence. Debré agreed: one had to invent the federation or else "overseas territories have no other means to know what this revision would be." The constitution should sketch "the broad lines of the federation": a president elected with the participation of overseas territories, a common assembly, and a list of federal competences. Debré had no illusions over what made might make the effort attractive: "what would create the solidarity of the Federation is the financial aid of the metropole."[33]

Initial proposals were for a relatively extensive list of competences for the federal president and federal assembly: defense, planning, commerce with foreign states, "harmonization of social expenditures," telecommunications, money, and customs duties. The territories should continue to be represented in the Assemblée Nationale and the Conseil de la République, "until the time when a true federal republic" could be established. The federal Senate would approve treaties with other states associating with it "by ties of a confederal character."[34]

At this point in the discussion, Senghor and Dia sent a note to Debré insisting that the nature of institutions should be spelled out: if the overseas populations were to affirm the engagement with France, "the conditions of this engagement must be known to them before the choice." They added, "It cannot be a question of a classic federalism, but only of a light and dynamic federalism." There should be a federal president and "a congress," that would connect the overseas assemblies to the metropolitan one, as well as a "court of justice" that would ensure respect of the constitution and "fundamental freedoms." They concluded, "The federal Constitution must recognize for territo-

---

of Africans came to Paris for Bastille Day, and de Gaulle made something of an effort to court them. *Le Monde*, 17 July 1958.

[32] Plantey, "Compte rendu de la réunion de groupe de travail," *Documents*, 1:402.

[33] Luchaire and Debré, *Documents*, 1:402–3.

[34] "Projet d'articles relatifs à la Fédération préparé par M. Max Querrien pour la réunion du groupe de travail," 10 July 1958, *Documents*, 1:407–8; "Note rédigée par M. François Luchaire pour M. Louis Jacquinot sur l'outre-mer," nd but late June 1958, *Documents*, 1:409–11.

ries or groups the right of self-determination." Their short proposal—six articles—stated that the Federal republic, to which each federated republic would adhere, would have a common politics in matters of defense, foreign affairs, justice, economic development, money, and higher education. The president would be elected by members of the legislative assemblies of the federated republics and administrative assemblies.[35]

The interministerial council and working groups submitted their suggestions to de Gaulle's Cabinet on 23 and 25 July 1958, and the sections on overseas France provoked immediate doubt. The proposed preamble stated, "The Republic offers to the people of the overseas territories who manifest the desire to adhere to it new institutions of a federal or confederal nature founded on the ideals of liberty, equality, and fraternity." The Cabinet promptly dropped the words "of a federal or confederal nature." The first article read "France is an indivisible, secular, democratic, and social Republic." Its second asserted that "national sovereignty belongs to the French people," but the Cabinet decided to drop the word "French."

Under the proposal to the Cabinet, all "French nationals and *ressortissants*, adults of both sexes, enjoy their civil and political rights." They would have the right to vote. The President of the Republic—also the President of the Federation—would be elected indirectly, by a college that included members of Parliament, regional councils in the metropole, and "the assemblies of the overseas territories." Territories could choose to remain in the republic—in their present status or as departments—or opt to leave it for the federation, and if they chose the latter, they would acquire "their autonomy and [would] freely manage their own affairs." The competence of the federation would be limited to foreign affairs, defense, strategic materials, money, common financial and economic policy, control of justice, and higher education. The federation would have a senate that would deliberate separately on matters concerning overseas France, with the participation of deputies from those territories. Until organic laws putting the federation into operation were in place, the overseas territories that had opted for the federation would continue to be represented in the Assemblée Nationale. In some sections reference was made to "territories, grouped or not among themselves"—leaving the door open to federalism à la Senghor without actually implementing it.[36]

---

[35] "Note rédigée par MM. L.S. Senghor et M. Dia pour M. Michel Debré proposant un projet de Constitution fédérale," nd early July 1958, *Documents*, 1:411–12.

[36] As Joseph-Roger de Benoist points out, the discussion of such a constitutional provision assumed that the AOF had already disappeared and "consecrates its suppression." *La balkanisation de l'Afrique occidentale française* (Dakar: Nouvelles Éditions Africaines, 1979), 225.

Territories might simply enter the Federation or they might negotiate specific accords about the terms of their entry. France would preside over a looser grouping of states based on what was initially referred to as "confederal accords," but at the first Cabinet meeting the concept of confederation was dropped. The text stated, "There can be formed between the Federation and the people who indicate the desire to bring together with it a community of free peoples in order to associate and to develop their civilizations." Then the Cabinet changed the expression "community of free peoples" to "community of states." Here was the hope—and little more—that Morocco, Vietnam, and other former members of the French Union would choose to rejoin a French community, leaving to negotiations what this "community" would actually be.[37]

The draft was immediately subject to a scathing critique from François Luchaire. The text, he pointed out, did not affirm the "the right of self determination of peoples." Of the options open to the overseas territories, exit was not included. Luchaire insisted that "to recognize the right to independence is now perhaps the only way to get them to renounce it." He found the article giving territories the right to keep their status within the republic "absolutely incomprehensible." Territories belonging to the federation had the right to manage their own affairs, but the metropole did not, for the National Assembly would include overseas members. As for the autonomy being promised members of the federation, he thought they already had it: "The status of members of the Federation will not bring them any new advantages." Federal institutions were being created by federal law, not by "a negotiated construction." He concluded that the constitution "maintains for the metropole a certain domination."[38]

We need not focus on the details of this draft but rather on its pathos. People from de Gaulle to Debré to Houphouët-Boigny, not to mention the trenchant jurist Luchaire, were casting about for a way to define a political structure that deliberately blurred the lines of sovereignty. The France of the draft constitution existed in multiple forms, as a republic, a federation, and a community of free states. The Republic was "indivisible" except that it contained nonequivalent parts, some

---

[37] "Avant projet de Constitution soumis au Conseil de Cabinet," 23, 25 July 1958, *Documents*, 1:473–94. Chérif Mecheri wrote to Senghor that the prospect of development might bring Morocco or Vietnam back into the fold: "All the territories of the former French empire can be classified as 'underdeveloped countries.' . . . They have realized that political independence has not brought them either economic development or regime stability." Ameliorating underdevelopment, with French help, could be the basis for community. Mecheri to Senghor, 25 July 1958, and "Note sur les conditions d'une relance d'une union," 25 March 1958, 4AG 528, ANF.

[38] "Observations sur l'avant projet de Constitution soumis au comité consultatif constitutionnel rédigées par M. François Luchaire," 29 July 1958, *Documents*, 1:529–37.

of which (overseas territories) had the right to turn into others, one of which (the metropole) did not, some of which had differing degrees of legislative and executive autonomy. It was vague on who or what was actually French. It responded, without saying so, to Senghor's plea to combine vertical and horizontal solidarities by permitting but not saying that territories could group themselves while remaining tied to a France that was still, as Luchaire pointed out, holding onto elements of domination. For the moment it seemed that the constitution writers agreed that France, or at least one of the Frances, was going to be federal. But once they tried to pin down what "federal" actually meant, federalism risked the danger that Herriot warned against in 1946 and the costs of which the authors of the loi-cadre of 1956 had intended to avoid. At this time, the possibility of another France being confederal—Senghor's argument—got the fleeting attention of the interministerial drafting committee but was too much for the Cabinet. Most people party to the discussion assumed that the overseas territories wanted to be part of either the republican France or the federal France. Since metropolitan opinion would not accept placing Algeria outside the Republic and Algerian opinion would not accept a place within it, the Algerian problem lay beyond the constitution writers, even though it was the Algerian crisis that had precipitated the new republic. And, as Luchaire pointed out, the authors of this draft lacked the courage to specify the option that might have made other options attractive to Africans—the right to independence.

When, a few days later, the draft came before the Comité Consultatif Constitutionnel (see above), the first question posed by an African committee member, Philibert Tsiranana, was, "Is the independence of the territories recognized in this Constitution?" The second, also by Tsiranana, was, "Since one speaks of federation, does this comprise states or simply territories?" The word "territory," he added, "begins to sound bad among us."[39] Raymond Janot, Commissaire du Gouvernement and de Gaulle's man in the juridical thickets, replied that independence (or joining the community of free people rather than the federation) was not mentioned in the document because it was not a good idea to say, "We are making a federation, but you can start by going elsewhere right away"; in other words, one did not talk about divorce while celebrating a marriage. His main point, repeatedly made, was that the constitution "represents in itself an offer . . . an offer made by the Republic to the peoples of the overseas territories." The answer revealed a way of thinking, but the idea of an "offer" was not very logical: the territories were supposedly *in* the Republic and were

[39] "Comité consultatif constitutionnel," Compte Rendu, session of 30 July 1958, *Documents*, 2:52. Gabriel Lisette, asking that the principle of self-determination be specifically affirmed, was making the same point as Tsiranana. *Documents*, 2:52–53.

involved in writing the constitution. On specific points—about the composition of the Senate, possibilities of changing status at a later date—he encouraged questioners to amend the text. Asked whether the repeated use of the word "federal" was accurate or the word "confederation" might be more appropriate, Janot admitted the terminology was ambiguous. But he made clear that the principal "offer" was that territories, if they so desired, could move from the Republic to the Federation.[40]

The draft constitution was made public on 30 July in its uncertain state, having moved back and forth among a bewildering array of committees and working groups.[41] Africans had been present present in some of these bodies, and politicians and the press were following the action with great attention.

The Constitutional Question in French West Africa

As the debates were going on in Paris, politicians in Africa were underscoring the stakes in newspaper articles, interviews, and political meetings. Mamadou Dia pointed to African concerns with the process: "We do not want a granted charter any more." He warned of the dangers of "a profound disappointment." No African political party would accept the constitution if it did not embody a federalist perspective, equality, self-determination, and "recognition of the national fact"—the last phrase moving beyond the notion of territorial autonomy. Sékou Touré emphasized the need to recognize the right to independence and the internal autonomy of the "federated states." For him, the status of "state" was as important as the notion of autonomy. He emphasized the goal of creating a "multinational federal community" and the possibility of resurrecting the "former federations." But noting the "role that France can play in the economic and cultural domains," he hoped that "the federation France-TOM [overseas territories] will thus be an intercontinental and multinational community of free and solidaristic peoples." True federalism was again evoked as the only solution to the Herriot problem, since as Mamadou Dia pointed out, absent a federal parliament, the alternative was for overseas representatives to sit in the French National Assembly in appropriate numbers, meaning that they would "in their turn colonize the metropole." He was willing to concede that the primary federation—the African federation—could be created after the federal constitution had been

[40] Janot, *Documents*, 2:54–55, 59.
[41] *Le Monde*, 30 July 1958.

accepted and the territories constituted as "autonomous states." The alternative to meeting these demands was "sooner or later, secession."[42]

Sourou Migan Apithy was now calling for full independence for each territory within a French ensemble, while remaining skeptical about an *African* political unit. The issue for him was how to reconcile "recognition of the sovereignty of each territory, that is its absolute right to independence, and on the other side the necessity which one feels inevitable for these territories to unite in a larger ensemble." He was not convinced that territories would accept "abandonments of sovereignty" to a federation or that the French Republic would accept "a confederal super-parliament . . . above its own assemblies." He thought bureaucracies at multiple levels would be a burden. So he came down in favor of a constitutional right to territorial independence, then giving the states time to decide if they wanted to group themselves into entities that could be recognized as independent. Whatever states were created could choose to form something that might be called the "Union of French Republics." But independence had to come first, and federation could only come later on the basis of agreement among sovereign states: "All the overseas peoples now want to be at home on the territory of their ancestors. But that in no way prevents them from understanding that they must collaborate to construct a larger ensemble to which they already belong on the basis of the French language and culture and economic ties." In Apithy's thinking, the territory and France both appear as units of sentiment and practice, African federation as a vaguely specified option for association among states.[43]

The words "state," "sovereignty," and "independence" were repeatedly spoken in Africa, and federation remained an open question. Some African politicians saw the possibility of getting what they wanted, given de Gaulle's federalism, and therefore being able to embrace a new constitution. Wrote the party newspaper of the Union Soudanaise-RDA, "The President of the Council is a federalist. Our elected representatives are, with greater or lesser nuances, also confederalists. . . . If the referendum guarantees us this equality, there is no reason why Africa cannot vote for it as a single man."[44]

As the first draft of the constitution was emerging, the PRA and RDA held a meeting in Paris that agreed in principle on a "common

[42]*Afrique Nouvelle*, 11, 18 July 1958, *Le Monde*, 24 July 1958. Journalist André Blanchet warned that there was a real danger of "active hostility to the Constitution" embracing Africans from Senghor to Sékou Touré. He feared there were too many compromises in the document, and that it constituted "federalism-light." "La France propose à ses territoires d'outre-mer un fédéralisme leger," *Le Monde*, 24 July 1958.

[43]Sourou Migan Apithy, "La revision du titre VIII de la Constitution," *Marchés Tropicaux*, 19 July 1958, 1738.

[44]*L'Essor*, 30 June 1958.

African action front." The presence of Senghor (PRA), Lisette (RDA), and others on the Consultative Committee would, the party leaders, hoped, lead to a common push for egalitarian federalism, the only way to save the "Franco-African Community." The leaders were conscious of pressures for radicalization coming from the "organizations of youth and trade unions." Not agreeing among themselves on an African federation, the two parties suggested that the option of territories grouping themselves be left open. They insisted that the constitution provide a right to independence in the future and that such an option should be exercised in cooperation with France, not as "secession" from it.[45]

The ante was upped at the meeting of the PRA in Cotonou, Dahomey, at the end of July in an atmosphere shaped by the unsatisfactory first draft of the constitution. In the discussions, there emerged "strong nationalist tendencies," which Senghor, the PRA's top leader, could barely contain. The difference between the argument for independence, pure and simple, set forth by Abdoulaye Ly and Senghor's federal-confederal structure was much debated. The conference ended in a compromise resolution calling for "immediate independence," while insisting that new African states would "enter with France into a confederation of free and equal peoples," a "French Commonwealth" in Senghor' phrase. France would have to recognize the "African national fact." If so, the territories having obtained independence would proceed directly to "voluntary abandonments of sovereignty" to create an African federation and a confederation including France, based on equality. The resolution called for the "unification of Black Africa and the disappearance of artificial borders." A constituent assembly for Africa would define the forms of "regrouping," and it would be this "new state" that would join France in a confederation.[46]

The "audacious positions" taken by the PRA, put pressure on the RDA since, commented Le Monde, "the word 'independence' has, to be sure, more radiance among the masses than that of 'internal autonomy.'" But at least some RDA leaders were wary of the independence plus confederation option suddenly embraced by its rival, fearing that it could be, literally, costly to African territories, and they remained

---

[45] Le Monde, 20–21 July 1958. Djibo Bakary was more categorical: "the majority of Africans will never accept a new cutting up of their territories on the pretext of later regroupment." Le Monde, 23 July 1958. The text of the joint statement is reprinted in Gabriel Lisette, Le combat du Rassemblement démocratique africain (Paris: Présence Africaine, 1983), 334–36.

[46] Afrique Nouvelle, 13 June, 28, 29 July, 1 August 1958; Le Monde, 29 July 1958. Even Abdoulaye Ly, while calling for "immediate independence," quickly added, "but we accept a multinational confederation with France, because of the existing, long-term ties." By holding the congress in Cotonou, fief of the RDA, the PRA was trying to signal how far beyond Senegal it could reach. Le Monde, 27–28, 29, July, 1 August 1958.

"partisans of a federation in which economic and financial solidarity will play a much more rigorous role than in a confederation."[47]

The PRA was not as polarized as was the RDA over an African federation, but the alternative of independence had been posed and Senghor and his allies—who had long wanted to have the right but not to exercise it—had been pressured to accept "decisions that they had not accepted only a few days before."[48] Senghor was trying to assimilate the appeal of the word "independence" to his notion that one claimed sovereignty in order to give up part of it. It would be an African federation that claimed sovereignty and ceded some of it to a Franco-African confederation. Senghor put the PRA's position in the context of recent history. France was always one reform behind, he said. Before the liberation of 1945, we wanted assimilation and were refused. After liberation, we wanted federation, but were offered assimilation. Then we asked for a federal republic and were offered federation. Now, we are asking for confederation—of a unified Africa with France. The PRA would continue juxtaposing its call for independence with its desire to join France in a "multinational Confederation of free and equal peoples."[49]

Senghor's multilevel politics had its limits: he could see Senegal as a part of a larger federation, but could not accept Senegal as itself a federal entity. The issue came up in relation to the Casamance, the part of Senegal south of Gambia. In his conflict with Lamine Guèye in the early 1950s, Senghor had enlisted the support of the Mouvement des Forces Démocratiques de Casamance (MFDC), whose members were allowed to affiliate with Senghor's BDS. The Casamance vote helped Senghor's party to win territorial elections. By 1954, as the BDS was consolidating its control and looked toward a fuller role in governing Senegal, regionalism began to seem more of a threat than an asset. As Dia put it, "If the BDS has the role of representing Senegal in its unity, one cannot see why certain zones would remain outside of its control." After the loi-cadre government was installed, the party of Senghor and Dia would no longer accept a regional affiliate. A Senegal under control of a unified party would campaign to be part of a federal Africa and a confederal France.[50]

[47] *Le Monde*, 31 July, 1 August 1958.
[48] Philippe Decraene, "Les trois thèmes majeurs du Congrès de Cotonou," *France Outre-Mer* 344 (1958): 8. The reporter's three themes were independence, confederation, and creation of a united states of Africa.
[49] *Paris-Dakar*, 29 July 1958; Direction des Services de Police du Soudan français, "Synthèse mensuelle de renseignements," August 1958, Bamako/Ambassade/1, ADN.
[50] Séverine Awenengo Dalberto, "Hidden Debates about the Status of Casamance in the Decolonization Process: Regionalism, Territorialism and Federalism at a Crossroads in Senegal," in Séverine Awenengo Dalberto and Camille Lefebvre, eds., *Tracing Uncertainty: Boundaries, Territoriality and Decolonization in Africa* (forthcoming).

It would be more accurate to describe official French opinion on African federation as wary rather than hostile, and some commentators—as we shall see—came to believe that an African federation was the best way of keeping African territories from going their own way as independent states. *How* African states came together was a serious concern. The High Commissioner's staff worried that the territories "risk federating themselves without any control and under the impulsion of the least moderate factions of the political parties." Alain Plantey thought that the French government should not interfere with negotiations among African leaders. There were risks, but he hoped that the "preventive control" of the High Commissioner in West Africa and the courts to be set up would ensure that the constitution was not violated.[51] But these officials were not suggesting that Africans should actively be prevented from federating—if that was what they wanted.

Constitution Writing Continues: The Debates over Independence, Federation, and Confederation

Senghor, returning to Paris and his seat on the Comité Consultatif, was well aware that he and other leaders could lose control of their followers if they did not have something attractive to show for their efforts at working within French structures. Even some stern figures of French authority like Roland Pré—Governor General of Cameroon and partly responsible for the repression of the UPC—recognized the problem posed by public opinion overseas.[52] But the committee meetings were revealing a double contradiction: metropolitan opinion wanted to keep authority and devolve it at the same time, African opinion wanted the benefits of inclusion while insisting on autonomy.

[51] Alain Plantey, "Note pour le Gouverneur Général, résumé de l'exposé de M. Plantey sur le regroupement des Territoires," nd [summer 58], "Note à l'attention de M. le Ministre sur les conditions d'application de la Constitution dans le groupe de territoires de l'AOF," 5 September 1958; Minister of FOM to High Commissioner, 22 September 1958, FPR 98, ANF. A Senator from the Côte d'Ivoire set out a pragmatic argument for federation: the "cutting up" of AOF would mean that state regulations on taxation and mineral rights would diverge and opportunities for corruption would flourish. Without associating poor and rich territories, France would get stuck with subsidizing the poor ones. "Note concernant le regroupement éventuel des Territoires d'AOF et la création éventuelle d'un exécutif fédéral à Dakar," by M. Delmas, Senateur de la Côte d'Ivoire, nd, c. June 1958; "Note sur les modalités du regroupement des territoires," nd [1958], FPR 98, ANF. The opposite argument in regard the AEF came from Leon M'Ba of Gabon. If AEF became a federation, he feared losing the profits derived from his wealthy territory to poor territories. *Le Monde*, 18 July 1958.

[52] Comité Consulatif, 30 July 1958, *Documents*, 2:61.

Metropolitan members of the committee wondered if French taxpayers would take on the burdens if they gave up the control.[53]

The problem was most acute in the version of federalism sought by de Gaulle and Houphouët-Boigny: Africans would not accept anything but a federation of equals, and French people would not want to pay for providing equal resources to all citizens. Senghor's version offered a way out of the dilemmas: "Because the metropole does not want a federal republic on the basis of equality, very good, we propose to it a confederation." He understood the French dilemma: "There is a difference in standard of living." Annual revenue per capita was 20,000 metropolitan francs in the overseas territories, 400,000 in the metropole. He was suggesting a trade-off: more independence for a more modest claim on French resources.[54]

Senghor had some notable support. Paul-Coste Floret and especially Pierre-Henri Teitgen (consistent with his position since 1956) both feared that federalism meant more French responsibility than France could afford. "On the contrary," said Teitgen, "in a confederal system France will be able to put in common what she wants, on agreement with the other states. There will be states distinct from each other, France being bound only by accords concluded with them." That argument met objections from those who feared ties would be "too weak," tempting Africans to push for secession, or worse still making them more susceptible to "political influences from the exterior." From an African perspective, Lisette continued to speak in favor of federation, even if it meant "that for a certain time it is inevitable that metropolitan France have a certain preponderance. He also thought that the federation must look ahead to an economic and social plan permitting the overseas populations to have a higher standard of living. This well-being would make it possible to avoid movements in favor of total independence."[55] Lisette's proposed trade-off was more resources for less independence.

The constitution makers were coming together and apart in curious ways: de Gaulle and Lisette were pushing federation, the former because he wanted to keep France at the center of a coherent ensemble, the latter because he wanted to claim the resources of that ensemble. Senghor and Teitgen were favorable to confederation, the former because he wanted to develop the distinct personality of African territories, the latter because he thought that confederation would imply less of an economic burden on France.

[53] For example, M. Malterre, 30 July 1958, *Documents*, 2:62.

[54] Senghor, *Documents*, 2:85.

[55] Lisette wanted a federal responsibility for "economic solidarity" inscribed in the constitution. Against Coste-Floret and Teitgen were also arrayed Marcilhacy, Blocq-Mascart, de Bailliencourt, and Pré, 1 August 1958, *Documents*, 2:121–22.

Some committee members kept trying to find a formula in the middle and proposed various texts to accomplish such a task—federal institutions with a confederal option, said one member.[56] As the debates in committee went on, there were hints in the press that even longtime supporters of French colonial rule like the journal *Marchés Tropicaux* were getting fed up with the whole thing. An editorial—following the Cartier thesis of 1956—grudgingly argued that if Africans wanted independence, they could have it: "The large majority of overseas elites, on which the masses have their eyes fixed and will follow, want independence, immediately or over time. Why not accord without delay independence to the overseas countries, to clarify a situation that would risk being equivocal for some and poisoning an atmosphere that we want to be one of friendship and loyalty?"[57] Whatever the editors of *Marchés Tropicaux* really thought about African independence, they were telling Africans that they should not consider themselves indispensable.

In early August, the options of federation and confederation were both in play in the texts under consideration, as was the possibility of leaving it up to the territories to decide whether they wanted to be grouped or not.[58] A proposal about citizenship, given little attention before, now entered discussions: "There exists only one federal citizenship. All citizens are equal in rights and duties, whatever their origin, race, or religion." That citizenship entailed rights gave rise to the question of what kind of judicial system would enforce them. Senghor was firmly federalist on this point: "M. Senghor believes . . . that justice must be part of common matters, so as to avoid the danger of biased local justice."[59] Here, he was saying, was a major advantage of a multilayered polity over a unitary one: by putting courts at a higher level, the pressure of immediate interests and immediate structures of power on judicial processes could be lessened. The committee seemed to agree.

The Consultative Committee's preference now seemed to be for relatively simple provisions on federal institutions; a president, a sen-

[56] Senghor and Lauriol, *Documents*, 2:122.

[57] *Marchés Tropicaux*, 2 August 1958, editorial, "Une communauté de Peuples Libres." 1833–35, 1834 quoted. The editorial made much of the "demagoguery" and "oneupmanship" of African politicians. Its worst fear seems to have been that African deputies would exercise real power within France. The journal came out in favor of a loose association of states in which France would have little explicit responsibility and accord Africans little power over collective decisions. The bitter tone of the article suggests a realization that such an association was the best deal colonial business interests could now get.

[58] Comité Consultatif, 1 August 1958, *Documents*, 2:123; 5 August 1958, *Documents*, 2:150; *Le Monde*, 6 August 1958. A working group on overseas France was chaired by Paul Alduy and Lamine Guèye. *Le Monde*, 2 August 1958.

[59] Comité Consultatif, 5 August 1958, *Documents*, 2:151.

ate elected by the legislatures of "Member States" (not de Gaulle's three-part senate with a chamber for corporate interests) and a cour d'arbitrage (court of arbitration). The federal senate would vote on the federal budget and laws applicable to the federation as a whole; it would approve economic plans and examine government reports on foreign policy and defense, formulating recommendations on those matters. The court would settle disputes among the federated states. Coste-Floret took the initiative in regard to the status of territories and groups: territorial assemblies would have the right to decide which of the statuses "offered" they wanted; territories could group themselves or not as they chose. Senghor wanted more specific wording, including the right for territories to change status and to "group themselves in primary federations."[60] The next day, the committee was working on how the federation would be governed. The federal government would consist of the "prime ministers of the Member States and the ministers in charge of enumerated matters." The President of the Republic would head the federal government. The older proposal for a "community of free peoples" was still on the table, and some wondered about the difference between it and a confederation.[61]

The working groups, as Coste-Floret admitted, had come up with a mix of federal and confederal principles. Within the federation, he was willing to refer to the territories as "federated states," but not to use words like independence or sovereignty. The working groups had decided that the territories would have four months to decide what status, among those "offered," they wanted. But now Coste-Floret conceded that the options should go "up to independence," but only once. "One cannot offer independence to the territories every day. When one is in a federation, or even in a confederation, one has agreed, by means of a contractual accord, on ties to other states, and one cannot by unilateral will go away every day." Territorial assemblies would have to choose to join the federation, and if, later, one wanted to leave the federation, the federal assembly would have to agree.[62] At this point, Senghor considered the proposal "catastrophic." It "balkanized" Africa and did not adequately provide for self-determination.[63]

De Gaulle was present at the committee meeting of 8 August. *Le Monde*'s headline read, "Controversy Develops between Partisans of Federation and Defenders of Confederation." Lamine Guèye addressed de Gaulle directly and at length.[64] He told de Gaulle about the meeting African deputies had had at the Palais Bourbon. His appeal

[60] *Documents, 5 August 1958,* 2:152–53.
[61] *Documents*, 6 August 1958, 2:193–200.
[62] *Documents* , 8 August 1958, 2:305–6.
[63] *Afrique Nouvelle*, 8 August 1958; *Le Monde*, 31 July 1958.
[64] Before de Gaulle's appearance at the committee, African leaders had private meetings with him. The RDA sent a delegation—Lisette and d'Arboussier, as well as

was historical and sentimental—to the man of Brazzaville, the leader of a government that had decided in 1945 that the colonies would be represented in the constitution-writing process. He claimed that no assembly or party in Africa wanted to abandon association with France. How wide, he wanted to know, would our options now be—status quo, department, federation, confederation, with the possibility of entering or leaving?[65] Tsiranana claimed that Africans wanted what Madagascar had always claimed: "an autonomous Malagasy Republic federated with France." But it was not obvious whether Madagascar belonged in a federation or a confederation.[66]

De Gaulle replied at length to his African interlocutors. What we are doing is "a great achievement; it is an absolutely new achievement . . . to put together an ensemble that is modern, that is adapted to the world in which we live." The referendum would place the endeavor "on the basis of spontaneous acceptance. . . . If one refuses this association that is proposed, by the draft constitution, it is understood that one wants independence, that one wants it with all the duties, expenses, dangers, and in that case, evidently, the metropole will draw the consequences." As of now, territories "are not states, that is they cannot take charge, on their own, of their defense, their foreign policy, their economic life, their currency, of all the prerogatives that are absolutely inevitable for a state, without which there is no state." One could discuss, he said, the line between federation and confederation, but he had opted for the word " 'federation,' because it says, I think, very clearly what we mean by it. . . . It is the constitution of an ensemble of people who wish to constitute it."

The constitution, de Gaulle went on, was "a whole," for the metropole as well as the territories. The territories would administer themselves; he used the phrase "self-determination, or, if you wish, the freedom to dispose of oneself." Both the overseas territories and the metropole would delegate power "to establish a domain common to all," encompassing foreign affairs, the overall economy, currency, justice, higher education, and other areas agreed upon through negotiations. He was convinced of the importance of solid federal institutions—a president and a "federal executive council" composed of the president of the federation, federal ministers, presidents of territorial governments. Territories would be represented in a senate.

Houphouët-Boigny—and they apparently reacted positively to the discussion. *Le Monde*, 7, 9 August 1958.

[65] Lamine Guèye, Comité Consultatif, 8 August 1958, *Documents*, 2:307–8.

[66] Ibid., 2:308. Tsiranana had earlier stated, "One thing is certain: our nation is too small to leave the orbit of France. We do not want to be the prey of great powers, and we also believe that for Madagascar independence is not currently viable." *Le Monde*, 28 June 1958.

He admitted that the line between federation and confederation was not clear, but he was engaged in an act of creation: "It is I, de Gaulle, who says to you, we do so very frankly, on a practical basis, and we believe it, on the most human bases that are conceivable." He came back to the referendum: "The referendum will be proposed to them as acceptance to be part of the ensemble that is now being proposed, or as a refusal to be part of it."[67] In posing the question in all or nothing terms, de Gaulle was setting the stage for the confrontation that would take place during his tour of Africa later that month.

As news of the encounter spread, *Paris-Dakar* reported that de Gaulle's intervention caused a strong reaction in Africa, particularly among the PRA, who interpreted de Gaulle's words as saying "You accept what we propose or we will cut off your livelihood." *Afrique Nouvelle* claimed that the RDA reacted positively to de Gaulle's intervention; the PRA's reaction was "mitigated."[68]

In Paris, the committee found itself unable to go along with de Gaulle's attempt to minimize the distinction between federation and confederation. *Le Monde* tried to explain the difference: a federation has "one citizenship" and "one face toward the exterior," and a confederation includes several states and "several citizenships" but can have a common diplomacy, currency, defense, and educational system. If federation meant a single government of equals, worried its reporter, might not one see "the policies of the metropole dictated, on the most important questions," by assemblies with substantial, if not majority, overseas representation? Here was the Herriot problem again—and a reason why the various committees were drifting away from the version of federalism that de Gaulle and Houphouët-Boigny had in mind.[69]

Teitgen tried to clarify the issue for the committee: federated states had no international existence, confederated states did—their relationship was regulated not by constitutions or laws but by treaties. States, federal or otherwise, could delegate some powers to a confederal body. De Gaulle's preference for federation, he worried, might cause some states to opt out, while leaving open the possibility of choice

[67] Comité Consultatif, 8 August 1958, *Documents*, 2:309–11. Robert Bourgi describes de Gaulle's option for federation as a decision in favor of Houphouët-Boigny's line over Senghor's. He also cites the influence of his counselor—soon to be the Monsieur Afrique of the Élysée Palace—Jacques Foccart. But de Gaulle had been talking federation since 1946. *Le Genéral de Gaulle et l'Afrique Noire: 1940-1969* (Paris: Librairie générale de droit et de jurisprudence, 1980), 340.

[68] *Paris-Dakar*, 16 August 1958; *Afrique Nouvelle*, 15 August 1958.

[69] Pierre Viansson-Ponté, "La controverse se développe entre partisans de la Fédération et défenseurs de la Confédération," *Le Monde*, 9 August 1958. In the end, the jurist Janot emphasized that the "true federal republic" was "difficult to make acceptable to metropolitan opinion." Press interview, 9 September 1958, *Documents*, 4:96.

might lead them to opt in. And he pointed out that in mentioning the complications regarding Togo, Cameroon, and Madagascar, de Gaulle was accepting a certain suppleness to federation—depending on accords—which brought his structure closer to that advocated by confederalists.[70]

But the intervention that had, at least as far as nomenclature was concerned, the strongest eventual impact came from Philibert Tsiranana of Madagascar. Instead of arguing about federation or confederation, he asked, why not think of another word? What we are creating, he said, was "the Franco-African community."[71]

As the meeting proceeded, Lamine Guèye objected to de Gaulle's take-it-or-leave-it approach to the referendum. Better than closing the door to whomever did not get their way on the federation-confederation question was leaving room for maneuver; otherwise, some African territories might back themselves into an independence that they could not afford. "That is why I beg our friends to consider this situation."[72] Senghor asserted that the PRA's view of independence in confederation had the support of Senegal, Niger, Dahomey, Ubangui, parts of Cameroon, and Guinea. That meant a lot of potential "no" votes if the constitution did not reflect their desires. Federation, moreover, would likely prove out of date within a few years as federated territories came to find it too restrictive: "It is essential that the constitutional project not block the future and that it gives us all the options." Confederation, he insisted, was a synonym of alliance, treaty, and by extension "marriage"; it was not separation. The two great ideas of the day were "the independence of peoples and, at the same time, the constitution of large ensembles. All great civilizations were the civilizations of cultural mixing, as you know." He wanted at all costs to avoid a "false dilemma," to accept what was being offered or to secede. "What we want is for this option for independence to be clarified here, in the constitutional text; at that moment we will vote for the Constitution, and then we will choose and conclude accords with France."[73] The discussion went around and around, bringing out major conceptual differences within the committee and serious incoherence in the text.[74]

Frustrated, the committee adjourned to let a small working group on the overseas territories, headed by Coste-Floret, try to draft a better text. In the late afternoon of 12 August, the group reported back,

[70] Comité Consultatif, 12 August 1958, *Documents* 2:368–69.
[71] Ibid., 2:370.
[72] Ibid., 2:371–72.
[73] Ibid., 2:372–74. Senghor described federation as "marriage under the regime of community property, confederation is marriage under the regime of separate property." But both were marriage. The separation of property was why Teitgen found confederation less burdensome than federation. Ibid., 2:378.
[74] Ibid., 2:378–89.

claiming to have found in the suggestion of Tsiranana a way out of the impasse. What was being created would not be called either federation or confederation, but "community."[75] The name stuck. The government's lead jurist, Raymond Janot, later told reporters that the commission debates between federalists and confederalists had been going nowhere, "It was awful!" He added, "The federal notion disappeared in the course of a heroic session of the Comité Consultatif Constitutionnel." Tsiranana had broken through by abandoning the words and postponing the decision, leaving in place different options as the Community evolved: "The institutions have within them the possibility of becoming institutions of a true federation, it is possible, but they also have the possibility of becoming the institutions of a simple confederation."[76]

Michel Debré, later on, was blunter: "The Community is not a federation," reversing de Gaulle's position of three weeks earlier.[77] But the basic problems would not go away, and the committee was quickly stuck on the same kinds of problems it had been debating before. Should the control of justice be a Community matter? Some argued—as had Senghor in a previous session—that the best way of ensuring an independent judiciary was to have at least the appeals jurisdictions be at the Community level, while others insisted that the "particularity of our morals and customs" meant that more local control was desirable. The government saw that an appeals jurisdiction at the Community level (practically everybody slipped into using the word "federation") was basic, but that with "evolution" more judicial autonomy could be devolved.[78]

Some members continued to worry that a federal assembly might impose laws on the metropole that its own assembly had not agreed to.[79] Africans worried that ministers taking charge of common matters like defense would always turn out to be metropolitans. Most committee members thought that the constitution had to allow for degrees of

[75] De Gaulle's legal aide Jean Foyer later stressed the importance of Tsiranana's contribution: "the confederalists heard no more talk about federation; the federalists lost nothing." *Sur les chemins du droit*, 88. Law professor R.-E. Charlier pointed out that the distinction between federation and confederation was far from absolute. A variety of "groups of states" was part of "the modern world," and the key point was to reach agreements over what different parts of government would do. *Le Monde*, 21 August 1958.

[76] Janot, press interviews, 5, 8, 9, 10 September 1958, in *Documents*, 4:12, 44–45, 84, 126.

[77] Allocution de M. Michel Debré to Assemblée Générale of Conseil d'État, 27 August 1958, *Documents*, 3:263. Debré also said that the Community was not a confederation: "there are too strong inequalities among the participants." Ibid.

[78] Interventions of Coste-Floret, Senghor, Lisette, Tsiranana, Janot, and Gilbert-Jules, Comité Consultif, 12 August 1958, *Documents*, 2:391, 393–97.

[79] Paul Reynaud, President of commission, *Documents*, 2:413; Teitgen, 2:416.

autonomy and common action to vary; the metropolitan role would be stronger at the beginning, as Lisette argued.[80]

The committee members, from African and European France, were engaging in a process of give-and-take—trying to establish what a Community would be that the Union was not, but they also seemed willing to accept a degree of uncertainty and changeability. African politicians may well have had on their minds the previous twelve years of political engagement that had produced frequent frustration, but also desirable results—the Code du Travail, universal suffrage, Conseils de gouvernement. They would continue to have to sort out differences among themselves and put pressure on their metropolitan colleagues. Many if not most of them thought that de Gaulle might well have a point when he warned them that with independence would come duties, costs, and dangers. Modibo Keita, for example, told a party meeting in the midst of the constitutional debates, "Independence presumes that the Sudan or AOF has its diplomatic corps, its army, its currency. Are we ready for that? Do we have on our own the means to solve all our problems, to construct roads, schools, dispensaries, to open work sites? Our lack of means imposes on us to associate with those who can help us, in this case, France."[81] By the 12th, the committee members were generally referring to its component parts as "États membres"—Member States. The use of word "state" in relation to a French Community that was in some respects a state but also a community of states suggests how important the layering of sovereignty was to the committee's thinking.

One of the basic premises of constitution writing—a condition of performing such a task under de Gaulle—was that the new republic have a stronger president than the old one. De Gaulle's position was a direct response to the uncertainties of state power that had characterized the Fourth Republic. But how did one reconcile presidential power with the complex sovereignty of the Community?

Not easily. The "keystone" of the Community, Michel Debré would later say, was the President.[82] The deputies realized that there would be eighteen Member States in the Community if all went as expected. Each would have a head of government responsible to a territorial assembly. The Community government would—everybody agreed—have a president, and the president would be the president of the French Republic, although elected by a college mostly consisting of representatives of the legislatures of the different states. To govern the Community, ministers with functional responsibilities would be nec-

[80] Interventions of Gilbert-Jules, Chazelle, Lisette, David, *Documents*, 2:397–403.
[81] *Paris-Dakar*, 18 August 1958.
[82] Allocution of Debré to Assemblée Générale of Conseil d'État, 27 August 1958, *Documents*, 3:264.

essary—a bone of contention with African committee members, who feared metropolitan dominance. There was talk of a two-level executive committee to administer the Community—one of prime ministers, the other of functional ministers—but it all began to sound too complicated, risking division between metropole and Member States. Here was where the idea of a "Conseil exécutif" (Executive Council) came in—the heads of state and/or heads of government of each Member State, the French Republic included, presided by the President.[83] The Conseil exécutif would turn out to be a key site where the last acts of the French Empire would play out.

The great fear on both sides of the Mediterranean was losing control of the political process. Africans remembered the ten years of trying to obtain universal suffrage and the single college. Metropolitans kept bringing up the Herriot problem. Former Governor General Roland Pré pointed to the fine line that had to be walked: in a "true federation," guarantees had to be given so that the metropole "does not feel itself to be a minority"; but taking too many attributes away would leave the federation with nothing of substance. Others thought economic and cultural ties was what would maintain "the solidity of the Federation," but the fact was that those ties were not symmetrical—perhaps giving the metropole too much power or burdens too large.[84]

There were warnings that de Gaulle's take-it-or-leave-it approach was risky. Teitgen agonized that territories voting "no" would feel "chased away, repudiated, sent back." Coste-Floret objected that voting against the constitution was the only way to choose independence. Tsiranana warned that a stark choice at the time of referendum would make it difficult for people like him to confront "extremists" in their own countries, making a "no" vote more likely. Le Monde journalist André Blanchet criticized the way de Gaulle was posing the choice: "It would be undignified for a great nation to appear to impose on its former colonies the choice between a defined political status and the renunciation of all material aid." He noted that de Gaulle was being accused in the Communist press of "condemning" Africa to independence.[85]

Some members of the committee suggested that more options could be proposed—for example letting territories that opted "in" have a chance to opt "out" every five or seven years. But the point that achieved general agreement was on the choices to be made after a territory voted to accept the constitution: it could decide by vote of the territorial assembly and/or referendum between departmental or

[83] Coste-Floret, Comité Consultatif, 12 August 1958, Documents, 2:410.
[84] Ibid., 2:416.
[85] Ibid., 2:424–29, 432–38; André Blanchet, "'Condamnés' à l'indépendance?" Le Monde, 19 August 1958.

territorial status within the Republic and becoming a federated state of the Community.[86]

Meanwhile, members wanted to give Morocco, Tunisia, and the states of Indochina—the now independent states of the former French Union—a chance to rejoin a postimperial Community.[87] By now, Sénghor's insistence that territories could join the Community either individually or in groups had general approval.[88] The committee did not know what to do about Algeria—a question de Gaulle wanted to leave in abeyance. That Muslim Algerians and settlers had such different views of their attachments to Algeria and to France did not fit well with the idea of exercising options by territory.[89]

Algeria was, of course, the elephant in the conference room even though there was little that constitution writers could do other than leave a place for it to occupy if the nationalist revolution and settler rebellion could be resolved. But one reason that de Gaulle and many others hoped to institute the Community was that it would be more plausible to integrate Algeria into a diverse Franco-African ensemble than into the French Republic. De Gaulle himself stated in July that Algeria would have "a choice place" in the Community, and in August he told Gabriel d'Arboussier, "It is for Algeria that I create the Community."[90] Some African leaders (including Dia) later suggested Africa could serve as a mediator in the Algerian conflict, but the Algerian nationalists rejected the move. At least one French observer thought "these Blacks are better qualified than we to address" the Algerian liberation movements.[91] Such hopes fit into a pattern dating back some years of thinking, as Todd Shepard argues, that Algeria's situation could best be dealt with by looking at it as part of a "grand ensemble," but French politicians and intellectuals thought of that en-

[86] *Documents*, 2:435–38. A proposal to confer an option of changing status every seven years (the legislative cycle) from M. Triboulet lost on a thirteen to eleven vote. Ibid., 2:437.

[87] Ibid., 2:424–25.

[88] Senghor and Paul Reynaud (committee president), ibid., 2:437.

[89] Ibid., 2:441. One member, Marc Lauriol (from Algeria), added to the discussion that if Algeria were integrated into the Republic, Muslim Algerians should be excluded from votes on matters pertaining to the civil code—an argument most of his colleagues found appalling. Ibid., 13 August 1958, 2:455–59.

[90] Quoted in Charles-Robert Ageron, "Les États africains de la Communauté et la guerre d'Algérie (1958–1960)," in Ageron et Marc Michel, eds., *L'Afrique noire française: L'heure des indépendances* (Paris: CNRS Éditions, 2010), 269–311, 271 quoted.

[91] Ibid., 288–89; exchange between journalist Jean Piat and government jurist Raymond Janot at the latter's press conference, 9 September 1958, *Documents*, 4:92. In fact, as Ageron argues, unity between sub-Saharan Africa and Algeria was as elusive as a Eurafrica embracing France and Africa.

semble as Eurafrican, while FLN leaders were more likely to think of it as Maghrebian, Arab, or Islamic.[92]

The Algerian problem was not going to be solved by writing a more inclusive constitution. But enough points about the grand ensemble were resolved or finessed to arrive at a text to send back to the Conseil interministériel on 14 August. Transmitting the draft to de Gaulle, Committee Chair Paul Reynaud (an old line conservative deputy), well aware of de Gaulle's advocacy of federation, called attention to the federation-confederation conflict and argued that both concepts were too abstract. The best method, he argued, was to agree on creating a Community, to label it as such, and to shape it in such a way as to take into account the different situations of its component parts and the need to "adapt oneself to the evolution of the world without presuming in advance the direction of the evolution."[93]

The committee's text kept intact the designation of "Member States." It allowed those states to group themselves if they so chose and—every five years—to opt for a new status, including that of "independent state within the Association of Free States." Until the institutions of the Community were in place, the Republic would take control of the issues specified as Community competences—guarantee of basic liberties, defense, foreign policy, strategic materials, "common economic policy," control of justice and the status of magistrates, higher education, common transport, and telecommunications. Until that point, the overseas territories would continue to be represented in Parliament. The President would preside over a "Conseil exécutif" consisting of the prime ministers of the Member States and ministers in charge of the enumerated domains. There would be a Senate and a high court to ensure respect of the constitution and treaties. The President was to consult with the Conseil exécutif on decisions on common matters, but as he controlled the institutions to implement decisions, it was far from shared governance. In practice, as we shall see below, the African members of the Council showed over the course of 1959 that they could at least exercise influence. The Senate was not expected to be an important decision-making body. It would meet only twice a year for a month, could have its say on constitutional revisions affecting the Community, and was otherwise expected to be an instrument "coordination and legislative harmonization," with the possibility that in the future, if things evolved that way, it could become "a true federal parliament."[94]

[92]Todd Shepard, "A l'heure des 'grands ensembles' et la guerre d'Algérie. L'État-nation' en question," *Monde(s): Histoires, Espaces, Relations* 1 (2012): 113–34.

[93]Reynaud to de Gaulle, 14 August 1958, *Documents*, 2:557–61.

[94]Text of draft constitution, *Documents*, 2:564–611. According to Georges Chaffard, Houphouët-Boigny thought the idea of a status revision every five years—supported by Senghor and Coste-Floret—was dangerous because it would give no stability to long-

Citizenship had not—unlike in 1946—been a controversial concept, and the committee's draft (earlier versions had said virtually nothing), stated, "There exists only one citizenship of the Community." Later, Raymond Janot, when asked by a reporter whether this provision meant that the people of any Member State were "French like the others," replied, "Yes, they enjoy the same rights and the same duties." There was virtually no discussion of the fact that, as in the 1946 constitution, they could keep their own personal status unless they renounced it.[95]

On the 18th, de Gaulle, Debré, Janot, and René Cassin worked on the text and presented a modified version to the Conseil interministériel.[96] Their version mentioned the possibility of "primary federations" alongside the Member States as part of the Conseil exécutif, as participants in the election of the President, and as places where a High Commissioner would represent the President of the Community. It included a provision on changing the status of Member States—on their initiative or on that of the Republic, requiring agreement from both the Parliament of the Republic and the territorial assembly in question, including the option "to accede to the condition of independent state. In this way, it ceases to belong to the Community."[97] De Gaulle promised that the compromise notion of "community" would be considered "with much care." On 20 August, de Gaulle left for Africa, his big trip to campaign for a yes vote on the constitution. Exactly what that constitution would say was still not entirely decided.[98]

De Gaulle's African Odyssey and the Referendum of 28 September

One important question, a sore point in 1946, was no longer an issue in 1958: universal suffrage. African citizens, just like their European counterparts, would be voting in the referendum to approve or reject the proposed constitution of the Fifth Republic. Universal suffrage was central to de Gaulle's notion of politics, and in this context he

---

term thinking or planning. Giving states an immediate choice was the way to "exorcise the demon of independence." Chaffard thinks Houphouët-Boigny persuaded de Gaulle to seek a definitive and immediate decision from each territory on accepting the constitution or becoming independent. *Les carnets secrets de le décolonisation* (Paris: Calmann-Lévy, 1967), 2:184–86. Janot made a similar argument. Press interview, 9 September 1958, *Documents*, 4:85. On the Conseil exécutif and the Sénat, see the commentaries on the text of the constitution assembled in *Documents*, 4:198–202.

[95] Janot, press interview, 8 September 1958, in *Documents*, 4:44.
[96] See the editorial notes in *Documents*, 2:623.
[97] Ibid., 2:635–37.
[98] *Paris-Dakar*, 20 August 1958.

looked to "the suffrage of all citizens, male and female, in the metropole and in the overseas territories."[99] It was in this light that his Africa odyssey of August 1958 took on such importance: he was appealing to Africans as citizens. But if Africans voted on the same basis as other citizens, their votes did not have the same consequence: if the citizens of any overseas territory rejected the text, that territory would cease to be French, while metropolitan citizens faced no such threat. That was how de Gaulle had insisted on posing the question: an inclusive appeal at one level, an ultimatum at another.

De Gaulle's appearance in some of the major capitals of French Africa put pressure on African politicians to commit themselves to a new constitution, and they had no middle ground between yes and no. The text was emerging only as de Gaulle traveled. The Conseil interministériel, working from the text of the Consultative Committee that had already been modified, issued its revised draft on 19 August. It then went to the Conseil d'État, the "sages," as they were often called, who were required to pass judgment on every text of law. That text was the object of a report, then a deliberation of the Commission Constitutionnelle of the Conseil d'État on 25 and 26 August. That committee issued its revised text, which went before the Assemblée Générale of the Conseil d'État on 27 and 28 August. It issued its opinion on 28 August. The text went back to the Conseil interministériel, which had been responsible for the first draft. Propositions for modifications were still coming in. A draft went before the Conseil des Ministres on 3 September, and the next day, at a ceremony, the text was presented to the public. On 28 September, citizens in metropolitan and overseas France would vote on its approval.

By then, de Gaulle had returned from Africa. In a short space of time, African politicians and voters across the continent were confronted with a choice of voting "oui" or "non" on a text of considerable complexity. The process that produced it had also been complex, and not entirely transparent, although several African deputies had made their voices heard.

De Gaulle's trip was a strangely imperial procession and it set off a storm—what happened in those few days merits a book in itself.[100] The man of Brazzaville basked in the adulation of crowds in Tananarive,

[99] Speech in Madagascar, 22 August 1958, cited in Philippe Foro, "Être citoyen selon Charles de Gaulle," in Claude Fiévet, ed., *Invention et réinvention de la citoyenneté* (Aubertin: Éd. Joëlle Sampy, 2000), 601–16, 603 quoted. De Gaulle made the same argument as in Madagascar in Algeria in June 1958: "France considers that in all of Algeria there is only one category of inhabitants; there are only full-fledged French people, with the same rights and the same duties." Ibid.

[100] Elisabeth Fink's doctoral research at NYU on elections and voting in AOF will include analysis of the campaigns over the referendum. See the coverage of de Gaulle's voyage in *Afrique Nouvelle*, late August 1958.

Brazzaville, and Abidjan. But the high drama took place in Conakry, on 25 August, when two men of vision, and sizeable egos—Charles de Gaulle and Sékou Touré—confronted each other over the process and the substance of the proposed new structure.

Beginning in Tananarive, de Gaulle set forth the case for "a Community in the federal mode." He told his audience, "tomorrow you will again be a state"—a politically astute reference to the claims of Malagasy, or at least those from the dominant elements, that they had been a state at the time of the French conquest of 1896.[101] Voting yes would both restore the political honor of Madagascar and bring the island into the contemporary world of states.

It was in Brazzaville where he revealed how far he was willing to go to obtain the consent of Africans. Apparently on the advice of Coste-Floret—who had taken in the strong words of Senghor and Lamine Guèye—he now made clear that even after the referendum, those territories that had voted "oui," now Member States, could later opt for independence without being considered to have seceded. There would have to be a vote by the territorial assembly and a referendum; the Community would "take note" and reach an agreement on how power was to be transferred.[102]

This was an important issue to Africans, and without this concession the PRA might well have backed a no vote. Gabriel d'Arboussier thought that after the Brazzaville speech, "the great Franco-African debates have found their solution. . . . There is no more Franco-African problem. . . . There remains an inter-African problem."[103] But the right to independence was still short of creating a confederation—independence within the Community—and a primary federation that Senghor and Sékou Touré wanted.

While de Gaulle was in Africa, the Conseil d'État was going over the draft constitution. From the start, its Commission Constitutionnelle saw the institution of the Community as central to its entire endeavor and wanted it mentioned up front: a Community "founded on the equality of the peoples who compose it." The "freedom of peoples to enter or to leave it from the start" was the great "novelty" of the Constitution. Such a statement would create a "psychological shock."[104]

---

[101] Le Monde, 24–25 August 1958.

[102] Bourgi states that the decision was made on 19 August. Le Général de Gaulle et l'Afrique Noire, 344. See also Chaffard, Carnets secrets, 2:192.

[103] Le Monde, 26 August 1958; L'Essor, 27 August 1958.

[104] Marcel Martin, reporter, Conseil d'État, Commission constitutionnelle, sessions of 26 and 26 August 1958, in Documents, 3:42–43. The members promptly got into a discussion of whether the people making the constitution were one or plural, or perhaps that the people of the Republic were one, those of the Community many. They ended up with a plural, then invoked the "solidarity of the peoples" who composed the Community, all the while worrying that "solidarity" implied too strongly "the idea of a right"—presumably a claim to material resources. Ibid., 3:43–47.

As that body debated the draft's distinction between a "territory" that chose to remain within the Republic and a "state" within the Community, the President of the Committee pointed out that "General de Gaulle, who just went to Madagascar, said to the inhabitants of the island, 'you will be a state.'" Because of that promise, the Conseil was stuck, although he and some of his colleagues wondered whether all the states of Africa had "the true level of civilization" for such a status.[105] The Conseil's Committee was clearly concerned about the implications of the word "state," for it seemed to mean a certain international status, a claim to sovereignty, the existence of a "head of state." How could the Community—which was to be in charge of foreign policy—act coherently when there were states within it? Was there enough difference between being in the Republic and being in the Community—both of which entailed simultaneously citizenship and autonomy—to justify a distinction in terminology? On the other hand, as M. Guldner pointed out, the word "territory" now seemed to imply "a status we could call 'colonial'"—although twelve years earlier the word had been deployed to mark a break with "colony." A member suggested "country," another "province." But if territories had to choose between "state" and something else, everyone, most members believed, would choose the more prestigious title of "state."[106] But the Committee, given de Gaulle's statement in Madagascar, did not have much choice; it ended up with the distinction between "territory" (in the Republic) and "state" (in the Community) much as it had been.

The Committee was open-minded about whether territories would be grouped or not. The territories themselves would have to come to an agreement and figure out how to make a federation, although members expressed doubt over whether an association of African states—or the Community for that matter—could actually be a federation in the juridical sense.[107] The Committee and the Assemblée Générale of the Conseil d'État, unlike the Assemblée Nationale Constituante of 1946, did not agonize over the question of the personal status of citizens. They closely followed the earlier text in allowing citizens of the Republic who did not have the "statut civil de droit commun" to keep their status unless they renounced it.[108] The discussions of 25 and 26 August

[105] Commission Constitutionnelle, *Documents*, 3:183. The President of the Commission was the distinguished jurist René Cassin.

[106] Ibid., 3:180–89. See especially the interventions of MM. Solal-Céligny, Blocq-Mascart, Hoppenot, Latournerie, Janot, Plantey, and Guldner. The complexities were not those of terminology, but of competences and organization, for instance how decisions about defense would be allocated between the Parliament of the Republic and the Senate of the Community, and whether the Republic's minister of defense would necessarily be the Community's. Ibid., 3:108, 175–78.

[107] Ibid., 3:181, 184, 186–88.

[108] Ibid., 3:176–79; Conseil d'État, Assemblée Générale, *Documents*, 3:417. The name of the status went from "statut civil français" to "statut civil de droit commun." The main

in the Commission Constitutionnelle and 27 and 28 August in the General Assembly were revealing above all of the concern in France to find a solid juridical basis for a Community that was in some sense French, in another united multiple peoples, that distributed sovereign powers over different levels, and was adaptable to future conditions, especially as Member States became ever more assertive of their autonomy. The big battle between federation and confederation had been finessed rather than decided. And, as the jurist Marcel Merle concluded, the difference between the two was not in theory absolute: both distribute powers over different levels, and in practice ambiguity was not a bad thing, allowing states leeway to negotiate their actual relationship while allowing nationalists "to utilize the magic word independence."[109]

But the main act was not taking place in the chambers of the Conseil d'État. It was taking place in Africa, in the debates and demonstrations set off by de Gaulle's imperial procession and by the efforts of parties to reach decisions and mobilize voters. Some of the leading actors were uncertain what they would do. And in Africa the voters were deciding not only whether they liked the constitutional draft, but also whether they would join the Community or secede from France.[110]

When de Gaulle came to Conakry, capital of Guinea, he probably did not realize how much he had alienated Sékou Touré by his take-it-or-leave-it statement of 8 August. On Radio-Dakar, Sékou Touré said on 9 August that "my amour propre for the dignity of Africa was shocked."[111] Yet underneath, the positions of de Gaulle and Sékou Touré were not poles apart. Sékou Touré had spoken consistently of his desire for continued association with France. He favored Senghor's position—for a primary federation in French Africa that would in turn be part of a confederal France. On that point—and in regard to his militant style and socialist leanings—his major opponent was Houphouët-Boigny, whose protégé he had been and with whom he tried to maintain cordial relations and sometimes compromise. But in de Gaulle's presence in Conakry on 25 August, Sékou Touré gave

---

question was whether the Parliament could legislate about diverse statuses, but allowing people to keep their status seemed like a sufficient resolution.

[109] *Le Monde*, 29 August 1958. Merle himself favored confederation. The ambiguity Merle saw between federation and confederation is not far from the complex and flexible way in which the political theorist Jean L. Cohen sees them. "Federation," on the website Political Concepts: A Critical Lexicon, www.politicalconcepts.org/2011/federation (accessed 21 July 2012).

[110] A point made by a member of the Conseil d'État, M. Latournerie. Assemblée Générale, *Documents*, 3:418.

[111] Chaffard, *Carnets secrets*, 2:190. See also Elizabeth Schmidt, *Cold War and Decolonization in Guinea, 1946–1958* (Portsmouth, N.H.: Heinemann, 2007), 146. According to *Le Monde* (27 August 1958), Conakry was the first place on his epic journey where de Gaulle encountered resistance to his arguments.

a speech that was militant in tone, even if it stopped short of calling for a no vote. His most quoted line—"we prefer poverty in freedom to wealth in slavery"—must have cut to the quick, since de Gaulle saw himself as having brought liberty to Africa. Sékou Touré wanted an African federation, a right to independence, and a "Franco-African Community" of fully equal states—a more consistent and far-reaching position than de Gaulle's, but not its opposite.[112]

Sékou Touré's speech itself, aside from the oft-quoted line, did not constitute a break with his previous positions: "Our heart, our reason, in addition to our most obvious interests, lead us to choose, without hesitation, interdependence and liberty in this union rather than to define ourselves without France and against France." He sounded like Senghor in saying, "We willingly accept certain abandonments of sovereignty in favor of a larger ensemble," and he mentioned defense, diplomatic relations, money, and higher education as domains where the Community could exercise jurisdiction. He went on, "We are Africans and our territories cannot be part of France. We will be citizens of our African states, members of the Franco-African Community. In effect, the French Republic, within the Franco-African association, will be an element just like the African states, [which] will be equally constitutive elements of this great multinational Community composed of free and equal states." He thought that the "right to divorce" was necessary for a marriage.

What had seemed like the two sticky points in the previous demands of Sékou Touré (and Senghor for that matter)—the right to independence and the right to constitute a group of African territories—had been conceded by de Gaulle, and some commentators insist that d'Arboussier and others had made sure Sékou Touré was informed, although others leave open the possibility of miscommunication. But Sékou Touré's words were ambiguous, and de Gaulle seems to have been affected as much by the tone of the speech and the reactions of the audience as by its contents. The two leaders had met only once before, and although de Gaulle's aides considered Sékou Touré a radical, his Minister of Overseas France, Bernard Cornut-Gentille, did not consider him lost to the "oui" cause. In any case, de Gaulle apparently felt personally humiliated and bitter, and refused from then on to talk to Sékou Touré. He withdrew his earlier offer to give the Guinean leader a ride on his airplane to the next stop on the tour, Dakar.[113]

[112]The text of the speech is in *Le Monde*, 27 August 1958, and is reprinted in, among other places, André Lewin, *Ahmed Sékou Touré (1922-1984). Tome 2-1956-1958* (Paris: L'Harmattan, 2009), 106–10. See also Chaffard, *Carnets secrets*, 2:197 and Schmidt, *Cold War and Decolonization*, 153–54. Foyer (*Sur les chemins du droit*, 91) commented, "That night, in Conakry, the Community in gestation died before it was born." He exaggerated; its death really came with the breakup of the Mali Federation in August 1960.

[113]Cornut-Gentille kept trying; he hoped to get Sékou Touré to talk to Houphouët-Boigny and Gabriel Lisette, who could reassure him about the constitutional provisions.

In the absence of further negotiations or assurances, Sékou Touré had made up his mind. But he kept insisting until the eve of the referendum that calling for immediate independence did not signify "a desire to break with France." On the contrary, he thought that a confederation of equals, including France, could be produced only once all parties were independent. But at the heart of Sékou Touré's position was a contradiction, or at least a gamble. He knew that other territories were likely to vote yes and remain in the Community, and if Guinea voted no and left the Community his great dream of African unity—and specifically of West African federation—would become all but unattainable. He was himself accused by his former comrades in the RDA of promoting the "balkanization" of Africa.[114]

De Gaulle replied to Sékou Touré in a way that only sharpened the break: Guinea could, on 28 September, claim its own independence, but "it would certainly feel the consequences." His speech, while claiming that he thought Guinea would still vote "oui," emphasized the "sacrifices" that France had made for Guinea and the "expenses" it had assumed: "All these expenses are considerable and, nevertheless, I believe that, from its angle, the metropole will say 'oui' to the Franco-African Community." He seemed to be embracing the thesis that Africa was costly to France, turning it into an argument for Africans to stay in the Community—or else be excluded from the benefits of French self-sacrifice.[115]

The clash of two egos, quick to take affront? Such an explanation may well be at the heart of the matter. But there is more to it. De Gaulle had already made a major concession in his Brazzaville speech: the right of a Member State to claim independence without being considered to have seceded. But on the Constitution, de Gaulle had

Minister, telegram to High Commissioner, Dakar, 10 September 1958, AP 2181, AOM. For somewhat differing but overlapping versions of the events in Conakry see Lewin, *Ahmed Sékou Touré*, 92–93, 95, 156; Ibrahima Baba Kaké, *Sékou Touré: Le héros et le tyran* (Paris: Jeune Afrique, 1987), 75–82; Ismael Barry, "Réflexions sur le NON de la Guinée cinquante ans après"; and Abdoulaye Diallo, "Et si Sékou Touré n'était que l'homme du 25 août 1958?," in Odile Goerg, Céline Pauthier, and Abdoulaye Diallo, eds., *Le NON de la Guinée (1958): Entre mythe, relecture historique et résonances contemporaines* (Paris: L'Harmattan, 2010), 29–42, 81–97.

[114] Press conference, 20 September 1958, in *Afrique Nouvelle*, 26 September 1958; Chaffard, *Carnets secrets*, 2:198; *Le Monde*, 5 September 1958. In another press conference, Sékou Touré said he did not want to withdraw from the franc zone or discourage French or other foreign investment. *Le Monde*, 23 September 1958.

[115] The text of the speech is in *Le Monde*, 27 August 1958. The Cartier thesis was at the time much discussed. See for example André Blanchet, "Condamnés à l'indépendance?" *Le Monde*, 19 August 1958. On the costs of either maintaining or breaking up the Community, see Jean Ehrhard, *Destin du colonialisme: essai sur la théorie et la politique économique dans les territoires sous-développés politiquement non autonomes* (Montpellier: Eyrolles, 1957) and Gilbert Mathieu, "L'ensemble économique franco-africain," *Le Monde*, 24, 25, 26 September 1958.

consistently maintained that a no vote meant secession and the termination of all help from France. He may have overinterpreted Sékou Touré's position as a no, and he may have been unwilling to make any concessions beyond what he had just done. So there is a logic to his stubbornness, even if it was a dysfunctional logic.

Elizabeth Schmidt argues that Sékou Touré's position had become more militant in the past months under pressure from workers, youth, women's organizations—a bottom-up campaign for independence much stronger than found in other countries of AOF. She has clear evidence for the militancy, but it does not refute an explanation that is more top-down. Had the vote in Guinea on the referendum been 55 or 60 percent "non," her emphasis on grassroots organizing might be persuasive, but it was 95 percent, and that starts to look like the electoral politics of the old Soviet Union. Guinea's "non" seems to have a lot in common with other territories' "oui," with similar percentages of the vote for the opposite side (except in Niger). On both sides, a party organization had used its control of resources since 1957 to marginalize opponents. And however real the grassroots pressure on Sékou Touré, he had no significant opponent to fear and had proved himself perfectly capable, as Schmidt notes, of purging his party of "Left deviationism."[116] In Schmidt's account, Sékou Touré, the responsive leader of a militant mass party, all of a sudden becomes a tyrant after September 1958; but there is much in her own telling to suggest that Sékou Touré's autocratic ways were not so new. Sékou Touré made some effort after the disastrous visit to find common ground, but de Gaulle would have none of it. In any case, the die was cast for Guinea's no vote—itself a response to de Gaulle's insistence that one either accepted his Constitution or exited from France.

At the next stop of the tour, the messages were mixed. The proindependence militants from UGTAN and the PAI had their anti-French

[116] Schmidt, *Cold War and Decolonization*, 134. See also her "Anticolonial Nationalism in French West Africa: What Made Guinea Unique?," *African Studies Review* 52, 2 (2009): 1–34. French sources may be self-serving—but are not inconsistent—in seeing top-down pressure: "many Africans would be favorable to the oui but would not dare vote in this way because of fear of the putting into place of a powerful politico-police force of the RDA Guinea." Genesuper to Ministry, 22 September 1958, telegram, AP 2181, AOM. Senghor wrote of the "iron discipline" that Sékou Touré imposed during the campaign. "*Les Cahiers de la République*, October 1958, reprinted in *Liberté II: Nation et voie africaine du socialisme* (Paris: Seuil, 1971), 230. French sources said much the same about the apparatus used to bring out the "oui" vote in Côte d'Ivoire. In Senegal, they noted the efforts of the heads of the Mouride and Tijani brotherhoods to get their disciples to vote yes. Governor, Côte d'Ivoire, to Ministry, telegram, 27 September 1958; Declaration of El Hadji Falilou M'Backe, Khalif Général des Mourides, Touba, 14 September 1958; Governor, Senegal, to Ministry, 17 September 1958, AP 2195/1, AOM; Affaires Politiques, Dakar, "Rapport sur le référendum du 28 Septembre en Afrique Occidentale Française," 25 October 1958, AP 221, AOM.

Figures 5a and 5b. The campaign for and against the referendum on
the Constitution, September 1958, Sudan and Senegal. ©AFP/Getty Images.

signs out when de Gaulle arrived in Dakar—giving him a "disagree-
able reception"—but other parts of the crowd were welcoming, even
enthusiastic. Senghor and Dia were nowhere to be seen. They lamely
claimed other engagements and poor communications, but the real
reason was undoubtedly that they had not formulated a common
position.[117]

[117] Some Senegalese leaders apologized for the behavior of the crowd. *Le Monde*, 28,
29 August 1958. Dia and Senghor replied weakly to accusations of "cowardice" for having absented themselves from Dakar. *Paris-Dakar*, 1 September 1958. In the absence of
Dia and Senghor, the government of Senegal was represented by Valdiodio N'Diaye,
Interior Minister, whose words were welcoming but equivocal: "The proposed choice
is not fully free." The constitution needed to take account of the "national sentiment
of African masses, their aspirations for unity, and their wish to enter the modern world

Figures 5a and 5b. (*continued*)

Senghor had seen his minimum demands met: an independence option, the possibility of territories grouping themselves. The PAI and other youth and student groups, UGTAN, and a dissident faction of the PRA advocated a no vote. Dia was agonizing. As he later told the story, he had initially opposed the constitution. Probably his

within a vast ensemble, which is the multinational confederation of free peoples, equal to France." *Le Monde*, 28 August 1958.

continued annoyance at the "semiautonomy" that he had experienced as Vice-Président (later Président) du Conseil in Senegal made him more eager for a break. And he thought that de Gaulle's challenge required a strong response: "It would be necessary to affirm our adulthood." But when he went to Senghor's retreat in Normandy, he heard his mentor warn against "adventure, anarchy." Dia felt that a break with Senghor would be "an irreparable catastrophe." He persuaded Senghor that Senegal would take no more than five years "to digest autonomy" and then take the option for independence. With "tears in my eyes," he gave in to Senghor's plea to support the yes vote.[118]

Once the party's position was decided, it overwhelmingly carried the day. Although Senegal was where the PAI—the party most explicitly identified with the independence-now position—was centered, where talented intellectuals like Abdoulaye Ly, Cheikh Anta Diop, and Amadou Mahtar M'Bow campaigned for a no vote, and where there was a considerable working class for the trade union federation UGTAN to enlist, the no vote still came to less than 2.5 percent.[119] There is a revealing footnote to the referendum story in Senegal. The French government intrigued with leaders of the regional party from Casamance, the MFDC, whose relationship with Senghor and Dia's bloc had become tenuous, suggesting that if Senegal voted against joining the Community, the government would support autonomy for the region, allowing it to remain within the Community even if the rest of Senegal did not. The intrigue became irrelevant when Senegal voted yes.[120]

In the Sudan, a faction of the PRA tried to outflank the Union Soudanaise-RDA—which came out for a yes vote—by arguing for a no.

[118] Mamadou Dia, *Mémoires d'un militant du tiers-monde* (Paris: Publisud, 1985), 91–92. Dia's public support for the "oui" is reported in *Paris-Dakar*, 13 September 1958. Three days before, he had not been willing to commit. The vote at a party conference in Senegal was 160 in favor of "oui," 29 opposed, and 47 abstentions. *Le Monde*, 23 September 1958. On Dia's hesitations, see also the memoirs of one of his top cabinet officials, Roland Colin, *Sénégal notre pirogue: Au soleil de la liberté. Journal de bord 1955–1980* (Paris: Présence Africaine, 2007), 101–3.

[119] Joseph Roger de Benoist, *L'Afrique occidentale française de 1944 à 1960* (Dakar: Nouvelles Éditions Africaines, 1982), 516. There were "riots" in Dakar on 21 September, according to *Le Monde* (23 September 1958) instigated by young men, supposedly spurred on by the "slogans" of UGTAN and Le Conseil de la Jeunesse, at a site where Senghor, Dia, and Lamine Guèye were supposed to speak. The support of leading marabouts for the yes vote no doubt weighed heavily in the outcome. So too perhaps did the argument Senghor made when he spoke in Senegal's peanut basin: independence would mean Senegalese farmers would have to sell their peanuts at the world price, much less than the subsidized price now expected. And the long history of France's connection to "old Senegal" was part of the picture too. *Le Monde*, 26 September 1958. The French government had deliberately sought the support of the top marabouts. Pierre Messmer, *Après tant de batailles: Mémoires* (Paris: Albin Michel, 1992), 237–38.

[120] Awenengo Dalberto, "Hidden Debates about the Status of Casamance."

But Keita insisted that the Community was a necessary step to African unity: "The most important problem to solve for us Africans is to bring to fruition the unity of our present federations. . . . We are performing the experiment of the Franco-African Union. We will mobilize all our energies for the construction of African unity." The recent concessions by de Gaulle influenced the radical Madeira Keita to assert that much of the African demands had been met, most importantly the "right to independence."[121]

The campaign in Niger revealed how far the French government would go to manipulate the vote. A militant faction led by Djibo Bakary had split off from the Niger branch of the RDA, forming the party Sawaba. By a thin majority, Sawaba won control of the Territorial Assembly. It affiliated with Senghor's PRA, of which Bakary became the general secretary. Like Senghor and Sékou Touré, Bakary vigorously opposed the "cutting up" of French Africa and insisted on "our right of self-determination." His thinking was shaped by his split with the RDA and Houphouët-Boigny's support for Bakary's RDA opponents. He was also influenced by his neighbors—the example Nigeria's path to self-government and independence programmed for 1960 and the war in Algeria, with which he hoped to build relations as part of the "confederal Union."[122] He thought that Niger had alternatives to economic relations with France—through its neighbors and other possible sources of aid (which he was careful not to mention); a break with France might be possible.

Djibo Bakary had exulted in the stance for independence, even if qualified, of the PRA's Cotonou meeting in July, but when the referendum came to be the central issue, the PRA was far from united. At a meeting of the PRA on 14 September, in Bakary's home base of Niamey, Senghor dominated the debate. His "realist" position was supported by heavyweights like Fily Dabo Sissoko of the Sudan, Zinsou and Apithy of Dahomey, Nazi Boni of Upper Volta, and Mamadou Dia. Bakary supported a "non," not least because he—like many colleagues—was appalled by de Gaulle's ultimatum. He also gave a notable critique of the contents and context of the constitutional draft. He saw the Community on offer as dominated by the "the all-powerful patron . . . who, alone, has the right to commit us on the double level

[121] Direction des Services de Police du Soudan français, Synthèse mensuelle de renseignements, September 1958, Bamako/Ambassade/1, ADN; *L'Essor*, 27 August, 1, 12, 19, 23 September 1958. Abdoulaye Diallo, a Sudanese who was once a leading light in communist trade union circles, then in UGTAN, opposed the Constitution, mainly on the issue of the African federation, but still claimed that UGTAN believed in "the Franco-African community." *L'Essor*, 5 September, 1 October 1958.

[122] Extrait du bulletin d'information de l'Agence France Presse, 18 July 1958, AP 2181/1, AOM; Djibo Bakary, *"Silence! On décolonise . . .": Itinéraire politique et syndicale d'un militant africain* (Paris: L'Harmattan, 1992), esp. 144–47, 169–70, 176–86.

of the Community and international relations." A Parliament in which African territories were no longer represented could make laws; African states would have no power over foreign affairs, defense, currency, political economy, strategic materials (Niger had uranium), justice, higher education, transport and telecommunications; Community appeals courts could reject decisions by African states. He also noted, "The African would see himself eternally refused all right to nationality because the Community includes only one citizenship: French citizenship." While advocating a no vote, he insisted that "the initiative for a break will never come from Africans, not from Niger in any case." He later insisted that neither he nor any other African leader of stature had advocated "secession," and he made clear his resentment at the acts of the "agents of M. Houphouët" in Niger. Bakary defined the choice as between "eternal slavery and liberation," and the referendum offered "the unique chance that France herself offers us to bring out the African personality in peace and concord."[123] Bakary later claimed that he was never told of the amendments regarding the right to independence that de Gaulle had accepted (blaming Houphouët-Boigny), although he had had a long interview with de Gaulle in Dakar on 26 August.[124] The Niamey meeting resolved only to let each territorial affiliate of the PRA make its own decision.[125] The appeal to African unity was not, it turned out, a unifying theme.

The French government was particularly concerned about a friendly and cooperative government in Niger, both because it bordered on Algeria and because it had uranium. But Bakary was pushing for a no vote—and therefore independence. Shortly before the vote, the French government installed a hard-line governor, Don Jean Colombani, and he reached into his bag of dirty tricks to influence the election: a government-sponsored propaganda machine, the manipulation of electoral lists, visible military presence, pressure brought through chiefs, support for RDA efforts, and, most likely, outright fraud in vote counting. Claiming Sawaba had abused its power, Colombani removed it from office in what Klaas van Walraven considers "Africa's first modern coup d'état"—nine days before the referendum vote. The "non" vote came to 22 percent of those voting—the least skewed of the

[123] Communiqué of Sawaba "à la population," enclosed in Direction des Services de la Police, Niger, Renseignements, 16 September 1958, AP 2181/1, AOM; Bakary, *"Silence!,"* 242.

[124] Bakary, *"Silence!,"* 195–96, 211–12. At the time, Bakary described his interview with de Gaulle in Dakar as "extrêmement fructueux." *Le Monde,* 30 August 1958. Jacques Foccart claimed that de Gaulle made clear to Bakary in Dakar that the territories choosing to join the Community could later become independent. *Foccart Parle: Entretiens avec Philippe Gaillard* (Paris: Fayard/Jeune Afrique, 1995), 1:166.

[125] Direction des Services de la Police, Niger, Renseignements, 15 September 1958, AP 2181/1, AOM; *Paris-Dakar,* 16 September 1958.

results in any of the territories—but Niger also had the lowest turnout (37 percent, versus 69 percent overall).[126] In Guinea, the French government did not even try to manipulate the results; elsewhere it apparently believed that African political parties were more effective than government intrigue in support of a yes vote.[127]

The outcome in Côte d'Ivoire was predicable from the start, but Houphouët-Boigny put together his arguments in September with clarity: "It would be to exit from History, to go against the current, if, in Africa notably, we had to limit our evolution to the narrow framework of a nation." He had called for a "federal Republic, a Republic with a central federal executive, a central federal parliament, and an arbitration court." We did not get our wishes, he said, but we did obtain "our right to self-determination, even independence." He claimed that the quest for dignity was consistent with joining the Community. He argued that Côte d'Ivoire lacked the financial resources for its own defense; it could not afford embassies in 90 countries; only cooperative relations with France and its European partners could "fertilize our latent riches"; and "the highest level" of courts was the best antidote to letting justice be distorted by "internal conflicts . . . tribalism." He seemed to be warning against what a political elite might do unless there were checks at another level: "How can you want to let a young state have the facility to send freely to the stake its political adversaries?"[128]

The results across the AOF were unambiguous in two directions: the "non" garnered 95 percent of the vote in Guinea, the "oui" between

[126] Klaas van Walraven, "Decolonization by Referendum: The Anomaly of Niger and the Fall of Sawaba, 1958–1959," *Journal of African History* 50 (2009): 269–92; de Benoist, *L'Afrique occidentale française*, 516. For Bakary's version, see *"Silence!,"* 213–30. Some PRA leaders, including Zinsou, who had campaigned for a yes vote, nevertheless complained to reporters about French tactics in Niger. Thomas F. Brady, "Africans Charge French Vote Curb," *New York Times*, 13 October 1958, clipping in AP 2195/1, AOM. Bakary's account is partially confirmed by his enemy, High Commissioner Pierre Messmer, who later wrote that the result of the referendum "was not set in advance" and to make sure that the desired result was obtained he had installed Colombani to replace a governor "thought to be too close to Djibo Bakary and intellectually too honest to 'demolish' him politically." Columbani led "an overt campaign in favor of the 'oui.'" Messmer, *Après tant de batailles*, 239–40.

[127] Alexander Keese argues that the French government could not go too far in manipulating elections for fear of provoking a scandal. "Rigged Elections? Democracy and Manipulations in the Late Colonial State in French West Africa and Togo, 1944–1958," in Martin Thomas, ed., *The French Colonial Mind* (Lincoln: University of Nebraska Press, 2011), 324–45.

[128] Discours prononcé au stade Géo-André 7 Septembre 1958, reprinted in Félix Houphouët-Boigny, *Anthologie des Discours 1946–1978. Tome I: 1946–1963* (Abidjan: Éditions CEDA, 1978), 195–208. RDA leaders claimed success in arguing for changes in the constitution: "The essential of the demands of their movement have been satisfied." They claimed that Sékou Touré had failed to understand the concessions de Gaulle made toward the end. *Le Monde*, 5 September 1958.

94 and 99.98 percent (Côte d'Ivoire) everywhere else, except for Niger (78 percent).[129] La République de Guinée was proclaimed a few days later.[130]

One can read these results in different ways, not inconsistent with each other. One is that the party apparatus had triumphed everywhere. The first leaders to gain positions of power—in the absence of local or provincial governments that could serve as platforms for building a political base independent of the center—were well placed to get out the vote for whatever cause they espoused. Student groups and youth organizations could affect political discourse, but not political outcomes. Second, while there was no tidal wave of opinion for "independence" as such, people in French West Africa saw something in politics: the voter turnout in AOF was 69 percent. Senghor called the results "a 'yes' for African unity, which will act to reconstitute itself in two federal states of AOF and AEF. It is also a 'yes' to African independence in refound unity. . . . Our 'yes' is finally a 'yes' to association with France. . . . We need its technicians and its culture as organizing and enriching elements: and France needs us." Dia hoped to renew ties with Guinea and "find again that unity which is for us a vital question." The tone turned more negative as the PRA accused Houphouët-Boigny and the RDA of contributing to the "balkanization" of Africa. The RDA continued to feud within itself over the question of the primary federation.[131]

Conclusion

However opaque the constitution-writing process had been, especially compared to that of 1946, African leaders had shaped the outcome. In May, Debré had categorically rejected a constitutional right to independence—the equivalent of "secession and the end of the French presence in Africa."[132] In August he and de Gaulle conceded just such a right. African political leaders had turned the disastrous first draft into something most of them could live with. De Gaulle's fed-

[129] De Benoist, L'Afrique occidentale française, 516. Before the vote, Gabriel d'Arboussier noted that the overseas territories would play a major role in the acceptance of the constitution: they had fifteen of the forty-five million possible voters. He favored a yes vote. *Afrique Nouvelle*, 26 September 1958.

[130] None of the leaders of the RDA congratulated Guinea on its independence. *Le Monde*, 3, 4 October 1958.

[131] *Paris-Dakar*, 30 September, 11, 16, 21 October, 20 November 1958. Gabriel d'Arboussier continued to push for the primary federation but admitted that territories, "inspite of their artificial creation have acquired a certain personality in the course of historical development." *Paris-Dakar*, 14 November 1958, and "Étude sur les fédérations primaires," mimeographed paper, Dakar, 10 November 1958, Dakar/Ambassade/345, ADN.

[132] *Marchés Tropicaux*, 31 May 1958, 1380.

eration became Tsiranana's Community. Territories acquired the title of "state" for themselves, although not the international recognition associated with the term; de Gaulle accepted that states could exit the Community and become independent on their own volition; references had been inserted to "territories, grouped or not," allowing the effort to forge an African federation to go on.[133] Africans had to accept a compromise document that was in some ways incoherent, and in many ways a reflection of one man's imperial stature. But if that man, and his fellow citizens, wanted to keep together the entity now called la Communauté, they knew that they had to give Africans reasons to want to stay within it.[134]

[133] Louis Delbez, professor of law at Montpellier and former deputy, saw the open door to independence as "one of the most remarkable dispositions of the Constitution, which underlines the extent to which any idea of constraint has been banned." Still, the Republic was a Member State whose power "exceeds significantly that of other Member States and which corresponds to its superiority, as a factual matter, over the other states, demographic, economic, financial, technical, cultural superiority." It deviated from "the literary theory of the federal states," because it was an "'inegalitarian' federalism, an 'open' federalism, and an 'evolving' federalism." "Un fédéralisme original: La Communauté," *Revue Politique des Idées et des Institutions* 48, 3 (February 1959): 72–85, 76, 80, 84 quoted.

[134] This was the point of an article published by Maurice Duverger, "Demain la Communauté?," *Le Monde*, 24 October 1958. The 1958 Constitution referred to "The Community," that of 1946 to "The *French* Union."

CHAPTER 7

UNITY AND DIVISION IN AFRICA AND FRANCE, 1958–1959

All the territories of French West and Equatorial Africa, with the exception of Guinea, were by late 1958 Member States of the French Community. They quickly moved within that framework to make claims—for fuller autonomy, for fuller recognition of their personalities. By 1959, some of their leaders were pushing one step further—for recognition of the nationalities of the Member States, all the while claiming the benefits of French citizenship.

But where did the nation lie? Africans insisted they wanted unity but were divided over what it meant. With more capacity for self-government, with more at stake in elections in each territory, the debate between those who advocated strong territories within a French Community and those who sought a strong African federation within a French Community became more immediate. Did African unity pass through Paris? Or could it be constructed in Africa itself?

France had accepted that the price of maintaining a "Community" was that it give up the notion that it was indivisible. But its leaders still believed that whatever the Community had become, it had to be held together. With the word "independence" more and more in the air, the possibility of redefining France as a multinational community slowly became for de Gaulle's government an imaginable possibility. In 1959, the question of what sort of unit would constitute the subjective and juridical basis of political belonging was being debated in both African and European France.

A Community of African Republics

By the end of November, the Sudan, Senegal, and other territories had each voted—under the terms of the new constitution—to become a republic. One of the first acts of the new republics was to vote to become Member States of the Community, giving up their place within the French Republic in favor of internal autonomy and a place in a broader ensemble. They insisted that "competences"—all the functions of government except those enumerated as Community domains in the Constitution (defense, foreign affairs, etc.) be transferred to the

Member States.[1] Each of those states would be governed by an elected assembly and a Conseil de gouvernement of its choosing, headed by a Président du Conseil. The French Republic would be represented in each Member State by a High Commissioner (not to be confused with the High Commissioner of the now-defunct AOF). Uncertainty about the division of capacities and the relationship between the High Commissioner and President of the Council would produce frictions that proved to be an impetus for African governments to take new steps of self-assertion.

The Community itself had a President—Charles de Gaulle—a Conseil exécutif consisting of the President, his Prime Minister, the heads of the governments of the Member States and heads of ministries relevant to community affairs, a Senate, and an Court of Arbitration. The latter two bodies took time to organize, so it was the Conseil and the President that mattered. The Executive Council met about once a month beginning in February 1959, most often in Paris, but twice in Africa, in Tananarive (Madagascar) and Saint-Louis (Senegal).[2]

According to a paper prepared for Mamadou Dia, Président du Conseil of Senegal, in January, no texts indicated how the Conseil exécutif would reach decisions or how they would be implemented. Senegal intended to insist that all states have an equal role in the Conseil. But of course France had the army, the ministries, and the purse strings, so absolute equality was not in the cards. Raymond Janot, jurist and government spokesman, told reporters that "the Conseil exécutif of the Community could become the embryo of a real government. But it is not a government."[3] It was a strange structure between a consultative and a decision-making body. But because Member States had the option of leaving, their leaders' voices were heard. The

[1] That some important competences, notably defense, were at the Community level did not at first bother most African leaders. Most states felt vulnerable to political and military meddling from other African states (Ghana and Guinea for instance), from communist powers, or from each other, and wanted to be part of a collective defense. They also wanted their countrymen to have opportunities for military careers. All of this was beyond their own financial means. See discussions at the July and September 1959 meetings and papers prepared by the Secretariat for those meetings, all in FPR 105 and FPR 107, ANF.

[2] Decisions are reported as coming from the President, usually after consultation with the Executive Council. *Journal Officiel de la Communauté. Recueil des Actes et Informations*, 15 February–15 December 1959. See also Paul Isoart, "Le Conseil exécutif de la Communauté," in Charles-Robert Ageron et Marc Michel, eds., *L'Afrique noire française: L'heure des indépendances* (Paris: CNRS Éditions, 2010), 209–27.

[3] "Projet: organisation de la Communauté," 3 January 1959, VP 131, Dossier for meeting of 2–3 February 1959, VP 133, AS; Raymond Janot, press interviews, 5, 9 September 1958, reproduced in France, *Documents pour servir à l'histoire de l'élaboration de la Constitution du 4 octobre 1958* (Paris: La Documentation française, 1987), 4:11, 96. On the limited power of the Conseil exécutif, see P.-F. Gonidec, "La Communauté et les relations internationales," *Penant* 70 (1960): 141–60, esp. 147–49.

Conseil operated throughout 1959, reaching in most cases, consensus. Later in this chapter, we shall trace the way it dealt with a delicate question, that of defining single or multiple nationalities within the Community.

For the new Republics and the Community, the asymmetrical relationship of Member States to France was a major issue. But so too was the relationship of Member States to each other. France's last High Commissioner in West Africa, Pierre Messmer, told the Grand Conseil de l'AOF at the beginning of January 1959 that "the unity of West Africa was created by France and it cannot continue to exist without France."[4] He was attempting to put advocates of African unity in their place. Although self-serving, the argument, sadly, proved correct. But Messmer could not see the opposite side of the coin: the French Community could not continue to exist without African unity.

Senegal tried immediately to use its new status as a Republic and Member State to push for an African federation. On 7 October 1958, barely ten days after the referendum, Dia appointed a committee, chaired by a Senegalese lawyer, Isaac Foster (later President of the Senegalese Supreme Court), with the dual charge of writing a constitution for Senegal and for the hoped-for primary federation. It was to ponder the relationship of both to France. Dia was well aware of the effects of territorialization under the loi-cadre, so he thought the new entity should have an "a fairly light federal apparatus."[5]

By late November, Foster's committee came up with a draft constitution for Senegal, a blueprint for a government based on democratic elections under universal suffrage, a parliamentary system, and a relatively strong executive. The committee produced a draft of a federal constitution as well, providing a federal executive, legislature, and judiciary. The federation's executive council would consist of the heads of government of each state; ministries would be distributed equitably among member states. The federal government would concern itself with commercial legislation, labor codes, the civil service, principles of état-civil (although individual states would apply it), education, health, transport, tax revenues, and penal procedures. Its preamble would guarantee "the freedoms without which citizenship of the Community would have no reason to exist." Gabriel d'Arboussier—the one-time RDA stalwart who had jumped ship to the PRA because of its embrace of an African federation—also submitted to Dia a study of primary federations, taking note that "the current of unity . . . today animates the African masses." Senghor added that one should proceed by steps and avoid for now speaking of either a "United States of Africa" or "total independence." Instead, constitution writers and

[4] Messmer, 5 January 1959, in Grand Conseil, *Bulletin*, 10.
[5] Dossier on the "Comité pour l'étude des problèmes institutionnels," VP 90, AS.

these leading activists were seeking a balance among different levels of government—territorial, federal, Community.[6]

By decree in December 1958, Senegal asserted its takeover of "the power previously exercised by the government of the French Republic or its representatives in AOF and Senegal," except those reserved for the Community.[7] The practicalities of running a Republic in the midst of a Community soon caused friction between Senegalese and French officials. High Commissioner Pierre Lami, the Community's representative in Senegal, accused its government of claiming attributions "unilaterally." One of the first clashes—before the Conseil exécutif had taken up the issue—concerned nationality. In January 1959, Lami expressed annoyance that some local officials were sending dossiers regarding the acquisition or loss of nationality to the Président du Conseil of Senegal or to his interior minister. These dossiers should go to the Minister of Justice in Paris, he said; nationality was a Community competence. Dia said no, it was a competence of Senegal, "because French nationality confers on those who benefit from it the rights of the citizen and in consequence political rights of which my government has the right to control the extension." There were several testy exchanges around December 1958 and January 1959. There was tension as well over security personnel, and it was not always clear who was supposed to pay for what. In the Sudan, territorial government and High Commissioner also battled over appointing local administrators.[8]

The new governments not only confronted the lingering presence of a French administration; they also had to govern a territory of citizens. How were *ressortissants* of ex-AOF using their citizenship? A full answer requires research territory by territory into how people voted, how parties recruited followers, how social and political organizations posed demands, and how governments both shaped and were influenced by

[6] Ibid.; draft constitution for Senegal, 21 November 1958, and dossier on federal constitution, nd; d'Arboussier, "Étude sur les fédérations primaires," 10 November 1958, and "Observations de Léopold Sédar Senghor," nd [November 1958], VP 90, AS. D'Arboussier also wrote a letter to de Gaulle warning that "excessive territorialization tends to awaken all the centrifugal forces of tribalism, which Africa has not yet undone. . . . We would commit an irreparable error by not reconstituting the former Federation of AOF with the territories that opted for the Community." De Gaulle replied that he appreciated d'Arboussier's note and he favored "rapprochement and constructive exchanges of views" among Africans but that their relationship with each other was for them to decide. D'Arboussier to de Gaulle, 7 November 1958, and de Gaulle to d'Arboussier, 15 November 1958, FM 112, AS.

[7] Decree of 2 December 1958, VP 127, AS.

[8] "Note de synthèse sur le transfer des compétences et les Services d'État," nd [December 1958], "Note au sujet des problèmes de transfert des compétences résultants de l'option pour le Statut d'État au Sénégal," 8 December 1958, Lami to Dia, 4 December 1958, VP 138, AS; Dia to Lami, 6, 10 December 1958, Dakar/Ambassade/271, ADN; Lami, Circular to Commandants de Cercle, 26 January 1959, and Dia to Lami, 30 January 1959, VP 136, AS; *L'Essor*, 29 May 1958.

actions and discourses. We can only suggest how some of these issues might be approached in the new context.

Dia and Senghor had recognized that the French Community, with its gestures toward a confederal view of its Member States, did not go as far as a federal or a unitary state in presupposing the equivalence, particularly in social and economic terms, of all its citizens. But people had the legal right to move anywhere in the Community, taking their citizenship with them. They would likely know about—and perhaps make a political issue of—the different living conditions across the Community, and as individuals they could use mobility to counter economic deprivation. So social citizenship did have a Community dimension.

Mamadou Dia could argue after 1957—and especially after October 1958—that his government, elected by the people of Senegal, was responsible for bringing up the standard of living of *all* Senegalese. The government of Senegal regarded itself as the arbiter among different claims to economic and social citizenship: between a deeply impoverished peasant society striving for a decent standard of living and organized labor, poor by comparison with workers in Europe, relatively well off by comparison with their rural relatives. Senghor and Dia's vision of a socialist future integrated classic European socialism with the moral economy advocated by people associated with social Catholicism in France and with a view of African culture as intrinsically communal and solidaristic. Early on, the Senegalese government set up committees—led by Catholic priest and economist Joseph Lebret (founder of the journal *Économie et Humanisme*)—to study the specific forms of economic organization in different regions of Senegal, with the idea of developing local strategies for economic development, in contrast to the one-size-fits-all approaches that some Western planners were bringing to African countries in the late 1950s.[9]

The aspirations of African governments quickly ran into the demands of labor that had been strongly articulated ever since 1945. Tensions came to a head in Senegal in January 1959, when a postal strike that began in December turned into a general strike among civil servants, especially auxiliaries. UGTAN was its principal organizer. Dia decided to fire strikers, and the military was put on alert. The crackdown struck some observers as extremely harsh, but it was consistent with Dia's new position: now that an African government

[9]Mamadou Diouf, "Senegalese Development: From Mass Mobilization to Technocratic Elitism," in Frederick Cooper and Randall Packard, eds., *International Development and the Social Sciences: Essays on the History and Politics of Knowledge* (Berkeley: University of California Press, 1997), 291–319. Senghor's thinking is spelled out in "Rapport sur la doctrine et le programme du Parti, Congrès constitutif du Parti de la Fédération Africaine," Dakar, 1 July 1959, reprinted in *Liberté II: Nation et voie africaine du socialisme* (Paris: Seuil, 1971), 232–70.

was in place, the kind of social movement whose claim making against France had once been a useful part of political mobilization had become a challenge. Senghor later made the same point to UGTAN leaders: "In Africa, the state is you, it is us."[10]

The Saint-Louis local of UGTAN defended the strikers in terms that suggest how much they had been thinking in terms of French citizenship and how difficult it was to accept that the politics of citizenship had changed: "We persist in believing that we are still French citizens, that there exists only one citizenship inside the Community, that we are to be judged in French courts and in the hypothesis whereby the government of Senegal would take us away from their jurisdiction, it should start by asking your assembly to constitutionalize laws of exception that should be spelled out only after a prior accord between the Senegalese state and the highest courts of the Republic."[11]

But the French government had no desire to have this crisis land in its jurisdiction. UGTAN leaders seemed aware of the irony of their situation: they had recommended a "no" vote on the referendum of 1958—wanting a clean break with French colonialism—but now an African government was refusing the kind of demands that had made headway under French rule and was repressing a social movement with a thoroughness new to Senegalese workers. The national conference of UGTAN in Senegal apologized for its "no" in 1958 and insisted that it was not working for "the defeat of governments that said yes to the Community." Perhaps it was necessary "to rethink the situation of our movement," to "make use of the political reforms that have intervened" while placing its demands "in the framework of trade union rights."[12] Senghor had already shown a hostility to UGTAN that did not bode well for it: he was furious at its venturing into the political realm to push for a "no" vote on the referendum, thought it had suffered "a crushing defeat," and asserted that the goal of its leaders was no longer "to raise the standard of living of the workers, but to obtain ministerial posts."[13]

[10] Security reports, 6 January 1959, and Dia's decree firing striking workers, dated 5 January 1959, 5D/13, SRAD; Senghor, report to conference of Parti de la Fédération Africaine, 1 July 1959, in *Liberté II*, 262. Over a year later—and now in his role inside the government of the Mali Federation—Dia was still pushing for "a firm attitude" toward a union seeking a pay increase. The other ministers, including Modibo Keita, agreed. Mali, Conseil des Ministres, Summary of meeting of 12 May 1960, FM 38, AS.

[11] UGTAN, Union locale de Saint-Louis, Comité permanent pour la réintegration des travailleurs licenciés pour faits de grève, to President and deputies of Assemblée Constituante du Sénégal, 21 January 1959, VP 355, AS. The Secrétaire Général of the CGT wrote to Dia on 19 February 1959 pointing out how harsh it was to fire three thousand workers and calling such action "a grave blow to trade union freedom, and in particular the right to strike." Ibid.

[12] Conférence Nationale Sénégalaise de l'UGTAN, Thiès, 9–10 May 1959, VP 355, AS.

[13] "Nations et voie africaine du socialisme," October 1958, reprinted in *Liberté II*, 229.

The tensions between a citizenship linked to an African state's effort to promote economic development and a citizenship linked to the French Community as a whole—but in practice favoring certain sectors of it—were not about to go away.[14] Each government faced them in different ways: Sékou Touré's Guinea, where citizenship was the most sharply bounded to territory, cracked down even more severely than Senegal on the autonomy of unions, or of any other social movement.[15]

Even more fundamental was the question of what sort of states Africa would have, and this leads us back to the familiar but ongoing question of the primary federation. In late 1958 and early 1959, the dispute was becoming increasingly acrimonious, dividing most sharply Senegal and Sudan on one side and Côte d'Ivoire on the other. The party newspaper of the Union Soudanaise-RDA envisioned a "West African Nation" in the making, sewn together by geography and common experience, including that of fifty years of colonization. The party insisted that an African federation was the only way to confront "an Africa that is still cut up, subject to old racial rivalries, where national consciousness only manifests itself by a common hostility to the dominating presence of Whites, where the economy is rudimentary." Sudan condemned the "isolationism" of Houphouët-Boigny and accused him of acting to "poison Franco-African relations."[16]

In the Côte d'Ivoire, the RDA was equally vehement on the opposite side, accusing the advocates of African federation of entering the Community with the intention of leaving it. The party was willing for African states to talk about coordination of policies, but "the Côte d'Ivoire will never agree to enter any such primary federation with a super-assembly and a super-government." Upper Volta's leaders seemed to be open to the possibility of an African federation, although its assembly was closely divided. Dahomey was split, initially favoring federation, but with Apithy—who had lost his earlier majority—leading the charge in February, the antifederal position gained influence and the legislature would agree to only a vague reference to the possibility of joining a federation. Senghor commented

[14]After the independence of Mali, the federal government continued to be annoyed at unions that remained "demanding." Keita, like Dia, thought that "workers, whether of the public or private sector, are privileged and they err if they think that the redistribution of national revenue should be done to their benefit. I intend, myself, that it be done for the benefit of truly disinherited classes, that is the down-and-out proletariat and the peasantry." Record of meeting of Conseil des Ministres of Mali Federation, 13 July 1960, FM 38, AS.

[15]Claude Rivière, "Lutte ouvrière et phénomène syndical en Guinée," *Cultures et Développement* 7 (1975): 53–83.

[16]*L'Essor*, 9 October 1958, 10 February 1959; Report on RDA meeting, Paris, 7–9 October 1958, in Direction des Services de Police du Soudan Français, Synthèse mensuelle des renseignements, November 1958, Bamako/Ambassade/1, ADN.

in April, "The former AOF now offers us the spectacle of disunited and even enemy states. The antifederalist states set the tone."[17]

Profederation leaders managed to bring together for a December meeting representatives of Senegal, Sudan, Dahomey, and Upper Volta, although Upper Volta was wavering. Niger, after hesitation, followed the lead of the Côte d'Ivoire and stayed away. The meeting resolved to call an Assemblée Constituante Fédérale to define federal institutions and competences.[18]

The Constituent Assembly met in Dakar between 17 and 19 January 1959, to discuss the federal constitution, working on the basis of Foster's and d'Arboussier's contributions. "The Federation of Mali is born on 17 January 1959," wrote the Union Soudanaise-RDA newspaper.[19] In taking the name of "Mali"—after an old empire that had once ruled a great swatch of Sahelian territory from the thirteenth to the sixteenth centuries—the new federation was making an imperial reference. Senghor spoke of the three great empires of West African history, Ghana, Mali, and Songhai, and he insisted "we want to enracinate the Federation in the African tradition. In a word, we want to resuscitate our past."[20]

Even reduced to four states, d'Arboussier asserted, the federation would be an important entity, with eleven million people and 56 percent of the budget resources of the former AOF. It stood for the "African personality," for economic solidarity, and for the harmonization of social policy. Mali would be "a state above the states that compose it."

[17]*Afrique Nouvelle*, 28 November, 5, 12, 26 December 1958; Bureau d'Études d'Outremer, Synthèse politique du Haut-Commissariat Général à Dakar, February 1959, FPR 265, ANF; *Le Monde*, 12 October 1958; Maurice Yaméogo to President of Community, 18 November 1959, FPU 1411, ANF; AFP, Bulletin d'information, 7 July 1959, FPR 109, ANF; Senghor to Georges Pompidou, director of de Gaulle's cabinet, 3 January 1959, FPR 102, ANF; Senghor, Speech to Assemblée fédérale du Mali, April 1959, in VP 81, AS. For Houphouët-Boigny's attacks on Senghor, see Frédéric Grah Mel, *Félix Houphouët-Boigny: Biographie* (Abidjan: CERAP, and Paris: Maisonneuve et Larose, 2003), 730–35.

[18]*Paris-Dakar*, 25, 26, 27, 28 November, 6, 10, 12, 13, 17, 13, 23 December 1958; *Afrique Nouvelle*, 17 October, 28 November, 5, 12, 19, 26 December 1958, 2 January 1959; Direction des Services de Police du Soudan français, "Synthèse mensuelle de renseignements," December 1958, Bamako/Ambassade/1, ADN.

[19]*L'Essor*, 19 January 1959.

[20]Transcript of Assemblée Constituante Fédérale, 17 January 1959, pp. 68–69 and meeting of its intercommission, 16 January 1959, p. 11, in FM 161, AS. Modibo Keita claimed that he was descended—albeit distantly—from the founder of the original Mali empire. William Foltz, *From French West Africa to the Mali Federation* (New Haven, Conn.: Yale University Press, 1965), 104n23. Senghor, in the Commission de Déclarations (14–16 January 1959, 9, FM 161, AS), set out the "purely African" origins of the name Mali: originally a town in Guinea, Mali gave its name to a kingdom, then to "a confederation, an empire." The story, he said, was similar to that of France, whose name derived from a Germanic tribe.

Senghor insisted, "The Federation will construct a sole people with a sole culture, renewed by French culture, a sole people animated by the same faith and heading toward the same goal, that is the realization of its collective personality."[21] Consistent with Senghor's notion of the nation (as distinct from the *patrie*), Mali was a product of human will, with French as well as African cultural roots, an ongoing effort.

Citizens were assumed to have already identified themselves: "Any citizen of the Community, regularly inscribed on the electoral list of the federated state to which he belongs" could vote for or be elected to the federal assembly. Voting, in the absence of a reliable état-civil, was itself the identifier of the citizen. Among the competences of the federal assembly was ensuring respect for "the rights and freedoms of citizens." Social legislation and economic solidarity would also be among its competences, but each state within the federation would safeguard its personality. All states of the Community could at a later date join Mali. As Maurice Yaméogo of Upper Volta stated, "We are entering the federation of four with the assurance that shortly the other states will come along."[22]

This Constituent Assembly reveals how much perspectives had changed since 1946, when Senghor and Lamine Guèye had put citizenship—French citizenship—at the center of their demands. Much—from universal suffrage to family allowances for workers—had been gained through a politics of citizenship. But now, at a meeting of a committee of the Assembly, Senghor replied to a colleague who referred to "citizenship of the Community" that citizenship was no longer the main problem, rather it was that the French government continued to exercise power—installing top administrators and creating institutions—in Member States:

> It is necessary that freedoms, that is collective and individual autonomy, be ensured inside the Community. It is that which is important, more so than the question of citizenship. Moreover, in regard to the second point, our friend Lamine Guèye has underlined that citizenship of the Community does not signify very much. That is why our committee asked for a declaration asking that citizenship be defined in a more precise manner. That is why we have suppressed citizenship of the Community, in order to say simply Community, which has its own significance.

Lamine Guèye chimed in, "Yesterday we were French citizens. Today, what are we citizens of? French citizens and at the same time citizens of Mali, this is not a very clear situation and requires specification." "We

---

[21] *Afrique Nouvelle*, 23 January 1959.
[22] Ibid.

could thus be Malians," said Senghor.[23] In these remarks, Senghor and Lamine Guèye seemed to be saying that individual and collective rights had already been won within the Community, and their focus was now making Mali into a proper nation with a proper citizenry.

In a committee debate, Lamine Guèye also pointed to uncertainty about locating citizenship: "The name of our citizenship is that of the Community. However, we are all citizens of our respective states. . . . I would like for us to agree on an interpretation which will be ours: Am I, today, a citizen of Senegal or of France?" Asked if there could be double citizenship, he said no. Another member (M. Djibode) simply stated, "We are citizens of the Community," but Senghor replied, "We are all citizens of states, independent of the French Republic." The discussion turned away.[24] While these exchanges did not add any precision to the nature of Federation citizenship—or its relation to Community and Senegalese citizenships—it did bring out the growing discomfort of African elites at being part of France and building states of their own.

Most of the constitution writers were well aware of the difficulties of creating a truncated federation. D'Arboussier put it this way: "We are creating this federation in the worst possible conditions. If we had been able to maintain the former AOF, we would have been in much better shape. That said, we have four territories and starting from concrete facts we will figure it out." Only one of the four had much in the way of economic assets; "the three others are poor, that is the concrete reality." The federation would allow for the pooling of resources. Joseph Ouedraogo of Upper Volta, one of the poorest territories, understood the implications clearly: "We must not forget that some territories are incapable, in the current situation, to balance their budgets. The Federation must, through its solidarity, succeed in helping them." D'Arboussier pointed out that the Côte d'Ivoire could have done more for Upper Volta than the Federation possibly could, underscoring the difficulty—the tragedy, ultimately—of the truncated federation.[25]

Senegal, Sudan, and Upper Volta ratified the constitution, but there was trouble in Dahomey. The assembly there—unlike that of other West African states—was divided politically, and Apithy led a mobilization against the profederation government (led by Emile Zinsou and Alexandre Abandé). The majority shifted. On 30 January, Dahomey took itself out of the Federation. Some saw the powerful

---

[23] Discussion at meeting of Intercommission of the Assemblée Constituante, 16 January 1959, 9–11, 33, FM 161, AS.

[24] Commission des Déclarations, 14–16 January 1959, 26–27, FM 161, AS.

[25] Ouedraogo also stated, "by the fact that the Côte d'Ivoire and Guinea are no longer part of the Federation, we are going to find ourselves much diminished." Commission des Institutions, 16 January 1959, Assemblée Constituante Fédérale, FM 161, AS.

hand of Houphouët-Boigny in Dahomey's defection, but Apithy had long before embraced the idea of the "patrie locale." A few days later, he resigned from the Dahomean branch of the PRA (Parti progressiste dahoméen) saying that the federal constitution amounted to "the abandonment of sovereignty."[26]

Upper Volta was the next to defect, voting first to approve the Mali constitution and a month later in favor of its own constitution that made no mention of Mali. For this landlocked, impoverished land, the influence of the richer neighbor—to which many citizens went to seek work—was obvious. The Moro Naba, king of the largest ethnic group in the country, lobbied against the Federation. Explaining his change of heart to his deeply divided legislature in February 1959, Yaméogo noted the close connections to Côte d'Ivoire, including the railway that linked his country not to Dakar but to Abidjan—"our port, our lungs." His country needed more aid than Mali could supply. He had changed his mind on the Mali Federation because he did not want "a screen between us and the Community." If the Federation constituted itself as a state, Upper Volta would not have direct representation in Community institutions like the Conseil exécutif or the Senate: "As you see, gentlemen, this would not be a delegation of sovereignty, it would be a veritable erasure."[27]

Meanwhile, committees appointed by the Fédération du Mali began to ponder the problems of actually governing a federal state that had not only federated states within it, but also people of great cultural diversity and different personal statuses. Leaders felt the need to have justice be as close to each community as possible, but they also faced the fact that "control of justice" was—still—a competence of the French Community, that Mali had few magistrates, and that it was essential to guarantee the independence and impartiality of justice. A committee presented an argument for a balance between Community and local control of justice, combining a diversity of tribunals, including appeals courts for customary matters at the federal level,

[26] *Afrique Nouvelle*, 6 February 1959; *Abidjan-Matin*, 3 February 1959; Direction des Services de Police du Soudan français, "Synthèse mensuelle de renseignements," February 1959, Bamako/Ambassade/1, ADN. There were protests among Dahomeans against Apithy and the antifederalist stance. *Afrique Nouvelle*, 13 February 1959. See also Foltz, *From French West Africa to the Mali Federation*, 111–12, and Ruth Schachter Morgenthau, *Political Parties in French-Speaking West Africa* (Oxford: Clarendon, 1964), 316–17.

[27] Georges Y. Madiéga, "Les partis politiques et la question des fédérations en Haute Volta (Burkina-Faso)," in Charles-Robert Ageron and Marc Michel, eds., *L'Afrique noire française: L'heure des indépendances* (Paris: CNRS Éditions, 2010), 431–57, quotations from 453; Joseph Roger de Benoist, "La Haute Volta, la Communauté française et l'Afrique occidentale française du référendum (28 septembre 1958) à l'indépendance," in Yénouyaga Georges Madiéga and Oumarou Nao, *Burkina Faso: Cent ans d'histoire, 1895-1995* (Paris: Karthala, 2003), 1003–30. See also Yaméogo's press conference, 8 June 1959, FPR 100, ANF.

employing professional magistrates and "customary notables." The committees wanted to allow for "the interpenetration of modern and customary law now that social evolution will tend to accelerate." Mali's governing elites concluded that inclusion in the French Community gave it the opportunity to use its different levels of government as safeguards, making possible "a solution that is both simple and more consistent with the principles of a healthy justice."[28]

Invested as President of the Assemblée Fédérale of Mali during its first sessions in April 1959, Senghor pointed, as he had before, to the distinction between "real independence" and "nominal independence" and emphasized the need to "reconstitute the former federations of AOF and AEF" as well as to build the "Franco-African Community." He took note of the "enemies" among other African states who wanted the effort to fail. Keita, sounding like Senghor, spoke of the effort of the "construction of a great African nation, proud of its freedom and prosperity, associated with France and which, nourished by French humanism and rehabilitating African humanism, will permit the irresistible radiance of Negro-African culture."[29]

The Conseil de gouvernement of Mali included equal numbers of Senegalese and Sudanese ministers, and its first President was Modibo Keita, with Mamadou Dia as Vice-President; both also headed the governments of their respective states. Senghor, as head of the PRA and then the Parti de la Fédération Africaine (PFA), held powerful political strings, as well as strong intellectual influence. French officials initially thought that both Sudanese and Senegalese leaders were politically fragile: Senghor and Dia subject to the challenges from more Islamic-oriented leaders, Keita to those from younger activists impatient for full independence. Yet their parties won overwhelming victories in the March elections; the party elites remained in control of the agenda.[30]

---

[28] "Rapport présenté par M. le Conseiller Arrighi au nom du sous-comité de l'organisation judiciaire de la Fédération du Mali," 23 February 1959, and "La Communauté et le Contrôle de la Justice," 28 February 1959, FM 165, AS.

[29] Fédération du Mali, *Journal Officiel: Débats Parlementaires de l'Assemblée Fédérale*, No. 2, 6 April 1959, 10–13.

[30] Pierre Lami, "Note strictement réservée à l'attention personnelle de Monsieur Foccart," 11 February 1959, FPR 265, ANF; Direction des Services de Police du Soudan français, "Synthèse mensuelle," May 1959, Bamako/Ambassade/1, ADN. French intelligence got a report that Dia had his doubts that a federation would be viable if it did not include at least the majority of the states of ex-AOF, whereas Senghor wanted to push on at all costs. Bulletin de Renseignements, 23 March 1959, AOF/Dakar/109, ADN. The High Commissioner in Bamako wrote that month that Keita was getting increasingly radical, pushed by "doctrinaire" members of his own government and by the "contagion effect" of Guinea's independence. High Commissioner Sicurani to Foccart, 16 March 1959, FPR 234, ANF. It would be more accurate to describe his attitudes as volatile.

The French state, over the course of 1959, had to redistribute personnel from its rolls to those of Mali or the other Member States, following upon the initial reallocation after the loi-cadre of 1956. The last of AOF's functions were wound down over 1959, and in December High Commissioner Pierre Messmer took his leave, wishing Mali well.[31] The closing of AOF bureaucracies caused problems to the budding West African states, for the State Services, run and paid for by France, could not absorb all the ex-AOF civil servants or other government workers, putting pressure on those states to pick up some of their nationals who lost their jobs. Reallocating civil servants strained the "unity" doctrine of leaders, whose own nationals might resent the competition of other Africans. Guineans—who were not in the Community—and Dahomeans, whose educational levels had given them prominence in certain AOF departments, caused anxiety to Malian leaders who were not sure how loyal such civil servants would be or how their own citizens would take to their continued presence.[32] Not only civil servants, but traders who plied routes all across AOF and intellectuals whose involvement in educational and civic life crossed territorial boundaries were affected by the dismantling of AOF, by the isolation of Guinea, and later by the breakup of the Mali Federation and the development of national systems of regulation and employment.[33]

Much was at stake—for the rest of Africa as well as the two federating states—in making a success of the Fédération du Mali. The Dakar archives, with minutes of cabinet meetings and other documents, display evidence of a real effort, from leaders from both of the federated states, to figure out how to run a federation and how to preserve its relationship to France. It would be a mistake to write the history of the Mali Federation as if its failure is the only point of interest.[34]

[31] Messmer's farewell letter was read to the Cabinet of Mali on 24 December 1959, FM 37, AS. As of February, the Service du Personnel in Dakar had under its charge 11,100 personnel dossiers, 5,200 of which were to be transferred to Mali, the rest to the "ungrouped" states. On personnel, see Haut Commissaire Général à Dakar, Service du Personnel, "Note sur la distribution du Service Commun du Personnel entre la Fédération du Mali et les États non Groupés," 6 February 1959, High Commissioner to President of Community, 21 February 1959, and transcript of Conférence des Chefs de Gouvernement, 5 March 1959, Bamako/Ambassade/8, ADN. The distribution of AOF property occupies numerous files in the series AP, AOM, and 18G, AS.
[32] Ministère de la Fonction Publique, Mali, circular letters to President of Government, heads of Ministries and others, 27, 28 May 1959, 8 January, 30 May, 11 August 1960, FM 106, AS.
[33] Morgenthau, *Political Parties*, 322–26.
[34] See for example the minutes of Cabinet meetings, concerned with the details of taxation, organization of ministries, and security. FM 37 and FM 38, AS. The most valuable existing scholarship on the federation includes Foltz, *From French West Africa to the Mali Federation*, and Guédel Ndiaye, *L'échec de la fédération du Mali* (Dakar: Nouvelles Éditions Africaines, 1980). Pierre Messmer, the last High Commissioner in Dakar, thought that "reduced to Senegal and the Sudan, Mali is much more solid that a federation of

Senghor opened a second front, establishing another political party to make the case for federation across French Africa. The Parti de la Fédération Africaine (PFA) was intended to overcome the splits over the referendum and other matters that had bedeviled the PRA and to bring together advocates of federation dispersed across the former AOF.[35] The new party could, hopefully, campaign in the name of African unity against the parties that had kept their Member States out of the federation and try to get those territories to change sides.

At the same time as they were trying to build an African federation, Senghor, Dia, and Keita were engaged in politics at the level of the Community. Their relationship to the French government became more tense in May 1959, when Mali wished to present itself as a single state to the Conseil exécutif, but was told that Senegal and Sudan were the Member States in question.[36] The issue grated particularly on Keita. It was eased slightly as de Gaulle acknowledged that the people representing Senegal and the Sudan were the same as those who governed Mali and could speak on its behalf, and he tried to suggest that the issue was juridical rather than political. Keita reported to his Council of Ministers that he had told de Gaulle that now "the mystique of unity was bigger than that of independence; but if the first is thwarted the second will irresistibly prevail among our peoples."[37] This aggravation was added to the tensions over the division of competences that had persisted since the loi-cadre days. In addition, African leaders found their desire to represent their interests in international organizations frustrated by their lack of sovereign status. In the give-and-take of negotiations, they got some of what they wanted: Member

---

four, which carried in itself the seeds of its disintegration." He thought Mali could cause France "difficulties," but "I do not think, all the same, that these are sufficient reasons to impose excommunication on Mali. In Africa, situations evolve, and not always for the worse!" Dia, he thought, had "turned toward the Community." Messmer to Foccart, 9 April 1959, FPR 229, ANF.

[35] *Afrique Nouvelle*, 3 April 1959; *L'Essor*, 27 March 1959. See also Léo Hamon, "Le Parti Fédéral Africain et le Rassemblement Démocratique Africain de la querelle fédéraliste à l'indépendance (1959–1960)," *Revue Juridique et Parlementaire d'Outre-mer* 14 (1960): 551–69.

[36] Some other African leaders did not help Mali's cause. Hamani Diori of Niger said in the Conseil exécutif that if Mali were to get an extra seat, others would group themselves and demand such a seat too. Tsiranana was not supportive either. After a long discussion, de Gaulle concluded that Mali was not a state "in the sense of the Member States of the Community." He claimed to have nothing against the Federation but was arguing on the basis of the Constitution. He added, however, that he thought it would be best for states "to acquire solid traditions of state before passing to a larger grouping." Record of meeting of 4–5 May 1959, FPR 107, ANF.

[37] *L'Essor*, 11, 19 May 1959; Keita reporting to the Council of Ministers of Mali on his trip to France, 22 May 1959, FM 37, AS. *L'Essor*, 11 May 1959, cited Dia as also decrying the nonrecognition of Mali, pointing out that Senegal and the Sudan had "delegated part of their sovereignty to the Federation of Mali."

States could send representatives to international organizations that were concerned with technical, not political, matters.[38]

It was also in May that the rivalries in West Africa took another step as Houphouët-Boigny announced that he was forming a rival to Mali: the Conseil de l'Entente, embracing Côte d'Ivoire, Niger, Upper Volta, and Dahomey, the latter two the defectors from the original plan for the Mali Federation. The Conseil de l'Entente did not claim to be a federation, but rather a coordinating body intended "to harmonize their relations on the basis of friendship, fraternity, and solidarity." However, Houphouët-Boigny laid claim to the mantle of African unity, arguing that the Mali Federation was likely to fail and that the only path forward was the one he had chosen, that is, for African states to maintain their direct ties to France and their cooperative relations with each other unencumbered by another layer of administrative and political apparatus that would be expensive, distant, and subject to divisive political tensions.[39] The act of giving Houphouët-Boigny's web of alliances a name made explicit that the French Community was split in two.

Interstate tension manifested itself in Africa in another way. In June, Modibo Keita decided to expel all "Dahomean civil servants in the services of Mali." Dahomey's betrayal of the federation weighed on his mind, and perhaps he did not think its people could loyally serve the federal state. Some Senegalese objected to this action. "Misplaced sentimentality," responded Keita. Civil servants of Guinean origin caused concern too; Keita thought they should be classified into those "who are with Mali and those who are against." The knife could cut the other way: Upper Volta expelled Malians from its territory, including some who according to French sources had been there thirty years. Expulsions took place from Côte d'Ivoire and Niger. French intelligence feared that such intra-African divisiveness could lead to the "weakening of this Community."[40]

[38] Présidence du Conseil du Sénégal, Affaires Extérieures, "Rapport à M. le Président du Conseil sur la réunion du comité des rapports de la Communauté avec les organisations internationales," 6–8 October 1958, VP 138, AS. French officials were particularly insistent that "there is one foreign policy of the French Republic and of the Community." High Commissioner (Messmer), note pour M. Chambon, Conseiller Diplomatique, 10 February 1959, AOF/Dakar/50, ADN; Relevé des decisions, Conseil exécutif, meeting of 7–8 July 1959, and Minister of Foreign Affairs to High Commissioner, Dakar, 18 August 1959, AOF/Dakar/49, ADN.

[39] *Abidjan-Matin*, 4, 11, 29, 30 May, 1 June 1959; record of "Réunion du Conseil de l'Entente," 29–30 May 1959, AOF/Dakar/108, ADN.

[40] Intelligence report, Dakar, 1 June 1959, AOF/Dakar/108, ADN; High Commissioner, Dakar, to President of Community, telegram, 12 November 1959, FPR 265, ANF; Transmission de Renseignements, by Bureau d'Études d'Outre-Mer, 25 June 1959, FPR 100, ANF, quoted. Malian officials told their Dahomean counterparts that the dismantling of AOF institutions required sending civil servants back to their terri-

Toward Independence, but Not the Nation-State

With the Community disunited, the argument for remaining in it was becoming weaker. Without giving up on the notion of retaining close ties to France, some of the leadership of the PFA was moving into the independence faction. Senghor and Dia were trying to hold them back, and Keita thought that by linking independence to confederation Mali could avoid a break with France. Senghor was most at pains to avoid disagreements turning into territorial independence, warning against the "uniformization of people" that was "one of the temptations of the nation-state." He continued to insist that the strongest states, including the United States, the Soviet Union, China, India, Canada, and Brazil owed their success to the "mixing" of peoples. France had gone too far in the other direction, Senghor thought, and its more lucid leaders realized that a supra-national polity was the best hope for France and Africa. Senghor's position had evolved toward putting more emphasis on an African nation but not on the nation-state. He was now advocating "national independence and a Negro-African nation within a multinational confederation." Dia warned that if an African community were not established *before* independence, the result could be the "cutting up of Africa and a break with France."[41]

French officials perceived in July and August a growing split between the impatient Sudanese and the more cautious Senegalese, as well as a deeper polarization between Mali and the Conseil de l'Entente. And that brings us to a remarkable admission, from the High Commissioner in Senegal, Pierre Lami, who had previously exchanged testy letters with Mamadou Dia. Now, the future of the Community seemed to him to depend on this one man. Dia, he wrote, is "the only statesman of French-speaking West Africa capable at the same time of moderating or slowing down the impatience of the Sudanese, stimulated by pressure from Guinea, and looking for and finding a terrain of compromise if not agreement between Mali and the Conseil de l'Entente. He feels that he is defending the fate of the Community at the same time as that of his government, of Senegal, and his

---

tories of origin and Mali had difficulty reabsorbing its own people affected in this way. Dahomey needed to understand "the consequences of the balkanization of ex-AOF to which, in the end, it consented." Record of meeting of Conseil des Ministres, 19 November 1959, FM 37, AS. On Guineans, see ibid., 22 October 1959, and "Situation des Guinéens ayant opté pour la Communauté," nd [early 1960], FPU 1677, ANF. A Senegalese who had lived in Niger wrote to Dia asking for a job because of "a climate of terror . . . against Senegalese" in Niger. Serigne N'Diaye to Dia, 15 October 1959, VP 23, AS.

[41]Congrès constitutif du PFA, "Rapport sur la doctrine et le programme du parti," by Senghor, 2–3 July 1959, FPR 265, ANF; "Note à l'attention de M. le Président de la Communauté," nd [July 1959], FPR 103, ANF.

own fate as a man of politics." After the two spoke, he wrote that Dia would not "let himself be trapped in the following alternative: intangible and unchangeable Community or else independence, synonym of secession."[42] Lami understood how much the French Community needed the Mali Federation.

But in August 1959 Mali existed as a federation of two states, was not yet recognized as a state in itself, and had yet to make itself into a nation. With some Malians ready to give up on a fractured Community and opt for independence, leaders of the PFA hit on the idea of modifying the version of independence that its predecessor, the PRA, had advocated the year before: rather than follow the procedures of Article 86 of the Constitution allowing a Member State to opt for independence—and out of the Community—by vote of its assembly, ratified by referendum, PFA leaders suggested that France transfer "competences" to Mali. Mali would become fully self-governing, with its own nationality and its own international personality, but it would do so without a sharp break. Dia and Senghor did not want to go the way of Guinea, which they saw troubled by isolation and extremism. Senghor told his party members, with Guinea in mind, "Whatever the friendship that links us to other independent or autonomous African states, our policies are not theirs. Our autonomy is not theirs. Our independence is not theirs."[43] Mali had its own ideas, and it understood that not all African states shared them. And not all in the PFA either: Madeira Keita—who had lived and worked in Sudan, Guinea, Senegal, and elsewhere in French Africa, veteran, former civil servant, leader of the more radical faction of the Union Soudanaise, future minister in the government of Modibo Keita—wanted to hold a referendum as soon as 15 October. But Modibo Keita sided with Senghor and Dia, and even thought of pushing Madeira Keita out of the PFA.[44]

The transfer of competences was the route the PFA chose to take, and on 26 September, after a session of its Comité Directeur, Dia, and Modibo Keita wrote to de Gaulle to communicate that decision, citing the agreement on the "evolving character" of the Community at

[42] High Commissioner to Secrétaire Général, 20 August 1959, FPR 265, ANF. Former AOF High Commissioner Messmer also recognized Dia's importance to the French Community. Messmer to Foccart, 9 April 1959, FPR 229, ANF.

[43] High Commissioner, Dakar, to Secrétaire Général, telegram, 23 September 1959, FPR 265, ANF.

[44] High Commissioner to Secrétaire Général, 22 September 1959, FPR 265, ANF. French intelligence also thought that Modibo Keita was having trouble with his "hardliners," including Madeira Keita. Renseignements, by Bureau d'Études d'Outre-mer, 25 June 1959, FPR 265, ANF. On Madeira Keita's political trajectory, see Gregory Mann, "Anti-Colonialism and Social Science: Georges Balandier, Madeira Keita, and 'the Colonial Situation' in French Africa," *Comparative Studies in Society and History* 55 (2013): 92-119.

the recent meeting of the Conseil exécutif.[45] In a communiqué, the Party placed its assertiveness in the context of how far Africans had moved beyond a colonial situation: "The colonial fact is behind us. It is not a question of abolishing the colonial fact, but of going beyond it. We are now free men, masters of our options, masters of our destiny. We are achieving decolonization by killing, in ourselves, the former man, by finishing with talk in order to act under the direction of our Party and our Governments."[46]

It remained to convince de Gaulle that France should change its rules once again to allow independence by transfer of competences without it implying leaving the Community. It was a measure of the nearly desperate desire of the French government to hold together something that resembled the Community created a year before that it was willing to consider such an option.[47]

Africa's leaders were continuing to think of inclusive ensembles even as the circumstances were changing. The independence track, since September 1958, had a francophone exemplar, Guinea, but there was a contradiction at its heart: Sékou Touré had been a vigorous advocate of African federation and unity, but now he was going it alone. Sékou Touré flirted with Kwame Nkrumah in Ghana, with the possibility in mind of a radical franco-anglophone federation, but such a dream did not come to fruition.[48] The PAI, youth movements, and some people inspired by Guinea argued for an immediate assertion of independence, but they were not getting very far. The most serious alternative to the Senghor-Dia-Keita position was still Houphouët-Boigny, and he had the influence—and his territory the affluence—to bring along his neighbors against the African federation. But his position was not the polar opposite of Senghor's. Both wanted a close relationship with France. Both thought the territorial nation-state a bad idea. Houphouët-Boigny, like Senghor and Dia, made clear that what he wanted was a "multinational state." But he wanted that state to be a solid federation, not a loose confederation—not a "commonwealth" he

[45] Dia and Keita to de Gaulle, 26 September 1959, FPR 233, ANF.

[46] Communiqué of Parti de la Fédération Africaine, 25 September 1959, Dakar/Ambassade/343, ADN.

[47] A memorandum in the Ministry of Foreign Affairs expressed its "strong worry" about the "idea that an African state can benefit at the same time from the powers of independence and the advantages of the Community." But it went on to say that France would probably have to accept that idea anyway. Confidential note, "Le project d'indépendance du Mali: éventualité d'une indépendance dans la Communauté," November 1959, Direction des Affaires Africaines et Malgaches, Mali, 2518, ADLC.

[48] As Meredith Terretta shows, the UPC in Cameroon sought an inclusive association with radical African states, but it faced not only French repression, but the self-interest of other African parties and states. "Cameroonian Nationalists Go Global: From Forest *Maquis* to a Pan-African Accra," *Journal of African History* 51 (2010): 189–212.

said at one point—and the federation would include, as equals, France and the African states.[49]

Houphouët-Boigny did not come to grips with the difficulty of persuading the French people to enter a federation of equals with African states: France's own jealousy over its own sovereignty, the cost of making equality an economic reality. Despite the limited place French Africa had obtained under the Treaty of Rome of 1957, Houphouët-Boigny still thought that "Eurafrica" remained a possibility, and the Ivorian newspaper *Abidjan-Matin* published in February 1959 a map showing Europe and Africa with arrows linking them, accompanied by the caption, "The horizontal solidarity of the peoples of Africa does not exclude vertical solidarity with Europe."[50] This was the language that Senghor had been using for a decade. The newspaper cited some of the same examples as Senghor of models of federal states: the United States, Soviet Union, Canada, Switzerland.[51] Senghor's solidarity was intended to produce a grand African nation, Houphouët-Boigny's nations directly linked to Paris. Both were thinking in terms of connections, not bounded national units.[52]

At a press conference on the occasion of a meeting of the Conseil exécutif in September, Modibo Keita pointed out the weak point in Houphouët-Boigny's argument: his version of federalism would not work because "we do not believe that France, with its traditions, history, and current vitality is able to accept its disappearance as a national entity." That left "multinational confederation" as the formula that could safeguard the "interests" and the "internal personality" of both France and the states of the Community as well as preserve "the sincere connections that have been woven between the metropole and the former colonies."[53]

Keita noted that the Conseil exécutif had no authority under the Constitution to decide whether Member States and the Republic

[49] Statement to press after July meeting of Conseil exécutif, AFP, Bulletin quotidien d'information, 7 July 1959, FPR 109, ANF. Officials in Paris interpreted the RDA position as the "organization of solidarity at the level of the Community (substituting for the currently existing bilateral aid)." Such an approach would have implied a strong claim from African Member States on French resources. Note for the President, September 1959, FPR 103, ANF.

[50] *Abidjan-Matin*, 19 February 1959.

[51] *Afrique Nouvelle*, 11 September 1959.

[52] Pierre Messmer, the last High Commissioner of AOF, noted that the Prime Ministers of the African states agreed on the need to reform the Community, but since "each government wants to be the sole master on the territory of its state, it wants itself to exercise there the powers of the Community. . . . In practice, this claim signifies the disappearance of the General Secretariat of the Community and that of the Hauts-Commissariats-Généraux." "Note sur l'état d'esprit des premiers ministres de l'ex-AOF," 7 September 1959, FPR 100, ANF.

[53] *L'Essor*, 14 September 1959. Senghor also said of France, "I understand that she fears becoming the colony of its colonies." *Paris-Dakar*, 3 October 1959.

would form a confederation or federation or to decide when and if a Member State would opt for independence. He announced, "President Mamadou Dia and I have presented our thesis and informed the Conseil exécutif of the decision of the Federation of Mali, comprising Senegal and the Sudan, to make use of our right to independence in the framework of a confederal association with France; the leaders of Mali will make the contacts necessary to attain this objective that was decided for them by the congress of the Parti de la Fédération Africaine." In a private conversation with de Gaulle, Keita told the press conference, he had made clear that he preferred a transfer of competences to a referendum, which would "take place with emotion and provoke alienation from France, which we do not desire at all."[54]

Keita was suggesting a method for France and Mali to reconfigure their relationship, and France had to take it seriously. He had also pointed out the fatal flaw of the leading alternative. Houphouët-Boigny's French federation would either be egalitarian—and unacceptable in France—or inegalitarian—and unacceptable in Africa.

In an undated and apparently unsent letter from sometime in 1959, Debré wanted to warn Houphouët-Boigny that continuing to insist on federation was not going to get the support of his government. One had to get beyond "an irreducible opposition between federalists and confederalists." Inside the French Republic, there was fear that fully incorporating Africans into a federal legislature would lead to an alliance of Africans with the "far left." So turning the Community into a "federal structure is not immediately realizable. It would demand beforehand the preparation of attitudes." One needed "a very supple structure." And he worried that if the RDA issued an ultimatum for federation or else secession, "the process of decomposition would not stop." Debré intended this text, filled with cross-outs, to be that of "a friend," not the Prime Minister.[55] The French government was continuing its evolution, already evident in the constitution-writing process of 1958, away from de Gaulle's preference for a French-led federation toward recognition that something closer to confederation was the most realistic alternative.

African politicians, in the fall of 1959, were still jockeying for position, sniping at each other, and trying to mobilize followers for their respective positions. Senghor explained that the PFA's decision would "permit Mali to attain its major objective: the transformation of our quasi-Nation into a Nation, the accession of Mali to independence in a confederal association with France."[56]

[54] *L'Essor*, 14 September 1959. Keita and Dia later referred in the following months to "prenegotiations" with France over independence. *Afrique Nouvelle*, 23, 30 October 1959.
[55] Draft letter [1959] in Debré Papers, 2DE 11, MD.
[56] Intelligence report, 25 September 1959, FPR 100, ANF; *Afrique Nouvelle* 25 September 1959.

Mamadou Dia put the process that had led to this demand in historical context during a seminar in October for political elites in Senegal:

> In the aftermath of the loi-cadre that reformed the structures of the Overseas Territories, we had the profound and sad conviction the one had just committed one of those major historical errors that can affect the destiny of a people. We had however fought to the possible limit to be spared. In spite of us, West Africa was balkanized, cut into fragments, putting in place a division based on the interests of certain political clans. . . . Since then, our principal reflex has been to lead the fight as good federalists, partisans of African Unity, to regain our national space. We still bear the weight of this error, or of this political miscalculation.

The original draft of the 1958 constitution, he claimed, had been catastrophic, but Africans had prevailed on de Gaulle to recognize their right to independence. Entering into governance, the task was "to build the nation." Now, the task was to take the nation to independence and to build a "human economy." The new African nation would reflect a geographic, civilizational, cultural, political, and economic community, and French West Africa had provided a framework in which such connections were forged. Like Senghor, he insisted that the African nation should espouse a socialism inflected by the communitarian values of Africa. And building a nation was still a question of will: "The national will exists: the enthusiasm with which the birth of Mali was greeted amply proves it." He concluded, "This is how Mali will be created, and that way we will better establish our consciousness, our Malian national will; I do not say Senegalese or Sudanese, because there can be no nation at the level of our states—I say our Malian will, and we have the steady conviction that the cause that we serve is the Malian cause, and thereby that of Africa."[57]

Even while calling for the construction of a nation, Dia and Senghor were leery of nationalism, an overly narrow, exclusionary view of what the nation was. Senghor wrote in October 1959, "Nationalism, I acknowledge, is an illness. It conquered European in the nineteenth century, Asia in the first half of the twentieth century; it now gnaws at

---

[57] "Discours d'ouverture et de cloture du Président Mamadou Dia au premier séminaire national d'études pour les responsables politiques, parlementaires, gouvernementaux," 26 October 1959 on "La construction nationale," VP 93, AS. The authorities Dia cited in his discussion of the concept of the nation were an eclectic lot, including the Soviet Africanist Potekhin, Teilhard de Chardin, and François Perroux and Joseph Lebret, the economists who had brought together Catholic humanism and socialist economics and who became advisors on Senegal's economic policy. *Afrique Nouvelle*, 6 November 1959. Similar sources and language were deployed in Senghor's report to the PFA congress, 2–3 July 1959, reprinted in *Liberté II*, 232–70.

Africa. France will not vaccinate Africa against nationalism without inoculating itself with a reasonable dose of nationalism—in the framework of Association." He was worried about the contagion effects of a series of independent states. France had to accept a degree of nationalist sentiment within the Community if it were to prevent the dangerous spread of the notion that each nation deserved exclusive authority over its territory.[58]

De Gaulle, in the fall of 1959, was not making himself into an obstacle to change, and he was willing to talk with Mali's leaders about a new relationship. In his early November press conference, he admitted that the idea of "self-determination . . . animates these peoples," affecting even "the countries that were, yesterday, colonizers." He apparently still had in mind the Cartier thesis, to which he had alluded in his Conakry speech in August 1958, for he stated, "These territories cost us much more than they bring in. If they want to leave us, they should do it." But that was not what he wanted to happen. France's policy toward the Member States was "to recognize their free disposition of themselves and at the same time to offer to build with them an ensemble in which they will find help. . . . In this Community, all the states that belong to it are there because they wanted to be and all, at any moment, can leave when they want to." There was a hint of bitterness—no doubt going back to August 1958 in Guinea—in his repeated references to people's leaving the Community. But the choice was up to the Member States.[59]

France's continued advocacy of Community citizenship reflected not only its desire to maintain a sense of belonging in a French Community, but also its need for assurance that French businessmen and professionals could remain in former colonies as rights-bearing individuals. Officials thought that if former territories—notably Mali—went their own way, investors would be wary. The Community, however, could provide "superguaranties" that property would be protected and that French businessmen would not be discriminated against.[60] So even as the French government contemplated Mali's demand for

[58] Senghor, "Note sur le référendum et la Communauté," with note of transmission of this document, 18 October 1959, from Georges Pompidou to Foccart, 18 October 1959, FPR 265, ANF.

[59] *Afrique Nouvelle*, 13 November 1959. The cost-benefit question was also taken up in 1959 by the noted political scientist Raymond Aron, who concluded that France's interest was in keeping its former territories in the franc zone and maintaining good relationships, not sovereignty. France had political, moral, and economic reasons to continue to provide aid whether or not territories became independent, but it had to make clear that its support would be limited. "Conséquences économiques de l'évolution politique en Afrique noire," *Revue Française de Science Politique* 9 (1959): 610–28, esp. 615, 620.

[60] The last argument is made frankly in R. Perrin, note to Jacques Foccart, 28 October 1959, FPR 229, ANF.

Figure 6. Mamadou Dia, Modibo Keita, and Léopold Sédar Senghor
arriving in Paris to discuss the independence of Mali with
Charles de Gaulle, 26 November 1959. ©AFP/Getty Images.

independence, it hoped that it would want to remain within the Community, but it could not be the same Community as that defined only recently by the Constitution of 1958.

The next meeting of the Conseil exécutif, in December 1959, would be crucial; Mali's demand for independence within the Community was to be discussed. But there was another item on the agenda that had been the object of controversy throughout most of 1959: the question of whether the French Community defined a single or multiple nationalities. Even as Mali had taken the lead in raising the possibility of independence, its leaders had joined other Africans in a yearlong argument over the meaning of nationality within the ambiguous unit in which they participated. That discussion too came to a head in December 1959.

Citizenship and Nationality in a Community of States

The 1958 Constitution stated that there was only one citizenship of the Community. During the writing of the constitution, there had been none of the controversy of 1946 on this subject. Nor was there debate over the continued existence of different status regimes.

The Constitution—like those that went before it—said nothing about nationality. If "the people" write a constitution, the constitution cannot define who the people are, although laws created under it can subsequently regulate who can acquire or lose their nationality. The arguments in 1959 over nationality offer a window onto different political actors' conceptions of what kind of polity the Community actually was, and how its thin institutional apparatus could handle a matter that was juridically complex and politically sensitive.

To appreciate the debates, however, let us look first at the question of the nation from two quite different perspectives, first Senghor's evolving writing on the meaning of "nation," and second an incident that took place in Abidjan in October 1958. Most French jurists (see below), aware of the circularity inherent in the notion of nationality, regarded it as a quality of belonging to a particular political unit that is recognized as such by other political units. They were concerned with distinguishing the French national from the Italian or German one. Colonies—even renamed colonies—did not have their own nationalities, only the French one. Any relationship of people in such a territory to a foreign power had to pass through the French state. Since foreign affairs was a Community function after October 1958, it made little sense in these terms to think of Member States as having nationality.

But that is not how all African leaders were thinking. In 1955 (chapter 3), Senghor had written that "African nationalism is willing to renounce the nation, but not the African *patrie*." He was holding onto the units of sentiment to which Africans attached themselves, but he was not turning them into a claim to undivided sovereignty. In 1958, he stated,

> a nation in formation promoted to autonomy must move past it and insert itself, at the last stage, in a larger ensemble: a confederation. She consents freely to abandonments of sovereignty; she dies at the absolute fiction of independence in order to enjoy real independence. And the more the confederated states are diverse in race and culture, the stronger the confederation is because its members are complementary.[61]

The importance of sovereignty was that one could relinquish part of it; the point of constituting a nation was to cement ties with other nations. Senghor was not, in 1958, alone in thinking this way about sovereignty. Behind the European Common Market was also the premise that a nation had "the possibility to delegate a portion of its sovereignty," and such a premise—as one of Europe's architects, Jean Monnet, insisted—could apply to "Eurafrica" as much as to Europe.[62] The most influential of Senghor's opponents—Houphouët-Boigny—did not see the French federation he advocated to be tied to a uniquely French nationality: "Many of us want to reconcile the life of our states and their personalities with those of the Community itself. It is at the same time a marriage of reason and of love. I believe in it, that is why we remain to the limit partisans of the multinational state."[63]

Now, in 1959, Senghor was still working with the distinction between "patrie" and "nation," but instead of renouncing or going beyond the nation, he was constructing it. In a report for the PFA, he elaborated on the categories of his thinking. The "patrie" had been inherited from the ancestors:

> One land, one blood, one language, at least a dialect, morals, customs, folklore, art, in a word a culture enracinated in territory

[61] Léopold Sédar Senghor, "Pour une République Fédérale dans une Union Confédérale," *Union Française et Parlement* 97 (1958): 5–11, 9 quoted. In 1959, Senghor applauded the Bandung conference's affirmation of the dignity of all humanity and its condemnation of colonialism, but he did not want anticolonialism to take too nationalist a turn. He worried that nationalism was "the myth" transmitted to ex-colonial nations by Europe. One had to look beyond the nation to federation, to the "Afro-Asian group" as a whole, and "universal civilization." "Les nationalismes d'outre-mer et l'avenir des peuples de couleur," *L'encyclopédie française*, 1959, reprinted in *Liberté II*, 271–82, 272, 273, 279, 282 quoted.

[62] See his contribution to *Le Monde*, 11 September 1958.

[63] *Abidjan-Matin*, 17 September 1959. The same phrase was used in a 1958 symposium organized by the journal *France Outre-Mer* 339 (1958): 18–25, with a somewhat different couple in mind: "L'Eurafrique . . . mariage d'amour ou de raison?" Senghor, Modibo Keita, and Robert Schuman were among the participants—an occasion for the Africans present to insist on a full role in governing Eurafrica.

and expressed by a race. In West Africa, the *patrie* is the Serer, Malinké, Songhai, Mossi, Baulé, Fon countries. The Nation, if it brings together the *patries*, it is to transcend them. It is not, like the *patrie*, a natural determination, an expression of its milieu, but rather the will to construct, or better to reconstruct. In terms of its realization, the Nation builds out of its provinces a harmonious ensemble. A single country for a single people, animated by the same faith and heading toward the same goal.

The state should express the will of the nation, but it was also a creator of the nation:

> The state is to the nation what the entrepreneur is to the architect. It incarnates itself in institutions: government, parliament, public services. The civil servants are the workers. It is that state that accomplishes the will of the Nation and ensures its permanence. Inside, it mixes together the *patries*, it kneads together individuals in the mold of the "archetype"; toward the exterior it defends the integrity of the Nation, which it guards against foreign intrigue.[64]

The new federal state would express and construct the African nation. It would do so within the Community. The nation could not be Senegalese or Sudanese, and Senghor hoped that the Mali Federation would be the first step to forging the African nation. The "patrie" that Senghor had wanted to preserve in 1955 had become a building block of something more substantial, more inclusive, more all-embracing in 1959. And Senghor, legislator as well as poet, thought that the nation would not simply construct itself. It needed institutions. Perhaps his increasing emphasis on the African federation as nation-in-the-making reflected the split among Africans; African unity was not about to happen by virtue of the fact of being African or of being part of the French Community. The only way out of the bind was to build the federation from those states willing to make the leap.

The party newspaper of the Union Soudanaise had made a similar argument some months earlier, putting more emphasis on the nation whose historical roots lay in colonization. It explained why the nation should be a specifically French West African one: "Fifty years of common subjection have created in West African under French domination the necessary and sufficient conditions for the stability of the West African nation and for its development." AOF met the criteria for constituting a nation: fifty years of stability, a shared French language, geographical contiguity, economic community, and a "cultural community" on a Negro-African basis. All this formed the basis of

[64] Report to congrès constitutif of Parti de la Fédération Africaine, reprinted in *Afrique Nouvelle*, 3 July 1959.

building a nation, but not everyone understood the situation in such terms. The party had work to do to make the West African nation into a reality.[65] That was where the problem lay for Senghor, Dia, Keita, and others who believed in an African federation: devising a constitution, turning its tenets into institutional reality, and giving the nation the kind of independence that might eventually make it into a pole of attraction for other African states-in-the-making. I will return to this subject. But one thing that the nation was not was French.

What the French nation was in 1959 was not entirely clear either—not that it had been at any time since 1789. If the Revolution in the metropole had seemed to line up nationality, citizenship, and the state, revolutions and conquests overseas had blurred the boundaries. Under a law of 1865, the notion of "un Français" embraced not only the self-minded French of the metropole, but Arabs and Berbers in Algeria and later the people of sub-Saharan Africa—even though most of the latter were denied citizenship. But the state, with the establishment of protectorates in Southeast Asia and North Africa, exercised its authority over people of Moroccan, Vietnamese, and other nationalities. After 1946, all nationals acquired citizenship, but not all citizens—of the French Union that is—were French nationals. Now, in 1959, the question of the relationship of state, citizenship, and nationality was open once again. Opinions differed as to whether the Members States of the Community were really states, or whether the Community was itself a state. They differed as well over whether the people of the Member States were citizens of them—although they were clearly citizens of France—and whether they were nationals of those states, or only of the French Community, or nationals of both a Member State and the French Republic and the Community. The Director of Political Affairs in the Secretariat of the Community thought that the members of the Community were "not nations, having an international personality, but rather states enjoying internal autonomy."[66] In such a logic, they were states without nationals, and depending how one interpreted the Constitution's assertion that there was only one citizenship, they could be states without citizens either. These conceptions were all subject to debate.

In October 1958, a grave incident took place in Abidjan, only a month after the referendum campaign that had ended so well for Houphouët-Boigny. Dahomean and Togolese residents in Abidjan

[65] *L'Essor*, 9 October 1958.

[66] Pignon, Directeur des Affaires Politiques, Secrétariat Général de la Communauté, Note for the Secretary General, 16 January 1959, 940167/14, CAC, plus attached note "Nationalité et citoyenneté." The note asserted that "any French national is not necessarily a citizen of the Republic" and that "any French national is not necessarily a citizen of a Member State." Here, however inconsistent the logic, was the thesis that the Community consisted of multiple states, multiple citizenships, and a single nationality.

were the victims of a pogrom led by an illegal organization called the "Ligue des originaires de la Côte d'Ivoire" (League of Original Inhabitants of the Côte d'Ivoire). Its members felt aggrieved that Dahomeans and Togolese—whose access to education had been better than that provided in the Côte d'Ivoire—were taking significant numbers of the better-paid jobs in the public and private sectors in Abidjan. The organizers of the Ligue referred to themselves as "authentic children of this territory" and workers from elsewhere in AOF as "invaders." The Ligue did not for the most part represent the downtrodden of Abidjan's unemployed, but educated Ivorians who felt themselves in competition with better educated people from elsewhere in AOF. Faced with threats, pillage, arson, and personal violence, some eight thousand Togolese and Dahomeans took refuge in the port, as government agents tried to protect them. Houphouët-Boigny denounced the instigators of the riots. Most of the victims apparently wanted to be repatriated "at any price," freeing the government of the Côte d'Ivoire from having either to deport them or to ensure their protection.[67] But the Abidjan riot was a warning that xenophobia could follow the lines of territorialization. Other incidents of nationals of one Member State being expelled from positions in another—despite the idea that there was no such thing as a foreigner within the Community—would soon take place.

With these complexities of social tensions and political theory in mind, let us turn to the Conseil exécutif of the Communauté to follow the yearlong debate over nationality.

In February 1959, the Executive Council met for the first time, in Paris. Among its decisions was one on nationality. The Community would recognize only one nationality, the French one, but a special kind of French nationality. The decision was not the object of a happy consensus, nor did it last. But it had been carefully thought out. In January, the Secretariat in charge of the Community had consulted with jurists and prepared a number of reports on the subject, confronting the problem that the Constitution had created a peculiar sort of entity whose international status was not self-evident. The Community, the reports concluded, was the successor to the Fourth Republic and inherited the latter's international personality. The Member States had no such status.

> [T]he Constitution, in terms of international public law, has created a complex ensemble, including two distinct personalities: the first, the French Republic is included within but mixed up

[67] *Afrique Nouvelle*, 31 October 1958; "Note sur les incidents d'Abidjan," October 1958, in FPU 215, ANF; Henri-Michel Yéré, "Citizenship, Nationality & History in Côte d'Ivoire, 1929–1999" (PhD diss., University of Basel, 2010), 88–93. The quotations from Ligue leaders are from Yéré, 90.

with the second, the Community. From this complex structure and the necessity of presenting itself to the exterior as a solidaristic unity, comes the necessity to constitute an entity: that of the *French Republic and the Community*. . . . In the name of this ensemble, only one nationality may be conferred: it cannot be different from French nationality. However, it cannot be French nationality only, for then the other Member States would have a basis for organizing their own regime of nationality. It is appropriate, therefore, that the common nationality be the *nationality of the French Republic and the Community*.[68]

Here was the sole nationality to be recognized within the Community—not that of the French Republic, but not that of the Member States.

The rules governing nationality would be set by the institutions of the Community. A non-national seeking to be naturalized could submit the case for investigation to a Member State, but the final say went to the President of the Community, and any court cases arising would go before the justice of the Community. As for the alternative hypothesis, "To accept the plurality of nationalities in the interior of the Community supposes that each state possesses its own international juridical personality. The states would probably be led to claim in this optic an enlarged participation in foreign policy, special consular representatives for their nationals, and the possibility of issuing passports."

But if this report was categorical about the unity of nationality, it was more open about citizenship: "Citizenship is the expression of the nature, of the enjoyment, and of the exercise of civil and political rights. It is regulated by Article 77 of the Constitution, which specifies that there exists only one citizenship of the Community. The expression does not exclude the existence of citizenships particular to Member States." Since each state determined *how* civic and political rights would be exercised within its territory, it made sense to consider that each state had its own citizenship. One could see Community citizenship "superposing itself over the particular citizenships of the states." Community citizenship meant, then, that someone resident in, say, Senegal, even if a citizen of Côte d'Ivoire or of metropolitan France, could exercise the same rights as a Senegalese. But Senegal, as an autonomous state, could decide the specific contents of political participation—for all citizens. In conclusion, community nationality was unique, community citizenship superposed on the citizenships of

[68] Secrétaire Général de la Communauté, "Aspects internationaux de la situation juridique de la République française par rapport à la Communauté," 29 January 1959, FPR 103, ANF.

Member States.[69] Nation and state, nationality and citizenship were thus not congruent.

Other opinions also held them to be incongruent, but in different ways. The heads of government of the Members States of AEF issued before the meeting of the Executive Council a joint declaration that "the *ressortissants* of a Member State of the Community have the nationality of that state." The Directeur des Affaires Politiques smugly told his colleagues in response, "The Member States of the Community (other than the French Republic) not having international competences or a personality recognized in the law of nations, the formula is perfectly empty and lacks any significance in the law of nations [droit des gens]."[70]

Mamadou Dia put in his views too, addressing them to the High Commissioner in Dakar in January: "There will be no nationality of the Community, in the sense in which the word is habitually used. There could only be the nationalities of the Member States (Senegalese, Dahomean, French). Naturalization in these conditions would be an act under the competence of the states, individuals being nationals of this or that state, and citizens of the Community."[71] Officials in Paris dismissed his argument.[72]

Dia's views were carefully considered. He had asked for and received an opinion from a leading French jurist, P.-F. Gonidec. Gonidec wrote that nationality and citizenship should not be confused. Up to 1946, most people overseas were French nationals but not French citizens. The 1946 constitution brought the two together, but not quite: inhabitants of the overseas territories were citizens of two different sorts, depending on personal status, and inhabitants of the Associated States were citizens of the French Union, not of France. Then he made an argument that ran counter to what the Community Secretariat's jurists were saying: the Community was not a state, and since nationality was a relationship of people to state, there could therefore be no nationality

[69] "Note relative à la nationalité et à la citoyenneté dans la Communauté," 1 February 1959, FPR 103, ANF; Directeur des Affaires Politiques, Ministère de la FOM, "Note pour M. le Secrétaire Général pour la Communauté, à l'attention de M. Plantey," 16 January 1959, FPU 215, ANF; "Nationalité et citoyenneté," enclosed with Affaires Politiques, "Note pour M. le Secrétaire Général pour la Communauté," 16 January 1959, 940167/14, CAC. Two French jurists later argued that under the Constitution of 1958 there existed "local citizenships," but they had "remained unorganized." Roger Decottignies and Marc de Biéville, *Les nationalités africaines* (Paris: A. Pedone, 1963), 25.

[70] Directeur des Affaires Politiques, Note pour M. le Secrétaire Général, 24 January 1959, in response to declaration of 17 January 1959, FPU 215, ANF. The Sudan made a similar argument to that coming from the states of the AEF. Conseil exécutif, Projet d'ordre de jour, 3 February 1959, FPR 105, ANF.

[71] Président du Conseil to High Commissioner, 5 January 1959, VP 133, AS.

[72] Directeur des Affaires Politiques, Note pour M. le Secrétaire Général, 26 January 1959, FPU 215, ANF.

of the Community. Gonidec asserted that a state had to be "politically organized," but the Conseil exécutif, meeting intermittently, was more "a sort of club" of prime ministers than the organ of a state; the Senate of the community discussed legislation but did not make it. And since the Member States were outside the French Republic, they could not have French nationality any more than Community nationality. Nationality was not mentioned among Community competences, so by default it must be a matter for Member States. He acknowledged that the Member States were not sovereign and that they did not provide diplomatic services, but he insisted—citing the examples of the Commonwealth, protectorates, and trust territories—that full sovereignty was not necessary to define nationality. To the objection that a single nationality would enhance the cohesion of the Community, he replied that a common citizenship served that purpose. He concluded that nothing in the Constitution of 1958 stood in the way of the Member States having competence in matters of nationality. The formula should be "a citizenship common to all nationals of the Member States of the Community, multiple, different nationalities depending on the state."[73]

The record we have of the discussion of nationality at the meeting of the Conseil exécutif, 3 and 4 February 1959, is an incomplete and largely illegible handwritten record. It records Léon M'ba of Gabon saying, "a single French citizenship and each state its own nationality." De Gaulle stated, "one citizenship, that of the Community . . . externally, the nationality of the Community." Debré spoke of "nationality of France and the Community." Dia insisted on "nationality of the state," but Apithy stated, "only one nationality, agreed."[74] We do not know how a decision emerged from this clash of opinions, but the official record of the outcome states, "There exists within the Community only one nationality, which is that of the French Republic and of the Community. In conformity with Article 77 of the Constitution, there is only one citizenship of the Community. The states are competent to determine the particular conditions of access to certain elected offices or certain public functions."[75]

The Secretariat set about trying to implement the decision. The French Ministry of Justice would handle naturalization applications,

[73] P. F. Gonidec, "Note sur la nationalité des ressortissants des États membres de la Communauté," written for the Government of Senegal in preparation for the meeting of the Conseil exécutif, 2–3 February 1959, VP 133, AS. French officials noted that Gonidec had changed his mind; he had argued in November 1958 that there was only one nationality. "Note sur la nationalité et la citoyenneté des ressortissants des États membres de la Communauté," 20 May 1959, FPU 215, ANF. The issue was considered further within Dia's office: "Projet: organisation de la Communauté," 3 January 1959, VP 131, AS.

[74] Notes on session of Conseil exécutif, 3 February 1959, FPR 105, ANF.

[75] "Relevé des décisions adoptées en Conseil exécutif de la Communauté au cours de la réunion de 3 et 4 février 1959," FPR 103, ANF.

which the President would have to approve. Member States could prepare dossiers, but not make decisions. The Community would have to approve any Member State legislation on nationality. States had to respect "the essentials of citizenship, such as the exercise of political rights," but they had some room for maneuver, for example in giving their own citizens privileged access to public employment or the exercise of some professions.[76] Passports would state that the bearer's nationality was "de la République française et de la Communauté."[77]

Nevertheless, in April Mamadou Dia was arguing for recognition of multiple nationalities, insisting that "the best jurists" were on his side and that "one can accept inside a community where reciprocity of civic rights is completely operative, a diversity of nationalities that translates the multiplicity of associated values."[78] At the July meeting of the Conseil exécutif, held in Tananarive, Madagascar, Modibo Keita made clear Africans' unhappiness with the idea of a single, French, nationality. Part of the problem was a question of dignity, and part of it was practical. Without recognized nationality, African Member States had no place in international organizations, including some, such as the UN's Economic Commission for Africa, in which Africans had a specific interest apart from those of "France."[79] Debré was not ready to change his mind, but recognized the political problem. The transcript of the meeting describes him as linking the unity of foreign policy with the singularity of nationality, but admitting that "there is a problem and he proposes that a technical committee meet to examine it. It was so decided."[80]

[76] "Note relative à la réunion du 25 mars 1959 concernant le problème de nationalité, and note sur la nationalité et la citoyenneté de la Communauté," by Alain Plantey, nd [1959], FPU 215, ANF. By May, officials were worrying that a single nationality might require a single form of compulsory military service—which they did not wish to impose—so the possibility of a more subtle approach started to creep in. "Note sur la nationalité et la citoyenneté dans la Constitution," from Ministère de la Justice, 30 May 1959, FPU 215, ANF.

[77] "Conférence du 23 avril 1959, avec M. Gaudart, sous-directeur de la règlementation intérieure," FPU 215, ANF.

[78] Speech of investiture to Assemblée législative of Senegal, 4 April 1959, reprinted in Sénégal, *La nation en construction*, published by Secretariat d'État à l'Information, à la Presse, et à la Radiodiffusion de la République du Sénégal, on occasion of meeting of Conseil exécutif, Saint-Louis, 11 December 1959.

[79] There was also the question of Member States' relations with their non-Community neighbors. Senegal wanted to have direct relationships, but its lack of international status made that technically impossible. Office of the Vice-President, "Note au sujet des Relations avec les États voisins," nd [summer 1959], and Dia to de Gaulle, 22 April 1959, VP 131, AS; Minister of Foreign Affairs to High Commissioner, Dakar, 18 August 1959, AOF/Dakar/49, ADN; Note for the President, nd [ca. July 1959], FPR 105, ANF.

[80] Record of meeting of Conseil exécutif, 7–8 July 1959, FPR 105, ANF. The Secretary General considered multiple nationalities to be a confederal notion and he opposed moving to confederalism via "an apparently secondary question like nationality."

Keita reported on the meeting to the Council of Ministers of Mali, "Nationality gave rise to impassioned debates between Debré and me. Happy intervention of Tsiranana. Question will be studied anew." But he added a discouraging note about the Conseil exécutif in general: "The leaders of the governments do not have the courage of their opinions in plenary session. It is depressing. General de Gaulle is conciliatory, tries to arrange things. Debré bridles him through his intransigent nationalism. In these conditions, the Community cannot survive apart from the total abdication of autonomous states."[81]

Debré reciprocated Keita's perception of intransigence. He feared a "crisis" in the Community. Privately, he wrote to de Gaulle that Keita was a "resolute adversary" of France, frequently sparring with Houphouët-Boigny, not immune to communist propaganda. However, by August Debré's views on nationality were opening up. He thought some African states had the depth of experience to lay claim to nationality, but others were more problematic. Most important, he now realized that the meaning of nationality was not so clear-cut after all and needed a fuller airing among African and French leaders:

> Apart from independence, the word "state" supposes contents of which he has not always been conscious. This is how the problem of nationality is posed, in a manner that is confused but will soon become clear. Neither Madagascar nor Senegal, to take two examples, can be considered to be states without a past, and, because of this fact, the reclamation of a Malagasy or Senegalese nationality already comes forth. It is necessary to pay attention because the problem of nationality automatically poses the problem of a certain international presence. These are seriously grave questions and it is necessary not to treat them lightly.

The tensions over nationality were part of the problem France was having, adapting to the new structures it had created: a Community secretariat responsible to the President instead of the old Ministère de la France d'Outre-mer, changes in personnel, uncertainty among old colonial hands about how to deal with states that were now autonomous. The French government needed, Debré thought, much closer contacts with "black ministers," especially the prime ministers of the states.[82] France, not just the emerging African states, had to learn how to live in a postcolonial situation.

African leaders' desire for recognition of their states as nations was one of the problems that had to be solved. A "working group" of the

"Note relative à la nationalité et à la citoyenneté dans la Communauté," 3 July 1959, FPU 215, ANF.

[81] Transcript of meeting of Conseil de Ministres, Mali, 20 July 1959, FM 37, AS.

[82] Debré, letters to de Gaulle, 3 August 1959, 2DE 29, MD.

Community Secretariat met and came up with a report in early August. This report, and a meeting chaired by Debré on 5 August, was the basis for a note prepared for Debré and de Gaulle reexamining the question that had supposedly been decided in February. One option was that Community citizenship be "superposed" over the citizenships of the Member States. Each state could define certain political and public rights, and any Community citizen could exercise those rights in that state. Community citizenship would affect the coverage of social, commercial, and tax legislation, although the note did not specify how. All citizens would enjoy "a privileged regime whatever solution is adopted in regard to nationality."

The note acknowledged that even those states that had expressed a preference for federalism over confederalism "demand 'multinationalities' within the Community." The allusion was clearly to the Côte d'Ivoire of Houphouët-Boigny, who advocated a Community that was both federal and multinational. Hence the second option: to give each territory "full liberty" to determine the rules for acquisition and loss of nationality. Fully vesting nationality in the states would have important implications under international law, including how states were represented externally. It entailed a new conception of the Community and perhaps could be seen as a step toward independence. The third option was in between: let each state define its own nationality, but with effect only within the Community. The nationality conferred by each state would automatically confer the nationality of the Republic and the Community. The rest of the world would see only "la nationalité de la République française et de la Communauté." Some measures would have to be taken to prevent "flagrant discords" regarding the conditions of acquisition and loss of nationality. There would be a passport for the community, but underneath the designation of the bearer as a national of the Republic and the Community would be a mention of the specific nationality of the bearer's state. The file even contained alternative mock-ups of how such a passport might look. Perhaps, the working group told de Gaulle and Debré, the third option would satisfy the states' desire to have their own nationality but preserve the international status of French nationality.[83]

The Conseil exécutif, meeting on 10 and 11 September 1959 in Paris, agreed to appoint a committee of experts to find a way to reconcile "the personality of the states and the assurance of the cohesion of the Community . . . based on the principle of a common nationality of the French Republic and the other states of the Community

[83] Report of "groupe de travail, sur les questions de la citoyenneté et de la nationalité dans la Communauté," 5 August 1959, FPU 215, ANF; Note, 5 September 1959, transmitted from Debré to de Gaulle, 5 September 1959, FPR 102, ANF; "Note pour M. le Président de la Communauté," 6 November 1959, FPU 215, ANF; *Le Monde*, 2, 6 August 1958.

superposed on the nationalities of each Member State." The General Secretary of the Community, Raymond Janot, told a press conference that the Council "recognized the need to respect, on the one hand, the growing national sentiment within each state and, on the other hand, the unity of all members of the Community in regard to relations with the exterior." De Gaulle acknowledged "the evolving character of the Community."[84]

In effect, two versions of a multinational community were being talked about in the fall of 1959—one for superposed nationality, the other, just put forward by Mali, for national independence softened by a confederal relationship with France. Even as the idea of the Community as a multinational entity became a discussable subject, Mali's leaders had their doubts about any version of Community nationality. Modibo Keita reported to his Council of Ministers after the September meeting of the Conseil exécutif that "everyone agrees" about a common citizenship of the Community, but there had been—again—"animated debates" about nationality. Debré had spoken in favor of the double system: multiple nationalities recognized within the Community "and a common external nationality." He went on to say, "Of course the representatives of Mali do not agree with this formula, which tends to deprive the states of any international personality." Finally the Conseil exécutif had decided to confide the study of this question to a special committee.[85]

But, Keita reported, things had gone further. De Gaulle had indicated his willingness to work toward a multinational "ensemble." Keita and Dia had been more specific: they wanted a "multinational confederation," and they told the meeting that they were ready to start the process of "transfer of competences." Dia pointed out the danger of "external influences that would be brought to bear on African states to push them toward secession." But there was disagreement among Africans on such a move. François Tombalbaye of Chad and David Dacko of the Central African Republic called the Mali position "demagogic." De Gaulle, according to Keita, was conciliatory, hoping that "the evolution of the Community takes place without passion." De Gaulle acknowledged to Keita the demand for independence via a transfer of competences but warned him of "the fragility of states" and

[84] Summary of decisions made at meeting of Conseil exécutif, 10–11 September 1959, FPR 104, ANF; "Synthèse politique concernant les États membres de la Communauté," September 1959, 5AG 1/16, ANF; *Afrique Nouvelle*, 18 September 1959. In October, a Secretariat "draft convention between the French Republic and the Republic of Senegal on nationality" used the plural to refer to "nationalities in the Community." The draft, dated 24 October 1959 (in FPU 215, ANF), is covered with cross-outs and handwritten changes; it was not acted on.

[85] Transcript of meeting of Conseil de Ministres de la Fédération du Mali, 19 September 1959, FM 37, AS. The Council approved Keita's handling of the controversy.

the "difficulties that would confront them in becoming independent." Keita replied, according to his report to his ministers, that "Mali had very seriously prepared itself for independence and that it was ready to take it."[86]

Mali's demand for a discussion of the transfer of competences—the substance of sovereignty—had been stated. It would be made formally the next week. Meanwhile, the issue of nationality came out in public, through the Sudanese party newspaper *L'Essor*:

> The Conseil exécutif evades the question in deciding to appoint a committee to resolve it while preserving the unity of the Community at the external level; to put it clearly, for the notion of nationality one tends to substitute that of citizenship and the operation will end up with a nationality of the Community. This will be, in the most beautiful manner, the suffocation of the personality of the states. It is a sign of the strangulation of the evolution of the Community toward the superior form of Associated States. The independence of states requires the existence of their own nationality and above all the existence of a personality the recognition of which cannot be exclusively within the Community and cannot be confused with the personality of a department.[87]

The reason the French government changed positions on the multinational nature of the Community was most likely its worry that all the states might go further and seek full international recognition of their sovereignty. But African leaders were still far from a consensus on how or whether they should strive for national independence.

Michel Debré wrote in his memoirs that the September meeting had left him with a sense of malaise in Africa. That some African countries, including Guinea, Togo, and Cameroon, were becoming independent put pressure on the others. He claims to have asked himself at the time, "This Community, desired by France, is it not a sort of prolongation of the colonial fact? Is not international personality the tangible sign of independence?" He claims to have asked de Gaulle to consider "this external form of sovereignty which is direct representation in the United Nations." He asked, "What does our policy of so-called internal autonomy signify, when it leaves heavy financial burdens on France and in compensation for influence hardly altered

[86] Mali, Conseil des Ministres, 19 September 1959, FM 37, AS.

[87] *L'Essor*, 18 September 1959. The High Commissioner in Bamako later commented that the Sudanese were particularly keen to "manifest or safeguard in all domains, including the common ones, the full sovereignty of the Sudanese Republic." High Commissioner, Bamako, to President of Community, telegram, 3 December 1959, Bamako/Ambassade/12, ADN.

by the new institutions deprives our territories and their leaders of the honor and joy that affirmation of an international personality represents?" De Gaulle, he wrote, was silent for a time, but then agreed that "our institutions and our community regulations are not appropriate." He wanted to allow further change without coming to "a rupture."[88] Debré seems to be claiming more prescience than he likely had, but the evolution in official thinking over the course of the year reflects these considerations. We will return to the questions of Community and independence as they played out, but meanwhile the French government was trying in earnest to solve the nationality problem.

Following the September meeting, a Committee of Experts was duly appointed. Meanwhile, the government was rethinking not just its position on nationality in the abstract, but its relationship to Mali. Just a few months previously, the new Mali Federation had been excluded from the Conseil exécutif on the grounds that it was Senegal and the Sudan that had the status of Member States. But now, in October, de Gaulle's counselor, Alain Plantey, argued the opposite position. Mali, he wrote, was in the process

> of forming a federal state and has effectively constituted one.... Mali has the attributes of a state: its territory is unified and belongs, in a general way, to the same geographic and climatic zone. Its population, although ethnically diversified, is by and large of the Muslim religion. It has its own government, its own legislative assembly, and its own justice; it has a flag. Mali has the structure of a centralized federal state; Senegal and the Sudan find themselves vis-à-vis Mali in a juridical situation comparable to that in which the federated states of the USA find themselves vis-à-vis the federal state.... The personalities specific to the Republic of Senegal and the Sudanese Republic tend to be effaced and dissolved into the personality of Mali.... The Federation of Mali, therefore, considering the facts of the last six months, has the attributes of a state and can be recognized as such.[89]

The "state" question was being steadily transformed as Mali *acted* like a state. It was becoming less and less plausible for France to insist that a national personality could exist only at the level of the Community.

Amid all this uncertainty, the French government, pulling back from its insistence on the undivided Frenchness of the Community, was trying to turn the nationality question into a juridical issue. The issue was for now in the hands of a committee chaired by Henri Battifol, law professor from Paris, with representatives of eleven Member States

[88] Michel Debré, *Gouverner. Mémoires 1958-1962* (Paris: Albin Michel, 1988), 326–27.
[89] Note by Plantey for de Gaulle, "Note au sujet de la nature juridique de la Fédération du Mali," October 1959, AOF/Dakar/108, ADN.

as well of relevant ministries and the Secretariat of the Community, plus additional jurists. The government's new thinking about the basis for a solution was already clear in the terms of reference given to the committee in early November: "a common nationality of the French Republic and the other states of the Community superposed on the nationalities of each Member State."[90]

It is apparent from a note circulated within the Secretariat just before the committee's first meeting how much the government had been influenced by the protests coming from African leaders: "The states have manifested the desire to possess their own nationality which appears to them to concretize their accession to autonomy and mark recognition of their new dignity. This sentiment was from the beginning particularly lively among the Malagasy and the Senegalese and Sudanese." The note also admitted that there was a "juridical basis" to the states' claims of "a conception of the Community with a confederal tendency. According to the governments, ever since the referendum of 28 September 1958 the states have had the object of independence and international sovereignty. They renounced it of their own free will in adhering to the Community and ceded to the Community certain enumerated competences but not their nationality, which was not included in the delegated matters."[91] Once again, politics had made a difference. The government of the Fifth Republic had reversed itself under pressure from leaders of the Member States.

The committee of experts met on 16 and 18 November 1959. The jurists decided that superposed nationality was "technically viable. . . . The specific nationalities would constitute the base. Conferred by the states, they would automatically entail: (a) the common nationality, whose effects will be felt externally where it would benefit indistinguishably all the nationals of the Member States; (b) the common citizenship, whose attributes would be attached to those entitled to it in all states of the Community."

Nowhere in the Community would any of its members "feel a foreigner." Moreover, the fact that there was only one citizenship of the Community did not exclude each state from having its citizenship, "the citizenship of the Community being a superposed citizenship." The rights referred to in the preamble to the Constitution would be considered inviolable in all states of the multinational Community. States could have their own rules about voting and officeholding, but those rules would apply to all citizens of the Community resident in the state on the same basis as to nationals of that state. All citizens

[90]Conseil exécutif de la Communauté, Comité des Experts chargés de l'étude des problèmes de la nationalité et de citoyenneté, meetings of 16 and 18 November 1959, Rapport, FPU 215, ANF.
[91]"Note relative à la nationalité," 14 November 1959, FPU 215, ANF.

would be eligible for civil service jobs anywhere, except that in "exceptional and temporary" circumstances a state could give priority to its own nationals "in order to ensure their social advancement"—what Americans call affirmative action. All citizens would enjoy "freedom and inviolability of the home, freedom of conscience and religion, freedom of expression and association. . . . The nationals of the Community would be free to enter and sojourn in the territory of all Member States on presentation of the national identity card provided by a state." The property of all citizens of the Community would be safeguarded, a clause that guaranteed protection to nationals of the French Republic doing business in Africa. States could set their own rules for naturalizations, but only within a certain spectrum to ensure a modicum of consistency, given that acquiring the nationality of any state automatically entailed Community nationality and citizenship. Passports would show the common nationality and on a lower line the "state of origin" of the bearer. The committee wanted a copy of declarations to the état-civil of each state to go to a representative of the Community.

The outside world would see a single nationality—of the Republic and the Community—and France would participate in international organizations as a single entity. Its diplomats would watch over all its citizens traveling abroad. But among themselves, the Member States would see themselves as part of a multinational Community.[92] The most controversial question within the committee was whether a state could expel a citizen who was the national of another state. Some thought such a provision negated Community citizenship, others that under tight judicial control it could serve a legitimate purpose.[93]

The report of the experts was to go before the Ministers of the Republic, but when it came in (rather late) the agreement among experts and the Member States was so complete that it went directly to the Conseil exécutif, meeting in Saint-Louis du Sénégal on 11 and 12 December 1959. There, de Gaulle, Debré, and the heads of the Member State governments approved the report. The experts would continue

[92] Comité des experts, Report, and transcript of discussions of 16 and 18 November 1959, FPU 215, ANF. Committee members voiced concern with the fact that the multiple nationalities were internal to the Community and that the Community as such had no international existence. Plantey argued that because of this situation, the Republic "serves in regard to the foreign world as the juridical support of the Community" (16 November). In this reasoning, neither the Member States nor the Community had sovereignty in an international sense, while a unit that existed within the Community (the French Republic) acted toward the outside world as if it were sovereign, while claiming to represent the entire French Community.

[93] The expulsion argument came about after the High Commissioner in Chad wrote the President (6 November 1959, FPU 215, ANF) about his concern regarding the presence of about thirty thousand non-Chadians, some from French territories, some not. He wanted to be able to naturalize some of them and get rid of the rest.

to work on the details, and an accord would be prepared for all Community members to sign that would make clear the rights of states to govern their own nationality consistent with only general rules.[94] De Gaulle, having recently agreed to call former territories, previously colonies, by the name of "state," had now conceded that the French Community would be multinational. Even more remarkably, superposing the nationality of the Republic and the Community on top of these different nationalities meant that a bureaucrat in Dakar or Abidjan could decide that someone had the right to live in Marseille, attend a French school (or a Dahomean school), and seek a job in the French civil service.[95]

The leaders of Member States could now claim that they had defended the dignity of the states as well as their autonomy. African leaders had obtained what they wanted. But it was not clear that all of them wanted it any more.[96]

Justice, Rights, and Social Progress in a Multinational Community

Nationality questions were among the many that might come before the judicial institutions of the Community. The draft accord that experts came up with after the December 1959 Executive Council meeting proposed a multilateral agreement that "any citizen of the Community enjoys public freedoms on the territory of each state of

[94] Note for the President, 3 December 1959, summary of decisions at meeting of 11–12 December 1959, FPR 103, ANF; Note for the President, 8 December 1959, FPU 216, ANF; Prime Minister to Minister of Justice, 14 January 1960, 940167/14, CAC. The expulsion question was again the only real source of controversy in the Conseil exécutif. Houphouët-Boigny wanted to be able to expel French communists; others wanted similar rights. Although French officials thought that expelling one's own nationals was contrary to international law and a threat to Community solidarity, Debré was willing to concede the point, conditional on judicial controls, but a final decision was put off to a future meeting. Record of Conseil exécutif, meeting of 12 December 1959, and note by General Secretary for President, nd [late 1959], FPR 113, ANF.

[95] Such a decision-making process was precisely what French police officials in Senegal had termed "unthinkable" a few months earlier. They did not like the fact that "non-metropolitan police, often poorly informed of our customs, and who might also have—in all honesty, we admit—opinions sharply divergent from ours on a national scale" would investigate nationality applications. Commissaire de Police, Section des Renseignements Généraux, Dakar, to Chef des Services de la Police de la Région du Cap-Vert, 1 June 1959, Dakar/Ambassade/482, ADN.

[96] One post-Saint-Louis dissent came from Mali's Minister of Public Works, Amadou Aw: "The Community was not a state, even less a nation. . . . We want to remain ourselves, and safeguarding our personality does not allow us to accept French nationality on the international level." Article in L'Essor, quoted in Direction des Services de Police du Soudan français, "Synthèse mensuelle," December 1959, Bamako/Ambassade/1, ADN.

the Community under the same conditions as the nationals of that state."[97] The Conseil exécutif had already adopted a report on "control of justice" that stated that it was the Community's duty "to ensure that the ideals of justice and freedom to which the peoples of the Member States have subscribed are continuously respected in both legislation and in juridical decisions." An implication of layered sovereignty was that liberties should be protected at a level above the give-and-take of ordinary political life.

Yet the Community also recognized that justice was plural. Different people had different personal statuses, whose regulation was a Member State competence. States could organize their own court systems. The Executive Council hoped to reconcile the plural and universal dimensions of justice by putting in place a Community appeals jurisdiction focused on basic rights and ensuring good relations among states. It wanted the Community to assist efforts to recruit and train magistrates throughout the Member States, including for service on appeals courts.[98]

Togo and Cameroon had already moved toward autonomy and independence at a pace ahead of that of the former overseas territories, and Togolese and Cameroonian nationalities had just been recognized. That posed a series of questions. Would their people lose whatever rights they had had as citizens of the French Union—an entity that no longer existed? Or would they—if their governments so chose—come into the looser category of Community? Such issues would have to be negotiated with Togolese and Cameroonian governments.[99]

As more and more people moved about in the Community, exercising their "droit de libre circulation" (right of free movement), they took with them rights and expectations of access to the institutions and resources of whatever state they were in, particularly the metropole. Officials in Paris, as they had in 1946, affirmed to each other that people from all the states of the Community had "a right to equal

[97] "Projet d'accord de la Communauté relatif à la citoyenneté de la Communauté et aux nationalités dans la Communauté, élaboré par le Comité des experts lors de sa réunion des 21 au 25 janvier 1960," sent by Lami to President of Government of Mali, 10 February 1960, AOF/Dakar/221, ADN. The committee that drafted this accord was also chaired by Battifol and included representatives of the Member States. Its report is in FPU 218, ANF.

[98] Dossier of meeting of 4–5 May 1959, adopting (with some changes) the "Rapport sur le contrôle de la justice," of the Comité des Ministres (Justice), 20 March 1959, FPR 103, ANF.

[99] Note by Directeur des Affaires Politiques, 23 March 1959, 950165/13, CAC; Secrétariat Général de la Communauté to High Commissioner, Fort Lamy, 9 May 1959; "Note relative à la nationalité," 14 November 1959, FPU 215, ANF. France was quite conscious that the eyes of the UN were on the trust territories. The revolt of the UPC had been put down, but officials were aware that the "moderates" they were backing needed something to show for their cooperation.

access to schools established in the whole of the Community and to the civil service as long as they meet the specified conditions without any discrimination on the basis of their origin." Michel Debré made a point of saying to the Conseil exécutif that "it is essential that the Africans and the Malagasy can accede to the cadres of the French Republic." Otherwise, "common citizenship would lose much of its significance."[100]

Mobility, meanwhile, implied that people would be exercising different sorts of personal rights outside of their places of origin. Personal status was to be regulated by Member States, but "any citizen of a Member State of the Community has the right to have his personal status applied as it is defined in his state of origin." In principle, a court in one state would have to apply rules of marriage or inheritance based on laws and customs specific to another state.[101] Member States were in charge of the état-civil, but as we have seen (chapter 5), the French government had bequeathed to the territories a very limited capacity to record life events. Ministers acknowledged the need to share information about individuals on a Community-wide basis, but did not get very far in figuring out how to do so.[102]

With state regulation of social life now the concern of Member States, Mamadou Dia appointed study committees to look into the problem in regard to Senegal. The committee on social welfare and family life included educators, health officials, representatives of unions, representatives of university students, a philosopher, and others. Dia was personally aware of the difficulties that ensued as aspirations for equality and progress met up with desires to recognize tradition and respect different modes of life. The transcript of the initial meeting of the social committee contains this intervention by Dia:

> In front of the enthusiasm of a member of the Committee who proposed the abolition and prohibition of polygamy, the President reminds us that the desire for progress must not prevent us from being very prudent and from making propositions that the country could vote for. There is another point, he said, to which

[100]Note for Minister from Affaires Politiques, 4 December 1959, 940161/219, CAC; Record of meeting of Conseil exécutif, 11 December 1959, FPR 113, ANF.

[101]Working document for meeting of ministers of justice of the Community, May 1960, FPU 215, ANF; "Rapport du Comité des Compétences sur la délimitation des compétences à l'intérieur du Domaine Commune," including Secrétaire Général to Foccart, 23 February 1959, FPR 102, ANF.

[102]Report of meeting of Ministres de la Justice des États de la Communauté, 10–14 May 1960; "Projet d'accord de communauté relatif à la citoyenneté de la Communauté et aux nationalités dans la Communauté," nd, FPU 215, ANF; "Note à l'attention de M. le Président de la Communauté," 26 June 1959, FPR 107, ANF; "Note d'information sur la réunion des Ministres de la Justice de la Communauté," 14 May 1960; "Note sur les conflits des lois dans les États de la Communauté," May 1960, FPR 122, ANF.

I want to draw your attention. It regards the protection of the African woman, let us say the Senegalese woman. You can feel my embarrassment to talk about this subject, I who am polygamous, I do not have the intention to turn our institutions upside down, but in spite of it all, I believe that in this domain there are some things to be done, some innovations to bring to it.[103]

Dia was discussing an institution that in much of French discourse epitomized the otherness of Africans. But one of those "others" was now the head of a government that had the authority to act on questions of marriage, justice, and nationality.

Saint-Louis and Beyond

The issues that had occupied—and often divided—African and French leaders in the aftermath of the Constitution of 1958 came together in the meeting of the Conseil exécutif held in Saint-Louis in December 1959. There was considerable uncertainty about the atmosphere that would prevail.[104] Mali's demand for a transfer of competences had been made, and at the same time the report recommending multiple nationalities with a superposed Community nationality was submitted for approval. De Gaulle not only met with his fellow heads of state while in Senegal, but also spoke to the Federal Assembly of Mali. He was gracious, if a bit wistful. He told Malians, "Independence, you take the responsibility and France accepts it with all its heart." France was ready to conduct "the federal state of Mali and the states of the Sudan and Senegal that compose it to a new situation." He preferred the expression "international sovereignty" to "independence" because no one was truly independent. "But things being as they are, the world being what it is, once again Mali will have to choose the direction it will take. . . . There is no international reality that is not first a national reality. It is necessary that a state that plays its role in the world takes the routes that allow it to do so, and those routes are that it first constitutes itself as a state." He concluded, "Vive le Mali! Vive le Sénégal! Vive le Soudan! Vive la France!"[105]

[103]Comité d'Études pour les Problèmes Sociaux, "Séance inaugurale commune des Comités d'études auprès de la Présidence du Conseil," 10 October 1958, VP 91, AS.

[104]Senghor, Dia, and Keita met with de Gaulle for two hours a couple of weeks before the Conseil exécutif meeting. *Paris-Dakar*, 27 November 1959.

[105]*Allocution prononcée à l'Assemblée fédérale du Mali par le Général de Gaulle, 13 décembre 1959* (copy in Bibliothèque Nationale de France); *Afrique Nouvelle*, 18 December 1959. In the meeting of the Conseil exécutif itself, de Gaulle stated that demands for the transfer of competences would be dealt with "without rupture, without separation." Transcript of meeting, 11 December 1959, FPR 113, ANF. On de Gaulle's evolving position on the Community after conversations with African leaders, see Debré, *Gouverner*, 328.

Mamadou Dia welcomed the negotiations that would lead to Mali's independence, but he made clear that his long-standing concerns were still with him:

> We are perfectly aware that we live in the time of great ensembles that can alone guarantee a real independence worthy of the name. We know that it would be pure folly for small states to pretend to organize the world on their own. Apparent and ephemeral success of seesawing and blackmail could only lead to catastrophe, that is to say the establishment of a very narrow economic dependence stifling the country and hidden under the shell of a pretend independence with an international facade.[106]

Senghor, as he saw Mali en route to independence, called for a "reinforced Community." He praised de Gaulle at length, fitting him into a grand narrative of liberation in which France transcended its enslaving and colonizing past. As he had in calling for citizenship before the Assemblée Nationale Constituante in 1946, Senghor cited the decree of 16 pluviôse An II (1794)—"the greatest act of political revolution that the world has ever known"—that had proclaimed ex-slaves in French colonies "free citizens, that is to say equal to and fraternal with the citizens of France." De Gaulle, he did not need to say, would not reverse such an act, as Bonaparte had done. Senghor concluded, "Long live de Gaulle! So that France and Mali live in freedom, but fraternally united!"[107]

As we have seen, it was at this meeting that the new policy on multiple nationalities was approved by the Conseil exécutif. By then, the decision was an anticlimax, although it would presumably apply to the rest of the Member States and to Mali until its independence was complete. The drama of the meeting was Mali's application for the transfer of competences. In the end, the Conseil could report that there had been agreement both to set out the rules for a common citizenship and multiple nationalities in the Community and to open negotiations over the independence of Mali.[108]

Houphouët-Boigny was apparently seething with resentment at the Saint-Louis meeting. The High Commissioner wrote Debré that "Houphouët returned from Saint-Louis dismayed" at de Gaulle's positive response to Mali's demands. He had thought himself close to de Gaulle, had served as a minister in his government, had shared his preference for a federal over a confederal structure for the Community,

---

[106] Text of speech by Dia, Saint-Louis, 12 December 1959, VP 138, AS.
[107] *Afrique Nouvelle*, 18 December 1959.
[108] *Paris-Dakar*, 14 December 1959.

and here his rival Senghor was having his federation and his vision of a Franco-African future consecrated by the General himself.[109]

Even as Mali moved toward independence on the last days of the 1950s, its leaders insisted on the necessity of remaining part of a "grand ensemble" that would link Africans to each other and to France. The leaders of France had already given up their control of the budgets and policies of the individual territories, their insistence on the indivisibility of the state, and the exclusiveness of the French nationality. They had conceded to Africans the very name of "state" and the right to determine if and when any state could leave the French Community.[110] Whether the Community was itself a state, an extension of the French state, or an ensemble of states was not certain or fixed. Most French and African leaders seemed to agree on one point: they wanted to remain together in some kind of community.

African leaders from AOF knew perfectly well that other colonies were turning into independent nation-states. The possibility of sharing in their status and joining them in international organizations was becoming attractive. But most of French Africa's political elite still wanted to follow another path, and now Mali's leaders were seeking the benefits of national recognition without a sharp break with the more inclusive French Community they had helped to shape.

The elites of European France were thinking about alternatives too. But while questions were being raised about the costs and benefits of overseas territories—especially in the face of the claims to social and economic equality made in the name of citizenship—most leaders still felt that France's stature depended on its presiding over a large ensemble. France too was trying to have things both ways: limiting its financial and other responsibilities while asserting that it would maintain the "participation of France in the uplift of peoples," as Pierre-Henri Teitgen put it in 1959.[111]

[109] High Commissioner Yves Guena to Debré, 11 January 1960, 2DE 73, MD. De Gaulle's advisor Jean Foyer states that Houphouët-Boigny was, after the Saint-Louis meeting, "ulcerated, he felt a veritable emotional wound." *Sur les chemins du droit*, 126, 158. Jacques Foccart noted the same reaction (*Foccart Parle*, 199).

[110] Djibo Bakary notes in his autobiography that what de Gaulle conceded in December 1959—a multinational confederation of free states—was not very different from what Bakary's political party, Sawaba, had advocated in July–September 1958, bringing on the French administration's campaign to eject Sawaba from Niger's government. Djibo Bakary, *"Silence! On décolonise…": Itinéraire politique et syndicale d'un militant africain* (Paris: L'Harmattan, 1992), 268.

[111] Pierre-Henri Teitgen, "La participation de la France à la montée des peuples," in Semaines Sociales de France, *La montée des peuples dans la communauté humaine: Compte rendu in extenso* (Paris: Librarie Gabalda, 1959), 313–36. The Semaines Sociales was a forum of socially minded Catholics. Its 1959 edition was addressed by politicians like Teitgen and Louis-Paul Aujoulat, the anthropologist Georges Balandier, and the economist François Perroux.

African leaders wanted to preserve the breakthrough of 1946, when the people of French Africa had acquired the rights of the French citizen and the possibility of exercising those rights anywhere in the French Union. As people moved around in increasing number within French African territories or to European France, those rights were given concrete meaning in the lives of ordinary people, and particularly in those of wage workers, who had the protections of the Code du Travail as well as the right of "free movement." But such movements were creating tensions as well as connections, as became apparent with the riots against Dahomeans and Togolese in Côte d'Ivoire in October 1958. There were nevertheless, at the end of 1959, reasons to believe that French citizenship was a useful and attractive notion to a significant portion of French Africans.

Throughout 1959, leaders from Sudan and Senegal were caught up in the hopes and difficulties of building the Mali Federation. Senghor, Keita, and Dia insisted that the nation was African, not Senegalese or Sudanese. It was intended to be a model that would attract new members. But other leaders from the former AOF did not share in this effort even if they agreed that some form of community was preferable to the isolation of the nation-state. Political parties had organized themselves within territorial boundaries, drawing on a variety of social connections and building their own networks across rural and urban spaces. Both the RDA and the PRA and its successor the PFA tried to mobilize across French Africa, but neither was able to turn the appeal of "African unity" into an effective, unifying political force. The RDA itself had split over the federation question. As the about-faces of Upper Volta and Dahomey in the midst of the effort to found the Mali Federation suggest, such a question could give rise to tension within a given Member State.

When Mali tried to put into practice its call for an African federation, its opponents made explicit the division by forming the Conseil de l'Entente. African leaders were finding horizontal solidarity—of Africans with each other—difficult to achieve. And while they agreed in principle that the relationship of France and Africa should be a relationship of equals, the reality was that France was rich and Africa was poor, and Africans' hopes for the resources they needed for economic and social development depended on continued—if restructured—forms of vertical solidarity. In December 1959, in Saint-Louis du Sénégal, it became clear to all concerned that French rule in Africa was coming to an end. But the relationship of independence and community—within and beyond Africa—was still in question.

CHAPTER 8

BECOMING NATIONAL

For all the political dynamism evident in late 1959, it was clear that none of the major actors would be able to obtain what he most wanted. De Gaulle had sought a federation with a strong center, a single citizenship and nationality, and a commitment from all those accepting the new constitution to remain in the French Community. He ended up with a structure that was neither federal nor confederal, with multiple nationalities, and with territories that could exercise their right to independence whenever they chose to do so. Houphouët-Boigny had seen his own version of federalism slip away during constitution writing, as his French colleagues realized that a federation of equal states would give Africans more power over the federation as a whole and a stronger position to demand resources than was acceptable to French voters. The Constitution of 1958 had put African political leaders in a position that was both awkward and powerful, an unsatisfying compromise between autonomy and subordination, but with an option for secession that enabled Member States to pose new demands.

Just as the strong federalism of de Gaulle and the egalitarian federalism of Houphouët-Boigny eluded their authors' grasp, so too did Senghor's most desired goal, an African federation. Only one territory had proved willing to join Senegal. As French West Africa split into two blocks, what held them together was not their Africanness but their relationship to France. If that relationship were to evolve, each faction would have to take the initiative in bilateral negotiations. Mali took the lead in such a negotiation, even as it kept trying to realize its own federalist ambitions.

The compromise that the PRA had reached in Cotonou in July 1958— as inconsistent as its call for independence and continued confederal relations with France seemed to be—became the framework in which negotiations took place. The constitutional provisions for a Member State to declare independence by vote of its assembly and a referendum were set aside. Mali instead demanded that the "competences" of a sovereign state be transferred to it. France would amend its own constitution to allow an independent state to remain in the Community—now referred to as "la Communauté renovée" (the renewed Community)—and Mali would agree to remain within it. De Gaulle's insistence on an all-or-nothing choice between independence and community had produced a bitter break with Guinea and a community structure that lasted only a year. After all the political maneuvering and juridical imagination that had gone into defining community and nation in 1958 and 1959, their significance would be reconfigured yet again in 1960.

The Mali Federation and the French Community: Negotiating Independence

The best hope for keeping the French Community together—and some of the wiser heads in Paris knew it—was the Mali Federation. If Mali could make a go of it, more territories might see the virtues of membership in a large ensemble. There were two immediate problems. One was Mali itself: whether a federation of two states—and of these two states in particular—was viable. The second was Houphouët-Boigny, who did not want Mali to become the vanguard of Africa's future. Once Mali had taken the initiative in seeking independence, he and is allies in the Conseil d'Entente had to follow suit.

The short history of the Mali Federation gets us to the heart of the problem of postimperial sovereignty. Up until 20 August 1960, the model of multilayered sovereignty—territorial, federal, Community— was an available option, if a difficult one to achieve. Afterward such an option was all but eliminated.

The December 1959 meeting of the Conseil exécutif of the Community in Saint-Louis du Sénégal had been a cause for celebration: the leaders of Mali had placed their demand to negotiate independence via a transfer of competences, and de Gaulle had accepted the demand. But even in December there had been signs of tension.

French intelligence had been hearing both before and after the Saint-Louis meeting that Modibo Keita and Madeira Keita had expressed hostility to a "common citizenship" in meetings with Senegalese colleagues. Just after the meeting, conflict had erupted between Dia and Modibo Keita. Keita reportedly claimed at a PFA meeting that he had agreed with de Gaulle on the independence process "the knife on the throat." He was thought to have said, "I do not see the need to maintain community institutions," including the Senate and common citizenship. He left his Senegalese colleagues "stupefied." French officials in Dakar thought that Mamadou Dia "revealed himself to be the last defender of the Community." Senghor and others tried to play down the significance of the term "common citizenship" while leaving open the possibility of negotiating its substance with the French government.[1] Perhaps Keita was still annoyed at the Conseil

[1] Telegram, labeled very secret, from High Commissioner, Dakar, to President of Community, 8, 17 December 1959, FPR 231, ANF; Report of informant on PFA meeting in Dakar, 18–20 December 1959, FPR 106, ANF.

exécutif for refusing to recognize Mali in July, hence his militant assertion of Mali as the sole focus of national identification. Modibo Keita may also have been reacting to the accusations by François Tombalbaye and David Dacko at the Conseil exécutif in September that the Malians had acted demagogically in asking for independence. In December, Keita allegedly told a party meeting that he could not abide sitting in the Conseil exécutif next to "ignoramuses like Léon M'Ba and Tombalbaye."[2]

But behind the aggravations of working in Community institutions were issues that had been simmering, especially among Sudanese. Conscious of their common border with Algeria, they did not want to get drawn into France's wars that they opposed.[3] The 1958 Constitution had given the Member States some voice in defense policy, but the ultimate decision was the President's, and the President was still prosecuting the war in Algeria.[4] The question of "common" institutions or common citizenship would be a key point of difference at the negotiations, but the very process of negotiation would redefine the issue: bilateral negotiations, not multinational institutions, were becoming the new reality.

The negotiations between France and Mali began on 18 January. The Malian delegation was led by Madeira Keita, the most adamantly nationalist of the leading politicians and now the Interior Minister of the Mali Federation. Senghor, Dia, and Modibo Keita were directly involved as well. At stake were the "competences" associated with sovereignty that would be transferred to Senegal and Sudan, some of which would immediately be ceded to the Mali Federation. Mali might conclude bilateral accords with France that would establish the terms of association, whether inside a "renewed community" or perhaps simply as treaties between two sovereign states.

One side of the argument over nationality and citizenship was articulated in a position paper for the PFA written by one of the party's

---

[2]Bureau de Synthèse, Renseignements, 28 December 1959, Dakar/Ambassade/419, ADN. See chapter 7 for the clashes of September. Keita's references are to François Tombalbaye of Chad, David Dacko of the Central African Republic, and Léon M'Ba of Gabon.

[3]Direction des Services de Police du Soudan français, "Synthèse mensuelle de renseignements," August 1958, Bamako/Ambassade/1, ADN; L'Essor, 14 September 1959; Keita, cited in transcript of meeting of Conseil exécutif, 21 March 1960, FPU 1408, ANF.

[4]The Conseil exécutif agreed in February 1959 that "the Army is one, whatever the origins and mode of recruitment of its constitutive elements." It decided in March that "the citizens of the states will participate in military service," but agreements among the states would decide the terms of that participation. "Rapport du Comité des Compétences sur la délimitation des compétences à l'intérieur du domaine commun" (after Conseil exécutif meeting of February 1959), Bamako/Ambassade/12, ADN; Extract from decisions of Conseil exécutif, 2–3 March 1959, VP 131, AS.

stalwarts, Léon Boissier-Palun—lawyer, former President of the Grand Conseil de l'AOF, son of a French administrator and a Dahomean woman, and a close ally of Senghor. Malians would soon have their own nationality and their own citizenship, he pointed out. But many people lived in and contributed to Mali who were not originally from there, and he worried about the dangers of "a dangerously xenophobic movement for the self-realization of the new state itself, inconsistent with the principles of a soundly led decolonization and of African solidarity and unity necessary to the advancement of Africans." He cited the example of the British Commonwealth in which "above local nationalities there exists a citizenship of the Commonwealth that correspondence to the maintenance of community ties." He was referring to the Nationality Act of 1948, which had defined such a citizenship, superposed—to use the term of French jurists—on the nationalities of the dominions and Great Britain (including its colonies). In France since 1946, the distinction between citizens of different personal statuses had been "steadily emptied of its political content." He took note of the recent agreement that the Community would show one nationality to the outside world but acknowledge multiple personalities of states within it. Nobody in the Community would be a foreigner in another state of the Community. Mali's citizenship, he argued, should not negate Community citizenship, for maintaining mutual rights among the states was essential to the "goals defined by the PFA and the pursuit of the regrouping of francophone African states that Mali considers fundamental."[5]

But Modibo Keita, as we have seen, wanted Malian citizenship to stand on its own, and he did not want to participate in Community institutions. In that circumstance, treaty negotiations would have to define whatever rights different nationals would have in each other's states. Or perhaps the negotiators could discuss the substance of mutual recognition of rights without using the name of Community citizenship. The Malian position was not fully agreed upon.

French negotiators, whatever they wanted, had to adapt to the positions that were uncertainly emerging from their Malian counterparts. Their shifting positions emerge from the papers of Jacques Foccart, presidential counselor and from March 1960 Secretary General of the Community, who was following the negotiations closely. By early 1960, French policy toward Africa was being directed by the General Secretariat of the Community, under the President's office. It fended off efforts to put Community affairs under the control of the Prime

[5] Report on "condition des personnes dans la perspective de l'indépendance du Mali," by Boissier-Palun, enclosed High Commissioner, Dakar, to President of Community, 8 December 1959, FPU 198, ANF. On Commonwealth citizenship, see Kathleen Paul, *Whitewashing Britain: Race and Citizenship in the Postwar Era* (Ithaca, N.Y.: Cornell University Press, 1997).

Minister or perhaps a new ministry. Africa policy was becoming a fiefdom under the direct control of the President and his Monsieur Afrique, Foccart.[6] For now, the Secretariat had charge of negotiating with Mali.

Although many of the position papers are not dated, one can infer where they come in the process. What French negotiators initially wanted for the postindependence Community was rather like what they already had. Preparing for negotiations, French officials thought that Mali's main motivation for independence was to have a seat in the UN. France was prepared to insist that "Mali must recognize that the President of the Republic is, by law, President of the Community; it must accept the existence of one citizenship of the Community; it must participate in a Council presided over by the President of the Community and whose essential attributions are foreign policy, defense, and certain aspects of economic policy. Its participation in the Senate and acceptance of the jurisdiction of the Court of Arbitration are less essential."[7] A section on nationality and citizenship made clear that French leaders wanted the treaty "to give [us] without saying so explicitly the best possible treaty of establishment for French people, to guarantee autochthonous elites a privileged situation in France, and to affirm in front of the world the cohesion of the Community." Mali would have its own nationality and would decide who would possess it; Malian nationality would automatically confer Community citizenship. But officials realized that superposed *nationality*—accepted only the month before—was no longer acceptable to Malians; they wanted to be Malians. An internal document of the Secretariat noted as early as 5 January 1960 that "the dispositions relative to superposed nationality should be abandoned." But Community *citizenship* would confer public and political rights, public liberties, the right to vote, access to public employment, private rights, the benefits of social legislation, and a nondiscriminatory tax regime. If Community citizens were assimilated to the nationals of the territory in which they resided, there would be little pressure on them to opt for one or another nationality. Officials thought that allowing Malians to "recover French nationality at any time" would actually encourage them to remain Ma-

[6]Jean-Pierre Bat, *Le syndrome Foccart: La politique française en Afrique, de 1959 à nos jours* (Paris: Gallimard, 2012), 106–7, 118–22, 128. Foccart's predecessor as General Secretary was Raymond Janot, who had played a key role in writing the Constitution of 1958.

[7]Papers in folder labeled "premiers entretiens avec les représentants du Mali," nd [mid-January 1960], FPR 106, ANF. Another paper in the same folder [nd] asserted (misleadingly), "This desire for external sovereignty takes pride of place over the desire to exercise, alone and above all at their own expense, the competences now in the hands of the Community."

lians, whereas opting for French nationality might exclude them from Malian political life.[8]

Another paper from early January added that loss of French nationality "would mark a very clean break with France" and mean that people would have to be allocated to one side or the other: "As soon as one starts to distinguish among nationals and put them into categories who will be treated differently, an arbitrary element intervenes: one is led to classify individuals according to certain norms." But now, Malians *were* French citizens; they were not choosing to secede from France but to acquire international sovereignty with France's consent. Should they be given a choice to retain a citizenship that was already theirs or to opt for the citizenship of the new state their representatives were creating for them? If the choice were given to each individual, French officials worried, some might choose to remain French out of "a reflex of security," but then their "loyalty will always be suspect" in Mali. And if they chose to abandon French citizenship, might they not resent France for making them do so? The problem was particularly acute for the people who were "the most French": métis, *originaires* of the Quatre Communes, civil servants in State Services, former soldiers, Malians who had renounced their personal status and chosen to come under the French civil code. The most pro-French of Malians would lose influence in the government of Mali; their place would be taken by "the most uncultivated and least evolved elements whose attachment to France is much looser and who can more easily be attracted to other political philosophies." One solution might be to allow, indeed to encourage, dual nationality. It was not the usual thing to do, but it was legally possible, and the British Commonwealth had allowed something of the sort after 1948.[9]

Such a move would not solve a major problem: what about citizens of the French Republic who wanted to remain in or move to Mali? Malian nationality—since it was new—would not be as attractive to them as French nationality would be to Malians. One had to use a different approach. The rights of French citizens in Mali would have to be protected by a "convention d'établissement"—a bilateral accord that would give French citizens in Mali the same rights as Malian nationals, and vice versa. Here we get to a point that sounds remarkable from today's vantage point, but was not in its time. Allowing Malians to keep French nationality—including the right to settle in France—would add no new obligations to France but would enhance French

---

[8]"Réunion du sous-groupe de travail, institutions de la Communauté au Secrétariat de la Communauté," 5 January 1960, FPU 1731, ANF; Annexe II to papers on "premiers entretiens," in FPU 1731, ANF.

[9]"Note relative à la nationalité," 9 January 1960, FPU 1731, ANF.

influence on independent Mali. "It seems on the contrary in the interest of the Republic to maintain close ties with the states, which will thus remain open in a privileged way to its citizens. Maintaining the French nationality of the nationals of the new states would translate juridically the desire of the French Republic and of Mali not to consider each other as foreign states."[10] The best minds of the Secretariat of the Community did not want independence to mean that France and Mali would become wholly separate states. They were still searching for a formula that would maintain at least overlapping citizenships.

And what of the Community as a constitutionally defined entity, with its own institutions? "The accession to international sovereignty of the Mali Federation must not bring about the dislocation of the Community. The loss of this notion would call into question the cohesion of French-speaking Africa."[11] Officials were thinking that the Conseil exécutif would continue to function by bringing together heads of state to work on matters of common interest, including foreign affairs and defense. But the Conseil could no longer "direct" Community affairs and might be compatible with independence only if decisions were unanimous. Some officials were admitting by mid-January that "centralized authority, even under a collegial form (Conseil exécutif) as it is now, appears hard to justify." They thought the Senate would stay in place, but would have to be restructured. It was particularly important to maintain the "community character" of justice "in regard to nationality and citizenship" and in criminal appeals. The Community Presidency, officials admitted, "is not strictly reconcilable with the new character" of the Community, but they wanted the French President to keep at least his "honorary and symbolic" role. Officials at least recognized that the "new Community" would be "contractual."[12] Yet contractual cooperation, officials wanted to believe, was not the same as a neat separation of two sovereign entities, Mali and France. They instead hoped that the new version of community "appears to facilitate the reconciliation of the notions of sovereignty and Community."[13] But even that cooperation would turn out to be less than hoped for; the March meeting of the Conseil exécutif would turn out to be its last.

Defense was a particular concern. "Our goal is to conserve for France essential strategic resources in Africa, indispensable for the se-

[10] Ibid.

[11] "Note" in folder on "Affaires étrangères," nd [January 1960], FPU 1731, ANF.

[12] Undated paper, January 1960, papers on "problèmes concernant la structure de la Communauté . . . le Conseil exécutif . . . le Sénat . . . le contrôle de la justice," 28 and 29 December 1959, and Secrétariat Général, "note pour le Général," 13 January 1960, FPR 106, ANF; "Note sur le Conseil exécutif et les comités," 16 January 1960, FPU 192, ANF.

[13] "Note sur le Conseil exécutif et les comités," 16 January 1960, FPU 192, ANF.

curity and for her place in the world. We must equally ensure the cohesion of the Community and the defense of its African territories." But officials knew they had a problem, since independence would mean that each state was entitled to use its resources as it wished and could refuse to participate in decisions it did not make. Officials worried about the "'balkanization' of defense," all the more so since not every Member State had moved toward independence and France needed to "bring about the cooperation in a single organization of states of different status." They slowly seemed to be coming to grips with the fact that the days of "there is only one defense" were over and that "cooperation" would be the new watchword. But France had to offer something to Mali—such as support for Mali's police, gendarmerie, and "a small national army." Officials hoped that Malians would want France to assume the burden of defense against external enemies.[14]

So also with justice. From Dakar, the High Commissioner warned that Mali was likely to ask for full control of justice, and he feared that such a move would not only complicate the adjudication of nationality but open the door to totalitarian politics: "In effect, the suppression of any route of recourse at the level of the Community risks to render inoperative the anticipated reciprocity of rights in regard to nationality. It risks above all to discourage definitively all political opposition and to favor antidemocratic and totalitarian tendencies that constitute the permanent temptation of young African states and Mali in particular."[15] In Paris, worry about losing control over justice was linked to a particular concern: that an entirely Malian judicial system would become less secure for persons and property of French citizens working or doing business in Mali. A Secretariat paper from January pointed to the danger of a transition from French to Malian justice: "One can think that the system would be much closer to customary type jurisdictions than to the French jurisdictions that France has tried to implant in these countries over several decades. This would be the immediate ruin of patient efforts to lead the people of these territories to a modern and liberal conception of justice to which an active minority has already rallied, not to mention the probable repercussions on the security of French citizens and their enterprises in this state." These officials wanted to keep—at least for a time—appellate jurisdictions in French hands and for France to play a transitional role in

[14]"Note sur les problèmes de la défense de la Communauté," nd [February 1960], and "Note sur une organisation nouvelle de défense de la Communauté," 8 January 1960, FPU 1735, ANF. P.-F. Gonidec pointed out that common defense was not just a matter of state, but an advantage to citizens from anywhere in the Community who could aspire to make a career and move through the ranks of the French military. P.-F. Gonidec, "La Communauté et les relations internationales," *Penant* 70 (1960): 151–53.

[15]High Commissioner (Lami) to President of Community, 22 January 1960, FPU 192, ANF.

lower jurisdictions while Malian magistrates were being trained. But they did not seem to have full confidence that they could get their way, for the document put particular emphasis on the hope that Malian jurists were inculcated with French ways: "The originality of French juridical conceptions, shared by nationals of the new state, would constitute a durable and solid link between the two states. . . . This close collaboration must permit Mali to put in place modern justice, of French conception, a non-negligible element of French influence, that will allow French citizens and enterprises to continue to exercise their activities in Mali and develop them under the best conditions."[16] Juridical assimilation and personal linkages were the slender hope on which the personal and property rights of French citizens in an independent African country might depend—whether those rights were specified under a common citizenship or by bilateral agreements.

But, as we have seen, Malian leaders—and particularly the head of the Federation's delegation, Madeira Keita—did not want common citizenship, common institutions, or common justice. By March, French negotiators were realizing they were not likely to get what they hoped for. Mali made clear that it would not participate in a Conseil exécutif and if there were any kind of senate, it would have a consultative role only. The Malians would not accept the proposed Arbitration Court, although there was some possibility that they might accept some form of arbitration for interstate disputes.[17] Malians were putting sovereignty first. Cooperation would remain a possibility, but common institutions making decisions about a set of common affairs would not.

Nor was there any consensus on Community citizenship. The Malian delegation "does not accept the existence of a citizenship of the Community." The Community Secretariat saw the Malian position as "an imperialist, pan-African tactic, based not on the notion of citizenship in its French conception, but on the desire for regrouping of West African states around the notion of Mali." To call the quest for an African nation "imperialist" was hyperbolic; French officials were reacting to Malian hopes to expand into something like the African federation Senghor had long advocated. But the Malians did not want to abandon all of the benefits of Community citizenship. They ap-

[16]Note relative à la justice, 11 January 1960, FPU 200, ANF. For more on the French government's anxiety on the security of the property of French citizens in an independent Mali, see Ministry of Foreign Affairs, Note pour M. Jacques Roux, 22 January 1960, Direction des Affaires Africaines et Malgaches, Mali, 2518, ADLC.

[17]Debré to de Gaulle, 19 March 1960, Notes for President of the Community, 21 March 1960, FPR, 106, ANF. Secretariat officials thought Mali did not want Community institutions that included both independent states (as Mali was about to become) and "autonomous states," so only "very light superstructures" would be possible for the Community. Note for President, nd [March 1960], FPU 1408, ANF.

parently agreed that the inhabitants of "all states of the Community could not be considered foreigners vis-à-vis each other." The French fallback position was to "reduce the multilateral accord on citizenship to a strict minimum."[18]

But even such an accord was not a sure thing. "In a more general way, it [the Mali delegation] does not agree to conclude a multilateral convention, but only a Franco-Malian convention of establishment." Such a convention—on conditions of the rights of citizens in each other's country—was a more ordinary part of interstate relations than the notion of Community citizenship.[19]

The French government was trying to salvage something. "In this situation, the French delegation, anxious to maintain citizenship of the Community, proposed a system that reconciles the existence of this notion and the establishment of certain bilateral relations between the states." States, both those that had become independent and those retaining their current degree of autonomy, would sign a minimal common agreement. It would provide all Community citizens "the guarantee of the enjoyment of public liberties; the right to enter and leave; access to courts; the right of reparations for damages incurred as a result of public catastrophes; protection against discrimination." Anything else would be left to bilateral agreements.[20]

The Foccart Papers include cryptic handwritten notes from the meeting of negotiators on 18 January and 19 March. In the earlier meeting, Debré laid out the original French line: there should remain the Presidency of the Community, a "council of leaders of the states, common citizenship." Senghor agreed on the need for coordination and "that we will not be foreigners." Dia said arrangements should be "contractual." Debré mentioned the common citizenship of the Commonwealth and repeated, "Malians and French people are not foreigners." Senghor replied, "Agreed on the fundamentals, facts and advantages. Problem of naming and form." Another Malian negotiator, Mahamane Haïdara, added, "We think that there will be a Malian nationality and citizenship. End of citizenship of the Community." Debré kept trying: "Citizenship of Commonwealth superimposed on nationality and citizenship." Modibo Keita replied, "Agreed on the contents, disagree on the term," and Senghor added, "Question of vocabulary linked to psychological problem." The subject changed, but it was clear from the negotiating session that common citizenship—so much a live topic in December—was a dead one in January. Yet both sides wanted something other than a neat separation of citizenships.[21]

[18]Notes for President of the Community, 21 March 1960, FPR 106, ANF.
[19]"Note sur les problèmes de citoyenneté et d'établissement," 19 March 1960, FPR 106, ANF.
[20]Ibid.
[21]Handwritten notes on meeting of 18 January 1960, FPU 1732, ANF.

By 19 March, Prime Minister Debré was ready to admit that Community citizenship "cannot be maintained." But he wanted some way of ensuring "rights and fundamental guarantees" in both states and he did not want former members of the Community to be "foreigners" in each other's countries. He sought, therefore, a "middle measure," part bilateral, part multilateral accord. Senghor said, "We can accept an agreement on reciprocal rights," and Modibo Keita added, "Convention of establishment is a good agreement." Dia seemed to want something broader, referring to the "principle of multilaterality." Debré acknowledged, "Your agreement is bilateral and contractual." Keita suggested that anything multilateral should be open to Africans generally, not just to the states of the Community. Debré promised to work on a text.[22] It was clear by then that Debré's text would have to be closer to what the Malians wanted than to his own initial position.

The story was similar with the other contentious issues: the Malians did not want whatever persisted of the Community to have much of an institutional armature. There was now pessimism in the Secretariat of the Community. Mali did not want the representative of the French government to Mali to have any special status. French officials feared that "this staking out of a position tends to eliminate the notion of Community, so that relations between France and Mali are bilateral."[23]

Negotiations indeed focused on a bilateral "accord d'établissement." The draft accord that was emerging in late March included a "good number of dispositions that could have found a place in a convention on common citizenship, the negotiation of which Mali has refused."[24] The draft agreement emphasized reciprocal rights for citizens residing in each other's territory and affirmed both parties' adhesion to the universal declaration of human rights, specifically mentioning protection of "cultural, religion, economic, professional or social activities, individual and public freedoms, such as freedom of thought, conscience, religion, culture, opinion, expression, and association, as well as trade union rights." Most important, perhaps, "the nationals

[22]Handwritten notes on meeting of 19 March 1960, FPU 1732, ANF. At the March meeting of the Conseil exécutif, Debré seemed to be saying that one could have the contents of Community citizenship without the name. Transcript of meeting of 21 March 1960, FPU 1408, ANF. Meanwhile, the principle of reciprocity was being used to weave connections among states. Cameroon, now independent, signed an agreement with the French Republic providing for equal treatment of Cameroonians in the Community and for Community citizens in Cameroon. Mali accepted that the agreement would apply to its "ressortissants." High Commissioner, Dakar, to Government of Mali, 15 January 1960, President of Mali to High Commissioner, Dakar, 24 February 1960, FM 159, AS.

[23]"Note sur l'état des négociations avec la Fédération du Mali," 28 March 1960, FPR 106, ANF.

[24]Note, "Project de convention franco-malienne d'établissement," 24 March 1960, FPR 106, ANF.

of each contracting party can enter freely into the territory of one and the other party, travel there, establish residence in their place of choice and depart from there."[25]

French officials were worried that such an accord would offer less protection than common citizenship to French citizens trying to live, work, or do business in Mali. The Malians were willing to accept that nationals from other states of the Community could exercise the same rights as Malians when in Mali, but they were insisting on an escape clause to allow either party to privilege its own nationals in conditions "imposed by the economic and social situation of one of the parties." At this very time, the French government was developing a related program in an effort to woo Muslim Algerians, notably by insisting that at least a minimum number of posts in the French civil service be designated for "français musulmans d'Algérie."[26] But with Mali resisting a Community-level court able to enforce rules on citizenship and nationality, French negotiators worried about unilateral evocation of this clause: "This disposition is clearly dangerous for our nationals residing in Mali."[27] That Mali might refuse a French citizen the right to open up a business in Mali worried the French negotiating team more than the danger of Malians turning up in Marseille.

Even if there was little chance of getting Malians to agree to a community-wide citizenship, French officials took the trouble to write a draft agreement, as if it would be agreed to by all the "republics," listed by name: France, the Central African Republic, Congo, Côte d'Ivoire, Dahomey, Gabon, Upper Volta, Madagascar, Mauritania, Niger, Senegal, Sudan, and Chad. It combined provisions of the 1958 constitution with the agreement on nationality from December 1959: "There exists only one citizenship of the Community; all citizens are equal in rights and have the same duties." The file contains a copy of part of this document, with the names of states other than France and Mali cut out and with the word "citizen" replaced by "national of the

<hr />

[25] Draft agreement, 15 March 1960, FPU 201, ANF. The draft attempted a general description of how each state would handle nationality: "The nationality of each of the Contracting High Parties can be attributed to birth, either by filiation or birth in the territory; it can be acquired after birth under the law or by naturalization as accorded by the public authority." But the key phrase of the proposed agreement came earlier: "The conditions of attribution or acquisition of nationality are determined by the law of each state, taking into account the following dispositions." Draft agreement, 15 March 1960, FPU 201, ANF.

[26] Todd Shepard, "Thinking between Metropole and Colony: The French Republic, 'Exceptional Promotion,' and the 'Integration' of Algerians, 1955–1962," in Martin Thomas, ed., *The French Colonial Mind* (Lincoln: University of Nebraska Press, 2011), 298–323.

[27] Note, "Project de convention franco-malienne d'établissement," 24 March 1960, FPR 106, ANF.

High Contracting Parties."[28] By the end of the month, negotiations with Mali and Madagascar had pointed to a multilateral accord that would guarantee fundamental rights of "any national of a state of the Community" without saying anything about a common nationality or citizenship.[29] The notion of community citizenship was almost literally being crossed out.

The issue of the état-civil came up alongside the idea of reciprocal rights: Mali and France would keep track of births, marriages, and deaths of each other's citizens, wherever they occurred, and would furnish the information to the partner state. Since Mali's citizens might come under different personal status regimes, marriage arrangements would have to be consistent with the "law governing their status of origin."[30]

Meanwhile, the transfer of competences was being worked out between the two parties. Essentially all the typical functions of government were being transferred to Mali (with the fiction that they were first passing through the states of Senegal and Sudan). But the accords included transitory provisions that eased Mali into statehood. As the negotiations reached their conclusion at the beginning of April, an exchange of letters between Michel Debré and Modibo Keita and Mamadou Dia specified that as soon as the independence of Mali was proclaimed, the two parties would sign accords defining "the modalities of cooperation freely put in place between the French Republic and the Mali Federation within the renewed Community, as well as the multilateral accord on the basic rights of nationals of states of the Community, the convention of establishment and the convention on conciliation and the Arbitration Court."[31] Mali had made some concessions too—and it was willing to accept multilateral agreements and the court (it never came into existence) because it was doing so as an independent state.

Debré's letter of 4 April—accompanied by a letter from Keita promising that Mali would accept its terms as soon as it had independent

[28] "Accord de Communauté relatif à la citoyenneté de la Communauté et aux nationalités de la Communauté," nd [spring 1960], FPU 201, ANF. Mali was also talking with other former French states about establishment accords. See President of Mali to High Commissiner, Dakar, 24 February 1960, FM 493, AS.

[29] "Accord multilatéral sur les droits fondamentaux des nationaux des États de la Communauté," 29 March 1960, Dakar/Ambassade/512, ADN.

[30] Paper on negotiations on "État-civil," nd [early April 1960], FPU 201, ANF; "projet d'accord de coopération en matière de justice," 14 March 1960, FM 522, AS; Garde des Sceaux to Secrétaire Général de la Communauté, 10 March 1960, 950236/2, CAC. René Pleven and Paul Coste-Floret kept proposing to the Assemblée Nationale bills to systematize the état-civil in Africa long after France had the power to do so. Note for Minister from Services des Affaires Politiques, Bureau de Législation Civile et Pénale, 27 May 1960, 940161/220, CAC.

[31] Debré to President of the Government of Mali, 4 April 1960, FPU 1732, ANF.

stature to do so—said that nationals of either country would have "a privileged status" in the other. Debré added, "The representative of Mali have reserved their agreement on the expression citizenship of the Community." Several "transitory dispositions" stated that France would ensure diplomatic protection for Malians abroad and would represent Mali whenever Mali could not represent itself. French armed forces would continue their present missions, while France helped the Malians to put in place their own armed forces. Mali, at least for now, would remain in the franc zone, and agreements on economic regulations and cooperation would remain in force. Until appeals jurisdictions were established in Mali, appeals would go to the Conseil d'État and Cour de Cassation in Paris. But Mali would be the ultimate master of its foreign policy, defense policy, and economic relations. Both parties recognized the President of France as the President of the Community (although Malians would not participate in his election), and Mali agreed to participate in a "periodic conference of heads of state and heads of government" and had the possibility of sending a delegation to a "Consultative Inter-parliamentary Senate" made up of delegates from the parliaments of the respective states.[32] Along with the bilateral accords, Mali accepted a multinational agreement—signed by Mali, Madagascar, and the French Republic but open to other states of the Community—that carefully avoided the word "citizenship" but provided for reciprocal recognition of the rights of citizens of each state on the other's territory.[33] Neither the conference of heads of state nor the Senate would have any real power—and that was what Mali wanted.

France, meanwhile, was in the process of revising its constitution—which was rapidly becoming more its own—to allow Member States to remain in the Community even after independence. In the debates in the Assemblée Nationale that made the necessary changes, Debré all but admitted that France had faced tough negotiations and was accepting the minimal power of Community institutions and the necessity of amending its own constitution because that was the best it could do. Mali could simply have withdrawn from the Community. Debré acknowledged "the mutation of former colonial empires and

[32] Exchange of letters between Prime Minister of France and President and Vice-President of the Government of Mali (also referred to as Presidents of the Conseil of Sudan and Senegal), 4 April 1960, FPU 201, ANF; paper marked "secret," nd, accompanying Debré to President of the Government of Mali, 4 April 1960, FPU 1732, ANF; "Accord particulier sur la participation de la Fédération du Mali à la Communauté," 4 April 1960, Dakar/Ambassade/512, ADN.

[33] The agreements were reported in Le Monde, 14 April 1960. They were effective 22 June 1960, and the texts were published in Journal Officiel de la Fédération du Mali, 1 August 1960, 505–6.

the evolution of the continent of Black Africa."[34] Mamadou Dia, at the end of the negotiations, commented about his opposite number, "We are in a position to say that M. Debré changed completely in the last months. He understood us and now shows himself to be up to the situation in what concerns African affairs."[35]

Returning to Bamako, Madeira Keita told interviewers from the party newspaper *L'Essor* that his delegation had got what it wanted: "This independence is real. Mali, in a few weeks, will solemnly declare its independence. There will be a Malian nationality, a Malian citizenship; we will be masters of our foreign policy, masters of our foreign commerce. All these contacts will be consultative and only consultative." Mali could ask France to represent its diplomatic interests where it could not mount an embassy or send a delegation, but there would be no common foreign policy. Mali had decided to stay in the franc zone, but it could have its own currency if it so chose. It would have its own army, but with French help to build it.[36]

Madeira Keita went on to make clear that Mali's continued membership in the French Community was the choice of an independent state: "The French, for reasons that we all understand, hang onto the word 'community.' The essential, for us, is that this renewed community, this transformed community, is only relevant from now on to the relationship which independent Mali will establish with the French Republic." No Community institution could "make decisions." In a later speech, he made much of the bilateral nature of the negotiations: "We refused in the course of all negotiations to give the impression to the French delegation that we were dealing with the Community. We made them accept that we were dealing only with the French Republic."[37] Mali agreed—via a "very short" bilateral accord as an independent state—to participate in the "Communauté contractuelle," but Madeira Keita regarded this as little more than a promise to cooperate with France. And, lest anyone forget, he made it clear that while Senegal and Sudan had been Member States of the Community at the start of the negotiations, what had emerged from them was Mali,

[34]Assemblée Nationale, *Débats*, 10 May 1960, 727–28, 765, 771. Jean Foyer, Secrétaire d'État aux relations avec les États de la Communauté, claimed that there would be "a defense Community" and an "economic community," but only as long as Mali agreed to coordinate policies and allow common use of military bases. Ibid., 724–25.

[35]Intelligence report, 5 April 1960, Dakar/Ambassade/386, ADN.

[36]*L'Essor*, 8 April 1960. As of June 1960, there were twenty thousand Malians in the French army, many fighting in Algeria. The Mali government wanted as many as possible to join the Malian army, although many of them were serving France "because of career advantages." Comments of Dia and Tidiani Traore to meeting of Conseil des Ministres of Mali, 16 June 1960, FM 38, AS.

[37]*L'Essor*, 8 April 1960.

"since we decided that the nation is situated at the level of the Federation of Mali."[38]

L'Essor now contended, "What can be called the renewed Community today is nothing more than the ensemble of bilateral accords that have recently been signed plus acceptance of the principle of conferences of heads of independent states."[39] On the transformed nature of citizenship, the Sudanese newspaper had this to say:

> One has epilogued a lot about the notions of dual citizenship and dual nationality. . . . The accords are clear in this regard: there is no more dual citizenship than dual nationality. Mali will have its own nationality with its own citizenship, the only one that prevails for a Malian as much inside the Federation as outside, that is to say in regard to international law. . . . It was only accepted that a Malian, in France, will not be treated as a foreigner, and reciprocally.[40]

The real work was now being done by the establishment agreements. Malians still had the right of "free circulation" in France, where they would enjoy the same rights as French nationals. As we will see below, French police officials were not altogether happy with such a situation, but for now there was little they could do about it. And French citizens still had rights in Mali, including that of doing business. In both countries, rights now came under a bilateral treaty, not a constitution, and treaties can be renegotiated or repudiated.

Modibo Keita and Léopold Senghor, coming home from the negotiations, were gracious toward their French negotiating partners and particularly toward de Gaulle, but they made clear the fundamental nature of the break: Mali had achieved, said Senghor, "true independence." It was not an independence that had been offered. "It is we who will proclaim the independence of the Mali Federation. And France will be the first to recognize it." He hoped that other states would follow Mali's route. He added, "The Community, which ceased to be constitutional to become contractual, will be, as I like to repeat, a Commonwealth à la française." Keita concluded his remarks,

[38] Exposé of Madeira Keita on Franco-Malian negotiations, fourth conference of cadres de l'Union Soudanaise, 28–31 May 1960, Dakar/Ambassade/386, ADN. The copy of accord in Dakar/Ambassade/512, ADN shows that the agreement was indeed very short.

[39] L'Essor, 29 April 1960.

[40] Ibid. Modibo Keita had earlier remarked in the course of summarizing the negotiations, "Mali did not accept citizenship of the Community. The principle of reciprocity will be assured to French people in Mali and Malians in France." Mali, "Compte Rendu de la réunion d'information," 5 April 1960, Dakar/Ambassade/511, ADN.

"Vive la France. Vive la Féderation du Mali. Vive les Communautés des peuples libres [long live the Communities of free peoples]."[41]

Debré wanted to emphasize the past that had led to the present—a past of attachment rather than of colonization: "The sovereignty acquired [by Mali] is not and cannot be secession. The former connections if they disappear with a page of history give way to new relationships which, beyond cooperation, express the will to profit in common from the work of the former endeavor to animate the renewed community."[42]

Mali's independence would be celebrated on 20 June. Parallel to the negotiations of France and Mali were negotiations between France and Madagascar. For all the painful history of the latter relationship— the rebellion of 1947 and its repression—the Malagasy negotiators were not so negative about community citizenship or about attenuated forms of Community institutions.[43] Once the die was cast for the independence of Mali and Madagascar, it was clear that the states of the Entente would follow suit (see below) and so would those of AEF. The latter had talked briefly about federating, but it was soon clear that they would not—for the usual reasons of rulers guarding their territorial bases and in particular the richest of those territories, Gabon (like the Côte d'Ivoire), not wanting to share its wealth with poor neighbors.[44]

Tensions of Independence

Even before Mali's independence, tensions between the leaders of Senegal and Sudan were growing and efforts were being made to overcome them. Conflict between Dia and Keita had manifested itself after the December Conseil exéctutif meeting in Senegal. French officials in Dakar—even while negotiations were going on in Paris—thought that problems between the two states were being exacerbated by continued economic difficulties: rising prices, lack of breakthroughs in eco-

<hr>

[41] *Afrique Nouvelle*, 6, 20 April 1960. The newspaper explained the contents of the agreements in its edition of 13 April 1960: "Finally a multilateral convention, similar to that previously signed with Madagascar, looks ahead to a Malian citizenship next to a French citizenship. It did not create a citizenship of the Community but since the current convention remains open to other African states, it in a sense takes its place. Because of this, French citizens in Mali and Malian citizens in France will enjoy equal rights."

[42] *Afrique Nouvelle*, 6 April 1960.

[43] The Madagascar negotiations can also be followed in the Foccart Papers. See especially FPU 222, ANF.

[44] Note for President on evolution of the states of Afrique Equatoriale, 22 February 1960, FPU 1408, ANF. On the Entente around this time, see the note for the President, nd [March 1960], in FPU 1408, ANF.

nomic development. They thought that organized labor in the Sudan was pushing its leaders toward taking a strong, potentially centralizing, position on economic affairs. They distinguished between a "centralizing, totalitarian tendency in Sudan, federalist, liberal in Senegal."[45]

Neither side fit so neatly in an ideological frame as the report suggests, and the French view from Bamako was that Modibo Keita, considering that the time was favorable for negotiations with France and worried that tensions with Guinea and the Conseil de l'Entente could get worse, was anxious to achieve consensus. He told the High Commissioner in Bamako that one had to proceed toward unity "bit by bit," with support "from the base" and "general consensus." Another influential Sudanese politician, Jean-Marie Koné, was also anxious to act: "If African unity among our countries—balkanized despite us—is not accomplished in 1960, the chances of unity will be very slim, even nonexistent."[46]

But there were real difference in party structure and leanings, and these tensions emerged in meetings in April over the form of federal government was to take and who was to occupy which posts. Mali was a federation, not a confederation. The rest of the world would see it as a single unity, rather like the United States one report put it. There would be only one citizenship, one nationality. The competences of the federal state would have to be specified and consultations between the federal and the federated states frequent and intense. Revenue would have to be allocated to the federal and federated states. Malian leaders understood all this quite well; a conference in early April made progress on some issues, agreed to put off others.[47]

But even within the notion of federalism, there were differences in orientation. Dia and Senghor wanted a large autonomy for each of the federated states; they hoped such an approach would attract new members, whereas "a unified Mali of six and a half million inhabitants will appear as a partner with which it is difficult to federate in the eyes of the other states of West Africa, whose population varies between one and three million." Insisted Dia, "Mali must be a *federal state* with an additional characteristic: a *federating state*," not yet "perfect and finished."[48]

[45] Monthly Report by High Commissioner Lami, February and March 1960, Dakar/Ambassade/161, ADN.

[46] High Commissioner, Bamako (Jean Sicurani) to Foccart, 10 March 1960, FPR 234, ANF; High Commissioner, Bamako, to President of Community, 18 March 1960, telegram, Dakar/Ambassade/419, ADN.

[47] Monthly Report by High Commissioner Lami, April 1960, Dakar/Ambassade/161, ADN; Bulletin de Renseignements, 4, 21 April 1960, Dakar/Ambassade/340, ADN.

[48] "Note sur le problème de l'évolution institutionnelle interne du Mali, au regard de l'indépendance," in information report, 16 March 1960, Dakar/Ambassade/482, ADN.

The Sudanese wanted a more centralized federal government, with a strong, single executive. The Senegalese worried that the Sudan, with a larger population (four million vs. two and a half), would dominate a state if the electorate were treated as a single body; the Sudanese worried that too weak a center would give the government insufficient levers to effect economic reform. Although Dia, Senghor, and Keita all considered themselves socialists, the Senegalese were more intent on preserving their "vertical" connection to France and skeptical about the viability of a more immediate or radical alternative. Senegal's budget was over twice that of Sudan's despite the population difference; it contained the port of Dakar; its population was better educated; it had, in short, better advantages for participating in international commerce, including attracting investment from French and other sources. Although Keita's and Senghor's parties (affiliated to each other via the PFA) dominated the political landscape in their respective states, the US-RDA had absorbed its major rival and it was virtually a single party. Madeira Keita even published an explicit argument for the single party, claiming that there were no fundamental differences in interests to be represented, that the fight against colonialism required unity, and that multiple parties would foster ethnic conflict. Senegal, in contrast, favored the principle of multiparty politics and its leaders had considerable experience in making it work for themselves.[49]

At a meeting of the Comité Directeur of the PFA in April, there was conflict between the "hard" and the "soft," unitarists and federalists, Madeira Keita and Mamadou Dia.[50] The High Commissioner in Dakar thought the conflict at the 14 and 15 April meeting "very seriously calls into question the solidity of Mali."[51]

[49] Madeira Keita, "La partie unique en Afrique," *Présence Africaine* 30 (February–March 1960): 267–73, reprinted in *Présence Africaine* 185–86 (2012): 169–93. The basic points of difference between Sudan and Senegal are well spelled out in the existing literature. Guédel Ndiaye, *L'échec de la Fédération du Mali* (Dakar: Nouvelles Éditions Africaines, 1980), 103–18; William Foltz, *From French West Africa to the Mali Federation* (New Haven, Conn.: Yale University Press, 1965); Alain Gandolfi, "Naissance et mort sur le plan international d'un État éphémère: La Fédération du Mali," *Annuaire Français du Droit International* 6 (1960): 880–906. Some of the weak points of the federation were noted early on by *Le Monde* correspondent Philippe Decraene (15, 16 January 1960), above all the tensions inherent in a two-state federation.

[50] High Commissioner, Dakar, to Community, Paris, telegram, 15 April 1960, Dakar/Ambassade/343, ADN. The Commissioner regretted that in the midst of their arguments with each other, neither side had anything to say about the French Community: "has it already disappeared not just from preoccupations, but also from the vocabulary?"

[51] High Commissioner, Dakar, to Community, Paris, telegram, 4 May 1960, Dakar/Ambassade/340, ADN. *Le Monde* (19 April 1960) also noted conflict between those favoring "a flexible federation" and proponents of "a very centralized state." At the April meeting, decisions were put off and no communiqué issued.

The French government, having in early April reached agreement over independence with Mali, was worried. It is possible to argue that France wanted a divided Africa—easier to manipulate—but the evidence is that it did not. It had worse things to fear than Mali, and indeed the Secretariat was well aware that if Africans were in conflict with each other, the French Community was dead. In a meeting within the Secretariat of the Community in February 1960, "The General insists on the interest there is in the states—even if of different status—remaining grouped. We must, he said, encourage them and we must show a preference for those that remain in the Community."[52]

One danger was that if Mali split up, Sudan would then try to unite with Guinea. It might take a more engaged position vis-à-vis Algeria, with which it had a long common border. If such a leftist, anti-French alliance developed, it would have "for its first result to eliminate Modibo Keita from the first rank in favor of Madeira Keita." So Modibo Keita, the High Commissioner thought, had to follow "a prudent path. . . . I am persuaded that he will do everything to avoid the breakup of Mali, the exit of Sudan from the Community." What the French government hoped for was a Senegalese-style federation but one acceptable to the Sudanese. The Senegalese were also in an awkward situation because Lamine Guèye "deals in secret with the Sudanese," presumably in the hope of undermining Senghor. And French officials feared that Senghor was so attached to his federation that he would compromise too much: "The least solid element in Senegalese resistance is Senghor, always ready, in the name of 'négritude' to sacrifice reality to fiction, without forgetting his personal ambitions, notably, as of now, the presidency of the Federal Republic."[53]

The issues themselves between Sudan and Senegal were not unresolvable. There could be compromises on the degree of power allotted to the federal and federated components of Mali and over who would take what position. By mid-April there were reports that the Sudanese were backing away from their insistence on "a strong federal state" and were acknowledging Dia's argument that "a flexible construction" would be more effective in attracting other states to join.[54] French sources, in early May, alternated between predictions that the "breakup" of Mali was imminent and that the controversy "seems to be evolving toward an armistice." Modibo Keita accepted that a Senegalese would become head of state, while he would be head of

[52] Summary of meeting of 23 February 1960, FPR 119, ANF. Note the references previously cited to Dia as the potential savior of the Community.

[53] High Commissioner, Dakar, to Community, Paris, telegram, 5 May 1960, Dakar/Ambassade/340, ADN.

[54] High Commissioner, Bamako, to Community, telegram, 14 April 1960, FPU 1677, ANF.

government. Dia would be minister of defense—and the control of the army might be insurance against Sudanese domination. But what had been agreed upon was "a precarious truce."[55]

The conflict, French officials thought, had caused "antisudanism" to develop in Senegal. But efforts were being made to smooth things over: getting jurists from both sides to talk with each other about government structures, looking ahead to more conferences. The Senegalese thought that they had at least a tentative agreement for a system that would be relatively decentralized. Keita told interviewers that a "détente" had been achieved. A committee got to work on the constitution for the independent federation.[56]

The Sudanese party newspaper in mid-May made a point similar to that made by Dia in March: "we must be careful, in practice, not to crystallize the Nation at the level of Mali, so that we will be able to associate ourselves, if possible, with other states." The article noted that the leaders of West African states, "found it was very difficult, after the creation of autonomous governments [under the loi-cadre], to retrocede afterward a part of their power to a government above them. . . . If, from now on, we do not take care, African Unity, despite all the declarations that can be made, will be definitively broken and we will end up effectively with the dust of small states, among whom the Cold War will be transmitted with all the risks that entails." Party leaders seemed to be a stepping away from their centralizing version of federalism in the interest of the long-term goal of African unity.[57]

But the next step would be tough: the two sides had agreed that a President would be chosen before the end of August, and while they had negotiated that the President would be Senegalese, they had not agreed who that person would be. Rumors were that Lamine Guèye, perhaps with support from Sudanese, might contest Senghor's aspirations for the post.[58]

Both before and after Mali's formal independence on 20 June, the federation's cabinet—with posts carefully divided between Senegalese and Sudanese—met regularly and resolved a variety of issues collectively. The ministers managed to agree on 13 June on revisions to the

[55] High Commissioner, Dakar, to Community, telegram, 5 May 1960, FPU 1677, ANF; High Commissioner, Dakar, to Community, Paris, telegram, 7 May 1960, Dakar/Ambassade/340, ADN; Bureau de Synthèse in Dakar, Bulletin, 3 May 1960, FPU 1677, ANF.

[56] High Commissioner, Dakar, to Community, Paris, telegram, 8, 10, 14 May 1960, Dakar/Ambassade/340, ADN. Malian politician Mahamane Alassane Haïdara, returning from Dakar, referred to "high level of the debates," which he considered frank and loyal, and he thought the results, in the end, were "very positive." L'Essor, 13 May 1960.

[57] L'Essor, 20 May 1960.

[58] High Commissioner, Dakar, to Community, Paris, telegram, 8, 14 May 1960, Dakar/Ambassade/340, ADN.

constitution of the federation appropriate for a country becoming independent. The constitution enshrined "fundamental rights," inspired by the French declarations of 1789 and 1848, and—most notably—declared that Mali would be "an open federation" that is open to other African nations that wished to join. Mali would be "secular, democratic, and social. She ensures equality before the law to all citizens without distinction of origin, race, sex, or religion."[59]

But at the moment when the top leaders of Mali seemed to be agreeing on their constitution, rumors started to fly about a "new start of the internal crisis of Mali." It was set off by the diffusion at the end of May of a tract by the Union des Jeunes du Soudan (Union of Sudanese Youth) insisting that the President of this largely Muslim federation must be a Muslim—an argument clearly targeting Senghor. Senghor did not see this move as a folly of youth, but as a "hostile current" against him. He tried to diffuse the issue by suggesting that Dia be the candidate for the Presidency, but Dia did not want to take the place of his mentor. French officials predicted that a crisis would erupt between 20 June, the date of independence, and 31 August, the deadline for choosing a President.[60]

While these tensions were developing in Africa, France took the final steps to allow independent African states to remain in the Community, or for other independent states to join. The votes in May in the Assemblée Nationale and the national Senate to modify the constitution in this manner were far from unanimous, and the dissent mainly concerned process. It was not clear that it was legitimate to amend the Constitution this way rather than by referendum. Others thought that France was giving up too much too soon. But de Gaulle's government was so anxious to keep some sort of Franco-African community in existence and unwilling to risk the uncertainties of a referendum that it strong-armed the modifications through.[61] Part of the procedure for a constitutional change affecting the Community was that the new

[59] Reports and drafts of the federal constitution from May and June 1960, FM 160, AS. The minutes of Cabinet meetings show that on many specific issues, agreements could fairly readily be reached. FM 37 and 38, AS. The constitution raised no serious controversies at the meeting of the federation's Conseil de Ministres, 13 June 1960, FM 38, AS.

[60] Note by High Commissioner Lami, 14 June 1960, for Secrétaire d'État chargé des relations avec les États de la Communauté, FPU 1740, ANF; intelligence report, 10 June 1960, Dakar/Ambassade/340, ADN.

[61] The vote in the Assemblée Nationale on amending the constitution in accordance with de Gaulle's wishes was 280 to 174. *Débats*, 11 May 1960, 774. During the debate, Maurice Schumann rather implausibly argued that the constitutional reform would both prevent the new states being tempted by pan-Africanism, pan-Arabism, or communism and be a step toward "the great hope that begins today, that of Eurafrica, conceived, oriented, and shaped by the double vocation, European and Africa, of France." Ibid., 774.

Senate of the Community had to approve. In this body, in early June, the constitutional revision had clear sailing.[62]

Juridically, the idea of independence within the Community, was not straightforward. If the Community was to be capable of doing something, it had to keep some competences. The fiction was that all competences had been ceded, but some retroceded by Mali acting independently. As P.-F. Gonidec pointed out, lawyers often considered independence to mean "the exclusivity, autonomy, and entirety of competence." But, insisted Gonidec, "these notions are not absolute, no more than is the notion of sovereignty." He compared what a state like Mali was doing to what France itself did in relation to the Common Market.[63] In short, France and Mali were both trying to innovate in regard to the notion of sovereignty, to mediate between independence and inclusion in some kind of "grand ensemble."

When the Community Senate pronounced in favor of the constitutional modification, it was accomplishing practically the only substantive action it ever undertook.[64] Debré, after the vote, was still insisting that "it is through the Community that France maintains its influence in Africa and a circle of friendships that reinforces its authority in the world." Coming close to acknowledging that the government's previous policy of devolving power to territories had gone too far, he now argued that the Community would alleviate "the quarrels born of the division [of Africa] into too many independent states." Moreover, the Community would counter external subversion and give Africa "the best chance to remain in close liaison, in association with the free world."[65] His arguments met a degree of skepticism among relatively conservative deputies, who pointed to the lack of solid institutional framework, the absence of a President within meaningful powers, the voluntary and revocable nature of Mali's membership in the Community, the ambiguity of Mali's commitment to support France's defense

[62] The vote in favor of the constitutional revision was 205 to 8. The Community Senate's committee on legislation reported that African states wanted the proposed change: "They reject 'independence-secession' and demand 'independence-association.'" Michel Debré evoked "our common patrimony from the time when we were citizens of the same *patrie*." Citizenship was now in the past tense. Paul Coste-Floret all but admitted how much France had to give up to retain its relationship with former colonies: "I do not say French Community. . . . I say 'the Community.'" Sénat de la Communauté, *Comptes Rendus des Débats*, 2 June 1960, 27–48, 31, 33, 47–48 quoted.

[63] P.-F. Gonidec, "La Communauté et les voies de l'indépendance," *Penant* 70 (1960): 8–9.

[64] At the opening of the session at which the constitutional revision was passed, Marius Moutet, Président d'âge, noted that in the ten months since the Senate's initial meeting—at which it did nothing but organize itself—there had been no meetings. After this session ended on 3 June, it did not meet again. Sénat, 30 May 1960, 2. See also Sénat, *Débats*, 15–31 July 1959, 1–48.

[65] Assemblée Nationale, *Débats*, 9 June 1960, 1219–20. The occasion for Debré's remarks was the debate over approval of the accords with Mali.

of the Community, and the lack of a court with authority to enforce the mutually agreed upon rights of citizens in states other than one's own.[66]

Once independent, Mali was free to finalize as a sovereign state the accords it had negotiated with France. The French Parliament also ratified the accords, with some reservations expressed (see below) that France was separating itself from some of its citizens. *Le Monde* explained to its readers the ratified accords, agreed to by Madagascar as well as Mali and a model expected to be followed by other overseas territories:

> It is a question first of all of bilateral conventions of establishment that specify that the nationals of each party can accede to public employment in the territory of the other and will be assimilated to the nationals of the latter in regard to the creation of any industrial, commercial, agricultural, or artisanal establishment similarly for accession to liberal professions, the possibility of obtaining concessions and agreements regarding public markets, representation in consular assemblies and economic organizations, civil rights, etc. . . . In addition, the accords—multilateral this time—on fundamental rights of nationals of different states of the Community guarantee to any national of one of the states the enjoyment of public liberties in the territory of other contracting states, as well as access to judicial institutions under the same conditions as nationals, the right to invest, acquire property, etc. Property and interests are subject to guarantees, in particular against eventual expropriation without prior indemnization.[67]

What had once been imperial citizenship, *Le Monde* was in effect saying, was becoming a relatively inclusive regime of reciprocal rights. Africans' right of free movement to France and the rights of French citizens to do business and secure their property in Mali were woven together.

As Mali was uneasily moving toward independence, Houphouët-Boigny surprised the French government by putting in his own claim, on 3 June. The other members of the Conseil de l'Entente followed in his footsteps.[68] These states wanted, in chronological order, independence, membership in the UN, and negotiation of accords with

[66] Pascal Arrighi, *Débats*, 9 June 1960, 1222–26.

[67] André Blanchet, "Les organes nouveaux de la Communauté auront un caractère essentiellement consultatif," *Le Monde*, 28 July 1960.

[68] As late as April, French officials did not think that Houphouët-Boigny was about to demand independence, but would wait and see what would happen with Mali and Madagascar. Note for the Secrétaire Général, 11 April 1960, by Joseph Bellat, based on a telegram from the High Commissioner, Abidjan, 9 April 1960, FPU 1672, ANF.

France as a sovereign nation.[69] By putting things this way, Houphouët-Boigny was saying that he did not want independence and accords to be simultaneous, as was the case with Mali, but for "independence without prior accord," as an Ivorian newspaper put it.[70]

Such an approach would in effect take these states, temporarily at least, out of the Community. Houphouët-Boigny's statement to the press made clear the element of resentment—against Mali and against France—behind his approach and in making the announcement on the eve of Mali's independence: "The renewed Community was put in place without us and contrary to our wishes for a federal organization. We were effaced during the negotiations between France and Mali although it was with the entire Community that Mali should have negotiated its independence." Now, he was exercising the constitutional right to demand independence, with the intention of remaining in the Community but on terms to be determined later.[71] He kept repeating over the next months his point: "It takes two to marry: in fact France did not want to go to the church. I remained in front of the church, fading flowers in my hands."[72]

The demands of the Entente states caused alarm bells to go off in France. Gaston Defferre asked in Le Monde, "Will the Community break up?" He pointed to the "differences in conception, even rivalries, among African statesmen," worried about one-upmanship in the demands for independence coming from those men, and concluded that the Community had been badly designed. He went on to assert that the Algerian war was leading Africans to align themselves against France while strengthening "Cartiérisme" in France itself. But he was not prepared to give up on Community, for without it, he wrote, France would become "a small country." A solution had to be found to the Algerian war and the Community reconstructed.[73]

So representatives of the four countries of the Conseil de l'Entente—Côte d'Ivoire, Dahomey, Upper Volta, and Niger—went to work with French leaders to arrange the transfer of competences. The pace was rapid: the independence ceremonies took place in Abidjan on 6 and

[69] Letters of Presidents of the États de l'Entente to de Gaulle, 3 June 1960, FPR 324, ANF. The letters asking for transfer of competences referred to the presidents' desire for "friendship" with France, but the only reference to the Community was that the letters were addressed to Charles de Gaulle, "Président de la Communauté."

[70] Fraternité, 10 June 1960. Le Monde (5–6 June 1960) saw these demands as "the contagion of independence."

[71] Press statement reported in Abidjan-Matin, 7 June 1960. Debré feared that Houphouët-Boigny was trying to outdo Mali and would complicate negotiations with Mali and Madagascar. Debré to de Gaulle, 31 May 1960, 2DE 29, MD.

[72] Fraternité, 10 June 1960. For other versions, see Abidjan-Matin, 11 June, 28 July 1960.

[73] Gaston Defferre, "La Communauté va-t-elle éclater?" and "Le vrai problème: la guerre d'Algérie," Le Monde, 9, 10 June 1960.

7 August.[74] French officials noted sadly that the French delegation to the ceremony received the "most modest" of welcomes. No hostility was expressed, but "on the other hand, membership in the Community was never recalled and there is no doubt that all the leaders, particularly M. Houphouët-Boigny, sought, as one could have expected, to take their distance in regard to France." The new President hinted that bilateral accords would be forthcoming, "but he remained silent about the intentions of the Conseil de l'Entente in regard to its participation in the Community."[75]

The sequence that Houphouët-Boigny insisted on threatened at least for a time France's hope for a soft letdown from Community citizenship. In the absence of a "transitional accord" or participation by the states of the Conseil de l'Entente in multilateral accords with the other states of the Community, the citizens of the new states "would be considered foreigners"—exactly what French leaders did not want. Independence without accords, even if not intended to be long term, led to a "legal void" in regard to passports, visas, and court jurisdictions.[76] Debré was extremely annoyed, fearing that Houphouët-Boigny was "a man who can destroy everything" because of "a disappointment that he believes he suffered and a conception that he has of his future role."[77]

The space would eventually be filled by bilateral negotiations allowing for reciprocal recognition of rights. But that was not the same as reforming the Community. Indeed, two Ivorian politicians, Philippe Yacé and Mamadou Coulibaly, drew the conclusion that the Community was "stillborn." Coulibaly went on to hint that the Community's stillbirth was linked to the French government's desire to let lapse its "fraternal, contractual solidarity with African and Malagasy partners of color" in favor of "reconciliation with former hereditary European enemies."[78]

[74] *Abidjan-Matin*, 25 June, 12 July, 28 July, 13 August 1960.

[75] Note for the President of the Community, 24 August 1960, FPR 324, ANF.

[76] Secrétaire d'État aux relations avec les États de la Communauté to High Commissioners, Côte d'Ivoire, Dahomey, Niger, Haute-Volta, 29 July 1960, FPU 200, ANF.

[77] "Note à l'attention du Général de Gaulle," 16 August 1960, 2DE 29, MD. Debré continued to complain that Houphouët-Boigny's "egocentrism and ambition manifest themselves for several months and lead him to take some quite particular pathways." Projet de note, bilan et programme, 26 September–17 October 1960, 2DE 29, MD. Jean Foyer later wrote that for Houphouët-Boigny, "it was necessary for the Entente to 'pass' Mali and destroy the renewed Community the way Mali caused the institutional Community to explode." Jean Foyer, *Sur les chemins du droit avec le Général. Mémoires de ma vie politique 1944–1988* (Paris: Fayard, 2006), 149–50.

[78] Philippe Yacé, cited in *Abidjan-Matin*, 8 June 1960; Mamadou Coulibaly, "La Communauté mort-née," *Fraternité*, 3 June 1960. A clipping of Coulibaly's article is in the Foccart Papers, marked "vu par le Général." FPR 324, ANF. Yacé was President of the Côte d'Ivoire's legislative assembly and Coulibaly served in the Senate of the Community.

Whereas Coulibaly was blaming France for abandoning Africa in favor of Europe, Mamadou Dia—who had not given up on Community—still used the word "Eurafrica," hoping it could produce "a harmonious equilibrium and not a second edition of the treaty of Berlin [the agreement to partition Africa among colonizing powers in 1884–85]." *Afrique Nouvelle* could still ask in a headline in 1961, "Is the Construction of Eurafrica Possible?" The article was about a meeting of European and African parliamentarians in Strasbourg. Some hundred Africans attended.[79] They did not produce Eurafrica, and the Franco-African community had by then come apart.

In short, the faction led by de Gaulle's closest African ally, Houphouët-Boigny, was in the summer of 1960 pronouncing the Community dead, a Community that had already been altered in the face of demands coming out of Africa. And the faction that had argued for an alternative to de Gaulle's Community was still willing to remain within it, albeit a version that contained neither the common citizenship nor the institutional armature that de Gaulle had wanted. Senghor had ended up with something like his "Commonwealth à la française," Houphouët-Boigny with an independence he had not desired. The Malians wanted to preserve some form of Community above all to keep alive the attempt to build an African federation. In the summer of 1960, the Mali Federation was the slender thread on which hung the possibility of reviving the French Community.

The Brief Life and Dramatic Fall of the Mali Federation

On 20 June 1960, Malians celebrated their independence, with expressions of pride and optimism, or at least a brave face. The cabinet was presided over by Modibo Keita, who was also Foreign Minister with Dia as Vice-President and Defense Minister. Keita was also the President of the Conseil de gouvernement of the Soudan, Dia his equivalent in Senegal. Speaking to the Assemblée fédérale, Keita emphasized "the affirmation of Mali's personality, with its characteristics of an independent nation, with an underdeveloped economy." He affirmed simultaneously its "particular relations with France, with which we participate in the construction of a multinational confederation, on the basis of equality" and "our presence, in this French-speaking West

[79]Mamadou Dia, "Le Mali: pôle d'attraction économique de l'Ouest africain," *Le Monde Diplomatique*, April 1960, clipping in Dakar/Ambassade/345, ADN; "La construction de l'Eurafrique est-il possible?" *Afrique Nouvelle*, 21 June 1961. See also Guia Migani, *La France et l'Afrique sub-saharienne, 1957–1963: Histoire d'une décolonisation entre idéaux eurafricains et politique de puissance* (Brussels: PIE Peter Lang, 2008) and Giuliano Garavini, *After Empires: European Integration, Decolonization, and the Challenge from the Global South 1957–1986* (Oxford: Oxford University Press, 2012).

Africa where there are our racial brothers, with whom so many historical and economic links unite us."[80]

The Malian ministries continued the work they had begun before the magic date of independence. The records suggest that the Cabinet was trying from April through July to develop regulations governing the civil service, to define competences between the federated and the federal states more clearly, to discuss "property reform," and to develop rules governing rural communities.[81] Mali even decided to send troops to the former Belgian Congo, to try to find an African solution to an African problem.[82]

One of the dossiers being worked on was a code of nationality for Mali. Since Mali—not Senegal or Sudan—was to be where the nation lay, such a code was a federal responsibility. A scheduling conference for the Cabinet said a draft of the code was ready to be discussed at the meeting of 21 July, but the Cabinet records do not indicate that in fact it was, nor have I been able to find a text of the draft. The coordinating conference among the ministries agreed that creating the code was "particularly urgent."[83] We do know what the Minister of Justice, Boubakar Guèye, told Modibo Keita in June about the state of the project:

> A draft of a Malian nationality code was elaborated by the Ministry of Justice. Its essential logic, while respecting the African mentality and the exigencies of neighboring states is to define who, at the moment of Mali's accession to independence, has Malian nationality and under what conditions, in the future, this nationality can be attributed, acquired, or lost. To take account of the objective of African unity, an important right to choose is anticipated for all *ressortissants* of the states of the Community and of the Republic of Guinea. . . . The superposition of nationalities is not expressly permitted, but this choice not being urgent, the search for solutions to conflicts is left to subsequent accords between Mali and these states.[84]

Malian thinking about nationality, then, was shaped by the ongoing aspirations to create an *African* nation.

---

[80] Speech to Asssemblée fédérale, June 1960, copy in FM 112, AS.

[81] Conférence interministérielle périodique de coordination, 26 April, 24 May, 18 June, 4 July, 12 July 1960, FM 32, AS. Roland Colin, who served in Dia's cabinet, notes that the Cabinet "functioned in a double register: Senegalese and Malian." Colin claims to have worked out "the articulation of responsibilities between the Senegalese state and the Federation." *Sénégal notre pirogue: Au soleil de la liberté. Journal de bord 1955–1980* (Paris: Présence Africaine, 2007), 155.

[82] Record of meeting of Conseil des Ministres, 18 July 1960, FM 38, AS.

[83] Conférence interministérielle périodique de coordination, 12 July 1960, FM 32, AS.

[84] Minister of Justice to President of Government, 10 June 1960, FM 159, AS.

When a French citizen wrote to the Minister of Justice about his worries over what might happen to him as a non-Malian national living in Mali, Guèye replied that while "the Malian nationality code has not yet been promulgated," the establishment convention between France and Mali "in general reserves the same consideration for nationals of both countries. No action on your part is therefore necessary to profit from these advantages."[85] Mali was in principle open to the possibility of inclusiveness in regard to Africa and reciprocity in regard to France.

There had been, as noted earlier, signs that attitudes toward fellow Africans might not be so open in practice: the worries expressed by Modibo Keita and others in 1959 that Dahomean and Guinean residents in Mali (many of them having worked for the government or private enterprise in the Dakar region) might not turn out to be loyal Malians. But the most dangerous tension was within.

Neither cabinet minutes nor newspapers from Bamako and Dakar suggest how serious the tensions were in July and early August. But French intelligence got wind of them. The near-split in May had been papered over, but in early July a meeting of the Senegalese branch of the PFA at which Sudanese leaders were invited guests resulted in an altercation between Modibo Keita and Senghor and Dia. In a discussion of government policy, Dia refused to cede to what he considered a demagogic policy of "Africanization at a discount" when there were not enough appropriately trained cadres. Keita gave a "strong critique" of this argument, insisting on the need to "Africanize politically." The verbal fisticuffs degenerated from that point, and Senghor and Dia were taken aback by the "harsh" words of Keita. Claude Hettier de Boislambert, who represented the French Republic in Mali, reported that Senghor was "furious" at Keita, accused him of trying to "colonize" Senegal, and went so far as to say, "better to break up Mali than to give in to the Sudan."[86] By 30 July, Hettier de Boislambert was warning Paris that his conversations with Senghor suggested that this longtime advocate of federation was "resigned to seeing the breakup of Mali."[87]

Then things got worse. Tensions crystallized around control of the army—the "affair of the colonels." Keita wanted Colonel Soumaré to be Chef d'État Major, while Dia wanted Colonel Fall (both colonels

[85] Minister of Justice to M. Claude LeGros, 21 July 1960, FM 493, FM, AS.

[86] Hettier de Boislambert to Foccart, 6 July 1960, FPR 238, ANF; Bureau de Synthèse, Fiche de Renseignements, 4 July 1960, FPU 1678, ANF. The bitter and personal nature of this clash is confirmed from by a noted author and "sage" close to Keita, Amadou Hampaté Ba, "Les heures sombres de la rupture entre le Sénégal et le Soudan," *Afrique Histoire* 2 (avril–juin 1981): 55–60, esp. 56.

[87] Haut Représentatif to Community, 30 July 1960, FPU 1678, ANF.

were Senegalese). At a stormy meeting on 23 July of the Conseil des Ministres, Keita and his allies insisted that Soumaré was entitled to the post by virtue of seniority; Dia asserted that Fall had been responsible for reorganizing the army and putting someone else in charge over him would be a "grave perturbation in our Army before it is even born." But the basic issue was that Dia, as Minister of Defense, believed the appointment was his to make, while Keita claimed ultimate authority. Having an ally or client in such a position could be crucial if push came to shove within the Federation. Keita got the majority of the Cabinet to support him, but Dia insisted that as Minister of Defense, he had to sign off on the appointment, and he refused to do so, saying he would rather quit his post. Keita said that would be impossible since it would require a decree and that "would be disastrous for the public." Dia backed down, but the damage was done.[88]

On 3 August, French sources reported a spat between Senghor and Keita. Senghor thought Keita was being too indiscriminate in signing accords of cooperation with different countries, and Keita asserted that Senghor had "overly francophilic sentiments." Keita apparently told Senghor that he thought the latter would "return Mali to France, if it [Mali] were confided to him." Senghor complained about this reproach to the leader of the Mourides (the Islamic brotherhood), Falilou M'Backé, and apparently said he "would bring about the breakup of Mali" if he were not allowed "his freedom of action." M'Backé, via an envoy, informed Keita of this conversation—a sign that intrigue was going on between Keita and people whom Senghor saw as his supporters. Keita seemed assured—dangerously assured—that Senghor could do nothing of what he threatened "since at the international level the independence of only one state is recognized, that of Mali."[89]

Senghor was sensitive to "the campaigns of denigration of which he is the object," and Dia complained of "constant obstacles" in his work as Defense Minister. Hettier de Boislambert reported that Senghor and Dia were thinking of secession, or of provoking the Sudanese

---

[88] Record of meeting of Conseil des Ministres, 23 July 1960, FM 38, AS. There had been a prior round of debate in the Conseil when Fall was put in charge of reorganizing the armed forces after having done preliminary work. For that job, Soumaré had his partisans, who made the seniority argument, but—with Keita absent that day—the Cabinet agreed that Defense Minister Dia "is thus free to choose his technical adviser." Ibid., 27 May 1960. For reports reaching French officials on the affair of the colonels, see Intelligence report, 2 August 1960, Dakar/Ambassade/340, ADN. These reports appear on the letterhead of the Haute Représentation de France auprès de la Fédération du Mali, Bureau de Synthèse.

[89] Record of meeting of Conseil des Ministres, 3 August 1960, FM 38, AS. Senghor was indeed upset at the contacts between Keita and M'Backé. Haut Représentatif de France auprès de la Fédération du Mali, to Community, telegram, 3 August 1960, FM 38, AS.

enough to demonstrate that cooperation was impossible. The Senegalese were indeed worried that they lacked the international status of Mali and that Mali might come under Keita's sole control.[90]

The next issue to surface was the Presidency of Mali, even though that post was more ceremonial and less substantive than that of the Président du Conseil, occupied by Keita. The President was to be chosen by an electoral college consisting of the federal assembly of Mali and the territorial assemblies of both federated states, slated to meet on 27 August.[91] French intelligence reported that Senghor, who felt himself entitled to the position, was threatened by intrigues from the Sudanese and dissenting Senegalese to put Lamine Guèye into the post. Arguments were being floated that Senghor should not have the post because he was married to a white woman, his sentiments were "too deeply French," he was too close to de Gaulle, and he was Catholic. Rumors were that if Senghor did not get the Presidency, Senegalese leaders would bring about the breakup of Mali.[92] Other reports came in that former Socialist partisans—members of Lamine Guèye's old party—were organizing Lébou people, a community in the Dakar region, against Senghor. Still more rumors suggested that the Sudanese were throwing money around in an effort to recruit Senegalese allies.[93]

Senghor went to Touba, headquarters of the Mouride brotherhood, to "firm up his ties to the great marabouts who have inspite of everything shown him an attachment and fidelity that constitute his principal asset in the face of Sudanese and even internal intrigues."[94] And while French sources did not think that Falilou M'Backé had gone over to Keita's side, they thought his brother might have and that Falilou was not hostile to Keita. Another politically active marabout with his own following, Cheikh Tidjiane Sy, supposedly had lined up with Keita.

In Touba, on the 13th, Senghor and Dia—who had long been denying their "Sénégalité"—now used the term "the Senegalese nation" and "Senegalese unity." Dia called Senegal "la Mère patrie," and according to French sources stated, "Before solidifying Mali, it is first

[90]Haut Représentatif de France auprès de la Fédération du Mali, to Community, telegram, 3 August 1960, FM 38, AS.

[91]On election procedures, see decree of 8 July 1960, FM 13, AS.

[92]Intelligence reports, 4, 5, 6 August 1960, Dakar/Ambassade/340, ADN. Another theory, perhaps a product of French paranoia, was that Keita wanted to bring Guinea into the Federation and considered that Senghor as president would block such a move. Haut Représentatif to Community, telegram, 6 August 1960, FPU 1678.

[93]This and the following paragraphs are based on Intelligence Reports, 6, 8, 10, 16 August 1960, Dakar/Ambassade/340, ADN; Monthly report of Haut Représentatif, 16 August 1960, Dakar/Ambassade/161, ADN; Haut Représentatif, "Note à l'attention de M. le Premier Ministre," 16 August 1960, FPR 230, ANF.

[94]Intelligence Report, 8 August 1960, Dakar/Ambassade/340, ADN.

necessary to think of Senegal." Senghor called upon Senegalese to "close ranks, to strengthen the unity of Senegal, to ensure the Senegalese personality. Mali cannot hold together if Senegal is divided."

Intelligence sources predicted a showdown on 20 August, when there was a meeting scheduled between Senegalese and Sudanese leaders to discuss the election to the Presidency. When Lamine Guèye apparently indicated he did not want to be considered, the Sudanese clan put forward Boubacar Guèye (his nephew), Minister of Justice of Mali and a Senegalese close to the Sudanese. Evidence of Sudanese intrigues with marabouts and "Laministes" raised the stakes for Senghor, who apparently felt that if he did not obtain the Presidency of Mali, his enemies would marginalize him altogether. With a two-thirds vote needed for election, Senghor's chances looked grim.[95]

Reports like these, of course, tell us more about the rumors flying around the milieu in which intelligence agents were operating than about acts actually taking place. But in a context like this one, rumors matter. Their circulation was speeding up as the end of August approached. Doudou Guèye, a former RDA stalwart in Senegal, now close to the Sudanese faction of the PFA, was reportedly at work in Senegal, drumming up support, passing out cash, and perhaps trying to get arms for "action committees."[96] Top Senegalese officials, notably Valdiodio N'Diaye, reportedly thought that Keita's operation had removed all possibility of electing Senghor President and that Dia was in danger as head of the government of Senegal. On 15 August, N'Diaye was reported to be organizing Senegal's security forces in case of the breakup of Mali on the 20th. French security heard that Senegal's leadership was prepared to "break with the Sudan, having realized the development of its tentacular hold over Senegal." But French officials still thought that Senghor was so attached to federation that he might give in if the Sudanese showed a little "suppleness."[97] And the Secretariat of the Community in Paris still seemed, on the 18th, to want to Federation to hold together: "In the current situation, it seems by far preferable that Senegal and the Sudan continue to get along, at the cost of some compromises on both sides."[98]

But suppleness was not what either side had in mind.[99] Coming to Dakar for the meeting of 20 August, Keita was greeted only by his

[95] Monthly report of Haut Représentatif, 16 August 1960, Dakar/Ambassade/161, ADN; Foltz, *From French West Africa to the Mali Federation*, 177–78.
[96] Intelligence Reports, 8, 14 August 1960, Dakar/Ambassade/340, ADN.
[97] Ibid., 13, 15, 16, 17 August 1960.
[98] Secrétaire Général, "Note sur la situation politique de la Fédération du Mali," 18 August 1960, FPU 1678, ANF.
[99] Nonetheless, the Conseil des Ministres of Mali went about its regular business—making decisions, issuing decrees—with general agreement on most. Even the meeting of 18 August 1960 seemed fairly routine. Record of meetings of 4 and 18 August, FM

acolytes. On the night of 19 August, he issued a decree firing Dia as Vice President of Mali's Council of Ministers and Defense Minister and ordered his new Chef d'État-Major, Colonel Soumaré, to have the Malian armed forces take strategic positions. But his move was too well anticipated, and he had the disadvantage of having to oper- ate in a capital city that was his rivals' turf.[100] He overestimated both the inroads he had made into the power base of Senghor and Dia and the legal advantages he had as leader of a recognized state. Dia and Senghor denied Keita the armed forces he needed and used their own muscle—the gendarmerie plus truckloads of supporters of Dia and Senghor who had been brought to Dakar in the morning in an- ticipation of trouble—to surround and isolate the Sudanese leaders in Dakar.[101] They were soon humiliated by being put on a train back to Bamako, after which the rail line was cut. The Senegalese Assembly— before the day was out on the 20th—voted to abrogate the law trans- ferring competences to the Federation of Mali and declare Senegal's independence.[102]

Keita was put in the embarrassing position of appealing to France— through French officers in Dakar, to Hettier de Boislambert, and di- rectly to de Gaulle—to intervene militarily.[103] He was not altogether

---

38, AS; file of decrees of Federation du Mali, including one dated 8 August creating "Air Mali" and several of 2 August on the civil service, FM 13, AS.

[100] Hettier de Boislambert claimed to have warned Keita on the eve of the coup at- tempt that the Gendarmerie of Senegal was under Senegalese control and he should not try anything. Haut Représentatif to Community, telegram, 19 August 1960, FPU 2856, ANF.

[101] The decree of 19 August 1960 firing Dia may be found in FM 38, AS. See AFP report, 20 August 1960, FPU 2856, ANF. While the Cabinet of Mali was meeting on the night of 19 August—in the absence of Senegalese ministers, except for Keita's ally Boubakar Guèye—Senegalese leaders were meeting with security officers, including Colonel Fall and the French Lieutenant-Colonel Pierre, head of the Senegalese gen- darmerie. The arrest of Keita's chief of staff Colonel Soumaré was ordered by Senegal's Minister of the Interior Valdiodio N'Diaye, and it was carried out by the gendarmerie, while Mali's forces remained in the barracks. See the narrative of Secrétaire Général de la Communauté to Secrétaire d'État aux relations avec les États de la Communauté, 31 August 1960, FPU, 2856, ANF, and Colin, *Sénégal notre pirogue*, 187–98, as well as *Afrique Nouvelle*, 24 August 1960, and *Le Monde*, between 21 and 26 August 1960.

[102] Senegal, Assemblée Territoriale, *Débats Parlementaires*, 20 August 1960, 3–4. The votes were unanimous, with no debate other than the statements of Dia and Senghor.

[103] There is a copy of Keita's decree of 19 August requisitioning Community troops in the Dakar region in FPR 230, ANF. See also Keita to de Gaulle, telegram, 20 August 1960, FPR 230, ANF. Such a request from Keita had been anticipated, and Hettier de Boislambert had said he would insist that Community forces could be used only against an external aggressor and "I would never allow myself to be used as an instrument of in- ternal political action." Haut Représentatif, Dakar, "Note à l'attention de M. le Premier Ministre," 16 August 1960, FPR 230, ANF. See also the list of orders done by Keita's Chef d'État Major, Colonel Soumaré, on the night of 19 August in an attempt to con- trol Dakar militarily—orders that were not obeyed—in Dakar/Ambassade/345, ADN.

wrong in arguing that France had pledged to support Mali by force of arms, and Mali was the only state with any claim to existence. The Mali Constitution mentioned no right to secession. "A break is constitutionally impossible," asserted Keita.[104] But the French government, even if it needed Mali to keep the Community alive, wanted Dia's Mali, not Keita's.[105] There was enough plausibility to the argument that the events of 19–20 August were internal matters that French forces did not intervene.[106]

Keita's attempt to rid the government of Mali of his rivals had failed. Trucks continued to arrive on the 21st from the interior with more supporters of the Senegalese leadership, but they were no longer needed and people were moving about the city normally. Radio Mali had become Radio Sénégal. Already on the 21st, Dia received ambassadors resident in Dakar and told them that Senegal wanted to be recognized "as an independent country as soon as possible." The next day Senegal informed the UN of the dissolution of Mali, although the UN refused to accept the report on the grounds that Senegal was not a country. That position did not remain viable for long.[107]

It remained to gain control of the history of the night of 19–20 August 1960. Both sides—long-term and vigorous proponents of federation—had gone against the basic tenets of federal government. Keita had attempted a palace coup, violating the norms of balance and consultation that federation depended on; Dia and Senghor had seceded from the Federation. Keita was confined to his residence for a few days and then preoccupied with his grievance against France for failing to intervene to preserve the Federation.[108]

[104] *Le Monde*, 26 August 1960. The preindependence version of the Federation's constitution contained a procedure for secession, but that clause was taken out in the version of 18 June 1960, apparently at the suggestion of Senghor. Hence Keita could assert "indissolubility of Mali." Secrétaire Général, note for President, 26 August 1960, FPU 1678, ANF.

[105] The Agence France Presse, apparently articulating official France's perceptions of the political scene, drew a contrast between Keita as "intransigent and authoritarian," versus Senghor, "deft politician and brilliant orator" and Dia's "realistic and moderate spirit." Clipping, 20 August 1960, in FPU 2856, ANF.

[106] The Community Secretariat in Paris sent around to French representatives in Africa Hettier de Boislambert's long telegram narrating the events of the night. He insisted that Keita's actions were unconstitutional and merited no military support. Telegram, 29 August 1960, Dakar/Ambassade/345, ADN.

[107] AFP clippings, 20, 21, 22, 23 August 1960, FPU 1678, ANF.

[108] Keita traveled to Paris to plead his case, telling a press conference that the Mali Federation continued to exist even if Senegal was no longer in it. De Gaulle immediately after the events asked both Dia and Keita to come to Paris. He said that France continued to recognize Mali, but that "Mali is no longer a federation but a state confounded with the Sudan." That did not please Keita, who considered that France's attitude "calls into question the application of the Franco-Malian agreements." Text of Keita's press conference at Orly Airport, 2 September 1960, de Gaulle to Keita, 21

Senghor had a good story, and he told it well. Already on the 23rd, he gave a press conference that was quickly printed and distributed by the government of Senegal. He argued that the difference between the two countries was less ideological than one of "method." The Sudanese methods were "more totalitarian." They wanted "a unitary state," the Senegalese "a very supple federal state." Senegal wanted a democratic regime, Sudan did not. Mali's Constitution, in Senghor's eyes, was "halfway between a classic federation and a confederation," but Keita acted as if it were a "unitary federation." Worst of all was "the intrusion of Modibo Keita into the internal affairs of the Republic of Senegal," when federalism imposed the "duty to respect the autonomy of federated states." The events of 19–20 August were "an aborted coup d'état." Senghor attempted to hold onto the high—federalist—ground: "Of course the federation remains an ideal. We are forced to admit that it remains a distant ideal. It cannot be realized if African states have not moved beyond their territorialism." He assured France that Senegal wanted to remain in the "contractual Community" and offered something conciliatory to his African neighbors who had refused to join the Mali Federation: "cooperation" and "association," something like what Houphouët-Boigny had proposed as an alternative to Senghor's primary federation. He concluded, "In a word, it is a question of reconciling independence and African cooperation."[109]

He was more forthright in a message to the Senegalese people at the beginning of September: "Woman and men of Senegal, for fifteen years I have often warned you against a certain sickness, inoculated by colonialism and which I called *Senegality*. It was a superiority complex." Now, "Senegalese independence is an African necessity. . . . But it is first of all a fact. . . . We have drawn the lesson, which is that Senegalese independence is a prerequisite for African cooperation." Senghor reviewed the Senegalese struggle against the *indigénat*, assimilation, and "balkanization." Senegal was a "hyphen" between "the black world and the Arabo-Berber world" and between "Europe and Africa," and it had been so for three hundred years. In the past fifteen years, Senegal had "grafted European socialism on the old subject of Negro-African *communalism*, as I say, on *Négritude*." He now recognized the difficulty of a "government of two" and the need to work for a larger but looser grouping of the former states of AOF, including

September 1960, and Keita to de Gaulle, telegram, 22 August 1960, FPU 1678, ANF; AFP, Bulletin, 21–22 August 1960, Bamako/Ambassade/13, ADN. Dia also traveled to Paris to see de Gaulle. *Le Monde*, 24 August 1960.

[109] "Conférence de Presse du 23 Août 1960 par Léopold-Sédar Senghor, Secrétaire Général de UPS," published by Ministère de l'information, de la Presse et de la Radiodiffusion de la République du Sénégal.

Figure 7. Léopold Sédar Senghor and Mamadou Dia in front of the National Assembly, 5 September 1960, shortly after Senegal became an independent republic. ©AFP/Getty Images.

Guinea. "The idea of federation is not yet ripe in the former AOF; micronationalisms have not yet been transcended."[110]

Senghor also wrote to Houphouët-Boigny, offering to work together for cooperation among the states of the former AOF and coming as close to eating crow as high-level politicians ever get: "*Naturally, it cannot be a question of 'Federation.' We are even agreed not to talk any more about 'Confederation.'* It would be a question, according to the formula of the Conseil de l'Entente, of a flexible association that would be founded on the principles of independence, equality, and cooperation in the financial, economic, cultural, technical, and social domains." Dia

[110] Message to the people of Senegal, sent by Hettier de Boislambert to Foccart, 7 September 1960, FPU 1685, ANF.

put it more simply, "We were wrong and M. Houphouët-Boigny was right."[111]

Try as he might to claim that he was still on the road to federalism, the immediate necessity for Senghor was national construction—of Senegal. The ideological apparatus heretofore devoted to making "Mali" and "Africa" was transferred rapidly to the task of making Senegal. The government of a federated state became within days a government of a sovereign republic, with Senghor as President, Dia as Prime Minister.

France's discrete handling of the breakup of Mali left Senghor with a political debt. Informed in early September of France's intention to recognize Senegal's independence, Senghor knew that a major juridical and political obstacle had been overcome, and he told Hettier de Boislambert, "You know that Senegalese politicians were among the first in Black Africa to fight for this decolonization. That is why, to be precise, they overcame the resentment of the formerly colonized. That is why we intend, now, to extend Franco-Senegalese cooperation from 'Atlantic Europe to the Urals.'" He was willing to pay his debt through the positions Senegal would take in international relations: although "partisan of the independence of Algeria," the new state would take care at the UN and elsewhere "not to annoy France."[112] France recognized Senegal on 11 September, Great Britain did so on 17 September, and Senegal was admitted to the UN on 28 September.[113]

On 22 September, the former Sudan proclaimed itself independent and "free of all engagements and political linkages with France." It kept the name Mali for itself—République rather than Fédération.[114] For some time, its relations with France were cold and its relations with Senegal frozen. It refused to have anything to do with "the renewed Community."[115] The rail line that had been the Sudan's prin-

[111] Senghor to Houphouët-Boigny, 21 September 1960, FPU 1678, ANF; *Le Monde*, 24 August 1960; Haute Représentation, Synthèse Politique, September 1960, Direction des Affaires Africaines et Malgaches, Senegal, 1959–72/1, ADLC.

[112] Haut Représentatif to Community, telegrams, 7, 11 September 1960, Note of Haut Représentatif, 28 October 1960, clipping from *Le Monde*, 7 December 1960, FPU 1685, ANF.

[113] Haute Représentation, Dakar, Synthèse Politique, September 1960, Direction des Affaires Africaines et Malgaches, Senegal, 1959–72/1, ADLC. See Dia to de Gaulle, 4 September 1960 (FM 203, AS), for Senegal's plea for his "personal intervention" in obtaining France's recognition of Senegal's independence. He made clear Senegal's desire to "adhere without reservation to a friendly association with France and the other states of the Community."

[114] *Le Monde*, 23 September 1960.

[115] Foyer, *Sur les chemins du droit*, 163. French officials—fearing that the Republic of Mali would establish a Conakry-Bamako axis, open the door to American connections, and/or fall under Soviet influence—professed a desire to avoid a "sharp break" and did not, as with Guinea, immediately pull out French teachers and functionaries or cut off all aid. Relations were tense, however, until they eased somewhat with agreements

cipal link to the sea was cut until September 1963—causing hardship not only for those who depended on exports and imports along the route, but for thousands of railway workers and merchants for whom "AOF" had been a meaningful category.[116] Keita would try to align himself on the left side of the African political spectrum—and make connections with the Soviet block—but until the conflict with Senegal eased, he depended on the more conservative Houphouët-Boigny to have access to a port.[117]

Houphouët-Boigny was, in any case, much solicited in the fall of 1960. He offered to cooperate with other African states in all ways, except those that entailed "supra-national political ties."[118] But Houphouët-Boigny had also given up his most cherished idea—for a close-knit federation of individual African states with France.

Senghor continued to insist throughout 1960 and even into 1962 that "we hold to the Community."[119] But there was not much to hold to. The Conseil exécutif had gone out of business after its March 1960 meeting; the interparliamentary Senate did not meet. Debré kept hoping into 1961 to re-create the "cohesion of a community," but although the Entente states were willing to make various agreements and sought French aid, they were not interested in "Community agreements."[120]

---

reached in early 1962. De Gaulle to Keita, 21 September 1960, FPR 239, ANF; Debré to de Gaulle, 16 October 1961, FPR 238, ANF; Haut Représentatif to Community, telegram, 25 August, 1 September 1960, FPR 230, ANF; Présidence, Note for President, 21 December 1960, FPU 1679, ANF; Note on accords franco-maliens, 2 February 1962, FPU 1416, ANF.

[116]The effect of the border closing on railway workers is a theme of the dissertation research of Brandon County of Columbia University.

[117]Amadou Hampaté Ba claims a personal role as go-between linking Houphouët-Boigny and Keita in setting up the transport link from Mali through the Côte d'Ivoire. "Les heures sombres." Houphouët-Boigny and Keita talked on 7 September and patched up some of their differences. Ambassador of France to Côte d'Ivoire, to Secrétaire d'État aux États de la Communauté, 25 November 1961, Dakar/Ambassade/419, ADN.

[118]Le Monde, 2 September 1960. Talking to Houphouët-Boigny five days after the events of Dakar, the French High Commissioner in Abidjan reported "I had in front of me a relaxed, brilliant, triumphant man." Telegram to Community, 25 August 1960, FPU 2856, ANF. Kwame Nkrumah was also solicited by both sides of the conflict. Le Monde, 11–12 September 1960.

[119]Clipping from Le Monde, 7 December 1960, FPU 1685, ANF; Présidence, Note for the President, 5 April 1961, FPU 1687, ANF. Senghor might not have just been engaging in wishful thinking but was also appealing to de Gaulle's lingering hope for French influence over a wider francophone world. Notes of interview between Senghor and de Gaulle, 21 April 1961, and Senghor to Debré, 6 January 1962, FPR 268, ANF. Senegal, Madagascar, Chad, the Central African Republic, the Congo, and Gabon formally remained in the Community—unlike the Entente states, Mauritania, and the Republic of Mali—even when its institutions did not function.

[120]Account of interview between Debré and Houphouët-Boigny, 16 January 1961, 2DE 64, MD.

Finally, in 1964, the Ministry of Foreign Affairs stopped referring to de Gaulle as "Président de la République française, Président de la Communauté."[121]

Well before then—as early as September 1960 in fact—some officials within the Secretariat seemed to wash their hands of the whole business by evoking another kind of expression. "The transfer of competences resolved a capital problem: that of decolonization," said an internal memo. The mission set out in 1946 was declared to have been accomplished: colonial rule had been brought to an end. The question was now to form relationships with the new states, for which the Community might be useful, but it was not "an absolute." The point was to avoid the "distancing" of African states and especially their "binding together with the Afro-Asian bloc or the red block."[122] The old Secretariat of the Community, operating directly under the French Presidency, came to specialize in the weaving of personal and discrete connections to African leaders under a master of networking, Jacques Foccart.[123] The separation of African states and France pushed the relationship into the realm of international relations, development aid, and personal networks.

The Mali Federation and the French Community failed together. Both France and its former territories had recognized the importance of shaping an "ensemble" that would in some way balance the individuality and the commonality of states. The Mali Federation was a last attempt to give community substance, limited by its two-state configuration, personal clashes, and the enmity of the Conseil de l'Entente. For a time, French leaders had thought that the one hope for preserving the Community was Mamadou Dia—who had the virtue of actually believing in such a role.

During the 1950s, much of what gave the French Union and then the Community substance was its common citizenship. The inhabitants of Senegal, Dahomey, or metropolitan France—if they had the means—could go anywhere within it as rights-bearing citizens. In principle at least, they had the protection of constitutional law and French courts against abuses of power, and if abuses took place, they could be

---

[121] Michel Debré, *Gouverner. Mémoires 1958-1962* (Paris: Albin Michel, 1988), 344–45; Foyer, *Sur les chemins du droit*, 167.

[122] Maurice Ligot, note for Secrétaire Général, 6 September 1960, FPU 182, ANF. For a related argument, see Todd Shepard, *The Invention of Decolonization: The Algerian War and the Remaking of France* (Ithaca, N.Y.: Cornell University Press, 2006).

[123] The workings of this apparatus are slowly becoming visible through access to Foccart's papers. See also Jacques Foccart, *Foccart Parle: Entretiens avec Philippe Gaillard* (Paris: Fayard/Jeune Afrique, 1997). Jean-Pierre Bat refers to Foccart's role in creating a "the indispensable 'short-circuit' between de Gaulle and his African homologues." Such relationships became known as "Françafrique" (with quite a different valence from Eurafrique). *Le syndrome Foccart*, 138. See also François-Xavier Verschave, *La Françafrique, le plus long scandale de la République* (Paris: Stock, 2003).

objects of debate. Neither Union nor Community let Africans engage in politics as equals, but they did provide space for Africans to engage in politics. Africans sometimes got their way.

Common citizenship had the advantage of *not* being defined or controlled by local governments. Senghor understood the risks of losing the layered quality of post-1946 citizenship: that it offered citizens protection from the worst instincts of politicians within each territory or state, which Senghor himself would later demonstrate (see the conclusion). The distancing of citizenship from territory was both its virtue and its liability. For Keita, at least after the debates in the course of 1959 over common nationality and citizenship, the problem was that the citizenship in question was too French, too much a denial of the "personality" of the individual state. His dilemma came from the fact that it was not just citizenship but unity among French-speaking Africans that passed through France. Keita was consistent in his campaign for African federation and African union, but when it came down to making decisions, he did not want to be bound by rules that were not his own, as he demonstrated in the firing of Mamadou Dia on the night of 19 August.

The compromise that African leaders had forced on de Gaulle and Debré in 1959 was that of superposed nationality and citizenship, but the compromise of 1960 was for reciprocity of rights via negotiation and treaty. The problem was that reciprocity offered no more than had collective citizenship within each political unit, and each unit had the chance of taking rights or institutions away. Both Senegal and Sudan acted unilaterally and outside of constitutional procedures in August 1960. In the 1970s, France acted unilaterally to undermine the right of "free movement" of former citizens into metropolitan France (see the conclusion). It was because citizenship operated as both a claim-making construct and a constraint on administrative power that it was a valuable notion in the postwar decade and a half. The transformation of *common* citizenship into bilaterally negotiated reciprocity left the former citizens of French Africa vulnerable not only to the whims of their own governments, but also to those of the one in Paris.

This point was recognized with particular clarity by Gabriel Lisette, RDA leader from Chad and participant in the constitution writing of 1958 (chapter 6). In May 1960, when Community and independence agreements were in play, he wrote that bilateral accords had to be supplemented by multilateral accords among the states. He favored federalism but would settle for confederation in acknowledgment of the "national prejudices" against "the cessions of sovereignty that a federal Republic would imply." But he feared that even this solution would not work, for many Africans were inclined to " 'flee' toward independence-isolation, I really mean 'flee,' because in claiming this immediate intellectual satisfaction, they would bare themselves before the real problems, that is to say Hunger, Culture, social Progress, and Human Solidarity."[124] But within a few months it was clear that he was writing not a program for Africa's future, but an epitaph for its past hopes.

The disputes between Mali and the Conseil de l'Entente and then Senegal and the Sudan and the tensions of a close but asymmetrical connection to France left African states with something they had been trying to avoid, a position of weakness in individual and bilateral relationships with France. But why did the quest for unity fail so quickly and so dramatically in the summer of 1960? The simplest thesis is the most convincing: the combination of real or perceived threats to each leader's political base, and the ambitions of some or all parties to secure control, to treat politics as a zero-sum game. As William Foltz remarks of Senghor, he in the end "chose to sacrifice his wider aims to preserve his territorial political power."[125] Keita, having established singularity of control within his party, the US-RDA, and through the party over the government of Sudan, was not able to accept a plurality of power within the Mali Federation. He had his goals and his plans. His big vision of African unity was not to be stopped by disunity within his political bloc or objections from his federal partners.

Gabriel d'Arboussier, who had long advocated an African federation, argued in a book published in 1961 that the problem was less the excess of ambition of political leaders or ideological incompatibility than "the confusion maintained between the two fundamental notions of state and nation." He felt that, in the aftermath of Mali's collapse and the aspirations of people for a better and freer life, regional and multinational association was more necessary than ever, and he optimistically thought that the failure of the federation of two would

[124] Gabriel Lisette, "Les pays africains d'expression française—du régime colonial à la Communauté rénovée," 31 May 1960, mimeographed paper in FPU 474, ANF. In another paper, Lisette worried about an "international class struggle between the West and the Third World" coming out of the Bandung movement. The only solution he saw was dialogue: "That means that the Third World must get beyond all its negative passions and resolutely envision means of cooperation with so-called bourgeois Nations." Africa needed to be part of "a true zone of solidarity." "L'Europe et l'Afrique: Continents solidaires," unpublished paper, 24 May 1960, in FPU 182, ANF.

[125] Foltz, *From French West Africa to the Mali Federation*, 179. Alternative theories—besides mutual accusations between Senegalese and Sudanese—include ideological differences (socialist Sudan vs. liberal Senegal) and French machinations. The evidence against the latter is considerable: French leaders needed Mali—or at least Dia's Mali—if the Community were to stand a chance. The former is more a question of degree, for neither Senegal nor the Sudan had the capacity to institute a centrally planned economy, while both actively sought to use state power for economic and social betterment. Different relations to international commerce and commercial enterprises played a part, but did not necessarily pose obstacles that were impossible to overcome.

lead to a "larger regrouping." But his most profound insight into the experience he had just lived through was into the deep uncertainty in which the crisis unfolded: "We are obliged to ask ourselves, in which framework do we want the nation to exist, at what level will the source of state sovereignty be situated, how, all the while claiming a national life, we can participate in a large ensemble, if that is in our interest." The collapse of the federation, however, clarified where nation and sovereignty lay, and it was not where d'Arboussier—or Senghor, Dia, Keita, Sékou Touré, or Houphouët-Boigny—wanted them to be.[126]

If the AOF—with its eight territories—had been turned from a unit of administration into a unit of politics, it is possible to imagine that the kinds of zero-sum politics that developed in Mali during the summer of 1960 could have been diffused. A federation of two or three is a more knife-edge proposition than a federation of many.[127] Senghor's warning that African unity needed to be established before independence had a strong basis. But the road toward territorialization had been opened by the institution of territorial electoral districts in 1945, furthered by the development of political parties on a territorial basis (despite repeated attempts to unify party structures), and solidified by the institution of territorial governments in 1956. And one cannot forget the context: extreme global inequality. African leaders lacked the resources to realize projects that their much wealthier former colonizer had found overwhelming. They knew, from their experience with labor unions between 1958 and 1960, that it was difficult for governments to meet the demands of citizens. That governments could stay in power by fulfilling promises for social betterment to their citizens was not as clear in Mali in 1960 as it was in European France, where questions of social policy were complicated enough. Senghor, Keita, and their colleagues all had good reason to be insecure about the territorial power base they had carefully erected and to fear others poaching on it. Yet the seriousness of the attempt to build federation stands alongside the obstacles that brought it down.

[126] Gabriel D'Arboussier, *L'Afrique vers l'unité* (Paris: Éd. Saint-Paul, 1961), 36–37, 58, 60. Foccart's judgment in early 1961 was that "I have the impression that the idea of unity that was very deep a year ago is disappearing bit by bit." He had some hope for modest, step-by-step cooperation around specific problems and that "we should favor these regroupings." Such efforts might not produce unity, but would give rise to "ensembles that hold." Réunion des Hauts-Représentants et Envoyés exceptionnels, 31 January 1961, AP 2230/3, AOM.

[127] Dia, in his speech of investiture as Président du Conseil of Senegal, made much of the obstacle posed by having a "a federation of two isolated states." He considered that in the absence of true African unity, the federation was "denatured, cut off from its initial vocation." Senegal, Assemblée Nationale, *Débats*, 7 September 1960, 36.

With the independence of Senegal and the other former French territories in Africa, the question arose of how to allocate the people living in or linked to each territory to the nationalities that had been created.[120] The answer was not obvious. All the people concerned, up to the day of independence, were French citizens. They were mobile; they might live at the time in metropolitan France or in a part of Africa other than where they were born or where their parents were born. There had already been riots in the Côte d'Ivoire over the presence of "Dahomeans" and "Togolese" even before there was such a thing as a Dahomean, Togolese, or Ivorian nationality. The majority of inhabitants of former AOF did not appear in any état-civil, although a large percentage of the adults voted somewhere, not necessarily where they wanted to be recognized as permanently belonging. In Senegal, the situation was complicated by the fact that not all Senegalese had been citizens in the same way. The "originaires" of the Quatre Communes had unambiguously been French citizens (with their own personal status) since 1916—some would say since 1848. Could such a history of citizenship be eliminated by a decision of a legislature or a constitution-writing committee? And since many people who thought of themselves as European also lived in Senegal—and some might want to stay there—it would also have to be decided which of them would end up French and which Senegalese. It would not be acceptable to allocate people to nationalities by the color of their skin, but there was a lot of cultural and social baggage associated with the way people looked and whom they associated with—all of which might bear on where they wanted to have their nationality assigned and how acceptable their choice might prove to be in the chosen nation. Would French nationality be redefined at the same time as Senegalese nationality was defined?[129]

Let us start in Senegal, where a new nationality had to be created. The problem existed from August 1960, but it was in early 1961 that

[128] For a survey of how the different countries emerging out of the French empire dealt with nationality, see Alexandre Zatzépine, Le droit de la nationalité des républiques francophones d'Afrique et de Madagascar (Paris: Librarie Générale de droit et de jurisprudence, 1963) and Roger Decottignies and Marc de Biéville, Les nationalités africaines (Paris: A. Pedone, 1963). The first nationality code was produced in Cameroon (November 1959). Guinea's was passed in March 1960, Côte d'Ivoire's in December 1961, Mali's in February 1962.

[129] The accords that gave citizens of France and the new states of Africa certain reciprocal rights were interstate agreements; they did not concern nationality, "this question belonging to the internal legislation of each independent state." Note for Gouverneur Bonfils by Secrétariat d'État aux relations avec les États de la Communauté, 25 November 1960, Dakar/Ambassade/396, ADN.

Gabriel d'Arboussier—the most cosmopolitan of Senegalese, now Minister of Justice—presented a report on the subject. As an independent nation, he wrote, Senegal had to "make consistent the juridical position of individuals and their actual situation." Senegalese nationality should be assigned to those "who are truly incorporated into the country." One could not do so by filiation because no one yet had Senegalese nationality and so no one could pass it on. One could start with jus soli of two degrees (a French precedent): someone born in the territory of someone born in the territory. But most people, let alone the previous generation, were not entered in the état-civil. One had to make presumptions. The goal was to identify "those people who normally reside in Senegal, that is who have established residence there and have made it the principal center of their material and moral interests." The measure was not an open door, but a presumption subject to evidence and perhaps contradiction, especially evidence of another nationality. Over time, one could move toward a system of filiation—jus sanguinis. Habitual residence would be considered to be ten years for someone born outside of Senegal, five years for someone born in the country. But as a temporary measure—for one year—the bill would suspend these delays for people born in the states of the former AOF and AEF, Togo, Cameroon, Madagascar, and Senegal's immediate neighbors. This provision was intended to allow civil servants and employees currently working in Senegal to continue to do so and to acquire Senegalese nationality. But the government had the right to oppose according nationality to someone "whenever the assimilation of the individual does not appear sufficient." Provision would be made for naturalization, but only for people "proving their perfect honorability."[130]

Behind Senegalese thinking was the notion that nationality should "correspond to being truly rooted in the country. . . . It is not because Senegal is independent that one defines a Senegalese nationality, but because there were Senegalese that Senegal has become independent." Never mind that d'Arboussier, Senghor, and Dia had previously tried to define the nation as more African than Senegalese. The law's object was "to define a preexisting nationality by means of criteria rooted in the past, in attachment to Senegal." But Senegalese nationality could be relatively open to people, notably African, who were losing their French nationality through independence.[131]

In the Assemblée Nationale of Senegal, the reporter for the committee on legislation, Khar N'Dofène Diouf, assured his colleagues

[130]"Rapport de présentation d'un projet de loi portant code de la nationalité," nd [early 1961], VP 226, AS.

[131]Ministre de la Justice, "Rapport sur la loi déterminant la nationalité sénégalaise," nd [1961], VP 121, AS.

that the nationality question had been discussed with "passion and ardor" and that the issue was not just how nationality was viewed by legal experts around the world but "Senegalese reality." Senegal had to consider that it was a "pole of attraction for foreign populations," giving rise to questions about the "uncertainty of definitive rootedness" on the part of new Senegalese and the danger of "the constitution of strong minorities posing to the young state many political and social difficulties." Senegal therefore had to be liberal, but not too liberal, standing somewhere in between jus soli and jus sanguinis. The state had to be careful not to accept as its own people "who are not healthy in spirit, those who because of their physical or mental state could constitute a burden or a danger for the collectivity."[132] The government would therefore have the right to oppose demands for naturalization or recognition of Senegalese nationality.[133]

Of special interest was the relationship of Senegalese to French nationality. France was leaving (see below) the door open to its ex-citizens to reassert their French nationality if they established residence within the current boundaries of France, even if they had another nationality. The majority of the committee rejected such a possibility for Senegal, which it termed nationality "in the refrigerator." They did not want Senegalese to use dual nationality as a fallback option should they not wish to remain Senegalese.[134] The law, in the end, left an ambiguity in place: "The Senegalese who voluntarily acquires a foreign nationality loses his Senegalese nationality." The text did not say "have recognized." Indeed, the French nationality law of July 1960 allowed French Africans born before independence to have their French nationality recognized under certain conditions. Accord-

<hr>

[132]Senegal, Assemblée Nationale, *Débats*, 21 February 1961, 139–41. A juridical commentator thought that the article in the law based on these ideas constituted "eugenicism" and pointed out that they had not been in the government's initial draft. "Note sur la promulgation de la loi determinant la nationalité sénégalaise," by Michel Aurillac, 3 March 1961, VP 226, AS.

[133]Other legislation had previously recognized the right—which Senegalese had had under the French Constitution—to keep their own civil status and for those statuses to be considered equal. A foreigner being naturalized would acquire the Senegalese status closest to "his original status." René Bilbao, "Statuts civils et nationalité," *Revue Sénégalaise de Droit* 5 (1969): 23–39.

[134]Senegal, Assemblée Nationale, *Débats*, 21 February 1961, 140–41. French officials were worried that the Senegalese law would force people to make hard choices between nationalities and give people of the Community "no particular advantage for accession to the local nationality." What worried them, of course, was not people of the Community in general but those from France. French people, they commented, were less well treated than Gambians; "this nationality is almost completely closed to *français de souche* [true French people]." Note for the Secrétaire Général, 8 March 1961, and note for the President, 14 March 1961, FPU 558 ANF.

ing to a literal reading of the texts, then, they would not be *acquiring* a foreign nationality.[135]

Following d'Arboussier's draft, the nationality law of 21 February 1961 pronounced, in its first article, that Senegalese nationality would go to anyone born in Senegal of Senegalese parents, and it took as evidence of such a fact "his normal residence on the territory of the Republic of Senegal and that he has at all times had the possession d'état of Senegalese." The concept of possession d'état implied that the individual had "continually and publicly comported himself as a Senegalese" and had "continually and publicly been treated as such by the Senegalese population and authorities."[136]

Senegal's eagerness to separate its nationality from the French one forced some people, particularly of elite status, to make hard choices. Civil servants and members of Parliament had to give up the French nationality, as did soldiers who had served in the French Army before entering the Senegalese armed forces. Lawyers had to have Senegalese nationality to be admitted to the bar.[137]

The nationality law presumed what Senghor and Dia had long insisted they did not want—"sénégalité." The government was giving itself a certain authority over deciding who in body and spirit was truly Senegalese. It was open, for a time at least, to people from neighboring countries. Given the weakness of the état-civil, subjective criteria would enter into consideration not just for candidates for naturalization, but for people who claimed to be originally from Senegal. And Senegalese in ambiguous situations would have to decide that Senegalese was what they wanted to remain; they were not supposed to keep another nationality in the "refrigerator."

That Senegal, in 1961, had to confront the fact that it did not know who lived in its territory takes us back to the failure of the French government to put in place an effective état-civil. Could the Senegalese state do better? It tried.

[135]This is the interpretation of the jurists Decottignies and de Biéville, *Les nationalités africaines*, 296. The quotation is from Article 18 of the law of 7 March 1961, Republic of Senegal, *Journal Officiel*, 15 March 1961, 351–54.

[136]Law of 7 March 1961, Republic of Senegal, *Journal Officiel*, 15 March 1961, Article 1. See also Ambassade de France à Dakar, "Étude sur le plan des principes de la législation sénégalaise depuis la rupture de la Fédération du Mali à la fin de l'année 1961," FPU 1686, ANF; Kéba M'Baye, "L'attribution de la nationalité 'jus soli' et l'option de nationalité dans la loi sénégalaise du 7 mars 1961," *Penant* 71 (1961): 347–53.

[137]Renseignments, 9 May 1961, and Minister of Foreign Affairs to Haut-Représentant, Dakar, 9 November 1961 (with enclosed memo), Dakar/Ambassade/396, ADN; "La situation des avocats français au Sénégal après le vote de la loi sur la nationalité," memo from a lawyer's organization in Dakar, 24 February 1961, Dakar/Ambassade/482, ADN. Some deputies in the Senegalese national assembly hesitated between losing their French nationality or their seats. High Commissioner, Dakar, to Community, telegram, 13 April 1961, FPU 558, ANF.

A few months after the Senegalese nationality act was passed, the état-civil had its turn before the legislature. In introducing a proposed law in June 1961, legislators and the Minister of Justice described it as putting an end to the "unacceptable distinction" that had previously existed between people assimilated to European status and everyone else. Insisting that "a modern state could not dispense with registering these acts [marriage, birth, death] of its citizens," it made the état-civil obligatory for all Senegalese. Such registration was necessary "both for sound family policy and for reasons of health, or at least, in a general statistical and demographic interest." But Senegal's rulers maintained that they would respect diversity. People could marry in different ways, but they had to inform the state that they had done so. If they did not, they would be fined.[138]

Before the bill passed the Assemblée Nationale, a debate ensued that revealed that some of the same questions that paralyzed the French government disturbed Senegalese deputies as well. The bill's reporter insisted that the measure was intended to record marriages, not define them. But there was more going on. His committee recommended dropping a proposed article that would have made part of the record a husband's declaration—strictly voluntary—that he would not marry a second wife (a binding declaration unless the marriage was dissolved). The opponents, who had prevailed in a close vote in committee, argued that this clause could be "a coercive means at the disposition of future wives to oblige their husbands to contract only one marriage. The temptation of women, if one believes the proponents of this thesis, would be great and with a tendency to generalize, given how true it is that the married woman is the most ferocious adversary of polygamy." The bill was also criticized by the deputy Boubakar Guèye for requiring that, after a Muslim marriage, both partners come before an officer of the état-civil to register the marriage and attest their consent. He thought the bill anti-Muslim, for it required a man who regarded himself as having followed the Koran's rules on marriage to be married twice, the second time "before someone secular, who moreover might be of Catholic faith." The bill's defenders retorted that its object was not "to elaborate Muslim law, but [to enact] legislation that takes account of Senegalese pluralism." Pressed on why the bill required attestation of consent—and that the bride herself go before the officer of the état-civil, not her father as some self-described Muslims wanted—the Minister of Foreign Affairs said, "If

[138] Projet de loi 17/ANS/61, "tendant à la création d'un état civil unique et sa règlementation," presented February 1961, VP 121, AS; Garde des Sceaux, circular to Prosecutors and Judges of the Peace, nd [June 1961], and Report, by Khar N'Dofène Diouf on behalf of Commission de la Législation, de la Justice et de l'Administration Générale, Assemblée Nationale du Sénégal, 15 June 1961, VP 226, AS.

we have demanded consent, it is from taking account of sociological conditions." Girls, he asserted, were being married against their will. Another deputy was even blunter: "Our concern is precisely that we do not have confidence in all the fathers." Insisting on consent came from "a concern with progress," said the Minister. So the act of recording a marriage was also an intervention in the process of marriage.[139]

In the end, concerns were assuaged with the dropping of the article that some thought threatened polygamy, and the bill passed. Muslims would have to go through a second process, not a second marriage but a check by an official of the state on the fact of the marriage and its consensual nature. Failure to register would not invalidate the marriage, but it would make the couple subject to a fine. The national state, for all the concerns among its legislators, expressed a will that the colonial government did not have to know its citizens and oversee, in however limited a fashion, some key events of their life cycle.[140] Speaking on Radio Senegal at the end of 1961 of the accomplishments of the Ministry of Justice, d'Arboussier placed first and foremost the laws on nationality and on the état-civil. He emphasized, as he had in presenting the nationality law, that Senegal was giving "a large place to foreigners from neighboring territoires who have become Senegalese by adoption" and that the état-civil was both an obligation and a tool for all Senegalese.[141]

The other states of the former AOF followed Senegal in enacting their own nationality legislation. The Republic of Mali did so in February 1962, attempting in the interests of African unity to make the recognition of Malian nationality relatively easy for anyone born in Mali of at least one parent "of African origin" (leaving ambiguous what that meant).[142] Both the Republic of Mali, whose relations with France were at the time quite bad, and Senegal, whose relations were

[139] Senegal, Assemblée Nationale, *Débats*, 16 June 1961, 458–77. The bill was presented by Khar N'Dofène Diouf, reporter for Commission de la Législation, de la Justice de l'Administration Générale et de la Fonction publique, and its most vocal critic was Boubakar Guèye. Also cited are the Minister of Foreign Affairs, Ousmanne Alioune Sylla, and Moustapha Touré.

[140] Note, "De l'état-civil sénégalais en matière de mariage coutumier," 6 December 1961, Dakar/Ambassade/312, ADN. Senegal would go on to adopt a national identity card. Loi sénégalaise instituant une carte nationale d'identité, adopted by Assemblée Nationale, 14 February 1962, VP 121, AS.

[141] "Les principales activités du Ministère de la Justice durant l'année judiciare 1960–1961," text for broadcast over Radio Senegal, 19 December 1961, VP 226, AS. On nationality laws in some other states of former AOF, see documents from 1961 and 1962 in FPU 557, ANF.

[142] There was controversy over whether the notion of African origins had racial implications, but the final language suggested that the concept was geographical. Pierre Decheix, "Le code de la nationalité malienne," *Penant* 73 (1963): 300–314.

good, wanted to mark their distance from French nationality and—unlike France—avoid letting people sit on the fence between the two.

In the Côte d'Ivoire, Houphouët-Boigny argued for a relatively open version of Ivorian nationality, one that would allow non-Ivorians—including people from neighboring countries, French citizens, and people of Syrian and Lebanese origin (who were a significant part of the business community)—to remain and work in Côte d'Ivoire. He expressed his interest, in late 1960, in an "eclipsing nationality," meaning that a migrant could take Ivorian nationality, then give it up when leaving the Côte d'Ivoire. Without going through naturalization procedures, such a person could serve in the Ivorian civil service.[143] The legislature would not go quite that far, but the next year, his government put forward a bill that, like Senegal's, took note of the weakness of the état-civil and the impossibility for most people to prove their ascendants' connection to the soil. The government proposed that children born to foreign parents living in the Côte d'Ivoire could become nationals by a simple declaration at age eighteen, while foreigners resident for five years could become Ivorian themselves. Anyone who had been living in the Côte d'Ivoire at the date of independence could declare himself or herself to be an Ivorian national and those who did not would nonetheless benefit from whatever rights that person had before that date, except for the right to vote or hold elected office. In December 1961, the Assembly approved the law, proud of its liberality.[144] Perhaps this inclusive vision reflected Houphouët-Boigny's political trajectory, notably his early campaign to develop the Côte d'Ivoire's agricultural economy with voluntary migrants from the poorer countries to the north.[145]

Houphouët-Boigny also took a page from the last phase of the debates over nationality in the French Community. In 1963, he proposed to the other states of the Conseil de l'Entente a version of "superposed nationality." Citizens of Dahomey, Niger, and Upper Volta, whenever they were in the Côte d'Ivoire, would have the same rights as Ivorian nationals, and vice versa. As he put it in regard to Upper Volta, "Voltaics in Côte d'Ivoire and Ivorians in Upper Volta will have the

[143] High Commissioner, Abidjan, to Community, Paris, telegram, 17 November 1960, FPU 557, ANF.

[144] Henri-Michel Yéré, "Citizenship, Nationality & History in Côte d'Ivoire, 1929–1999" (PhD diss., University of Basel, 2010), 121–27; Ambassador to Secrétaire d'État, Affaires Étrangères 2 December 1961, FPU 557, ANF.

[145] As the bill moved forward, a committee of the legislature acknowledged "the presence on our soil of non-native elements which will have the possibility, under certain conditions, to melt into the national crucible, in order to pursue their activities without having to renounce their nationality of origin." Report of Commission des Affaires Générales et Institutionnelles of Assemblée Nationale de la Côte d'Ivoire, 8 November 1961, copy in FPU 557, ANF.

same rights and duties without, however, renouncing their respective qualities."[146] With five hundred thousand Voltaics living and working in Côte d'Ivoire, integration seemed to Houphouët-Boigny a better solution than marking them as foreigners. Their rights would include access to the civil service, the vote, and ministerial office. But there was opposition, coming especially from relatively young Ivorian professionals, who considered themselves entitled to the positions and privileges involved. They worried especially about competition from Dahomeans who had a head start in education and who had been the object of jealousy and ethnic chauvinism going back to the 1958 riots. Talk of an "invasion" of the Côte d'Ivoire sprang up. The proposal caused tension in Upper Volta as well, where the government of Maurice Yaméogo was tottering (and soon fell). In Dahomey, enthusiasm for superposed nationality was muted by "the vivid memory of xenophobic acts for which Abidjan was the theater in 1958." In any case, Dahomey's government under Sourou Migan Apithy was overthrown by a coup in 1965. Superposed nationality—West African style—did not come into being, victim of inward-looking, self-serving politics of certain elements inside Côte d'Ivoire and instability elsewhere.[147]

Houphouët-Boigny's idea of an inclusive nationality went further than most African leaders were willing to go. Two French jurists wondered what happened to the spirit of African unity when it came to writing nationality laws: "Jealous of a recently acquired sovereignty, fortified by the international rule that gives nationality a purely unilateral character, each state established its own law without caring about the measures taken by its neighbors."[148]

And what of France? As former territories became independent, France was shedding a significant portion of its nationals, some of whom had claims to being French dating to the seventeenth century, others of whom had acquired French nationality with the conquests of the late nineteenth century, and most of whom had had the rights of French citizens since 1946. The French government was not eager to get rid of its overseas citizens, even if wanted to rid itself of the burdens of colonies.[149] One of the objections to the government's policy

[146] Houphouët-Boigny's speech of December 1964, in Yéré, "Citizenship, Nationality & History," 134.

[147] Yéré, "Citizenship, Nationality & History," 128–42; AFP, report on meeting of Conseil de l'Entente, 31 December 1965, Abidjan/Ambassade/13, ADN; Bulletin de Renseignements, 27 April 1965, Abidjan/Ambassade/13, ADN.

[148] Decottignies and de Biéville, Les nationalités africaines, 28.

[149] The idea that independence meant cutting people off from French nationality "seemed too brutal," wrote P.-F. Gonidec, "La nationalité dans les États de la Communauté et dans les États 'marginaux,'" Annuaire Français de Droit International 7 (1961): 814–35, 834 quoted.

of negotiating independence was in fact that the agreements would cause "free men to lose all at once, against their will, French nationality and French citizenship. That's a lot at the same time."[150] Replying to this argument in the Assemblée Nationale, Debré announced the government's intention to let the citizens of France from all over the French Community "reclaim without other formality" the citizenship that they might be losing or had already lost. He went on to put citizenship at the center of what he claimed France had done for its empire and the world: "France, by bringing citizenship to men and women living in very diverse latitudes, has given—we can proudly proclaim—a notion of equal citizenship to men belonging to very different races and religions." It had "given the word citizen an exceptional moral value." For those people who had been French "it is indispensable to maintain for those who so wish not only the rights attached to citizenship as we know it but also, I insist, French citizenship itself." He promised recognition of French citizenship "to all who have benefitted from it, to all who benefit, and to all who would like to continue to benefit, as well as their descendants." And to those who did not want to remain French, he claimed to have provided a model: "We have passed on to the states that are taking their independence the elevated conception of citizenship that is ours."[151]

Debré's elegy for French citizenship and his promises did not settle the issue. No less a figure than Georges Bidault, speaking at the debate over ratification of the accords with Mali, was blunt about what France and its overseas territories had terminated: "Common citizenship? It no longer exists." That, he thought, was in its historical context a betrayal: "I remind you that the citizens of the Quatre Communes of Senegal have been French since Louis XIV and maybe since Louis XIII and French citizens since the Revolution. . . . It seems to me that in law—I say 'in natural law,' not wanting to offend a jurist of positive law—French nationality cannot be suppressed by a state decision. . . . Up to the present, French nationality was an inheritable patrimony: when one was French, there was no need to ask to remain French, even less to ask to become French again."[152]

[150] René Moatti, Assemblée Nationale, *Débats*, 10 May 1960, 741. Moatti was an Algerian Jew, resistance veteran, and Gaullist.

[151] Debré, Assemblée Nationale, *Débats*, 11 May 1960, 765–66. The French representative in Dakar expressed around this time the desire to offer "to interested people the solution that allows them to remain French while having, if they wish, Malian nationality." Haut Représentatif to Adolphe Diagne, premier conseiller du Haut Commissaire, 27 May 1960, and draft letter from Lami to Dia, 28 May 1960, Dakar/Ambassade/482, ADN.

[152] Assemblée Nationale, *Débats*, 9 June 1960, 1234–35. The accords, in the end, were approved by a vote of 379 to 72. Ibid., 1248.

Both Bidault's and Debré's interventions reveal how much the citizenship concept was internalized among France's governing elite. Two French politicians were arguing over who was going further to recognize Africans as full members of a French polity and to give them the opportunity to honor their sense of belonging to the French nation—this at a time when African leaders were pulling away from their claims to being French.

The law that Debré promised—it became the nationality act of 28 July 1960—turned out to be less welcoming than promised, but it was still quite open precisely in regard to what became the point of closure a decade later: allowing France's former overseas citizens to enter and settle in France. Africans born before independence could have their French nationality "recognized" if and only if they established residency within the current boundaries of the French Republic.[153] There were a few extra possibilities: people who were descended from an "originaire"—a rather interesting usage of a term once applied to Senegalese from the Quatre Communes—of the République française could retain French nationality without the residency requirement. The terminology avoided inscribing a racial connotation, but it referred to people descended from a person from the current French Republic; it was mainly métis who would benefit from this provision. People who were refused nationality in a former state of the Community or who found themselves resident in a country of the former Community other than their own—a Senegalese in Chad for example—could also claim French nationality, in an apparent effort to avoid letting decolonization give rise to apatrides. Algerians could retain French nationality without settling in France if they were of French civil status; if they had kept their personal status they would have to reside in the Republic in order to claim French nationality. The law both acknowledged that the residents of France's former colonies had gone their own way and opened the door for them to live in what remained of France and to reclaim their French nationality.[154]

---

[153] Pierre Carous, reporting on the proposed law for the Commission des Lois Constitutionnelles, worried that unless the legislature passed a new nationalities act any French person, perhaps including someone of metropolitan origin, could find himself or herself pushed into the nationality of the state in which he or she was then resident. Ibid., 11 July 1960, 1844.

[154] Loi No. 60-752 du 28 juillet 1960 portant modification de certains dispositions du code de la nationalité, *Journal Officiel de la République Française*, 30 July 1960, 7040; Note attached to Minister of Foreign Affairs (Directions des Affaires Africaines et Malgaches) to Ambassador to Dakar, 9 November 1960, and Ministère des Affaires Étrangères, circular to Agents Diplomatiques et Consulaires de la France à l'Étranger, 23 November 1960, Dakar/Ambassade/396, ADN; High Commissioner, Madagascar, to President of Community, 6 February 1960, FPU 558, ANF. The French law did not exclude dual nationality. François Terré, Conseiller technique in Secretariat for relations with the États

These provisions gave rise to a mix of sentiments and anxieties in the years immediately following independence.[155] That the law allowed for an influx of former citizens caused little commentary. The break between the imperial citizenship of 1946 to 1960 and the national citizenship of the postcolonial era was deliberately muted. The political elite in France seemed more concerned about losing citizens than being inundated with Africans claiming French citizenship. The Secretariat of the Community—even as the Community was tottering in late 1960—insisted that France should have a liberal approach to nationality and to establishment accords with former Member States in the interest of the "cohesion of the Community."[156] Secretariat officials expressed particular concern about people with "French" civil status or of métis origin, and especially about African elites who might have an attachment to France that could prove useful now that Africans were running their own governments. One sees in the early 1960s a lingering desire for a relatively inclusive French nationality and the prolongation of certain citizenship rights via accords as ways of binding a large and diverse overseas population to France and French interests. As one official frankly put it in 1966, "The fundamental idea guiding the legislator of 1960 was to avoid forcing a rapid choice on Africans

de la Communauté, "La Double Nationalité," nd [late 1960] Dakar/Ambassade/396, ADN.

[155] The law said nothing about personal status; regulating such statuses had already become a concern of Member States. But what about someone who did not have French civil status but lived in France and acquired French nationality under the law of 28 July 1960? It was not clear whether France could recognize any status other than the "French" one, since it could not enforce the laws of other states. But the French Constitution gave people from the overseas territories the right to keep their status and nothing said that such a right disappeared with the exit of those territories from French sovereignty. Some French officials noted that the social consequences of not recognizing diverse personal statuses could be serious for polygamous families—"an extraordinary disruption of the family situation of those whom the law of 28 July 1960 accords the favor of remaining French." Note pour M. Le Chef du Bureau du Contentieux de la Nationalité, 26 July 1961, 950236/24, CAC. But the Minister of Justice opined that "customary rules have lost their obligatory force in France," so that a person whose French nationality was recognized did so under the "statut civil de droit commun." Minister of Justice to Haut Représentatif, Dahomey, 20 March 1962, 950236/24, CAC. For the views of jurists on the complexities and uncertainties of a new world of multiple nationalities, multiple statuses within some of them, and multiple connections across the space of the former empire, see Pierre Lampué, "La diversité des statuts de droit privé dans les États africains," 1–10, François Terre, "La reconnaissance de la nationalité française," 17–23, and René Bilbao, "La nationalité française et l'accession à l'indépendance des anciens territoires d'outre-mer," 517–22, all in *Penant* 71, 685 (January–March 1961). The complexities of multiple statuses are still relevant to the French territories of Mayotte and New Caledonia. Norbert Rouland, "Les statuts personnels et les droits coutumiers dans le droit constitutionnel français," in Anne-Marie le Pourhiet, ed., *Droit constitutionnel local: égalité et liberté locale dans la constitution* (Paris: Economica, 1999), 145–225.

[156] Note for Gouverneur Bonfils by Secrétariat d'État aux relations avec les États de la Communauté, 25 November 1960, Dakar/Ambassade/396, ADN.

favorable to France and to allow them to 'play the game' inside their new states without burning their bridges behind them."[157]

There was an ironic coda to the efforts of the early 1960s to retain some of the effects and spirit of earlier conceptions of imperial citizenship. Some officials wondered if people from the Quatre Communes would have special consideration in retaining French nationality. The answer from the government was no, they did not.[158] Their citizenship had ceased to be unique in 1946. Indeed, it had been the Senegalese model of citizenship that had been applied to overseas France generally.

It was a politician from one of these Communes, Assane Sylla, a leader from the Lébou community of the Dakar region, who made the argument that his constituents should have special recognition for their historic position. He allegedly tried to "incite the *originaires* of the Quatre Communes to ask for French nationality and demand the respect of the statutes by which the Quatre Communes are attached to France." He thought that France's arrangements with old Lébou families provided better guarantees of property than would Senegalese law. He was in part claiming a legal right—France's prior recognition of the originaires' citizenship could not be undone—in part asserting the continued usefulness of a colonial relationship. For him, tacit, long-standing understandings between local elites and colonial officials counted for more than the legalisms, majoritarian orientation, and perhaps biases against "traditional" elites of a new, democratically elected Senegalese government.[159]

France was no longer playing this type of politics with leaders of Sylla's orientation. It was still playing variations on the vertical connections characteristic of imperial politics. It was now trying to cement relations with a new kind of African elite: political leaders, senior civil servants, people well educated in the French system. It was, in the summer of 1960, still making gestures toward "Community," but the

[157]"Note à l'attention de M. Alain Plantey," by Yves Jouhaud, 6 December 1966, FPU 557, ANF. A similar argument was made earlier in regard to Madagascar by Foccart: "France's interest appears to be that its French nationals can without separating themselves from Malagasy society by an inopportune choice continue to exercise influence favorable to our country in the milieu from which they came." Foccart to Foyer, 28 December 1960, FPU 558, ANF.

[158]"Note sur la loi No. 60–752 de 28 Juillet 1960 portant modifications de certaines dispositions de la code de la nationalité," and Secrétaire d'État aux relations avec les États de la Communauté to Haut Représentatif, 10 November 1960, Dakar/Ambassade/482, ADN.

[159]Sylla's initiative is described in Note for Haut-Représentatif by H. L.Touze, Consul Général, 3 November 1960, Dakar/Ambassade/482, ADN; Renseignements, 3 October 1960, Dakar/Ambassade/396, ADN. This effort to obtain French citizenship persisted into 1961, opposed by other Lébou who wanted to show their confidence in Senegal. Renseignements, 27 February 1961, Dakar/Ambassade/396, ADN.

reality of the political situation was that relations were increasingly bilateral and focused on direct ties of France to African heads of state. When negotiations with the states of the Conseil de l'Entente were at a delicate phase in June, Debré expressed his faith in the familiar figure of Houphouët-Boigny and in the generally friendly orientation of the leaders of these states.[160]

But most African states, as we have seen, were more concerned than France to establish an exclusive nationality. In the middle of the 1960s, a study of immigrant African workers in France showed that few—despite being resident in France—bothered to exercise their right to have their French nationality recognized, because they already had the right of free movement under the accords of 1960 with the new African governments.[161]

For French leaders, the price of ensuring that a French business-man could operate securely in Abidjan was that a Senegalese had the right to seek a job at the Renault factory in Boulogne-Billancourt.[162] The relationship with Algerians was more tense—and the failure of the French government to allow *harkis*, the Muslim Algerians who had fought on the French side during the war, to take refuge in France in 1962 against the vengeance of the victors in the war cost thousands of lives and brought shame onto France. Meanwhile, virtually the entire settler population of Algeria left (contrary to the expectations of the French government) and were able, with some difficulty, to settle in metropolitan France with the full rights of citizens.[163]

Because the treaties with West African states as well as Algeria gave former French citizens the right to enter France, police complained about their inability to track and keep control of such migrants. Although many of the large number of Muslim Algerians resident in metropolitan France during the war of 1954 to 1962 returned home to help build the new nation, the civil war that erupted almost immediately in Algeria produced a new wave of movement to France,

---

[160] Debré, Statement at Assemblée Nationale in debate on accords with Mali, 9 June 1960, 1219.

[161] J. Trillat, "Aspects généraux de l'immigration des travailleurs africains en France," in *Etudes Sociales Nord Africaines*, special issue on "Approches des problèmes de la migra-tion noire en France," nd [1965], copy in F/1a/5135, ANF.

[162] Even as the French government was reconciling itself to the need to negotiate the independence of Algeria with the FLN, it was more concerned with preserving the rights of people of French origin in Algeria than in cutting off the rights of Muslim Algerians to retain the rights they had had in France as citizens. See "projet de déclara-tion" in folder dated December 1961 and note on nationality for the Prime Minister, by Pierre Racine, 13 December 1961, 2DE 88, MD.

[163] Jean-Jacques Jordi, *1962: L'Arrivée des Pieds-Noirs* (Paris: Autrement, 2002). Despite the treatment of harkis, the door remained ajar for Algerians who established residence in France to obtain French nationality. See Patrick Weil, *Qu'est-ce qu'un Français? Histoire de la nationalité française depuis la Révolution* (Paris: Gallimard, 2005).

and labor-hungry France was eager to have them. Some 263,000 Algerians came to France in 1963. The Ministry of the Interior reported—unhappily—in 1964 that "immigration of Algerian workers in France was not regulated. The Evian accords create a French obligation to ensure the free movement of people from one side of the Mediterranean to the other." Both the French and the Algerian governments, however, soon moved against the ambiguous middle ground of nationality. Algerian officials often destroyed migrants' French papers when they returned to Algeria to visit—giving them no option but Algerian nationality—and France negotiated with the Algerian government in 1964 to ensure that Algerians would be admitted to France only under Algerian identification documents, unless they had opted definitively for French nationality.[164]

For workers coming to France from sub-Saharan Africa, the regime of "free movement" also did not suddenly come to an end with independence. Officials by 1963 were expressing anxieties that would become familiar over the years: over poorly educated migrants, not necessarily with skills adapted to the French labor market, living in bad conditions, under no surveillance, possibly leading to "an unassimilable subproletariat of African origin."[165] But there was not much to be done, given the independence treaties and relations of France with its former colonies: "For obvious political reasons, it would not be possible, in the absence of agreements, to proceed to massive repatriations of people who, by virtue of the dispositions in effect, are simply required to present a passport or a national identity card to be admitted to France" and who are not required to have a "carte de séjour."[166] Bilateral agreements with African countries—who did not want to see their countries drained of manpower—were the preferred

[164] Ministre de l'Intérieur, circular letters to prefects, 26 October 1963, 23 April 1964, FA/1a/5048, ANF; Conseillers techniques pour les affaires musulmanes, "Synthèse des rapports trimestriels," third and fourth quarters, 1962, 760133/14, CAC. Alexis Spire argues that despite the law, police (many with Algerian experience) found ways to keep their eyes on, if not harass, Algerians in the metropole. *Étrangers à la carte. L'administration de l'immigration en France (1945-1975)* (Paris, Grasset, 2005), 195–222.

[165] Ministre de la Coopération to Prefet de la Seine, 15 February 1962, F/1a/5136, ANF.

[166] Ministre de l'Intérieur, Note pour M. le Directeur Général des Affaires Politiques et de l'Administration du Territoire, Services des Affaires Musulmanes, 9 April 1963, F/1a/5136, ANF. Officials admitted that Senegal was in a position to restrict the right of French citizens to work in Senegal, so it would be risky to restrict Senegalese immigration to France. Note Documentaire, 20 December 1961, enclosed Chargé d'Affaires de France, Dakar, to Ministre de la Coopération, 21 December 1961, Dakar/Ambassade/512, ADN. Gregory Mann points out that not only were the requirements for documentation for former French Africans relatively modest, but migrants developed networks for forging and recycling documents, so that many more West Africans actually entered France than the government knew about. Unofficial sources put African migration (mostly Malian, Senegalese, and Mauritanian) at 40,000 in 1963, rising to

route to regulate the flow. Police complained that given the regime of free entry, they lacked the means to observe "immigrants." They did not even know how many of them there were but presumed they were numerous: "In the street or, here in the metro, they are conspicuous." But however much they appeared ill prepared to live in a European country, the African migrants were supposed to be "treated in this regard as if they were French citizens in regard to labor legislation."[167]

Migration into France was a reality that was both historically rooted in the regime of "libre circulation" and useful in the present. So in the years immediately following the end of French colonial rule in Algeria and sub-Saharan Africa, the boundary between a truly national France and a more inclusive France—of former subjects who had in 1946 acquired the rights of citizens—had still not hardened. It would do so in the 1970s.

Conclusion

Triumph and despair marked 1960. The states of French West Africa became independent, sovereign, internationally recognized political units. Modibo Keita in February 1960 asked Africans to grasp the significance of the end of colonialism:

> African comrades, you must cure yourself of a complex, the complex of the colonized. I know that intellectuals, all young people, are elated when one denounces colonialism, imperialism, capitalism. But where is colonialism now? You can look for it, you will not find it. So, is it worth wasting time, burning energy to vituperate against something that no longer exists? For now on, if one does so, it is because one has kept the mentality of the colonized. . . . We have nothing to blush at for having been colonized. Look around you. There is no country that has not passed through a colonial regime. Gaul, before becoming France, was Roman Gaul. We know that England has experienced the Normans. And the powerful United States were once an English colony. Why would you want, as Africans, for colonization to be a purely African fact? But no, it is a fact of history. It is a universal fact. We therefore have nothing to blush about for

---

over 200,000 in 1969. "The End of the Road: Nongovernmentality in the West African Sahel" (Manuscript), chap. 4.

[167] Préfecture de la Police, Seine, Reports, 5 September 1963, 19 February 1964, Statement of le Prefet Mamassoure, representing Ministère de l'Intérieur, to meeting of Conseil Économique et Social, Section du développement économique et social des pays autres que la France et de la coopération technique, meeting of 6 February 1964, F/1a/5136, ANF.

having been colonized, unless we consider that the black race is an inferior race, a race incapable of controlling a situation that the entire world has known.[168]

De Gaulle, in retrospect, was much cooler about the dénouement of overseas France than he had been when he was trying to hold together by one means or another some sort of supranational French community: "It is a fact: decolonization is in our interest and therefore our policy. Why should we hang onto costly domination, bloody and with no escape, when our country should be renewed from top to bottom, when all underdeveloped countries, beginning with those that depended on us and which today are our preferred friends, ask our help and cooperation?"[169]

But neither France nor its former colonies achieved the decolonization each had sought. The French Community that de Gaulle had advocated so vigorously in 1958 was emptied of substance in 1960. Another form of Community was preserved by constitutional rewriting, only to become a dead letter within months of its rebirth in "renovated" form. The idea of "African unity"—proclaimed by practically all leaders and political movements in AOF throughout the 1950s—ended up in a truncated Mali Federation, which negotiated successfully with France to achieve independence, largely on the terms it sought, only to explode two months after its creation as an independent nation. The common citizenship that had been the basis of political, social, and economic claim making by Africans since 1946 turned into a series of bilateral agreements, more easily repudiated or modified by either side than the constitutional provisions of 1946 or 1958. African politicians, over the course of 1959, successfully sought recognition of the national personality of their states, then rejected the "superposed nationality" of the Community that they had recently agreed to fold themselves into. The attempts to forge an African nationality failed with the breakup of Mali in 1960. Houphouët-Boigny was unable to bring about his own version of superposed African—or even Conseil de l'Entente—nationality in 1963–64. The nationality codes of new African states made gestures toward allowing other Africans to acquire their nationality, but covered those options with time limits and insistence on demonstrations of attachment—to the territory in principle, but perhaps to its rulers in fact.

What African states obtained was sovereignty. What their citizens lost was common citizenship—in an entity, whether African or Franco-African, larger than a nation-state. They, for a time, retained some of the rights and privileges they had had as French citizens, including

---

[168] Speech of Modibo Keita at conférence régionale de Ségou, 19–20 February 1960, Dakar/Ambassade/345, ADN.

[169] News conference, 11 April 1961, quoted in *Afrique Nouvelle*, 19 April 1961.

the right of free movement between their home states and France. But those rights were fragile. There were disturbing hints, going back to the Abidjan riots of 1958, of xenophobic attitudes among some Africans, especially it would seem, among the better educated. And the legislation of France and African countries was pushing people to choose between claiming French nationality in France or an African nationality in an African country. Meanwhile, the social and economic claims that Africans had made as citizens on France—with considerable success through at least 1956—were turning into requests for foreign aid. France's continued quest for influence in the world led its government to soften the break—continuing to allow African migrants to enter and seek work in its country, hoping the ruling elites of African states would in one way or another maintain their personal attachments to France, offering funds and technical personnel to former French territories, and from time to time intervening militarily to support its African allies. But those decisions were made in France by French nationals. The place of Africans in decision-making bodies in France—always minoritarian, sometimes influential—was gone. Meanwhile, Léopold Senghor and Mamadou Dia, who had insisted into the summer of 1960 that they wanted to build an African or a Malian nation, began on the morning of 20 August to construct a Senegalese nation.[170]

[170] Senegal chose to celebrate its independence, beginning in 1961, not on 20 August, but on 4 April—the date of the signing of the independence agreement with France, even though it was Mali, not Senegal, that signed. The first celebration partly followed plans that had been drawn up before the breakup to mark the declaration of the Federation of Mali (17 January 1959). Several African heads of state, including Houphouët-Boigny, the Vice President of the United States, and high French officials (but not the President) were present. Susann Baller, "Les fêtes célébrées et supprimées: Les indépendances de la Fédération du Mali et du Sénégal" (unpublished paper, 2012); Afrik.com, "Indépendance du Sénégal: Quelle date fêter?," www.afrik.com /article22493.html (accessed 6 August 2012).

CONCLUSION

The spectrum of ideas through which the leaders of African and European France approached politics between 1945 and the early 1960s was much wider than a dichotomy of colonial empire and independent nation-state. The meanings of citizenship, nationality, and sovereignty were not set. They were the object of political contestation, not just the subject of treatises of jurists or philosophers. The stakes in how they were defined were high, for a Senegalese seeking better pay in Dakar or a job in Lyon, for a political leader trying to mobilize a constituency in Bamako or in the suburbs of Marseille.

The historian is inevitably confronted with the temptation to trace a line that leads inexorably to the present. In contrast, we spend much of our political energies in the present dealing with unknowns and contingencies. In the story I have told, people acted in relation to the possibilities they perceived in their time, and they sought to widen—or to constrict—the openings they had. We have been repeatedly told that the nation has been the preeminent unit of political imagination since the revolutions of the late eighteenth and early nineteenth centuries, that "modern" sovereignty is necessarily territorial and indivisible, that citizenship in a republic entails a relationship of individual to state unmediated by distinctions of status or community. The actors in the story told here—French and African—thought otherwise.

This has been a story of politics in action, of people convincing others to do things they did not initially want to do, of issues being reframed as they were debated. A tiny number of African and Caribbean deputies in the assemblies that wrote the French Constitution of 1946 compelled their colleagues to engage in a serious discussion of what kind of polity France was and could be. The citizenship provisions of the constitution in turn positioned African political and social movements to insist on the social, economic, as well as political equivalence of all French citizens. They faced the resistance of defenders of colonial privileges and more consistently the qualms of people who acknowledged the need to make France more pluralistic but could not bring themselves to see African society and culture as equivalent to their own. Reform of French political institutions—largely because of the resistance of well-connected settler elements in Algeria and the inertia of the French political system—remained blocked for a decade, but more and more Africans became voters and political parties organized themselves into relatively effective electoral machines.

Political leaders from the colonies were able, despite opposition and setbacks, to make their metropolitan colleagues agree that citizenship had to become more open in a double sense: subjects had to be made into citizens, and France had to accept that one could be a citizen in different ways. African leaders insisted that France transform itself into a polity that was multicultural as well as egalitarian. From political leaders as different as Léopold Sédar Senghor and Sékou Touré, Charles de Gaulle and Félix Houphouët Boigny came proposals for different variants of federalism and confederalism as alternatives to colonial empires.

Particularly in regard to social questions, African movements won important victories between 1946 and 1956: improvements in wages and benefits, equalization of civil service benefits, a new labor code, and demonstrations that African organizations would have their say on key decisions. In rural areas, African parties challenged the old hierarchy of administrators and chiefs. The demands for social equality, above all, pushed French officials and politicians by the mid-1950s to rethink their centralizing tendencies and concede real power to African territorial assemblies, the only way that African political leaders could be induced to refocus their ambitions from equality with European France to the development and distribution of resources at the territorial level.

African political leaders were able to make the leaders of European France shift ground again. In 1958, de Gaulle's (and Félix Houphouët-Boigny's) desire for a federal structure with a strong center gave way over the course of the constitution-writing process to something closer to Senghor's confederal vision, with Member States having the right to demand independence at any time. The French government's insistence that there could be only one nationality in the Community—the French one—evaporated in the face of African opposition, ending up with the notion of the French Community as a multinational entity, with French nationality superposed on Senegalese, Ivorian, and other African nationalities. And as the Mali Federation asserted its right to independence, the French government was so eager to keep it in the French fold that it changed its own constitution to allow an independent, sovereign state to remain in the Community.

The citizenship provisions of 1946 had been the focus of political confrontation; by the time of the 1958 constitution they were no longer controversial. France's African population got something quite important out of this succession of concessions and reconfigurations: the rights of the French citizen. The rights to free speech and assembly and to equal justice—and by 1956 universal suffrage—were no small victories for people whose political voice had been denied and who had been subject to arbitrary punishments by French administrators. The right of "free movement" was no small matter either, for it gave the individual a means of countering the disadvantages of living in a poor state with a heritage of colonial neglect and exploitation: to seek livelihood elsewhere in the former empire.

The formal repudiation of racial discrimination and the juridical inscription of universal citizenship after 1946 did not mean that the concentration of political power in Paris and invidious discrimination in Africa disappeared, but it did mean that Africans had access to key institutions and media to force debate over social equality and political participation. These—often frustrating—debates took place in the space of what had been the French Empire, then the French Union, then the French Community. The fact that Malagasy, Algerians, and Cameroonians were French citizens did not prevent the government from engaging in brutal repression—and in labeling entire categories of people as putative terrorists—when political movements acted outside of certain boundaries. In other contexts, the repressive arm had to be restrained and understandings reached with African political movements, as in the Côte d'Ivoire in 1950.

How can we explain the fact that the ambitious and intelligent leaders of European and African France ended up in 1960 with a form of political organization—the territorial nation-state—that few of them had sought in 1946 and which all but Guinea had rejected in 1958? My emphasis in this book has been on narrating a process, since "independence" was neither an event nor a condition to be explained by identifying a cause. Alternatives were in play and at several key points, the choices made reconfigured what was possible, impossible, or difficult in ensuing moments. What was going on beyond France and French Africa—the attainment of sovereignty in Indonesia, India, Ghana, and elsewhere, the Cold War, the changing structure of the world economy—shaped conditions of possibility. The key actors in this story knew what others were doing, but tried to do something different; Houphouët-Boigny even bet Nkrumah that his strategy would prove the better. If we presume the overarching narrative of a global, long-term transition from empire to nation-state, we might not even ask the question posed above.

Advocates of federal and confederal political structures—French and African—were repeatedly caught between a politics of what they wanted and a politics of what they could get. The territorial basis for elections to French and territorial legislatures from the fall of 1945 onward led African political parties to create specific mechanisms of mobilization, patronage, and networking, slowly extending deeper into African social structures as suffrage expanded between 1946 and 1956. The loi-cadre was both a concession to Africans' demands for political reform and an attempt to deflect responsibility for social citizenship away from the metropolitan taxpayer. For African leaders it was simultaneously a political victory and a trap, crystallizing power at the territorial level even as Senghor and Sékou Touré were trying to add legislative and executive authority to the larger political entity of French West Africa and as the French government was losing its grip on Africa.

From their territorial bases, African political leaders, despite efforts to find common ground, could not agree on what they would sacrifice or risk in order to achieve the goal of unity that most supported. The unresolved conflict between the advocates of African federation—Senghor, Dia, Sékou Touré, Modibo Keita—and the opponents—Houphouët-Boigny, Apithy—reflected both political calculation and uncertainty over whether the "petite patrie," the territorial state that had emerged from colonization, or "Negro-African civilization" should be the focus of political identification. Meanwhile, the regime of semi-autonomy under the loi-cadre brought out French-African tensions over where power lay, while African leaders became increasingly sensitive to pressures from youth and other radicals and the alternative model of national independence.

Yet in 1958, different possibilities were still open. Africans had their say on the new constitution; they continued to debate what the concepts of federation, confederation, nation, sovereignty, and independence could mean for the people of French Africa. But with Guinea, the Mali Federation, and the states of the Conseil de l'Entente going separate ways and with the possibilities of international recognition and participation in international organizations becoming clearer, the "grand ensemble" looked more and more problematic and the possibility of achieving independence without giving up the benefits of the French connection became more appealing. The Mali Federation represented the last opportunity for the leaders of former French West Africa to give institutional basis to an inclusive African polity and to create a pole of attraction for other African nations. Its breakup in August 1960 was the final blow both to the dream of African unity and to the French Community.

Whatever the alternative pathways coming out of any of these turning points, the inevitability of the route taken only appeared—certainly to most of the activists involved—in retrospect. African leaders, after independence, were eager to rewrite their history with themselves as fathers of the nation, even though the nations they now led were not the nation they had previously sought to create. At the same time, memories of the struggle to make French citizenship into something socially, politically, and culturally meaningful to a diverse population were written out of French history as thoroughly as was, until recently, France's record of colonial domination and oppression. Bringing that story back in might help us think anew about the relationship of republican citizenship to cultural difference and of the colonial past to exclusion and discrimination in the present. And if Africans might from one perspective lament the loss of the vitality of the politics of citizenship in the 1940s and 1950s, from another angle memories of these struggles might broaden the range of what is imaginable politically.

After independence, Africans' claims to social and economic equivalence with other French people no longer could be posed within the framework of French citizenship. They had to be made within territorially distinct nation-states and more abstractly in appeals for rights and resources at the level of humanity. France could choose to respond to demands for aid and technical assistance, but the choice of when and to whom to provide them was no longer made by institutions in which Africans were represented.

In acquiring sovereignty, African states made an apparently clean break with the colonial past. But Senghor and others had sought a sovereignty that one could claim and then give some of it back in return for the advantages of belonging to a larger political unit. After the collapse of the Mali Federation and the French Community, the ruling elites of African states found that sovereignty was the strongest asset they had. They were anxious to define and assert the nationalities they had recently acquired. France sought for a time to soften the break with its former citizens, and one of the most important dimensions of citizenship after 1946—the right of free movement—remained in place by treaties until the 1970s. Meanwhile, France chose to "abandon," to use Senghor's term, some of its sovereignty, but it did so to make a "European," not a "Eurafrican," community.

Politics in Africa between 1945 and 1960 built on and deepened a democratic ideal: elections, party mobilization, the expansion of suffrage, and efforts to eliminate discrimination in the allocation of seats in assemblies in France and in Africa. After the ordeal of World War II and Vichy rule, a wide spectrum of the French public wanted representative government for themselves; the question was who would be included. African politicians worked within such a framework from the Assemblée Nationale Constituante through independence, while pushing it in new directions. African parties did what parties usually do: build patronage networks, work through brokers, put together coalitions. This process could in some cases draw on and reinforce structures of inequality within communities—as with the control by Mouride and other marabouts over their followers in Senegal or the privileged positions of cocoa planters in southern Côte d'Ivoire—but the gradual expansion of suffrage between 1946 and 1956 and then elections under universal suffrage and the single college after that subjected parties to the discipline of voting. The French government played its games—a repressive campaign against the Ivorian RDA from 1948 to 1950 and against Sawaba in Niger in 1958, the elimination of the UPC in Cameroon—but it too was constrained by the rules it had helped to establish.

The form that independence took brought an end to the multiple levels of institutions in which issues were debated and decisions made. Despite the efforts of many Africans to uphold democratic principles and to campaign for a more just society, the politics of postindependence French West Africa in the 1960s and 1970s moved away from an electoral focus that counterbalanced the tendencies toward personal and clientelistic politics that exist in all systems. Single-party domination and the long-term and authoritarian rule of an individual—thirty-three years in the case of Houphouët-Boigny, twenty-six for Sékou Touré, twenty for Senghor—came to be basic features of francophone African politics.

Senghor was caught in the trap he had warned against: a bounded national state, unchecked by federal connections either above it (an African federation, the French Community) or below it (strong local or provincial governments). Not least of the problems was the leadership's perception—widely felt with good reason across Africa—that the state did not have the resources to win the support of its citizens by meeting their aspirations for social and economic progress.

Much as we can delve into the intense debates among African political actors about the future of their territories, we know much less about how ordinary citizens in French West Africa—farmers, traders, workers—thought about the ambiguity of their position as French citizens. Future researchers will find out how much can be learned about the idioms and connections through which people in Africa's varied contexts practiced politics. We do know that even as the late-colonial state tried to slot its citizens into institutions concerned with social order, welfare, and surveillance, Africans tried to use such mechanisms in their own way, ignoring for example the état-civil except when they needed to make themselves known to the state to get a child into school, vote, collect social benefits, or obtain papers required for travel to European France.

We also know that student and youth organizations mobilized in favor of a complete break with the colonial past and present. Yet even in Senegal—where such movements were particularly well organized—activists were better able to stage an impressive demonstration during de Gaulle's visit in August 1958 than to bring out voters in September. Parties were able to channel, for a time, diverse forms of political mobilization into electoral machines.[1] They worked through vertical networks and brokers, putting together coalitions, agglomerating and transcending local social contexts. Such networks extended deep into rural communities and, for a time, co-opted trade unions and other urban elements. Senghor and Houphouët-Boigny were masters at this type of politics, even as they engaged with universalistic ideas and French institutions.

[1] Aristide Zolberg argued some time ago that West African political parties were more like political machines than mass parties. *Creating Political Order: The Party States of West Africa* (Chicago: Rand McNally, 1966).

The politics of citizenship played out in the form of collective attempts to forge institutions capable of giving life to multiple levels of belonging and sovereignty, but also to individual assertion of rights. For individuals, the possibility of taking advantage of "libre circulation" to seek opportunities in different parts of the French Union or Community was of particular importance. Many people sought to build a life for themselves on both sides of the Mediterranean. People in motion had to confront the tensions of cultural ambivalence and the realities of meager resources and enduring discrimination, but confronted these tensions as rights-bearing citizens.

Mobilizations should not be read into a single narrative of "nationalism." Labor movements, for example, were largely focused on classic issues of wages and benefits, and their claim making drew effectively on the rhetoric of equality among French citizens. By the late 1950s, however, political elites were trying to channel diverse social movements into the quest for national development under the aegis of the states that were coming under their control. The social tensions that accompanied the move toward independence brought out the anxieties of governing elites about the depth of their control in the face of the claims of citizens.

French West Africa's route out of empire, complex as it was, was one among others. In Algeria, settlers with the backing of key elements in metropolitan politics and the military, used their citizenship rights to prevent Muslim citizens from fully exercising theirs. Because Algeria was defined as an integral part of the French Republic—although one part of its population was more integral than the other nine-tenths—the possibility of ending or transforming Algeria's situation in relation to France was fraught. Its Muslim population had experienced land-grabbing, exploitation, and routine humiliation with an intensity found in only certain times and places in AOF, and nationalist movements developed earlier in Algeria than in sub-Saharan Africa. The French state—itself under pressure from settlers and their metropolitan allies, the military, and even leftist politicians in France who thought they knew best how to bring about social progress—did not develop the kind of give-and-take with Algerian politicians that it did with their West African counterparts and by 1956 was escalating repression in a way that ensured that Algeria's route out of empire would be violent and bitter.

In Morocco and Tunisia—former protectorates—inhabitants had not been French nationals and did not necessarily want such a status. They came under a particular citizenship regime, as citizens of the French Union. There were significant settler populations in Morocco and Tunisia as well, and postwar politics there was beset by confrontation, violence, and repression. But the juridical distinction was important to the trajectory of these states toward complete independence in 1956: there was no "Maroc français" comparable to "l'Algérie française." The refusal of the Sultan of Morocco and the Bey of Tunis, as sovereigns of their own nations, to cooperate in the institutions of the French Union after 1946 helped to doom the strategy of differential incorporation into that ensemble. The fiction of protection was easier to abandon than the fiction of integration, and the political networks of settlers in Morocco and Tunisia were less prominent than those of Algerian colons in French politics, leaving the government freer to act pragmatically when the challenge of anticolonial movements escalated in the early 1950s. Algeria, Morocco, and Tunisia, and the territories of French West Africa followed distinct trajectories, but they all ended up as territorial states, whether or not that was what their people wanted most.

What follows are three vignettes to illustrate the extent to which the issues raised in this book have shaped the postindependence history of Africa and of France. These vignettes serve to illustrate the zigs and zags in trajectories out of empire—in France as much as in Africa—and the long-term consequences of the emergence of national orders from the multiple possibilities that were in play between 1945 and 1960.

Epilogue 1: Senegal, 1962

The biggest danger that threatens the Community in Black Africa
is the institution of the single party, of dictatorships that do not
even have the merit of being anti-racist.

—*Léopold Senghor, 1958*[2]

After December 1962, Senghor's Senegal became what he had warned against, a single-party regime, dominated by its leader, chasing its opponents not only from the arena of politics, but into prison. The prime victim was Senghor's longtime comrade, Mamadou Dia. The crisis and its repressive aftermath were indicative of the political tensions intrinsic to the states that had emerged out of decolonization from 1956 to 1960: a bounded political domain, leadership conscious of its fragile hold on power, few material resources, and an elite's acute need to control the networks by which those resources were distributed.

Senghor and Dia had shared an aspiration to build a socialism that was both African and humanist. The Senegalese government sought to improve the livelihood of Senegal's rural population and to develop rural cooperatives to give peasants more power relative to local elites.

[2] From an interview given in Paris, "L'indépendance dans l'association," *Afrique Nouvelle*, 14 November 1958.

It provided technical assistance through young activists, a program known as "rural animation." There was little difference in theory between Senghor and Dia, but there was a difference in political perspective. Dia was Prime Minister, charged (ever since the implementation of internal autonomy in 1957) with running the daily work of government, while Senghor was President, the head of state but also the center of the political networks that kept their political party in power.

By 1961, Dia was deeply frustrated with the obstacles to change, and he insisted on pushing more vigorously. Among the obstacles were the marabouts, who dominated rural Senegal and the peanut economy.[3] Dia, a Muslim, came into increasing conflict with the rural Muslim elite, but it was Senghor, a Christian, who had constructed over the previous fifteen years an electoral apparatus that worked through those elites, making state resources available to them. The Senegalese National Assembly included people with commercial interests (some linked to France, most to the marabouts) who were worried about Dia's efforts to give a government agency a fuller role in peanut production and marketing, to turn rural cooperatives into a countervailing force against the brotherhood leaders, and to centralize and professionalize development planning.[4] Tensions grew throughout 1961, with Senghor trying to maintain a distant posture but aware that his government's policy threatened to undermine his most important supporters.

Behind the tensions was the basic situation Senegal shared with many other countries emerging from colonial rule: a monocrop economy, poor infrastructure, narrow channels of commercialization controlled by local elites within the country and foreign elites at the point of exportation. The problems were exacerbated by the failure of federation: Dakar had gone from being the headquarters of AOF and the potential capital of a large African federation to being the capital of a small nation-state.[5]

The crisis came to a head in 1962 as the Senegalese Assembly tried to censure Dia for his unpalatable policies. Dia argued that, under

[3]The pioneering study of the marabouts' importance to economy and politics is Donal Cruise O'Brien, *The Mourides of Senegal: The Political and Economic Organization of an Islamic Brotherhood* (Oxford: Clarendon, 1971).

[4]Dia saw the goal of rural reform as "a modern and progressive communal movement, putting in place that way and in depth the basis of the socialism we have chosen." Senegal, Assemblée Nationale, *Débats*, 4 April 1961, 262. Dia noted the hostility of leading marabouts to his government in *Mémoires d'un militant du tiers-monde* (Paris: Publisud, 1985), 146–47.

[5]French Ambassador Claude Hettier de Boislambert pointed to this problem. He also noted the "hardening of the authority of the state." Ambassador to Senegal to Secrétaire d'État aux Relations avec les États de la Communauté, 5 January, 6 February 1962, Dakar/Ambassade/304, ADN.

emergency regulations in place since the collapse of the Mali Federation over two years previously, the Assembly had no right to do so.[6] Dia tried to get the party to back him against the deputies, failed, and then decided to seal off the assembly meeting and prevent a vote. But Senghor had the military behind him, and he had Dia and ministers loyal to Dia—including Ibrahima Sarr, hero of the 1947–48 railway strike—arrested.[7] Each side accused the other of staging a coup. Much of the story remains murky.[8]

Dia spent twelve years in prison. The bureaucracy was purged; the agenda of rural reform was abandoned; the brotherhoods consolidated their control. Senghor abolished the post of prime minister and moved to a presidential regime. After winning a suspicious 98 percent of the votes in the 1963 elections, Senghor's party moved to eliminate all rivals, and soon Senegal was a one-party state. Trade unions were repressed.[9] Just as Senghor, in the summer of 1960, gave up federalism in the face of challenges to his political base, in the winter of 1962, he moved to a more authoritarian form of politics for the same reason.

[6] *Le Monde* ("La coopération entre MM. Senghor et Dia est de nouveau menacée," 16–17 December 1962) concluded that the basis of the conflict was not ideological difference, but Senghor's efforts "to protect Muslim notables—the marabouts—against the social reform movement" initiated by Dia.

[7] The population of Dakar was apparently little involved in the crisis, except for some efforts of Senghor's organization to turn out supporters. For a journalist's narration of the events, see Jean Lacouture, "Comment s'est nouée la crise," *Le Monde,* 18 December 1962. See also his commentary on the two protagonists, "Deux Africains," *Le Monde,* 19 December 1962 and the reporting of Philippe Decraene, *Le Monde,* 19–22 December 1962.

[8] Some commentators—including part of the French press at the time—took Senghor's side, arguing that Dia had become dangerously radical and authoritarian. Others saw the heavy hand of French neocolonialism working for Senghor. As we have seen, French opinion through independence was pro-Dia. By mid-June 1962, however, Hettier de Boislambert, reported that Senghor was complaining about Dia's move to the left and his headstrong character. The Ambassador even thought—in a notable misreading of character—that Senghor might want to return to France and "resume his professorial career." Note of Secrétaire d'État aux Relations avec les États de la Communauté on "La situation intérieure au Sénégal," enclosed Debré to de Gaulle, 3 May 1961; Ambassador, notes on conversation with Senghor, 8 June 1962, FPR 268, ANF. Dia later wrote that Debré had warned him during a visit to Paris a month before the events of December 1962 that Senghor was plotting with Mouride leaders against him. *Mémoires d'un militant*, 147.

[9] This account is partly based on Edward J. Schumacher, *Politics, Bureaucracy and Rural Development in Senegal* (Berkeley: University of California Press, 1975), 63–67; Catherine Boone, *Merchant Capital and the Roots of State Power in Senegal 1930–1985* (New York: Cambridge University Press, 1992), 91–94; Mamadou Diouf, "Le clientélisme, la 'technocratie' et après?," in Momar-Coumba Diop, ed., *Sénégal: Trajectoires d'un État* (Dakar: Codesria, 1992), 250–52. Dia's version is in *Mémoires d'un militant*, 143–75.

Epilogue 2: France, 1974

On 3 July 1974, the Council of Ministers of the French Republic an-nounced that most immigration was suspended. The suspension was said at the time to be provisional, but it proved long-term. Certain derogations were later granted and other provisions hardened. In the interest of promoting the social stability of people previously admit-ted, certain family members of settled immigrants were allowed to join them. Another set of circulars in October and November 1974 in ef-fect ended the regime of "free movement" for citizens from the former states of French Africa. They could get a carte de séjour (residence per-mit) only if they presented a work contract before departure, and of-ficials knew that such contracts would be hard to get. Africans already in France—but who had not obtained French nationality—were given a chance to regularize their situation by obtaining a carte de séjour, but when it expired (after three years, five in the case of Senegalese), they would be in the same situation as foreigners.[10] The government claimed that it was anxious to improve the social situation of immi-grants already in France at the same time that it wished to stop those seeking work from coming. Over time, it became more difficult still for the children of France's former citizens to enter France—student visas would become hard to come by for instance—and by the 1980s a xenophobic politics had become part of the French scene, featur-ing the public invocation of demeaning stereotypes of Muslims and sub-Saharan Africans, insistence that the barriers against immigration be raised higher, and calls for systematic expulsions, if not of all Mus-lims, at least of those deemed by authorities to be in an "irregular situation."

Some observers have argued that the 1974 measures reflected the economic downturn, itself a consequence of the world recession that followed a spike in oil prices and brought to an end the "trente glorieuses"—the thirty years of economic expansion in France—leading the government to anticipate growing unemployment in the summer of 1974. Sylvain Laurens has cautioned against too mechani-cal an interpretation. He sees the evidence of economic turndown and unemployment coming after rather than before the fact. He thinks a change in the composition of high officialdom in France, particularly in the newly inaugurated government of President Giscard d'Estaing, changed the way of thinking about immigration, not least because

---

[10]Catherine Gokalp, "Chronique de l'immigration," *Population* 30, 4–5 (1975): 889–96.

France's colonial past and the people whom that past had linked to France were of diminishing importance to the governing elite, compared to more immediate market-centered concerns.[11]

But the most important point is so obvious that it is rarely stated: the people of former French Africa who had obtained or were seeking jobs in France had *become* immigrants. They had been citizens, and after 1960 those born before independence had had the right of free circulation, under the treaties that softened the separation of nationalities. In the 1970s, they were the object of political calculation by French officials, politicians, and citizens, and they had no say in regard to the policies that concerned them. Such were the—delayed—consequences of the separating of citizenships.

Those Africans who had or could acquire French nationality now had strong incentives to attach themselves definitively to France. "Sans papiers" (undocumented immigrants) who were living under the radar in France had even more reason not to leave, for they might not get back in. The problem of immigration became the problem of immigrants, whose social conditions and ways of life became the object of concern to reformers and a focus of xenophobic sentiments for others.

Patrick Weil points out that as late as 1973, the French government was relatively open to allowing its former citizens born before independence to either obtain French nationality or enjoy some of its benefits without the status. In that year, a new law ensured the equality of men and women in the naturalization process, and the principal author of that law, Jean Foyer—one of de Gaulle's legal aides during the independence negotiations—underscored that France was "a land of immigration. . . . From Gallo-Roman and Germanic peoples she made a French people. The amended project that we propose to you will facilitate this action with other ethnic groups. Racism is an odious stupidity that has brought about the worst crimes of History." Only a few months later, Weil observes, "the immigration of new foreign workers was interrupted, and the words of Jean Foyer quickly forgotten."[12] But not by everyone. Government efforts to expel Algerians and Africans and subsequent immigrant-bashing words and actions were resisted by organizations of African immigrants and their French sympathizers in churches, unions, and rights-oriented organizations. It is no more clear that the forces of xenophobia and Islamophobia won in

[11] Sylvain Laurens, "'1974' et la fermeture des frontières: Analyse critique d'une décision érigée en *turning point,*" *Politix* 21, 82 (2008): 69–94.
[12] Patrick Weil, *Qu'est ce qu'un Français? Histoire de la nationalité française depuis la Révolution* (Paris: Grasset, 2002), 161–63, 163 quoted.

the 1980s (or today) than it was clear that openness and tolerance were universal norms in 1973—or 1946.[13]

Yet the very plausibility of the anti-immigrant politics that established itself—with its idea of a clearly defined French nation defending itself against outsiders—required erasing not just a long history of colonization, but a brief yet important period between 1945 and 1960 when different versions of a plural France had been debated, during which power had been divided across different layers of government and different notions of sovereignty had been contemplated, when different forms of civic life were juridically recognized, and when influential political figures could put forth the radical claim that those different forms were compatible with political and social equality.

Epilogue 3: Côte d'Ivoire, 2011

While I was working on this book in March and April of 2011, a horrendous battle was raging in Abidjan. At one level, it was another sad story of an African dictator, Laurent Gbagbo, refusing to leave office—ten years after winning a five-year mandate and after losing an election most outside observers regarded as legitimate. At another level, it was the playing out of a story that had begun with the riots of 1958 in Abidjan, directed against Togolese and Dahomean workers, but now focused on people with roots in Burkina Faso and other countries to the north of Côte d'Ivoire, mostly Muslims, many of whom had lived within its current borders for generations and who had contributed vitally needed labor to the great economic expansion of the Ivorian economy after 1946, a boom that has since dissipated. Seen over the period 1958 to 2011, the story is also one of reversing previous patterns, and above all it is a story of the dangerous consequences of dividing people into national containers, as the advocates of more supple conceptions of sovereignty had warned.

Those advocates included not only Senghor, Dia, and Sékou Touré, but also Félix Houphouët-Boigny. Houphouët-Boigny had built his political career on developing an alternative to the regime of settler farming and forced labor, helping to redirect the flow of workers from the north to African cocoa and coffee planters in the southern Côte d'Ivoire. He retained his sense of Côte d'Ivoire's connectedness even as he opposed Senghor's primary federation. He proposed various measures to allow people from the countries of the Conseil de l'Entente to live for short or long periods in Côte d'Ivoire with most of the rights

---

[13] For one view of the shift, see Miriam Feldblum, *Reconstructing Citizenship: The Politics of Reform and Immigration in Contemporary France* (Albany: State University of New York Press, 1999).

of national citizens. It was relatively educated "Ivorians"—in the narrow, territorial sense of the word—who opposed Houphouët-Boigny's plans, even as the other states of the Conseil de l'Entente, caught up in their own intraelite conflicts and efforts to consolidate national control, refused to buy into them.[14]

As the Côte d'Ivoire's export boom continued after independence, people of northern origin—overwhelmingly Muslim—became more deeply entrenched in the prosperous south and the social and cultural dividing line between the northern Côte d'Ivoire and its northern neighbors remained quite blurred. Communities of Muslims took root throughout the country, including in Abidjan.[15] The decline of world cocoa prices and a sharp downturn in the Ivorian economy and the death of Houphouët-Boigny in 1993—after thirty-three years in power and little effort to organize an orderly succession—fragilized the system of personal rule and patronage that kept the edifice together. In a zero-sum struggle for power among politicians lacking Houphouët-Boigny's stature, the card of xenophobia was played more and more. Rather than an inclusive Ivorian nationality, a vision of the nation that excluded those of foreign descent, not just foreign birth, came into play, dividing northern and southern portions of the national space itself. When Alassane Ouattara was denied the right to run for President in 2000 on the grounds that his parents were from Burkina Faso, the die was cast for struggles for personal power to map onto efforts to define "ivoirité." The state in 2002 tried to implement a "National Operation of Identification" to mark people by their "origin." Youth gangs turned themselves into enforcers.[16]

Through a series of rigged elections, military coups, and outright civil war—punctuated by outside interventions in the name of peace or democracy—the Côte d'Ivoire plunged into a cycle of ethnic cleansing and efforts on the part of those being cleansed to organize their own means of violence. When Gbagbo overstayed his term in office, and then—in large part due to outside pressure—found himself in another electoral contest with Ouattara, whom he tried to portray as a noncitizen, the organization of ethnicized political support networks and militias accelerated. The interventions of the UN, the African Union, the European Union, and France to insist that the election of 2010 take place and that it be conducted in accordance with some set of rules were variously characterized as an effort to promote democ-

[14] Henri-Michel Yéré, "Citizenship, Nationality & History in Côte d'Ivoire, 1929–1999" (PhD diss., University of Basel, 2010).

[15] Marie Miran, *Islam, histoire et modernité en Côte d'Ivoire* (Paris: Karthala, 2006); Sean Hanretta, *Islam and Social Change in French West Africa: History of an Emancipatory Community* (Cambridge: Cambridge University Press, 2009).

[16] Peter Geschiere, *The Perils of Belonging: Autochthony, Citizenship, and Exclusion in Africa and Europe* (Chicago: University of Chicago Press, 2009), 98–100, 109.

racy and prevent massive violence and as neocolonial intervention. The initial winner of the election was Ouattara, but Gbagbo's personally appointed electoral commission declared that there had been irregularities in northern provinces and thereby excluded them from the count—disenfranchising all people in those regions and tilting the count in Gbagbo's favor. Although these arguments convinced few people outside of his own camp, Gbagbo was willing to plunge Côte d'Ivoire into a civil war to remain in power. The Ouattara clan's armed supporters proved just as capable of mayhem and looting as those of Gbagbo, and the result was widespread atrocities, in which ethnicized conflict, patronage relations, and venality ran together. With help from outside, including French military forces, Ouattara's militias gained the upper hand and deposed and arrested Gbagbo. Ouattara became the internationally recognized President, but whether he can stitch together a Côte d'Ivoire that was torn apart by nearly two decades of debate and violence over the question of who was truly an Ivorian national is still in question.[17]

As with the definition of the "immigrant" in France, the definition of an "Ivorian" is not a given, but a product of history. The people who, in the 1990s and 2000s, were being defined *out* of the Côte d'Ivoire were part of a regime of free movement in the 1950s that embraced people from Upper Volta going to southern Côte d'Ivoire as much as Senegalese going to Marseille. There were tensions—witness the riots of 1958—but tensions can sometimes be managed. Some Ivorians, notably its first President, thought that a relatively inclusive view of nationality, blurring the boundaries of the nation-state, had much to offer the Côte d'Ivoire after independence. But others wanted to narrow and harden those boundaries in a quest to keep power and resources in their hands. Building an Ivorian nation came to be confounded with an effort on the part of a powerful portion of its elite "to achieve an impossible purification."[18]

---

[17] Giulia Piccolino, "David against Goliath in Côte d'Ivoire? Laurent Gbagbo's War Against Global Governance," *African Affairs* 111 (2012): 1–23; special section on the Côte d'Ivoire in *African Affairs* 110 (2011): 457–89; Mike McGovern, *Making War in Côte d'Ivoire* (London: Hurst, 2011). Gbagbo and his supporters tried to develop a narrative of Ivorian history that claimed a radical—anti-French—heritage, set against both Houphouët-Boigny's version of the past and France's alleged meddling in the present. The best evidence of the radical current came from the episode of rural mobilization described in chapter 4, in which Houphouët-Boigny was in fact active until he decided to compromise. Konstanze N'Guessan, "'Independence is Not Given, It Is Taken': The Ivorian Cinquantenaire and Competing History/ies of Independence," *Nations and Nationalism* 19 (2013): 276–95.

[18] This phrase is from Geschiere, *Perils of Belonging*, 114. See also Sara Dorman, Daniel Hammet, and Paul Nugent, "Introduction: Citizenship and Its Casualties in Africa," in *Making Nations, Creating Strangers: States and Citizens in Africa* (Boston: Brill, 2007), 3–26, and

Senghor might have seen the irony of the "Franco-African Community" becoming a Euro-European Community, and his compatriots felt the pain of the barriers erected around the continent to exclude the sons and daughters of the people France had once tried to keep within its imperial embrace.[19] If Europe got its Common Market, Africans got the territorial state. Firmly located within territorialized space, the first generation of rulers strove to keep resources in their own hands and out of any potential opponents'. Almost all of the ruling elites of former French Africa did away, at least for a time, with multiparty elections and co-opted or imprisoned the leaders of trade unions, farmers' organizations, or student associations. They made sovereignty into an exclusive claim because it was the most important resource they had.

At first glance, the end of colonial rule meant that horizontal solidarity had triumphed over vertical. The racial and political hierarchies of colonial rule were gone; African states took their place as the juridical equals of all other states. But the vertical remains an important axis of politics. The politics of patronage within most former French African states and the forging of clientelistic relations between African elites and French rulers flourished in the context of the enormous wealth gap between African and European states. The kinds of institutions— territorial assemblies, the Grand Conseil of French West Africa, or French legislative bodies—that in the 1950s provided relatively visible structures for debate and criticism were largely dismantled.[20] Shadowy personal networks became an important part of the relationship of French and African elites. Would the multiple levels of government that Senghor and Dia advocated have provided more checks on the

---

Francis B. Nyamnjoh, "From Bounded to Flexible Citizenship: Lessons from Africa," *Citizenship Studies* 11 (2007): 73–82.

[19] Some scholars argue that a "postnational" citizenship now characterizes the European Union, as many people, especially migrant workers, derive rights to work, participate in collective bargaining, obtain welfare benefits, gain access to education, and sometimes vote in local elections, even without national citizenship. In such terms, citizenship, like sovereignty, is a divisible concept and serves as a basis of claim making, whose effectiveness depends on the circumstances. The story told in this book suggests that there are different ways of thinking about citizenship beyond the nation-state— imperial and postimperial as well as "postnational." See Yasemin Nuhoğlu Soysal, *Limits of Citizenship: Migrants and Postnational Membership in Europe* (Chicago: University of Chicago Press, 1994); Stéphane Caporal, "L'Europe et le citoyen," in Michel Ganzin, ed., *Sujet et Citoyen: Actes du colloque de Lyon (11-12 Septembre 2003)* (Aix: Presses Universitaires d'Aix-Marseille, 2004), 441–63.

[20] I have used the concept of "gatekeeper state" to underscore the tendency of African rulers to base their power on the interface between national space and the world economy and to guard that position as best they could. Frederick Cooper, *Africa since 1940: The Past of the Present* (Cambridge: Cambridge University Press, 2002).

untrammeled exercise of power by the first generation of African rulers? Might such a scheme at least have provided a framework where claim making could take place? Perhaps. But we do know that Senghor himself, like most of the rulers of the former states of French West Africa, fell—or leaped—into the trap he had predicted would ensue from what he had called balkanization.[21]

The claim to power is often underscored by an exclusionary linkage of the territory to cultural authenticity—an assertion now directed more against other Africans than against former colonizers. Such conceptions are inconsistent with the interaction and movement that have long characterized African history, and they cast aside the efforts of a generation of African leaders to find in their historical connections a basis for common action among Africans and for a critical but realistic understanding of the ways in which Africans continue to make their way in a highly unequal world. Nevertheless, a politics of citizenship has periodically reappeared in African countries, not least in Senegal, where in 2000 and 2012 incumbent presidents lost elections and accepted their defeats and where in 2012 youthful activists mobilized in the streets of Dakar to prevent a change in electoral laws intended to protect the current leadership.

In France today, many intellectuals and political leaders insist that a Republic cannot tolerate distinctions among its citizens; others assert that those inhabitants who do not accept a homogeneous citizenship have no place within France. They do not recall that in a period not so long ago French and African leaders were engaged in a profound—at times bitter—debate over the ways in which France could keep within its polity diverse peoples who aspired to social equality and political voice.

We can only speculate whether a colonial situation could have been turned into a truly federal, multinational, egalitarian France—if only European French politicians had been willing to pay the bills, if only African politicians had not been so concerned with their territorial political bases. The interest of this story lies in recapturing the sense of possibility during an uncertain time in world history. And a basic question remains with us, in Europe, in Africa, and around the world: can we devise the means to reconcile aspirations to equality and democracy with the diversity of humanity?

[21] Robert Fatton, Jr., "Clientelism and Patronage in Senegal," *African Studies Review* 29 (1986): 61–78.

BIBLIOGRAPHY

Archives, France

ARCHIVES NATIONALES DE FRANCE (ANF)

3AG, 4AG, 5AG Presidential Papers
72AJ Papers of Henri Laurentie
560AP Papers of René Pleven
BB Papers of Ministry of Justice
C// Records of Committees of the Assemblée Nationale, Conseil de la République, and Assemblée de l'Union française
F/1a Papers on Muslim Workers in France
F/60 Legislative Papers
FPR Papers of Jacques Foccart, Private Papers. Classified within Fonds 5AG (Presidential Papers)
FPU Papers of Jacques Foccart, Public Papers (Archives du Secrétariat Général pour les Affaires Africaines et Malgaches, 1958–1974). Classified within Fonds 5AG (Presidential Papers)

ARCHIVES DIPLOMATIQUES, LA COURNEUVE (ADLC)

Afrique-Levant, 1953–1959
Afrique-Levant/Afrique-Généralités
Cabinet du Ministre/Couve de Murville
Direction des Affaires Africaines et Malgaches
K. Afrique 1944–1952, Généralités

ARCHIVES DIPLOMATIQUES, NANTES (ADN)

AOF/Dakar
Abidjan/Ambassade
Bamako/Ambassade
Dakar/Ambassade

ARCHIVES D'OUTRE-MER, AIX-EN-PROVENCE (AOM)

19PA Personal Archives, Robert Delavignette
28PA Personal Archives, Marius Moutet
100APOM Papers of Comité de l'Empire français
AE Affaires Économiques
AP Affaires Politiques
CAB Papers of the Cabinet of the Minister of France d'Outre-mer
IGT Inspection Générale du Travail

CENTRE D'ARCHIVES CONTEMPORAINES, FONTAINEBLEAU (CAC)

Dossiers 760133/14, 770623/83, 940167/14, 940161/219, 940227/80, 940227/81, 950165/13, 950236/1, 950236/2, 950236/24

FONDATION NATIONALE DES SCIENCES POLITIQUES, PARIS
GM Papers of Gaston Monnerville
MD Papers of Michel Debré

CENTRE DE RECHERCHE ET DE DOCUMENTATION AFRICAINE, PARIS
PDG (9)

Archives, Senegal

ARCHIVES DU SÉNÉGAL, DAKAR (AS)

Archives of the Gouvernement Général de l'Afrique Occidentale Française

17G Political Affairs
18G Administrative Affairs
20G Elections
21G Police
23G État-civil
K Labor

Archives of the Government of Senegal

D Government of Senegal
VP Office of the Vice President

Archives of the Mali Federation

FM Fédération du Mali

SERVICE RÉGIONAL DES ARCHIVES–DAKAR (SRAD)
B/20, 1D, 2D, F

Legislative Records and Other Government Publications

FRANCE
Assemblée Consultative Provisoire. *Compte rendu analytique officiel*, 1943–45
Assemblée Nationale (1946–60). *Débats, Documents*
Assemblée Nationale. *Impressions, projets de lois propositions, rapports, etc. tome CXX-VII, Session de 1950, No. 11348, "Incidents de la Côte d'Ivoire."* Paris: Imprimerie de l'Assemblée Nationale, 1951.
Assemblée Nationale Constituante (first and second, 1945–46). *Débats, Documents*
Assemblée Nationale Constituante (first), Commission de la Constitution. *Comptes Rendus Analytiques*
Assemblée Nationale Constituante (second), Commission de la Constitution. *Comptes Rendus*
Assemblée de l'Union Française (1948–58). *Débats, Documents*

Comité national chargé de la publication des travaux préparatoires des insti-
tutions de la Vè République. *Documents pour servir à l'histoire de l'élaboration de la
Constitution du 4 octobre 1958.* Paris: La Documentation française, 1987. 4 vols.
La Conférence Africaine Française. Brazzaville 30 janvier-8 février 1944. Brazzaville:
Editions du Baobab, 1944.
Conseil de la République (1946–60). *Débats*
Journal Officiel de la République

COMMUNAUTÉ FRANÇAISE

Journal Officiel de la Communauté. Recueil des Actes et Informations
Sénat de la Communauté, *Comptes Rendus des Débats*

AFRIQUE OCCIDENTALE FRANÇAISE

Governors General (Bernard Cornut-Gentille and Gaston Cusin), speeches
to Grand Conseil de l'AOF. Copies in library of Archives d'Outre-mer.
Grand Conseil de l'Afrique Occidentale Française. *Bulletin*

SENEGAL

Assemblée Nationale. *Débats*
"Conférence de Presse du 23 Août 1960 par Léopold-Sédar Senghor, Secré-
taire Général de UPS," published by Ministère de l'information, de la
Presse et de la Radiodiffusion de la République du Sénégal
Journal Officiel
Sénégal, *La nation en construction*, published by Secretariat d'État à l'Information,
à la Presse, et à la Radiodiffusion de la République du Sénégal, 11 Decem-
ber 1959

MALI FEDERATION

Journal Officiel
Journal Officiel: Débats Parlementaires de l'Assemblée Fédérale

Newspapers and Magazines

Abidjan-Matin (Abidjan)
L'A.O.F. (Dakar)
L'Afrique Nouvelle (Dakar)
Climats (Paris)
La Condition Humaine (Dakar)
L'Essor (Bamako)
Le Figaro (Paris)
Fraternité (Abidjan)
Libération (Paris)
Marchés Coloniaux (later *Marchés Tropicaux*, Paris)
Le Monde (Paris)

Paris-Dakar (Dakar)
Le Populaire (Paris)
Renaissances (Algiers)
Réveil (Dakar)
Union Francaise et Parlement (Paris)
L'Unité (Dakar)

Legal Treatises

Bilbao, René. "La nationalité française et l'accession à l'indépendance des anciens territoires d'outre-mer." *Penant* 71, 685 (January–March 1961): 517–22.

———. "Statuts civils et nationalité." *Revue Sénégalaise de Droit* 5 (1969): 23–39.

Borella, François. *L'évolution politique et juridique de l'Union française depuis 1946.* Paris: Librarie Générale de Droit et de Jurisprudence, 1958.

Brin, Henri-Louis. *La nationalité française dans les Territoires d'Outre-mer (décret du 24 février 1953).* Paris: Recueil Sirey, 1954.

Camerlynck, G.-H. "De la renonciation du statut personnel." *Revue Juridique et Parlementaire de l'Union Française* 3 (1949): 129–45.

Coste-Floret, Paul. "Jus sanguinis, jus soli et statut personnel dans les rapports de la Métropole, de l'Algérie et de l'Étranger." *Revue Critique du Droit International* 34 (1939): 201–14.

Decheix, Pierre. "Le code de la nationalité malienne." *Penant* 73 (1963): 300–314.

Decottignies, Roger. "L'application du code de la nationalité française dans les Territoires d'Outre-mer (décret du 24 février 1954)." *Annales Africaines 1954,* 49–90.

———. "La condition des personnes au Togo et au Cameroun." *Annales Africaines 1957,* 7–52.

———. "L'état civil en AOF." *Annales Africaines 1955,* 41–78.

Decottignies, Roger, and Marc de Biéville. *Les nationalités africaines.* Paris: Pedone, 1963.

Delbez, Louis. "Un fédéralisme originale: La Communauté." *Revue Politique des Idées et des Institutions* 48, 3 (February 1959): 72–85.

Gonidec, P.-F. "La Communauté et les relations internationales." *Penant* 70 (1960): 141–60.

———. "La Communauté et les voies de l'indépendance." *Penant* 70 (1960): 8–9.

———. "Une mystique de l'égalité: le code du travail des territoires d'Outre-Mer." *Revue Juridique et Politique de l'Union Française* 2 (1953): 176–96.

———. "La nationalité dans les États de la Communauté et dans les États 'marginaux'." *Annuaire Français de Droit International* 7 (1961): 814–35.

———. "L'Union française et l'Europe." *Union Française et Parlement* 52 (1954): 6–10.

Gouet, Yvon. "L'Article 82 (paragraphe 1) de la Constitution relatif à l'option de statut et l'élaboration de la 'théorie des statuts civils' de droit français moderne." *Penant* 67 (1957), section doctrine, 1–94.

———. "Le nouveau statut des originaires des territories d'outre-mer dans l'Union française." *Penant* 57, 555 (1947): 71–78.

———. "Remarques sur une réorganisation éventuelle de l'état-civil dans les parties d'outre-mer de la France qui connaissent le régime de la pluralité des états civils et dans les territoires sous tutelle." *Revue Juridique et Politique de l'Union française* 8 (1954): 492–585.

Hamon, Léo. "Le Parti Fédéral Africain et le Rassemblement Démocratique Africain de la querelle fédéraliste à l'indépendance (1959–1960). " *Revue Juridique et Parlementaire d'Outre-mer* 14 (1960): 551–69.

Lampué, Pierre. "La citoyenneté de l'Union française." *Revue Juridique et Politique de l'Union Française* 4 (1950): 305–36.

———. "La diversité des statuts de droit privé dans les États africains." *Penant* 71, 685 (January–March 1961): 1–10.

———. "L'Union française d'après la Constitution." *Revue Juridique et Parlementaire de l'Union Française* 1 (1947): 1–39, 145–94.

Lavigne, Pierre. "La Constitution de l'Union Française." *Penant* 57, 558 (1947): 89–102.

Luchaire, François. "Le champ d'application des statuts personnels en Algérie et dans les territoires d'outre-mer." *Revue Juridique et Parlementaire de l'Union Française* 9 (1955): 38–44.

M'Baye, Kéba. "L'attribution de la nationalité 'jus soli' et l'option de nationalité dans la loi sénégalaise du 7 mars 1961." *Penant* 71 (1961): 347–53.

Pautrat, René. "Formes et conditions de la renonciation au statut personnel particulier." *Revue Juridique et Politique de l'Union Française* 12, 2 (April–June 1958): 350–57.

———. "Les vicissitudes du statut personnel." *Annales Africaines 1957*, 331–61.

Penant 65, 626–27 (1955): 67–82. Text of decision of Conseil d'État, 18 March 1955.

Peureux, Gérard. *Le Haut-Conseil de l'Union française.* Paris: Librairie Générale de Droit et de Jurisprudence, 1960.

Revue Juridique et Politique de l'Union Française 12, 2 (1958): 350–52. Text of decision of Conseil d'État, 22 November 1955.

Rolland, Louis, and Pierre Lampué. *Précis de droit des pays d'outre-mer (territoires, départements, états associés).* Paris: Dalloz, 1952.

Rouland, Norbert. "Les statuts personnels et les droits coutumiers dans le droit constitutionnel français." Pp. 145–225 in Anne-Marie le Pourhiet, ed., *Droit constitutionnel local: égalité et liberté locale dans la constitution.* Paris: Economica, 1999.

Solus, Henry. *Traité de la condition des indigènes en droit privé. Colonies et pays de protectorat (non compris l'Afrique du Nord) et pays sous mandat.* Paris: Société anonyme du "Recueil Sirey," 1927.

Terre, François. "La reconnaissance de la nationalité française." *Penant* 71, 685 (1961): 17–23.

Thiam, Doudou. *La portée de la citoyenneté française dans les territoires d'outre-mer.* Paris: Société d'Éditions africaines, 1953.

Zatzépine, Alexandre. *Le droit de la nationalité des républiques francophones d'Afrique et de Madagascar.* Paris: Librairie Générale de Droit et de Jurisprudence, 1963.

Other Printed Primary Sources

Alduy, Paul. *L'Union française: Mission de la France*. Paris: Fosquelle Éditeurs, 1948.

Aron, Raymond. "Conséquences économiques de l'évolution politique en Afrique noire." *Revue Française de Science Politique* 9 (1959): 610–28.

Ba, Amadou Hampaté. "Les heures sombres de la rupture entre le Sénégal et le Soudan." *Afrique Histoire* 2 (avril–juin 1981): 55–60.

Bakary, Djibo. *"Silence! On décolonise . . .": Itinéraire politique et syndicale d'un militant africain*. Paris: L'Harmattan, 1992.

Boisdon, Daniel. "La citoyenneté de l'Union Française." *Union Francaise et Parlement* 28 (1951): 12–13.

——. *Les institutions de l'Union française*. Paris: Berger-Levraut, 1949.

Cartier, Raymond. "En France noire avec Raymond Cartier." *Paris-Match* 383 (11 August 1956): 38–41, 384 (18 August 1956): 34–37, and 386 (1 September 1956): 39–41.

Catroux, Georges (General). "L'Union française, son concept, son état, ses perspectives." *Politique Etrangère* 18, 4 (1953): 233–66.

Colin, Roland. *Sénégal notre pirogue: au soleil de la liberté. Journal de bord 1955–1980*. Paris: Présence Africaine, 2007.

Coste-Floret, Paul, Amadou Diop, Fily Dabo Sissoko, Yvon Gouet, Henri Guissou, Iba-Zizen, Marie-Hélène Lefaucheux, René Maran, Jean Scelles, and Maurice Viollette. "Un programme pour une nouvelle politique française outre-mer." *Union Française et Parlement* 69 (January 1956): 5–11.

Culmann, Henri. *L'Union française*. Paris: Presses Universitaires de France, 1950.

D'Arboussier, Gabriel. *L'Afrique vers l'unité*. Paris: Éd. Saint-Paul, 1961.

de Gaulle, Charles. *Allocution prononcée à l'Assemblée fédérale du Mali par le Général de Gaulle, 13 décembre 1959* (copy in Bibliothèque Nationale de France).

Debré, Michel. *Gouverner. Mémoires 1958–1962*. Paris: Albin Michel, 1988.

Decraene, Philippe. "Les trois thèmes majeurs du Congrès de Cotonou." *France Outre-Mer* 344 (1958): 8.

Delavignette, Robert. *Service Africain*. Paris: Gallimard, 1946.

——. "L'Union française à l'échelle du Monde, à la mesure de l'homme." *Esprit* 112 (July 1945): 227–28.

Dia, Mamadou. *Mémoires d'un militant du tiers-monde*. Paris: Publisud, 1985.

Dronne, Raymond. "La querelle du double collège et du collège unique en Afrique noire." *Union Française et Parlement* 67 (November 1955): 19–20.

Duverger, Maurice. "Une course contre la montre." *La Nef* Cahier 9 (June 1955): 212–22.

Éboué, Félix. *La nouvelle politique indigène pour l'Afrique Équatoriale Française*. Paris: Office Français d'Édition, 1945.

Ehrhard, Jean. *Destin du colonialisme: essai sur la théorie et la politique économique dans les territoires sous-développés politiquement non autonomes*. Montpellier: Eyrolles, 1957.

"États Généraux de la Colonisation." Mimeographed document including speeches and declarations of meeting, 5–8 September 1945 (copy in Bibliothèque Nationale de France).

Fauchon-Villeplée, A. *Constitution et Union française*. Paris: Berger-Levrault, 1953.

Foccart, Jacques. *Foccart Parle: Entretiens avec Philippe Gaillard*. Paris: Fayard/Jeune Afrique, 1995.

Foyer, Jean. *Sur les chemins du droit avec le Général. Mémoires de ma vie politique 1944–1988.* Paris: Fayard, 2006.

Houphouët-Boigny, Félix. "A mes frères métropolitains." *Union Française et Parlement* 89 (1957): 2–4.

Jacqmin, René. *États-Unis de France: Ce que doit être l'Union française.* Paris: Larose, 1953.

Juglas, Jean-Jacques. "Faut-il reviser le Titre VIII de la Constitution?" *Union Française et Parlement* 60 (1955): 6–7.

Lamine Guèye. *Itinéraire africain.* Paris: Présence africaine, 1966.

Lapie, P.-O. "Conception unitaire ou conception pluraliste de la Communauté française." *Politique Étrangère* 19 (1954): 437–44.

Lecaillon, Jacques. "L'intégration de l'Union française dans l'Union européenne et les enseignements de la théorie économique." *Annales Africaines 1954*, 19–48.

Lemaignen, Robert, Léopold Sédar Senghor, and Prince Sisonath Youtévong. *La communauté impériale française.* Paris: Alsatia, 1945.

Lisette, Gabriel. *Le combat du Rassemblement démocratique africain.* Paris: Présence Africaine, 1983.

Messmer, Pierre. *Après tant de batailles: Mémoires.* Paris: Albin Michel, 1992.

Mitterrand, François. "Paradoxes et promesses de l'Union française." *La Nef* Cahier 9 (June 1955): 223–31.

——. *Présence française et abandon.* Paris: Plon, 1957.

Moussa, Pierre. *Les chances économiques de la Communauté Franco-Africaine.* Paris: Colin, 1957.

Pleven, René. "L'avenir de l'Union française." *Union Française et Parlement* 84 (1957): 1–9.

——. "The Evolution of the French Empire towards a French Union." Address to the Anti-Slavery Society, 21 July 1949, published by the Society.

Ramarony, Jules. "La Constitution de l'Union française doit être repensée avec les États intéressés et cimentée par une citoyenneté commune." *Union Française et Parlement* 60 (1955): 12–13.

Schuman, Robert. "Unité européenne et Eurafrique: Politique révolutionnaire." *Union Française et Parlement* 79 (1957): 1–3.

Semaines Sociales de France. *Peuples d'Outre-mer et civilisation occidentale.* Lyon: Chronique Sociale de France, 1948.

Senghor, Léopold Sédar. "L'avenir de la France dans l'Outre-mer." *Politique Étrangère* 19, 4 (1954): 419–26.

——. "Pour un accord conciliant." *Union Française et Parlement* 104 (1959): 5–6.

——. "Pour une République fédérale." *Politique Étrangère* 21 (1956): 165–74.

——. "Pour une République Fédérale dans une Union Confédérale." *Union Française et Parlement* 97 (1958): 5–11.

——. "Pour une solution fédéraliste." *La Nef* Cahier 9 (June 1955): 148–61.

Servoise, René. "Introduction aux problèmes de la République française." *Affaires Étrangères* 19 (1954): 379–418.

——. "L'Union française devant l'intégration économique européenne." *Politique Étrangère* 18 (1953): 277–306.

Teitgen, Pierre-Henri. "Le Fédéralisme moderne est un mariage sous le régime de la communauté." *Union Française et Parlement* 64 (1955): 1–4.

———. "La participation de la France à la montée des peuples." Pp. 313–36 in Semaines Sociales de France, *La montée des peuples dans la communauté humaine: Compte rendu in extenso*. Paris: Librarie Gabalda, 1959.

Tévoédjrè, Albert. *L'Afrique révoltée*. Paris: Présence Africaine, 1958.

Tillion, Germaine. *L'Algérie en 1957*. Paris: Éd. de Minuit, 1957.

XXX [Anonymous], "Union française et institutions européennes." *Politique Étrangère* 18 (1953): 267–76.

Document Collections

CAMP (Comparative African Microfilm Project). "West African Political Ephemera, 1948–62." University of Wisconsin, microfilm 2169.

de Gaulle, Charles. *Discours et messages 1940–1946*. Paris: Berger-Levraut, 1946.

Houphouët-Boigny, Félix. *Anthologie des discours 1946–1978. Tome I: 1946–1963*. Abidjan: Éditions CEDA, 1978.

Senghor, Léopold Sédar. *Liberté II: Nation et voie africaine du socialisme*. Paris: Seuil, 1971.

Secondary Sources

Adelman, Jeremy. *Sovereignty and Revolution in the Iberian Atlantic*. Princeton: Princeton University Press, 2006.

Ageron, Charles-Robert. "Les États africains de la Communauté et la guerre d'Algérie (1958–1960)." Pp. 269–311 in Ageron et Marc Michel, eds., *L'Afrique noire française: L'heure des indépendances*. Paris: CNRS Éditions, 2010.

———. "L'idée d'Eurafrique et le débat franco-allemand de l'entre-deux-guerres." *Revue d'Histoire Moderne et Contemporaine* 23 (1975): 446–75.

Agnew, John. *Globalization and Sovereignty*. Lanham, Md.: Rowman & Littlefield, 2009.

Anderson, Benedict. *Imagined Communities: Reflections on the Origin and Spread of Nationalism*. London: Verso, 1983.

Arendt, Hannah. *Origins of Totalitarianism*. New York: Harcourt Brace Jovanovich, 1951.

Awenengo Dalberto, Séverine. "Hidden Debates about the Status of Casamance in the Decolonization Process: Regionalism, Territorialism and Federalism at a Crossroads in Senegal." In Séverine Awenengo Dalberto and Camille Lefebvre, eds., *Tracing Uncertainty: Boundaries, Territoriality and Decolonization in Africa*. Forthcoming.

Baller, Susann. "Les fêtes célébrées et supprimées: Les indépendances de la Fédération du Mali et du Sénégal." Unpublished paper, 2012.

Banerjee, Sukanya. *Becoming Imperial Citizens: Indians in the Late-Victorian Empire*. Durham, N.C.: Duke University Press, 2010.

Barry, Ismael. "Réflexions sur le NON de la Guinée cinquante ans après." Pp. 29–42 in Odile Goerg, Céline Pauthier, and Abdoulaye Diallo, eds., *Le NON de la Guinée (1958): Entre mythe, relecture historique et résonances contemporaines*. Paris: L'Harmattan, 2010.

Bat, Jean-Pierre. *Le syndrome Foccart: La politique française en Afrique, de 1959 à nos jours*. Paris: Gallimard, 2012.

Bayart, Jean-François. *Les études postcoloniales. Un carnaval académique.* Paris: Karthala, 2010.

Beaud, Olivier. *Théorie de la fédération.* Paris: Presses Universitaires de France, 2009.

Bendix, Reinhard. *Nation-building and Citizenship: Studies of Our Changing Social Order.* Berkeley: University of California Press, 1977 [1964].

Benton, Lauren. *A Search for Sovereignty: Law and Geography in European Empires 1400-1900.* Cambridge: Cambridge University Press, 2010.

Bernault, Florence. *Démocraties ambiguës en Afrique Centrale: Congo-Brazzaville, Gabon: 1940-1965.* Paris: Karthala, 1996.

Bertrand, Romain. *Mémoires d'empire: La controverse autour du "fait colonial."* Paris: Éd. du Croquant, 2006.

Bitsch, Marie-Thérèse, and Gérard Bossuat, eds. *L'Europe unie et l'Afrique: de l'idée d'Eurafrique à la convention de Lomé I.* Brussels: Bruylant, 2005.

Blanchard, Emmanuel. *La police parisienne et les Algériens (1944-1962).* Paris: Éd. Nouveau Monde, 2011.

Blanchard, Pascal, Nicolas Bancel, and Sandrine Lemaire. *La fracture coloniale: la société française au prisme de l'héritage colonial.* Paris: La Découverte, 2005.

Blévis, Laure. "Sociologie d'un droit colonial: Citoyenneté et nationalité en Algérie (1865-1947): une exception républicaine?" Doctoral thesis, Institut d'Études Politiques, Aix-en-Provence, 2004.

Boehm, Max Hildebert. "Federalism." Pp. 169-72 in Edwin R. A. Seligman and Alvin Johnson, eds., *Encyclopedia of the Social Sciences*, Vol. 5. New York: Macmillan, 1937.

Boone, Catherine. *Merchant Capital and the Roots of State Power in Senegal, 1930-1985.* Cambridge: Cambridge University Press, 1992.

Bourgi, Robert. *Le Genéral de Gaulle et l'Afrique Noire: 1940-1969.* Paris: Librairie générale de droit et de jurisprudence, 1980.

Branche, Raphaëlle. *La torture et l'armée pendant la guerre d'Algérie 1954-1962.* Paris: Gallimard, 2001.

Brocheux, Pierre, and Daniel Hémery. *Indochine: La colonisation ambiguë 1858-1954.* Paris: La Découverte, 1995.

Brubaker, Rogers. *Citizenship and Nationhood in France and Germany.* Cambridge, Mass.: Harvard University Press, 1992.

Burbank, Jane, and Frederick Cooper. "Empire, droits et citoyenneté, de 212 à 1946. " *Annales: Histoire, Sciences Sociales* 63, 3 (2008): 495-531.

———. *Empires in World History: Power and the Politics of Difference.* Princeton: Princeton University Press, 2010.

Caporal, Stéphane. "L'Europe et le citoyen." Pp. 441-63 in Michel Ganzin, ed., *Sujet et Citoyen: Actes du colloque de Lyon (11-12 Septembre 2003).* Aix: Presses Universitaires d'Aix-Marseille, 2004.

Chafer, Tony. *The End of Empire in French West Africa: France's Successful Decolonization?* Oxford: Berg, 2002.

Chaffard, Georges. *Les carnets secrets de la décolonisation.* 2 vols. Paris: Calmann-Lévy, 1965-67.

Chatterjee, Partha. *The Nation and Its Fragments: Colonial and Postcolonial Histories.* Princeton: Princeton University Press, 1993.

———. *Nationalist Thought and the Colonial World: A Derivative Discourse?* London: Zed, 1986.

Cohen, Jean L. "Federation." Political Concepts: A Critical Lexicon. www .politicalconcepts.org/2011/federation.

———. "Whose Sovereignty? Empire versus International Law." *Ethics and International Affairs* 18 (2004): 1–24.

Colas, Dominique. *Citoyenneté et nationalité*. Paris: Gallimard, 2004.

Collins, Michael. "Decolonisation and the 'Federal Moment.'" *Diplomacy and Statecraft* 24 (2013): 21–40.

Conklin, Alice. *A Mission to Civilize: The Republican Idea of Empire in France and West Africa, 1895–1930*. Stanford: Stanford University Press, 1997.

Cooper, Frederick. *Africa since 1940: The Past of the Present*. Cambridge: Cambridge University Press, 2002.

———. "Conditions Analogous to Slavery: Imperialism and Free Labor Ideology in Africa." Pp. 107–50 in Frederick Cooper, Thomas Holt, and Rebecca Scott, *Beyond Slavery: Explorations of Race, Labor, and Citizenship in Postemancipation Societies*. Chapel Hill: University of North Carolina Press, 2000.

———. *Decolonization and African Society: The Labor Question in French and British Africa*. Cambridge: Cambridge University Press, 1996.

———. "'Our Strike': Equality, Anticolonial Politics, and the French West African Railway Strike of 1947–48." *Journal of African History* 37 (1996): 81–118.

———. "The Senegalese General Strike of 1946 and the Labor Question in Post-War French Africa." *Canadian Journal of African Studies* 24 (1990): 165–215.

Coquery-Vidrovitch, Catherine. "Nationalité et citoyenneté en Afrique occidentale français: Originaires et citoyens dans le Sénégal colonial." *Journal of African History* 42 (2001): 285–305.

Cruise O'Brien, Donal. *The Mourides of Senegal: The Political and Economic Organization of an Islamic Brotherhood*. Oxford: Clarendon, 1971.

de Benoist, Joseph Roger. *L'Afrique occidentale française, de la conférence de Brazzaville (1944) à l'indépendance (1960)*. Dakar: Nouvelles Éditions Africaines, 1982.

———. *La balkanisation de l'Afrique occidentale française*. Dakar: Nouvelles Éditions Africaines, 1979.

———. "Le désapparentement et ses lendemains." Pp. 389–407 in Rassemblement Démocratique Africain, *Actes du colloque international sur l'histoire du RDA, Yamoussoukro, 18–25 octobre 1985*, Vol. 1. Abidjan: CEDA Hatier, 1987.

———. "La Haute Volta, la Communauté française et l'Afrique occidentale française du référendum (28 septembre 1958) à l'indépendance." Pp. 1003–30 in Yénouyaga Georges Madiéga and Oumarou Nao, *Burkina Faso: Cent ans d'histoire, 1895–1995*. Paris: Karthala, 2003.

Deschamps, Damien. "Une citoyenneté différée: sens civique et assimilation des indigènes dans les Établissements français de l'Inde." *Revue Française de Science Politique* 47 (1997): 49–69.

Diallo, Abdoulaye. "Et si Sékou Touré n'était que l'homme du 25 août 1958?" Pp. 81–97 in Odile Goerg, Céline Pauthier, and Abdoulaye Diallo, eds., *Le NON de la Guinée (1958): Entre mythe, relecture historique et résonances contemporaines*. Paris: L'Harmattan, 2010.

Dickens, Ruth. "Defining French Citizenship Policy in West Africa, 1895–1956." PhD diss., Emory University, 2001.

Dimier, Véronique. "For a Republic 'Diverse and Indivisible'? France's Experiences from the Colonial Past." *Contemporary European History* 13 (2004): 45–66.

Diop, David. "La question de la citoyenneté dans *l'Encyclopédie* de Diderot et de d'Alembert: de l'irreductibilité de l'individualisme 'naturel' dans la société civile." Pp. 137–53 in Claude Fiévet, ed., *Invention et réinvention de la citoyenneté*. Aubertin: Éd. Joëlle Sampy, 2000.

Diouf, Mamadou. "Le clientélisme, la 'technocratie' et après?" Pp. 233–78 in Momar-Coumba Diop, ed., *Sénégal: Trajectoires d'un État*. Dakar: Codesria, 1992.

———. "The French Colonial Policy of Assimilation and the Civility of the Originaires of the Four Communes (Senegal): A Nineteenth Century Globalization Project." *Development and Change* 29 (1998): 671–96.

———. "Senegalese Development: From Mass Mobilization to Technocratic Elitism." Pp. 291–319 in Frederick Cooper and Randall Packard, eds., *International Development and the Social Sciences: Essays on the History and Politics of Knowledge*. Berkeley: University of California Press, 1997.

Dorman, Sara, Daniel Hammet, and Paul Nugent. "Introduction: Citizenship and Its Casualties in Africa." Pp. 3–26 in Dorman, Hammet, and Nugent, eds., *Making Nations, Creating Strangers: States and Citizens in Africa*. Boston: Brill, 2007.

Dramé, Papa, and Samir Saul. "Le projet d'Eurafrique en France (1946–1960): quête de puissance ou atavisme colonial?" *Guerres mondiales et conflits contemporains* 216 (2004): 95–114.

Dubois, Laurent. *Avengers of the New World: The Story of the Haitian Revolution*. Cambridge, Mass.: Harvard University Press, 2004.

———. *A Colony of Citizens: Revolution and Slave Emancipation in the French Caribbean, 1787-1804*. Chapel Hill: University of North Carolina Press, 2004.

Evans, Martin. *Algeria: France's Undeclared War*. Oxford: Oxford University Press, 2012.

Fall, Babacar. *Le travail au Sénégal au XXe siècle*. Paris: Karthala, 2011.

Fatton, Robert, Jr. "Clientelism and Patronage in Senegal." *African Studies Review* 29 (1986): 61–78.

Feldblum, Miriam. *Reconstructing Citizenship: The Politics of Reform and Immigration in Contemporary France*. Albany: State University of New York Press, 1999.

Foltz, William. *From French West Africa to the Mali Federation*. New Haven, Conn.: Yale University Press, 1965.

Foray, Jennifer. "A Unified Empire of Equal Parts: The Dutch Commonwealth Schemes of the 1920s–40s." *Journal of Imperial and Commonwealth History* 41 (2013): 259–84.

———. *Visions of Empire in the Nazi-Occupied Netherlands*. Cambridge: Cambridge University Press, 2012.

Foro, Philippe. "Être citoyen selon Charles de Gaulle." Pp. 601–16 in Claude Fiévet, ed., *Invention et réinvention de la citoyenneté*. Aubertin: Éd. Joëlle Sampy, 2000.

Gamble, Harry. "La crise de l'enseignement en Afrique occidentale française (1944–1950)." *Histoire de l'Éducation* 128 (2010): 129–62.

Gandolfi, Alain. "Naissance et mort sur le plan international d'un État éphémère: La Fédération du Mali." *Annuaire Français du Droit International* 6 (1960): 880–906.

Garavini, Giuliano. *After Empires: European Integration, Decolonization, and the Challenge from the Global South 1957–1986*. Oxford: Oxford University Press, 2012.

Gratien, Jean-Pierre. *Marius Moutet: Un socialiste à l'Outre-Mer*. Paris: L'Harmattan, 2006.

Genèses. Dossier on "Sujets d'empire." 53 (2003–4).

Genova, James. "Constructing Identity in Post-War France: Citizenship, Nationality, and the Lamine Guèye Law, 1946–1953." *International History Review* 26 (2004): 55–79.

Geschiere, Peter. *The Perils of Belonging: Autochthony, Citizenship, and Exclusion in Africa and Europe*. Chicago: University of Chicago Press, 2009.

Gokalp, Catherine. "Chronique de l'immigration." *Population* 30, 4–5 (1975): 889–96.

Gorman, Daniel. *Imperial Citizenship: Empire and the Question of Belonging*. Manchester: Manchester University Press, 2006.

Goscha, Christopher. *Going Indochinese: Contesting Concepts of Space and Place in French Indochina*. 2nd ed. Copenhagen: Nordic Institute of Asian Studies, 2012.

Goswami, Manu. "Rethinking the Modular Nation Form: Toward a Sociohistorical Conception of Nationalism." *Comparative Studies in Society and History* 44 (2002): 770–99.

Guèye, Omar. *Sénégal: histoire du mouvement syndical: la marche vers le code du travail*. Paris: L'Harmattan, 2011.

Hanretta, Sean. *Islam and Social Change in French West Africa: History of an Emancipatory Community*. Cambridge: Cambridge University Press, 2009.

Hecht, Gabrielle. *Being Nuclear: Africans and the Global Uranium Trade*. Cambridge, Mass.: MIT Press, 2012.

Héricord-Gorre, Alix. "Éléments pour une histoire de l'administration des colonisés de l'Empire français. Le 'régime de l'indigénat' et son fonctionnement depuis sa matrice algérienne (1881–c. 1920)." Thèse de doctorat, European University Institute, 2008.

Herzog, Tamar. *Defining Nations: Immigrants and Citizens in Early Modern Spain and Spanish America*. New Haven, Conn.: Yale University Press, 2003.

Hodeir, Catherine. *Stratégies d'Empire: Le grand patronat colonial face à la décolonisation*. Paris: Belin, 2003.

Howland, Douglas, and Luise White, eds. *The State of Sovereignty: Territories, Laws, Populations*. Bloomington: Indiana University Press, 2009.

Isoart, Paul. "Le Conseil exécutif de la Communauté." Pp. 209–27 in Charles-Robert Ageron and Marc Michel, eds., *L'Afrique noire française: L'heure des indépendances*. Paris: CNRS Éditions, 2010.

James, C.L.R. *The Black Jacobins*. New York: Vintage, 1963 [1938].

Jayal, Niraja Gopal. *Citizenship and Its Discontents: An Indian History*. Cambridge, Mass.: Harvard University Press, 2013.

Johnson, G. Wesley. *The Emergence of Black Politics in Senegal: The Struggle for Power in the Four Communes, 1900–1920*. Stanford: Stanford University Press, 1971.

Jones, Hilary. *The Métis of Senegal: Urban Life and Politics in French West Africa*. Bloomington: Indiana University Press, 2013.

Jones, James. *Industrial Labor in the Colonial World: Workers of the Chemin de Fer Dakar-Niger, 1881–1963*. Portsmouth, N.H.: Heinemann, 2002.

Jordi, Jean-Jacques. *1962: L'Arrivée des Pieds-Noirs*. Paris: Autrement, 2002.

Joseph, Richard. *Radical Nationalism in Cameroun: The Social Origins of the UPC Rebellion*. Oxford: Oxford University Press, 1977.

Kaké, Ibrahima Baba. *Sékou Touré: Le héros et le tyran*. Paris: Jeune Afrique, 1987.

Keese, Alexander. "A Culture of Panic: 'Communist' Scapegoats and Decolonization in French West Africa and French Polynesia (1945–1957)." *French Colonial History* 9 (2008): 131–45.

———. "Rigged Elections? Democracy and Manipulations in the Late Colonial State in French West Africa and Togo, 1944–1958." Pp. 324–45 in Martin Thomas, ed., *The French Colonial Mind*. Lincoln: University of Nebraska Press, 2011.

Kelly, John, and Martha Kaplan. "Nation and Decolonization: Toward a New Anthropology of Nationalism." *Anthropological Theory* 1 (2001): 419–37.

Konaré, Alpha Oumar. "Le RDA, l'Union soudanaise et le désapparentement." Pp. 173–88 in Rassemblement Démocratique Africain, *Actes du colloque international sur l'histoire du RDA, Yamoussoukro, 18–25 octobre 1985*, Vol. 1. Abidjan: CEDA Hatier, 1987.

Laurens, Sylvain. "'1974' et la fermeture des frontières: Analyse critique d'une décision érigée en *turning point*." *Politix* 21, 82 (2008): 69–94.

Lawrence, Adria. *Imperial Rule and the Politics of Nationalism: Anti-Colonial Protest in the French Empire*. Cambridge: Cambridge University Press, 2013.

Le Cour Grandmaison, Olivier. *La République impériale: politique et racisme d'État*. Paris: Fayard, 2009.

Lewin, André. *Ahmed Sékou Touré (1922–1984). Tome 2–1956–1958*. Paris: L'Harmattan, 2009.

Lewis, James I. "The MRP and the Genesis of the French Union, 1944–1948." *French History* 12 (1998): 276–314.

———. "The Tragic Career of Marius Moutet." *European History Quarterly* 38 (2008): 66–92.

Lewis, Mary Dewhurst. *Divided Rule: Sovereignty and Empire in French Tunisia, 1881–1938*. Berkeley: University of California Press, 2013.

Louis, W. R. *Imperialism at Bay: The United States and the Decolonization of the British Empire, 1941–1945*. New York: Oxford University Press, 1978.

Ly, Abdoulaye. *Les regroupements politiques au Sénégal (1956–1970)*. Dakar, Paris: CODESRIA/Karthala, 1992.

Madiéga, Georges. "Les partis politiques et la question des fédérations en Haute Volta (Burkina-Faso)." Pp. 431–57 in Charles-Robert Ageron and Marc Michel, eds., *L'Afrique noire française: L'heure des indépendances*. Paris: CNRS Éditions, 2010.

Magnette, Paul. *Citizenship: The History of an Idea*. Trans. Katya Long. Colchester: ECPR Press, 2005.

Mamdani, Mahmood. *Citizen and Subject: Contemporary Africa and the Legacy of Late Colonialism*. Princeton: Princeton University Press, 1996.

Manchuelle, François. *Willing Migrants: Soninke Labor Diasporas, 1848–1960*. Athens: Ohio University Press, 1997.

Mann, Gregory. "Anti-Colonialism and Social Science: Georges Balandier, Madeira Keita, and 'the Colonial Situation' in French Africa." *Comparative Studies in Society and History* 55 (2013): 92–119.

———. "The End of the Road: Nongovernmentality in the West African Sahel." Manuscript.

———, *Native Sons: West African Veterans and France in the Twentieth Century*. Durham, N.C.: Duke University Press, 2006.

Mann, Gregory, and Baz Lecoq. "Between Empire, *Umma*, and the Muslim Third World: The French Union and African Pilgrims to Mecca, 1946–1958." *Comparative Studies of South Asia, Africa and the Middle East* 27, 2 (2007): 367–83.

Marr, David. *Vietnam 1945: The Quest for Power*. Berkeley: University of California Press, 1995.

Marseille, Jacques. *Empire coloniale et capitalisme français: Histoire d'un divorce*. 2nd ed. Paris: Albin Michel, 2005.

Martens, Georges. "Le syndicalisme en Afrique occidentale d'expression Française: de 1945 à 1960." *Le Mois en Afrique* 178–79 (1980): 74–97 and 180–81 (1980 81): 53–83.

Mazower, Mark. *No Enchanted Palace: The End of Empire and the Ideological Origins of the United Nations*. Princeton: Princeton University Press, 2009.

Mbembe, Achille. *La naissance du maquis dans le Sud-Cameroun, 1920–1960: Histoire des usages de la raison en colonie*. Paris: Karthala, 1996.

McDougall, James. *History and the Culture of Nationalism in Algeria*. Cambridge: Cambridge University Press, 2006.

———. "The Secular State's Islamic Empire: Muslim Spaces and Subjects of Jurisdiction in Paris and Algiers, 1905–1957." *Comparative Studies in Society and History* 52 (2010): 553–80.

McGovern, Mike. *Making War in Côte d'Ivoire*. London: Hurst, 2011.

Mel, Frédéric Grah. *Félix Houphouët-Boigny: Biographie*. Abidjan: CERAP, and Paris: Maisonneuve et Larose, 2003.

Migani, Guia. "L'Association des TOM au Marché Commun: Histoire d'un accord européen entre cultures économiques différentes et idéaux politiques communs, 1955–1957." Pp. 233–52 in Marie-Thérèse Bitsch and Gérard Bossuat, eds., *L'Europe Unie et l'Afrique: de l'idée d'Eurafrique à la Convention de Lomé I*. Brussels: Bruylant, 2005.

———. *La France et l'Afrique sub-saharienne, 1957–1963: Histoire d'une décolonisation entre idéaux eurafricains et politique de puissance*. Brussels: PIE Peter Lang, 2008.

Miran, Marie. *Islam, histoire et modernité en Côte d'Ivoire*. Paris: Karthala, 2006.

Mongia, Radhika. "Historicizing State Sovereignty: Inequality and the Form of Equivalence." *Comparative Studies in Society and History* 49 (2007): 384–411.

Montarsolo, Yves. *L'Eurafrique, contrepoint de l'idée de l'Europe: Le cas français de la fin de la deuxième guerre mondiale aux négociations des Traités de Rome*. Aix-en-Provence: Publications de l'Université de Provence, 2010.

Morgenthau, Ruth Schachter. *Political Parties in French-Speaking West Africa*. Oxford: Clarendon, 1964.

Ndiaye, Guédel. *L'échec de la fédération du Mali*. Dakar: Nouvelles Éditions Africaines, 1980.

N'Guessan, Konstanze. "'Independence Is Not Given, It Is Taken': The Ivorian *Cinquantenaire* and Competing History/ies of Independence." *Nations and Nationalism* 19 (2013): 276–95.

November, Andras. *L'évolution du mouvement syndical en Afrique occidentale.* Paris: Mouton: 1965.

Nyamnjoh, Francis B. "From Bounded to Flexible Citizenship: Lessons from Africa." *Citizenship Studies* 11 (2007): 73–82.

Ollivier, Anne-Laure. "Entre Europe et Afrique: Gaston Defferre et les débuts de la construction européenne." *Terrains et Travaux* 8 (2005): 14–33.

Palayret, Jean-Marie. "Les mouvements proeuropéens et la question de l'Eurafrique, du Congrès de La Haye à la Convention de Yaoundé (1948–1963)." Pp. 185–229 in Marie-Thérèse Bitsch and Gérard Bossuat, eds., *L'Europe unie et l'Afrique: de l'idée d'Eurafrique à la convention de Lomé I.* Brussels: Bruylant, 2005.

Paul, Kathleen. *Whitewashing Britain: Race and Citizenship in the Postwar Era.* Ithaca, N.Y.: Cornell University Press, 1997.

Piccolino, Giulia. "David Against Goliath in Côte d'Ivoire? Laurent Gbagbo's War Against Global Governance." *African Affairs* 111 (2012): 1–23.

Pinto, Michelle. "Employment, Education, and the Reconfiguration of Empire: Africanization in Postwar French Africa." PhD diss., New York University, 2013.

Pocock, J.G.A. "The Ideal of Citizenship since Classical Times." Pp. 29–52 in Ronald Beiner, ed., *Theorizing Citizenship.* Albany: State University of New York Press, 1995.

Public Culture 23, 1 (2011). Special issue on colonial studies and postcolonialism in France.

Rassemblement Démocratique Africain. *Actes du colloque international sur l'histoire du RDA, Yamoussoukro, 18–25 octobre 1985.* Abidjan: CEDA Hatier, 1987.

Rice, Louisa Claire. "Reframing Imperialism: France, West Africa, and Colonial Culture in the Era of Decolonization, 1944–1968." PhD diss., Rutgers University, 2006,

Rivet, Daniel. *Le Maghreb à l'épreuve de la colonisation.* Paris: Hachette, 2002.

Rivière, Claude. "Lutte ouvrière et phénomène syndical en Guinée." *Cultures et Développement* 7 (1975): 53–83.

Roche, Christian. *Le Sénégal à la conquête de son indépendance 1939-1960.* Paris: Karthala, 2001.

Rosanvallon, Pierre. *Le sacre du citoyen: Histoire du suffrage universel en France.* Paris: Gallimard, 1992.

Ruz, Nathalie. "La force du 'cartiérisme.'" Pp. 328–36 in Jean-Pierre Roux, ed., *La guerre d'Algérie et les français.* Paris: Fayard, 1990.

Saada, Emmanuelle. *Empire's Children: Race, Filiation, and Citizenship in the French Colonies.* Trans. Arthur Goldhammer. Chicago: University of Chicago Press, 2012.

Sahlins, Peter. *Unnaturally French: Foreign Citizens in the Old Regime and After.* Ithaca, N.Y.: Cornell University Press, 2004.

Schmidt, Elizabeth. "Anticolonial Nationalism in French West Africa: What Made Guinea Unique?" *African Studies Review* 52, 2 (2009): 1–34.

————. *Cold War and Decolonization in Guinea, 1946-1958.* Portsmouth, N.H.: Heinemann, 2007.

————. *Mobilizing the Masses: Gender, Ethnicity, and Class in the Nationalist Movement in Guinea, 1939-1958.* Portsmouth, N.H.: Heinemann, 2005.

Schumacher, Edward. *Politics, Bureaucracy and Rural Development in Senegal.* Berkeley: University of California Press, 1975.

Sheehan, James J. "The Problem of Sovereignty in European History." *American Historical Review* 111 (2006): 1-15.

Shepard, Todd. "A l'heure des 'grands ensembles' et la guerre d'Algérie. L'État-nation' en question." *Monde(s): Histoires, Espaces, Relations* 1 (2012): 113-34.

————. *The Invention of Decolonization: The Algerian War and the Remaking of France.* Ithaca, N.Y.: Cornell University Press, 2006.

————. "Thinking between Metropole and Colony: The French Republic, 'Exceptional Promotion,' and the 'Integration' of Algerians, 1955-1962." Pp. 298-323 in Martin Thomas, ed., *The French Colonial Mind.* Lincoln: University of Nebraska Press, 2011.

Shipway, Martin. "Thinking Like an Empire: Governor Henri Laurentie and Postwar Plans for the Late Colonial French 'Empire-State.'" Pp. 219-50 in Martin Thomas, ed., *The French Colonial Mind.* Lincoln: University of Nebraska Press, 2011.

Smith, Etienne. "'Senghor voulait qu'on soit tous des Senghor': Parcours nostalgiques d'une génération." *Vingtième Siècle. Revue d'Histoire* 118 (2013): 97-100.

Smith, Lahra. *Making Citizens in Africa: Ethnicity, Gender and National Identity in Ethiopia.* Cambridge: Cambridge University Press, 2013.

Smith, Tony. "A Comparative Study of French and British Decolonization." *Comparative Studies in Society and History* 20 (1978): 70-102.

Smouts, Marie-Claude, ed. *La situation postcoloniale: Les Postcolonial Studies dans le débat français.* Paris: Les Presses de Sciences Po, 2007.

Sorum, Paul Clay. *Intellectuals and Decolonization in France.* Chapel Hill: University of North Carolina Press, 1977.

Soysal, Yasemin Nuhoğlu. *Limits of Citizenship: Migrants and Postnational Membership in Europe.* Chicago: University of Chicago Press, 1994.

Spire, Alexis. *Étrangers à la carte: L'administration de l'immigration en France (1945-1975).* Paris: Grasset, 2005.

————. "Semblables et pourtant différents. La citoyenneté paradoxale des 'français musulmans d'Algérie' en métropole." *Genèses* 53 (2003): 48-66.

Stora, Benjamin. *La gangrène et l'oubli: La mémoire de la guerre d'Algérie.* Paris: La Découverte, 1998.

Terretta, Meredith. "Cameroonian Nationalists Go Global: From Forest *Maquis* to a Pan-African Accra." *Journal of African History* 51 (2010): 189-212.

Thiemeyer, Guido. "West German Perceptions of Africa and the Association of the Overseas Territories with the Common Market 1956-1957." Pp. 253-85 in Marie-Thérèse Bitsch and Gérard Bossuat, eds., *L'Europe Unie et l'Afrique: de l'idée d'Eurafrique à la Convention de Lomé I.* Brussels: Bruylant, 2005.

Thompson, Elizabeth. *Colonial Citizens: Republican Rights, Paternal Privilege, and Gender in French Syria and Lebanon.* New York: Columbia University Press, 2000.

Tronchon, Jacques. *L'insurrection malgache de 1947: essai d'interprétation historique.* Paris: Maspero, 1974.

Tshimanga, Charles, Didier Gondola, and Peter J. Bloom, eds. *Frenchness and the African Diaspora: Identity and Uprising in Contemporary France.* Bloomington: Indiana University Press, 2009.

Urban, Yerri. "Race et nationalité dans le droit colonial français 1865–1955." Doctoral thesis, Université de Bourgogne, 2009.

Vaillant, Janet. *Black, French, and African: A Life of Léopold Sédar Senghor.* Cambridge, Mass.: Harvard University Press, 1990.

van Walraven, Klaas. "Decolonization by Referendum: The Anomaly of Niger and the Fall of Sawaba, 1958–1959." *Journal of African History* 50 (2009): 269–92.

———. *The Yearning for Relief: A History of the Sawaba Movement in Niger.* Leiden: Brill, 2013.

Verschave, François-Xavier. *La Françafrique, le plus long scandale de la République.* Paris: Stock, 2003.

Wall, Irwin. *French Communism in the Era of Stalin: The Quest for Unity and Integration, 1945–1962.* Westport, Conn.: Greenwood, 1983.

Weil, Patrick. *Qu'est-ce qu'un Français? Histoire de la nationalité française depuis la Révolution.* Paris: Gallimard, 2005.

Weinstein, Brian. *Éboué.* New York: Oxford University Press, 1972.

White, Owen. *Children of the French Empire: Miscegenation and Colonial Society in French West Africa 1895–1960.* Oxford: Clarendon, 1999.

Wilder, Gary. *Freedom Time: Negritude, Decolonization, and the Future of the World.* Forthcoming.

———. *The French Imperial Nation-State: Negritude and Colonial Humanism between the Two World Wars.* Chicago: University of Chicago Press, 2005.

Woolf, Greg. *Becoming Roman: The Origins of Provincial Civilization in Gaul.* New York: Cambridge University Press, 1998.

Yéré, Henri-Michel. "Citizenship, Nationality & History in Côte d'Ivoire, 1929–1999." PhD diss., University of Basel, 2010.

Zolberg, Aristide. *Creating Political Order: The Party States of West Africa.* Chicago: Rand McNally, 1966.

———. *One-Party Government in the Ivory Coast.* Princeton: Princeton University Press, 1969.

INDEX

Page numbers in *italics* refer to figures.

Abandé, Alexandre, 335

Abbas, Ferhat: and 1946 Constitution, 61n103, 98–103, 109–20; attempt to reconcile nationalist claims with participation in French Union, 112, 212; and the double college, 116, 135–36; on federalism, 30, 109, 112, 135–36; France's hopes for agreement with, 30, 112; and intergroup, 98n108, 116, 118; separatism rejected, 102; and Sétif, 31, 61; on two-tier citizenship, 99, 113; and women's suffrage, 136

Abdul, Olympio, 29

Abidjan: in 2011 conflict, 443–45; anti-outsider riots in (1958), 340, 352–53, 371, 414, 421, 443–44; importance of to Upper Volta, 336; independence ceremony in, 396–97; RDA and 1949 riots in, 172; strike on Abidjan-Niger Railroad, 179. *See also* Côte d'Ivoire

Académie des Sciences Coloniales, 75, 94

Adotevi, Léonard, 29

AEF. *See* French Equatorial Africa

African federation: and 1958 Constitution, 294–98, 313; after 1958 referendum, 328–29, 332–39; Apithy's opposition to, 234, 237, 252, 295, 332, 335–36; Conseil de l'Entente as rival to, 340, 371; continued conflict over, 434; d'Arboussier's views on, 412–13, 434; Dia's support of, 294–95, 346; Houphouët-Boigny's opposition to, 11, 256, 257, 332, 336; as nation-in-the-making, 351–52; RDA's divisions over, 256–57, 280–81, 332, 333, 340, 351–52; Sékou Touré's support of, 256, 257, 281–84, 343; Senghor's support of, 196, 279, 283, 296–97, 328–29, 332–34, 340, 351–52, 372, 406–8. *See also* African unity; confederation; Conseil de l'Entente; Mali Federation

Africanization. *See* civil service: Africanization of

African unity: and African parties, 257–58, 339–40, 371; calls for, 256–62, 277–80, 316, 321–24, 340, 346, 351, 389, 392, 399, 412–13; and economic unity, 281; and Mali Federation, 419; Messmer on French role in, 328; Overseas Ministry's fears of, 204; and trade unions, 246–50; weakening case for, 252, 316, 326, 371, 392, 421, 429, 434. *See also* African federation; Conseil de l'Entente; Eurafrica; Mali Federation

Afrique Équatoriale Française. *See* French Equatorial Africa

Afrique Nouvelle, 237, 246–47, 251, 303, 398

Afrique Occidentale Française. *See* French West Africa

Alduy, Paul, 198–99, 231, 234

Algeria: and 1958 Constitution, 288–89, 293, 308–9; and citizenship rights of Muslims, 15–16, 18, 21, 29–30, 55, 65, 68, 75–78, 82–83, 88, 115, 121, 433; civil service posts for Muslims in, 383; colonization of, 15–16; constitutional referendum vote (1946), 92, 121; double college in, 74, 135–36, 138, 140, 145, 164, 231, 272; état-civil indigène in, 154–55; and Eurafrica, 203–4, 208, 265, 268; and the European Economic Community, 268; and federalist conceptions, 41, 43, 96, 111–12, 135, 194–95, 213, 275, 283, 288, 308, 321; France's role in modernization of, 4, 109, 132, 213, 228, 437; "French Muslims of Algeria" as official category, 272, 383; independence/autonomy sought, 43, 78, 212–13; map, *22*; Napoleon III on, 15–16; nationality in, 16, 21, 31, 96, 129, 352, 423, 433; near–coup d'état in, 280, 283; post-independence, 423, 426–28; relationship to Community of, 308; relationship to French Union of, 21; representation in the constituent assembly, 61; repressive violence in, 4, 30–31, 111, 437; ruled under "special" laws, 82–83, 111; settler politics in, 149, 213, 228, 437; students from, in French universities, 196–97; voting rights of Muslims in, 61, 74, 85, 92, 135–36, 138; war in, 23–24, 212–13, 228, 253, 262–63, 265, 275, 280, 308–9, 322, 374,

Algeria (*continued*)
396, 408, 426–27, 437; workers from, in France, 31, 74, 131, 426–27, 442. *See also* Abbas, Ferhat; Bendjelloul, Mohamed; Front de Libération Nationale
"Amis du Manifeste" (Abbas, 1943), 30
ANC. *See* Assemblée Nationale Constituante
Anderson, Benedict, 9–10n14, 23n44
Antilles (French colonies and departments): citizenship and slavery before 1848, 14–15, 21, 369; constitutional referendum vote in, 92; department status granted to, 78, 237n57; exterior provincial status, 43; map, *19*; status in French Empire and Union, 21, 41, 43; students from, in French universities, 196–97; voting rules in, 71; women's suffrage in, 45–46. *See also* department; Guadeloupe; Martinique; Saint-Domingue
AOF. *See* French West Africa
L'AOF (Senegalese newspaper), 50, 104, 146
Apithy, Sourou Migan, 51–52; and 1958 Constitution and referendum, 295, 321; and African federation question, 237, 252, 295, 332, 335–36; and Algerian crisis, 283; on citizenship and nationality, 71; and Conseils de gouvernement, 241; in constituent assembly, 67, 70; de Gaulle presidency supported, 284; deposed, 421; equality defended, 57; and European cooperation, 209–10; and *loi-cadre*, 229–30, 234, 241, 244, 245; on nationality, 356; proposals for the French Union, 98, 237; and the RDA, 166, 167; and the territorial assembly issue, 139–40, 229–30
Aron, Raymond, 347n59
Assemblée Consultative Européenne, 203
Assemblée Consultative Provisoire, 54–56, 60–61
Assemblée Nationale: and 1956 elections, 236; and Algerian war, 228; citizenship of *originaires* designated by, 16–17; constitutional revision called for in, 201–2, 274–76; debates over overseas representation in, 71–72, 74–75, 83–86, 97, 110, 114, 118, 127, 131, 135–40, 286, 290; election laws debated in, 143–45, 163–64; and European cooperation, 205–6, 210; and

French-Malian negotiations, 385–86; investigation into RDA/administration clashes, 172–74, 176; labor code passed, 181–83; and *loi-cadre*, 216, 231–35, 240–45; party politics in, 132–33, 186, 190, 275; powers of, debated, 83–86, 118, 131; pro-settler factions in, 143, 214, 233; role reconsidered, 227; sovereignty of, 83, 131, 190, 200, 221, 254–55; and territorial assemblies, 134
Assemblée Nationale Constituante (ANC; 1945–1946): election debated in, 90–91, 135–40; first constitution debated and drafted, 67–87; first constitution defeated, 91–92; forced labor and indigénat abolished, 67–68; "free consent" doctrine approved, 77; Lamine Guèye law passed, 88–90; overseas representation in, 26, 54–57, 61–64, 67, 79; powers limited regarding the protectorates, 151; pro-settler factions in, 70, 99, 102, 110, 114, 138; role of, 45; second constitution debated and drafted, 91–124. *See also* Constitution of 1946
Assemblée de l'Union française: citizenship's effects debated, 190–92, 216; commencement of, 146; double college debated in, 145–46; elections to, 116, 135n35, 146; and European cooperation, 267–68; and federation debates, 216–17, 226, 267–68; and the labor code, 182; limited power of, 109, 112, 192, 274; and *loi-cadre*, 230–31; Morocco and Tunisia's refusal to participate in, 149, 212; proposals regarding, 101, 109, 112; and registration and personal status, 156, 159–60, 271; and Senegalese capital's move to Dakar, 255
assimilation: arguments over, 75, 96, 109, 161; citizenship and, 211; and nationality in independent Senegal, 415; Senghor on, 35–36, 81, 187, 195, 261, 297, 406; vs. "separation," 75; as social and economic equality, 218, 223, 232
Associated States (protectorates): applicability of 1946 Constitution to, 114, 149–50, 212; citizenship question in, 75–76, 90, 96–97, 102, 108, 115, 119, 121, 127–28, 150–51, 191, 437; and constituent assembly's jurisdiction, 79, 99; inhabitants' nationality, 18–20,

44, 75; participation in National Assembly, 71–72, 74–75, 127–28; position of, in French Union, 21, 71–72, 101, 149–50, 212; post-independence relations with France and the Community, 274–75, 285, 289, 292, 308; in Senghor's notion of confederation, 196; sovereignty of, 18–20, 85, 96–97, 101; status of, under Pleven plan, 44. *See also* Morocco; Tunisia; Vietnam

Association des Étudiants du RDA, 197

Ateba, Tobie Gaston, 29

Aubame, Jean-Hilaire, 207–8

Aujoulat, Louis-Paul, 67, 72, 92, 114, 192

Auriol, Vincent (President of France), 179, 186–87

authoritarian rule, 436, 438–40, 447

Baidy Ly, Tidiane, 258

Bakary, Djibo, 321–23

balkanization of Africa: and AOF, 237–46, 251–63, 346; Dia on, 238, 274, 346; federalism vs. balkanization in the late 1950s, 251–63; Houphouët-Boigny and RDA accused of, 324; Koné on, 389; Sékou Touré accused of, 316; Senghor on, 214, 230–31, 237, 243, 258, 279, 301, 406

Bandung meeting (1955), 220, 233–34, 267, 275, 350n61, 412n124

Bardoux, Jacques, 75

Barry, Diawadou, 230, 284

Barthes, René (Governor General of AOF): on Africanization of cadres, 185; on citizenship, 131; defeated constitution supported, 95; double college seen as alienating by, 133–34; and the railway strike, 179

Bastid, Paul, 102, 110, 117

Battifol, Henri, 362–63

BDS. *See* Bloc Démocratique Sénégalais

Belgium, 265, 269

Bell, Alexander Douala Manga, 67

Bendjelloul, Mohamed: appeal for inclusion by, 56; citizenship sought for Muslim Algerians, 30, 55, 78, 82–83; in constituent assembly, 78, 82, 85–86; double college opposed, 85–86; in Provisional Consultative Assembly, 54–56

Benin. *See* Dahomey

Bey of Tunis, 101, 114, 212, 438. *See also* Tunisia

Bidault, Georges, 115, 117, 422–23

births, registration of, 57, 62, 89, 130, 153, 156–57, 384, 418. *See also* état-civil

Blanchet, André, 295n42, 307

Bloc Africain, 51

Bloc Démocratique Sénégalais (BDS), 188–90, 238, 251, 297

Bloc Français, 51

Bloc Populaire Sénégalais (BPS), 251

Boisdon, Daniel, 77, 128, 160–61, 230–31

Boissier-Palun, Léon, 375

Boni, Nazi, 321

Borna, Bertin, 237

Brazzaville: conference in (1944), 27–28, 64, 69–70; de Gaulle's visit to (1958), 312. *See also* Congo (Congo-Brazzaville); French Equatorial Africa

British Commonwealth, 40, 227, 375, 377

Burkina Faso. *See* Upper Volta

Buron, Robert, 244

Cambodia, 18–20, 149–50, 196, 274, 289. *See also* Associated States (protectorates); Indochina

Cameroon: and 1958 Constitution, 304; applicability of Lamine Guèye law to, 90, 97, 111; *colons'* interests in, 64; Conseil de gouvernement established, 221; demands for independence from, 259, 361, 366; double college in, 143; mandate status, 20, 21; nationality and citizenship in, 20–21, 71–72, 97, 127–28, 244–45, 366, 433; relationship to Community of, 289; representation in French assemblies, 61, 67, 128; status in Pleven plan, 44; UPC in, 178, 221, 259, 298, 435. *See also* Aujoulat, Louis-Paul; mandated territories; Pré, Roland

capacitaires, 91, 137–38. *See also* voting rights

Capitant, René, 76

Caracalla, edict of, 13, 30n11, 65, 77–78

Caribbean colonies/departments. *See* Antilles

Cartier, Raymond, 270. See also *cartiérisme*

cartiérisme, 270, 300, 347, 396

Casamance (region of Senegal), 297, 320

Cassin, René, 41, 310

Catroux, Georges (Gen.), 29n9, 199

Colonial Ministry, 30, 38. *See also* Commissioner of Colonies; Overseas Ministry

colonies: cost of maintaining, 219, 270; and federalism, 33–34; governing structure of French African colonies, 23; international trusteeship debated, 20–21; Laurentie on, 37–38; "old colonies" given department status, 78; proposals for representation in the Union, 34, 36, 42–45, 71–72, 83–85, 93–94, 97–98, 101, 112–13; as "provinces" in Pleven's vision, 34–35; representation in constituent assembly, 26, 54–57, 61–64, 67. *See also* colonialism; French Empire; territories; *and specific colonies and regions*

Colonna, Antoine, 114

colons. See settlers

Comité Consultatif Constitutionnel. *See* Consultative Constitutional Committee of 1958

Comité de Coordination des Unions Territoriales des Syndicats de l'AOF et de l'AEF, 183

Comité de l'Empire Français, 64–65, 93, 94

Comité d'Etudes Franco-Africaines, 171

Commission Constitutionnelle. *See* Constitutional Committee (1946)

Commission de la France d'Outre-mer. *See* Overseas Committee

Commissioner of Colonies, 45–46, 49. *See also* Colonial Ministry

Committee on Overseas France. *See* Overseas Committee

Communauté. *See* Community (1958–64)

La Communauté impériale française (Lemaignen, Senghor, and Youtévong), 35–37

Communist Party (PCF): and 1946 Constitution, 82, 87, 102, 119; and 1958 referendum, 307; ambivalent on colonialism, 119, 133; CGT linked to, 104, 247; excluded from government (1947), 132, 172; and RDA, 167, 176–77, 197. *See also* Confédération Générale du Travail; Rassemblement Démocratique Africain

Community (1958–64): 1958 referendum on, 295, 302–4, 307, 310–24; and citizenship, 310, 330–37, 354–56, 359,
363–67, 371, 373–77, 380–84, 410–11; and defense policy, 374, 378–79; demise of, 396, 398, 409–10, 412–13, 425–26, 429, 434; French power in Member States, 329, 334; future questioned, 361–62, 396; governmental structure, 306–7, 309, 327, 358, 378, 385; judicial system, 305, 327, 336–37; and Mali Federation, 339, 341–43, 345, 360–61, 372–88, 391, 403; and Member States' independence, 307, 309, 339–40, 344–45, 393–98; as multinational community, 357, 360, 364–70; name proposed, 304, 305; nationality in the context of, 349–65; nature of, 305; personnel redistributed to Member States, 338; presidential power in, 306–7, 309, 374–76, 378, 385; Secretariat of, 355, 358, 363, 375–77, 380–82, 403, 410, 424; statehood granted to territories, 325, 326; as successor to Fourth Republic, 353–54. *See also* confederation; Conseil exécutif; Constitution of 1958; de Gaulle, Charles; federation; Member States

Conakry, Guinea, 312, 314–17. *See also* Guinea

La Condition Humaine, 187–88, 215–16

confederation: and Associated States, 195, 201; in debates over 1958 Constitution, 292–96, 305, 312; defined, 11; de Gaulle on, 302–3, 305, 345; European or Eurafrican, 202–10, 227, 264, 270; vs. federation, 11–12, 194–96, 240, 252, 260, 294–305, 314, 343–45, 389, 406–7, 411, 434; and independence, 296–97, 316, 360, 398; Senghor's proposals for, 11, 194–96, 201, 227, 251, 279, 283, 296–97, 299, 304, 341, 350, 406–7. *See also* European cooperation; federalism; federation

Confédération Générale du Travail (CGT), 104, 182, 247–48. *See also* labor movement

Confédération Générale du Travail-Autonome (CGTA), 247–48. *See also* labor movement

Congo (Belgian), 265, 269, 399

Congo (Congo-Brazzaville), 21–23, *22*, 67. *See also* Brazzaville; d'Arboussier, Gabriel; Félix-Tchicaya, Jean; French Equatorial Africa

Conseil de l'Entente: freedom of movement among member states, 420–21, 443–44; independence sought by member states, 388, 395–98, 426; as rival to Mali Federation, 340–41, 371, 373, 395; superposed nationality proposed for, 420–21. *See also* Côte d'Ivoire; Dahomey; Houphouët-Boigny, Félix; Niger; Upper Volta

Conseil d'État: and 1958 Constitution, 286, 311–14; and double college, 140; on freedom of movement, 130–31, 151; judicial appeals handled by, 385; on personal and French civil status, 159, 163, 271–72

Conseil exécutif (Executive Council of the Community), 307, 309, 327; African leaders' effectiveness, 327–28; and citizens' rights, 365–66; demise of, 378, 409; and Mali's demand for independence, 345, 349, 368–69, 373, 378, 380; Mali's representation in, 339, 362, 376, 380; and Member States' independence, 339–40, 344–45, 349, 368–70, 373, 378; Member States' representation in, 307, 309, 327, 339, 362; nationality and citizenship debated, 353–65; Saint-Louis meeting of (Dec. 1959), 368–69, 373

Conseil interministériel (Interministry Council), 284–86, 309–11

Conseil de la République (Senate), 112, 145, 235, 290. *See also* legislative institutions

Conseils de gouvernement (governing councils): for AOF, 239; and the civil service, 229; cooperation with Governor needed, 225, 243; jurisdiction and composition of, 241–42, 245, 253, 266, 274; labor and, 242, 248, 250; of Mali and its federated states, 337, 398; of Member States, 327; politics changed by, 251; proposed, 221, 228–30; as term, xv; Vice-President's role and authority, 241, 243

Conseil de l'Union française, 83–84, 86

Constituent Assembly. *See* Assemblée Nationale Constituante

Constitutional Committee (Commission Constitutionnelle, 1946): of first constituent assembly, 73–82; representation on, 69; of second constituent assembly, 98–104, 107–12, 115–17. *See also* Constitution of 1946

Constitution of 1946: ambiguity of, 10–11, 122–23; Article 80, 121, 126, 130–31; Article 81, 121, 127–28, 150–51; Article 82, 121, 129, 158, 159, 211; calls for revision of (Title VIII), 190–93, 195, 199–202, 216, 252, 262–63, 274–76, 284; diversity recognized in, 5, 71, 122; empire evoked in discussions of, 77; first rough draft, 57–58; first version defeated, 91–93; first version written, 67–91; Intergroup walkout, 116; method for drafting, 45; not imposable on Associated States, 114, 149–50, 212; overseas representation in drafting, 26, 45, 54–56; overseas subjects ineligible to vote on, 86; preamble of, 122, 150; preliminary debates over, 53–66; second version approved, 122–23; second version written, 91–124. *See also* Assemblée Nationale Constituante; Constitutional Committee; French Union

Constitution of 1958: and African federation, 294–98, 313; ambiguity and uncertainty in, 10–11; and citizenship, 300, 310, 349, 363–64; and defense policy, 374; drafted, 284–94, 298–314, 346; and nationality, 322, 354–55, 356; referendum on, 295, 302–4, 307, 310–24, 331, 352, 363; resulting position of African leaders, 372; revised, 385–86, 393–94. *See also* confederation: in debates over 1958 Constitution; Member States

Consultative Constitutional Committee (Comité Consultatif Constitutionnel, 1958), 285–86, 293–94, 298–310

Convention Africaine, 257

Cornut-Gentille, Bernard, 183n54, 222, 225–26, 288, 315

Coste-Floret, Paul: and 1946 constitution, 84, 86, 98–99, 100–104, 109–10, 112–13, 116–20; and 1958 Constitution, 300, 301, 304–5, 307, 312; appointed Overseas Minister, 172; and citizenship issues, 110, 119–20, 217–18; on confederation, 276, 299; and double college debate, 143; on federalism, 98–99, 103, 111–13, 122, 217–18, 276; on the labor code, 183; and RDA, 172

Cot, Pierre, 75, 83, 110, 115, 136

Côte d'Ivoire: and 1958 referendum, 323, 324; and African federation question, 255–56, 332, 335; anti-foreigner mobilization in, 340, 352–53, 371, 414, 421, 443–44; budget, 238, 240, 323; *colons* in, 64; and founding of Conseil de l'Entente, 340; independence of, 323, 395–98; Lamine Guèye law defended in, 95–96; nationality legislation, 420–21; as part of AOF, 21–23, *22*; power struggles in (1993–2011), 443–45; RDA and administrative repression in, 167, 172–78; representation in constituent assembly, 62, 67; SAA's mobilization in, 170–71; territorial assembly of, 156, 251; wealth of, 23, 238, 256, 335, 378, 420. *See also* Conseil de l'Entente; Houphouët-Boigny, Félix; Rassemblement Démocratique Africain

Coty, René, 283

Coulibaly, Mamadou, 256, 397

Coulibaly, Ouezzin, 173, 176, 245, 252

Cournarie, Pierre (Governor General), 45–46, 47–48

Court of Arbitration (of the Community), 327, 376, 380

Cros, Charles, 48, 49

Culmann, Henri, 197–98

currency, 302, 303, 322, 385, 386

Cusin, Gaston (High Commissioner of AOF), 254, 263, 281

customary laborers, 181–84

Dacko, David, 360, 374

Dahomey: and 1958 Constitution, 304; agitation for citizenship in, 51–52; civil service in, 240, 282; and Conseil de l'Entente, 340, 420–21; Dahomean civil servants in other states, 338, 340, 371, 414; independence of, 396–97; labor confrontation in, 249; and Mali Federation, 332–36, 371; as part of AOF, 21–23, *22*; poverty of, 222; representation in constituent assembly, 67; territorial assembly of, 237–38, *239*, 251. *See also* Apithy, Sourou Migan; Zinsou, Emile

Dakar, Senegal: and breakup of Mali Federation, 402–5; de Gaulle's visit to, 315, 317–18, 322; as federal capital, 23, 225, 233, 238, 240, 256–57, 280, 390, 439; politics in, 50–51, 402, 425, 447; Senegalese capital moved to, 255; strike in, 52–53; women's suffrage

protests in, 45–50. *See also* Quatre Communes; Senegal

Dara, Almamy Ibrahima Sory, 160

d'Arboussier, Gabriel, 62–63; and 1958 Constitution, 312, 315; and African federation, 328, 333, 412–13; and Algerian crisis, 283; in constituent assembly, 61–63, 67, 71–72; and de Gaulle, 308; frustration felt by, 146; and Mali Federation, 333, 335; as Minister of Justice in Senegal, 415, 419; on nationality and citizenship, 415, 419; on nation and sovereignty, 413; and RDA, 166, 169, 173, 176, 260

deaths, registration of, 156–57. *See also* état-civil

Debré, Michel: and 1958 Constitution, 284, 289, 290, 310, 324; and breakup of the Community, 409; and citizenship and nationality, 356–60, 364, 367, 381–82, 422–23; on the Community, 305, 306–7, 345, 361–62, 394; on contacts with African leaders, 358; and French-Malian negotiations, 381–82, 384–86, 388; on Houphouët-Boigny, 397, 426

decentralization: Africans' calls for, 190, 192, 195, 201, 262; debates over, in AOF, 108, 190, 200–201, 217, 233, 241, 252; fears of excessive, 42, 92, 200–201, 216, 224–26; French calls for, 87, 107, 142–43, 164, 190–93, 200–201, 214, 216–17, 228, 230, 276, 378, 432; under *loi-cadre*, 234–42; and Mali Federation, 362, 389–90, 392. *See also* independence; *loi-cadre*; territorial assemblies

Declaration of the Rights of Man and of the Citizen (1789), 14

decolonization: Boissier-Palun on, 375; conservative argument for, 270; de Gaulle on, 429; Keita on, 342–43; Secretariat of Community claims to have resolved, 410; Senghor on, 251, 408. *See also* colonialism; independence; self-determination

defense: as Community jurisdiction, 315, 326, 374, 376; in a confederation, 303; European defense pact, 205, 209–10; federal government and, 84, 87, 195, 288, 290–91, 301, 309; France in charge of, 36, 42, 58, 147–48, 229–30, 322; independence and, 323, 378–79, 385; Malian independence and, 374,

defense (*continued*)
378–79, 385, 400–401, 404; territories not yet capable of, 302, 323

Defferre, Gaston: and the Community, 396; and Eurafrica, 208, 264–66; and *loi-cadre*, 228–30, 234–35, 241, 243–44, 266

de Gaulle, Charles: and 1946 constitution, 92–93, 106; and 1958 Constitution, 285, 299, 301–4, 307–8, 310–12, 314–18, 324, 346, 432; and 1958 referendum, 302–4, 307, 310–12, 314–18, 322, 372–73; AEF's loyalty to, 7–8, 18, 27; and Algerian conflict, 280, 308; at the Brazzaville conference (1944), 27–28; and citizenship and nationality, 29, 356, 359–60, 364–65; on decolonization, 429; federal system espoused, 1–2, 44–45, 147–48, 192, 285, 287, 299, 302–4, 372, 432; Keita on, 358; and Mali Federation, 339, 342–43, 347, 360–61, 368, 391, 404; as Président du Conseil, 280, 284, 306; as President of the Community, 327, 409, 410. *See also* Community (1958–64); Constitution of 1958

Delavignette, Robert, 38, 54, 77, 170

democracy: African demands for, 190, 238, 283–84; arguments about Africans' capacity for, 145, 263; and Associated States, 114, 150; as French principle, 83, 183; of "groups," 84, 112, 122, 276. *See also* universal suffrage; voting rights

Deniau, Roger, 55–56

department (overseas): as component of French Union, 57–58, 72, 103, 127; as component of possible confederation, 194–95, 262, 275; department status granted to "old colonies," 71, 78, 237n57; and Eurafrica, 206, 208, 265; opposition to departmental status, 361; as part of French Republic, 21, 202; as possible status for overseas territories, 41, 84, 109, 187, 291, 302, 307–8. *See also* Antilles; French Union; territories

development. *See* economic development

Dia, Mamadou, *348*; and 1958 Constitution and referendum, 285, 290–91, 294, 318–20, 321, 324; and Algerian conflict, 308; arrested and imprisoned, 438–40; on balkanization of West Africa, 238, 274, 346; capital moved to

Dakar, 255; and Community politics, 339–40, 341–42, 410; on dangers of electoralism, 245–46; on de Gaulle's coming to power, 284; education of, 23; and Eurafrica, 266–67, 344, 350, 398; federalism of, 215–16, 238, 251–52, 407–8; and independence, 341–42, 369; and the labor movement, 250, 330–31; and *loi-cadre*, 244–45, 252–53; and Malian-French negotiations, 342–43, 345, 369, 373–74, 381–82, 384, 386; in Malian government, 337, 398, 401; and Malian tensions, 388–92, 400–405; and Mali Federation's creation, 328, 346, 360; and Mali's representation in the Conseil exécutif, 339–40; on the multinational state, 1, 216; on nationality, 329, 352, 355–56, 357; and personal status issues, 367–68; as savior of French Community, 341–42, 410; and Senegalese independence, 402–5, *407*, 430; and Senegal's economy, 330; as Vice-Président du Conseil, 252–53, 320

Diagne, Blaise, 16–17

Diallo, Boubakar, 29

Diallo, Saifoulaya, 235

Diallo, Saliou, 29

Diallo, Yacine, 67, 166

Diarra, Tiémoko, 148–49

Dimbokro, Côte d'Ivoire, 173

Diop, Cheikh Anta, 197, 258, 320

Diop, Fatou, 48–49, 50

Diouf, Khar N'Dofène, 415–16

diversity: and citizenship, 5–6, 17, 44, 71, 77–78, 191; and empire, 34–38, 43–45, 71; and equality, 5–6, 164, 447; in Senghor's vision, 261–62, 304, 341. *See also* personal status; racism and racial discrimination

Djibode, M., 335

double college. *See* electoral colleges

Duclos, Jacques, 119

Éboué, Félix, 7–8, 18, 27. *See also* French Equatorial Africa

Éboué-Tell, Eugénie, 120

École William Ponty, 23, 167, 191, 215

economic cooperation, 302, 303, 322, 385, 386. *See also* Eurafrica; European cooperation

economic development: 1958 Constitution and, 290; European cooperation and, 264–65, 268–69; funding for, 68, 189, 218, 277; under *loi-cadre*, 235; in Senegal, 330; territories responsible for, 254; vertical solidarity required for, 371. *See also* decentralization; metropole: costs borne by; poverty; standard of living

elections: in 1945, 51; in 1946, 92, 94, 139; in 1956, 236; in 1957, 151–52, 248, 258–59, 337; in AEF, 62; colonialist opposition to, 64, 70; and electoral laws, 86, 88–91, 103, 132–41, 143–46, 155–56, 182; French manipulation of, 60, 177, 193, 322, 435; frequency of, 146; and *loi-cadre*, 230, 236, 248; and Mali Federation, 334; and mobilization of citizens, 132, 165, 171, 177–78, 435; practical difficulties of, 57, 61–62, 73, 90–91, 155; for president (France), 83, 287, 289, 310, 385; for president (Mali), 403; referendum on 1946 Constitution (May), 45, 77, 86, 88, 91–92; referendum on 1946 Constitution (October), 122; referendum on 1958 Constitution, 295, 302–4, 307, 310–24, 331, 352, 363; referendum on independence, debates over, 282–84, 307, 342, 345, 372, 393; suppression of in independent Africa, 446; territorial basis of, 433; voter participation in, 139, 146, 193, 236, 323, 324; and women in Senegal, 47–49. *See also* electoral colleges; état-civil; universal suffrage; voting rights

electoral colleges: double vs. single college, 57, 60–61, 72–74, 85–86, 90–91, 93–94, 114–17, 133–38, 140–46, 158, 164, 217, 231; single college under *loi-cadre*, 229–31, 233, 235. *See also* elections; universal suffrage; voting rights

electoralism, dangers of, 246

empire. *See* citizenship: imperial; French Empire

equality: 1958 Constitution and, 288, 291, 295, 299, 312, 327; and access to public jobs, 89, 128, 130, 189, 364, 367, 395; and Algeria's status, 82–83, 135–36; among citizens, 5, 14, 24, 50–51, 57, 60, 80, 87, 98, 121–22, 134, 141, 191, 211, 217–18, 221, 278, 433; and diversity, 5–6, 152, 164, 443, 447; of justice, 224; Lamine Guèye law and, 88–89, 146–47; and legislative representation, 36, 40–42, 63, 72–75, 105–6,

194, 227; and Mali Federation, 393, 398; Overseas Ministry on, 125; in pay and benefits, 50, 52, 121, 179, 182–85, 189, 223, 232, 245–47; in Provisional Consultative Assembly debate, 55–56; among races and peoples, 51, 55, 57, 137, 188, 198, 209, 223–24; Senghor on mystique of, 24, 183, 206, 279; of standard of living, 24, 80, 185, 204, 218, 232–33, 252, 344, 413; among states, 201–3, 274, 282, 288, 296, 407; and voting rights, 57, 60, 70, 72–73, 130, 136–40; of women, 45–50, 136, 150

L'Essor (party newspaper of Union Soudanaise), 332, 351–52, 361, 386–87

état-civil: after independence, 364, 384, 414, 417–20; compulsory registration in, 89, 152–54, 156–57, 418; defined, xv; état-civil indigène, 62, 154–57, 271; French hesitations about, 154–56, 270–71; and individuality, 153, 158; and *jugements supplétifs*, 154, 157, 273; and *loi-cadre*, 235, 241–42, 271; need for, 62, 152–54, 217, 230–31, 235; and noncitizens, 5–7, 57, 61, 62; practical challenges of extending, 129–30, 141, 154–57, 193, 273; and renunciation of personal status, 158–63, 271–72; territorial responsibility for, 235, 242, 271; used by Africans as needed, 157, 235, 271, 273, 436; and voter identification, 57, 61–62, 73, 130, 137, 153–54, 193, 230–31, 334, 414. *See also* personal status

États Généraux de la Colonisation, 64–65, 93

L'Étudiant d'Afrique Noire, 220

Eurafrica (Eurafrique), 202–10, 263–78, 309, 344, 350, 393n61, 398, 435

Euratom, 268–69

European cooperation, 202–10, 263–79, 344, 350, 397–98, 435

European Defense Community, 205, 209–10

European Economic Community (Common Market), 206, 264–68, 350

European Union, 202, 210, 266, 444

évolués: and civil service, 185; co-optation of, 32, 57, 185; desire for citizenship of, 44; as representatives of other Africans, 27–28, 60; as unrepresentative, 94; use of état-civil by, 271; as voters, 73, 137

Executive Council. *See* Conseil exécutif

Fagbamigbe, Guillaume, 249
Fall (Col.), 400–401
Fall, Alsine, 49–50
Fall, Ely Manel, 54, 62
family allowances, 183, 184, 262
farm workers. *See* customary laborers
Faure, Edgar, 227
federalism: of Catroux, 199; Coste-
    Floret and, 98–99, 103, 111–13, 122,
    217–18, 276, 299; of de Gaulle, 1–2,
    44–45, 147–48, 192, 285, 287, 299,
    302–4, 372, 432; of Dia, 215–16, 238,
    251–52, 407–8; of Herriot, 105; of
    Houphouët-Boigny, 238, 286, 299,
    343–45, 369–70, 372, 409, 432; IOM's
    advocacy of, 190; of Laurentie, 96;
    loi-cadre and, 237–46; *Marchés Coloniaux*
    version of, 93–94; Moutet on, 75; of
    MRP, 97–98, 166; overseas' depu-
    ties compromise on, 82; poverty an
    obstacle to, 224–25; risks to French
    power of, 42, 44, 74, 104–5, 217, 277,
    289, 299, 344–45; as route out of
    empire, 8–12; of Senghor, 11, 103–4,
    112, 194–96, 199, 203–4, 215, 217,
    227, 251–52, 262, 274–75, 350; of
    Teitgen, 102, 216–17, 226, 299. *See also*
    confederation; Constitution of 1946;
    Constitution of 1958; federation;
    French Union
federation: 1958 Constitution and,
    286–305, 312; AOF and, 1–2, 9–11,
    237–46, 251–63; vs. confederation,
    11–12, 194–96, 240, 252, 260, 294–305,
    314, 343–45, 389, 406–7, 411, 434;
    defined, 11; Houphouët-Boigny's
    plan for, 343–45; jurists' critique of,
    58–59; Lapie's argument for, 33–34;
    Luchaire's version, 288–89; Pleven
    commission and, 40–44, 84; prin-
    ciple of representation supported,
    63–64; Senghor's plan for, 11,
    36–37, 275; Viard's proposals, 34. *See
    also* Community (1958–64); European
    cooperation; federalism; French
    Union
Federation of Mali. *See* Mali Federation
Félix-Tchicaya, Jean: and 1946 constitu-
    tion, 67, 110; and Algerian crisis, 283;
    and electoral laws, 136–37, 145; and
    RDA, 166; on territorial assemblies,
    139–40
Le Figaro, 111
FLN. *See* Front de Libération Nationale

Foccart, Jacques, 375–76, 381, 410. *See
    also* French Republic: Mali's negotia-
    tions with
Foltz, William, 412
Fonlupt-Esperaber, Jacques, 76
forced labor: abolished by Houphouët-
    Boigny law, 8, 67–68, 93, 171; colonial
    Africa to be weaned from, 27; interdic-
    tion as a right, 72; routine use of, 7;
    SAA as alternative to, 171
Foreign Ministry (Ministère des Af-
    faires Étrangères): on citizenship, 78;
    concern with international opinion,
    38–39; and demise of the Commu-
    nity, 410; jurisdiction over protector-
    ates, 96; on Lamine Guèye law in
    mandates, 97; on long-term goals for
    Africa, 220; and problem of Associ-
    ated States, 149; report on political
    situation, 220
Foyer, Jean, 442
France: as Muslim power, 148–49; weak-
    ness of (1945), 7, 32; as world power,
    12, 202, 209; in World War II, 7–8,
    20, 26, 137, 435. *See also* Community
    (1958–64); French Empire; French
    Republic; French Union; metropole
Franco-African community, 304; and
    1958 Constitution, 296, 304, 304;
    balkanization vs. federalism and,
    251–60; de Gaulle's desire for, 316,
    393; diverse notions of, 12, 220, 253,
    265, 275–80, 283; efforts to create,
    275–77, 280–83, 296, 304, 337; Euro-
    pean cooperation and, 265, 268, 393,
    446; Houphouët-Boigny on, 252, 256;
    Keita on, 260n128, 268, 321, 337; and
    Mali Federation, 337; Mitterrand on,
    275; RDA split over, 256–60; Sékou
    Touré on, 257, 281, 315; Senghor on,
    251, 258, 275; and sovereignty, 260,
    265. *See also* African unity; Community
    (1958–64); confederation
franc zone. *See* currency
Frédérix, Pierre, 148
freedom of movement: guaranteed un-
    der 1946 Constitution, 130–31; iden-
    tity papers and, 273; immigration to
    France suspended (1974), 411, 441–
    43; Lamine Guèye law and, 125–26; as
    means of protecting other rights, 74,
    432, 437; and Moroccans, 151; under
    Ordinance of 7 March 1944, 31; under
    proposed French Union citizenship,

65–66; as right within the Community, 330, 364, 366–67; under treaties, 383, 387, 395, 426–28, 435

French civil code and civil status. *See* état-civil; personal status

French Community. *See* Community (1958–64)

French Empire: and "citizenship of empire," 36, 54, 58, 64; compared to other empires, 77–78, 108, 237; forms of governance in, 18–21; maps (ca. 1945), *19, 22*; preservation of, 35, 46, 56, 60, 92, 93, 104–5, 276; as starting point for reform, 21–26, 30–40, 43, 45, 54–64, 79, 81, 83, 87–88, 93, 106, 111, 147n73, 149–50, 196, 198, 220, 432–33, 437. *See also* colonialism; French Union

French Equatorial Africa (AEF): and 1958 referendum, 312; administrative centralization in, 200–201; citizenship in (1945), 39; composition and governance of, 21–23, *22*; double college in, 136–38, 143; independence of former territories, 388; inhabitants seen as primitive, 41; maps, *19, 22*; representation in constituent assembly, 61, 67; status under Pleven plan, 44; students from, in French universities, 196–97; during World War II, 7–8, 18. *See also* Chad; Congo; Éboué, Félix; Gabon; Governor General of the AEF; Ubangui-Chari

French of metropole: and business and residence in independent former territories, 375, 377, 379–80, 383, 387, 395; independence and French nationality, 376–78, 387, 414–17, 420–30, 441–42; people included/excluded as, 21, 75, 127, 244, 352; special representation for (white) overseas citizens, 72–73, 110, 114–16, 118, 140. *See also* nationality; settlers

French North Africa, 7, 8. *See also* Algeria; Morocco; Tunisia

French Republic: and Algeria, 24, 30–31, 212–13, 308, 437; citizenship of (vs. citizenship of French Union), 65, 107, 116, 121; Fifth, 284, 310, 363; Fourth, 8, 26, 124, 133, 193, 211, 213, 280, 287, 306, 353; immigration suspended by (1974), 441–43; issue of separating citizenships of France and its former territories, 335, 352,

367, 377, 421–25; Mali's negotiations with, 372–88, 394–95, 404–5, 432; Member States' relationship to, 307–8, 326, 328, 338; and nationality after African independence, 423, 441; "nationality of the French Republic and of the Community," 354–60, 363, 378; as "one and indivisible," 4, 40, 109, 221, 232, 279; in projects for 1958 constitution, 279, 286–87, 295, 306–7, 315; relationship to Empire of, 21; relationship to French Union of, 90, 95, 100, 122, 129; relationship to proposed federation/confederation of, 194–202, 204, 212, 238, 252, 260, 262, 345, 352–54, 384–86; and republican ideals, 3, 37; Senegal's independence recognized by, 408; separation of African states from, 326, 329, 335; Third, 7, 87. *See also* Community (1958–64); Constitution of 1946; Constitution of 1958; French Union; metropole

French Revolution, 7, 13–15, 64, 80, 103

French Sudan. *See* Sudan

French Union: the Community as successor to, 353–54; composition of, 21–23, *22*, 30; crisis of, 149–50, 152, 194, 199, 207–9, 212, 215, 251–52, 275–76; de Gaulle's concept of, 1, 2, 44–45, 147–48; and European cooperation, 202–10; "free consent" doctrine in, 71, 77, 106, 121; governmental structure debated (1944–46), 33–37, 40–45, 53–54, 57–60, 71–72, 82–86, 93–94, 97–109, 112, 118; name debated, 58–59; RDA and, 166; reform of, debated, 187–88, 190–93, 199–202, 215–19, 252, 262–63, 274–76, 284; rethinking sovereignty in, 194–202, 209–10; Senghor's vision for, 186–88, 261–62; as state or super-state, 198–99, 212; transition from Empire to, 10–11, 26–45, 83. *See also* citizenship of the French Union; confederation; Constitution of 1946; decentralization; federation; French Republic; *loi-cadre*; sovereignty; *and specific territories, protectorates, and trust territories*

French West Africa (AOF): and 1958 Constitution and referendum, 294–98, 310–24; administrative centralization in, 22–23, 200–201; arguments over executive and legislative authority for, 11, 229–30, 234, 237, 241, 244,

Guyana, 43. *See also* Éboué, Félix; Monnerville, Gaston

Hadj, Messali, 30
Haïdara, Mahamane, 381
Haiti (Saint-Domingue), 14–15
Haut Conseil de l'Union française, 101, 112, 149–50, 212
Herriot, Edouard, 105–6, 120, 194, 227; and Herriot problem (danger of overseas majority), 111, 194, 227, 277, 289
Hettier de Boislambert, Claude, 400–402, 404
High Commissioner of AOF: on African unity, 328; authority diminished, 229, 263; vs. Conseil de gouvernement, 221, 253; as coordinator of services, 100, 200; and Dia, 253; efforts to preserve power of, 201, 226; farewell of, 338; and implementation of *loi-cadre*, 239; on independence, 254, 281; misunderstanding of citizenship categories by, 127, 272; and potential African federation, 298; title, xv; on viability of territories, 222. *See also* Chef de Territoire; Cusin, Gaston; Governor General of AOF; Messmer, Pierre
High Commissioners (in Member States of Community), 327, 379; on crisis in Mali Federation, 390–91; and Dia, 329, 341; on Houphouët-Boigny, 369. *See also* Hettier de Boislambert, Claude; Lami, Pierre
Ho Chi Minh, 32–33, 59, 79, 99. *See also* Vietnam
horizontal solidarity: as Africans' connections with one another, 11, 23, 188; Dia on, 238; difficulties of achieving, 371; and Eurafrica, 203, 258, 264; and French Union, 213; Houphouët-Boigny on, 344; and independence, 446–47; IOM on, 190; need to combine with vertical solidarity, 11, 23, 188, 203, 213, 258, 293, 446–47; Senghor on, 11, 188, 203, 258; Zinsou on, 237–38. *See also* African federation; African unity; vertical solidarity
Houphouët-Boigny, Félix, *63*; and 1958 Constitution, 283–84, 286, 321, 323, 432; and Abidjan riots, 353; and African federation question, 11, 256, 257, 332, 336; after Mali Federation's

demise, 407, 409; authoritarian regime of, 436; bet with Nkrumah, 433; and Conseil de l'Entente, 340, 420–21, 426, 429, 443–44; in constituent assembly, 62, 67, 165, 171; death of, 444; and de Gaulle's government, 284, 369; discrimination decried, 110; division and racism warned against, 115–16; and European cooperation, 210, 266–67; on the experiment of the French Union, 278; federal system espoused, 238, 286, 299, 343–45, 369–70, 372, 409, 432; forced labor opposed, 68, 72, 170–71; on Franco-African Community, 251–52, 280; and Ivoirian independence, 395–98; Keita and, 358; and labor movement, 179, 247; Lamine Guèye law defended, 95–96; and *loi-cadre*, 238–39; and Mali Federation, 373, 395; and nationality issues, 420–21; on personal status, 160; political acumen of, 436; and RDA, 166, 172–78; on risks of universal suffrage, 193; and SAA, 95–96, 170–71; and Sékou Touré, 314; special representation opposed, 116; and territorial assemblies, 139–40, 141; on voting along racial lines, 72. *See also* Conseil de l'Entente; Rassemblement Démocratique Africain
Houphouët-Boigny law, 8, 67–68, 93, 171

identification documents: difficult to obtain, 235; establishing voter identity via, 73, 137–38, 155–56; French vs. Union citizenship on, 272; right to, 153, 273. *See also* état-civil; voting rights
immigration: into Africa, fears of, 202–3, 267; and anti-"foreigner" mobilization, 340, 352–53, 371, 414, 421, 430; and citizens' rights of movement, 31, 125, 131, 273, 426–28; into Côte d'Ivoire, 170–71, 420, 430, 443–44; French restrictions on, 442–41; as historically defined, 445. *See also* freedom of movement; migration, labor
Indépendants d'outre-mer (IOM), 190, 201–2, 234
independence: 1958 Constitution and, 288, 295–96, 301, 307, 309–24, 372,

independence (*continued*)
385, 393–94; Bendjelloul on, 83; and
Community, 361–62, 393–98; costs
and risks of, 277, 302, 306, 323; and
defense policy, 323, 378–79, 385; dis-
avowed by IOM, 190; first put forth
as goal, 258; global context of, 262–63,
275, 433–34; High Commissioner
Cusin on, 281–82; and justice, 379–80;
Keita on, 285, 306, 341–43, 398–99,
428–29; nationality and citizenship
after, 414–28; overview of factors
leading to, 433–34; PAI and, 258;
PFA and, 341, 342; PRA and, 260,
296–97; RDA and, 259–60, 296–97;
"real" vs. "nominal," 259, 261, 284,
337, 350, 369, 386; right to, under the
1958 Constitution, 292–93, 295–96,
301, 307, 312, 315–16, 321–24, 346;
Senghor on, 187–88, 259–61, 279,
283, 296–97, 341–42, 402–6, 412, 430;
sought by Conseil de l'Entente states,
388, 395–98, 426; via transfer of competences, 342–43; youth movement's
calls for, 220, 258–59. *See also* Mali
Federation; secession; self-
determination; *and specific countries*
indigénat (colonial justice system), 7,
67–68, 80, 95, 118, 168, 170
Indochina: citizenship in, 71; federation
in, 30; and the French Community,
308; map, *19*; not represented in the
constituent assembly, 61; position of,
in French Union, 21, 30, 149; status
under Pleven plan, 43; students from,
in French universities, 196–97. *See also*
Cambodia; Laos; Vietnam
Inspecteur Géneral du Travail, 249
Intergroup (in Assemblée Nationale
Constituante), 70–72, 98, 100, 116, 118
international opinion: French concern
with, 21, 38–39, 134, 193, 221, 408
IOM. *See* Indépendants d'outre-mer
Islam: and brotherhoods, 189, 401,
439–40; and citizenship in Associated States, 150; in Côte d'Ivoire,
444; and France as Muslim power,
148–49; and French fears of nationalism, 30, 135–36, 138; and personal
status, 6, 15–16, 29, 116, 129; and
pilgrimage to Mecca, 148; and politics in Mali Federation, 337, 362, 393,
401–2; in Senegal, 48, 189, 401, 418–

19, 439–40; and Senghor-Dia relationship, 439–40. *See also* Algeria;
originaires; personal status
Ivory Coast. *See* Côte d'Ivoire

Jacquinot, Louis, 192–93, 199–200
Janot, Raymond, 293–94, 305, 310, 327,
360
Jews, 16
judicial system: advantage of federal
judiciary, 300; of the Community,
290–91, 300, 302, 305, 322–23, 327,
336–37, 354, 356, 362, 364–68, 376–
80, 385; *indigénat*, 7, 67–68, 80, 95, 118,
168, 170; in Mali Federation, 399–400,
403; in Senegal, 415, 419
jugements supplétifs, 154, 157, 273
Juglas, Jean-Jacques, 99–100, 113
Jullien, Jean, 119
justice. *See* judicial system; rights

Kamara, Mamadou, 156
Kassi, Ernest Sampah, 162–63
Keita, Madeira: and the 1958 referendum, 321; and French-Malian negotiations, 342, 373–74, 380, 386; and
Malian tensions, 390
Keita, Modibo, 167, *348*; and 1958
referendum, 321; and Algerian crisis,
283; and breakup of Mali Federation, 388–92, 400–406, 411–12; and
Community politics, 339–40, 344–45;
de Gaulle presidency supported, 284;
education of, 23; on end of colonialism, 428–29; on Eurafrica, 268; and
independence, 285, 306, 341–43, 361,
428–29; and *loi-cadre*, 240, 242; and Malian citizenship/nationality, 360, 411;
and Malian-French negotiations, 339,
342–43, 345, 360–61, 373–75, 381–82,
384–85, 387–88; and Malian nation-
building, 352; as Malian Président du
Conseil, 337; Mali Republic led by,
409; on Mali's independence, 398–99;
on nationality and citizenship of Community, 357–58, 360, 381; on "Negro-
African civilization," 337; and Union
Soudanaise/RDA, 167–69, 240, 342
Kir, Félix, 232
Konaté, Mamadou, 168, 169
Koné, Jean-Marie, 252, 257, 389

nation: vs. *patrie*, 195–96, 341, 344–45, 349–51, 381, 402; relationship to state, 351, 355. *See also* independence; multinational state/nation; nationalism

National Assembly. *See* Assemblée Nationale

National Constituent Assembly. *See* Assemblée Nationale Constituante

nationalism: at 1958 PRA meeting, 296; Abbas on, 112; Apithy on, 209–10, 234; and assumption that anticolonial politics is nationalist, 4, 9, 437; Aujoulat on, 114; in Cameroon, 178; French views of, 200, 204, 220, 358; Houphouët-Boigny's critique of, 238; IOM's critique of, 190; Keita's critique of, 189n72; as outdated, 189, 200, 238; Senghor's critique of, 189–90, 195, 346–47, 358, 406; in Vietnam, 82. *See also* independence; nationality

nationality: and 1958 Constitution, 322, 354–55, 356; in Associated States, 18–20, 44, 75; and citizenship, 75–76, 90, 96, 322, 352, 354–57, 359, 363–65; within context of the Community, 329, 349–65, 432; defining and allocating after independence, 377, 414–26, 429, 435, 445; dual nationality, 377–78, 416–17; expulsion of "other" nationals, 340, 352–53; in France, after territorial independence, 416–17, 421–26, 441–43; in French Union, 21, 352; Malian independence and, 259–61, 374–78, 381–87, 399–400; in Mali Federation, 360, 399–400; in Mali Republic, 419–20; naturalization, 355, 356–57, 364, 415, 416, 420, 442; in Senegal, 414–17; sovereignty and, 356–58, 361, 435; superposed, 363, 368, 369, 371, 411, 420–21, 429, 432

Nationality Act of 1948 (Great Britain), 375

nation-state: Dia's critique of, 1, 216; vs. multinational state, 216, 343, 350, 429, 435, 445; as political norm, 1–2, 9, 124, 214, 237, 275, 370–71, 431, 433; Senghor on, 341

N'Diaye, Valdiodio, 403

La Nef, 194–96

négritude, 17–18, 36, 262, 391, 406

"Negro-African" civilization, 9, 187, 189, 261, 337, 341, 351, 406, 434

Netherlands, the, 2n2, 41

New Caledonia, 41–42, 43

New Hebrides, 44

Niger: and 1958 Constitution and referendum, 304, 321–24; and African federation question, 333; civil servants from other states expelled, 340; and Conseil de l'Entente, 340, 420–21; independence of, 396–97; as part of AOF, 21–23, 22; poverty of, 23, 222; Sawaba party in, 321–22, 435; territorial assembly elections (March 1957), 251; uranium in, 268–69, 322. *See also* Bakary, Djibo

Nigeria, 321

Nkrumah, Kwame, 177, 193–94, 343, 433

notables évolués. See *évolués*

nuclear energy, 268–69. *See also* uranium

Ordinance of 7 March 1944 (on citizenship in Algeria), 29

originaires (Quatre Communes): citizenship status of, 6–8, 15–17, 103, 414, 422, 425; use of term in French nationality law, 423; voting rights of, 6–7, 45–50. *See also* Quatre Communes

Orselli, Georges (Governor of Côte d'Ivoire), 172

Ottoman Empire, 198

Ouattara, Alassane, 444–45

Ouédraogo, Joseph, 335

Overseas Committee (of Assemblée Nationale): and constitutional revision, 275; and double college, 141, 146; and European cooperation, 209–10; and *loi-cadre*, 226–30, 240–41; and reform of French Union, 274–76

Overseas Committee (of Assemblée Nationale Constituante): and 1946 constitution, 68–74, 97–100, 104, 107; and election laws, 136, 139; overseas representation in, 68–69; universal suffrage debated by, 70–71, 226–27

Overseas Ministry (Ministère de la France d'Outre-mer): and citizenship, 97, 121, 126–27, 128, 272; and composition of and elections to territorial assemblies, 139–40; and constitutional revision, 201–2, 275–76; decentralization's risks and benefits weighed by, 200–202, 216–17, 219–26; on dangers of African unity, 204; on double and single colleges, 134, 136–37, 140, 142–43, 164; and état-civil, 152–53, 156, 272–73; and European cooperation, 202, 207, 264–65, 269; on France as Muslim power, 148–49; and labor code, 181; and Lamine Guèye law, 88, 97, 125–26; and *loi-cadre*, 227–35, 239–41, 262–63; loss of control feared by, 101, 172, 175, 207; "particular laws" clarified by, 130; and personal status, 129, 159, 161, 163; on possible elimination of Governments General, 225; and RDA, 175, 176; and second constitutional draft, 106–7; and Senegalese capital's move to Dakar, 255; universal suffrage favored, 164. *See also* Colonial Ministry; Coste-Floret, Paul; Jacquinot, Louis; Mitterrand, François; Moutet, Marius; Teitgen, Pierre-Henri

Pacques, Georges, 64
pacte colonial, 142, 188, 192, 261, 269
PAI. *See* Parti Africain de l'Indépendance
Paris-Dakar, 303
Paris-Match, 270
Parliament. *See* Assemblée Nationale; Conseil de la République; legislative institutions; legislature
Parti Africain de l'Indépendance (PAI), 258–59, 263, 317–20, 343
Parti Communiste Français. *See* Communist Party
Parti Démocratique de la Côte d'Ivoire (PDCI), 167, 170–78, 263. *See also* Houphouët-Boigny, Félix; Rassemblement Démocratique Africain
Parti Démocratique de Guinée (PDG), 247, 263. *See also* Rassemblement Démocratique Africain; Sékou Touré, Ahmed
Parti de la Fédération Africaine (PFA): and African unity, 340; establishment of, 257, 339; and Mali Federation, 341–43, 345, 390, 400, 403; Senghor's influence through, 337
Parti de Regroupement Africain (PRA): and 1958 Constitution, 284, 295–97, 303–4, 319, 372; and 1958 referendum, 312, 320–21; and African unity, 340; Apithy's resignation from, 336;

conflict with RDA, 283, 324; Cotonou conference of (1957), 296–97, 304, 321, 372; established, 257, 282; and independence, 260, 296–97, 304, 321, 342. *See also* Parti de la Fédération Africaine; Senghor, Léopold Sédar
passports, 31, 113, 127, 272, 357, 364, 397
patrie, 195, 234, 349–51
pays, as category in Pleven plan, 43
PCF. *See* Communist Party
PDCI. *See* Parti Démocratique de la Côte d'Ivoire
PDG. *See* Parti Démocratique de Guinée
Péchoux, Laurent (Governor of Côte d'Ivoire), 172–73, 175, 176
personal status: and Algeria, 16, 29, 55, 85, 155, 423; arguments for citizenship with difference statuses, 6, 29, 55, 60, 69–71, 74, 76, 84–85, 89, 103, 108, 120–21, 129, 158, 191; and citizenship of French Union, 65, 74, 82, 108, 127, 150, 191, 272; in Constitution of 1946, 8, 117–18, 121, 127–28, 355, 375; Constitution of 1958 and, 310, 313; electoral laws and, 74, 85, 117, 128–29, 135–40, 156, 158; and the état-civil, 89, 130, 152–57, 270–73; and justice in a multinational community, 366–67, 375, 384, 424; and labor code, 184n59; Lamine Guèye law and, 89, 117, 138; marriage and, 156, 161–62, 384; officials' confusion over, 127, 272–73; and *originaires*, 6–7, 8, 15–17, 29, 414; and principle of equality, 89, 130, 138, 141, 161, 164, 191; as rationale for refusing citizenship, 7, 16, 82, 164, 191; renunciation of, 6, 16, 117, 119, 121, 129, 158–64, 271–72, 377; and two-tier citizenship, 161
PFA. *See* Parti de la Fédération Africaine
Philip, André, 70
Plantey, Alain, 290, 298, 362
Pleven, René, 34–35, 40–41, 84–86, 271. *See also* Pleven commission
Pleven commission (Commission chargée de l'étude des mesures propres à assurer aux Colonies leur juste place dans la nouvelle constitution française), 40–44
Poinboeuf, Marcel, 55
political parties: and African unity, 279–80; chiefs' authority challenged,

political parties (*continued*)
95, 167–69, 171, 174, 181, 432; con-
solidation across territories, 257; electoral competition among, 161, 246,
251, 257, 259, 321, 371, 436; growing
power of, 433; influence on 1958
referendum results, 317–24; single-
party domination, 170, 263, 390, 436,
438–40; territorial basis of, 161, 278,
412–13; unification of, called for, 246,
257, 282. *See also* elections; *specific parties*
political repression: in independent
Côte d'Ivoire, 443–45; in independent
Guinea, 250, 332, 436; in independent
Senegal, 438–40; limits to, 169–70, 323;
against RDA, 173–75, 177; against
striking workers, 180, 248, 250; voter
rolls interfered with, 175, 177. *See also*
Algeria; Cameroon; Madagascar
political violence, 443–45; in Cameroon,
233; and colonialism, 36; in Côte
d'Ivoire, 171–75, 353, 443–45; French
fears of, 47–48, 104; relative lack of in
AOF, 233; Senghor's rejection of, 243.
See also Algeria
Politique Étrangère, 199
polygamy, 129, 156, 159–62, 367–68,
418–19
Popular Front, 18
poverty: in AOF, 2, 23, 222; as burden
on French government, 24, 224, 232,
299; and development, 224, 290, 299;
federalism made difficult by, 224–
25; and horizontal and vertical solidarities, 188; and independence, 2,
261; Sékou Touré on, 315. *See also*
economic development; standard of
living
PRA. *See* Parti de Regroupement
Africain
Pré, Roland, 298, 307
President of Mali, 402
President of the Republic: as head of
the federal government, 291, 301; as
President of the Community, 306–7,
309, 374, 378, 385, 409. *See also* de
Gaulle, Charles
property rights, 158–59, 191, 288, 364,
380, 395. *See also* French of metropole:
and business and residence in independent former territories
protectorates. *See* Associated States
Provisional Consultative Assembly,
54–56, 60–61

"quality" of citizen. *See* citizenship:
quality of
Quatre Communes: citizenship in, 6–8,
15–17, 21, 41, 53, 80, 191, 377, 414,
422, 425; citizens of 1946 looked down
upon by, 142; as Lamine Guèye's
political base, 50–51, 188–89; women's
suffrage in, 45–50. *See also originaires*
Quilici, François, 135–36, 138

racism and racial discrimination: and
1958 Constitution, 300; and African
attitudes toward colonialism, 109,
113, 428–29; and African racial unity,
48, 388–89; and Africans' demands for
equality, 48, 51–53, 57, 69, 72, 110–11,
113, 137–38, 141, 145, 184–85, 187–
88, 238, 256, 278; and banning of
discriminatory practices, 126, 191–92;
in civil service and railroad employment, 179, 184–85, 191, 223–24; in
constitutional debates (1946), 55–57,
69, 72–73, 104, 110–18, 122; and
continued racist arguments, 42, 105,
113, 138, 145, 148, 208, 289; dual état-
civil system as, 154; and evocation of
"Negro chiefs," 42; and French fear
of losing dominance, 105, 148, 289;
French repudiation of, 30, 35, 38, 69,
74, 126, 208–9, 422, 433; and "immigration" issue in France, 442–43; and
labor code, 184; and Mali Federation's
constitution, 393; Saller on legislators'
racism, 145; Senghor on, 104, 105,
113, 116, 187, 189, 203, 227, 350–51,
438; and special representation for
whites, 57, 60, 72–73, 110–18, 132–46;
and white vs. African cocoa planters,
170–71. *See also* African unity; civil
service: Africanization of; colonialism;
electoral colleges; *négritude*; personal
status
railway strike (1947–48), 179–80
Ramadier, Paul, 212
Ramette, Arthur, 138
Raseta, Joseph, 67
Rassemblement Démocratique Africain
(RDA): and 1958 Constitution,
295–97, 303; and African federation
question, 256–57, 280–81, 332, 340;
and African unity, 166, 256, 316, 322,
340, 371, 389, 412, 429; clashes with
PRA, 283; Community federation

urged, 345; electoral laws criticized by, 141; founding and manifesto, 96, 166; French campaign against, 172–78, 435; in Guinea, 180–81; and independence, 259–60; and the labor movement, 179–80, 249; and *loi-cadre*, 234, 235, 239; organization of, 167; as parallel administration, 167–69, 171, 173–75; regroupment debated by, 282; relationship to PCF of, 167, 176–77, 197; Sékou Touré criticized by, 316; student branch of, 197; in territorial assembly elections (March 1957), 251; territorial parties affiliated with, 277. *See also* d'Arboussier, Gabriel; Houphouët-Boigny, Félix; Keita, Modibo; Lisette, Gabriel; Parti Démocratique de la Côte d'Ivoire; Parti Démocratique de Guinée; Sawaba; Sékou Touré, Ahmed; Union Soudanaise-RDA

Rassemblement de Gauche, 141–42
Rassemblement des Jeunesses Démocratique Africaines, 219–20
Ravoahangy, Joseph, 67, 137
RDA. *See* Rassemblement Démocratique Africain
referenda: on 1946 Constitution (May), 45, 77, 86, 88, 91–92; on 1946 Constitution (October), 122; on 1958 Constitution, 295, 302–4, 307, 310–24, 331, 352, 363
renewed Community (la Communauté rénovée). *See* Community (1958–64); Constitution of 1958: revised
Republic of Mali (formerly Sudan), 408–9, 419–20
ressortissants, xv. *See also* citizenship; subjects
Réveil, 138
Reynaud, Paul, 309
rights: as claim-making notion, to, 8, 12, 437; claims to under 1946 Constitution, 129–47, 158, 198–99, 211, 217, 227, 245, 278, 432; claims to under 1958 Constitution, 291, 300, 310, 329, 354, 363, 432; from constitutional to treaty protection of, 377–84, 387, 395, 410–11, 422–24, 430; differential allocation of, 17, 29, 44; evocation of in constitutional debates (1946), 70–122; free speech, 127, 432; under French Union citizenship, 65–66, 76, 96–97, 127–29, 150–51; to independence, 77,

93, 102, 259–60, 274, 282, 285, 292–96, 312, 315, 321–24, 345–46, 372, 432; and Mali Federation, 334–35, 375, 393; and monarchs of Associated States, 97, 114, 150–51; in a multinational community, 365–68; personal status not an obstacle to exercising, 120, 130; portability of, 347, 354, 359, 365–67, 371, 376, 387, 437; property rights, 142, 158–59, 191, 288, 364, 380, 395; social rights, 80, 178, 181–84, 189, 219, 229, 232, 331. *See also* Constitution of 1946; Constitution of 1958; freedom of movement; independence; self-determination; universal suffrage; voting rights

Rocher, M., 168, 169
Roman Empire, 13, 77–78, 108
Ruais, Pierre, 60

SAA. *See* Syndicat Agricole Africain
Said Mohamed ben Cheikh Abdallah Cheikh, 67, 276
Saint-Domingue (Haiti), 14–15
Saint-Louis (Senegal), 46–48, 50–51. *See also* Quatre Communes; Senegal
Saller, Raphaël, 145
Sarr, Ibrahima, 179, 189, 440
Sator, Kaddour, 135–36
Sawaba (political party), 321–22, 435
Scelle, Georges, 111
Schmidt, Elizabeth, 181, 317
secession: and demand for inclusion in Eurafrica, 208; fears of, 40, 99, 104–5, 113, 222, 295, 299, 345; vs. "independence" (1958), 296, 324–25, 342, 360, 372, 388, 394; from Mali Federation, 401–2, 405; 'No' vote on 1958 referendum as, 302–4, 314, 317; rejection of, 102, 286, 322; right of, 77, 102; separate electoral colleges and, 74. *See also* independence; referenda: on 1958 Constitution
Seck, Verkha, 47
Sékou Touré, Ahmed: and 1958 Constitution, 294, 312, 314–17; and African federation question, 256, 257, 280–84, 312, 315–16, 343, 433–34; and African unity, 260, 316, 343; authoritarian rule of, 332, 436; on civil service, 230, 234, 243; confrontation with de Gaulle (1958), 314–17; on de Gaulle's investiture, 284; on état-civil, 235; and

Sékou Touré, Ahmed (*continued*)
  Franco-African community, 280, 281,
  315; and Guinea's independence,
  314–17; and Houphouët-Boigny, 2,
  256–57, 314; and labor movement,
  180–81, 184, 243, 247–50, 332; and *loi-
  cadre*, 230, 234–35, 242–43; and RDA,
  257, 281–83; on right to independence, 294, 315
self-determination, 291, 294, 301–2, 321,
  323. *See also* independence
Sénat de la Communauté (Senate of
  the Community), 309, 327, 378, 380,
  394, 409
Senegal: and 1946 Constitution, 67, 80,
  95, 104, 115; and 1946 referendum,
  92; and 1958 Constitution, 304; and
  1958 referendum, 317–20, *318*, 436;
  authoritarian tendencies in, 436,
  438–40, 447; budget, 390; capital
  moved to Dakar, 255; Casamance
  region, 297, 320; citizenship in (before
  1946), 6–8, 15–17, 21, 414; conflict between French and Senegalese officials,
  255, 329; and Conseil exécutif, 327,
  339–40, 362; constitution of, 328; economic development in, 330; elections
  of 2000 and 2012 in, 447; état-civil in,
  154, 417–19; French president's visit
  to, 179, 186–87; independence of,
  402–6, *407*, 408; international status
  of, 408; labor movement in, 52–53,
  178–80, 247, 250, 282, 330–31; Lamine
  Guèye law in, 95, 131, 146–47; and
  Mali Federation, 328–29, 332–35, 337,
  341, 362, 386–93, 401–6, 411; map,
  22; as model for 1946 Constitution,
  29; National Assembly of, 415–18,
  439–40; and nationality, 358, 363,
  414–18; as part of AOF, 21–23, *22*;
  personal status issues in, 367–68; political mobilization in, 50–51; political
  parties in, 46, 51, 167, 188–89, 238,
  251, 258–59, 297, 317, 319–20, 440;
  population of, 46, 390; postindependence crisis in, 438–40; regionalism
  in, 297; representation in constituent
  assembly, 61, 62, 67; single college
  maintained, 140; standard of living of,
  330; statehood of, 326, 358; student
  movement in, 197; suffrage and voting rights in, 45–51, *236*; Territorial
  Assembly of, 141, 239, 251; women in,
  45–51, *236. See also* African federa-

tion; Bloc Démocratique Sénégalais;
  Dia, Mamadou; Lamine Guèye;
  Mali Federation; Parti Africain de
  l'Indépendance; Quatre Communes;
  Senghor, Léopold Sédar; Socialist
  Party of Senegal
Senegality, 189–90, 402, 406, 417
Senghor, Léopold Sédar, *144*, *407*; and
  1946 Constitution, 62, 67, 69–81,
  95–120, 165; and 1958 Constitution,
  284, 286, 290–91, 296, 298–301, 304,
  308, 312, 432; and the 1958 referendum, 304, 318–24; advocacy of
  Community-level judicial system, 300;
  advocacy of socialist economic policy,
  187–88, 261–62, 330, 439; on African
  empires, 333; on African federation,
  279, 283, 296–97, 301, 308, 312, 315,
  328–29, 332–34, 340–41, 344, 351–52,
  372, 391, 403, 406–8; on African unity,
  324, 328, 372, 413; and Algerian crisis,
  283, 408; as Assemblée Nationale
  deputy, 143–55, 183, 240, 274–75;
  on assimilation, 35–36, 81, 187, 195,
  261, 297, 406; authoritarian rule of,
  436, 438–40, 447; on balkanization
  of Africa, 214, 230–31, 237, 243, 258,
  279, 301, 333, 406; and breakup of
  Mali Federation, 389, 391, 400–406,
  412; break with Lamine Guèye, 188;
  on building Senegalese nation, 408,
  430; on citizenship, 36–37, 51, 71, 81,
  89, 100, 102, 108, 113, 115, 334–35,
  373, 381–82, 411; on colonialism, 36,
  408; on Commonwealth à la française, 387, 398; and Community, 300,
  339–40, 409; on confederation and
  federation, 11, 37, 188, 194–96, 199,
  203–4, 217, 227, 251–52, 259, 262,
  274–76, 283, 290–91, 293, 296–99,
  301, 304, 328–29, 332–34, 350–52,
  369, 406–7, 413, 432–34; conflict with
  Houphouët-Boigny, 11, 343–44, 350,
  369–70, 407, 443; and creation of
  Mali Federation, 328–29, 332–35, 337,
  351, 369, 389; defense of AOF, 230,
  240–41, 243–45; on de Gaulle, 284;
  and Dia, 215, 319–20, 393, 438–40; vs.
  double college, 72, 116, 143; on
  Eurafrica, 202–4, 206–8, 210, 267–68;
  on executive authority for territories,
  192, 221, 227, 241; and Franco-African
  community, 12, 280, 446; on Frenchness of Senegalese, 76, 207; and

independence, 187–88, 259–61, 274, 279, 283, 296–97, 304, 337, 341–42, 350; and labor movement, 247, 331; and *loi-cadre*, 229–31, 240–45; and Malian-French negotiations, 339–40, 369, 373–74, 381–82, 387; and marabouts, 189, 251, 401–2, 404, 439; on mixing of civilizations, 81, 262, 304, 341; and Monnerville Committee, 56, 57; on mystique of equality, 24, 183, 206; on mystique of unity, 279; on nation, *patrie*, and state, 196, 341, 344–45, 349–51, 381, 402; on nationalism, 189–90, 195, 346–47, 406; on "Negro-African civilization," 9, 17–18, 81, 187, 189, 261, 341, 391, 406, 434; and political parties, 167, 188, 257–59, 277–78, 296, 337, 339, 390; power base of, 189, 251, 401–2, 404, 412–13, 439–40; and PRA conference (1957), 296, 304, 372; and presidency of Mali, 391–93, 402–3; and presidency of Senegal, 408, 439–40; racism denounced, 104, 105, 113, 116, 187; vs. RDA, 257–58, 282, 284, 295–96; on reform of French Union, 187, 190, 192, 194–96, 199, 201, 227, 274–76; vs. regionalism, 297; report on French Union (1946), 80–81, 110; report on modifying Constitution (1955), 227; and Senegalese independence, 402–6, *407*, 412, 430; on sovereignty, 38, 260, 279, 297, 350–51, 411, 413, 435, 446; on universal suffrage, 51, 70, 155, 193, 231; on vertical and horizontal solidarity, 11, 24, 188, 203, 258; walkout from constituent assembly by, 116; and youth groups, 197. *See also* Bloc Démocratique Sénégalais; *Condition Humaine*; confederation; federalism; Indépendants d'Outre-mer; Parti de la Fédération Africaine; Parti de Regroupement Africain

Servoise, René, 218–19, 270

Sétif, 31

settlers (*colons*): and 1946 constitution, 92, 93, 114; in Algerian politics, 149, 213, 228, 437; in Côte d'Ivoire, 62, 170–72, 443; and French party politics, 92, 132, 141–42; interests defended, 18, 58, 64, 92–94, 99, 102, 141–42, 149, 213–14, 431, 437–38; in Morocco and Tunisia, 437–38; representation in constituent assembly

of, 61, 114, 119; special representation demanded for, 72–73, 110, 114–16, 118, 135, 138, 140, 143; universal citizenship opposed, 64–65; white cocoa planters privileged over Africans, 62, 64, 170–71. *See also* Algeria; electoral colleges

Sheehan, James, 10

Shepard, Todd, 308

Sikasso, Sudan, 167–68

Singly, Pierre, 146

Sissoko, Fily Dabo, 67, 166, 167, 217–18, 321

slavery, 14–15, 21, 80, 369

social Catholics, 92, 132, 182, 184–85, 330. *See also* Aujoulat, Louis-Paul; Dia, Mamadou; Teitgen, Pierre-Henri

Socialist Party: and 1946 Constitution, 82, 87, 102; leadership, *89*; *loi-cadre* supported by, 231; and party politics in France, 132–33; progressive empire supported, 119; vs. RDA, 167. *See also* Defferre, Gaston; Mollet, Guy; Moutet, Marius; Socialist Party of Senegal

Socialist Party of Senegal, 51, 167, 188. *See also* Lamine Guèye; Senghor, Léopold Sédar

social security system, 181, 182

Solus, Henry, 58

Somalia (French Somalia), 44

Soumah, David, 250

Soumaré (Col.), 400–401, 404

sovereignty: and 1946 Constitution, 72, 79, 83, 85, 96–98, 101, 114, 118, 122, 127, 150–51, 194, 255; and 1958 Constitution, 291–92, 295, 306–7, 432; of African states/territories, 248, 260, 274, 295, 301, 313, 336, 339, 356, 361, 363, 368, 372–78, 388, 395–96, 411–13, 421, 429, 435, 446; of the Assemblée Nationale, 70, 79, 83, 118, 131, 199–200, 254–55; in Associated States, 18–20, 23, 44, 72, 85, 96–97, 101, 114, 127–28, 149–52, 194–96, 199, 212, 438; and concepts of federation and confederation, 10–12, 85, 194–99, 210, 227, 260, 276, 279, 295–96, 336, 350, 378, 411–13; divisibility of, 10, 12, 21, 38, 40–41, 79, 98, 122, 151, 210, 243, 269, 274, 292, 295–97, 306, 313–15, 350, 366, 373, 394, 435; European cooperation and, 202–10, 260, 264, 266, 269, 279, 435; under French Empire, 18–21; and French Union, 149–52,

sovereignty (*continued*)
194–202, 210, 212; international, 212, 363, 368, 377–78; inviolability of French sovereignty asserted, 1, 28, 31, 35, 65, 118, 131, 147, 192, 200, 279, 344; and *loi-cadre*, 253–54; of the Mali Federation, 336, 373–74, 377–78, 380, 387–88, 394–96; of mandates, 20; and monarchical rulers, 43, 114, 149–51; and nationality, 356, 435; reciprocal limitations on, 122, 194, 198–99; representatives of French sovereignty in African territories, 243, 253–54, 327; of Senegal, 408; services of, 229, 233, 243; and transformation of empire, 10, 23–24, 83, 98–99, 101, 118, 147, 165, 194–202, 207, 210, 373; UN representation and, 361. *See also* Community (1958–64); confederation; Eurafrica; federalism; French Union; independence

standard of living: and overcoming disparities among citizens, 11, 80, 185, 204, 218, 232–33, 252, 299; in Senegal, 330. *See also* economic development; poverty

state(s): citizenship as individual-state relationship, 4–5; Madagascar's status as state, 78–79, 302, 312–13, 358; Mali's status as state, 362, 399; nation vs. *patrie* vs. state, 194–96, 341, 344–45, 349–52, 355, 381, 402; relation of nationality to state debated, 349–65; Senegal's status as state, 355; whether Community is a state debated, 299–307, 352, 355–56, 370; whether French Union is a state debated, 107, 109, 198; whether "Member States" are states debated, 306, 313, 344–45, 352, 355–56, 387. *See also* Associated States (protectorates); confederation; federalism; federation; independence; Member States; multinational state/community; nationality; nation-state; self-determination; sovereignty

state services, 240, 241, 243–44, 254, 338. *See also* civil service

strikes, 52–53, 178–84, 248–49, 330–31

student groups: African, in Paris, 196–97, 219–20; independence as goal of, 258–59, 436; 'no' vote advocated in 1958 referendum, 319; political influence of, 324. *See also* Parti Africain de l'Indépendance

subjects: Africans as, through 1945, 6–7, 21; in Algeria, 24, 55, 82–83, 85–86; citizenship debated for, 8–9, 24, 40–41, 58, 64–65, 69–70, 81–83, 85–87, 97, 103, 432–33; citizenship granted under 1946 Constitution, 121, 190–91, 428; electoral rights of, 60–62, 86; inclusion of in body politic, 27–28, 32–33, 41–43, 53–66, 81–89, 97–99, 122–23; lack of rights of, 7; of Morocco, 150, 151n84; path to citizenship of (before 1945), 28–29, 162; political voice of former subjects, 133; representation in constituent assembly of, 27–28, 55–57, 60–64; representation in legislative institutions debated, 40–43, 55, 58, 64, 72–73, 83–87, 97–99; right to make claims acquired by, 8–9. *See also* citizenship; *indigénat*; universal suffrage; voting rights

Sudan (French Sudan): and 1958 referendum, *319*, 320–21; and African federation question, 332–33; civil service strikes, 249, 282; conflict between French and Sudanese officials in, 329; and Conseil exécutif, 339–40, 362; independence of as Mali Republic, 408; labor movement in, 389; and Mali Federation, 332–35, 337, 341, 362, 386–87, 388–93, 411; as Member State of Community, 326; as part of AOF, 21–23, *22*; population of, 390; post-independence foreign relations of, 408–9; poverty of, 23, 222; representation in constituent assembly of, 67, 168; representation in National Assembly of, 168, *169*; territorial assembly elections (March 1957), 251. *See also* Keita, Madeira; Keita, Modibo; Mali Federation; Sissoko, Fily Dabo

Sultan of Morocco, 149–50, 212, 438

superposed citizenship. *See* citizenship: superposed

superposed nationality. *See* nationality: superposed

Sy, Cheikh Tidjiane, 402

Sylla, Assane, 425

Syndicat Agricole Africain (SAA), 95–96, 170–71. *See also* Houphouët-Boigny, Félix; Parti Démocratique de la Côte d'Ivoire

Tananarive, 311–12. *See also* Madagascar

taxation: and economic development, 68, 218, 277, 299; overtaxation of peasants, 27; RDA and, 173; state's ability to collect, 70; and state services, 241; territorial assemblies and, 90, 223–24, 235, 243

Teitgen, Henri, 103

Teitgen, Pierre-Henri: and 1958 Constitution, 299, 303–4, 307; and European cooperation, 265; federalism of, 216–17, 226, 299; on France's role in the Community, 370; and *loi-cadre*, 228–29, 231–33, 240–41, 243–44, 246; response to African demands, 216

territoires d'outre-mer, 38. *See also* territories

territoires-unis, 58. *See also* territories

territorial assemblies, 253–54; in 1946 constitutional debates, 103–4, 107–9, 112–13; elections for (March 1957), 236–37, 248, 251; electoral system for, 134, 139–40; and état-civil, 235, 242; and executive power (Conseils de gouvernement), 221, 228–29; fiscal responsibilities of, 219, 222–24, 243; and Grand Conseil, 146, 252, 332; limited powers of, 118–19, 142, 192, 200; and *loi-cadre*, 216, 241–42, 253–54; possibility of conceding more power and autonomy to, 148, 216–17, 222–26, 228–30; and right of self-determination, 301; Senegal assembly's protest, 141; special representation for whites in, 134, 140; status choices under 1958 Constitution, 301; and taxation, 90, 223, 224, 235, 243; Territorial Assemblies law (1946), 90–91. *See also* French Union: structure debated; voting rights; *and specific territories*

territories: and 1958 referendum, 310–24; authority over civil service of, 229–31, 240–41, 243, 246, 282; autonomy proposed for, 166, 228–35, 253, 255; autonomy's risks for, 200–201; cost of maintaining/developing, 219, 222, 232, 241, 270, 277, 299, 316; de Gaulle on, 147; difficulties of self-governance, 261; economic viability of, 216; and état-civil, 271, 273; and European cooperation, 202–10, 263–70; evolution toward department or Associated State, 90, 99, 103, 187; executive and legislative power proposed for, 21,

192, 225–29, 234, 236, 244, 255; governor's power over, 221; included in Republic, 21, 101; Lamine Guèye law in, 88–90; poverty of, 2, 23, 222, 224, 299; readiness for statehood questioned, 313; representation in the constituent assembly, 26, 54–57, 61–64, 67; representation of, in Union legislative bodies, 34, 36, 42–45, 71–72, 83–85, 93–94, 97–98, 101, 112–13; right of secession, 77, 102; in Senghor's confederation, 194–95; status within the Community, 244, 307–10, 312–13, 325–26; term disliked, 293, 313. *See also* colonies; French Union; *loi-cadre*; mandated territories; Member States; territorial assemblies; *and specific territories*

Thiam, Doudou, 211

Title VIII. *See* Constitution of 1946: calls for revision of

Togo: applicability of Lamine Guèye law to, 90, 97, 111; Conseil de gouvernement established, 221; federal territory status, 44; government reformed, 193–94; mandate status of, 20, 21; nationality and citizenship in, 20–21, 71–72, 97, 127–28, 244–45, 366; relationship to Community of, 289; representation in constituent assembly, 61, 67; representation in Union legislative bodies, 128; workers in Côte d'Ivoire threatened, 352–53, 371, 414. *See also* Apithy, Sourou Migan; mandated territories

Tombalbaye, François, 360, 374

trade unions. *See* labor movement

transfer of competences, and independence of Mali Federation, 341–43, 345, 349, 360–61, 368–70, 372–78, 394–95, 398–99, 410

Traoré, Tidjani, 256

trust territories, 71–72, 90, 97, 127–28, 149. *See also* Cameroon; Togo

Tsiranana, Philibert: and 1958 Constitution, 286, 293, 302, 304–5, 307; and nationality issue, 358

Tunisia: and 1946 constitution, 61, 114; and citizenship of French Union, 121, 150–51, 437–38; and the Community, 308; independence of, 151, 214, 228; inhabitants not French nationals, 75; Lamine Guèye law not applicable to,

Tunisia (*continued*)

102; map, *22*; more autonomy proposed for, 41; nationals not included in Monnerville Committee or constituent assembly's purview, 56, 61; post-independence relations with France, 274, 275, 289; protectorate status, 21, 23, 149–50; refusal to participate in Union institutions, 149–50, 212, 438; in Senghor's confederation plan, 196; sovereignty of, 72, 101; status under Pleven plan, 44; students from, 196–97. *See also* Associated States

Ubangui-Chari, 21–23, *22*, 304. *See also* Dacko, David; French Equatorial Africa

UGTAN. *See* Union Générale des Travailleurs de l'Afrique Noire

Union Générale des Travailleurs de l'Afrique Noire (UGTAN), 247–50, 317–20, 330–31

Union des Jeunes du Soudan (Union of Sudanese Youth), 393

Union des Populations du Cameroun (UPC), 178, 221, 259, 298, 435

Union Progressiste Mauritanienne, 251

unions. *See* labor movement

Union Soudanaise-RDA: and 1958 Constitution and referendum, 295, 320–21; and African federation question, 332–33, 351–52; chiefs' authority challenged, 167–69; membership of, 169; near-monopoly on power held by, 390, 412. *See also* L'Essor; Keita, Madeira; Keita, Modibo; Koné, Jean-Marie; Rassemblement Démocratique Africain

Union des Syndicats, 95, 247

Union des Syndicats du Sénégal et de la Mauritanie, 104

United Nations (UN), 39, 376, 395, 408, 444–45

United States (US): and criticisms of colonialism, 38–39; as federal model, 11, 40, 77, 341, 344, 362, 389; as former colony, 428; as major power, 269, 277

United States of Africa, proposed, 203–4, 328

universal suffrage: and 1958 referendum, 310–11; advocated by Monnerville Committee, 56–57; calls for, in 1945, 50–52, 57, 60–63; continued struggle for (1950s), 147, 163–64, 193, 214,

226–27, 231, 307, 432; debated in constituent assembly (1946), 70–71, 73, 100, 103; in de Gaulle's political conceptions, 310–11; difficulties of implementing, 42, 61, 73, 90–91, 155, 193, 230–31; in electoral law debates, 90–91, 141–43, 226–27; and état-civil, 155, 193, 230–31, 235; franchise extended gradually, 132, 137–39, 156, 435; Laurentie on, 91; under *loi-cadre*, 214, 229, 230–31, 235, 277; in Mali's constitution, 328; in metropole, 14, 26; Moutet on, 134; need for transition to, 61, 73, 123, 132, 143, 145; and political parties' strategies, 279; risk of administrative manipulation of, 193; and territorial assemblies, 255; women's suffrage, 14, 45–50. *See also* citizenship; elections; electoral colleges; état-civil; voting rights

UPC. *See* Union des Populations du Cameroun

Upper Volta: and Conseil de l'Entente, 340, 420–21; independence of, 396–97; Malians expelled from, 340; and Mali Federation, 332–36, 340, 371; migration from, 23, 170, 420–21; migration to Côte d'Ivoire from, 23, 443–45; and nationality question in Côte d'Ivoire, 420–21; as part of AOF, 21–23, *22*; political clashes in, 283; poverty of, 222, 223, 335; territorial assembly elections (March 1957), 251. *See also* Conseil de l'Entente

uranium, 268–69, 322

US-RDA. *See* Union Soudanaise-RDA

USSR, 38

Valentino, Paul, 82

van Walraven, Klaas, 322

Varenne, Alexandre, 101, 107, 111

Varenne committee (Comité Interministeriel pour le Statut de l'Union française), 101–2

vertical solidarity: as Africans' connections to France/Europe, 11, 23, 188; and clientelistic politics, 425, 446–47; Dia on, 238; and Eurafrica, 203, 258, 264; and French Union, 213; Houphouët-Boigny on, 344; and independence, 372, 446–47; IOM on, 190; need to combine with horizontal solidarity, 11, 23, 188, 203, 213, 258,

293, 446–47; Senghor on, 11, 188, 203, 258; Zinsou on, 237–38. *See also* Eurafrica; horizontal solidarity

Viard, Paul-Emile, 34, 74, 75, 87, 136

Vietnam: as amalgam of territories, 127–28; French war in, 212; independence declared by, 32–33, 59, 79; inhabitants not French nationals, 75; Monnerville Committee and, 56, 57; relationship to French Union of, 72, 79, 92–93; in Senghor's confederation plan, 196; sovereignty of, 72, 79. *See also* Associated States; Indochina

Violette, Maurice, 217

Voix de l'Afrique Noire, 197

voting rights: under 1958 Constitution, 291, 310–11; categories eligible for, 27–28, 60, 91, 137–38; and French civil status, 158, 272; and identification issue, 57, 61–62, 73, 91, 130, 137–38, 153–56, 193, 230–31, 235; and *loi-cadre*, 226, 229–32; Mali Federation referendum, 334; of Senegalese *originaires*, 6–7, 45–50; statistics of registration and voting, 139, 236; and territories' ineligibility to vote in 1946 referendum, 86; voter rolls interfered with, 175; of women, 14, 45–50. *See also* citizenship; elections; electoral colleges; état-civil; universal suffrage

wages, 52–53, 89, 182, 189. *See also* civil service: equal pay and benefits; labor movement

Weil, Patrick, 442

whites, special representation for, 72–73, 110, 114–16, 118, 140. *See also* racism and racial discrimination; settlers

women: demonstrations by, 40–50, 173; equality of, 150; Muslim Algerian women disenfranchised, 136; and polygamy, 418–19; and railway strike, 179–80; suffrage achieved in France, 14, 45; voting in Senegal, 45–51, *236*. *See also* polygamy

workers: African, in metropolitan France, 31, 125, 131, 273, 426–29, 430, 441–43; Algerian, in metropolitan France, 31, 74, 131, 426–27, 442. *See also* civil service; forced labor; freedom of movement; labor code; labor movement; strikes; wages

World War II, 7–8, 18

xenophobia. *See* immigration: and anti-"foreigner" mobilization; racism and racial discrimination

Yacé, Philippe, 397

Ya Doumbia, 191–92

Yaméogo, Maurice, 334, 336, 421

youth movements, 219–20, 319, 324, 343, 393, 436. *See also* Parti Africain de l'Indépendance; student groups

Zinsou, Emile, 237–38, 321, 335

CPSIA information can be obtained
at www.ICGtesting.com
Printed in the USA
BVOW06s0336130118
505250BV00002B/56/P